THEODORE ROOSEVELT

THEODORE ROOSEVELT

LETTERS AND SPEECHES

THE LIBRARY OF AMERICA

The paper used in this publication meets the
minimum requirements of the American National Standard for
Information Sciences — Permanence of Paper for Printed
Library Materials, ANSI z39.48 — 1984.

Distributed to the trade
in the United States by Penguin Putnam Inc.
and in Canada by Penguin Books Canada Ltd.

Library of Congress Catalog Number: 2004044205
For cataloging information, see end of Index.
ISBN 1–931082–66–9

———

First Printing
The Library of America — 154

Manufactured in the United States of America

LOUIS AUCHINCLOSS
IS THE EDITOR OF THIS VOLUME

Contents

President, 1901–1909

FORMER PRESIDENT, 1909–1919

Selected Speeches

EARLY PUBLIC CAREER
1881–1898

To Anna Roosevelt

Zermatt, August 5, 1881

Darling Bysie,

Day before yesterday, at nine in the morning, I started off, accompanied by two guides, to make the ascent of the Matterhorn. I was anxious to go up it because it is reputed very difficult and a man who has been up it can fairly claim to have taken his degree as, at any rate, a subordinate kind of mountaineer. At 6 o'clock in the evening we reached the small hut, half a cavern, where we spent the night; it was on the face of a cliff, up which we climbed by a rope forty feet long, and the floor was covered with ice a foot deep. The mountain is so steep that snow will not remain on the crumbling, jagged rocks, and possesses a certain sombre interest from the number of people that have lost their lives on it. Accidents, however, are generally due either to rashness, or else to a combination of timidity and fatigue; a fairly hardy man, cautious but not cowardly, with good guides, has little to fear. Still, there is enough peril to make it exciting, and the work is very laborious being as much with the hands as the feet, and (very unlike the Jungfrau) as hard coming down as going up. We left the hut at three-forty and, after seeing a most glorious sunrise which crowned the countless snow peaks and billowy, white clouds with a strange crimson irradescence, reached the summit at seven, and were down at the foot of the Matterhorn proper by one. It was like going up and down enormous stairs on your hands and knees for nine hours. We then literally *ran* down the foot hills to Zermatt, reaching it at half past three. It had been excessively laborious and during the journey I was nearer giving out than on the Jungfrau, but I was not nearly so tired afterwards, and in fact felt as fresh as ever after a cup of tea and a warm bath; went to table d'hote as usual and afterwards over to see the Gardiners, and coming back we spent the rest of the evening with Mrs Baylies, Miss Cornelia & Edmund. *Your Loving Brother*

To Corinne Roosevelt

Brussels, August 24, 1881

Darling Pussie,

Our trip through the Netherlands has been of necessity short, but very pleasant. What we have chiefly enjoyed, I think, has been looking at the country, the towns and the people themselves; and our regular "sight-seeing" time has been devoted mainly to pictures. I know nothing atall, in reality, of art, I regret to say, but I *do* know what pictures I like. I am not atall fond of Rubens. He is eminently a fleshly, sensuous painter; and yet his most famous pictures are those relating to the Divinity. Above all, he fails in his female figures. Ruben's women are handsome animals, excellent as pictures of rich flemish housewifes; but they are either ludicrous or revolting when meant to represent either the Virgin or a saint. I think they are not much better as heathen goddesses; I do'n't like a chubby Minerva, a corpulent Venus and a Diana who is so fat that I know she could never overtake a cow, let alone a deer.

Rembrandt is by all odds my favourite. I am very much attracted by his strongly contrasted colouring, and I could sit for hours examining his heads, they are so lifelike and expressive. Van Helst I like for the sake of the sake of the realism with which he presents to you the bold, rich, turbulent dutchmen of his time. Vandykes heads are wonderful; they are very lifelike and powerful — but if the originals were like them I should hardly have admired one. Perhaps the pictures I really get most enjoyment out of are the landscapes, the homely little dutch and flemish interiors, the faithful representations of how the people of those times lived and made merry and died, which are given us by Jan Steen, Van Ostade, Teniers and Ruysdaal. They bring out the life of that period in a way no written history could, and interest me far more than pictures of saints and madonnas. I suppose this sounds heretical, but it is true. This time, I have really tried to like the Holy pictures but I ca'n't; even the Italian masters seem to me to represent good men, and insipidly good women, but rarely anything saintly or divine. The only pictures I have seen with these attributes are Gustav Doree's! He alone represents the Christ so that your pity for him is lost in intense admiration and reverence. *Your Loving*

"HONOR ME WITH YOUR VOTE"

To Voters of the 21st Assembly District

New York, November 1, 1881

Dear Sir,

Having been nominated as a candidate for member of Assembly for this District, I would esteem it a compliment if you honor me with your vote and personal influence on Election day. *Very respectfully*

AN ELECTORAL VICTORY

To Charles Washburn

New York, November 10, 1881

Dear Charley,

Too True! Too True! I have become a "political hack."

Finding it would not interfere much with my law I accepted the nomination to the assembly, and was elected by 1500 majority, heading the ticket by 600 votes. But do'n't think I am going to go into politics after this year, for I am not.

With warmest regards to your mother and father, and from Mrs R. I am *Your True Friend*

"THE BILL WAS A STEAL"

To Henry Hull

New York, October 24, 1882

My Dear Sir:

To my great regret I have no copy of my speech, which was of necessity short, each speaker being limited to two minutes. *It is sheer nonsense* for any man to pretend that he voted on that bill without being fully aware of its character. It was put through under the gag law of the previous question, which cut off all debate, and which was of itself enough to excite the suspicions of any man of reasonable intelligence. Then, when my turn came to vote, I spoke with the greatest emphasis, stating and showing beyond doubt that the bill was a steal, and the motives of its supporters dishonest. Mr. Robb, a New York Democrat of unimpeachable character and ability, took the same stand that I did, so that Mr. Searl did not have even the poor excuse of partisanship; yet immediately afterwards, and in spite of the fact that our words had produced an immediate change in the current of the voting, Mr. Searl voted for the bill. *Very truly yours*

"A REPUBLICAN, PURE AND SIMPLE"

To Jonas Van Duzer

New York, November 20, 1883

My dear Sir,

I was very glad to get your letter; permit me to say that it was the most interesting and *practical* one I have received.

In answer to your questions I would state that, after having passed through Harvard College, I studied for the bar; but going into politics shortly after leaving college, and finding the work in Albany, if conscientiously done, very harassing, I was forced to take up some out-of-doors occupation for the summer, and now have a cattle ranch in Dakotah. I am a

Republican, pure and simple, neither a "half breed" nor a "stalwart"; and certainly no man, nor yet any ring or clique, can do my thinking for me. As you say, I believe in treating all our business interests equitably and alike; in favoring no one interest or set of interests at the expense of others. In making up the committees I should pay attention, first, to the absolute integrity of the men, second, to their capacity to deal intelligently with the matters likely to come before them — for in our present anything but ideal condition of public affairs, honesty and common sense are the two prime requisites for a legislator.

As writing is, at best, unsatisfactory work, I shall try to see you in person before the session begins.

With great regard, I am *Very truly yours*

MOURNING WIFE AND MOTHER

To Carl Schurz

Albany, February 21, 1884

Dear Mr. Schurz,

Your words of kind sympathy were very welcome to me; and you can see I have taken up my work again; indeed I think I should go mad if I were not employed.

I will try to act in public so as to deserve what you have said of me; though I have not lived long, yet the keenness of joy and the bitterness of sorrow are now behind me; but at least I can live so as not to dishonor the memory of the dead whom I so loved. *Ever Faithfully Yours*

"MY IDEAL . . . IS RATHER A HIGH ONE"

To Simon Dexter North

Albany, April 30, 1884

Dear Mr. North:

I wish to write you a few words just to thank you for your kindness towards me, and to assure you that my head will not be turned by what I well know was a mainly accidental success. Although not a very old man, I have yet lived a great deal in my life, and I have known sorrow too bitter and joy too keen to allow me to become either cast down or elated for more than a very brief period over any success or defeat.

I have very little expectation of being able to keep on in politics; my success so far has only been won by absolute indifference to my future career; for I doubt if any man can realise the bitter and venomous hatred with which I am regarded by the very politicians who at Utica supported me, under dictation from masters who were influenced by political considerations that were national and not local in their scope. I realize very thoroughly the absolutely ephemeral nature of the hold I have upon the people, and a very real and positive hostility I have excited among the politicians. I will not stay in public life unless I can do so on my own terms; and my ideal, whether lived up to or not is rather a high one.

For very many reasons I will not mind going back into private for a few years. My work this winter has been very harassing, and I feel both tired and restless; for the next few months I shall probably be in Dakota, and I think I shall spend the next two or three years in making shooting trips, either in the far West or in the Northern Woods — and there will be plenty of work to do writing. *Very truly yours*

AN AUTOBIOGRAPHICAL SKETCH

To an Unknown Correspondent

Albany, May 1, 1884

Dear Sir,

I do not know where you would find a sketch of my life. I will give you an outline myself. Do you wish me to send you a photograph of myself? Some are much worse than others. I will send you one if you wish.

I was born in New York, Oct 27th 1858; my father of old dutch knickerbocker stock; my mother was a Georgian, descended from the revolutionary Governor Bulloch. I graduated at Harvard in 1880; in college did fairly in my studies, taking honors in Natural History and Political Economy; and was very fond of sparring, being champion light weight at one time. Have published sundry papers on ornithology, either on my trips to the north woods, or around my summer home on the wooded, broken shore of northern Long Island. I published also a "History of the Naval War of 1812 with an account of the Battle of New Orleans," which is now a text book in several colleges, and has gone through three editions. I married Miss Alice Lee of Boston on leaving college in 1880. My father died in 1878; my wife and mother died in February 1884. I have a little daughter living.

I am very fond of both horse and rifle, and spend my summers either on the great plains after buffalo and antelope or in the northern woods, after deer and caribou.

Am connected with various charitable organizations, such as the Childrens Aid Society, Orthopaedic Hospital, National Prison Association, and others, in which my father took a leading part.

I was elected to the Assembly from the 21st district of New York in the autumn of 1881; in 1882 I served on the Committee on Cities. My chief work was endeavouring to get Judge Westbrook impeached on the ground of malfeasance in office and collusion with Mr. Jay Gould, in connection with railroad litigation.

Was reelected and in 1883 when the Republicans were in a

minority was their candidate for speaker, thus becoming their titular leader on the floor. My main speech was on the report of the democratic committee giving Sprague (Republican) the seat wrongly held by Bliss (Democrat), which report was reversed by the action of the Democratic house. Was again reelected. The republicans were in the majority; was a candidate for the speakership, and in the caucus received 30 votes to the 42 received by the successful candidate Mr Sheard, who was backed by both the halfbreeds who followed Senator Miller, and the stalwarts of President Arthurs train. This winter my main work has been pushing the Municipal Reform bills for New York City; in connection with which I have conducted a series of investigations into its various departments Most of my bills have been passed and signed.

In the primaries before the Utica Convention, I led the independents in my district, who, for the first time in the history of New York City Politics, won against the machine men, though the latter were backed up by all the Federal and municipal patronage. At Utica, I led the Edmunds men, who held the balance of power between the followers of Blaine and of Arthur; we used our position to such good effect as to procure the election of all four delegates as Edmunds men, though we were numerically not over 70 strong, barely a seventh of the total number of men at the convention. Am fairly well off; my recreations are reading, riding and shooting. *Very Respy*

THE NOMINATION OF BLAINE

To Anna Roosevelt

St. Paul, June 8, 1884

Darling Bysie,

Many thanks for your sweet note. Can you tell Douglass to get me files of the "Times" and "Sun" for the week ending June 7th? Also of the "Post." I would like to see them. I am now on my way to the Little Missouri; I shall probably be back about July 10th, but will write or telegraph to you before;

perhaps I shall be back much earlier, as I intend to take quite a long hunting trip this fall, there being now no necessity of my taking part in the political campaign.

Well, the fight has been fought and lost, and moreover our defeat is an overwhelming rout. Of all the men presented to the convention as presidential candidates, I consider Blaine as by far the most objectionable, because his personal honesty, as well as his faithfulness as a public servant, are both open to question; yet beyond a doubt he was opposed by many, if not most, of the politicians and was the free choice of the great majority of the Republican voters of the northern states. That such should be the fact speaks badly for the intelligence of the mass of my party, as well as for their sensitiveness to the honesty and uprightness of a public official, and bodes no good for the future of the nation — though I am far from thinking that any very serious harm can result even from either of the two evils to which our choice is now limited viz: — a democratic administration or four years of Blaine in the White House. The country has stood a great deal in the past and can stand a great deal more in the future. It is by no means the first time that a vast popular majority has been on the side of wrong. It may be that "the voice of the people is the voice of God" in fifty one cases out of a hundred; but in the remaining forty nine it is quite as likely to be the voice of the devil, or, what is still worse, the voice of a fool.

I am glad to have been present at the convention, and to have taken part in its proceedings; it was a historic scene, and one of great, even if of somewhat sad, interest. Speaking roughly the forces were divided as follows: Blaine 340, Arthur 280, Edmunds 95, Logan 60, Sherman 30, Hawley 15. But the second choice of all of the Logan and Sherman and of nearly half the Arthur men, was Blaine, which made it absolutely impossible to form a combination against him. Arthurs vote was almost entirely from office holders, coming mainly from the south, and from the great cities of the north. Except among a few of the conservative business men he had absolutely no strength at all with the people. The votes for Logan, Sherman and Hawley represented nothing but the fact that Illinois, Ohio and Connecticut each had a "favorite son." The Edmunds vote represented the majority of the Republicans of

New England, and a very respectable minority in New York, New Jersey, and the three states of Wisconsin, Michigan and Minnesota. It included all the men of the broadest culture and highest character that there were in the convention; all those who were prominent in the professions or eminent as private citizens; and it included almost all the "plain people," the farmers and others, who were above the average, who were possessed of a keen sense of personal and official honesty, and who were accustomed to think for themselves.

Blaines adherents included the remainder, the vast majority of those from the middle and eastern states, and some from New England. These were the men who make up the mass of the party. Their ranks included many scoundrels, adroit and clever, who intend to further their own ends by supporting the popular candidate, or who know Mr Blaine so well that they expect under him to be able to develope their schemes to the fullest extent; but for the most part these Republicans were good, ordinary men, who do not do very much thinking, who are pretty honest themselves, but who are callous to any but very flagrant wrongdoing in others, unless it is brought home to them most forcibly, who "do'n't think Blaine any worse than the rest of them," and who are captivated by the man's force, originality and brilliant demagoguery.

About all the work in the convention that was done against him was done by Cabot Lodge and myself, who pulled together and went in for all we were worth. We achieved a victory in getting up a combination to beat the Blaine nominee for temporary chairman, who was also supported by the Logan men. To do this needed a mixture of skill, boldness and energy, and we were up all night in arranging our forces so as to get the different factions to come in to line together to defeat the common foe. Many of our men were very timid; so we finally took the matter into our own hands and forced the fighting, when of course our allies had to come into line behind us. White, Curtis and Wadsworth were among the weak kneed ones; but when we got in Curtis made a good speech for us. I also made a short speech, which was listened to very attentively and was very well received by the delegates, as well as the outsiders; it was the first time I had ever had the chance of speaking to ten thousand people assembled together.

Some of the nominating speeches were very fine, notably that of Governor Long of Massachusetts, which was the most masterly and scholarly effort I have ever listened to. Blaine was nominated by Judge West, the blind orator of Ohio. It was a most impressive scene. The speaker, a feeble old man of shrunk but gigantic frame, stood looking with his sightless eyes towards the vast throng that filled the huge hall. As he became excited his voice rang like a trumpet, and the audience became worked up to a condition of absolutely uncontrollable excitement and enthusiasm. For a quarter of an hour at a time they cheered and shouted so that the brass bands could not be heard at all, and we were nearly deafened by the noise.

Tell Uncle Jimmie that I may write to him to send me out money for my cattle ranche to the German American Bank, St. Paul; and if Chas. P. Miller wishes two thousand dollars he is to have it. *Yours always*

HUNTING GRIZZLY BEARS

To Anna Roosevelt

Fort McKinney, Wyoming, September 20, 1884
Darling Bysie,

For once I have made a very successful hunting trip; I have just come out of the mountains and will start at once for the Little Missouri, which I expect to reach in a fortnight, and a week afterwards will be on my way home. I hope to hear from you there.

It took sixteen days travelling (during which I only killed a few bucks) before I reached the foot of the snow capped Bighorn range; we then left our wagon and went into the mountains with pack ponies, and as I soon shot all the kinds of game the mountains afforded, I came out after two weeks, during which time I killed three grizzly bear, six elk (three of them have magnificent heads and will look well in the "house on the hill") and as many deer, grouse and trout as we needed for the table; after the first day I did not shoot any cow or calf elk, or any deer at all, except one buck that had unusual antlers; — for I was more anxious for the quality than for the quantity of my bag. I have now a dozen good heads for the hall. Merrifield killed two bears and three elk; he has been an invaluable guide for game, and of course the real credit for the bag rests with him, for he found most of the animals. But I really shot well this time.

We met a heard of a dozen parties either of English or Eastern amateurs, or of professional hunters, who were on the mountain at the same time we were; but not one of them had half the success I had. This was mainly because they hunted on horseback, much the easiest and least laborious way, while Merrifield and I, in our moccasins and buckskin suits hunted almost every day on foot, following the game into the deepest and most inaccessible ravines. Then again, most of them would only venture to attack the grizzly bears if they found them in the open, or if there were several men together, while we followed them into their own chosen haunts, and never but one of us shot at a bear. Merrifield, indeed, who is a perfectly fearless and reckless man, has no more regard for a grizzly than he has for a jack rabbit; the last one we killed he wished to merely break his leg with the first shot "so as to see what he'd do." I had not atall this feeling, and fully realized that we were hunting dangerous game; still I never made steadier shooting than at the grizzlies. I shall not soon forget the first one I killed. We had found where he had been feeding on the carcass of an elk; and followed his trail into a dense pine forest, fairly choked with fallen timber. While noiselessly and slowly threading our way through the thickest part of it I saw Merrifield, who was directly ahead of me, sink suddenly to his knees and turn half round, his face fairly ablaze with excitement. Cocking my rifle and stepping quickly forward, I found myself face to face with the great bear, who was less than twenty five feet off — not eight steps. He had been roused from his sleep by our approach; he sat up in his lair, and turned his huge head slowly towards us. At that distance and in such a place it was very necessary to kill or disable him at the first fire; doubtless my face was pretty white, but the blue barrel was as steady as a rock as I glanced along it until I could see the top of the bead fairly between his two sinister looking eyes; as I pulled the trigger I jumped aside out of the smoke, to be ready if he charged; but it was needless, for the great brute was struggling in the death agony, and, as you will see when I bring home his skin, the bullet hole in his skull was as exactly between his eyes as if I had measured the distance with a carpenters rule. This bear was nearly nine feet long and weighed over a thousand pounds. Each of my other bears, which were smaller, needed two bullets apiece; Merrifield killed each of his with a single shot.

I had grand sport with the elk too, and the woods fairly rang with my shouting when I brought down my first lordly bull, with great branching antlers; but after I had begun bear killing other sport seemed tame.

So I have had good sport; and enough excitement and fatigue to prevent over much thought; and moreover I have at last been able to sleep well at night. But unless I was bear hunting all the time I am afraid I should soon get as restless with this life was with the life at home.

I shall be very, very glad to see you all again. I hope Mousiekins will be very cunning; I shall dearly love her.

I suppose all of our friends the unco' good are as angry as ever with me; they had best not express their discontent to my face unless they wish to hear very plain English. I am sorry my political career should be over, but after all it makes very little difference.

If any Englishman named Farquahr, Lee or Grenfell calls get Douglass or Elliott to do anything they can for them; I met them hunting. Tell Douglass to write me when the last day of registry comes *Your Loving Brother*

CONSOLING A FRIEND

To Henry Cabot Lodge

New York, November 7, 1884

Dear old fellow,

I just did not have the heart to write you before. It is simply cruel; and I do not dare trust myself at present to speak to an

Independent on the subject; I wrote an open letter to Godkin but I tore it up afterwards; we must not act rashly.

Of course there seems no use of saying anything in the way of consolation; and probably you feel as if your career had ended; that is *not so*: you have certainly received a severe blow; but you would be astonished to know the hold you have on the party at large; not a man in New York have I seen (Republicans I mean, of course) who does not feel the most bitter indignation at your defeat. They will never forget you and come back in time you must and will.

Now a word of advice; don't let the Independents see you express any chagrin; be, as I know you will be, courageous, dignified, and above all *good tempered*; make no attacks at present; at any rate write me first. This is merely a check; it is in no sense a final defeat; and say nothing, even to the fools who hurt you, without cool thought.

I wish I could be with you. It may be some comfort to know that the Independents draw no distinction between your defeat and my retirement. You have a hold on the party that I can not have; and beyond question you will in time take the stand you deserve in public life.

Here everything is at sixes and sevens. I shall be happy if we get clear without bloodshed; thanks to the cursed pharisaical fools and knaves who have betrayed us.

Remember that your wife and yourself have promised to visit us this winter. *Always your friend*

DAVIS AND BENEDICT ARNOLD

To Jefferson Davis

New York, October 8, 1885

Sir:

Mr. Theodore Roosevelt is in receipt of a letter purporting to come from Mr. Jefferson Davis, and denying that the character of Mr. Davis compares unfavorably with that of Benedict Arnold. Assuming the letter to be genuine Mr. Roosevelt has only to say that he would indeed be surprised to find that his views of the character of Mr. Davis did not differ radically from that apparently entertained in relation thereto by Mr. Davis himself. Mr. Roosevelt begs leave to add that he does not deem it necessary that there should be any further communication whatever between himself and Mr. Davis.

GUARDING THIEVES AND READING TOLSTOI

To Corinne Roosevelt Robinson

Dickenson, Dakota, April 12, 1886

Darling Pussie,

I wrote Elliott about my successful trip after the three thieves, and so will not give you the particulars. I have been absent just a fortnight. It has been very rough work, as we got entirely out of food and had an awful time in the river, as there were great ice gorges, the cold being intense. We captured the three men by surprise, there being no danger or difficulty about it whatever, as it turned out; and for the last ten days I have hung to them, through good and evil fortune, like a fate, rifle always in hand. The last two days I have been alone, as Seawall and Dow went on with the boats down stream, while I took the prisonners on to here overland; and I was glad enough to give them up to the Sheriff this morning, for I was pretty well done out with the work, the lack of sleep and the strain of the constant watchfulness, but I am as brown and as tough as a pine knot and feel equal to anything.

I took Anna Karénine along on the trip and have read it through with very great interest. I hardly know whether to call it a very bad book or not. There are two entirely distinct stories in it; the connection between Levines story and Annas is of the slightest, and need not have existed atall. Levines and Kitty's history is not only very powerfully and naturally told, but is also perfectly healthy. Ann'as most certainly is not, though of great and sad interest; she is portrayed as being a prey to the most violent passion, and subject to melancholia, and her reasonning power is so unbalanced that she could not possibly be described otherwise than as in a certain sense insane. Her character is curiously contradictory; bad as she was however she was not to me nearly as repulsive as her brother Stiva; Vronsky had some excellent points. I like poor Dolly — but she should have been less of a patient Griselda with her husband. You know how I abominate the Griselda type. Tolstoi is a great writer. Do you notice how he never comments on the actions of his personages? He relates what they thought or did without any remark whatever as to whether it was good or bad, as Thucydides wrote history — a fact which tends to give his work an unmoral rather than an immoral tone, together with the sadness so characteristic of Russian writers. I was much pleased with the insight into Russian life. To think, by the way, of there being a Russian whose life business is the same as Lizzie Stewart's, but who rejoices in the name of Korsunsky!

What day does Edith go abroad, and for how long does she intend staying? Could you not send her, when she goes, some flowers from me? I suppose fruit would be more useful, but I think flowers "more tenderer" as Mr. Weller would say.

Today I go to Medora where I *hope* to receive some letters — hope, mark you, and underscored, oh scoffer among women. *Yours ever*

POLITICAL CAMPAIGN EXPENSES

To Corinne Roosevelt Robinson

Medora, Dakota, April 15, 1886

Sweet Pussie,

It would be difficult to write briefly about Legitimate Campaign Expenses; and I have not the time to send a regular essay. If a campaign is honestly carried on the expenses, though heavy, are less so than is commonly supposed. There is some indispensable work to be done which has to be paid for. Tens of thousands of ballots have to be printed, folded and sent out to every voter in the district; no light labour. At every polling place there ought to be at least one man especially charged with the interests of the candidate singly and provided with his ballots only, so as to give members of the opposite party a chance, if they wish it, to vote for him without the rest of the ticket. This man has to have a booth, ballots, posters etc. which again costs money. Then there must be some advertisement in the papers, and some pasting of placards. If there are political processions a candidate will bear his share in defraying the expenses; also, if for an important position, he must have rooms hired for headquarters, and if he speaks will have to pay for the hall etc.

But whenever possible volunteers should be chosen instead of paid workers; they are much more effective. Any form of bribery is not only criminal but is also, unless done by an old hand, useless; what is known as a "bar room" canvass is, for a gentleman, especially ineffective; the loafers and vagabonds will take anyones money, or drink with him, but will vote against him just the same. In my three campaigns I never paid for a drink or entered a saloon; and my whole expenditures were under the items enumerated above, together with a subscription to the local political association, to defray the printing and other general expenses of the party ticket on which I ran. Hiring wagons for voters, paying great numbers of men to work etc. are generally, although not always, merely thinly disguised forms of bribery. In districts where crooked work is feared detectives must be hired. Some districts are so rotten that it is almost impossible to win without bribery; in such cases a gentleman should go in simply with the expectation of defeat; no form of bribery is ever admissible. *Yours*

I enclose a card to send with the flowers to Edith when she starts off.

P.S. Will it bother you awfully to have an apothecary send me three or four cakes of that nice transparent soap? I have nothing but castile soap here. Express it to me.

CAPTURING HORSE THIEVES

To Henry Cabot Lodge

Medora, Dakota, April 16, 1886

Dear Cabot

I think the Harvard speech a first rate one (bar the allusion to me; did you see the N.Y. *Herald* on this latter point?); and was also greatly pleased with the editorials on Dawes and Indiana Civil Service Reform — especially the latter. Black must be quite a pill for the civil service people, by the way; what perverse lunatics the mugwumps are anyway. The St. Paul *Pioneer Press*, a very liberal paper, had a stinging article on them the other day. Your Hamilton is a work which was most assuredly well worth doing.

I got the three horsethieves in fine style. My two Maine men and I ran down the river three days in our boat and then came on their camp by surprise. As they knew there was no other boat on the river but the one they had taken and as they had not thought of our building another they were taken completely unawares, one with his rifle on the ground, and the others with theirs on their shoulders; so there was no fight, nor any need of pluck on our part. We simply crept noiselessly up and rising when only a few yards distant covered them with the cocked rifles while I told them to throw up their hands. They saw that we had the drop on them completely and I guess they also saw that we surely meant shooting if they hesitated, and so their hands went up at once. We kept them with us nearly a week, being caught in an ice jam; then we came to a ranch where I got a wagon, and I sent my two men on down stream with the boat, while I took the three captives overland a two days journey to a town where I could give them to the Sheriff. I was pretty sleepy when I got there as I had to keep awake at night a good deal in guarding, and we had gotten out of food, and the cold had been intense.

The other day I presided over the meeting of the Little Missouri Stockmen here, preserving the most rigid parliamentary decorum; I go as our representative to the great Montana Stockmeeting in a day or two.

Can you tell me if President Harrison was born in Virginia? I have no means of finding out here. I hope he was; it gives me a good sentence for Benton.

I am as brown and as tough as a hickory nut now. *Yours always*

READING "WAR AND PEACE"

To Anna Roosevelt

Medora, Dakota, June 19, 1886

Darling Bysie,

The round up has stopped for a day or two, and on riding into town I was delighted to find your two letters; they told me just what I wanted to hear, about the jolly parties at Sagamore, and all the rest of it. I have never considered myself a very social personage; but I do wish I could have been present at some of the sprees; and I simply can not say how much I wish to see you and to kiss and pet darling baby. Did you ever receive my letter in which I asked if you could conveniently send me some toys (blocks, a ball, a woolly dog, a rag doll etc) for the forlorn little mite of a Seawall child? I shall probably be home about October 1st; perhaps a fortnight sooner, perhaps not until two or three weeks later; make all your plans without reference to me, and I will fit into them somehow.

I enclose a letter which I wish you could get Mrs. Butler to answer. I can't make out the signature, nor the sex of the writer nor whether a friend or a stranger.

I am very glad you had Mrs. Lee to stay with you — I can say darling martyr Bi and the interminable grabage — and that she enjoyed herself so much, as she says in a long sweet letter to me.

La Guerre et La Paix, like all Tolstoi's work, is very strong and very interesting. The descriptions of the battles are excellent, but though with one or two good ideas underneath them, the criticisms of the commanders, especially of Napoléon, and of wars in general, are absurd. Moreover when he criticises battles (and the iniquity of war) in his capacity of author, he deprives himself of all excuse for the failure to criticise the various other immoralities he portrays. In Anna Karénine he let each character, good or bad, speak for itself; and while he might better have shown some reprobation of evil, at least it could be alleged in answer that he simply narrated, putting the facts before us that we ourselves might judge them. But when he again and again spends pages in descanting on the wickedness and folly of war, and passes over other vices without a word of reproach he certainly in so far acts as the apologist for the latter, and the general tone of the book does not seem to me to be in the least conducive to morality. Natacha is a bundle of contradictions, and her fickleness is portrayed as truly marvellous; how Pierre could ever have ventured to leave her alone for six weeks after he was married I can not imagine. Marie as portrayed by him is a girl that we can hardly conceive of as fascinating Rostow. Sonia is another variety of the patient Griselda type. The two men André and Pierre are wonderfully well drawn; and all through the book there are touches and descriptions that are simply masterpieces.

The round up has been great fun. If I did not miss all at home so much, and also my beautiful house, I should say that this free, open air life, without any worry, was perfection and I write steadily three or four days, and then hunt (I killed two elk and some antelope recently) or ride on the round up for as many more.

I send the enclose slip from a criticism of my book on account of the awful irony of the lines I have underscored; send it to Douglass when you write him. *Ever your loving brother*

"THESE HARUM-SCARUM ROUGHRIDERS"

To Henry Cabot Lodge

Medora, Dakota, August 10, 1886

Dear Cabot,

Just a line, to make a request.

I have written on to Secretary Endicott offering to try to raise some companies of horse riflemen out here in the event of trouble with Mexico. Will you telegraph me at once if war becomes inevitable? Out here things are so much behind hand that I might not hear the news for a week. I haven't the least idea there will be any trouble; but as my chance of doing anything in the future worth doing seems to grow continually smaller I intend to grasp at every opportunity that turns up.

I think there is some good fighting stuff among these harum-scarum roughriders out here; whether I can bring it out is another matter. All the boys were delighted with your photographs — except the one in which you left the saddle, which they spotted at once. They send a very cordial invitation to come out here; though they don't approve of bobtailed horses.

I sent the Benton ms. on to Morse yesterday; I hope it is decent, but lately I have been troubled with dreadful misgivings.

Remember me particularly to Nannie and tell her that the opening lines of "Childe Harold to the dark tower came" (in Browning, I mean) now always excite pensive memories in my gentle soul. *Always yours*

"CRUDE AND VICIOUS THEORIES"
To Denis Donahue Jr.

New York, October 22, 1886

Sir:

I have received the communication addressed to me by your body on Oct. 21, and am much struck by the reckless misstatements and crude and vicious theories which it contains. The mass of the American people are most emphatically not in the deplorable condition of which you speak, and the "statesmen and patriots of to-day" are no more responsible for some people being poorer than others than they are for some people being shorter, or more near-sighted, or physically weaker than others. If you had any conception of the true American spirit you would know we do not have "classes" at all on this side of the water. For example, you say I belong to

the "landlord class," whereas, in reality, I own no land at all
except that on which I myself live. Your statement that I wish
rents to be high and wages low is a deliberate untruth. Your
next statement that I would like to have all the inhabitants of
this city my tenants and wage-workers is a ridiculous untruth.
Your third statement as to what I would do in that contin-
gency is as preposterous as it is absurd. I have worked both
with hands and with head, probably quite as hard as any
member of your body. The only place where I employ many
"wage-workers" is on my ranch in the West, and there almost
every one of the men has some interest in the profits, either
because he is partly paid by a share out of them or else because
he has invested a portion of his surplus earnings in the business with me.

Some of the evils of which you complain are real and can
be to a certain degree remedied, but not by the remedies you
propose; others are imaginary, and others, though real, can
only be gotten over through that capacity for steady, individual self-help which is the glory of every true American, and
can no more be done away with by legislation than you could
do away with the bruises which you receive when you tumble
down, by passing an act to repeal the laws of gravitation. *Very
truly yours*

MARRIAGE AND THE MAYORAL RACE

To Henry Cabot Lodge

New York, November 1, 1886

Dear Cabot,

I have written Nannie telling her that on Saturday next I
sail for England to marry Edith Carow. The chief reason I was
so especially disappointed at not seeing you both this fall was
because I wished to tell you in person. You know, old fellow,
you and Nannie are more to me than any one else but my own
immediate family. The engagement is not to be announced,
nor a soul told, until the 8th.

I only pray you may succeed. Here, I have but little chance, I have made a rattling canvass, with heavy inroads on the Democratic vote; but the "timid good" are for Hewitt. Godkin, White and various others of the "better element" have acted with unscrupulous meanness and a low, partisan dishonesty and untruthfulness which would disgrace the veriest machine heelers. May Providence in due season give me a chance to get even with some of them! *Yours always*

TOURING ITALY

To Anna Roosevelt

Milan, February 12, 1887

Darling Bysie,

We ended up Venice by having a real snow storm, giving the place a very picturesque but wholly unlooked for aspect. Our stay there though short was very pleasant; there is no other Italian town that has such a charm for me — it gives me the feeling of being in the presence of vanished, old world splendour as neither Rome nor Florence does, and is tenfold as strange and romantic.

Here, also, I am very fond indeed of the Cathedral at any rate; I think it impresses me more than any other building I have ever seen, more even than St Peters (I do'n't include the old Eguptian and Greek temples) The lofty aisle, with its rows of towering columns, white and shadowy, and the fretted, delicate work above, all seen in the dim half light that comes through the stained glass windows, really awes me; it gives me a feeling I have never had elsewhere except among very wild, chasm-rent mountains, or in the vast pine forests where the trees are very tall and not too close together. I think I care more for breath, vastness, grandeur, strength, than for technique or mere grace or the qualities that need artistic sense or training to appreciate. Thus I honestly confess I do'n't care a rap for the preraphaelites except as curiosities; just as I care for the Egyptian tomb paintings; but I am very fond of the

Sistine Chapel and of Rafaels great wall paintings in the Vatican; still more of such statues as the Dying Gladiator; most of all of such very different buildings as Karnak, Baalbek, the Parthenon and this very Milan Cathedral. But perhaps on the whole I will always come back to my beloved woods and mountains and great lonely plains.

We sail from Liverpool on March 19th; I suppose I shall be about three weeks in the west soon after I return. I won't buy any claret in Paris after all.

Can you find out, without too much trouble, what furs of mine Gunther has, and in especial if he has my mink skin over coat?

I so long to see Sagamore Hill again, with my rifles, in your gun case, my heads and all. I shall fit up the top room as my study; the library is too disturbed; and so I shall have up there as my sanctum to which people are not to come — not even the guests, unless I specially invite them. With many kisses for baby, *Your loving*

"YOUR WORKS STAND ALONE"

To Francis Parkman

Oyster Bay, April 23, 1888

My dear Sir;

I suppose that every American who cares at all for the history of his own country feels a certain personal pride in your work — it is as if Motley had written about American instead of European subjects, and so was doubly our own; but those of us who have a taste for history, and yet have spent much of our time on the frontier, perhaps realize even more keenly than our fellows, that your works stand alone, and that they must be models for all historical treatment of the founding of new communities and the growth of the frontier, here in the wilderness.

This — even more than the many pleasant hours I owe you — must be my excuse for writing.

I am engaged on a work of which the first part treats of the extension to our frontier westward and southwestward during the twenty odd years from 1774 to 1796 — the years of uninterrupted Indian warfare during which Kentucky and Tennesee were founded and grew to statehood, under such men as Daniel Boone and George Rogers Clark, John Sevier, James Robertson and Isaac Shelby. I have gathered a good deal of hitherto unused material, both from the unpublished mss. of the State Department, and from the old diaries, letters and memoranda in various private libraries at Louisville, Nashville, Lexington &c.

This first part I have promised the Putnams for some time in 1889; it will be in two volumes, with such title as "The Winning of the West and Southwest," and perhaps as a subtitle "From the Alleghenies to the Mississippi."

I should like to dedicate this to you. Of course I know that you would not wish your name to be connected in even the most indirect way with any but good work; and I can only say that I will do my best to make the work creditable. William Everett, John Morse or Cabot Lodge can tell you who I am.

I do not know if you have ever seen a little series published in Boston, the "American Statesmen"; if so, the first chapter in the "Benton" will give you an idea of the outline I intend to fill up. *Yours very truly*

A POLO FALL AND A MISCARRIAGE

To Anna Roosevelt

Oyster Bay, August 8, 1888

Darling Bysie,

Your telegram was characteristic of you, you darling sister; it was just like you to send it.

Unfortunately, we will not have to take advantage of it; for Edith has just had a miscarriage. She is getting on all right now. The mischief of course came from my infernal tumble at the polo match. The tumble was nothing in itself; I have had

twenty worse; but it *looked* bad, because I was knocked perfectly limp and senseless, and though I was all right in an hour,
the mischief had been done to Edith, though we did not know
it for over a week. So I shall not go out west for a fortnight,
and perhaps not then.

Dora is our here now, and is having a great time; she loves
being with the children. We had a terrible storm a couple of
days ago, and among other feats it took the roof clean off the
bathing houses. *Your aff brother*

"A BIT OF A SPAR WITH GERMANY"

To Cecil Spring-Rice

New York, April 14, 1889

Dear Cecil,

Last fall's campaign being now a thing of the long past, I
venture to write you again. Besides, just at present our statesmen seem inclined to abandon the tail of the lion, and instead
are plucking vigorously at the caudal feathers of that delightful war-fowl, the German eagle — a cousin of our own bald-
headed bird of prey. Frankly, I do'n't know that I should be
sorry to see a bit of a spar with Germany, the burning of New
York and a few other seacoast cities would be a good object
lesson on the need of an adequate system of coast defences;
and I think it would have a good effect on our large german
population to force them to an ostentatiously patriotic display
of anger against Germany; besides, while we would have to
take some awful blows at first, I think in the end we would
worry the Kaiser a little.

Clough (who lunches here today) dined here the other
night to meet the Cleavlands Whitneys and a few other, as we
did up all our democratic friends; I doubt if he knew exactly
what to make of the ex-president. Mrs. Whitney said all sorts
of nice things about you. Whitney himself is certainly a very
able man. Harrison does not yet seem to have a very firm grip;
it is still quite on the cards that Cleavland may come in again

in '92. I think our new minister, Bob Lincoln, is a very good fellow.

By the way, when Geo Haven Putnam goes to London this spring I shall give him a note to you, though I suppose you will remember him; he is among the salt of the earth. His wife goes with him this year; she is a decidedly bright woman, but very far short of his standard in every respect — my own wife and sister dread her very presence, so you had best proceed cautiously about her. But he himself is a trump.

I hope the first two volumes of my book on the west will be out by June. By the way, do you know Andrew Lang? he must be a bright fellow.

Do come over here soon; we are all really anxious to see you again, old fellow. *Your friend*

"LITERATURE MUST BE MY MISTRESS"

To Francis Parkman

Washington, July 13, 1889

My dear Mr Parkman

I am much pleased that you like the book.

I have always had a special admiration for you as the only one — and I may very sincerely say, the greatest — of our two or three first class historians who devoted himself to American history; and made a classic work — not merely an excellent book of references like Bancroft or Hildreth. I have always intended to devote myself to essentially American work; and literature must be my mistress perforce, for though I really enjoy politics I appreciate perfectly the exceedingly short nature of my tenure. I much prefer to really accomplish something good in public life, no matter at what cost of enmity from even my political friends than to enjoy a longer term of service, fettered by endless fear, always trying to compromise, and doing nothing in the end.

I thought it really necessary to hit Gilmore a rap; his work is very dishonest. I am not quite sure how the Kentuckians and Tenneseeans will take my book; they have the dreadful habit of always writing of themselves in the superlative tense.

Mr. Draper unfortunately thinks one bit of old ms. just exactly as good as any other *Very sincerely yours*

STRUGGLING AGAINST A SEDENTARY LIFE

To Douglas and Corinne Robinson

Washington, July 28, 1889

Dear Douglass and Pussie,

I think I am very good to write you, for I have heard nothing from either of you, and I did not even know how the Orangemen had done at polo until I met Nell (poor, dear old Nell; I suppose it is useless to wish that he would put himself completely under a competent physician; I did my best to get him to). Douglass has worked his team up wonderfully; but he must always choose a first-rate man when he plays doubles. As for my polo, it is one of the things that have been; witness the enclosed check, which is for Cranford; and I am trying to sell Diamond. How I hate to give it up! Struggle as I will, my life seems to grow more and more sedentary, and I am rapidly sinking into a fat and lazy middle age. When I am home I always want to spend the time with Edith and the children; and of course what is exercise for them is not exercise for me. But our rowboat serves both purposes; Edith and I have spent lovely days in her this summer. Alicey and Ted are sweeter than ever. Ask Teddy Douglass if he remembers how I took all the children down to the pond, and made them walk out on a half sunken log, where they perched like so many sandsnipe. Small Ted never forgets me at all, even when I am away for three weeks, and dances a clumsy little tarantalla of baby-joy when I come back, and take him down to feed the ponies and see the chickies.

Putnam says my book is selling well and he thinks there will soon have to be another edition. A week from tomorrow I leave for the west. I take a mild Ferghie with me, and leave him on the ranch while I go on for a hack at the bears in the Rockies. I am so out of training that I look forward with acute physical terror to going up the first mountain.

I have mortally hated being so much away from home this summer; but I am very glad I took this place, and I have really enjoyed my work. I feel it incumbent on me to try to amount to something, either in politics or literature, because I have deliberately given up the hope of going into a money-making business. Of course however my political life is but an interlude — it is quite impossible to continue long to do much, between two sets of such kittle-cattle as the spoilsmen and the mugwumps. *Yours*

DEFENDING CIVIL SERVICE EXAMINATIONS

To William Warland Clapp

Washington, August 7, 1889

I have just been reading your interesting editorial upon competitive examinations in England, in which you speak of certain objections that have recently been brought up against the system as managed in Britain. I am keenly aware of the shortcomings inevitably attendant upon this as well as upon every other system. I do not suppose that any one believes that we are getting ideal candidates for Government positions under the new method. We see that this method has certain disadvantages. Some of these we think we can do away with, for others we have not yet found a satisfactory solution, but I most emphatically assert that with all its shortcomings the merit system is an immeasurable advance upon the old spoils system. Moreover, some of the objections that apply in England do not apply here. In reference to the objection that by the competitive system we do not get the fittest person, all I can say is that this is probably true, but we come a good deal nearer to getting the fittest than we did under the spoils system. If, for instance, Mr. Bell, the head of the railway mail service, were left absolutely free to manage that service on

purely business methods, if it were understood that no matter
how Administrations changed, that for the term of his natural life, until he become incapacitated by disease or otherwise,
and that as long as he gave satisfaction he was to be continued in charge of the service, and to be left absolutely unhampered under this and succeeding Administrations, as to
his choice of subordinates, then it would be perfectly safe to
leave this choice entirely in his own hands. But, as a matter of
fact, under the old system Mr. Bell did not appoint his subordinates at all. They were parceled out among all the Congressmen of his party, and a few other prominent politicians;
each being given so many places to fill, and each being furi-
ously indignant if any question was made as to the candidates
whom he chose. Without doubt a number of the Congressmen choose men who are most excellent public employes;
doubtless they choose them with a view to the interests of the
public service, but a very large number certainly choose them
also with a view to the political exigencies in their own districts, and the employes thus chosen naturally consider that
they owe their first duty to the politician by whom they are
appointed, and their second duty only to the public service.
One of Mr. Bell's assistants remarked to me the other day that
on the whole, since the civil service rules have been extended
to the railway mail service, the result had been very beneficial;
for they got fully as good a class of men under the new system,
and, moreover, were entirely at liberty to dismiss any of those
obtained who did not behave themselves; whereas, of those
obtained under the old method, it was necessary to take account, not only the man's misconduct, but also the nature of
his political backing, before dismissing him. The result was,
he stated, that after a few months of service those employes
furnished by the Civil Service Commission were at a positive
advantage, in point of efficiency, as compared with those furnished by the old spoils system.

The next point made in England against the system is that
the health of candidates is affected by the strain of competitive examinations. This certainly is not true here, and the difference is owing to the entirely different kinds of examinations
held in England and held here. Ninety-five per cent. of our examinations are for places like carrier, clerk and copyist. There

rtion that they were asked of some clerk or letter carrier. the other day I happened to overhear a very prominent litician from one of the Middle States openly assert, as a oof of the ridiculousness of the system, that one of the questions asked a letter carrier was, how many rings there were to Saturn. Every now and then it is necessary to answer a fool according to his folly, and as a bet seems to be the only argument that some people understand, I offered this gentleman to bet him one hundred dollars to ten, or similar odds in any shape he chose, that he could not show that such a question had ever been asked a letter carrier, clerk or copyist. He declined to bet. At first he insisted that his statement was true, then gradually admitted that it was made by a friend and that he thought it was true, and finally confessed that he was uncertain about the whole matter. As a matter of fact he had taken a question asked in an examination for assistant astronomers, and spoke as if it was asked a carrier.

The third point, that competitive examinations for the public service injure the educational system, certainly does not apply in America for the very reasons given above. For as far as our examinations are not tests of a man's general good sense, they are simple tests of such knowledge as he would now get in our common schools.

My four months in Washington have made me more than ever a most zealous believer in the merit system. I do not see how any man can watch the effects of the spoils system, both upon the poor unfortunates who suffer from it and upon the almost equally unfortunate men who deem that they benefit by it, without regarding the whole thing in its entirety as a curse to our institutions. It is a curse to the public service and it is a still greater curse to Congress, for it puts a premium upon every Congressman turning spoilsmonger instead of statesman. A large number of our Congressmen remain statesmen, and do most admirable work, but it is in spite of not because of the spoils system.

In conclusion, let me as a straightout Republican and a strong civil service reformer thank The Journal most heartily for the invaluable assistance it has rendered and is rendering the merit system and the Republican party. I firmly believe that patronage is the one thing which just at present en-

is comparatively little chance for cram[...]
nations. The examinations are perfectly s[...]
practical character already, and we are try[...]
more practical day by day. A bright, sharp, [...]
usually about thirty years old, is shown by tha[...]
experience, to be the man most apt to succeed i[...]
nations. The boy fresh from school or college doe[...]
so good a chance. This is contrary, as I am well awar[...]
statements usually made by the interested advocates of [...]
spoils system; but it is conclusively shown to be the truth[...]
our records, by which it appears that the average age of su[...]
cessful candidates is thirty-one years. We lay great stress, for
instance, upon the kind of letter a candidate writes; and in
writing such a letter a man's general sense and intelligence are
the things that count. It would be quite impossible for him to
cram up on such a subject. So in examining for the railway
mail service, very great weight is put upon a person's skill and
quickness in reading addresses from a package of cards. This
is a practical test in the very line of the man's duty, and not a
subject on which much can be accomplished by cramming. So
with the copyist or clerk, very great stress is laid on penman-
ship, and here again the man cannot cram. The questions in
spelling and arithmetic are of a perfectly simple nature, and
while cramming here could do something, again the general
intelligence will count for more. We think it right that every
American citizen who wants to enter the public service should
know a little about the geography and history of his native
land, and our questions on these points are perfectly simple,
and the total mark to be given for them counts for but five per
cent of the whole. So that even if a man failed on them utterly
he could still get ninety-five per cent, on the examination.
There are, of course, a few positions like that of assistant astronomer, or of assistant geologist, or of computer in the nau-
tical almanac office, where very special knowledge is needed.
Here we examine men on abstruse and difficult subjects, such
as astronomy, geology and the calculus. In no other way could
we get the men we need. But these examinations form an insignificant fraction of the whole. One of the most common
forms that the attack on the merit system takes is the quotation of questions asked in these special examinations with the

dangers Republican supremacy, and as a citizen and as a party man alike I feel that I and those who think as I do owe a positive debt of gratitude to The Journal for the stand it has taken. *Very truly yours*

DEFENDING "THE WINNING OF THE WEST"

To Charles A. Dana

Washington, September 25, 1889

Sir:

In your issue of last Sunday there appeared a letter signed "Cumberland," occupying four columns of your valuable space. As one or two of it's misstatements seem to need an answer, I may as well reply to the others also; and I respectfully request that you print this letter in your next Sunday edition, that the refutation may circulate as widely as the original document.

Cumberland's letter is nominally a criticism of my "Winning of the West"; it is really written on behalf of Edmund Kirke (James R. Gilmore), in an effort, more malevolent than successful, to take vengeance because in my book I was forced, much against my will, to demolish the very unsubstantial structures which it had pleased Mr. Kirke to style "histories" of the early Tennesee leaders.

I will not touch upon Cumberland's expressions of opinion, for his opinion is to me a matter of profound indifference; but I will discuss his statements of fact seriatim.

In the first place, in his entire four columns he is able to produce just two errors that I have committed — once in speaking of the diameter, instead of the circumference, of a tree, and once in alluding to the novelist Kennedy as Robert L. instead of John P. Of course these were both mere slips of the pen, which have already been corrected in my second edition, now out or about to come out.

His first column is occupied mainly with quotations to prove that I criticised unfavorably portions of the writings of the western historians. He omits the favorable criticisms; and his historical and critical knowledge is evidently much too limited for him to see that every criticism I have made is absolutely just. He sums up by saying that I "cast aside as worthless" the work of my predecessors. This is a falsehood. I have merely done what neither Cumberland, nor yet his alter ego Edmund Kirke, is capable of doing — that is I have discriminated between narratives that are true and narratives that are false, and, in the same narrative, between the parts that are trustworthy and those that are not.

He then comes to the defence of Mr. Gilmore, complaining that I let off Ramsey "scot free," and yet distrust the accuracy of Gilmore "who assumes to be scarcely more than the mouthpiece of Ramsey"; and, again, that I "stigmatize as 'oral tradition gathered one hundred years after the event' information which Mr. Gilmore expressly declares that he derived from" Ramsey. In the first place even accepting Mr. Gilmore's modest claim to be only a mouthpiece, there is a world of difference between the credit attaching to the statements made by Ramsey in his history, with the original documents before him, and the credit to be given statements by the "mouth piece" which he asserts are based on what he was told by Ramsey when the latter was ninety years old about matters that happened long before those ninety years had begun. In the next place, the "mouthpiece" claim is a mere afterthought. Mr. Gilmore's own words, in the preface to his first volume, are: "a large part of my material I have derived from what may be termed original sources — old settlers, whose statements I have carefully verified and compared with one another." In other words a large part of his material is oral tradition gathered a hundred years after the event.

In his next column Cumberland comes to the material on which I base much of my book. Concerning this he says "The truth is that of the manuscripts and documents which he (Mr. Roosevelt) enumerates as unpublished there is not one that has not been repeatedly examined by historians, and no fact of any historical importance is contained in any one of them which has not been already published. A claim made at this late date to the discovery or use of any valuable original document relating to early Tennesee or Kentucky is, on the face of it, too absurd for serious refutation." Choosing almost at random from among the many manuscripts which I quote in my book, I now challenge Cumberland to specify the printed history of date prior to my own in which is to be found for instance the journal of Floyds first trip to Kentucky, or the original account, as I give it, of the treaty of the Sycamore Shoals, or the petition for the erection of Kentucky and Illinois into a state in 1780, or the account of Hamilton's march from Detroit to Vincennes, or the original journal of Clark's siege of Vincennes, (which was intercepted by the British), or the journal of Hickman's visit to Kentucky, or the letters from Colbert and Cameron in reference to the Chero- kee wars in Tennesee, or Colbert's letter about the flotilla which went down the Tennesee eight months before Donel- son's, or the British partisan McKee's account of the fights with Floyd and Squire Boone, or the British official reports of the Battle of the Blue Licks and the seiges of Boonsboro and Bryants Station, or the petition of the French creoles to Congress, etc., etc., etc. If he can not specify the histories wherein these, and many others like them, (such as the accounts in the Virginia State Papers of Seviers campaigns, and in the American archives of the Cherokee campaigns of 1776) are to be found — and I well know that he can not so specify — then I denounce him as having penned a deliberate falsehood.

Cumberland goes on to speak of Collin's history, and says "In Collins work may be found all the facts which Mr. Roo- sevelt credits to the McAfee manuscripts and also all that are contained in what he calls the Campbell manuscripts which have any reference to either Tennesee or Kentucky." Again choosing almost at random I challenge him to name the volume and page of Collins wherein are to be found the facts concerning the McAfees' characteristic adventure with the es- caped bondservant, or with the buffalos at the lick, or the ac- count of the attack on Piqua, or their census of Kentucky in 1777, all of which I give from the McAfee manuscripts; or Arthur Campbell's account of the battle of Boyd's Creek, or David Campbell's account of the Holston settlers, or the let- ters of Preston and Shelby concerning the battle of the Great Kanawha, which I take from the Campbell manuscripts. If

Cumberland can not so specify volume and page — and of course he can not — I denounce him as having penned another deliberate falsehood.

Cumberland then devotes a column to irrelevant matter concerning the historians Ramsey and Haywood, ending with an unimportant misstatement, carefully put in vague language, concerning my relations to Putnam's history.

He then has an enigmatical sentence about the American State Papers, which I do not use at all in my two published volumes; I presume he refers to what I have called the State Department Mss, of which he apparently does not so much as know the existence. I again challenge him to specify the places where the documents I quote (such as the letters of Colbert, Tait, the Creoles etc) are printed.

Following this comes a delicious bit of unconscious humour; for with comic gravity Cumberland puts aside the Haldimand manuscripts as "merely the British account of events that have been often told and no doubt as truthfully by American writers." He is evidently in full sympathy with the famous judge who refused to hear the evidence except on one side, for fear it would unsettle his convictions.

He ends his third column by discussing the Gardoqui papers, to which I merely alluded in my printed volumes. In my next two volumes I shall discuss them at length, and I may mention incidentally that when I come to the couple already printed by Mr. Kirke I shall also discuss an antic of Mr. Kirke in the way of history making which is even more noteworthy than any on which I have hitherto touched.

So far all that Cumberland asserts can be shown to be false from my book itself. I have met him on every point he has raised, have made the issue specific, and have challenged him to show that what he says is true. His assertions are sweeping generalities; so in each instance I have given him a number of definite cases; and each instance admits of a definite answer. If his assertions are true then he can point out the book and the page where the documents which I have specified above are to be found; and if he can not point them out (and most assuredly he can not) then he stands convicted of repeated and deliberate falsehoods. Let him answer definitely one way or the other; and let him answer over his own name, and no longer skulk behind a thin disguise — for there is no difficulty in guessing who he really is.

But in his fourth column he makes a charge which there might be difficulty in answerring from the printed volumes alone; and it is solely because of this that I have answered his article at all. The charge is in substance that the most valuable part of my book was not written by me but by some person unknown. It is a charge which if true would convict me of gross deceit; and which, as it is false, stamps the maker as a person unfit to associate with any honorable man.

He wishes to show that I did not begin to work on the book until too late to really write it; and he begins with the gratuitous falsehood that I did not visit Tennesee until late in September 1888. In reality I visited it in March, and did not go there again during that year. He continues "It would have been simply impossible for him (Mr. Roosevelt) to do what he claims to have done in the time that was at his disposal. . . . The most that could have been done in that brief period was to submit the completed manuscripts on proof sheets already composed from printed authorities to some western scholar familiar with the original documents and to employ him to verify the facts and incidents by a comparison with the old manuscripts. This was probably the course pursued, and the evidence of it is in the notes of the book themselves, which supply very many facts not in the text of the book — facts that would naturally have found place there had both text and notes been written by the same hand." I hereby offer a thousand dollars, which I will pay at once to Cumberland, or Edmund Kirke or Mr. Gilmore or any one else who can show that the above statement is true, in whole or in part, about so much as a single page of my book; or to any one who can show that ten lines of it, notes or text, were written by any one but myself. I wrote it all either in New York, or at my Long Island home, with before me, as I worked at each chapter, the original manuscripts, or exact copies of them, or else the rough notes and abstracts I had myself made of them. As well as I recollect no man saw a line of it until it was printed, except the publishers and possibly my friend Cabot Lodge. The matter is fortunately easily settled. The original manuscript of the book is still in the hands of the Publishers, the Messrs Putnams, 27 West 23d St New York; a glance at it will be sufficient to show that from the first chapter to the last the text and notes are by the same hand and written at the same time. I shall be pleased to have any reputable man whom the Editor of the Sun may designate call and examine the manuscript.

I challenge Cumberland to come out over his own name and substantiate his charge — a charge all the meaner because it is as much inuendo as direct assertion; and until he does thus substantiate it I brand him as a coward who dares not sign his name to the lying slander he has penned.

CONTINUING A CONTROVERSY

To Charles A. Dana

Washington, October 10, 1889

Sir:

In last Sunday's edition of the Sun, Mr. Jas. R. Gilmore at length casts aside his various aliases and appears over his own proper signature; and I must trespass on your space to answer him.

Mr. Gilmore's attack was nominally a criticism of my "Winning of the West," but in reality an effort to avenge himself for a private grievance. This he practically acknowledges by devoting one of the two columns which his last letter occupies solely to a correspondence that took place between himself and myself. This has no bearing whatever on the accuracy of my work or the inaccuracy of his; but I shall discuss it briefly before taking up the more important matters.

As I distinctly stated in the appendix to volume I of my work I was at the outset, when I first read them, charmed with Mr. Gilmore's books. I had then no suspicion of their utter untrustworthiness, and I wrote freely to Mr. Gilmore. As soon as I came to study them I found that if I intended to write an honest book I would needs have to condemn his as dishonest; and I then instantly ceased all communication with him, and have never written him since: the fact is simply that in preparing my book I wrote to some hundreds of men all over the country, requesting information on different points. A few of these men answered me refusing the information; a great many did not answer at all. Others answered promising me what I asked; I thanked them most warmly; and when the assistance was actually given (as by Judge Lea, Col. Durrett, Col. Brown, Mr. Warfield, etc. etc. etc.) I specifically acknowledged my obligations in my book. Yet others promised assistance in even heartier terms; again I thanked them warmly, and when they failed to make good their promises I simply said nothing more about it, one way or the other. Mr. Gilmore comes in the latter class. He promised me more than any other correspondent I had; he utterly failed to keep his promise. Literally all he did was to forward me a letter to Judge Lea, to whom I had already written, and who had already answered my letter promising me every assistance in his power — a promise which unlike Mr. Gilmore he kept. When I forwarded him Mr. Gilmore's letter he wrote back that it was quite needless. When I first read Mr. Gilmore's books I was already familiar with the printed Tennesee histories, and I hailed Mr. Gilmore as a writer who was doing a really remarkable work; for I saw at a glance that he had introduced a mass of material that was not to be found in the old histories, and it never occurred to me for a moment that this new material was invented. I supposed that he must have a quantity of newly found manuscripts, and, as his own books were of sketchy character, I thought he might be willing to let me have such of these manuscripts as he was not going to use. The exact words of my request were, as he quotes them, for the "material for which you no longer have use, that on which you in part based your life of Sevier and your recent sketch of Robertson." In response Mr. Gilmore wrote promising with the utmost effusiveness that he would place at my disposal "all his material." I was extremely pleased and very grateful, and wrote a most warm letter of thanks. Then I waited patiently several weeks, but never received the promised material, and never found it in any of the depositaries through which I hunted; and gradually it dawned on me that he could not keep his promise to give me the new matter for the very good reason that the new matter did not exist. Mr. Gilmore never sent me a page or a document of any kind, he never gave me any information that I did not already have, or which, on being followed up did not prove worthless, he never sent me a line to any one in Kentucky; literally all he did was to send me a letter to Judge Lea with whom I was already in correspondence, and to promise me very valuable aid which he never gave. When he so freely made me this promise I supposed of course that he both could and would keep it; and I thanked him in the heartiest languge I could muster. My thanks proved to have been wasted; and when I found this out I kept silent; but I certainly did not feel under any obligations to falsify history so that his own falsifications might pass uncondemned. In order to write truthfully it was necessary to prick Mr. Gilmore's historical bubble; and accordingly I pricked it in passing. He well knows that he can not answer a single criticism I have made on his books. Be it remembered that the criticisms are neither vague nor general; they are definite and precise, challenging Mr. Gilmores truthfulness, and to leave them unanswered is to confess the absolute untrustworthiness of what it has pleased his fancy to call "histories" of early Tennesee events.

Now, to come down to Mr. Gilmore's criticism of my "Winning of the West." His vague general charges I must perforce content myself with merely denying. For instance he says that when I come to Tennesee matters my book is a mere "rewriting" of the older Tennesee histories. This charge is a simple falsehood. Some of my chapters, as chapter VII of volume I, and chapters XI and XII of vol II, are based mainly, though by no means exclusively, on the old Tennesee historians; and this I expressly and fully state, on pp 170 and 185 of vol I, and pp 342, 348, 355 and 364 of vol II. In other chapters, as VII, IX, and XI of vol I, and X, of vol II, the old writers are a hindrance rather than a help, and I had to carefully unravel their errors, show the inaccuracy of their statements and for the first time give the real history, basing it on the original documents in the American Archives, the Campbell Mss, the Virginia State Papers, etc. If Mr. Gilmore were a competent critic he would know this; were he an honest one he would say it. As for his assertion that I copy from his works some "facts" which are to be found nowhere else, if he will point them out I will not only be surprised but grateful, and will promptly proceed to strike them from my pages; for I do not wish my book to contain any "facts" that are not authentic.

But I have no idea of letting Mr. Gilmore take refuge, as he seeks to, in generalities. He made certain sweeping and definite statements; I promptly furnished a number of instances by which their truth or falsehood could be tested; and to these I intend to pin him. He first stated that every single document I quoted that was of any historical importance was already to be found in the printed histories. I instantly named a dozen, challenging him to tell in what printed history they were to be found. This he does not even attempt to do; but makes a rambling series of really very funny excuses. He first says I only furnish a "meagre list" of examples. I gave him a dozen; I could quite as easily have given him a hundred; but a dozen was enough to convict him of untruth just twelve times over. He says that the hitherto unknown British accounts of the different battles are unimportant because "they are probably not more truthful than the American." On the same principle Grant's official reports would be valueless because "probably not more truthful than Lee's." Similarly he deems the letters of the British Indian agents valueless because the pioneers would like to have hanged the men who wrote them! Really Mr. Gilmore's mental processes seem to be akin to those of the White Queen in Alice Through the Looking Glass. It makes one almost ashamed to be in a controversy with him. There is a half-pleasurable excitement in facing an equal foe; but there is none whatever in trampling on a weakling.

On the first count Mr Gilmore thus stands guilty on his own showing. It is exactly so with the next, which relates to his similar statements about the State Department Mss. He simply shuffles round. For instance in answer to the challenge to point out the printed volume containing the letters I quote from Colbert he says Colbert took no part in the Cherokee wars until 1792. If he will turn to pages 89 and 334 of my second volume he will see he was taking a very active part in 1779.

As regards Mr Gilmore's similar charge about the matter I quoted from the Macafee and Campbell papers being in Collins

I gave him eight instances. As to five of these he makes no effort to show that he told the truth, and thereby admits that he did not. But for the remaining three quotations he gives references in Collins. I shall set him a good and much needed example by at once acknowledging that in one case, that of the escaped bondservant, his reference is right. Again in the second case, that of the buffalos at the lick the adventure as given in Collins is somewhat but not very markedly different from the adventure as quoted by me from the original mss. In the third, and very much the most important, case, the fight at Piqua, Mr Gilmore deliberately seeks to cover up his first misstatement by giving false references. I for the first time described the fight at length and in detail, making much use of the McAfee mss; Mr. Gilmores references are not to quotations from the McAfee mss. at all, but merely to bare notices of the fight, a couple of lines in length, such as all the Kentucky historians, from Filson down, had already given. That the two accounts have but the slightest relation to one another can be seen by turning to the references Mr. Gilmore gives, Collins, II, pp. 138, 139 & 449, and then to my account in the "Winning of the West," volume II, page 104 to 111.

Therefore Mr. Gilmore fails to clear himself on any one of my counts; and so by his second letter he stands convicted of having penned a string of untruths in his first.

I now finally come to his most serious charge, which was in effect that I had not written my book myself, but that the most important part must be by "another hand." I promptly met this perfectly gratuitious slander by offerring Mr. Gilmore a thousand dollars if he could prove it, in whole or in part, of so much as a single page. I also offerred to have the manuscript, which is at the Messrs. Putnams examined by any responsible man the Sun's Editor might name, to show that the text and notes are written at the same time and by the same hand, or else any one who wishes can write Mr. Geo. Haven Putnam on the subject and publish his reply. From the first line to the last every word was written by me. Mr. Gilmore makes no effort whatever to substantiate his accusation in his second letter. He simply says it was "impossible" for me to write my book in the time elapsing after my return from Tennesee in March. As a matter of fact I began the actual writing somewhere about the first of May, and finished the second volume about the first of April following, when much of the first volume was already in press; two months or over were taken out, while I was away on my ranch, or on the stump in the political campaign; so that the actual writing occupied a scant nine months — and a good part of the time I reproached myself for idleness. Of course my rough notes and manuscripts were already carefully arranged when I began and I had been for years saturating myself with the subject.

I therefore speak with guarded moderation when I denounce Mr. Gilmore for having penned a particularly mean and malicious falsehood. Is Mr. Gilmore ignorant of the ordinary rules of common decency and common honesty? Does he not know that to make so foul and wanton an accusation, and then to fail to back it up by so much as a scintilla of proof, is to brand himself as infamous? Out of his own mouth he stands convicted; and henceforth all honorable men are warranted in treating any statement he may make with contemptuous indifference.

PRAISE FOR "A NAVAL CLASSIC"

To Alfred Thayer Mahan

Washington, May 12, 1890

My dear Captain Mahan,

During the last two days I have spent half my time, busy as I am, in reading your book, and that I found it interesting is shown by the fact that having taken it up I have gone straight through and finished it.

I can say with perfect sincerity that I think it very much the clearest and most instructive general work of the kind with which I am acquainted. It is a *very* good book — admirable; and I am greatly in error if it does not become a naval classic. It shows the faculty of grasping the meaning of events and their relations to one another and of taking in the whole situation. I wish the portions dealing with commerce destroying could be put in the hands of some of the friends of a navy, and that the whole book could be placed where it could be read by the navy's foes, especially in congress. You must read the two volumes of Henry Adams history dealing with the war of 1812 when they come out. He is a man of infinite research, and his ideas are usually (with some very marked exceptions) excellent.

With sincere congratulations I am *Very cordially yours*

FAMILY LIFE

To Gertrude Tyler Carow

Washington, October 18, 1890

My dear Mrs. Carow,

I have rarely seen Edith enjoy anything more than she did the six days at my ranch, and the trip through the Yellowstone Park; and she looks just as well and young and pretty and happy as she did four years ago when I married her — indeed I sometimes almost think she looks if possible even sweeter and prettier, and she is as healthy as possible, and so young looking and slender to be the mother of those two sturdy little scamps, Ted and Kermit. We have had a lovely year, though we have minded being away from Sagamore so much; but we greatly enjoyed our winter at Washington, and our months trip out west was the crowning touch of all. Edith particularly enjoyed the riding at the ranch, where she had an excellent little horse, named wire fence, and the strange, wild, beautiful scenery, and the loneliness and freedom of the life fascinated and appealed to her as it did to me. Did she write to you that I shot a deer once while we were riding together? Are not you and Emily coming over here next summer? It will be over two years since you have seen Edith; and Kermit will be older than Ted was when you left. Of course I do not know what your plans are, nor how you find it necessary to shape them; but I should think that any extra expense entailed by the voyage over and back would be made up by the fact that you would be at Sagamore pretty much all the time you were here. Edith does want to see you both very much. If there are two ponies here she and Emily could ride together while I was away.

The children are darlings. Alice has grown more and more affectionate, and is devoted to, and worshipped by, both the boys; Kermie holds out his little arms to her whenever she comes near, and she really takes care of him like a little mother. Ted eyes him with some suspicion; and when I take the wee fellow up in my arms Ted clings tightly to one of my legs, so that I can hardly walk. Kermie crawls with the utmost rapidity; and when he is getting towards some forbidden spot and we call to him to stop Ted always joins in officiously and overtaking the small yellow-haired wanderer seizes him with his chubby hands round the neck and trys to drag him back — while the enraged Kermie endeavours in vain to retaliate. Kermie is a darling little fellow, so soft and sweet. As for blessed Ted he is just as much of a comfort as he ever was. I think he really loves me, and when I come back after an absence he greets me with wild enthusiasm, due however, I fear, in great part to knowledge that I am sure to have a large paper bundle of toys — which produces the query of "Fats in de bag," while he dances like an expectant little bear. When I come in to afternoon tea he and Alice sidle hastily round to my chair, knowing that I will surreptitiously give them all the icing off the cake, if I can get Edith's attention attracted elsewhere; and every evening I have a wild romp with them, usually assuming the rôle of "a very big bear" while they are either little bears, or "a raccoon and a badger, papa." Ted has a most warm, tender, loving little heart; but I think he is a manly little fellow too. In fact I take the utmost possible enjoyment out of my three children; and so does Edith.

I really enjoy my work as Civil Service Commissionner; but of course it has broken up all my literary work. *Faithfully yours*

RESPONDING TO A SENATOR'S "UNTRUTHS"

To Arthur Gorman

Washington, March 1, 1891

Sir:

On Feb. 23d last you commented with some temper upon me for having in a letter to you, and also in public speeches "called you to account very severely" for what you said on the floor of the Senate, a couple of years ago, in criticising the action of the Civil Service Commission; and you further remarked that you had at the time "sought to correct a great evil" which had arisen owing to our "stupidity"; and that I had "gone beyond the bounds of propriety" and been guilty of "audacity" because as you said, I had found fault with you for having "attempted to correct the defects growing out of (the Commissioners) want of ability to enforce the Civil Service law in a practical and fair way." You added that you had neither answered nor taken any notice of my letter, deeming my action outrageous and insolent.

Permit me to refresh your memory as to the facts in the case. In a speech in the Senate in 1889 you criticised the alleged extraordinary and impractical questions which the Commission propounded to applicants and gave an account of a (purely imaginary) "outrage" perpetrated by our local board in Baltimore upon a friend of yours "a bright young man" who tried to pass the letter carriers' examination. You said "They wanted him to tell them what was the most direct route from Baltimore to Japan, and, as he said, he never intended to go to Japan, he had never looked into that question, and he failed to make the proper answer. They then wanted to know the number of lines of steamers plying between the United States and Liverpool or London. . . . They then branched him off into geometry. . . and passing over everything that looked to his qualifications he was rejected." There is not one word of truth in this statement from beginning to end; each individual assertion is a falsehood. No such questions and none even remotely resembling them have ever been asked in any of our examinations for letter carriers, whether at Baltimore or elsewhere. In these as in all our other examinations the questions asked are practical and are relevant to the duties to be performed in the place sought for.

Later in the same year you substantially reiterated these statements in interviews in the press and they were widely quoted and used as arguments against the Commission. Your high official position, which gave them currency and credence, made it imperative that they should be answered.

As there was not a word of truth in your allegations it was evident either that you were wilfully stating what you knew to be false, or else that you had been grossly deceived by your friend "the bright young man." I acted on the latter supposition, and wrote you a perfectly respectful letter, pointing out that we had never asked any such questions as you alleged, and offerring to show all the letter carrier examination papers we had ever used either to you, or if you had not the time, to some one whom you might appoint to examine them at his leisure. You received this letter but never answered it. Be it remembered that my offer to you to examine all our letter carriers' examination papers is still open. Or you can give us the name of the "bright young man," if he has any name, or if you have forgotten his name, you can state to us the time at which he was examined, and we will send to you or make public any examination papers we then used.

It was then evident, after you refused to answer and failed to retract your statements, that whether you had originally erred through ignorance or not you had no intention of withdrawing the untruths you had utterred. The only course left me was to publish an authoritative and flat contradiction of your statement, with an account of my dealings with you. This was the course I followed. That it should have irritated you I do not wonder. Your position was not a pleasant one, and it is no pleasanter now. *Yours*

REREADING CHAUCER

To Thomas Raynesford Lounsbury

April 28, 1892

My Dear Mr. Lounsbury:

The praise of a layman can count but little in relation to a book on a subject requiring special and peculiar knowledge. Still, I cannot refrain from writing you to tell you how much I have enjoyed your "Chaucer." Of course there were parts that would appeal most to the professed scholar of Chaucer's works, but much the greater part of each of your three volumes cannot but please even the multitude like myself, not only because of the extremely interesting matter which they contain, but because of the delightful style in which they are written. But having just reread Chaucer in consequence of your book, I must protest a little against some of his tales, on the score of cleanliness. It seems to me that the prologue to the Sompnour's tale, and the tale itself, for instance, are very nearly indefensible. There are parts of them which will be valuable to the student of the manners of the age simply from the historical standpoint, but as literature I don't think they have a redeeming feature. On the other hand, I must confess that it was only on account of what you had said that I ever cared for the prologue to the tale of the wife of Bath and the tale itself. I have always regarded them with extreme disfavor, knowing that, as a matter of fact, among the men I knew, of every ten who had read them nine had done so for improper reasons; but after reading what you said I took them up and read them from a changed point of view, and am now a convert to your ideas.

Did you see the *Atlantic* review of your book? I was much amused at the start of horror the reviewer gave at your eminently wise proposition in relation to the modernization of the spelling. Your touch about the extra "u" in words like honor was delicious.

By the way, I was a little irritated at the extreme colonialism of *Harper's Weekly* in congratulating you, and America generally, upon the favorable article in the *Saturday Review*.

Hoping soon to have the pleasure of meeting you again, I am, *Cordially yours*

TEACHING DEVOTION TO THE FLAG

To Osborne Howes

Washington, May 5, 1892

My Dear Sir:

I have just received your letter and the cut of the editorial, for which please accept my thanks. I was already familiar with the editorial. It is a little difficult to answer you, my dear sir, when you ask for my candid opinion of the editorial, taken as a whole, without seeming to use harsh language. Yet, as you have requested an answer, and as I can answer but in one way, I will say that it does seem to me that the views expressed in that editorial are very, very unfortunate and I should feel a pretty lively despair of the future of our country if I believed that these views had obtained any great currency among our best classes. I think them especially dangerous because of the character of the constituency which is appealed to through so influential a paper as the Boston *Herald*. As far as the school question is concerned would you permit me to refer you to an excellent article on the youthful tenement house population of New York, written by Mr. Jacob Riis, in the last *Scribner's*, if I remember right? He therein incidentally mentions the use of the flag in our schools, and I think shows very clearly what a good thing it is. If there is one thing more than another which we need to have impressed upon the children of immigrants who come hither it is that they must forget their Old World national antipathies and become purely Americanized, and in no way can this result be better achieved than by teaching them early a genuine and fervid devotion to the flag. I very firmly believe that if you could persuade our people that the flag is nothing but a mere textile fabric, and that there should be no acceptance of it as a symbol and ideal that you would have gone a long way to darken the future of this country. We emphatically do want to get rid of all foreign influence. We want to make our children feel, as they ought to feel, that the mere fact of being American citizens makes them better off than if they were citizens of any European country. This is not to blind us at all to our own shortcomings; we ought steadily to try to correct them; but we have absolutely no ground to work on if we don't have a firm and ardent Americanism at the bottom of everything. It may possibly be that patriotism is only a middle stage in the development of mankind precisely as it may possibly be that this is true of property and marriage. Mr. Winwood Reade, for instance, very strongly insisted in his later scientific works that the custom of monogamous marriage was reprehensible and showed great selfishness, and that as the race became really unselfish it would drop it. I need hardly mention the innumerable men, of excellent intentions, who believe that property is theft. At the same time, as things now are, I regard the man who holds up to admiration adultery and robbery, for instance, as being but an indifferent moral teacher. In the same way, I feel that the lack of patriotism shows an absolutely fatal defect in any national character. I don't think that the present age is in danger of suffering from too little breadth in its estimate of humanity. I think, on the contrary, that we suffer altogether too much from the ill-regulated milk and water philanthropy which makes us degrade or neglect our own people by paying too much attention to the absolutely futile task of trying to raise humanity at large. Our business is with our own nation, with our own people. If we can bring up the United States we are doing well; yet we can't bring it up unless we teach its citizens to regard the country, and the flag which symbolizes that country, with the most genuine fervor of enthusiastic love. Frankly, I think that the denationalized philanthropist who does not regard his country in a different way from the way he regards all other countries is in a fair way to lose all the robuster virtues. If he thinks his country is not as good as some other countries let him go and live in one of the latter; but if he believes, as I believe, and as I feel most people who live here do and ought to believe, that America is, on the whole, a notch higher in the scale than any other country, and an infinite number of notches higher than most other countries, he had better allow his feelings to have fair expression.

I do not think that there is anything that so tends to minimize the influence of the highly educated classes in this country as does the queer lack of Americanism which occasionally appears among them. From Washington and Lincoln to Parkman and Lowell no man has ever been able to do a stroke of work worth doing who did not do it merely purely as an American, and at a time when he was saturated through and through with the most ultra-American spirit of patriotism.

With great respect, *Very truly yours*

IDEAS FOR MAGAZINE ARTICLES

To Richard Watson Gilder

Washington, April 1, 1893

Dear Gilder:

Lodge came to me the other day with the proposal that he and I jointly write an article for the *Century* upon what the last census has shown concerning immigration, — that is, the distribution of the immigrants throughout the country, with the curious differences shown in the different localities to which the different races go, the number of paupers and criminals that they furnish, and the general bearing of the statistics upon the problem of controlling immigration. Would you care for such an article, and if you do care for it would you care to publish it within a reasonable length of time? The census of course is not an annual serial story, but still the lessons it teaches grow less valuable the further one goes from the date of its publication. In the next place, on my own hook, I have simmering in my mind an article which I thought I would like to submit to you apropos of the recent comparison by Andrew Lang, wherein he said it was "not critical" to speak of a certain three verses of Lowell's magnificent war poetry as better than any three verses of the *Song of Roland* for instance. Now, of course they *are* infinitely better, and I thought I might use this as a text to speak of the fetiches of the irrational adoration of things merely because they are old, using certain of Lowell's poetry and two or three of the speeches of Abraham Lincoln, and possibly one or two of the fights in Napier's *Peninsular War*, as illustrating what I mean. There is nothing in Demosthenes or Cicero which comes up to Lincoln's Gettysburg speech and second inaugural, and I don't believe there is much that surpasses the speeches of Burke and Webster. My idea would be to have an article of four or five pages in length only. Would this be enough in your line to warrant my setting to work on it and submitting the piece to you to reject or accept? I wish you would ask your brother, by the way, whether he received something I sent to him for the *Critic* in reference to the *Sewanee Review*. I haven't had any answer to it.

I suppose my cowboyland article will be out in your May number, will it not? From what Putnams write me I gather that their book will be ready sometime in May. However, of course, it could be put off until the first of June. *Cordially yours*

TAXONOMIC QUESTIONS

To Madison Grant

Washington, March 3, 1894

My Dear Grant:

Many thanks for your letter. I am at present at work on the third and fourth volumes of my *Winning of the West*, but they will only take me down through Wayne's victory and the treaties of Jay and Pinckney. The next volumes I take up I hope will be the Texan struggle and the Mexican War. I quite agree with your estimate of these conflicts, and am surprised that they have not received more attention.

I think your suggestion for an article for our next volume just the thing, and I am almost sorry I have you on the moose article now, for I would like to start you at it; but don't you think you and I and Grinnell could get the article on the names of our game up together and have it put in unsigned as editorial matter?

Our species certainly are distinct from those of Europe as a rule; but speaking scientifically, I think you will find I am correct in what I say of their close relationship. The best zoologists nowadays put North America in with North Asia and Europe as one arctogeal province, separate from the South American, Indian, Australasian, and South African provinces, which have equal rank. Our moose, Wapiti, bear, beaver, wolf, etc., differ more or less from those of the Old World but the difference sinks into insignificance when compared with the differences between all these forms, Old World and New, from the tropical forms south of them. The wapiti is undoubtedly entirely distinct from the European red deer; but I don't think the difference is as great as between the black-tail and white-tail deer. It's normal form of antler is, as you describe, six points, all on the same plan, without any cup on top, and the fourth or dagger point having a prominence which it does not have at all in the European red deer; but occasionally, especially in Oregon and Washington, elk are found with this cup, and when a rather undersized Oregon elk possessing this cup is compared with one of the big red deer of Asia Minor, which are considerably larger than those of Europe, the difference is less by a good deal than the difference between the black-tail and white-tail. But all of these points can very interestingly be treated in the article to which you refer; and, as I say, I think it would be admirable, and we must certainly adopt it and put it into execution. Do send me your moose piece as soon as you can. *Cordially yours*

P.S. The moose, caribou and wapiti, for instance are very close indeed to their old-world relatives, when either are compared with the South American or Indian deer.

DINNER WITH KIPLING

To Anna Roosevelt

Washington, April 1, 1894

Darling Bye,

Your letters are just dear. Do tell us about all the funny people you meet; and do you see anything of the Fergies? Last Monday the Kiplings came to dinner, with the Brooks Adams,

Langley, Miss Pauncefote, Willie Phillips & Emily Tuckerman. It was very pleasant. Kipling is an underbred little fellow, with a tendency to criticise America to which I put a stop by giving him a very rough handling, since which he has not repeated the offence; but he is a genius, and is very entertaining. His wife is fearful however.

I had to go to Philadelphia for a couple of days, on a fruitless investigation. My 4th volume is making laboriously painful progress.

Yesterday, Sunday, Edith and I, with Ted, Alice, John Lodge, and various assorted friends took a long scramble up Rock Creek. Edith walked so well, and felt so well, that it was a pleasure to see her. Over some of the worst rocks I let down the children with a rope; and did much climbing myself. The spring is later than I have ever seen it in Washington.

Tell Helen how we all look forward to seeing her for a good long visit at Sagamore. *Your loving brother*

MODERN WARFARE

To Charles Henry Pearson

Washington, May 11, 1894

Dear Sir,

I take the liberty of forwarding you herewith a copy of the *Sewanee Review*, in which I had the pleasure of writing a review of your book, as it may possibly interest you to know how much effect your work has had even in places so remote from where it was written. All our men here in Washington who read that kind of thing at all were greatly interested in what you said. In fact, I don't suppose that any book recently, unless it is Mahan's *Influence of Sea Power*, has excited anything like as much interest or has caused so many men to feel that they had to revise their mental estimates of facts; and I say this, although I don't myself altogether agree with your forecast. I took so much pleasure in reading it that I was very glad to have a chance of saying something about it in print, and I had to keep a rigid check upon myself not to say a good deal more than I did.

There are one or two points that I would like to suggest to you. In the first place, where you speak of the comparative mercifulness of modern warfare as being one reason why the inferior races will not be exterminated or dispossessed bodily by the superior, don't you think that this mercifulness would disappear instantly if any of the inferior races began to encroach on the limits of the superior? What occurs in our own Southern States at the least sign of a race war between the blacks and whites seems to me to foreshadow what would occur on a much bigger scale if any black or yellow people should really menace the whites. An insurrectionary movement of blacks in any one of our Southern States is always abortive, and rarely takes place at all; but any manifestation of it is apt to be accompanied by some atrocity which at once arouses the whites to a rage of furious anger and terror, and they put down the revolt absolutely mercilessly. In the same way an Indian outbreak on the frontier would to this day mean something approaching to a war of extermination, as after one or two massacres by the Indians the frontier men, in retaliation, would begin to put to death man, woman and child, exactly as if they were crusaders; indeed, as the soldiers did generally during those dismal years included in the "ages of faith." Of course the central or home population, which is unaffected by the massacres, would always clamor against the retaliation by the borderers, but if the movement became sufficiently strong to jeopardize white control I think this clamor would be hushed, and it would certainly be disregarded.

In the next place, have you ever thought that there are certain modern trades which entail the exercise of the manlier virtues to a degree that hardly any trade ever did formerly? Take the immensely developed business of railroad men, including the superintendents of division, etc. down to the brakemen, switchmen, conductors, yardmen, and the like. The last time I dined with General Sherman he expressed his belief that an army composed of railroad employees would be the most efficient in the whole world, because the men practice a profession which beyond any other necessitates the exercise of hardihood, daring, self-reliance, and physical strength and endurance, so as to train a man's moral, mental, and physical qualities, while the hours being irregular peculiarly fit a man for the irregular and hazardous work of the campaign; and obedience is taught, as well as the necessity for individual initiative. It does not seem to me that any mediaeval trade, or indeed any trade practiced by men advanced beyond the pastoral stage, has ever so tended to develop the hardier, manlier, more soldier-like virtues in the way that our railroad business has tended. All that the men who follow it lack is that preliminary acquaintance with arms which can be gained only by the man skilled in private war, or by the hunter, but which is of course far less necessary in teaching a man how to handle a rifle than in teaching him how to handle a sword or a lance.

I wish much we could see you some time on this side of the water. There are many of us who would like to have the pleasure of telling you in person of the enjoyment which we owe to reading your book. *Very truly yours*

HAMLIN GARLAND AND HENRY JAMES

To James Brander Matthews

Washington, June 29, 1894

Dear Brander:

I think the cutting about Mahan's book was one of the most delicious things I have ever read. It circulated freely throughout Washington, from Lodge on. Sometime or other I shall write an article on James Stuart, the Hanoverian Pretender, or on the Duke of Cumberland, the well-known Jacobin leader who fell at Culloden.

I am very glad the immigration has come to a standstill for the last year. We are getting some very undesirable elements now, and I wish that a check could be put to it.

I shall be ranching in September. Up to that time I shall alternate between Sagamore Hill and this hot city. I shall get back from the West early in October and report at 121 promptly.

After receiving your letter I got Hamlin Garland's book and read it. I think you are right about Garland, excepting that I should lay a little more stress upon the extreme wrong-headedness of his reasoning. For instance, he is entirely wrong in thinking that Shakespeare, Homer and Milton are not permanent. Of course they are; and he is entirely in error in thinking that Shakespeare is not read, in the aggregate, during a term of years, more than any ephemeral author of the day. Of course every year there are dozens of novels each one of which will have many more readers than Shakespeare will have in the year; but the readers only stay for about a year or two, whereas in Shakespeare's case they have lasted, and will last quite a time! I think that his ignorance, crudity, and utter lack of cultivation make him entirely unfit to understand the effect of the great masters of thought upon the language and upon literature. Nevertheless, in his main thought, as you say, he is entirely right. We must strike out for ourselves, we must work according to our own ideas, and must free ourselves from the shackles of conventionality, before we can do anything. As for the literary center of the country being New York, I personally never had any patience with the talk of a literary center. I don't care a rap whether it is New York, Chicago, or any place else, so long as the work is done. I like or dislike pieces in the *Atlantic Monthly* and the *Overland Monthly* because of what they contain, not because of one's being published in San Francisco or the other in Boston. I don't like Edgar Fawcett any more because he lives in New York, nor Joel Chandler Harris any the less because he lives at Atlanta; and I read Mark Twain with just as much delight, but with no more, whether he resides in Connecticut or in Missouri. Garland is to me a rather irritating man, because I can't help thinking he has the possibility of so much, and he seems just to fail to realize this possibility. He has seen and drawn certain phases of the western prairie life with astonishing truth and force; but he now seems inclined to let certain crude theories warp his mind out of all proper proportion, and I think his creative work is suffering much in consequence, I hate to see this, because he ought to be a force on the right side.

By the way, have you seen that London *Yellow Book*? I think it represents the last stage of degradation. What a miserable little snob Henry James is. His polished, pointless, uninteresting stories about the upper social classes of England make one blush to think that he was once an American. The rest of the book is simply diseased. I turned to a story of Kipling's with the feeling of getting into fresh, healthy, out-of-doors life.

I think your vignettes are really admirable, and I am much pleased that in your last you allowed a more cheerful ending than you sometimes do, and that when the bullet struck the young lady it should have only made a flesh wound in her arm. There is more than one particular in which that vignette struck a high note. I think that Dan Wister has been doing some very good work.

Give my warm regards to Mrs. Matthews. *Faithfully yours*

PLAYING IN A HOLLOW TREE

To Anna Roosevelt

Washington, July 29, 1894

Darling Bye,

All the early part of the week I was at Sagamore. On Monday I took blessed little Kermit in to see Dr. Schaeffer, who is yet unable to say whether, as he hopes, the affair is one of the knee cap merely, or whether it is in the bone itself, in which case the poor little fellow may have to wear the instrument a couple of years. It tells on him, and makes him peevish. Ethel, who is a perfect scamp, and as cunning as she can be, and who does everything and manages everybody, has fearful fights with Kermit; they celebrated my homecoming by a row in which Ethel bit him, and he then stood on his head and thumped her with his steel leg. Alice and Ted have been revelling in Corinnes children, with whom they are now devoted friends. We have found a large hollow tree, the hollow starting from a huge opening twenty feet up; the other day, with much labor I got up the tree, and let each child in turn down the hollow by a rope. Ted is such a blessing! he is very manly and very bright — but he is clumsy in spite of his quickness. How impossible it is to tell how any of them will turn out! Archie is such a wee, merry baby, and lies on his back on the bed waving his little arms.

Corinne is so dear; and also Douglass. But I do wish Corinne could get a little of my hard heart about Elliott; she can do, and ought to do, nothing for him. He can't be helped, and he must simply be let go his own gait. He is now laid up from a serious fall; while drunk he drove into a lamp post and went out on his head. Poor fellow! if only he could have died instead of Anna!

On Friday I left with Springy, who for four weeks has led the life of a Sagamore Hill Trappist, and with Trent, the University of Sewanee man, for whom I have much regard. I made an address in Philadelphia that evening, and came on to this sweltering place yesterday. I am now practically living with the ever-delightful Caboty.

Darling Bye, I know how dreadfully you feel about dear Alice Lippencott's death; I feel it much for myself too; I valued greatly her loyalty and straightforward honesty. *Your loving brother*

REMEMBERING A BROTHER

To Corinne Roosevelt Robinson

Washington, August 29, 1894

My darling little sister,

My thoughts keep hovering round you now, and I love you so. There is one great comfort I already feel; I only need to have pleasant thoughts of Elliott now. He is just the gallant, generous, manly boy and young man whom everyone loved. I can think of him when you and I and he used to go round "exploring" the hotels, the time we were first in Europe; do you remember how we used to do it? and then in the days of the dancing class, when he was distinctly the polished man-of-the-world from outside, and all the girls, from Helen White and Fanny Dana to May Wigham used to be so flattered by any attentions from him. Or when we were off on his little sailing boat for a two or three days trip on the Sound; or when he first hunted; and when he visited me at Harvard.

I enclose Uncle Jimmie Bulloch's letter — rather solemn and turgid — because I think he would like me to.

Give my love to all. *Your loving brother*

RELIGION AND POLITICS

To John Joseph Keane

Washington, October 15, 1894

My Dear Bishop Keane:

On Sunday morning Mrs. Storer showed me your letter to her in which you state that you had received the facts from Mr. Gardiner, the secretary of the Democratic committee. I went this morning up to the Republican committee rooms and saw Mr. McKee. He informs me in the strongest and un-equivocal language that there is not one word of truth in Mr. Gardiner's assertions, and that the Republican committee has not in any shape, way, or fashion helped in the circulation of A.P.A. documents. Moreover, he informs me that as a matter of fact no A.P.A. people, or people with A.P.A. proclivities, have asked him for such documents, and that such requests that have come to him have always come from Democratic decoys; one, who he has every reason to believe was sent by Senator Gorman, doing his best to lure one of the subordi-nates of the committee into compromising himself in some manner. Moreover, the Republican committee is, as a matter of fact, extending precisely the same help to Republican can-didates who are Catholics, of whom there are several, as it is to Republican candidates who are Protestants; and its actions are supervised by the National committee, one of whose mem-bers at least, Mr. Kerens of Missouri, is a Catholic.

Now, my dear sir, I am sure I need not tell you that I am as heartily opposed to the A.P.A. or to anybody that seeks to attack a man politically because of his creed, or to bring questions of religion into American politics, as anyone can possibly be. If the Republican committee has been doing this I will do my best to see it stopped, and if it is not stopped will publicly denounce it. On the other hand, it is infamous to accuse a committee of doing anything of this kind if it has not done it, and Mr. Gardiner is bound immediately to produce proof of his assertion, or else to retract it in the most public manner and to express his regret at what he has done. I will be delighted to go up to the Republican committee rooms with you and with any witnesses whom Mr. Gardiner has or can produce and to confront the Republican committeemen with them in your presence.

As you know, I am a straightout adherent of our nonsectarian public school system. I have always opposed any division of the school fund or any compromise whatever about the school system, and I am against the system of appropriations for sectarian institutions of any kind wherever it is possible for the State to do the work it has undertaken; but when I use the words "nonsectarian" I mean them. I don't mean that I will stand up for Protestant against Catholic, any more than for Catholic against Protestant; and I feel just the same indignation at any discrimination, political or otherwise, against a Catholic, because of his religion, that I feel if a Protestant is discriminated against for similar reasons; and I should pay no heed to party considerations in denouncing any man or body of men who thus in a political contest discriminated against Catholics or against Protestants. Similarly, if a man tries to use this feeling for party purposes, and tries to excite it by false accusations for momentary partisan gain, he, it seems to me, is acting as badly as it is possible for anyone to act. I therefore beg you that you will get Mr. Gardiner to produce his witness so that we may find out where the truth lies. *Very faithfully yours*

SCOTTISH CUSTOMS

To John William Fox

Washington, October 23, 1894

My Dear Mr. Fox:

I am delighted that you liked the *Winning of the West*. In a few weeks my third volume will be out.

Now, as to your questions. I haven't got my authorities here, and I am answering rather from memory than otherwise. First, as to the fighting, the Scotch have always been rough-and-tumble fighters, and it has been one of the most marked of the points of difference between them and the English, who have for some centuries, certainly since the days of Queen Elizabeth, fought regularly with their fists. Smallett mentions how the bystanders would not allow his hero to smash and thump his antagonist when he was down, as he would have done in Scotland. In Borrows delightful "Gypsy" book *Lavengro*, he comments on this difference between the Scotch and English schoolboys; fist-fighting, according to the English system being unknown, while the Scotch boys scuffled, wrestled with, hit, and tore at, one another.

Among the other habits of thought that I alluded to was the tendency to a rigid Sabbath observance among those backwoodsmen who were religious at all, this Sabbath being kept in the Scotch fashion, and the fact that the backwoodsmen so invariably took to the Presbyterian religion, and not to the English form of worship, until the Methodists and Baptists began to make their way there. There were other habits but I should have to look them up in the books now.

Now, about the feuds. I don't think that these were developed in the way that the modern feuds are, but I think that the rudiments of the modern feud system were very visible. Milfort, the Frenchman, who hated the backwoodsmen, describes with horror their extreme malevolence and their murderous disposition toward one another. He says that whether a wrong had been done to a man personally or to his family, he would, if necessary, travel a hundred miles and lurk round through the forests indefinitely to get a chance to shoot his antagonist. He wrote just after the Revolution. By turning to the published accounts in Draper's *King's Mountain*, and in the lives of Shelby and William Campbell, you will see how the war between Whig and Tory rendered immensely bitter the personal hostilities between the different backwoodsmen; and it seems evident that many of these backwoodsmen took sides in the contest according to their antipathy to one another, rather than with reference to their real political feelings.

I wish I could answer you more fully. *Faithfully yours*

CIVIL SERVICE APPOINTMENTS

To Henry Childs Merwin

Washington, December 18, 1894

Dear Mr. Merwin:

Many thanks for your letter. I am very glad you are going to be here in March, when I shall have a chance to see you. Let me know a few days in advance about your coming.

First, as to your letter proper, I most cordially agree with what you say. I can't believe that we haven't got in Harvard as much natural athletic talent as they have in Yale. During the last nine years our freshmen football teams, baseball nines and crews have won a fair share of victories from the Yale freshmen, while during the same time there have been but one winning nine, one winning eleven and one winning eight from the University itself. Unquestionably the evil development of Harvard is the snob, exactly as the evil development of Yale is the cad; and upon my word of the two I think the cad the least unhealthy, though perhaps the most objectionable person. The trouble with the Bostonian professor is emphatically that he is out of touch with nature. I am a man with no New England blood in me, yet I get on better with and perhaps have more admiration for New Englanders than for any other of our people; but the New Englander can't really "think continentally," as Washington used to phrase it, until he has spent a good deal of time west of the Mississippi.

I think President Eliot's attitude in some respects a very unfortunate one for the College. His opposition to athletics and
his efforts to Germanize the methods of teaching work real
harm. The main product we want to turn out of our colleges
is men. Incidentally let them be professors, chemists, writers,
anything you please, but let them be men first of all, and they
can't be turned out if we don't have the instructors themselves
men, and not bloodless students merely. All of this I want to
talk over with you when we meet.

Now for your friend's letter.

1. The rule that after one year's service in an excepted place
the holder could be transferred to the classified service without competitive examination was a very bad one. The Commissioner has denounced it for the last six years in the various
annual reports which I have written, pointing out that this
was a back door of entry to the service, and that only harm
could result from keeping it open. At last we succeeded in getting the President to take our view and shut it. But your friend
is entirely in error when he thinks that "messengers, watch-
men, sweepers, and cleaners of cuspidors" could be promoted
under this rule. Such men do not occupy *excepted* positions at
all; they are in the *unclassified* service, and your friend in dealing with these is thinking of an abuse abolished five years ago.
When I came into office I found that there was a provision allowing promotion of people such as those mentioned from
the unclassified to the classified service after being two years
in office. This opened a door to such gross abuses that we
got President Harrison to abolish it forthwith, so that not a
single promotion of "messenger, watchman, sweeper, or
cleaner of cuspidors" has been made for the last five years. The
distinction is a very important one, because the number of
excepted positions is small, and the abuse therefore comparatively small also; whereas the number of unclassified positions, including messengers and the like, is very large. During
the last four years in the departmental service here at Washington there have been only thirty appointments made in this
way by transfer from excepted places, as against 1658 made
from our regular lists after competitive examination. Of these
thirty appointments I agree with your correspondent that the
majority, although I should not say as high a proportion as

90 per cent, were transferred mainly for political reasons. It was a back door that we did our best to get closed, and finally did get closed; but as you will see by the figures given above it was very far from being as wide or as important as your friend supposed. Thus in the last four years I don't think that it has resulted in what he calls a "practical nullification" of the law in more than say about twenty of the thirty cases which is a small per cent when we take the whole number of 1658 appointments.

2. In all probability there have been in the past instances of evasion of the law by calling upon the Commission for eligibles from special lists, as bookkeeper, French translator, German translator, etc., but about the only instances to which I could actually point were in the Sixth Auditor's Office during Mr. Cleveland's first administration, when, undoubtedly, the Sixth Auditor, McConville, got friends of his from Ohio to take the bookkeeper examination, and then made calls for bookkeepers. In the case of French translator your informant is all wrong, for the instances of abuse in this, instead of being common, must have been very rare. No person has been appointed from this register in 1894. In 1893 there was but one appointment; in 1892 but one, and in 1891 but one, out of some fifty applicants. When there is such a large number of applicants of course only the persons standing at the very head can get appointments; and when there are in four years but three appointments from a register which at any one time contains from ten to fifty names there is hardly any chance of political favoritism being shown. Moreover, these appointments were actually made from the heads of the lists. Your informant is all wrong also in his supposition that French is not actually used in the Departments aside from the Department of State. It is continually used in the Bureau of Pensions, in the Statistical Bureau of the Treasury, and in the Surgeon General's Office of the War Department; and of recent years all our appointments from this register have been to these three Departments. I think that it has been a number of years since any person was appointed for political reasons from this French register. I think however, although I could not prove it, that there was one such case where a woman was appointed from Alabama from this French register early in Harrison's

administration on the recommendation of Senator Morgan, although Senator Morgan was a Democrat. Even in this case, however, I doubt very much if Morgan did more than inform the Department that the woman was thoroughly competent, and as it happened she was so competent that she stood at the very head of the register there was no way of preventing the appointment. In another instance I think that a man was appointed from the Scandinavian register simply to please a Scandinavian Congressman. In probably fifty instances we have found out that there were efforts of this kind being made and have stopped them [   ] As for the bookkeepers' register now, almost all the people that stand high on it get chosen, precisely as they do from the stenographers' register, and to an even greater extent from the registers of special pension examiners and Patent Office examiners. Unquestionably any man with political influence who can pass any one of these four special examinations will have a first-rate chance of appointment, simply because any man without political influence who passes them also has a first-rate chance of appointment. In the past about nine-tenths of the people who have passed the examinations for Patent Office examiner and special pension examiner, and all of those who have passed the examination for stenographer and typewriter, and fully three-fourths of those who have passed the bookkeepers' examination, have received appointments. They receive these appointments quite regardless of whether they do or do not have political influence, since the days of Mr. McConville, of whom I spoke, and even when he was in office, though undoubtedly many of his friends from Ohio took the examination and were appointed from it, all of the other people who took it got their appointments also. We advertise the fact in our circulars that there is a need of applicants for these various special registers, and that the chances of appointment are good from them, because we find it difficult to get men with the requisite capacity to pass them in sufficient numbers to supply the needs of the service. Of course when this is the case a politician who is shrewd enough to pass them and has the requisite capacity gets a place, just exactly as if he wasn't a politician; but I think you will agree with me that under circumstances such as these the chance for fraud is really infinitesimal.

One trouble is that always a certain number of the men who take the examinations are men with political backing. Of these a large number fail, and a large number who pass are never certified or appointed, as they stand too low; but of the proportion that do get appointed a number think they owe their appointments to political *influence*, when as a matter of fact they have simply been appointed right along in the order of their standing precisely like the rest of their associates on the list. Thus, once, about three years ago, Pennsylvania happened to be reached for a certification at a time when there was a demand for female copyists, and the two highest copyists on her list of a hundred names were appointed. To my intense amusement this was soon followed by a visit from Senator Cameron of Pennsylvania to know why we had made two appointments for Senator Quay and none for any other member of the Pennsylvania delegation. I couldn't understand what he meant at first, but diligent cross examination revealed the fact that the two girls in question were school teachers of very unusual ability who wanted to enter the Government service, and took it for granted from what they had read in the newspapers that they had to have Senator Quay's influence with the Civil Service Commission. They had accordingly written to Senator Quay when they took the examination. Quay made the response, as is usual with nineteen out of twenty politicians, that he would do the best he could for them, and when they got their appointments they wrote thanking him, and he answered that he was glad to have been of any service to them. Of course as a matter of fact he hadn't even known when they were certified or when they were appointed, and I pointed out to Cameron that the other people in whom he was interested and in whom the other members of the Pennsylvania delegation were interested simply hadn't passed high enough, and that if they had they would have been certified. The good faith of the Department in the matter was shown by the fact that they chose the first and second of the four names submitted to them for the appointments; but I doubt if I ever persuaded the other Pennsylvanians that something or other had not been done for Quay, and it took them about three years, during which time none of Quay's friends ever got within measurable distance of the head of the register, before they led up to the fact that all of the other people appointed from Pennsylvania, with the exception of these two, were persons with whom none of the Congressional delegation were acquainted. Of course in quoting my letter please don't quote this incident. Lodge was acquainted with it at the time.

We have to have special registers for branches of the service in which an unusually high degree of capacity is needed; but where few people take these special examinations there is always an opportunity for a man of influence who has the high degree of technical ability necessary to enable him to pass the examination to get an appointment, but, as I said above, I really don't think that this is an evil of sufficient size to merit any attention. It is perfectly true that bookkeepers, stenographers, etc., are often set to work at other than their special work, but this is merely because in many offices, while it is indispensable to have a man with bookkeeping knowledge or with capacity to write shorthand, yet there isn't enough of this work to keep him employed exclusively at it.

3. I believe that there have been rare instances in which the appointing officer has sought to discover, and has discovered, the politics of some of the people on the certifications submitted to him, but I think this is *very* rare, because in the first place, as a matter of fact the appointments are usually made within a couple of days and because all *must* be made within three days, after the certification is sent up. It is an absolute impossibility for an appointing officer within these three days to find out, save in wholly exceptional cases, the politics of men in States at all remote from Washington. Until he receives the certification he hasn't the slightest idea from what State the applicants come, so he finds himself with the names of three people from a State which may be Texas, or may be Massachusetts, or Oregon, and with only three days in which to find out about the three persons. It is possible that in some wholly exceptional instances he has found out, but I doubt if it occurs once in five hundred times, and I am not sure that it occurs at all. Moreover, we find as a matter of fact that in nineteen cases out of twenty, or thereabouts, the men are appointed exactly in their order. Under the law three out of every five men certified must be taken; but as a matter of fact

almost always four, and generally five, are taken, so that as you can see the room for this kind of misconduct is exceedingly limited.

As your correspondent very justly says, evasion takes many forms. Sometimes it is successful, but it does not defeat the main purpose of the law. I question very much if in the departmental service at Washington or in one of our big post offices all the kinds of evasion taken together would affect one per cent of the appointments, and I believe that during the last six years we have steadily, year by year, diminished even this small percentage.

Undoubtedly there is some transgression of the law against levying assessments. I am inclined to think that there is a good deal of transgression. Within the last year we have procured convictions against a postmaster in Ohio for violating this law and against a few collectors of internal revenue in Kentucky, and have had all of them heavily fined. We haven't succeeded in putting a complete stop to political assessments, and we have taken particular pains in our last report to point out this; but we have very greatly diminished the number of political assessments. Unfortunately promotions and reductions are not touched by the law at all, and we have nothing to do with them. The fact that they are made so generally for political reasons affords an excellent reason why the law should be extended to cover them. In both of our last annual reports, and also in a special report to the Senate last fall, we have shown that there is every reason to suppose that there has been transgression of the law as regards the matter of dismissals and forced transgressions in certain bureaus here at Washington, and in certain small post offices; but in the departmental service, taken as a whole, I don't think these cases of dismissal or forced resignations amount to more than half a per cent a year, and I am practically certain that they do not amount to one per cent a year. In most of the big post offices the proportion is no bigger, and the same is the case in the railway mail service and the one or two biggest custom houses. In some of the smaller offices, however, I believe that very great abuses have occurred, notably in Indiana and Mississippi, and we have called these abuses pointedly and repeatedly to the attention of the Post Office Department, both privately and publicly, and have worked to have the law amended so as to give us power to deal with them.

Don't you think that on the whole this makes a really good showing of the law? *Faithfully yours*

PATROLLING NEW YORK

To Anna Roosevelt

Oyster Bay, June 16, 1895

Darling Bye,

Twice I have spent the night in patrolling New York on my own account, to see exactly what the men were doing. My experiences were interesting, and the trips did good, though each meant my going forty hours at a stretch without any sleep. But in spite of my work I really doubt whether I have often been in better health. It is very interesting; and I feel as though it was so eminently practical; it has not a touch of the academic. Indeed anything more practical it would be hard to imagine. I am dealing with the most important, and yet most elementary, problems of our municipal life. The work has absorbed me. I have not tried to write a line of my book since I took the office; and a rather melancholy feature of it is that I do'n't see very much of the children. In the morning I get little more than a glimpse of them. In the evening I always take a romp with Archie, who loves me with all his small silly heart; the two little boys usually look over what they call my "jewel box" while I am dressing; I then play with cunning Ethel in her crib; and Alice takes dinner with us.

Emily's visit has made a very great difference to Edith. *Lovingly yours*

A SURPRISE ENGAGEMENT

To Anna Roosevelt

Oyster Bay, July 4, 1895

My own darling Bye,

To say that your cable and letter surprised us is a hopelessly inadequate way of saying what we felt. We were dumbfounded. But we were sincerely, very sincerely, glad. In Washington, and especially from Teresa Richardson, we had heard high praise of Captain Cowles; and I have always felt it a shame that you, one of the two or three finest women whom I have met or known of, that you, a really noble woman, should not marry. Then, I am so glad it was'n't an Englishman! I should have hated that. And I am glad it *was* a naval officer. I have a very strong feeling for the navy; I wish one of my boys could enter it; and I am very glad your husband is to be an officer in our navy. By the way, tell me his exact rank; is he a captain or a commander?

But there is one thing about which I feel dreadfully. I can not by any possibility leave my work here at this time. It would be dishonorable for me. I have plunged the Administration into a series of fights; to leave now would be to flinch; when you appreciate the situation here you will be the first to say that I could not honorably have left. It is the greatest imaginable sorrow — a real sorrow — to me not to be with you, my darling sister, at this moment. I should, moreover, so like to see you in the flush of your triumph in London, where you have done so well; and to have met all the people you have known, whom I should so have liked to meet, and have seen them with you — especially with the Lodges & Corinne & all. Even apart from my longing to be with you now, this is the time of all others I should like to have been in London. But I *can* not as an honorable man leave this work now.

My darling sister how I love you! *Your own brother*

ENFORCING THE SUNDAY LIQUOR LAW

To Carl Schurz

New York, August 6, 1895

My dear Mr. Schurz:

It is a very easy task, although not a very pleasant one, to answer the editorials you quote from the *Staats-Zeitung*. I regret to have to say that both what the writer of the editorials says about the alleged increase of crime in New York City, and what he says when he purports to be quoting my remarks, are absolute and willful untruths. I earnestly hope that Mr. Ottendorfer will soon return from abroad so that his paper may again become one which respectable men can read.

In the first place I will take up the *Staats-Zeitung's* statement that there is less protection against crime than formerly. This is a willful and deliberate falsehood on the part of the Editor of that paper; because when he wrote that, I had already published the figures showing that since we have taken control of the Board the number of felonies committed had shrunk; and the number of arrests for felonies had increased compared with what went on under the old Board. Thus, taking six weeks from June 1st, as compared with a corresponding length of time last winter we find that in the six weeks of June and July there were but three hundred and fifteen felonies reported to the Police Department in New York; whereas, for the six weeks in the winter there were three hundred and seventy-nine (379). This shows a decrease of sixty-six (66) felonies committed during the six weeks of our administration as compared with any average six weeks before. During the same period that there was this shrinkage the number of arrests for felonies increased just about twenty-six (26); that is, sixty-six (66) fewer felonies were committed and twenty-six (26) more men were arrested for felonies.

The statements that the *Staats-Zeitung* makes as to my position are just as false. I have never varied in any way from the position I took at the outset, which was that I declined to state my own opinions on the question of the Sunday Liquor Law; that I stood fairly and squarely on the platform of the honest enforcement of law. I have never made any public statement of my position as to the Sunday Excise Law, because I do not intend to allow the issue to become confused.

We stand for the honest enforcement of law; the *Staats-Zeitung* has taken the ground that we ought to be guilty of corrupt connivance at its violation. When the *Staats-Zeitung* says that I hit mainly the poor man, the *Staats-Zeitung* is again guilty of deliberate falsehood. The same is true of its statement that I openly favor class legislation. What it means by such mendacious nonsense I do not know. I suppose it is dishonestly referring to my statement, that we really benefit the poor man who is in the liquor traffic because we prevent his wealthy and unscrupulous rival from driving him out of the business by means of the corrupt favoritism of the Police. I also said that the poor man who is prevented from getting drunk on Sunday is benefited by our course. Of course he is benefited, precisely as the rich man is, and my statement was merely an answer to the dishonest clamor of such men as this writer, who insisted that we were "hurting the poor man." When they untruthfully state such to be the case the only way to meet them is to truthfully tell what the facts are.

I published the statistics showing that drunkedness had decreased in consequence of our enforcement of the Excise Law; only because our opponents had been loudly insisting, through the newspaper press, that drunkedness had increased. If the *Staats-Zeitung* does not believe that I am right when I say that it is better for a man to take his wife and children to some place where they can all enjoy themselves, no matter whether he gets beer there or not, than for him to spend his week's earnings himself drinking at a bar, why, I can only say, that the *Staats-Zeitung* is welcome to its opinion.

I have the honor to be with great respect, *Faithfully yours*

P.S. I hope this will do; if you want me to make my statement more direct I will gladly do it. I think you are right about my not speaking too often. I have promised the Catholic Temperance Society I would speak for them, and I must do it; exactly as I spoke before the German G. G. Club, which passed resolutions demanding Sunday opening. I would speak before any Organization which is with us in this fight for Law and Order, whether it favors opening or closing; but at present I agree with you. I had better not talk much more; I will keep as quiet as I can.

To Preble Tucker

New York, October 22, 1895

Dear Sir:

Of course, I have all along appealed to the conscience vote. Equally certainly whenever the conscience vote acts without common sense I am all separate from it. If you read a full report of what I said, you would have seen that I spoke most highly of the conscience vote and of the purity of the motives of the Good Government Club men; but emphasized the fact, which is familiar to every student of history, as well as to every practical politician, that when conscientious men act in a silly manner they may be quite as noxious as the basest foes of good government.

If you will study the effect of the action of the political prohibitionist in this country you will not only see what I mean, but you will understand the extreme danger to which you and your friends are exposing, not only the cause of good government in New York, but your own Good Government Clubs. I am a little at a loss to meet your argument, because, frankly, it is difficult to understand how anyone can seriously compare the causes of a public official who keeps his oath of office and enforces the law with the course of a political organization which deliberately chooses to help the enemies of law by dividing the forces of the adherents of decent government. I cannot but think that such an argument shows a radical misunderstanding either of the duties of a public officer or of the proper functions of bodies like the Good Government Clubs.

Of course the argument of expediency cannot enter into any ordinary case of the enforcement of law. The honest enforcement of law by public officials lies at the foundation of civilized government; but no civilized government can ever succeed if its politicians, its public men, and its citizens interested in public affairs, do not pay full heed to questions of expediency, both practical and political, no less than to questions of principles.

Do you know how our Constitution was formed? Have you ever read the Federalist? If so, you know that the Constitution could not have been formed at all if questions of expediency had not been given full weight no less than questions of principle. You also know that Alexander Hamilton, the chief champion in securing the adoption of the Constitution, was entirely opposed to most of the provisions incorporated in it. Had he obeyed your principle, and because he could not get everything, refused to support the best of the only two practicable courses, he would have been a mere curse to the country.

You say you are obliged to support the principle of non-partisanship in local offices. Now, in your own ticket you have been careful to nominate men of both parties; to have the candidate for County Clerk a Republican, and the candidate for Register a Democrat, and to divide as nearly as possible, the Judgeships between the two parties. You have deliberately striven to bring about a representation of the two parties. Your ticket falls short of your own ideal; perhaps the fusion ticket may not come quite as near to this ideal; but it is a very good ticket; it does represent a union of Democrats and Republicans, and it is the only ticket which there is a chance of electing. It comes quite as near the principles for which you contend as did the ticket which you supported last year.

If you construe your pledges to mean that you never will support any ticket which has any chance of election, why, of course, you have no excuse for existence. I hope that in the end you can educate the people of this city up to the highest standard in non-partisanship in local affairs, but the course you now are following is of all others the most effectual to prevent them from being thus educated. At times it may be necessary to run a ticket simply as a protest against the action of the machine, but when the machine does well such a course is ludicrous.

If the Republican Party had run a straight ticket this year, I would myself doubtless have supported any respectable fusion ticket; but when the Republicans agree to put into the field a fusion ticket which is on the whole excellent, which is indorsed by the best Democrats, and which has the cordial approval of the Committee of Fifty, opposition to it is simply harmful to the best interests of the city.

You either misunderstood my allusion to the Abolitionists or you have forgotten the incident to which I referred. I spoke of the abolition vote in 1864. Lincoln was then running for re-election to the Presidency. He stood for the principles of National unity and of liberty for the slaves. The Abolitionists nominated a third ticket, the only effect of which was to help the opponents of union and liberty, exactly as the only effect of your ticket is to help the enemies of decent government in this city.

The judgment of every competent historian is that the action of the Abolitionists in 1864 when they ran the separate ticket showed that that particular conscience vote had gone mad. Common sense without conscience will at times breed criminality, but conscience without common sense may also at times breed a folly which is but the handmaid of criminality. *Very truly yours*

UPHOLDING NATIONAL HONOR

To the Harvard Crimson

New York, January 2, 1896
Sirs:

I have seen a newspaper statement that various professors and students of Harvard have urged through your columns the Harvard graduates and undergraduates to bring such pressure as they could upon Senators and Congressmen in order to prevent their upholding the honor and dignity of the United States by supporting the President and the Secretary of State in their entirely proper attitude on the Venezuelan question. I do not believe that any considerable number either of Senators or Congressmen would consent to betray the American cause, the cause not only of national honor but in reality of international peace, by abandoning our position in the peace, by abandoning our position in the Venezuelan matter; but I earnestly hope that Harvard will be saved from the discredit of advising such a course.

The Monroe Doctrine had for its first exponent Washington. In its present shape it was in reality formulated by a Harvard man, afterwards President of the United States, John Quincy Adams. John Quincy Adams did much to earn the gratitude of all Americans. Not the least of his services was his positive refusal to side with the majority of the cultivated people of New England and the Northeast in the period just before the war of 1812, when these cultivated people advised the same spiritless submission to improper English demands that some of their intellectual descendants are now advising.

The Monroe Doctrine forbids us to acquiesce in any territorial aggrandizement by a European power on American soil at the expense of an American state. If people wish to reject the Monroe Doctrine in its entirety, their attitude, though discreditable to their farsighted patriotism, is illogical; but let no one pretend that the present Venezuelan case does not come within the strictest view of the Monroe Doctrine. If we permit a European nation in each case itself to decide whether or not the territory which it wishes to seize is its own, then the Monroe Doctrine has no real existence; and if the European power refuses to submit the question to proper arbitration, then all we can do is to find out the facts for ourselves and act accordingly. England's pretentions in this case are wholly inadmissable and the President and Secretary of State and the Senate and House deserve the highest honor for the course they have followed.

Nothing will tend more to preserve peace on this continent than the resolute assertion of the Monroe Doctrine; let us make this present case serve as an object lesson, once for all. Nothing will more certainly in the end produce war than to invite European aggressions on American states by abject surrender of our principles. By a combination of indifference on the part of most of our people, a spirit of eager servility toward England in another smaller portion, and a base desire to avoid the slightest financial loss even at the cost of the loss of national honor by yet another portion, we may be led into a course of action which will for the moment avoid trouble by the simple process of tame submission to wrong. If this is done it will surely invite a repetition of the wrong; and in the end the American people are certain to resent this. Make no mistake. When our people as a whole finally understand the question they will insist on a course of conduct which will uphold the honor of the American flag; and we can in no way more effectively invite ultimate war than by deceiving foreign powers into taking a position which will make us certain to clash with them once our people have been fully aroused.

The stock-jobbing timidity, the Baboo kind of statesmanship, which is clamored for at this moment by the men who put monetary gain before national honor, or who are still intellectually in a state of colonial dependence on England, would in the end most assuredly invite war. A temperate but resolute insistence upon our rights is the surest way to secure peace. If Harvard men wish peace with honor they will heartily support the national executive and national legislature in the Venezuela matter; will demand that our representatives insist upon the strictest application of the Monroe Doctrine; and will farther demand that immediate preparation be made to build a really first-class Navy. *Yours truly*

DEFENDING POLICE TACTICS

To Francis Markoe Scott

New York, February 11, 1896

Sir:

In accordance with the suggestion of Assistant Corporation Counsel John Proctor Clarke, I write to call the attention of your office to the bill, introduced in the Assembly by Mr. Butts on Jan. 4, (No. 165,) to prevent the employment of spies, that is, of detectives, in the administration of justice. More or less similar bills have been introduced by Mr. Davidson, and possibly by others. The passage of bills of this character would greatly lessen the labor of the police, for it would relieve them at once of all responsibility for the numerous kinds of crime which are conducted in secret behind closed doors, and which can never be successfully interfered with by policemen in uniform.

The "Molly Maguires" who terrorized a large section of Pennsylvania through murder, arson, and violence of every kind, were only broken up by the employment of the very means which these bills would forbid the police force of New York to employ. Moreover, there are certain kinds of crime which can be reached only by the use of detective methods — gamblers, keepers of disorderly houses, and law-breaking liquor dealers can hardly ever be touched otherwise. It would be almost useless to try to enforce the law against any of them if we were confined to employing uniformed police. To a certain degree this is also true of green-goods men and bunko steerers.

We find that, as a matter of fact, we cannot get convictions against these criminals unless the complainant can testify to the commission of some definite act of wrong-doing. In the case of a liquor dealer who violates the law, for instance, we can hardly ever get a conviction on a mere charge of exposure for sale, and rarely get a conviction unless the complainant can testify that he himself bought, paid for, and tasted the liquor. It would be far better to repeal the laws against gambling, keeping disorderly houses, and selling liquor at forbidden hours, than to nominally keep them on the statute books and yet to pass other laws forbidding us to take the only possible methods of obtaining evidence against the law breakers.

I do not know that it is necessary to point out that the stories related by certain unscrupulous persons to the effect that policemen sometimes lure liquor sellers and the like into committing crime are also, without exception, sheer fabrications, invented either by the law-breaker or by his friends. Many such charges have been made during the past nine months. In each case the board has immediately investigated them, and has found that they were entirely false. We have not come across a single well-authenticated case.

A policeman merely goes into a place where liquor is being sold to every one who is admitted and tenders the money exactly as others are tendering it, and receives liquor exactly as they have received it. He makes a tender and receives a liquor, as I have said, simply because we find that, as a matter of fact, no other course secures conviction. Of course the law-breaker when caught invents any story which he thinks will appeal to the public. In one instance which was widely reported the liquor dealer alleged that the officer had procured the liquor under the pretense that it was for a sick child. On investigation we found that he had bought two glasses of beer. It need not be pointed out that it would be a very credulous man, indeed, who would believe that two glasses of beer were purchased for the use of a sick child. In another case a liquor seller complained that the officer had persuaded him to sell the liquor under pretense that he had a pain in his stomach. On investigation the officer, as in the former case, promptly denied the charge and proved that at the time of making the arrest there were seven other persons in the saloon, all getting liquor also. Again, in this case it seems unlikely that even the most innocent saloon keeper would believe that eight men at one time would all wish to buy liquor solely because they had pains in their stomachs.

The same denial holds good for the alleged "child-spy" system. There is not, and never has been, any such system in vogue in the Police Department, and the outcry about it is absolutely baseless. It is difficult to know exactly what some of the loudest complainants of the system believe to be the fact. A few newspapers apparently regard any member of the force from the Captain of a precinct to a policeman of the Broadway squad as a child spy the minute he makes an excise arrest. So far as the outcry can be said to have any basis at all, it presumably refers to a single case of the use of the evidence of a minor to whom liquor had been sold in trying to procure the punishment of the man who had illegally sold liquor to very many other children, a man of a class which in some cases make large fortunes by their peculiarly infamous form of traffic.

It is only on behalf of this type of criminals that the outcry can be raised. Apparently some people really believe that the police have, in a large number of cases, used such evidence. As a matter of fact, of the 6,000 arrests for violation of the Excise law made since the present Police Board came into power, in but one single instance has the evidence of a minor to whom liquor was sold been used. In that case it was used without the knowledge of the board by a couple of policemen who had been doing very efficient work in arresting excise violators, and who, in dealing with a notorious law-breaker, who made a practice of selling liquor to children of tender years, finally secured his arrest through the testimony of the minors, to whom he had long been accustomed to sell liquor. On investigating the case the board found the conduct of the policemen had been proper. Such testimony is never to be used save by the authorization of the board, and only after every other means to arrest a wrong-doer has been tried, both by the board and by the Gerry Society, with which the board always cordially co-operates. As above said, the incident has occurred precisely once during the nine months we have been in office. It may never occur again; but the board will not allow any liquor dealer who practices this particularly revolting form of debauching children to feel that in the last resort they would refrain from using against him the evidence of one of his victims in order to save both that victim and the hundreds of other children upon whose lives he preys. *Yours truly*

"THE WORK WAS HERCULEAN"

To Anna Roosevelt

New York, February 25, 1896

Darling Bye: —
I have just come home from a tumultuous whirl at Chicago. I have recently been steadfastly refusing to make any speeches, but on Washington's birthday I did consent to make the great Chicago speech under the auspecies of the Union League Club at the Auditorium. McKinley addressed the meeting last year and Tom Reed the year before. I was received with the utmost enthusiasm, and indeed was made the lion of the hour in Chicago; and during the thirty-six hours that I was there I had to make not less than seven speeches. Chicago looks at me through the perspective of space which

is almost as satisfactory as looking through the perspective of time; and, as she does not feel my rule, was loud in her denunciation of New York for not being grateful to me.

I have had my hands full as usual with both my regular police work and with politics since I last wrote you. Gradually and in spite of great difficulties with two of my colleagues I am getting this force into good shape; but I am quite sincere when I say that I do not believe that any other man in the United States, not even the President, has had as heavy a task as I have had during the past ten months. In itself the work was herculean, even had I been assisted by an honest and active public sentiment and had I received help from the Press and the politicians. As a matter of fact public sentiment is apathetic and likes to talk about virtue in the abstract, but it does not want to *re*tain the virtue if there is any trouble about it. The papers of the widest circulation have been virulent against me. The democrats of course oppose me to a man so far as their public representatives are concerned, and the republican machine is almost as bitterly hostile. Governor Morton in a feeble way would like to stand by me but he does not dare to antagonize Platt; he is now so miserable over having to decide whether or not he will veto the bill putting me out that he is almost sick. As yet they are not sure of his consent. They have not yet brought the bill in, but I think that in the end they will bring it in. However, I can afford to look at the result with a good deal of equanimity; they can't put me out much before I have finished my year's term of service; I will then have practically done the great bulk of our work, that is the reorganizing of the Department; we will leave the Force immeasurably improved compared to the Force we found; and, with all the worry and hard work, I have heartily enjoyed it. It has been emphatically a man's work, worth doing from every aspect. I feel I have been a useful citizen, and, though this is a point of very much less importance, I think that in the end decent people will realize that I have done a good deal. I am writing to you with frank egoism. My excuse must be that I have not worked in any way egotistically, for I can conscientiously say that not one single step I have taken has been influenced by any considerations save by those which I have deemed for the public good.

Politically, I have been rather unhappy because I have of course to support Morton and I want to support Reed. I think, however, that Reed thoroughly understands the case as I have taken no steps without his sanction.

Edith has a load off her mind because Mame's operation went off all right, and Mame is now on the high road to recovery. It was very trying to Edith as she had to take her down to Bellevue and be in an adjoining room all the time; but Edith went through it all with the absolute conscientiousness and sense of duty that she always shows. To my intense regret it had to be done the very day I was in Chicago. The children are all getting along well, and Edith is utilizing all the advantages of New York to the full for them in the way of dancing schools and the like. Archie is as pretty as a picture and a darling. I only wish that the future was a little more certain as far as they are concerned for while Edith is as much convinced as I am that we should live in the country as long as we can't both live in town and the country, there are serious disadvantages connected with the children's education when we have to be in the country during winter.

Give my love to Will. *Yours always*

"UNINTELLIGENT, COWARDLY CHATTER"

To Henry Cabot Lodge

New York, April 29, 1896

Dear Cabot: —

It was very good of you to send that letter to Laura, and she was deeply touched.

Did you see in *Scribner's* of this month the opening sentences in reference to yourself by the man who was writing about the Consulates? such a purely incidental tribute speaks more than all the resolutions of the Civil Service Reform Association for the good work you have done.

I was deeply interested in both the volumes by Gustave LeBon. He is really a thinker — not the kind of "thinker" whom the Mugwumps designate by that title — and his books are most suggestive. At the same time I think he falls into fundamental errors quite as vicious in their way as Brooks Adams', especially when he states positively and without qualification a general law which he afterwards himself qualifies in a way that shows that his first general statement was incorrect. I was rather amused at seeing that while his last summing up contained a sweeping prophecy of evil quite as gloomy as Brooks', it was based on exactly the opposite view. One believes that the mass, the proletariat, will swallow up everything and grind capital and learning alike into powder beneath the wheels of socialism. The other believes that the few men on top, the capitalists, will swallow up everything, and will reduce all below them to practical vassalage. But what LeBon says of race is very fine and true.

I see that President Eliot attacked you and myself as "degenerated sons of Harvard." It is a fine alliance, that between the anglo-maniac mugwumps, the socialist working men, and corrupt politicians like Gorman, to prevent the increase of our Navy and coast defenses. The moneyed and semi-cultivated classes, especially of the Northeast, are doing their best to bring this country down to the Chinese level. If we ever come to nothing as a nation it will be because the teaching of Carl Schurz, President Eliot, the *Evening Post* and the futile sentimentalists of the international arbitration type, bears its legitimate fruit in producing a flabby, timid type of character, which eats away the great fighting features of our race. Hand in hand with the Chinese timidity and inefficiency of such a character would go the Chinese corruption; for men of such a stamp are utterly unable to war against the Tammany stripe of politicians. There is nothing that provokes me more than the unintelligent, cowardly chatter for "peace at any price" in which all of those gentlemen indulge.

Give my best love to Nannie. *Always yours*

"THAT MORAL SPRING"

To Cecil Spring-Rice

New York, August 5, 1896

Dear Cecil: —

You would have been well repaid for your trouble in writing if you had seen the eagerness with which Mrs. Roosevelt and I read and reread your letter, and repeated parts of it to the children. As you know we are not fond of many people, and we are very fond of you; and if you don't come back to America for ten years, yet, whenever you do, you will find us just as anxious to see you as we always were in the old days at Washington. Funnily enough just about four days prior to the arrival of your letter we were talking you over, apropos of Willie Phillips, who was spending a week with us in the house, and were saying that he, Bob Ferguson and perhaps Grant LaFarge, were the only people who approached you in our minds as being guests whom we really liked to have stay for no matter how long a time in the house. Mrs. Roosevelt always refers to your last visit as one during which she got steadily to be more and more glad that you were in the house, so that she felt as if one of the family had gone when you left.

Ted has been learning to shoot with a Flobert rifle. We have a Scotch terrier, an offspring of the Lodge's Peter, with two beautifully forked & pointed ears, and an exceedingly stiff tail; the other day she stood end-on at some little distance looking at us, so that the tail appeared like a bar between the forked ears, and Ted remarked with pleased interest "doesn't Jessie look just exactly like a rifle sight." He rides on pony Grant, when that aldermanic little beast seems less foundered than usual. Alice is as tall as Mrs. Roosevelt now, and just as good as she can be. Archibald, the Cracker, is a darling, although I suppose that to all people but his parents, both his temper and his intelligence would seem to leave much to be desired. Kermit has his brace off, and the little fellow is very happy. He fights with Ethel a good deal, but they are rather more peaceful than formerly. I think I wrote you that both the little boys, in the interest of economy, were clad, over their regular clothes, in the beautiful and simple national garb of the American hired man, that is, blue overhauls with a waist under the armpits.

Ted is as much at home in the water as a duck. Mrs. Roosevelt and I ride a good deal on the two black ponies and we also row now and then, sometimes for a whole day on the water.

Did I tell you that Speck spent three days at our house last winter? One of his duties was to get up a report as to America's strength and weakness in the event of his Government finding it necessary to take a smash at us; he was going about it, and discussed it with me, with his usual delightfully cold-blooded impartiality.

The bulk of my work here is over; the worry will not be over until I leave. The fight has been against terrific odds, and it has been made up of innumerable petty conflicts in which I have lost about as often as I have won; and I could not begin to express the wearing anxiety of the incessant battles now against the Tammany Comptroller, now against the press, now against the machine Republican legislature, now against the dishonesty and scoundrelism of one of my colleagues, with, the whole time, the ingrained and cynical corruption of the Force we inherited from Tammany, as a ground on which all these influences can act. Nevertheless, while I have come very far short of doing what I would like to do, and what I am sure I could have done, had the conditions rendered it possible for any man to do it, yet, I think I can say that we have done a good deal, and that the standard of efficiency and honesty has been immeasurably raised so far as the administration of this Force is concerned.

If Bryan wins, we have before us some years of social misery, not markedly different from that of any South American Republic. The movement behind him is most formidable, and it may well be that he will win. Still, I cannot help believing that the sound common sense of our people will assert itself prior to the election, and that he will lose. One thing that would shock our good friends who do not really study history is the fact that Bryan closely resembles Thomas Jefferson; whose accession to the Presidency was a terrible blow to this nation. Cabot has been one of the men who was instrumental in forcing the gold plank into the Republican platform.

I quite agree with what you say as to the effect that the military training of a whole nation must in the end have on that nation's character; and I also entirely agree with what you say as to Brooks Adams' book, & of these threadbare comparisons of modern nations with the Roman Empire. As long as the birth rate exceeds the death rate, and as long as the people of a nation will fight, and show some capacity of self-restraint and self-guidance in political affairs, it is idle to compare that nation with the dying empire which fell because there sprang from its loins no children to defend it against the barbarians.

On this side the real danger is either that we shall stop increasing, as is true now of parts of New England, exactly as it is true of France, or else that we shall become so isolated from the struggles of the rest of the world, and so immersed in our own mere material prosperity, or lack of prosperity, so that we shall become genuinely effete, and shall lose that moral spring, which no matter how bent will straighten out a really great people in adversity, if it exists in them.

But there is one inexplicable thing about military training and its effect as instanced by the immigrants we see here. I am entirely unable to detect any improvement in the Germans as fighting policemen, because of the military training that their fathers for the last generation have been receiving in the old world. I cannot on any philosophical ground explain why the average Irishman certainly makes a better policeman in an emergency than the average German. We appoint hundreds of both races, and while there are scores of exceptions on both sides, yet as a general rule the fact remains as I have said. It is so in the Police of Chicago and Minneapolis; likewise, it was so with our soldiers of the Civil War. After one, or at most two generations the difference dies out. The children and grandchildren of the German and Irish immigrants, whom we appoint on our Force, are scarcely distinguishable from one another, and the best of them are not distinguishable from the best of the appointees of old American stock. But it certainly does seem to take a generation to make the German, in point of fighting capacity, come up to the Irish, or native American.

The other side of the Police Force amuses me much, and I shall have lots to tell you about it when, if ever, we meet.

Bob Ferguson spent a day with us before going abroad. I think he is coming back to New York next winter.

You will remember Captain Robert Evans? He was in here with the *Indiana*, which is a splendid ship. Kipling, by the way, went all over it, and he and Evans got on capitally together. Harry Davis was here with the *Montgomery*. He spent a day with us in the country. He has the *Montgomery* at a very high pitch of efficiency, especially in the drill of her guns; and when questioned about her, I was much amused to see the struggle in his mind between his ingrained tendency to state that everything was and must be wrong everywhere, and as bad as could possibly be; and his deep-seated pride and belief that nothing of her size really could be better than his own vessel.

Good bye, old man! Mrs. Roosevelt sends you her love, so do Alice and Ted. Do write us now and then for your letters are always very welcome. *Faithfully yours*

P.S. Indeed Russia is a problem very appalling. All other nations of European blood, if they develop at all, seem inclined to develop on much the same lines; but Russia seems bound to develop in her own way, and on lines that run directly counter to what we are accustomed to consider as progress. If she ever does take possession of Northern China and drill the Northern Chinese to serve as her Army, she will indeed be a formidable power. It has always seemed to me that the Germans showed shortsightedness in not making some alliance that will enable them to crush Russia. Even if in the dim future Russia should take India and become the preponderant power of Asia, England would merely be injured in one great dependency; but when Russia grows so as to crush Germany, the crushing will be once for all. The growth of the great Russian state in Siberia is portentous; but it is stranger still nowadays to see the rulers of the nation deliberately keeping it under a despotism, deliberately setting their faces against any increase of the share of the people in government.

Well, just at this moment, my country does not offer a very inspiriting defense of democracy. This free silver, semianarchistic, political revolutionary movement has the native American farmer as its backbone; it is not the foreign-born people of the great cities; who work for wages and have no property, but the great mass of farmers who own their freeholds, and are of old American stock, that form a menace to the country in the present election; and the Immigrants who back them are the Scandinavians, Scotch & English, not the Irish; while the Germans are among the chief props of sound money.

RESPONDING TO A REVIEWER

To Frederick Jackson Turner

New York, November 4, 1896

My dear Mr. Turner: —

I was very much pleased and interested in your reviews of my fourth volume, both in the *Nation* and the *American Historical Review*. You are a master of the subject, and therefore you can write the only kind of review I care to read. I fear I must agree with what you say about regarding history as a more jealous mistress, and giving more time and greater thoroughness of investigation to the work. I have in return no excuse to offer; but an explanation. I have been worked very hard indeed for the last eight years, and it was a physical impossibility to neglect my duties as Civil Service Commissioner or as Police Commissioner, so I either had to stop historical work entirely, or do just as I have done. As I say this is no excuse at all, it is merely an explanation.

Will you let me make one or two pleas however? I think my judgment *was* sober. I cannot imagine it possible for Jefferson to have been ignorant of the real desires of Michaux, and his absolutely tortuous dealings with Genet at the same time, show the lengths to which he was willing to go in deceiving Washington and supporting France. I feel that while one should be sober in judgment, one should avoid above all things being colorless in dealing with matters of right and wrong. In my estimation Jefferson's influence upon the United States as a whole was very distinctly evil; and, still more, he represented without influencing the very tendencies which have made for evil in our character. He did some very good things, and he of course did not begin to travel as far in the wrong direction as Messrs. Bryan, Altgeld, Peffer and the like; but there are some very unpleasant points of similarity between them.

When a thoroughly good study of a special subject has been made, it seems to me a more general writer can often with advantage use it rather than himself again thrash out the straw, so I did not try to get any manuscript sources for the travels of Lewis, Clark and Pike. In the Louisiana purchase it seems to me that I must have failed to make clear my effort to accentuate the most important point in the whole affair, and the very point which Henry Adams failed to see, namely that the diplomatic discussion to which he devotes so much space, though extremely interesting, and indeed very important as determining the method of the transfer, did not at all determine the fact that the transfer had to be made. It was the growth of the Western settlements that determined this fact. There is no need of additional work on the diplomacy of the this Louisiana cession. But you are quite right as to the need of exploiting the Spanish, English and French archives about the treaties of Jay and Pinckney. I did not dwell on the Kentucky resolutions, because they seemed to me not directly connected with my subject, as much as they derived their importance from the Virginia resolutions, and have their proper place in a treatise of the history of the national parties at that time. They were not frontier matters.

There! I have not written another critic of my work; but with you it is interesting to enter into a discussion.

Pray let me know if you come to New York. *Sincerely yours*

"I AM A . . . 'CUBA LIBRE' MAN"

To Anna Roosevelt Cowles

Oyster Bay, January 2, 1897

Darling Bye,

On Xmas the ever-delightful Captain Stoots arrived, looking like a queer sea-growth from among his own clams, and sent in an envelope with the outside "merry Xmas" and inside, his bill!

I am a quietly rampant "Cuba Libre" man. I doubt whether the Cubans would do very well in the line of self-government; but anything would be better than continuance of Spanish rule. I believe that Cleveland ought now to recognize Cubas independence and interfere; sending our fleet promptly to Havanna. There would not in my opinion be very serious fighting; and what loss we encountered would be thrice over repaid by the ultimate results of our action.

Xmas week here was lovely; heavy snow, bright, cold weather, and out of door sport from morning to night. It is now mild, with everything thawing. We can go up and down both the front and back roads, and wheels are supplanting runners. Ted and I yesterday found we could no longer use skis, and have gone back to chopping. I hate to leave the country; but for the next two or three months it will be better for me to be in town, because of my work. In the Police Department we make progress at the cost of the same ceaseless worry and interminable wrangling. I shall have about five million things to talk over with you and Will when I see you. *Yours always*

REMAINING AT HIS POST

To John Davis Long

Washington, April 26, 1897

My dear Mr. Secretary:

I was much pleased at receiving your note this morning. All right, I will look into the matter at once and give you the results of my investigation, to aid you in your decision when you come on.

I went on to New York after finishing my morning's work on Saturday and came back yesterday afternoon, and I wasn't easy a single hour I was away, and never again shall I leave this city when you are not here, unless you expressly order me to. I told Mrs. Roosevelt that I guessed I should have to give up even the thing I care for most — seeing her and the children at all until next fall when they come on here; this because I don't wish again to be away when there is the slightest chance that anything may turn up.

By the way, remember that I don't need any thirty or even twenty days holiday.

I shall have made out against your and the President's return a full list of the ships which are now available to be sent to the East, and what one or two could be sent, which would be a formidable force, and yet leave a force which would be available at twenty-four hours' notice in the event of things in Cuba taking an unexpected turn. I do this in obedience to a request made to me by the President this morning. *Very sincerely yours*

NAVAL STRATEGY

To Alfred Thayer Mahan

Personal and Private

Washington, May 3, 1897

My dear Captain Mahan:

This letter must, of course, be considered as entirely confidential, because in my position I am merely carrying out the policy of the Secretary and the President. I suppose I need not tell you that as regards Hawaii I take your views absolutely, as indeed I do on foreign policy generally. If I had my way we would annex those islands tomorrow. If that is impossible I would establish a protectorate over them. I believe we should build the Nicaraguan canal at once, and in the meantime that we should build a dozen new battleships, half of them on the Pacific Coast; and these battleships should have large coal capacity and a consequent increased radius of action. I am fully alive to the danger from Japan, and I know that it is idle to rely on any sentimental good will towards us. I think President Cleveland's action was a colossal crime, and we should be guilty of aiding him after the fact if we do not reverse what he did. I earnestly hope we can make the President look at things our way. Last Saturday night Lodge pressed his views upon him with all his strength. I have been getting matters in shape on the Pacific coast just as fast as I have been allowed. My own belief is that we should act instantly before the two new Japanese warships leave England. I would send the *Oregon*, and, if necessary, also the *Monterey* (either with a deck load of coal or accompanied by a coaling ship) to Hawaii, and would hoist our flag over the island, leaving all details for after action. I shall press these views upon my chief just so far as he will let me; more I cannot do.

As regards what you say in your letter, there is only one point to which I would take exception. I fully realize the immense importance of the Pacific coast. Strictly between ourselves, I do not think Admiral Beardslee quite the man for the situation out there, but Captain Barker, of the *Oregon*, is, I believe, excellent in point of decisions, willingness to accept responsibility, and thorough knowledge of the situation. But there are big problems in the West Indies also. Until we definitely turn Spain out of those islands (and if I had my way that would be done tomorrow), we will always be menaced by trouble there. We should acquire the Danish Islands, and by turning Spain out should serve notice that no strong European power, and especially not Germany, should be allowed to gain a foothold by supplanting some weak European power. I do not fear England; Canada is a hostage for her good behavior; but I do fear some of the other powers. I am extremely sorry to say that there is some slight appearance here of the desire to stop building up the Navy until our finances are better. Tom Reed, to my astonishment and indignation, takes this view, and even my chief, who is one of the most high-minded, honorable and upright gentlemen I have ever had the good fortune to serve under, is a little inclined toward it.

I need not say that this letter must be strictly private. I speak to you with the greatest freedom, for I sympathize with your views, and I have precisely the same idea of patriotism, and of belief in and love for our country. But to no one else excepting Lodge do I talk like this.

As regards Hawaii I am delighted to be able to tell you that Secretary Long shares our views. He believes we should take the islands, and I have just been preparing some memoranda for him to use at the Cabinet meeting tomorrow. If only we had some good man in the place of John Sherman as Secretary of State there would not be a hitch, and even as it is I hope for favorable action. I have been pressing upon the Secretary, and through him on the President, that we ought to act now without delay, before Japan gets her two new battleships which are now ready for delivery to her in England. Even a fortnight may make a difference. With Hawaii once in our hands most of the danger of friction with Japan would disappear.

The Secretary also believes in building the Nicaraguan canal as a military measure, although I don't know that he is as decided on this point as you and I are; and he believes in building battleships on the Pacific slope. *Faithfully yours*

SPECIES AND SUBSPECIES

To Henry Fairfield Osborn

Washington, May 18, 1897

Sir:

I have been greatly interested in Dr. Merriam's article as to discriminating between species and subspecies. With his main thesis I entirely agree. I think that the word "species" should express degree of differentiation rather than intergradation. I am not quite at one with Dr. Merriam, however, on the question as to how great the degree of differentiation should be in order to establish specific rank. I understand entirely that in some groups the species may be far more closely related than in others; and I suppose I may as well confess that I have certain conservative instincts which are jarred when an old familiar friend is suddenly cut up into eleven brand new acquaintances. I think he misunderstands my position, however, when he says, "Why should we try to unite different species under common names?" He here assumes, just as if he were a naturalist of eighty years ago, that a "species" is always something different by its very nature from all other species;

whereas the facts are that species, according to his own show-ing in the beginning of his article, are merely more or less arbitrary divisions, established for convenience's sake by our-selves, between one form and its ancestral and related forms.

I believe that with fuller material Dr. Merriam could go on creating new "species" in groups like the bears, wolves and coyotes until he would himself find that he would have to begin to group them together after the manner of the ab-horred "Campers". His tendency to discover a new species is shown by the allusion in the last part of his article to the "un-known form of wapiti" which has been exterminated from the Allegheny country. The wapiti was formerly found in the Al-legheny regions; there it was beyond a doubt essentially the same animal that is now found in the Rockies. Probably it agreed more closely with the wapiti of Minnesota, which still here and there survives, than the latter does with those of Oregon. It may have been slightly different, just as very pos-sibly a minute study of wapiti from the far South, the far North, the dry plains, the high mountains, and the wet Pacific forests might show that there were a number of what Dr. Merriam would call "species" of wapiti. If this showing were made, the *fact* would be very interesting and important; but I think it would be merely cumbrous to lumber up our zoo-logical works by giving names to all as "new species." It is not the minor differences among wapiti, but their essential like-nesses, that is important.

So with the wolves. Dr. Merriam has shown that there are different forms of wolf and coyote in many different parts of the country. When he gets a fuller collection I am quite sure he will find a still larger number of differences and he can add to the already extensive assortment of new species. Now, as I have said before, it is a very important and useful work to show that these differences exist, but I think it is only a darkening of wisdom to insist upon treating them all as a new species. Among ordinary American bipeds, the Kentuckian, the New Englander of the sea coast, the Oregonian, the Ari-zonian, all have characteristics which separate them quite as markedly from one another as some of Dr. Merriam's bears and coyotes are separated; and I should just as soon think of establishing a species in the one case as in the other.

Some of the big wolves and some of the coyotes which Dr. Merriam describes may be entitled to specific rank, but if he bases separate species upon characters no more important than those he employs, I firmly believe that he will find that with every new locality which his collectors visit, he will get new "species," until he has a snarl of forty or fifty for North America alone; and when we have reached such a point we had much better rearrange our terminology, if we intend to keep the binomial system at all, and treat as a genus what we have been used to consider as a species. It would be more convenient and less cumbersome; and it would be no more misleading.

Dr. Merriam states that the coyotes do not essentially resemble each other, or essentially differ from the wolves. It seems to me, however, that he does, himself, admit their essential difference from the wolves by the fact that he treats them all together even when he splits them up into three supra-specific groups and eight to eleven species. He goes on to say that there is an enormous gap between the large northern coyote and the small southern coyote of the Rio Grande, and another great gap between the big gray wolf of the north and the big red wolf of the south, while the northern coyote and the southern wolf approach one another. Now I happen to have hunted over the habitats of the four animals in question. I have shot and poisoned them, and hunted them with dogs, and noticed their ways of life. In each case the animal decreases greatly in size, according to its habitat, so that in each case we have a pair of wolves, one big and one small, which, as they go south, keep relatively as far apart as ever, the one from the other. At any part of their habitat they remain entirely distinct; but as they grow smaller toward the south a point is of course reached when the southern representative of the big wolf begins to approach the northern representative of the small wolf. In voice and habits the differences remain the same. As they grow smaller they of course grow less formidable. The northern wolf will hamstring a horse, the southern carry off a sheep; the northern coyote will tackle a sheep, when the southern will only rob a hen-roost. In each place the two animals have two different voices, and as far as I could tell, the voices were not much changed from north to south. Now, it seems to me that in using a term of conven-

ience, which is all that the term species is, it is more convenient and essentially more true to speak of this pair of varying
animals as wolf and coyote rather than by a score of different
names which serve to indicate a score of different sets of rather
minute characteristics.

Once again let me point, out that I have no quarrel with
Dr. Merriam's facts, but only with the names by which he
thinks these facts can best be expressed and emphasized.
Wolves and coyotes, grizzly bears and black bears, split up into
all kinds of forms; and I well know how difficult it will be,
and how much time and study will be needed, to group all
these various forms naturally and properly into two or three
or more species. Only a man of Dr. Merriam's remarkable
knowledge and attainments and ability can ever make such
groupings. But I think he will do his work, if not in better
shape, at least in a manner which will make it more readily understood by outsiders, if he proceeds on the theory that he is
going to try to establish different species only when there are
real fundamental differences, instead of cumbering up the
books with hundreds of specific titles which will always be
meaningless to any but a limited number of technical experts,
and which, even to them, will often serve chiefly to obscure
the relationships of the different animals by overemphasis on
minute points of variation. It is not a good thing to let the
houses obscure the city.

HUNTING IN WYOMING AND MONTANA

To Frederick Courtney Selous

Washington, May 18, 1897

Dear Mr. Selous:

The other day I sent you a copy of *Science* containing some
remarks of mine on scientific nomenclature. I thought you
might possibly be interested in it.

I am very sorry you shouldn't have had better luck with
your Asiatic stags. However, I am pretty well hardened to bad
luck myself. I think I read Buxton's account of his shooting

that giant stag. It must have been well up to the size of an ordinary wapiti. I am sorry not to see you in August, but shall look forward to seeing you in October.

I have been made Assistant Secretary of the Navy, and you had better address me here at the Navy Department in Washington after this. Give me as much warning as possible when you are coming to New York, because I may not be there unless I am warned well in advance, as my duties keep me in Washington most of the time.

I enclose the map of Wyoming, and also one of Montana, and I have drawn out my own course. Unfortunately I can't give you definite information about the passes of which you speak, because I have never come into the country quite the way in which you will have to come into it; but Archibald Rogers has two or three times been over the Stinking Water with a pack train, so that I know you could get in from that side. I have not shot on the Big Horn mountains for thirteen years. Elk were then very plentiful. They afterwards grew very scarce, and am told now are fairly plentiful again. You will get into camp at exactly the right time. I should not myself venture to advise you to go to the Big Horn, for I know nothing about it now except by hearsay, while I do know the country south of the Yellowstone Park and around the headwaters of the Snake, and there the elk are certainly abundant, but Montcrieffe will undoubtedly have your hunting grounds carefully looked out for you. You must remember that it is quite a trip down from the Big Horn mountains into and across the Big Horn valley and up to the Jackson's Lake country, and if you are satisfied there is no game on the Big Horn mountains I should leave them as early as practicable. I take it for granted, however, that Montcrieffe will furnish you with a guide who will know the passes. When I was in the Big Horn I had to explore my way, as I did also on the Two Ocean Pass [   ], but there is no need for such exploration now.

Let me know if there is any change in your plans, or anything further where I can be of the least assistance to you. *Very truly yours*

P.S. I send herewith two big maps of Wyoming and Montana, and a few small county maps from the Geological Survey. The latter would be very useful to you if I could get enough of them, but unfortunately there are only a few sheets completed. I have marked with a red pencil my routes, but the marking is done from memory without my journals being on hand, and can only be taken as illustrating the general direction. For instance, I cannot at the moment call to mind exactly where I forded a given stream, which I sometimes did a dozen times in a day. Moreover, I was traveling largely by guess and always without any map, so that I am not perfectly certain, when you come to the smaller creeks marked on the map, which of two close together it was that I went up.

The greatest variety of game I got was in southwestern Montana, where you will see by my red trail that I hunted about a good deal, making three different trips. In northwestern Montana I also did a good deal of hunting, as you will see, and I took a separate hunt, chiefly, however, for the purpose of coursing wolves, in the western central part, along the Sun River region.

My ranch was in North Dakota, close to the eastern edge of Montana, and I could not begin to put on the map all my travels around there. I made two trips to the Big Horn, although only in one did I really penetrate the mountains and make a regular hunt. The other time I was buying horses. Nowhere did I find wapiti so plentiful as south of the Yellowstone Park, and moreover my hunt there was the last I have taken in the mountains. The very little shooting I have been able to do for the last five years was after deer, antelope, and very rarely, sheep, in the neighborhood of my ranch, or southward up the Little Missouri to the Black Hills.

Since I hunted on the Kootenai a railroad has been built there, and another railroad crosses the line of my travels with the Big Horn over what was then an entirely wild country in 1884.

The best place I know for sheep is just east of the Yellowstone Park.

I am afraid this information will seem a little vague, but I hope at least the maps will be of some use. When you can tell me a little more definitely about your trip I will get letters for you from the Secretary of War and the Secretary of the Interior, not only to all their subordinates generally, but to the Commanders of any special posts near which you are apt to be.

"THE WARFARE OF THE CRADLE"

To Cecil Spring-Rice

Washington, May 29, 1897

Dear Cecil:

Your letter made amends for all your silence.

First, as to myself and my belongings. I have been a month in office now, and I heartily enjoy the work. I was very sorry to leave the New York Police Force for some reasons, because it was such eminently practical work, and I very strongly feel that if there is going to be any solution of the big social problems of the day, it will come, not through a vague sentimental philanthropy, and still less through a sentimental parlor socialism, but through actually taking hold of what is to be done and working, right in the mire. We have got to take hold of the very things which give Tammany its success, and show ourselves just as efficient as Tammany; only, efficient for decency. During my two years on the Police Force I felt I accomplished a substantial amount of good. It was nothing like what I would have liked to accomplish, but it was something, after all. However, I came to about the end of what I could do, and this was an opening for four years at something in which I was extremely interested, and in which I believe with all my heart. I think that in this country especially we want to encourage, so far as we can, the fighting virtues, and it is a relief to be dealing with men who are simple and straightforward, and want to do well, and strive more or less successfully to live up to an honorable ideal. There is a great deal of work to be done here, and though my position is of course an entirely subordinate one, still I can accomplish something. I have been busy enough so far, for the Secretary, who is a delightful man to work under, has been sending me around to various navy yards, and during the hot weather I am expecting to stay here steadily.

By the way, I have just sent Laird Clowes my contribution to his history of the British Navy. It deals with the War of 1812. Mahan does the Revolutionary War for him. I don't suppose my part will be out for a year.

For the last five weeks I have been staying with the dear Lodges, as my house won't be ready until June, and my family are not coming on until the fall. The Lodges are just the same as ever, but Mrs. Lodge is very much depressed at the moment because poor Willie Phillips was drowned two weeks ago. You knew him a little when you were here. He was a man of whom we became steadily fonder and fonder, and I hardly know any one who would have left so real a gap in so many households. Mrs. Roosevelt always used to say that he and you were the two guests whom she would like to have stay any length of time at her house.

Mrs. Roosevelt herself is well. I have never seen her so well as she was this winter, in looks, in health, in spirits and everything. Alice is taller than she is now, and has become a very sweet girl indeed. Ted is an excessively active and normally grimy small boy of nine. He is devoted to Kipling's stories and poems, and has learned to swim, ride and chop quite well. He and Kermit go to the Cove School, where they are taught by the daughter of Captain Nelse Hawkshurst, one of the old-time baymen. Ethel is a cunning, chubby, sturdy little thing of five, and Archie is just three, and is treated by the entire family as a play-toy. I can't say much for either his temper or his intelligence; but he is very bright and cunning, and we love him dearly. The one thing I mind about this place is being absent from my wife and children and my lovely home at Sagamore.

Poor little Speck! The day after I received your letter I got one from him, a pathetic, wooden letter, just like the little man himself. I am awfully sorry about it.

What you say about Brooks Adams' book is essentially true. I would have written my review very much more brutally than I did, but really I think the trouble is largely that his mind is a little unhinged. All his thoughts show extraordinary intellectual and literary dishonesty; but I don't think it is due to moral shortcomings. I think it really is the fact that he isn't quite straight in his head. For Heaven's sake don't quote this, as I am very fond of all the family. His fundamental thesis is absolutely false. Indeed, the great majority of the facts from which he draws his false deductions are themselves false. Like the Roman Empire in the Second Century — like the Greek dominions in the Third Century before Christ — our civilization shows very unhealthy symptoms; but they are entirely different symptoms, and the conditions are not only different, but in many important respects directly opposite to those which formerly obtained. There seems good ground for believing that France is decadent. In France, as in the later Roman world, population is decreasing, and there is gross sensuality and licentiousness. France is following Spain in her downward course, and yet from entirely different causes, and along an entirely different path of descent. The bulk of the French people exist under economic conditions the direct reverse of those which obtained in Rome, for in France the country is held by an immense class of small, peasant proprietors instead of being divided among the great slave-tilled farms of later Rome; and in France there is no such tendency to abnormal city growth as in the English-speaking countries.

I quite agree with you that the main cause of Rome's fall was a failure of population which was accompanied by a change in the population itself, caused by the immense importation of slaves, usually of inferior races. Our civilization is far more widely extended than the early civilizations, and in consequence, there is much less chance for evil tendencies to work universally through all its parts. The evils which afflict Russia are not the same as those which afflict Australia. There are very unhealthy sides to the concentration of power, at least of a certain kind of power, in the hands of the great capitalists; but in our country at any rate, I am convinced that there is no real oppression of the mass of the people by these capitalists. The condition of the workman and the man of small means has been improved. The diminishing rate of increase of the population is of course the feature fraught with most evil. In New England and France the population is decreasing; in Germany, England and the Southern United States it is increasing much less fast than formerly. Probably some time in the Twentieth Century the English-speaking peoples will become stationary, whereas the Slavs as yet show no signs of this tendency, and though they may show it, and doubtless will in the next century, it certainly seems as if they would beat us in the warfare of the cradle. However, there are still great waste spaces which the English-speaking peoples undoubtedly have the vigor to fill. America north of the Rio Grande, and Australia, and perhaps Africa south of the Zambesi, all possess a comparatively dense civilized population, English in law, tongue, government and culture, and with English the dominant strain in the blood. When the population becomes stationary I shall myself feel that evil days are probably at hand; but we need to remember that extreme fecundity does not itself imply any quality of social greatness. For several centuries the South Italians have been the most fecund and the least desirable population of Europe.

It certainly is extraordinary that just at this time there seems to be a gradual failure of vitality in the qualities, whatever they may be, that make men fight well and write well. I have a very uneasy feeling that this may mean some permanent deterioration. On the other hand, it may be merely a phase through which we are passing. There certainly have been long stretches of time prior to this when both writers and fighters have been few in number. The forty years following the close of the first decade of the Eighteenth Century is a case in point.

Proctor, whom you remember, sends you his regards. He is listening to me as I dictate these closing sentences. He is a confirmed optimist. I am not quite so much of a one, but I am not a pessimist by any means. *Always yours*

TAKING HAWAII

To Alfred Thayer Mahan

Personal

Washington, June 9, 1897

My dear Mahan:

I have shown that very remarkable letter to the Secretary. Yesterday I urged immediate action by the President as regards Hawaii. Entirely between ourselves, I believe he will act very shortly. If we take Hawaii now, we shall avoid trouble with Japan, but I get very despondent at times over the blindness of our people, especially of the best-educated classes.

In strict confidence I want to tell you that Secretary Long is only lukewarm about building up our Navy, at any rate as regards battleships. Indeed, he is against adding to our battleships. This is, to me, a matter of the most profound concern. I feel that you ought to write to him — not immediately, but sometime not far in the future — at some length, explaining to him the vital need of more battleships now, and the vital need of continuity in our naval policy. Make the plea that this is a measure of peace and not of war. I cannot but think your words would carry weight with him.

He didn't like the address I made to the War College at Newport the other day. I shall send it to you when I get a copy.

I do not congratulate you upon the extraordinary compliment paid you by the Japanese, only because I know you care more for what we are doing with the Navy than for any compliment. *Sincerely yours*

ARRANGING A VISIT

To Franklin Delano Roosevelt

Washington, June 11, 1897

Dear Franklin:

We shall be very glad to see you at Sagamore Hill on either the 2d or 3d of July, for as long as you can stay. One train leaves Long Island City for Oyster Bay (our station) at 11 o'clock, and another at 2. You take the East Thirty-fourth Street Ferry about 15 minutes earlier. Let us know the day before which train you are coming on. *Sincerely yours*

EDITING A HUNTING STORY

To George Bird Grinnell

Washington, August 2, 1897

My dear Grinnell:

I have read through the article which I return. How old is young Pierce? He writes as if he was not more than 14. Nevertheless there is much of the article that is really interesting, notably photographing the deer while it was held from the canoe, and some of the accounts of the distances at which the game was shot; but it needs merciless pruning. Wherever the young idiot speaks of papa, father should of course be substituted, and, if possible, the allusion should be left out altogether. It is not advisable to put in nursery prattle. In the next place all of the would-be funny parts must be cut out ruthlessly. If there exists any particularly vulgar horror on the face of the globe it is the "funny" hunting story. This of course means that we shall have to cut down the piece to about half its present length; but if that is done I think it will be good.

In two or three days I shall send you my piece. Did you get the annotated list of the Boone and Crockett books? *Sincerely yours*

GERMANY AND RUSSIA

To Cecil Spring-Rice

Washington, August 13, 1897

Dear Cecil:

Your letter was very interesting. I find the typewriter a comfort, and indeed when I have to carry on so much official correspondence it is the only way I have to write at all at length. I don't know whether I sent you a copy of my address at Newport, so I send one to you now. I don't think that even you can complain of the way I speak of England, and with a change of names it seems to me to be just the kind of doctrine that you preach to your people. I am very certain that both of our peoples need to have this kind of view impressed upon them.

I have not seen Bay. If he has sufficiently recovered from the Brooks Adams influence to be rational I should much like to talk with him, for he is an able young fellow.

You happen to have a mind which is interested in precisely the things which interest me, and which I believe are of more vital consequence than any other to the future of the race and of the world; so naturally I am delighted to hear from you, and I always want to answer your letters at length.

Did I tell you that I met such a nice Englishman here, named Spencer Walpole? He also is interested in the same problems.

In a couple of months I shall send you the collection of my essays, simply because I want you to read my reviews of Pearson's book, and of Kidd's *Social Evolution*. I have not heard from Laird Clowes since I sent him my piece on the War of 1812 for his book, so I don't know whether he thought it satisfactory or not. *I* did! or I would not have sent it.

Before speaking of the Russians and of their attitude toward us, a word about the Germans. I am by no means sure that I heartily respect the little Kaiser, but in his colonial plans I think he is entirely right from the standpoint of the German race. International law, and above all interracial law, are still in a fluid condition, and two nations with violently conflicting interests may each be entirely right from its own standpoint. If I were a German I should want the German race to expand. I should be glad to see it begin to expand in the only two places left for the ethnic, as distinguished from the political, expansion of the European peoples; that is, in South Africa and temperate South America. Therefore, as a German I should be delighted to upset the English in South Africa, and to defy the Americans and their Monroe Doctrine in South America. As an Englishman, I should seize the first opportunity to crush the German Navy and the German commercial marine out of existence, and take possession of both the German and Portuguese possessions in South Africa, leaving the Boers absolutely isolated. As an American I should advocate — and as a matter of fact do advocate — keeping our

Navy at a pitch that will enable us to interfere promptly if Germany ventures to touch a foot of American soil. I would not go into the abstract rights or wrongs of it; I would simply say that we did not intend to have the Germans on this continent, excepting as immigrants whose children would become Americans of one sort or another, and if Germany intended to extend her empire here she would have to whip us first.

I am by no means sure that either your people or mine have the nerve to follow this course; but I am absolutely sure that it is the proper course to follow, and I should adopt it without in the least feeling that the Germans who advocated German colonial expansion were doing anything save what was right and proper from the standpoint of their own people. Nations may, and often must, have conflicting interests, and in the present age patriotism stands a good deal ahead of cosmopolitanism.

Now, the reason why I don't think so much of the Kaiser is that it seems to me Germany ought not to try to expand colonially at our expense when she has Russia against her flank and year by year increasing in relative power. Of course if Germany has definitely adopted the views which some of the Greek States, like the Achaean League, adopted toward Rome after the second Punic War, I have nothing to say. These Greek States made up their mind that Rome had the future and could not be striven against, but they decided to take advantage of whatever breathing space was given them by warring on any power which Rome did not choose to befriend, hoping that Rome might perhaps spare them, and that meanwhile they would stand high compared to all the States but Rome. If Germany feels this way toward Russia, well and good; but if she does not feel this way, then every year she waits to strike is just so much against her. If the Kaiser were a Frederick the Great or a Gustavus Adolphus; if he were a Cromwell, a Pitt, or, like Andrew Jackson, had the "instinct for the jugular," he would recognize his real foe and strike savagely at the point where danger threatens.

A few years ago Germany could certainly have whipped Russia, even if, in conjunction with Austria and Italy, she had had to master France also. Of course it would be useless to whip her without trying to make the whipping possibly permanent by building up a great Polish buffer State, making Finland independent or Swedish, taking the Baltic Provinces, etc. *This* would have been something worth doing; but to run about imprisoning private citizens of all ages who do not speak of "Majesty" with bated breath seems to me foolish, at this period of the world's progress. That the Germans should dislike and look down upon the Americans is natural. Americans don't dislike the Germans, but so far as they think of them at all they look upon them with humorous contempt. The English-speaking races may or may not be growing effete, and may or may not ultimately succumb to the Slav; but whatever may happen in any single war they will not ultimately succumb to the German, and a century hence he will be of very small consequence compared to them.

Of course the Kaiser objects to liberalism in his country. Liberalism has some great vices, and the virtues which in our opinion outweigh these vices might not be of weight in Germany.

Now, about the Russians, who offer a very much more serious problem than the Germans, if not to our generation, at least to the generations which will succeed us. Russia and the United States are friendly, but Russians and Americans, in their individual capacity, have nothing whatever in common. That they despise Americans in a way is doubtless true. I rather doubt if they despise Europeans. Socially, the upper classes feel themselves akin to the other European upper classes, while they have no one to feel akin to in America. Our political corruption certainly cannot shock them, but our political institutions they doubtless both despise and fear. As for our attitude toward them, I don't quite take your view, which seems to be, after all, merely a reflection of theirs. Evidently you look upon them as they think they should be looked upon — that is as huge, powerful barbarians, cynically confident that they will in the end inherit the fruits of our civilization, firmly believing that the future belongs to them, and resolute to develop their own form of government, literature and art; despising as effete all of Europe and especially America. I look upon them as a people to whom we can give points, and a beating; a people with a great future, as we have; but, a people with poisons working in it, as other poisons, of similar character on the whole, work in us.

Well, there is a certain justification for your view, but the people who have least to fear from the Russians are the people who can speak English. They may overrun the continent of Europe, but they cannot touch your people or mine, unless perhaps in India. There is no such difference between them and us as there was between the Goths and Byzantines; it will be many a long year before we lose our capacity to lay out those Goths. They are below the Germans just as the Germans are below us; the space between the German and the Russian may be greater than that between the Englishman and the German, but that is all. We are all treading the same path, some faster, some slower; and though the Russian started far behind, yet he has traveled that path very much farther and faster since the days of Ivan the Terrible than our people have traveled it since the days of Elizabeth. He is several centuries behind us still, but he was a thousand years behind us then. He may develop his own art and his own literature, but most assuredly they will be developed on European models and along European lines, and they will differ from those of other European nations no more than Macaulay and Turner differ from Ariosto and Botticelli — nor will his government escape the same fate. While he can keep absolutism, no matter how corrupt, he will himself possess infinite possibilities of menace to his neighbors; but as sure as fate, in the end, when Russia becomes more thickly populated, when Siberia fills with cities and settled districts, the problems which in different forms exist in the free republic of the United States, the free monarchy of England, the free commonwealths of Australia, the unfree monarchy of Prussia, the unfree Republic of France and the heterogeneous empire of Austria, will also have to be faced by the Russian. The nihilist is the socialist or communist in an aggravated form. He makes but a small class; he may temporarily disappear; but his principles will slowly spread. If Russia chooses to develop purely on her own line and to resist the growth of liberalism, then she may put off the day of reckoning; but she cannot ultimately avert it, and instead of occasionally having to go through what Kansas has gone through with the populists she will sometime experience a red terror which will make the French Revolution pale. Meanwhile one curious fact is forgotten: The English-speaking people have never gone back before the Slav, and the Slav has never gone back before them save once. Three-quarters of a century ago the Russians meant that Northwestern America should be Russian, and our Monroe Doctrine was formulated as much against them as against the other reactionaries of continental Europe. Now the American has dispossessed the Russian. Thirty years ago there were thirty thousand people speaking more or less Russian in Alaska. Now there are but a few hundreds. The American — the man of the effete English-speaking races — has driven the Slav from the eastern coast of the North Pacific.

What the Russian thinks of us — or indeed what any European thinks of us — is of small consequence. What we *are* is of great consequence; and I wish I could answer you with confidence. Sometimes I do feel inclined to believe that the Russian is the one man with enough barbarous blood in him to be the hope of a world that is growing effete. But I think that this thought comes only when I am unreasonably dispirited.

The one ugly fact all over the world is the diminution of the birth rate among the highest races. It must be remembered, however, that Ireland has shown conclusively, as Italy still shows, that a very large birth rate may mean nothing whatever for a race; and looking at the English-speaking people I am confident that as yet any decadence is purely local.

The growth of liberalism undoubtedly unfits us for certain work. I don't like the look of things in India for instance. It seems to me the English position there is essentially false, unless they say they are there as masters who intend to rule justly, but who do not intend to have their rule questioned. If the English in India would suppress promptly any native newspaper that was seditious; arrest instantly any seditious agitator; put down the slightest outbreak ruthlessly; cease to protect usurers, and encourage the warlike races so long as they were absolutely devoted to British rule, I believe things would be much more healthy than they are now.

As for my own country, it is hard to say. We are barbarians of a certain kind, and what is most unpleasant we are barbarians with a certain middle-class, Philistine quality of ugliness and pettiness, raw conceit, and raw sensitiveness. Where we get highly civilized, as in the northeast, we seem to become civilized in an unoriginal and ineffective way, and tend to die out. Nevertheless, thanks to the men we adopt, as well as to the children we beget, it must be remembered that actually we keep increasing at about twice the rate of the Russians, and though the commercial and cheap altruistic spirit, the spirit of the Birmingham school, the spirit of the banker, the broker, the mere manufacturer, and mere merchant, is unpleasantly prominent, I cannot see that we have lost vigor compared to what we were a century ago. If anything I think we have gained it. In political matters we are often very dull mentally, and especially morally; but even in political matters there is plenty of rude strength and I don't think we are as badly off as we were in the days of Jefferson, for instance. We are certainly better off than we were in the days of Buchanan. During recent years I have seen a great deal of the New York Police Force, which is a very powerful, efficient and corrupt body, and of our Navy, which is a powerful, efficient and honorable body. I have incidentally seen a great deal of the constructors who build the ships, and the public works, of the civil engineers, the dock builders, the sailors, the workmen in the iron foundries and shipyards. These represent, all told, a very great number of men, and the impression left upon my mind, after intimate association with the hundreds of naval officers, naval constructors, and civil engineers, and the tens of thousands of seamen and mechanics and policemen, is primarily an impression of abounding force, of energy, resolution and decision. These men are not effete, and if you compare the Russians with them (and of course exactly the same thing would be true if you compared the Russians with corresponding Englishmen) I think you would become convinced that the analogy of the Goth and the Byzantine is forced. These men would outbuild, outadminister and outfight any Russians you could find from St. Petersburg to Sebastopol or Vladivostock — if that's the way you spell it. I doubt if our Presidents are as effete as the average Czar or Russian minister. I believe our Generals and Admirals are better; and so, with all their hideous faults, our public administrators. Of course both the English and the Americans are less ruthless, and have the disadvantages of civilization. It may be that we are going the way of France, but just at present I doubt it, and I still think that though the people of the English-speaking races may have to divide the future with the Slav, yet they will get rather more than their fair share.

To drop from questions of empire to those of immediate personal interest, I am immensely interested in my work here. I think on the whole I enjoy it rather more than anything I have ever done. It is a cool summer. We have a very nice house just opposite the British Embassy. Mrs. Roosevelt has been spending ten days here furnishing it with fragments fifty or sixty years old from our ancestral houses — said fragments representing the haircloth furniture (or unpolished stone) period of New York semicivilization.

Aside from my work I have been able to do two or three things which gratify me immensely, for I was mainly instrumental in getting Proctor retained as Civil Service Commissioner, and in having Rockhill kept in the diplomatic service as Minister to Greece.

I spent three weeks at Oyster Bay and had a lovely time. Counting my own children and their little cousins, there are now sixteen small Roosevelts there, and one day I took the twelve eldest on a picnic. *Always yours*

P.S. Mrs. Roosevelt sends you her love, and wishes to know whether you would be very good and write out the lovely ballad of "Hurry my Johnny, the jungle's afire" for her? The children are always asking for it.

REVIVING THE ARMY-NAVY GAME

To Russell Alexander Alger

Washington, August 17, 1897

My dear General Alger:

For what I am about to write you I think I should have the backing of my fellow-Harvard man, your son. I should like very much to revive the football games between Annapolis and West Point. I think the Superintendent of Annapolis, and I dare say Colonel Ernst, the Superintendent of West Point, will feel a little shaky because undoubtedly formerly the academic routine was cast to the winds when it came to these matches, and a good deal of disorganization followed. But it seems to me that if we would let Colonel Ernst and Captain Cooper come to an agreement that the match should be played just as either eleven plays outside teams; that no cadet should be permitted to enter or join the training table if he was unsatisfactory in any study or conduct, and should be removed if during the season he becomes unsatisfactory; if they were marked without regard to their places on the team; if no drills, exercises or recitations were omitted to give opportunities for football practice; and if the authorities of both institutions agreed to take measures to prevent any excesses such as betting and the like, and to prevent any manifestations of an improper character — if as I say all this were done — and it certainly could be done without difficulty — then I don't see why it would not be a good thing to have a game this year.

If you think favorably of the idea, will you be willing to write Colonel Ernst about it? *Faithfully yours*

FOREST CONSERVATION

To George Bird Grinnell

Washington, August 24, 1897

My dear Grinnell:

Beyond one or two slight verbal changes I have nothing serious to suggest about the preface, excepting on one point. This is in reference to the forestry business. I wish to say in substance exactly what you have said, but I think there should be a more just division of praise. It was a serious matter taking this great mass of forest reservations away from the settlers. That it needed to be done admits of no question, but the great bulk of the people themselves strongly objected to its being done; and a great deal of nerve and a good deal of tact were needed in accomplishing it. I am exceedingly glad that President Cleveland issued the order; but none of the trouble came on him at all. He issued the order at the very end of his administration, practically to take effect in the next administration. In other words he issued an order which it was easy to issue, but difficult to execute, and which had to be executed by his successor. This is a perfectly common thing; in civil service matters, for instance, I have seen it done by Presidents Arthur, Harrison and Cleveland; in fact by every outgoing President since the civil service law went into effect. At present it seems to be about the only way we can get ahead on certain lines; for the President who is not willing to do the thing himself, is glad enough to direct that his successor shall do it; and the latter, who probably would not have the nerve to do it, in his turn makes the excuse to the foes of the reform that he can't go back on what his predecessor did. I think that credit should be given the man who issues the order, but I think it should be just as strongly given to the man who enforces it. Cleveland had issued the order without consulting the Senators and Congressmen who were all powerful in the matter of legislation, and if he had stayed in power the order would have been promptly nullified. President McKinley and Secretary Bliss took the matter up, and by great resolution finally prevented its complete overthrow. It was impossible to expect its going into effect at once. Not a dozen men in the Senate were for it, and all of these were from the far west. Now, the point I want to make is that quite as much is owing to McKinley as to Cleveland in the matter, and I think that either we should not mention either of them, or we should mention both. What Cleveland did was very easy to do; for it is not at all difficult to say that your successor must be virtuous. McKinley had to encounter real opposition. If this country could be ruled by a benevolent czar we would doubtless make a good many changes for the better, but as things are, if we want to accomplish anything, we have got to get the best work we can out of the means that are available. All of this is a needless homily. The only point is that I wish you would revise the sentence about that reservation, so as either to make it more general or more fully specific.

If you will send me on Pierce's article I will slash it up into about a third of the space it now occupies, and send it back to you.

I also made a slight change in what you say about hunting stories, as you will see; your endorsement of the camels was a trifle strong. I think many of our scientific people don't put enough stress upon hunting, and upon the habits of big game. For instance, in Donaldson Smith's book on African explorations, if he had given us in full detail an account of the habits and chase of some of the big game encountered, he would really have contributed a work of more value than by collecting beetles and the like, or by working over the geology of the country. The geology and the beetles will remain unchanged for ages, but the big game will vanish, and only the pioneer hunters can tell about it. Hunting books of the best type are often of more permanent value than scientific pamphlets; & I think the B. & C. should differentiate sharply between worthless hunting stories, & those that are of value. Writings by "Chipmunk," [   ] etc., are not very valuable; but your piece on the buffalo is worth more than any but the very best scientific monographs about the beast. *Sincerely yours*

P.S. — Speaking of the buffalo reminds me that I don't know whether you have anything in about the Yellowstone Park. Have you a piece about it which shows the diminution of the buffalo. We have made such a point of the Yellowstone Park in our two previous volumes that I think we ought to dwell on it in this one, even if only to the extent of a paragraph in the preface. If we have no piece on the subject I wish you could put in just a paragraph on the Park, mentioning particularly the great destruction of the buffalo.

RAISING A REGIMENT

To Francis Vinton Greene

Washington, September 15, 1897

My dear Colonel Greene:

There is always a possibility, however remote, that we will have war with Spain, and now that the cool weather is approaching that would probably mean not merely a naval war, but a considerable expeditionary force. I suppose you would be going, would you not? I shall certainly go myself in some capacity. What I should like to do if it were possible would be to go under you. I suppose we should have to raise a regiment, with you as Colonel, and with me as Lieutenant Colonel. My military experience is strictly limited; I was a captain in the National Guard for three years; nevertheless I know that under a man like yourself I could do first-class work, and I would have what assistance the administration could give in getting up the regiment, etc. Would this suit you should the need arise? I don't suppose there is any chance of the need arising, and very possibly you have totally different arrangements in mind, but I want to take time by the forelock so as to have my plans all laid and be able to act at once in case there is trouble.

Remember me warmly to Mrs. Greene. I have really accomplished a good deal in this place. *Faithfully yours*

"THE MAJESTY OF OUR SHIPS"

To Frederic Remington

Washington, September 15, 1897

My dear Remington:

I wish I were with you out among the sage brush, the great brittle cottonwoods, and the sharply-channeled, barren buttes; but I am very glad at any rate to have had you along with the squadron; and I can't help looking upon you as an ally from henceforth on in trying to make the American people see the beauty and the majesty of our ships, and the heroic quality which lurks somewhere in all those who man and handle them.

Be sure to let me know whenever you come anywhere in my neighborhood. *Faithfully yours*

"ANY MAN WITH ANY SELF-RESPECT"

To John Hay

Washington, September 21, 1897

My dear Mr. Ambassador:

Just a line to say that I saw it rumored that you have been asked to interest yourself in getting the British to give back to us the frigate *President*, which they captured in 1815. I earnestly hope that you will refuse to have anything to do with so preposterous and undignified an effort. How any man with any self-respect can ask you to do such a thing I don't see. To beg to be given back, as a favor, what was taken from us by superior prowess, would be to put us in a position of intolerable humiliation. When the British ask us to give back the flags and guns of the frigates and sloops which we took in the War of 1812, then it will be quite time enough for us to ask to get the *President* back. The *President* is of value to the British Navy. She represents a prize which rewarded their foresight, diligence and prowess. She is of no more value to us than the *Macedonian* or *Guerrière* or *Java* would be to the British if we were able to return them. There are no heroic memories connected with her — very much the reverse. All the *President* could teach us by her past deeds is what to avoid.

This account of the proposed effort to get the ship may be all a fake, in which case I must ask your pardon for bothering you.

Remember me warmly to Mrs. Hay, and any other friends of mine — if such exist.

My chief has been taking a holiday for two months, so I have been steadily in Washington, but I have really greatly enjoyed it for I have been able to do two or three things in the Department which I have long really wished to do. *Faithfully yours*

A PROPOSAL FOR EXPANDING THE NAVY

To John Davis Long

Washington, September 30, 1897

Sir:

The steady growth of our country in wealth and population, and its extension by the acquisition of non-contiguous territory in Alaska, and at the same time the steady growth of the old naval powers of the world, and the appearance of new ones, such as Germany and Japan, with which it is possible that one day we may be brought into contact, make me feel that I should respectfully, and with all possible earnestness, urge the advisability of the Navy Department doing all it can to further a steady and rapid upbuilding of our Navy. We cannot hope to rival England. It is probably not desirable that we should rival France; while Russia's three-fold sea front, and Italy's peculiar position, render it to the last degree improbable that we shall be cast into hostile contact with either of them. But Japan is steadily becoming a great naval power in the Pacific, where her fleet already surpasses ours in strength; and Germany shows a tendency to stretch out for colonial possessions which may at any moment cause a conflict with us. In my opinion our Pacific fleet should constantly be kept above that of Japan, and our naval strength as a whole superior to that of Germany. It does not seem to me that we can afford to invite responsibility and shirk the burden that we thus incur; we cannot justify ourselves for retaining Alaska and annexing Hawaii unless we provide a Navy sufficient to prevent all chance of either being taken by a hostile power; still less have we any right to assert the Monroe Doctrine in the American hemisphere unless we are ready to make good our assertion with our warships. A great navy does not make for war, but for peace. It is the cheapest kind of insurance. No coast fortifications can really protect our coasts; they can only be protected by a formidable fighting navy. If through any supineness or false economy on our part, we fail to provide plenty of ships of the best type, thoroughly fitted in every way, we run the risk of causing the nation to suffer some disaster more serious than it has ever before encountered — a disaster which would warp and stunt our whole national life, for the moral effect would be infinitely worse than the material. We invite such a disaster if we fail to have a sufficiency of the best ships, and fail to keep both our matériel and personnel up to the highest conditions.

I believe that Congress should at once give us six (6) new battleships, two (2) to be built on the Pacific and four (4) on the Atlantic; six (6) large cruisers, of the size of the *Brooklyn*, but in armament more nearly approaching the Argentine vessel *San Martin*; and seventy-five (75) torpedo boats, twenty-five (25) for the Pacific and fifty (50) for the Atlantic. I believe that we should set about building all these craft now, and that each one should be, if possible, the most formidable of its kind afloat.

We should at once build new dry docks. With the additions which are outlined above we should need to have one more dry dock for the largest battleships on the Pacific coast, and three more on the Atlantic coast; that is, four extra, although we probably could get along with only two extra.

Many of our cruisers and battleships are armed, in part, with the slow-fire six-inch gun, a weapon which is now obsolete. It would be cruel to pit these vessels against hostile vessels nominally of the same type, but armed with modern rapid-fire guns. The vessels could be doubled in effectiveness by substituting the converted rapid-fire six-inch guns for the old style guns as rapidly as possible. There are ninety-five of these old style guns in the service. The conversion would cost about $1,000 per gun. We should have guns for all auxiliary cruisers; we now have almost none. The greatest need at the moment is smokeless powder. Smokeless powder would greatly increase the power and rapidity of the fire, and would be of great tactical advantage. We should get two million pounds at once, in order to completely outfit our ships. This would probably cost $1,500,000. For $100,000 all our armor-piercing shell should be capped, loaded and fused. We should provide a reasonable reserve supply of projectiles (about nine thousand in all) so as to permit a complete refill of all the ships.

If we stop building up the Navy now it will put us at a great disadvantage when we go on. The greatest difficulty was experienced when we began our work on the new Navy in 1883. We had to train the workmen and the designers; we had to build factories, and make tools. The difference between such a vessel as the *Texas* and such a vessel as the *Indiana* will illustrate the cost to the country of carrying on such an experiment. We are now in a situation to build up a navy commensurate with our needs, provided the work is carried on continuously, for the era of experiment has passed, and we possess designs suitable for our own use, with types of vessels equal to those of any other power. But if the work is interrupted, and new vessels are not begun, we shall soon find it necessary to start all over again, as we did in 1883, and to re-instruct the men and manufacturers and re-educate the officers and designers and re-experiment with the designs. It would be difficult to calculate the course we should incur by such a proceeding; and meanwhile we should be exposing the country to the possibility of the bitterest humiliation. *Very respectfully*

BENEFITS OF WAR WITH SPAIN

To William Wirt Kimball

Washington, November 19, 1897

My dear Mr. Kimball:

When will you be at Savannah or at Brunswick, Georgia? I am afraid I am not going to be able to make it, but if I can I shall. If I fail, then I shall join you at one of the gulf ports later. I don't think it will be possible for me to get to Charleston.

I will sound Captain Crowninshield to find out what the intentions are as to that submarine boat, but I don't want to interfere unless I see a fair opening.

Now, about the Spanish war. In the first place it is always a pleasure to hear from you. In the next place to speak with a frankness which our timid friends would call brutal, I would regard a war with Spain from two standpoints: first, the advisability on the grounds both of humanity and self-interest of interfering on behalf of the Cubans, and of taking one more step toward the complete freeing of America from European dominion; second, the benefit done our people by giving them something to think of which isn't material gain, and especially the benefit done our military forces by trying both the Navy and Army in actual practice. I should be very sorry not to see us make the experiment of trying to land, and therefore feed and clothe, an expeditionary force, if only for the sake of learning from our own blunders. I should hope that the force would have some fighting to do. It would be a great lesson, and we would profit much by it. I expressed myself a little clumsily about the transport question. Of course if we drift into the war butt end foremost, and go at it in higgledy-piggledy fashion we shall meet with occasional difficulties. I am not the boss of this Government; (and I want to say that I do think President McKinley, who is naturally desirous of keeping the peace, has combined firmness and temperateness very happily in his treatment of Spain); from my own standpoint, however, and speaking purely privately, I believe that war will have to, or at least ought to, come sooner or later; and I think we should prepare for it well in advance. I should have the Asiatic squadron in shape to move on Manila at once. I would have our squadron in European waters consist merely of the *Brooklyn, New York, Columbia* and *Minneapolis*; and of course I should have this, as well as the Asiatic squadron, under the men whom I thought ought to take it into action. All the other ships in the Atlantic I would gather around Key West before the war broke out. I should expect it would take at least a fortnight before the Army could get at Tampa or Pensacola the thirty or forty thousand men who should land at Matanzas. During that fortnight I should expect that our Navy would have put a stop to the importation of food to Cuba and would have picked up most of the Spanish vessels round about. At the end of that time I believe it would be safe to gather an ample number of vessels for the transport of the army. This ought not to take them more than a week or ten days from their legitimate duties. Meanwhile I believe that plenty of arms and a considerable number of men would go over to Cuba on private ventures, and that the Cuban insurrection would be infinitely more formidable than it is now.

With thirty or forty thousand men at Matanzas, re-enforced from time to time, I believe that the Navy could for the most part resume its duties, and that, while it would be the main factor in producing the downfall of the Spaniards, the result would be much hastened by the Army.

I didn't think the *Cosmopolitan* article worth paying much heed to. A writer who knows so little of naval affairs as to think that the *Columbia* would be unable to get her men to quarters or fire a gun before she was sunk by Spanish cruisers which she had previously descried, is hardly to be taken seriously.

Let me hear from you at any time. It is always a pleasure. *Very sincerely yours*

HARVARD FOOTBALL

To Norman Winslow Cabot

Washington, November 23, 1897

My dear Captain Cabot:

I would like to write to you, and through you to the members of your team, to say that my opinion is that the Harvard team did very well this year. Of course our hindsight is better than our foresight, and I suppose we all feel that with slight changes here and there we could have won against Yale. As for Pennsylvania, I don't think it was on the cards for us to beat her. At any rate, I feel that the team made an entirely creditable showing, and if the men don't get discouraged, and go in just as heartily next year with perhaps a trifle more attention to aggressiveness in attack, we will have good reason to expect a triumphant season. I want to see Harvard play hard, snappy football in attack. Nobody could condemn mean or vicious playing more than I do; I would rather see the game stopped than have it indulged in; but I do want to see the attack made with all the energy and aggressiveness possible. Fight with "devil," as they say in the boxing ring.

The only thing I did not like about this year was taking off the H after the Yale game. Our men had done well; not quite as well as we had hoped, but still well; and I think it as great a mistake to show undue sensitiveness in defeat, or after failure to achieve victory, as it is to be indifferent about it. It is very bad to be overconfident or overelated, and it is very bad to be too much cast down. It is exactly as in the great world. One never cares for the nations who, after a defeat, want to sacrifice somebody, to atone for their own mortification and wounded vanity. The French and the Greeks try to depose any government under which they have lost; but our people stood by Lincoln, just as they stood by Washington, through years of defeat, until we came out on top. They never lost their resolution to win, and they never were daunted by temporary disaster.

If you get time I wish you would drop me a line as to who of the team will be back next year. I am very sorry that you are going out, but I am glad of the election of Captain Dibblee. Tell him how pleased many of us are to see a Californian again prominent in our athletics. When I was at Harvard our crew beat Yale three out of four times, and the best man our class contributed to the crew was a Californian.

Pray give my regards to all the members of the eleven. *Yours truly*

VANISHING HUNTING GROUNDS

To Frederick Courtney Selous

Washington, November 30, 1897

Dear Mr. Selous:

Your letter made me quite melancholy — first, to think I wasn't to see you after all; and, next, to realize so vividly how almost the last real hunting grounds in America have gone. Thirteen years ago I had splendid sport on the Big Horn Mountains which you crossed. Six years ago I saw elk in bands of one and two hundred on Buffalo Fork; and met but one hunting expedition while I was out. A very few more years will

do away with all the really wild hunting, at least so far as bear
and elk are concerned, in the Rocky Mountains and the West
generally; one of the last places will be on the Olympic peninsula of Oregon, where there is a very peculiar elk, a different
species, quite as big in body, but with smaller horns which
are more like those of the European red deer, and with a
black head. Goat, sheep and bear will for a long time abound
in British Columbia and Alaska.

Well, I am glad you enjoyed yourself anyhow, and that you
did get a sufficient number of fair heads — wapiti, prongbuck,
blacktail and whitetail. Of course I am very sorry that you
didn't get a good sheep and a bear or two. In the northeastern part of the Park there is some wintering ground for the
elk; and I doubt if they will ever be entirely killed out in the
Park; but in a very short while shooting in the West, where it
exists, will simply be the kind that can now be obtained in
Maine and New York; that is, the game will be scarce, and the
game laws fairly observed in consequence of the existence of
a class of professional guides; and a hunter who gets one good
head for a trip will feel he has done pretty well. You were in
luck to get so fine a prongbuck head.

Do tell Mrs. Selous how sorry I am to miss her, as well as
you. I feel rather melancholy to think that my own four small
boys will practically see no hunting on this side at all, and
indeed no hunting anywhere unless they have the adventurous temper that will make them start out into wild regions to
find their fortunes. I was just in time to see the last of the real
wilderness life and real wilderness hunting. How I wish I
could have been with you this year! but, as I wrote you before,
during the last three seasons I have been able to get out West
but once, and then only for a fortnight on my ranch, where I
shot a few antelope for meat.

You ought to have Hough's *Story of the Cowboy* and
VanDyke's *Still Hunter*. Also, I think you might possibly
enjoy small portions of the three volumes of the Boone and
Crockett Club's publications. They could be obtained from
the *Forest and Stream* people at 346 Broadway, New York, by
writing. Have you ever seen Washington Irving's *Trip on the
Prairie* and Lewis and Clark's Expedition? And there are two
very good volumes about [   ] now out of print, by a lieu-

tenant in the British Army named Ruxton, the titles of which
for the moment I can't think of, but I will look them up and
send them to you. He describes the game less than the trap-
pers and hunters of the period; men who must have been
somewhat like your elephant hunters. When I was first on the
plains there were a few of them left; and the best hunting trip
I ever made was in the company of one of them, though he
was not a particularly pleasant old fellow to work with.

Now, to answer your question about ranching; and of
course you are at liberty to quote me.

I know a good deal of ranching in western North Dakota,
eastern Montana, and northeastern Wyoming. My ranch is in
the Bad Lands of the Little Missouri, a good cattle country,
with shelter, traversed by a river, into which run here and
there perennial streams. It is a dry country, but not in any
sense a desert. Year in and year out we found that it took
about 25 acres to support a steer or cow. When less than that
was allowed the ranch became overstocked, and loss was certain to follow. Of course where hay is put up, and cultivation
with irrigation attempted, the amount of land can be reduced;
but any country in that part of the West which could support
a steer or cow on 5 acres would be country which it would pay
to attempt to cultivate, and it would, therefore, cease to be
merely pastoral country.

Is this about what you wish? I have made but a short trip
to Texas. There are parts of it near the coast which are well
watered, and support a large number of cattle. Elsewhere I do
not believe that it supports more cattle to the square mile than
the northwestern country, and where there are more they get
terribly thinned out by occasional droughts. In Hough's book
you will see some description of this very ranching in Texas
and elsewhere.

Do give my warm regards to Buxton when you meet him.
I am very sorry that it has been so long since I have seen him;
and I really grudge the fact that you and Mrs. Selous got away
from this side without my even getting a glimpse of you.
Faithfully yours

REFORM IN NEW YORK

To Rudyard Kipling

Washington, January 5, 1898

My dear Kipling:

As you say you will be in Cape Town, and as I don't know where to write you, I send you this care of Scribner's, and I hope that ultimately it will catch up with you somewhere.

It was very pleasant to hear from you. Of course I shall be glad to do everything I can for Sidney Low. I know of him very well, and shall be glad of the chance of meeting him. I'll get Reed and Lodge and one or two others to dine with him here, and shall see that he has full opportunity to go through our navy yards and the like. I guess I can put him through all right, although I am sorry I am no longer in the Police Board, for that gave me a chance to show anyone, who really wished to see, the inside of New York matters. In spite of all the worry, and although I didn't accomplish more than half of what I wanted to accomplish, and often by no means as much as this, yet I wouldn't have given up my two years as President of the Police Board for a great deal. In the first place I did accomplish a good deal, and, in the next place, it was exceedingly interesting, alike from the executive, the political, the sociological and the ethnic standpoints. (Imagine my successor, Mr. Bernard York's feelings if he saw that sentence!)

In New York there are rather over half a million voters. There is a very appreciable percentage which delights in bad government. Counting in the liquor sellers, who, for the most part, are obliged by their associations to connive at a great deal of wickedness, and indeed to champion it, this might be from ten to twenty per cent. There is a still larger percentage of voters so very ignorant that they are quite indifferent to any appeal to their consciences, though they can sometimes be reached by an appeal to their emotions — an appeal which the average reformer, who is a somewhat bloodless person, never makes. Then we have the two classes of the very good and the pretty good, which together make a majority, but which generally are either split up by a line running through both classes, or, as on the present occasion, by a line running between them. The pretty good people don't like the grosser forms of corruption, but are apt, like most of us, to resent excessive and arrogant virtue, especially if it touches on puritanism. The very good people, or at least the theoretically very good, include a number of little groups, each group usually laying stress on some one virtue. The Methodist, for instance, believes in honesty, but can much less easily be roused on that score than on some issue which involves the suppression of what is technically termed vice, or the support of a non-sectarian school system. The Episcopalian on the other hand is usually very liberal in excise matters, and cares but little for gambling, but wants in his public service not only honesty, but the open profession of honesty; sometimes he accepts the latter in lieu of the former. This year Tammany was bound to come in. The republican machine, representing the pretty good people, and the straight-out reformers, representing the very good people, had quarreled among themselves and hated each other worse than they did Tammany; and it wasn't on the cards to make a winning combination. Moreover, Tammany had been out of power some time, and its misdeeds were not fresh in the public mind, whereas every slip-up of the reformers and every misdeed of the Republican machine was fresh and vivid. So we got whipped. But Tammany won't be quite as bad as it was — at any rate for some time to come; and in many matters she will strive to take exactly the position taken by those she supplants. We have gained something; and whenever the chance comes by which we may be able to make another successful alliance or coalition of the shifting and heterogeneous anti-Tammany elements we will gain a little more; and then when we do gain such a victory, it will, as on this occasion, be followed by another defeat, which will rob us of most, but not of all, that has been gained.

This navy work is extremely interesting. I am quite absorbed in it. Last summer, by the way, I got Remington down for a three days' cruise with the squadron. He was very nearly blown up through incautiously getting too near the blast line of one of the 13-inch guns when it was fired; but he enjoyed himself nevertheless. Your friend Captain Evans has been one of my right hand men. The peaceful soul is now fretting his life out because he doesn't think it likely he will have any chance at Spain; so at the moment he has gone off duck shooting with ex-President Cleveland instead, and has just sent me a dozen canvasbacks. I was to have gone with him, but couldn't, for the Secretary is away, and I am misguiding the Department in his absence.

We were all very much pleased and touched at your dedicating "The Feet of the Young Men" to Hallet Phillips. The afternoon before he was drowned he was at the Lodges, and was reading to us part of the poem, which you had sent him in manuscript. I do not know when I can recollect a man whose death left so great a gap in so many families. He was always so thoughtful and so unselfish that we miss him at every turn. Mrs. Lodge and Mrs. Roosevelt felt literally as if they had lost a brother.

I saw by the papers that you had a son. I now have four, and two daughters, the last baby being five weeks old. Remember me cordially to Mrs. Kipling. *Very sincerely yours*

PREPARING FOR WAR

To John Davis Long

Washington, January 14, 1898

Sir:

In one way it is of course proper that the military and naval branches of the Government should have no say as regards our foreign policy. The function of the military arm is merely to carry out the policy determined upon by the civil authorities.

Nevertheless, sir, it will be absolutely impossible to get the best results out of any military policy unless the military authorities are given time well in advance to prepare for such policy. At present the trouble with Spain seems a little less acute, but I feel sir, that I ought to bring to your attention the very serious consequences to the Government as a whole, and especially to the Navy Department, (upon which would be visited the national indignation for any check, no matter how little the Department was really responsible for the check) if we should drift into a war with Spain and suddenly find ourselves obliged to begin it without preparation, instead of having at least a month's warning, during which we could actively prepare to strike. Some preparation can and should be undertaken now, on the mere chance of having to strike. In addition to this, when the blow has been determined upon we should defer delivering it until we have had at least three weeks or a month in which to make ready. The saving in life, money, and reputation by such a course will be very great.

Certain things should be done at once if there is any reasonable chance of trouble with Spain during the next six months. For instance the disposition of the fleet on foreign stations should be radically altered, and altered without delay. For the past six or eight months we have been sending small cruisers and gunboats off to various ports of the world with a total disregard of the fact that in the event of war this would be the worst possible policy to have pursued. These smaller cruisers in the event of war would be of use only on one or two points. If scattered about the high seas they would be worse than merely useless; for they would inevitably run the risk of being snapped up by the powerful ships of the enemy which they cannot fight, and from which they are too slow to run; and every such loss would be an item of humiliation for the Department and for the nation. If we have war with Spain there will be immediate need for every gunboat and cruiser that we can possibly get together to blockade Cuba, threaten or take the less protected ports, and ferret out the scores of small Spanish cruisers and gunboats which form practically the entire Spanish naval force around the Island. Probably a certain number of our smaller cruisers could be used with advantage in the Asiatic Squadron for similar work around the Philippines. In these two places the unarmored cruisers would be very valuable. Everywhere else they would simply add an element of risk and weakness to our situation.

We have now in home waters on the Atlantic Coast, the *Marblehead*, *Montgomery* and *Detroit*, three thoroughly efficient ships for the work we would need around Cuba. We also have the *Vesuvius*, which could be used for the same purpose, although its field of usefulness would be limited. We also have ready the *Nashville*, *Annapolis*, *Newport* and *Vicksburg*, and the *Princeton* is almost ready. These four vessels are of the so-called gunboat class, and if used instantly on the outbreak of war, together with others of their kind, they would practically root out the small Spanish vessels in the Cuban waters. If there was a delay of two or three weeks some of these small Spanish vessels might inflict serious depredations in the way of attacks on our merchant marine or on our transports, especially if the Army was sent to Cuba. The *Princeton* should be pushed to immediate completion. The *Nashville* should not be allowed to leave our shores, the *Newport* should be recalled to Key West; and the *Vicksburg* sent there.

On the South Atlantic Station we have the *Cincinnati*, a very efficient fighting cruiser of small coal capacity, and two gunboats the *Wilmington* and *Castine*. If we have a war now these ships should all be recalled. It will take them thirty days to get home, and they will reach here without any coal. In other words for the first five or six most important weeks of the war these vessels will be absolutely useless, and might as well not be in existence. In my opinion they should tomorrow be ordered to Pernambuco. When they get there a week or two hence, we can then tell whether to bring them back to Key West or not. They should be at Key West and filled with coal and in readiness for action before the outbreak of hostilities. The presence of the *Cincinnati* might make the difference of being able to reduce Matanzas at the same time we blockade Havana. The presence of the two gunboats might make the difference of destroying a Spanish flotilla, or of driving out the Spanish garrison from one end of the Island.

More urgent still is it to take action with regard to the vessels in Europe. These include the *San Francisco*, a good cruiser, of not very great coal capacity, and with slow-fire six-inch guns; the *Helena*, a small gunboat, and the *Bancroft*, a still smaller gunboat. The *Helena* and *Bancroft* should be brought back from Europe today if there is the slightest chance of war with Spain. Against any fair-sized cruiser they could make no fight, and they are too slow to escape. The best that could happen in the event of war, would be that they would be shut up in a European port, if they stay where they now are. They would run great risk of capture, which, aside from the loss, would mean humiliation. If brought back however, they would aid materially in the reduction of Cuba for the reasons given above. I should also bring the *San Francisco* immediately back the minute a chance of war came. The *San Francisco* is a respectable fighting ship. She could aid not merely in the blockade of Cuba, but in the attack on some of the less protected towns; but, like the *Philadelphia*, she is not fit to oppose a first-class modern cruiser, thoroughly well armed. Her coal capacity, although respectable, is not very great, and she is probably not swift enough to insure her escape if pursued. For these reasons I do not think that she should form a part of the flying squadron, the sending out of which into Spanish home waters I regard as one of the most essential elements in the plan of campaign yesterday submitted to you. Accordingly she should be brought home.

On the Asiatic station Commodore Dewey will have the *Olympia*, *Boston*, *Concord* and *Petrel*. This will probably be enough to warrant his making a demonstration against the Philippines, because he could overmaster the Spanish squadron around those islands. At the same time the margin of force in his favor is uncomfortably close, and I should advise in the event of trouble with Spain that the *Baltimore*, *Bennington*, *Marietta*, and possibly the *Wheeling*, be sent to him in advance. If we had trouble with any power but Spain I should not advise Hawaii being left unprotected, but with Spain I do not think we need consider this point.

One of the most important points in our scheme of operations should be the flying squadron. This should especially be the case if we are not able to bombard Havana. To my mind the chief objection to bombarding Havana is to be found in the lack of ammunition, of which we are so painfully short. I believe we could reduce Havana, but it might be at the cost of some serious loss, and, above all, at the cost of exhausting our supply of ammunition. If we bombard Havana we must make it a success at any cost for the sake of the effect upon the people. If we do not bombard it, then we must do something else, for effect on the people, and upon the Navy itself. This something else can partly take the shape of the capture of Matanzas and other towns and the rooting out of the Spanish cruisers around Cuba; but we especially want to keep the

Spanish cruisers at home to prevent depredations on our own coast. In fighting efficiency the Spanish fleet is about double what it was so late as last April. They now have seven battleships, which, in average strength, are about equal to the *Maine* and *Texas*. We could beat these seven battleships if we could get at them, but they could cause us trouble if we allowed them to choose the time and place of attack. If, however, we send a flying squadron, composed of powerful ships of speed and great coal capacity, to the Spanish coasts we can give the Spaniards all they want to do at home, and will gain the inestimable moral advantage of the aggressive. The ships to be sent in this squadron should be the *New York* and *Brooklyn*, the *Minneapolis* and *Columbia*, and two of the auxiliary steamers like the *St. Paul* and *New York* of the American line, which steamers could be fitted in about ten days. The squadron should start the hour that hostilities began; it should go straight to the Grand Canary, accompanied by colliers. At the Grand Canary they should coal to their limit and leave coal there, if possible under some small guard. They should then go straight up, say through Gibraltar by night and destroy the shipping in Barcelona, returning immediately to the Grand Canary. If the Spaniards had occupied the Grand Canary in force, they could then go home. If not, they could replenish with coal, and strike Cadiz; then go off the coast and strike one of the northern seaports on the Bay of Biscay. Probably after this they would have to return home. Such an enterprise would, in all human probability, demoralize the Spaniards, and would certainly keep their fleet in Spanish waters, for they would be "kept guessing" all the time. Only the vessels I have named above would be fit to take part in the enterprise. The *Columbia* and *Minneapolis* are now laid up. It would take them three weeks to get ready. They are only valuable for just such an operation, and the operation would itself be of most value at the very outset of the war. They should therefore be got ready at once and kept in readiness so long as there is the least danger of war with Spain. Their captains should be assigned them, not because it is any man's turn to be assigned, but with a view to the fact that we will need for this flying squadron the very best men in the Navy. I should strongly advise, in the event of war, your substituting one or two men who now have no ships in the place of one or two of those who have ships; but in any event when the *Columbia* and *Minneapolis* are commissioned they should be sent to sea under a couple of the very best men whom you now have ashore.

Our most urgent need is ammunition. If there is any prospect of war, steps should be taken in advance to get this ammunition. We should have to accept a less high grade of powder than we now demand, and should have to get the companies to work night and day.

We also need more men. The battleships left on the Pacific could perhaps be depleted of most of their men, who should be sent east; and we could fill their places, temporarily at least, by the naval militia on the California coast. At the same time we should draw on the best of the naval militia on the Atlantic coast, and on any force that we can get from the Revenue Marine and Coast Survey; and this in addition to the extra men who should be immediately provided for by Congress. Our best ships are now undermanned. In the event of war I wish to reiterate what I have said in two or three former reports, that we should increase the number of officers on the battleships.

The work should be pushed with the utmost energy on the *Puritan* and *Brooklyn*. If war came tomorrow we should have no ships ready to put in this flying squadron except the *New York*.

Well in advance we should get every vessel we may possibly need, and especially an ample supply of colliers. It is extraordinary how many of these vessels would be needed under the conditions of actual sea service in time of war with a modern fleet, and lack of coal will reduce the Navy to immediate impotence. As soon as war broke out we could of course no longer get coal in foreign ports.

Some of the steps above advised should be taken at once if there is so much as a reasonable chance of war with Spain. The others it is not necessary to take now, but they should be taken well in advance of any declaration of war. In short, when the war comes it should come finally on our initiative, and after we had had time to prepare. If we drift into it, if we do not prepare in advance, and suddenly have to go into hostilities without taking the necessary steps beforehand, we may have to encounter one or two bitter humiliations, and we shall certainly be forced to spend the first three or four most important weeks not in striking, but in making those preparations to strike which we should have made long before. *Very respectfully*

THE SINKING OF THE *MAINE*

To John Davis Long

Washington, February 16, 1898

Sir:

In view of the accident to the *Maine*, I venture respectfully, but most urgently, to advise that the monitors, instead of being laid up, be put in commission forthwith. If we had gone to war with Spain a year ago we should have had seven armored ships against three; and there would be no chance of any serious loss to the American Navy. Month by month the Spanish Navy has been put into a better condition to meet us. A week ago it would have been seven seagoing armored ships against seven. Today it would be six against seven. When the *Numancia* is ready, as she soon will be, it will be six against eight. By adding the three monitors and the Ram *Katahdin* we can make it ten to eight. We have lost in peace one of our battleships, a loss which I do not believe we would have encountered in war.

I would not intrude on you with any suggestion or advice did I not feel, sir, the greatest regard and respect for you personally, no less than a desire to safeguard the honor of the Navy. It may be impossible to ever settle definitely whether or not the *Maine* was destroyed through some treachery upon the part of the Spaniards. The coincidence of her destruction with her being anchored off Havana by an accident such as has never before happened, is unpleasant enough to seriously increase the many existing difficulties between ourselves and Spain. It is of course not my province to in any way touch on the foreign policy of this country; but the Navy Department represents the arm of the government which will have to carry out any policy upon which the administration may finally determine, and as events of which we have not the slightest control may, at any moment, force the administration's hand, it seems to me, sir, that it would be well to take all possible precautions. If ever some such incident as the de Lome affair, or this destruction of the *Maine*, war should suddenly arise, the Navy Department would have to bear the full brunt of the displeasure of Congress and the country if it were not ready. It would in all probability take two or three weeks to get ready vessels laid up in reserve, and these two or three weeks would represent the golden time for striking a paralyzing blow at the outset of the war.

I would also suggest that the Merritt Wrecking Company, or else some other as good, be directed at once to make preparations to get the *Maine* up.

I note Captain Sigsbee and Consul General Lee advise against a warship going to Havana at present. It seems to me they would not thus advise unless they felt that there was at least grave suspicion as to the cause of the disaster. In any event I hope that no battleship will be again sent there. In point of force it is either too great or too small. The moral effect is gained as much by the presence of any cruiser flying the American flag, a cruiser such as the *Marblehead*, for instance. If there is need for a battleship at all there will be need for every battleship we possess; and the loss of a cruiser is small compared to the loss of a battleship.

I venture again to point out how these events emphasize the need that we should have an ample Navy. Secretary Tracy, in his address at Boston the other day, was able to show that he had no responsibility for our present inadequate Navy; that he had given advice which, if followed by Congress, would have insured us at the present moment, a Navy which would have forbid any danger of trouble with either Spain or Japan. The question of economy is very important; but it is wholly secondary when compared with the question of national honor and national defense. An unsuccessful war would cost many times over more than the cost of the most extravagant appropriations that could be imagined. Congress may, or may not, adopt your recommendations, if you recommend, in view of what has happened, the increase of the Navy to the size which we should have, but at any rate the skirts of the Department will then be cleared; and it is certain that until the Department takes the lead, Congress will not only refuse to grant ships, but will hold itself justified in its refusal. For a year and a half now we have been explaining to Spain that we might and very probably would, in certain contingencies interfere in Cuba. We have therefore been giving her ample notice, of which she has taken advantage to get ready all the fleet she could, until the margin of difference between our force and hers has become so small that by the sinking of the *Maine* it has been turned in her favor so far as the units represented by the seagoing armorclads on the Atlantic are concerned. It is of course true that the Department will be blamed for extravagance if it recommends that the Navy be increased, as it should be increased, and as the interests of the nation demand; but this blame will be baseless, and we can well afford to stand it, whereas it may be held against us for all time to come, not merely by the men of today, but by those who read history in the future, if we fail to point out what the naval needs of the nation are, and how they should be met. *Very respectfully*

DEFENDING THE NAVY

To J. Edward Myers

Washington, February 21, 1898

My dear Sir:

It is a little difficult to answer your letter with proper moderation. I am not ashamed of the Navy, but I am heartily ashamed that there are any Americans who should feel as you do; and I am quite unwilling to think that any considerable portion of them in your city or elsewhere so believe. If you had taken the trouble to read the accounts of the disaster, you would have known that the reason the crew suffered compared to the officers, was because the explosion occurred under them and in the forward part of the ship, and not in the after-part of the ship, where the officers were. Captain Sigsbee was the last man to leave the ship. I am happy to say that this is the first suggestion that has been made that this fact reflected upon the officers, because the making of such a suggestion reflects not in the least upon the officers, but upon the man who makes it. Recently, on one of the torpedo boats, one of the two officers perished in a gale, and not a single member of the 35 enlisted men; but no man with a particle of manliness in his nature would state that this reflected upon the enlisted men.

As for what you say about carelessness being shown by our officers, and inability to protect the vessel, you had better wait until the official inquiry is made. It will be full and ample. You further ask whether, in view of this disaster, it would not be well to have no Navy. This shows on your part precisely the spirit shown by those men who, after the battle of Bull Run, desired to abandon the war and allow the Rebellion to succeed. When men get frightened at the loss of a single ship, and wish to seize this as an excuse for abandoning the effort to build a navy (and this no matter what may be the reason for the disaster) they show that they belong to that class which would abandon war at the first check, from sheer lack of courage, resolution, and farsightedness.

I have purposely written this letter in strong terms, for they were called for by yours. *Yours truly*

THE DANGERS OF LITERARY POPULARITY

To William Peterfield Trent

Washington, February 23, 1898

My dear Mr. Trent:

As soon as you find out how much time you will have in Washington on Sunday the 6th let me know. I can almost surely arrange to see you. Indeed I must, for I do want to have a talk with you so very much.

I am glad you did not go to Cleveland. I feel just as you do; that is, when you receive a thoroughly advantageous offer, both in money and in position, you are bound, in justice to yourself and family, to accept it; but where there is a doubt, then give the benefit of it to Sewanee. You speak to the southern young men of the best type in a manner, and with a weight, belonging to no one else of the South; and probably you yourself will never know exactly how much you have done.

You touch on one of what I believe to be the most serious obstacles in the way of doing good literary work in the present generation, when you speak of the press and bustle of city life, and especially of the tendency to write "timely" articles, and the like. It is not necessary to be a mere recluse in order to do good work as a poet, a novelist, or even as a historian or a scholar; but it is absolutely necessary to be able to have the bulk of one's time to one's self, so that it can be spent on the particular study needed. Nowadays it is rather difficult to get such leisure, and indeed it can be gotten only by a man of some means and of great determination of character, if he has any widespread popularity. Prof. Lounsbury can work as a scholar should, very largely because his countrymen, as a whole, do not in the least appreciate him and his work; but if a man becomes at all popular the conditions of modern life render it the easiest thing in the world for thoughtless people to intrude upon his time, and for the man himself to fall into temptations which will interfere with his work. Even more important and more harmful is the fact that the enormous increase in the half-educated reading public, and in the half-educated caterers to this reading public, tends to divert every man capable of doing good work from that good work; because as my own experience tends to show, one's literary work is very apt to be remunerated in inverse proportion to its value. The minute that a man like Moses Coit Tyler writes a serious work on our early literature, a work which attracts attention and gives him a name, he receives all kinds of requests to do second-rate work, and unless he is very well-to-do, and very much accustomed to saying No, and to treating temporary popularity with indifference, it is exceedingly difficult for him not to yield.

I don't suppose I could ever have made the *Winning of the West* a big historical book, and a good deal of my active life has helped me in making it even what it is; but I know that if

I had had more leisure I could have done much better with it; and now I have to be adamantine in refusing innumerable requests to write a manual on western history for one publisher, a manual on naval wars for another, a little book on the cowboy for a third, some articles on our navy for a newspaper syndicate, some sketches of New York police life for the magazines, etc., etc., etc. There is a plausible reason for writing each one, but if I should go into any of them while I am at work as I am in the Navy Department, it would mean the absolute surrender of the purpose of going on with *The Winning of the West*, and that I am not willing to do if it can be avoided.

There! You see what you have brought on yourself by writing me as you did. My boy Ted is much better. Mrs. Roosevelt, however, improves so very slowly that I am still exceedingly anxious about her.

Give my warm regards to Mrs. Trent. *Faithfully yours*

ORDERS TO THE ASIATIC SQUADRON

To George Dewey

Cablegram

Washington, February 25, 1898

Dewey, Hong Kong:

Order the squadron, except the *Monocacy*, to Hong Kong. Keep full of coal. In the event of declaration of war Spain, your duty will be to see that the Spanish squadron does not leave the Asiatic coast, and then offensive operations in Philippine Islands. Keep *Olympia* until further orders.

To John Davis Long

Washington, March 25, 1898

Sir:

Mr. Walcott, Director of the Geological Survey, has just been in to see me, having seen the President. He has shown me some interesting photographs of Professor Langley's flying machine. The machine has worked. It seems to me worth while for this government to try whether it will not work on a large enough scale to be of use in the event of war. For this purpose I recommend that you appoint two officers of scientific attainments and practical ability, who in conjunction with two officers appointed by the Secretary of War, shall meet and examine into the flying machine, to inform us whether or not they think it could be duplicated on a large scale, to make recommendation as to its practicability and prepare estimates as to the cost.

I think this is well worth doing.

This board should have the power to call in outside experts like R. H. Thurston, President Sibley College, Cornell University and Octave Chanute, President of American Society of Civil Engineers, at Chicago. *Very respectfully*

To William Sturgis Bigelow

Washington, March 29, 1898

Dear Old Man:

Cabot handed me your letter yesterday, and I was deeply touched by it, as I always am by your repeated proofs of sincere interest. It is very hard for me to have to follow a course to which Cabot and you are opposed. I can only assure you that I adopted it after having given most careful consideration to all that both you and many other friends have said to me on the other side; and whether I am mistaken or not my action will be due to my conscientious belief and to really careful thought.

I do not know that I shall be able to go to Cuba if there is war. The Army may not be employed at all, and even if it is employed it will consist chiefly of regular troops; and as regards the volunteers only a very small proportion can be taken from among the multitudes who are even now coming forward. Therefore it may be that I shall be unable to go, and shall have to stay here. In that case I shall do my duty here to the best of my ability, although I shall be eating out my heart. But if I am able to go I certainly shall. It is perfectly true that I shall be leaving one duty, but it will only be for the purpose of taking up another. I say quite sincerely that I shall not go for my own pleasure. On the contrary if I should consult purely my own feelings I should earnestly hope that we would have peace. I like life very much. I have always led a joyous life. I like thought, and I like action, and it will be very bitter to me to leave my wife and children; and while I think I could face death with dignity, I have no desire before my time has come to go out into the everlasting darkness. Moreover, I appreciate thoroughly that in such a war disease, rather than the enemy's rifles, will be what we shall have to fear, and that it will not be pleasant to die of fever in some squalid hospital without ever having seen an armed foe. So I shall not go into a war with any undue exhilaration of spirits or in a frame of mind in any way approaching recklessness or levity; but my best work here is done. In time of peace I can push forward reforms and urge the President and Secretary to action in a way impossible to any line officer, because I can afford to incur resentments and to hazard my place, and as a matter of fact have done so repeatedly, but in time of war, the danger in advocating military measures will be past. There will be no question then of supine reluctance to do what is needed because it is hoped that the need may not arise, and no question of frowning on and resisting the man who agitates the proper measure. Then the officers of the Navy at headquarters will assume their proper importance and will be the real directors of military operations. Already Captain O'Neil, for instance, is doing everything that can be done with the ordnance, and

Captain Bradford with the equipment, while Captan Crown-inshield, whose position is the most important of all, is as fully alive as I am to the needs of the moment, and it is under him, and not under me, that the control of the officers will lie, save in so far as the Secretary takes the matter into his own hands. My office is essentially a peace office. The Assistant Secretary has properly nothing to do with military operations. They are decided by the Secretary on the advice of his naval subordinates. Whatever influence I have exerted or may exert was or would be due simply to the fact that I took upon myself the responsibility of interfering with what was not my business, and was permitted so to interfere. As a matter of fact I am not, save in exceptional places, allowed thus to interfere, and the things that I have done have usually been done when I was Acting Secretary. I shouldn't be allowed to be Acting Secretary in time of war.

Moreover, a man's usefulness depends upon his living up to his ideals in so far as he can. Now, I have consistently preached what our opponents are pleased to call "jingo doctrines" for a good many years. One of the commonest taunts directed at men like myself is that we are armchair and parlor jingoes who wish to see others do what we only advocate doing. I care very little for such a taunt, except as it affects my usefulness, but I cannot afford to disregard the fact that my power for good, whatever it may be, would be gone if I didn't try to live up to the doctrines I have tried to preach. Moreover, it seems to me that it would be a good deal more important from the standpoint of the nation as a whole that men like myself should go to war than that we should stay comfortably in offices at home and let others carry on the war that we have urged. This doesn't apply to a man in very high civic position. It does apply to men in low civic position.

When am I to see you here, that I may tell you all this more at length by word of mouth? *Faithfully yours*

ROUGH RIDER,
GOVERNOR,
VICE-PRESIDENT
1898–1901

To Henry Cabot Lodge

San Antonio, May 19, 1898

Dear Cabot:

Will you tell Gussie that I know he will pardon me for not writing. I am told that he is with Wilson's staff, and much appreciate his sending me the note. Here we are working like beavers and we are getting the regiment into shape. It has all the faults incident to an organization whose members have elected their own officers — some good and more very bad — and who have been recruited largely from among classes who putting it mildly, do not look at life in the spirit of decorum and conventionality that obtains in the East. Nevertheless many of our officers have in them the making of first rate men, and the troopers, I believe, are on the average finer than are to be found in any other regiment in the whole country. It would do your heart good to see some of the riding. The Eastern men are getting along very well. You would be amused to see three Knickerbocker club men cooking and washing dishes for one of the New Mexico companies. We have a number of Indians, who are excellent riders and seem to be pretty good fellows. The bulk of the men are quiet and self-respecting, often men of very considerable education and I think generally men of some property. The order has been excellent; we have had but one fight and one case of drunkenness. —— is turning out only fairly well as a major. I have been drilling his squadron and one of the others this afternoon. The dust, heat and mosquitoes prevent existence being at all sybaritic. I am heartily enjoying it nevertheless, and as the Spanish squadron has so far eluded our people, I think this regiment will be in trim to move whenever the advance on Cuba is to be made; but you can have no conception of the interminable delays of the Ordnance and Quartermaster's Departments.

I have a couple of scrawny horses, which they say are tough. I hope so, as otherwise I shall probably have to eat them and continue my career on foot.

I feel pretty homesick, of course. If it were not for that, I should really be enjoying myself thoroughly.

Wood is doing splendidly and the amount of work he has accomplished is incredible.

Give my best love to Nannie, and do not make peace until we get Porto Rico, while Cuba is made independent and the Philippines at any rate taken from the Spaniards.

I have given a note of introduction to you to a big stockman from Texas, Simpson, formerly of Forrest's cavalry, who went with us last trip on the gold issue. *Yours ever*

WAITING TO SAIL FOR CUBA

To Anna Roosevelt Cowles

On Board U.S. Transport *Yucatan*,
Port Tampa, June 12, 1898

Darling Bye,

This is our sixth day sweltering on this troop ship under the semitropical sun in Tampa harbor. It is not a large ship and has a thousand men aboard. We have given up the decks to the men, so that the officers are confined to the cabin, but even so it is far easier for us than for them. If the authorities in their wisdom keep us much longer in this ship, we shall certainly have some epidemic of disease. Why in the name of Heaven we should have been put on the transports before sailing I cannot tell. However, I won't complain if only we *do* start and get into the fun. I suppose Will has left New York by this time. The navy has had all the fun so far, and I only hope that peace will not be declared without giving the army a chance at both Cuba and Porto Rico as well as the Philippines.

Bob is along and so far perfectly healthy. Poor Billy Tudor was under the weather and to his bitter regret had to be left behind for the second expedition. The delay is most irritating and the enforced idleness and crowding tells on the morale of the men. Nevertheless, they have stood it astonishingly well and taken it in very good part so far.

I cannot say what a pleasure it was to see Edith for the four days, and I only hope the trip did her no harm. The post office is so hopelessly behind-hand here that we do not begin to get our mail. *Ever yours*

FIGHTING IN CUBA

To Corinne Roosevelt Robinson

On Board U.S. Transport *Yucatan*,
In the Gulf of Mexico, June 15, 1898

Today we are steaming southward through a sapphire sea, wind-rippled, under an almost cloudless sky. There are some forty-eight craft in all, in three columns, the black hulls of the transports setting off the gray hulls of the men-of-war. Last evening we stood up on the bridge and watched the red sun sink and the lights blaze up on the ships, for miles ahead and astern, while the band played piece after piece, from the "Star Spangled Banner" at which we all rose and stood uncovered, to "The Girl I Left Behind Me." — But it is a great historical expedition, and I thrill to feel that I am part of it. If we fail, of course we share the fate of all who do fail, but if we are allowed to succeed (for we certainly shall succeed, if allowed) we have scored the first great triumph in what will be a world movement. All the young fellows here dimly feel what this means; though the only articulate soul and imagination among them belong rather curiously, to ex-sheriff Captain "Buckey" O'Neil of Arizona. We have school for the officers and under-officers, and we drill the men a couple of hours in the manual, especially for firing. Everyone seems happy, now that we are going; though our progress is so slow that we may be a week before we reach Santiago, if we are going there. Thanks to the folly of having kept us a needless six days on board there will probably be some sickness among the men.

Monday, June 20th '98, Troop Ship nearing Santiago.

We didn't stop anywhere after all, so you'll get this letter with my last one, I suppose. Until yesterday we sailed slowly

but steadily south of east, against the trade wind that blew all
the time in our faces. The weather was always fine; there were
vexatious delays, thanks to a schooner, which, by an act of
utter folly at Washington, or here, is being towed, stopping
the whole fleet, and by an act of further folly our steamer,
which has no tow rope, was sent back to bear it company and
all the rest of the fleet are out of sight ahead. If the Spaniards
had any enterprise they would somewhere or other have cut
into this straggling convoy especially when Gen. Shafter left
us as stragglers in the rear; but they haven't any and so we are
safe and nearly in sight of Santiago; wondering very much
whether that city has fallen, in which case our expedition is
wasted, or whether it will fight, and if so how hard. All day
we have steamed close to the Cuban Coast, high barren looking mountains rising abruptly from the shore, and at this distance looking much like those of Montana. We are well within
the tropics, and at night the Southern Cross shows low above
the horizon; it seems strange to see it in the same sky with the
friendly Dipper. There has been very little to do, but we drill
the men in the manual of arms each day, and hold officers'
school in the evening. On Sundays I "support" the chaplain
at church.

Las Guasimas, June 25th '98.

Yesterday we struck the Spaniards and had a brisk fight for
2½ hours before we drove them out of their position. We lost
a dozen men killed or mortally wounded and sixty severely or
slightly wounded. Brodie was wounded; poor Capron and
Ham. Fish were killed. Will you send this note to Fish's
father? One man was killed as he stood beside a tree with me.
Another bullet went through a tree behind which I stood and
filled my eyes with bark. The last charge I led on the left using
a rifle I took from a wounded man; and I kept three of the
empty cartridges we got from a dead Spaniard at this point,
for the children. Every man behaved well; there was no flinching. The fire was very hot at one or two points where the men
around me went down like ninepins. We have been ashore
three days and were moved at once to the front without our
baggage. I have been sleeping on the ground in the mackin-
tosh, and so drenched with sweat that I haven't been dry a
minute, day or night. The marches have been very severe. One

of my horses was drowned swimming through the surf. I haven't seen Marshall. My bag has never turned up, like most of our baggage, and it is very doubtful if it ever does turn up, and I have nothing with me, no soap, toothbrush, razor, brandy, medicine chest, socks or underclothes. Will you ask Douglas to get me the articles as by enclosed list, and express them to my regiment at Tampa at once? I shan't be very comfortable until I get them. Richard Harding Davis was with me in the fight and behaved capitally. The Spaniards shot well; but they did not stand when we rushed. It was a good fight. I am in good health.

June 27th '98 Camp 5 miles from Santiago.

The day after our skirmish we stayed in camp, and to my great relief, my bundle came up. A number of our officers never got theirs at all. Also poor Marshall turned up, too sick to be any use to me. I am personally in excellent health, in spite of having been obliged for the week since I landed, to violate all the rules for health which I was told I must observe. I've had to sleep steadily on the ground; for four days I never took off my clothes, which were always drenched with rain, dew or perspiration, and we had no chance to boil the water we drank. We had hardtack, bacon and coffee without sugar; now we haven't even salt; but last evening we got some beans, and oh! what a feast we had, and how we enjoyed it. We have a lovely camp here, by a beautiful stream which runs through jungle-lined banks. So far the country is lovely; plenty of grass and great open woods of palms both sago and [   ], with mango trees and many others; but most of the land is covered with a dense tropical jungle. This was what made it so hard for us in the fight. It was very trying to stand, or advance slowly, while the men fell dead or wounded, shot down from we knew not whence; for smokeless powder renders it almost impossible to place a hidden foe. The morning after the fight we buried our dead in a great big trench, reading the solemn burial service over them, and all the regiment joining in singing "Rock of Ages." The vultures were wheeling overhead by hundreds. They plucked out the eyes and tore the faces and the wounds of the dead Spaniards before we got to them, and even of one of our own men who lay in the open. The wounded lay in the path, a ghastly group; there were no supplies for them; our doctors did all they could, but had little with which to do it; a couple died in the night, and the others we took back on improvised litters to the landing place. One of them, a Mexican cowpuncher, named Rowland, shot through the side, who had returned to the firing line after his wound caused him to fall out, refused to go aboard the hospital ship, and yesterday toiled out here to rejoin us. I really don't see how he ever walked with such a wound. One of the mortally wounded, Heffner, got me to prop him against a tree, and give him his water canteen and rifle, and continued firing until we left him as we went forward. The woods are full of land crabs, some of which are almost as big as rabbits; when things grew quiet they slowly gathered in gruesome rings around the fallen.

I am glad I asked for Douglas to send me those things, though my own have now turned up; for I shall need them anyhow.

SHAFTER'S INCOMPETENCE

To Henry Cabot Lodge

Outside Santiago, July 5, 1898

Dear Cabot:

Not since the campaign of Crassus against the Parthians has there been so criminally incompetent a General as Shafter; and not since the expedition against Walcheren has there been grosser mismanagement than in this. The battle simply fought itself; three of the Brigade Commanders, most of the Colonels, and all the regiments individually did well; and the heroism of some of the regiments could not be surpassed; but Shafter never came within three miles of the line, and never has come; the confusion is incredible. The siege guns have not yet been landed! The mortars have not been started from the landing place. Our artillery has been poorly handled. There is no head; the orders follow one another in rapid succession, and are confused and contradictory to a degree. I have held the extreme front of the fighting line; I shall do all that can be done, whatever comes; but it is bitter to see the misery and suffering, and think that nothing but incompetency in administering the nation's enormous resources caused it. The fighting has been very hard. I don't know whether people at home know how well this regiment did. I am as proud of it as I can be; and these men would follow me anywhere now. It was great luck for me to get the command of it before this battle.

Best love to Nannie. *Yours ever*

SICKNESS AND SUPPLY SHORTAGES

To Henry Cabot Lodge

Santiago, July 19, 1898

Dear Cabot:

It was the greatest pleasure to receive your two letters of the 24th and 25th, which came in inverse order, a couple of days ago. Wood was immensely flattered at your sending him your regards in so kind a way, and I was, naturally, deeply touched, old man, by the whole tone of your note and especially by your thinking now that I was justified in coming. Somehow or other I always knew that if I did not go I never would forgive myself; and I really have been of use. I do not want to be vain, but I do not think that anyone else could have handled this regiment quite as I have handled it during the last three weeks and during these weeks it has done as well as any of the regular regiments and infinitely better than any of the volunteer regiments, and indeed, frankly, I think it has done better than the regulars with the exception of one or two of the best regular regiments. We have moved up to the foothills, but fever is making perfect ravages among us. I now have left less than half of the six hundred men with whom I landed; but the gallant fellows struggle back to me from the hospital just as soon as their wounds are healed or the fever or dysentery lets up a little.

Well, the fight is over now and we have won a big triumph, so there is no use in washing dirty linen, except that surely we ought to profit by our bitter experiences in the next expeditions. Even now with Santiago taken and our ships in the bay and with a month in which to have gotten ample transportation, food and medical supplies, our condition is horrible in every respect. I have over one hundred men down with fever in my own camp out of my regiment of four hundred, 200 having previously died or having been sent to the rear hospitals. The mismanagement of the hospital service in the rear has been such that my men will not leave the regiment if they can possibly help it; yet here we have nothing for them but hardtack, bacon and generally coffee without sugar. I cannot get even oatmeal and rice except occasionally by paying for it myself, which seems a little needless in as rich a government as ours. I have to buy the men canned tomatoes and tobacco. The regiment was moved yesterday and I was given one wagon in which to transport everything, which simply meant a night of exposure for the men and a couple of very scanty meals, while as Gen. Shafter made us move at midday we had fifty cases of heat prostration, the tropical sun working its will upon men weakened by poor food, constant exposure and the grinding hardship of labor in the trenches. Curiously enough the part in which we have broken down has been the administrative and business part, and to a less extent in the mechanical part, while we have been saved by the dogged fighting of the individual regiments. The engineers and artillery have done poorly and the hospital division worse. But the prime difficulty has been lack of transportation, including lack of means to land from the ships. We should have had a great number of barges, lighters and small steam craft as a matter of course. During the month that has passed, Gen. Shafter should have insisted upon having a sufficiency of wagons, mule trains and small craft of the kind mentioned above. Even now we keep the wagons idle while the ships are in the bay, and our men half starved and in tatters. If only I could get decent food for my men! — rice, cornmeal, canned fruit, dried meat. I hope you will not think I grumble too much or am too much worried; it is not in the least for myself; I am more than satisfied even though I die of yellow fever tomorrow, for at least I feel that I have done something which enables me to leave a name to the children of which they can rightly be proud and which will serve in some sense as a substitute for not leaving them more money. But, as any honorable man must, I feel very keenly my share of the responsibility for this army and especially my responsibility for this regiment. I am deeply touched by the way the men of the regiment trust me and follow me. I think they know I would do anything for them, and when we got into the darkest days I fared precisely as they did. Certainly in battle or in the march or in the trenches I never went anywhere but I found them eager to follow me. I was not reckless; but with a regiment like this, and indeed I think with most regiments, the man in command must take all the risks which he asks his men to take if he is going to get the best work out of them. On the day of the big fight I had to ask my men to do a deed that European military writers consider utterly impossible of performance, that is, to attack over open ground unshaken infantry armed with the best modern repeating rifles behind a formidable system of entrenchments. The only way to get them to do it in the way it had to be done was to lead them myself. Now, naturally, I feel terribly to see them suffering for lack of plain food, to see my sick men in high fever lying in the mud on their soggy blankets without even so cheap a comfort as a little rice or even sugar for their tea or coffee.

Lt. Day was promoted for conspicuous gallantry. He was sent to the rear wounded with some of our men. They were kept in the hospital 48 hours before they were given a mouthful of food, and as for water they had to depend upon those of their number who could walk. My men's shoes are worn through; two of them went into the last battle barefooted. Their clothes are in tatters. They have not changed their underclothes since they landed a month ago; yet do what I can I cannot get them spare clothing.

However, enough of grumbling. Did I tell you that I killed a Spaniard with my own hand when I led the storm of the first redoubt? Probably I did. For some time, for your sins, you will hear from me a great many "grouse in the gunroom" anecdotes of this war. I am just wild to see you and spend an evening telling you various things. For the first hour of the last battle we had a very uncomfortable time. We were lying in reserve under orders, where the bullets of the enemy reached us, and man after man was killed or wounded. I lay on the bank by Lieut. Haskell, talking with him. Finally he did not answer some question of mine; I turned to find that he had been shot through the stomach. I gave an order to one of my men, who stood up and saluted and then fell over my knees with a bullet through his brain. But then came the order to advance, and with it my "crowded hour"; for there followed the day of my active life. I got my men moving forward, and when the 9th regiment of regulars halted too long firing, I took my men clean through it, and their men and younger officers joined me. At the head of the two commands I rode forward (being much helped because I was the only man on horseback) and we carried the first hill (this was the first entrenchment carried by any of our troops; the first break in the Spanish line; and I was the first man in) in gallant shape and then the next and then the third. On the last I was halted and for 24 hours I was in command, on the extreme front of the line, of the fragments of the six cavalry regiments, I being the highest officer left there.

Two of my men have died of yellow fever, but we hope to keep it out of the camp, and if we succeed we also hope we shall soon be ordered to Porto Rico.

Remember that I do not hear any news and do write me about anything, especially about Bay, Harry and Gus. You have done everything where you are. You have been more useful than any General, for you occupy the larger field; it would have been criminal for you to leave your task.

Warm love to Nannie. *Ever yours*

THE INDEPENDENT NOMINATION

To John Jay Chapman

Oyster Bay, September 22, 1898

My dear Mr. Chapman:

I hesitate to write to you while the independent nomination has not been formally offered me, but I am now receiving so many questions as to my intentions in the matter that I am not willing to wait longer.

My name will probably be presented for Governor at the Republican state convention at Saratoga on the 27th. If I am nominated then it will be on the same ticket with those who are named for the other state offices. The Republican Party will also have congressional and legislative tickets in the field. National issues are paramount this year; very few municipal officers are to be elected. The candidates will be my associates in the general effort to elect a Republican Governor, Republican congressmen to support President McKinley, the cause of sound money, and a Legislature which will send to the Senate a Republican United States Senator.

It seems to me that I would not be acting in good faith toward my fellow candidates if I permitted my name to head a ticket designed for their overthrow, a ticket moreover which cannot be put up because of objections to the character or fitness of any candidates, inasmuch as no candidates have yet been nominated.

I write this with great reluctance, for I wish the support of every Independent. If elected Governor, I would strive to serve the State as a whole and to serve my party by helping it serve the State. I should greatly like the aid of the Independents, and I appreciate the importance of the Independent vote, but I cannot accept a nomination on terms that would make me feel disloyal to the principles for which I stand, or at the cost of acting with what seems to me to be bad faith toward my associates.

Again expressing my hearty appreciation of the honor you wish to confer upon me, and my regret that it comes in such a shape that I do not see my way clear to accept it, I am *Very sincerely yours*

"THIS SUMMER I WAS LUCKY"

To Cecil Spring-Rice

Oyster Bay, November 25, 1898

Dear Cecil: —

Of course, I was delighted to get your cable, and I knew you would be pleased with my success. I have played it in bull luck this summer. First, to get into the war; then to get out of it; then to get elected. I have worked hard all my life, and have never been particularly lucky, but this summer I *was* lucky, and I am enjoying it to the full. I know perfectly well that the luck will not continue, and it is not necessary that it should. I am more than contented to be Governor of New York, and shall not care if I never hold another office; and I am very proud of my regiment, which was really a noteworthy volunteer organization.

Mrs. Roosevelt is now almost as well as ever she was and the children are well too. I am up to my ears in work and have time only to send you a line.

Isn't it nice to think how closely our two nations have come together this year? We must make every effort to see that they stay together. Do you recollect a letter I wrote you last year about Germany and especially Russia?

Mrs. Roosevelt sends you her love. Did you know that my sister Anna Cowles had a baby? *Faithfully yours*

AN ELECTORAL VICTORY

To James Bryce

Oyster Bay, November 25, 1898

My dear Bryce:

I have delayed answering your letter for a long time in the hope of being able to write you more at length, but I see no immediate prospect of a letup in my work and so I shall just send you a line anyhow.

I have had a distinctly interesting summer. As you know I believed with all my heart in the war with Spain, and I would have been very discontented if I had not been able to practice what I preached. I had a corking good regiment, although the men were only volunteers. When I came back the Machine, which was decidedly chastened by the Low-Tracy failure last year, took me up and nominated me. They would not have nominated me if I had not been a straight Republican, one who while always acting ultimately on his own best judgment and according to his own beliefs in right and wrong, was yet anxious always to consult with and if possible come to an agreement with the party leaders. In other words I had what the Mugwump conspicuously lacks, and what the Frenchman, and in fact all people who are unfitted for self-government, likewise lack, namely the power of coming to a consensus with my fellows. But, of course, the Machine never dreamt of asking a promise of me of any kind or sort. I had a big burden of scandals, both of the National and State administration, to carry; and I was opposed by the professional Independents, like Carl Schurz, Godkin, Parkhurst, and the idiot variety of "Goo-Goos," partly because they objected to my being for the war with Spain, and partly because they feared lest somebody they did not like might vote for me. However, we took the aggressive, and got a great many not only of the Independents proper but of the Independent Democrats, away from them; and, after a very close, uphill fight, we won. I have now a hard task before me. I do not think that there is much in the way of constructive legislation to be done; at least, I do not see much that is needed. Just at present, all that seems to be necessary is honest administration, save that some change will have to be made ultimately in the State civil service laws; and the factory legislation must be enforced.

Give my warm regards to Mrs. Bryce. *Faithfully yours*

To Helen Kendrick Johnson

Albany, January 10, 1899

My dear madam:

I had already read your book and was much interested in it. If you will pardon me for saying so, I think you confound two phases of the struggle for what are rather vaguely called "Woman's rights." I do not wonder at this at all, for the advocates of the movement not only do the same thing, but the noisiest of them usually lay all the stress on the very undesirable side; in other words, the professional woman's rights people contain in their number altogether too many representatives of the same intellectual and moral type as the bulk of the professional abolitionists. The antislavery cause was eminently just, and even the professional abolitionists probably on the whole did good; but the more one reads of these professional abolitionists (I do not mean men like Birney, but the men who advocated disunion or anarchy and who betrayed a foolish and feeble violence in dealing with all practical questions), — the more one feels that they were about as undesirable a class of people as the country ever saw. But it would have been literally criminal folly to wish to perpetuate slavery because so many of the extreme professional antislavery champions were noxious members of the body politic, or because most of their ideas were wrong, or even because the slaves would not do as well when free as was hoped.

The extreme advocates of any cause always include fanatics, and often fools, and they generally number a considerable proportion of those people whose mind is so warped as to make them combine in a very curious degree a queer kind of disinterested zeal with a queer kind of immorality. A great many self-styled woman's champions revolt, not against the laws of man, but against the laws of nature. It certainly seems to our finite minds a great injustice of nature that the hardest lot in life should fall to the weakest half of the human race. On the average the woman has a harder time than the man, and must have, from the mere fact that she must bear, nurse and largely rear her children. There is no use in blinking this fact. It must simply be accepted as war or any necessarily hazardous profession must be accepted. The first duty of woman is the duty of motherhood, just as the first duty of the man is breadwinning — homemaking. Marriage is, of course, just as much the duty of one as of the other. There are exceptional men and women who need not or ought not to marry, just as there are exceptional men and women who need not or ought not to work, or to go to war; but these are exceptions, sometimes to be honored and sometimes to be pitied. The normal, healthy man should always count upon working hard and should hold himself ready at any time to go to war, or to go into any occupation, no matter how hazardous — like that of a miner, a deep-sea fisherman, a railroad man or a fireman, — while the normal, healthy woman should be a mother. Our race is unfit to cumber the earth, if its men do not work hard, and are not always ready, if there is need, to fight, and, of course, a race is neither fit to cumber the earth nor able to do so, unless its women breed. Work — fight — breed — a race may do all these things, and yet be worthless; but unless it does them, it certainly *must* be worthless.

So far then as the movement for woman's rights represents a revolt against either common sense or morality, it should be smashed. But we are no more justified in opposing it because there is this element in it, than we would have been in championing slavery because there was a similar element in the abolition movement. It is not necessary to say that I entirely agree with you about the home and its all-importance. Remember that the very evils which the opponents of the present movement most dread exist to their fullest extent in societies where that movement has absolutely no footing. In France the race has begun to decrease and the nation is decaying mainly because of the way in which men and women look upon the relations between the sexes, upon family life and upon having children. But France is the very country where the legal and social attitude of the body politic on questions like divorce, the property of women, headship of the man, the different standards of morality for the man and the woman, political rights of the woman etc. is the least progressive and is the most medieval and most divergent from the views taken by the advocates of the betterment of woman's condition. The worst results that could follow the adoption of the ideas of the new champions of woman, could no more than equal the results that have happened in France, where those ideas have never gained the least foothold.

Sane advocates of woman's rights would bring about, I am confident, a great betterment in her status, while at the same time simply causing her better to perform every duty she now performs. Just the same arguments that were advanced against giving women the suffrage are or were advanced in favor of keeping the man the absolute tyrant of the household. As a rule the headship of the man is most complete the lower we go in the social and ethnic scale (heroic Greece to the contrary notwithstanding), and the higher and nobler the race is, the more nearly the marriage relation becomes a partnership on equal terms — the equality, of course, consisting not in the performance of the same duties by the two parties, but in the admirable performance of utterly different duties, and in mutual forbearance and respect.

I do not for a moment believe that the suffrage will do all that is claimed for it, whether for women or for men, and I should always introduce it tentatively in new groups of either sex. There are great bodies of women who are unfit for it, just as unquestionably, taking the world as a whole, (including Asia and Africa for instance), the great majority of men are unfit to exercise it. Only in the highest country, like our own, is it wise to try universal suffrage. In our own country the gradual betterment of woman's condition has been due to the working of forces which may or may not ultimately find expression through the suffrage. But I think the suffrage would accomplish something. If you will read such a story as Mary E. Wilkins's "The Revolt of Mother," you will appreciate how even in our country there are enormous bodies of, on the whole, pretty good people, where women are shamefully wronged because they are not treated as equals. What we need is to teach the woman self-respect, and the man to respect the woman; for in the last resort I hardly know whether to despise most the being who neglects his or her duties, or the being who fails to assert his or her rights. If the woman were a voter, if the woman were in the eye of the law a citizen with full rights of citizenship, it would undoubtedly on the whole have a tendency to increase her self-respect and to wring a measure of reluctant respect for her from man. There never was an extension of the suffrage yet which was not accompanied by some evil results, but on the whole, in the present state of society, the only way to ensure the proper regard for the rights of any particular section of a community like ours seems to be to let that section have a voice in the general affairs. Practically I may mention that in my own little school district admission of women to the franchise for school matters has resulted distinctly well. I should like by degrees to increase the sphere in which the women of New York State can exercise the suffrage, doing it very cautiously and by degrees, and seeing how each extension practically works. *Very truly yours*

STRENGTH AND GENTLENESS

To Edwin Kirby Whitehead

Albany, January 13, 1899

My dear Sir:

Replying to yours of the 10th inst.

I won't say that I used exactly the language you quote, for I would not wring a boy's neck; but I certainly would thrash him heartily for cruelty and have once or twice followed exactly this course. I am as intolerant of brutality and cruelty to the weak as I am intolerant of weakness or effeminacy. I want to see boys able to box, wrestle, play football and hold their own stoutly, not only in games, but when called upon to fight or resist oppression; and I also want them brought up to feel that it is incumbent upon every true man to be gentle and tender with the weak — with women and young children, and with dumb animals. *Very truly yours*

P.S. Be sure and put in both sides of this statement. It strengthens it.

CONSIDERING A CAPITAL PARDON

To Jacob Riis

Albany, February 8, 1899

Dear Friend:

I have your letter of the 6th instant and will support the bill you refer to. Now as to the case of Mrs. Place. I have not yet heard from her lawyers who together with certain other of her champions are to argue before me. Remember this is not my first case. I have already refused to pardon a negro convicted of wife murder. This is a woman convicted of a very cruel murder of another woman. I have exactly the same feeling that you have about womanhood and about the burdens which nature has placed upon women and the duty of man to make them as light as possible. For instance, where a poor seduced girl kills her child to hide her shame, I would infinitely rather punish the man who seduced her than the poor creature who actually committed the murder. But there are some fiends among women, and I hardly think, old man, that we help womanhood by helping these exceptions. However, I shall go into it with the utmost care and with the very highest sense of my own responsibility.

Am I to see Mrs. Kelley and Miss Addams on the afternoon of the 17th? *Faithfully yours*

CIVIL WAR HISTORY

To George F. R. Henderson

Albany, February 14, 1899

My dear Colonel Henderson:

I do not believe I have ever enjoyed a book dealing with the Civil War as much as I have yours, and so, my dear sir, you must pardon my writing to tell you how much pleasure you have given me. I am delighted, incidentally, to find out the author of the *Study of the Battle of Fredericksburg*. As you rec-ollect, you did not put your name to it. I think that you simply put on the title page that it was "By a Line Officer." It struck me at the time as being perhaps, in the proper sense of the word, the most scientific effort — that is, the most intelligent and truth-desiring effort, to get at the facts and learn the les-sons of a given battle, that I had seen in the literature of the Civil War. It may possibly interest you to know that I strove to apply some of the lessons it taught in dealing with my own regiment in the late Spanish War.

But your present book is what your little study of course could not be; that is, it is literature, just as Napier and Mahan are literature. There are some points which I should like to go over with you if it were ever my good fortune to meet you in person, (and if you come to this side again I trust you will not fail to visit me). But these are not in any way essential to your history itself. For instance, though Lord Wolseley has in many ways done such excellent work both in the practice and theory of his profession, I do not believe that his utterances on our civil war have any particular value. Some years ago I studied one of his pieces upon Lee, and I found he simply did not know the facts; and no matter how good a man is, if he does not know the facts and does not think it necessary to be sure of them before writing an essay, his opinion is not worth much.

If you will allow me to say so, I rather wish you had left out the footnote about *Uncle Tom's Cabin*. My mother was a Georgian; one of my uncles built the *Alabama* and another fired the last gun from her before she went down; and I am yet supporting one or two venerable black impostors who were slaves in the family before the war. I know what a good side there was to slavery, but I know also what a hideous side there was to it, and this was the important side. *Uncle Tom's Cabin* I think was essentially true so far as the whites were con-cerned. As for the blacks described, they were true also; but they were the exceptions and not the rule. One of the revolt-ing features of slavery to me was the fact that the large class of mulatto slaves were practically sold into slavery by their own fathers. I have myself known of a white brother selling his half sisters. However, I did not intend to go into this. My own belief is that there never was a war in which the right was so wholly on one side, and yet that there never yet was a war in which the wrong side believed so absolutely that it was fighting for righteousness and justice; and I agree with you as to the comparative prowess of the two parties.

By the way, your book was brought to my attention by General Bradley T. Johnson, who was spending a few days with me here in Albany. He is a fine old boy, if there ever was one, valiant, kindly, simplehearted.

I suppose you have seen Ropes' second volume. I am a little disappointed in it. In making his study concise, he has nevertheless been unable to resist keeping in altogether too many proper names of persons and places, and his book has to be studied as one would study a chess problem.

It always seems to me a pity that, when a man finds the work which he can do better than anyone else, he should not finish it. If Mahan's first volume had not been followed by his study on the Naval Wars of the French Republic and Empire, his work would have been incomplete. I most earnestly hope that you will now go on and write a history of Lee's campaigns after the death of Jackson. In the life of Jackson you have practically covered all that Lee did up to and including Chancellorsville. It would hardly be worth your while going over the same ground, but it would be emphatically worth while, at least from the standpoint of us outsiders, to have you finish your work by writing of Lee's campaigns during the two years that followed Jackson's death. What a happy death Jackson's was after all! Of course, the finest of all epitaphs is "Here lies Wolfe Victorious." And Jackson deserved just such an inscription.

By the way, when I feel very impatient over the maladministration and blundering during the Spanish-American war, I take a certain amount of consolation in remembering what occurred in 1812 and 1861. During the first year of the Civil War not one of the great men of the war made any real mark. Lee had accomplished nothing; Jackson had suffered a defeat; Farragut was only preparing for his first stroke; and though Grant had taken Fort Donelson, he had been defeated at Belmont and surprised at Shiloh, where he was only saved from utter disaster by Buell.

However, I did not mean to take up so much of your time. I can only say again how much I enjoyed your book. *Very sincerely yours*

PROTECTING BIRDS

To Frank Michler Chapman

Albany, February 16, 1899

My dear Mr. Chapman:

I need hardly say how heartily I sympathize with the purposes of the Audubon Society. I would like to see all harmless wild things, but especially all birds protected in every way. I do not understand how any man or woman who really loves nature can fail to try to exert all influence in support of such objects as those of the Audubon Society. Spring would not be spring without bird songs, any more than it would be spring without buds and flowers, and I only wish that besides protecting the songsters, the birds of the grove, the orchard, the garden and the meadow, we could also protect the birds of the sea shore and of the wilderness. The loon ought to be, and, under wise legislation, could be a feature of every Adirondack lake; ospreys, as everyone knows, can be made the tamest of the tame; and terns should be as plentiful along our shores as swallows around our barns. A tanager or a cardinal makes a point of glowing beauty in the green woods, and the cardinal among the white snows. When the bluebirds were so nearly destroyed by the severe winter a few seasons ago, the loss was like the loss of an old friend, or at least like the burning down of a familiar and dearly loved house. How immensely it would add to our forests if only the great logcock were still found among them! The destruction of the wild pigeon and the Carolina paraquet has meant a loss as severe as if the Catskills or the Palisades were taken away. When I hear of the destruction of a species I feel just as if all the works of some great writer had perished; as if we had lost all instead of only part of Polybius or Livy. *Very truly yours*

THE PHILIPPINE INSURRECTION

To William Bayard Cutting

Albany, April 18, 1899

My dear Mr. Cutting:

I have yours of the 17th inst. Don't you think it would be just as well to read my entire speech before condemning it? I distinctly stated that any man could be opposed to the movement in entire sincerity.

As for the incident you mention — if true (which I very much doubt, having had some experience of stories of this kind in Cuba) it is a lamentable incident of a type that happened hundreds of times in our warfare against the Indians right up to 1890 and which has happened hundreds of times in the warfare of the English against the black fellows of Australia and the Kaffirs of the Cape. If your argument is good in one case it is good in the other; and there is no right to keep a foot of territory on this continent, in Australia or South Africa for the white race save in accordance with the view which not only justifies but requires our presence in the Philippines. The talk of the "just consent of the governed," — aye, and the talk about "humanitarianism" is just exactly what I described it; and the case as regards its "righteousness" stands precisely parallel between the Philippines and the Apaches and Sioux. My doctrine is what I preached in my *Winning of the West*, for instance. In a fight with savages, where the savages themselves perform deeds of hideous cruelty, a certain proportion of whites are sure to do the same thing. This happened in the warfare with the Indians, with the Kaffirs of the Cape and with the aborigines of Australia. In each individual instance where the act is performed it should be punished with merciless severity; but to withdraw from the contest for civilization because of the fact that there are attendant cruelties, is, in my opinion, utterly unworthy of a great people. At the San Juan fight, by the accident of my presence at a certain part of the trenches, I was able to save the life of a captured Spaniard. By the accident of the absence of any officer from another part of the trenches, a certain captured

Spaniard was killed. To use either case as a reason for abandoning the attack on Santiago would not have seemed to me wise. *Faithfully yours*

To Thomas Collier Platt

Albany, May 8, 1899

My dear Senator:

I received your letter yesterday afternoon, and have taken 24 hours to consider it deeply before replying.

In the first place, my dear Senator, let me express my sense of the frankness, courtesy and delicacy with which you write and with which you have invariably treated me ever since my nomination. The very keen sense that I have of this makes it more unpleasant than I can say to have to disagree with you. As I have told you, and as I have told very many others, you have treated me so well and shown such entire willingness to meet me half way, that it has been the greatest possible pleasure for me to agree with you and to try to carry out your ideas, and it has caused me real pain when I have had to disagree with you. I am peculiarly sorry that the most serious cause of disagreement should come in this way right at the end of the session.

I remember well all the incidents of our meeting which you describe, and I knew that you had just the feelings that you mention; that is, apart from my "impulsiveness," you felt that there was a justifiable anxiety among men of means, and especially men representing large corporate interests, lest I might feel too strongly on what you term the "altruistic" side in matters of labor and capital and as regards the relations of the State to great corporations. I very earnestly desired to show that this was not to any improper degree the case. My dear Senator, I cannot help feeling that I *have* shown it. Now, I do not like to say this when you think I *have not*, because you have infinitely more experience than I have in matters of this sort, and in most of such cases your judgment is far better than mine; but pray do not believe that I have gone off half-cocked in this matter. I should have been delighted to have escaped the need of taking action at all, and I only did take action when it was forced upon me, after an immense amount of thought and worry.

I appreciate all you say about what Bryanism means, and I also know that when parties divide on such issues, the tendency is to force everybody into one of two camps, and to throw out entirely men like myself, who are as strongly opposed to populism in every stage as the greatest representative of corporate wealth, but who also feel strongly that masses of these representatives of enormous corporate wealth have themselves been responsible for a portion of the conditions against which Bryanism is in ignorant, and sometimes wicked, revolt. I do not believe that it is wise or safe for us as a party to take refuge in mere negation and to say that there are no evils to be corrected. It seems to me that our attitude should be one of correcting the evils and thereby showing that, whereas the populists, socialists and others really do not correct the evils at all, or else only do so at the expense of producing others in aggravated form, on the contrary the Republicans hold the just balance and set our faces as resolutely against improper corporate influence on the one hand as against demagogy and mob rule on the other. I understand perfectly that such an attitude of moderation is apt to be misunderstood when passions are greatly excited and when victory is apt to rest with the extremists on one side or the other; yet I think it is in the long run the only wise attitude. I believe that in the long run here in this State we should be beaten, and badly beaten, if we took the attitude of saying that corporations should not, when they receive great benefits and make a great deal of money, pay their share of the public burdens; and that on the other hand, if we do take this attitude we shall be all the stronger when we declare that the laborers shall commit no disorder and that we are utterly against any attack on the lawful use of wealth. For instance, when trouble was anticipated just now in Buffalo, I at once sent Major General Roe out there and got the whole brigade of National Militia in the neighborhood in shape to be used immediately. The labor men came up to protest. I told them instantly that

I should entertain no protest; that the militia would not be called out unless the local authorities stated that they needed them; but that the minute this condition was found to exist, they would be called out, and that I should not consider for a moment the protest that this was "intimidating the laboring men," because it would intimidate no one unless he was anxious to commit lawlessness, and that in that case it would be my especial care to see that he *was* intimidated.

Now, let me take up this particular franchise tax bill. I wish that its opponents would recollect that it is by no means a revolutionary measure. Franchises are taxed in very much the same way in Connecticut and have been for many years. They are taxed in a somewhat different way in Pennsylvania. They are taxed much more severely in many parts of Great Britain. Where they have escaped taxation the result has been as in Detroit, Toledo and Chicago, to make the citizens generally join in such a revolt that they have swung to the opposite extreme of municipal ownership and have forbidden the granting of any franchises. I think we wish to be careful about taking a position which will produce such a revolt. And as regards the effect on the party, I believe that the killing of this bill would come a great deal nearer than its passage to making New York democratic a year from next fall. If we run McKinley against Bryan the big corporate influences must in self-defense go for the former; and on the other hand, we shall have strengthened the former by strengthening the republican party among the mass of our people and making them believe that we do stand squarely for the interests of all of the people, whether they are or are not connected in any way with corporations. When I sent in my first taxation message to the Legislature it did not seem as if any bill could be passed or agreed upon by the legislature; and I was then told that this Committee would be appointed and that a serious effort would be made to tax franchises. In the message itself you will remember I took the most positive ground in favor of thus taxing them. Without any notification to me the Senate suddenly took up and passed the Ford bill. I then began to study it pretty carefully and the more I studied it, the more convinced I became that it was along the right lines; that is, that franchises should be taxed as realty, according to the Connecticut plan.

Now, as to the inference about my yielding to the yellow
journals and public clamor. I have not this year to my knowledge seen a copy of the *Journal*. I doubt very much if I have
seen a copy of the *World* twice and certainly I have never
looked at its editorial page; and it would be an overestimate
to say that I have seen a dozen editions of the *Herald*. I have,
however, read the *Tribune* quite often and the *Sun* very often.
These are almost the only papers I have seen except the Albany
Evening Journal. I feel the most profound indifference to the
clamor of the yellow papers. I think I showed it in my attitude on the Mrs. Place matter; in my veto of the *World's* labor
bill; in putting the militia in readiness in Buffalo to meet the
strike; also in my attitude on the 71st Regiment business. I
appreciate absolutely that any applause I get from any such
source would be too evanescent for a moment's consideration.
I appreciate absolutely that the people who now loudly approve of my action in the Franchise Tax bill will forget all
about it in a fortnight, and that on the other hand, the very
powerful interests adversely affected will always remember
it — certainly to my disadvantage, which is unimportant, and
not impossibly to the disadvantage of the party, which *is* important. But I feel that we should be put in the wrong if the
bill failed to become a law.

However, to return to the thread of the narrative of the bill.
It got into the House and everybody agreed that some action
in reference to taxation would have to be taken this session;
that is, that the principle of taxing franchises would have to
be recognized in some shape or form so as to give the Committee something to work on. As I told you that morning at
breakfast, and as I have reiterated to Odell on his last visit
here, I was anxious to accept any bill, whether I approved of
it in all its details or not, provided it met your approval, and
recognized substantially the principles sought to be attained.
When Odell was up here the Monday and Tuesday before the
legislature adjourned, I went over this matter with him. He
agreed with me in the most unequivocal manner that some
measure taxing franchises must be passed — indeed treated
this as a matter of course. At first on looking over the Rodenbeck and Ford bills, he said he preferred the Ford bill, but
that an amendment should be inserted giving the taxing power

to the State authorities. I think he said the State Assessors, but otherwise the Comptroller. To this I cordially agreed. That same afternoon he told me he preferred the Rodenbeck bill. I said, very well; that although I did not think it much of a measure, I would cordially back it if that was what the Organization wanted. Accordingly I summoned the different senators, Ellsworth, Raines, Higgins, Stranahan and others and asked them whether they would take up the Rodenbeck bill. They positively refused to do so and said that the Ford bill was what everyone wanted. I then saw Nixon and Allds and found that they were bent upon the Rodenbeck bill. I asked the leaders of the two houses to consult together and come to an agreement. They failed to reach any agreement; in my presence Ellsworth told Nixon that they must pass the Ford bill. I then wrote to Ellsworth and Nixon personal letters explaining that something ought to be passed; that though I did not like the Rodenbeck bill, I was entirely content to take it, but that the two houses ought to agree on some measure. Finally the day before adjournment Nixon and Allds called upon me and said they could no longer withstand the pressure; the people wanted the Ford bill (Allds used the words that he had "received orders not to pass it,") and they could not withstand the pressure any longer and would have to pass it, but wished it to be understood that they were not solely responsible for it — that is, I understood that they wished that I would share the responsibility. They explained that they knew they could not get the Rodenbeck bill through the Senate and did not think they could get it through the House. The senators had also told me by this time that they could not pass the Rodenbeck bill, and that if any amendment was made to the Ford bill, they thought that at that late day in the session it simply meant its death. Accordingly after Nixon and Allds went out and after Fallows had come in to state that without an emergency message they could not pass the bill, I sent them down the emergency message. Nixon says, and then said, that it was absolutely necessary for us to pass the bill; Ellsworth said it had to be passed, Nixon said my message was needless, and my message was never read. Exactly what became of it after it left my messenger's hands and passed into the custody of the Assembly, I do not know; I believe it was torn up. At any rate, the course was followed of refusing to entertain it; the objection being frankly made to the passage of the bill by Mr. Kelly, among others, that it could not be passed because Mr. Brady (he who deluged these counties last year with the money to beat our ticket) was against it. The representatives of the corporations here were perfectly frank in stating that they did not intend to have any legislative recognition of the principle that franchises should be taxed; that they were against it in any and every shape; that they were perfectly willing to have a committee appointed, because they would take care that that committee made its report in such shape as to prevent franchises being interfered with, but that no substantial action recognizing their taxation should be taken. They also urged upon me that I personally could not afford to take this action for under no circumstances could I ever again be nominated for any public office, as no corporation would subscribe to a campaign fund if I was on the ticket and that they would subscribe most heavily to beat me, and when I asked if this was true of republican corporations, the cynical answer was made that the corporations that subscribed most heavily to the campaign funds subscribed impartially to both party organizations. Under all these circumstances it seemed to me that there was no alternative but to do what I could to secure the passage of the Ford Bill without amendment — not that I altogether liked it, but that I thought it a great deal better than inaction under these conditions. I accordingly sent in my second message.

The serious objection to this bill is that the levying and assessing of the tax is made by the local authorities. It seems to me right that the payment should be to the local authorities, but the levying and assessing should be done by the State authorities. In its essence the tax is right. It should be a tax as realty and not as personalty. I question very much if we could by law secure at the outset the right method of getting at the exact money value of these franchises. It seems to me that it would be wiser to leave that question to a board of assessors. Nevertheless if the opposite course is deemed desirable, I am perfectly willing to acquiesce. If the Mazet Committee brings out, as you tell me it will, the utter corruption of Tammany in laying these taxes, my own idea would be, subject to your

approval, that we should use that as a justification for requesting speedy action by the Joint Committee of the two Houses
in preparing a proper tax bill, and I am then entirely willing
if it is deemed best to call together the legislature and have
the present bill amended, or have it repealed by the passage of
a full and proper tax bill; it being always understood, of
course, that this tax bill shall contain provisions under which
these franchises will be taxed in reality and genuinely and not
nominally, so that they shall pay their full share of the public
burdens.

I have just received a telegram from Odell saying that he
cannot come up here to spend the night with me. I shall ask
him up for tomorrow night and will submit my memorandum
on the bill to him.

I would come down to see you but it is simply impossible
to leave the thirty-day bills at this time. *Faithfully yours*

PASSING THE FRANCHISE TAX

To Henry Cabot Lodge

Albany, May 27, 1899

Dear Cabot: —

I was delighted to get your letter, as was Edith. I greatly
envy you your trip to Sicily. For some reason Sicily (which
I have never seen) has always peculiarly attracted me. I suppose it is because the history of the island gratifies to the full
my taste for ethnic contests and the struggle of wholly alien
civilizations.

You will be pleased to know that the regular army men seem
to take to your history; I was with a group of them the other
day and was interested to hear them mentioning that yours
was the best account that had appeared of the general military
operations of the war.

By the way, a perfectly preposterous incident of contemporary popular delusion is that Admiral Schley on his way
through the west is being lionized with a mad enthusiasm.

Since I wrote you I called an extra session of the legislature, and after a very doubtful and anxious struggle, won a complete triumph. Platt, as was to be expected, bitterly and frantically opposed the Ford bill taxing franchises. As with every other political leader of his type where the boss system obtains, his power rests in great part upon the money contributed by the corporations. He was influenced to defend them partly by this consideration and partly by his honorable desire to acknowledge the benefits he had received from them; and partly because like most old men he is very conservative in such matters, and fails to see that to meet a just popular demand is often the best possible way of preventing a perfectly unjust popular demand, and that to do justice in the one case strengthens one in resisting injustice in the other. He and Depew and the rest were crazy to have me veto the bill. To this I would not consent. But the bill was crude in form and there were two or three extremely desirable amendments, notably one which would give the State the power of making the assessment, and I offered to call the legislature together for the purpose of making these amendments. At first they could not decide whether the corporations would be willing to have the amendments made; for not a few of them preferred to be blackmailed by Tammany rather than pay their just dues to an honest Board of State Assessors. Finally, however, the best made up their minds to try for honesty, and Platt then told me he wished the extra session called. Thereupon we began to prepare a new bill, and here the attorneys for the corporations (including Frank Platt) tried to sell me a gold brick, by putting in seemingly innocent provisos which would have made the taxation a nullity. I told them that unless they passed the bill exactly as I wished it, I should sign the Ford bill; for having the Ford bill in my hands gave me the complete mastery of the situation. They then all went in in good faith to pass my amendments. The demagogues and Tammany now became my opponents; but we held every republican vote in the Senate, which was the close and doubtful body, and gained three democrats, and the net result is that we have on the statute books the most important law passed in recent times by any American State Legislature; and we have to our credit a perfectly clean record in appointments and legislation for the session and a great deal of positive work of a good character accomplished. Moreover the break that was threatened between myself and the machine over the Ford bill has been healed by the passage of the amendments. I do not mean to say that they will entirely forgive me, or that they won't cut my throat when the time comes, but they will act with me, so far I can now see, during my term, so that I will have the chance of making a success rather than a failure.

I am very tired, for I have had four years of exceedingly hard work without a break, save by changing from one kind of work to another. This summer I shall hope to lie off as much as possible. Edith is very well and so are all the children. I hope Nannie received the copy of my book which I sent her. *Ever yours*

THE DREYFUS AFFAIR

To Albert Seligman et al.

Albany, June 10, 1899

Gentlemen:
I feel the most heartfelt joy over the action now taken in relation to Captain Dreyfus, and the attempt partially to redress the hideous wrong done him. I trust also that we shall not forget the splendid courage and disinterested patriotism and loyalty of gallant Colonel Picquart. *Faithfully yours*

POLITICAL AMBITIONS

To Henry Cabot Lodge

Oyster Bay, July 1, 1899

Dear Cabot: —
On receiving your first letter about the Duffield incident, I looked up the official reports, and so was very glad to get your second. What you said was known by everybody to be

the exact truth. I doubt if there was a man in the army who did not know that Duffield and his Michigan regiments let themselves be stopped by a resistance so trivial as to be contemptible. He had the greatest chance of the war, for if he had chosen to have pushed home, I verily believe he could have taken Morro, or at least could have put himself in shape to guarantee a detachment of the army taking it. But he and Shafter arranged matters so that the official report holds Duffield blameless.

Incidentally, let me say that I think your last chapter on the war is almost the best. Everyone has agreed that yours is the only good history of the war that has yet come out.

I have just come back from a week in the west where I went to attend my regimental reunion at Las Vegas. It would really be difficult to express my surprise at the way I was greeted. At every station at which the train stopped in Indiana, Illinois, Wisconsin, Iowa, Missouri, Kansas, Colorado and New Mexico, I was received by dense throngs exactly as if I had been a presidential candidate. My reception caused some talk, so I thought it better to come out in an interview stating, that of course I was for President McKinley's renomination, and that everyone should be for it, and giving the reasons. Equally of course I am for Hobart's renomination, if he will take it.

Now as to what you say about the Vice-Presidency. Curiously enough Edith is against your view and I am inclined to be for it. I am for it on the perfectly simple ground that I regard my position as utterly unstable and that I appreciate as well as anyone can how entirely ephemeral is the hold I have for a moment on the voters. I am not taken in by the crowds in the west or by anything else in the way of vociferous enthusiasm for the moment. It would be five years before it would materialize and I have never yet known a hurrah to endure five years; so I should be inclined to accept any honorable position; that the Vice-Presidency is. As a matter of fact, I have not the slightest idea that I could get it, if I did decide to take it, and I should feel like talking any honorable position that offered itself. On the other hand, I confess I should like a position with more work in it. If I were a serious possibility for 1904, I should feel there was very much in what you say, but I do not think we need concern ourselves over the chances of the lightning striking me at that time rather than any other one of a thousand men. Meanwhile I could do more work in two years of the governorship, although I might get myself in a tangle. What I should really most like would be to be re-elected governor with a first-class lieutenant governor, and then be offered the secretaryship of war for four years. Of course it would be even better if I could become United States Senator, but of that I do not see any chance. Of all the work that I would like to undertake, that of Secretary of War appeals to me most. There I think I really could do something, but of course I have no idea that McKinley will put me in the position.

Last night I dined with Wood and Greene and we went over at length the problems in Cuba and the Philippines. I have been growing seriously concerned about both, and this morning I decided to send to John Hay a letter of which I enclose a copy. Having just come out in an interview for the President's renomination, I thought he might tolerate a little advice. I do not suppose it will do the least good, but I wrote on the off chance.

The President's civil service order was justifiable in part, and in part very unjustifiable. More than the matter, it was the manner of doing it that hurt, and especially the way in which it was trumpeted by Kerr, Grosvenor and similar cattle.

By the way, I particularly liked what you said about the attitude of the Germans and French in the last war. It is just as well those gentry should have a reminder now and then as to the effect of their conduct. Did I tell you that Captain Coghlan came out and took lunch here the other day? He was most amusing. I told him that there were no reporters present and that like the old Chancellor with Mr. Pell, he might "damn himself in confidence."

My week's railroading in the west put the finishing touch and I am now feeling completely tired out. I hope to have six weeks of practically solid rest before me, for I have worked pretty hard during the last four years.

Give my best love to Nannie and the boys. Occasionally we see cables in the papers about you. *Ever yours*

PRESIDENTIAL CHANCES

To Charles E. S. Wood

Personal

Albany, October 23, 1899

My dear Mr. Wood:

You are exceedingly kind to have written me and I shall write you with absolute frankness in return. I wish you would tell Senator Simon how I appreciate his interest and that I very much wish he would speak with Senator Lodge as soon as the Senate meets. Lodge is my closest friend and he would do anything possible for me.

I absolutely agree with what Senator Simon says as to the fact that my chance would come now if at all. This was a very small war and two years is the absolute outside limit of duration for any reputation made in it, nor is there anything whatever to be expected by me, or by anyone else for that matter, from McKinley and the McKinley crowd in the way of support after his second term. By that time the kaleidoscope will have shifted completely and the odds are that an entirely new set of men and set of issues will be at the front. Moreover, to change the metsphor, the chances are strong that the pendulum will have swung back and that a Democratic victory will be in order. By that time we shall either have failed definitely or have succeeded definitely in the Philippines. If the former, we shall be swept out because of our failure; if the latter, they will cease to be an issue and room will be made for some other issues.

If I hadn't happened to return from the war in a year when we had a gubernatorial election in New York, I should probably not now be Governor. If, on the other hand, I had returned at the end of the second instead of the first term of the existing President, I should have had a fair show for the nomination. But as things are now it does not seem to me as though there was a show. I have no Hanna; there is no person who could take hold of my canvass and put money in it and organize it, and the big corporations who supply most of the money vary in their feeling toward me from fear to tepid dislike. I have never won any office by working for it by the ordinary political methods and if I should try now I should probably merely fail and be humiliated. I don't think I can play the game that way. The result would be that my usefulness would go. From Tom Reed down and up, how many men have I seen ruined by getting the presidential bee in their bonnets. I have confined myself to trying to be a middling decent Governor. Of course I should like to be renominated and reelected and I shall be very glad if this comes about. If not, why I have had a first-class run for my money anyhow. I am not in the least taken in by the present wave of enthusiasm for me for I know that such waves always mean that the crest is succeeded by the hollow. Senator Simon's words are among the very few indications that there would be serious talk of making me President. In the middle west while there is immense shouting for me it almost always takes the form of "1904," which means in the first place that at present they want McKinley; and furthermore means nothing whatever, as shouting for a date five years ahead is the veriest waste of lung power that can be imagined. I think the organizations have stacked the cards for McKinley's nomination in all of the big states and of course with the southern delegations; and it has never looked to me as if any other outcome were possible unless there is a complete change between now and next spring. I have managed my own course absolutely without regard to the McKinley people as a Governor, and before that time; save in so far as I have of course acted as a good Republican. My course has been shaped to suit myself; and I believe that in great crises it is often necessary not merely to follow but to lead. In consequence you will not find the machine favorable to me.

I would not know how to organize a canvass for myself. If I did start doing it I should probably fail and I should certainly cease to be of much use as a public man. Whatever good I can accomplish is largely accomplished because I am not nervously calculating the chances as to my future.

Do let me say how really touched I am by the interest you have shown me. I deeply appreciate it. *Faithfully yours*

THE BOER WAR

To Hermann Speck Von Sternberg

Albany, November 27, 1899

My dear Speck:

I have just received yours of the 3rd on my return to Albany after several days absence. I send this to the German Embassy at Washington as you say you will be there so soon. I am perfectly delighted that you are to be on this side. We are not in the country this year, so I do not suppose you would care to come to us for Christmas; but we would be delighted to have you if you could come up here to Albany.

What you say about the Kaiser is most interesting. He is far and away the greatest crowned head of the present day. He is a Monarch — a King in deed as well as in name, which some other Kings are not. He is a fit successor to the Ottos, the Henrys, and the Fredericks of the past.

I take just the view you do of the Boer war. I have great sympathy for the Boers and great respect and liking for them, but I think they are battling on the wrong side in the fight of civilization and will have to go under. I have not been a bit surprised at the English defeats. You had told me what you thought of their practical military knowledge of the present day, and in reading of their Indian campaigns by their own best critics, I had been struck by the fact that they nearly encountered disaster again and again under circumstances which would have meant, if pitted against a formidable foe, just exactly the disasters that actually happened. Their victories seem to me to have been won by their disciplined courage, their numbers, and perhaps their artillery, in spite of the superior individual fighting, and for the matter of that, fighting as a whole, of the Boer riflemen. I had been told, moreover, that their military organization was only a little better than ours, and though this was an exaggeration, it had in it an element of truth. At Santiago the courage of our enlisted men and the good conduct of the junior officers could not be surpassed, but after what I saw of the higher officers, and the utter breakdown in administration, I am most heartily thankful that we did not have against us so formidable an enemy as General White has encountered at Ladysmith.

In great haste, *Ever faithfully yours*

CIVILIZED AND BARBARIAN VIRTUES

To Granville Stanley Hall

Albany, November 29, 1899

My dear Dr. Hall:

I must write you to thank you for your sound common sense, decency and manliness in what you advocate for the education of children. Oversentimentality, oversoftness, in fact, washiness and mushiness are the great dangers of this age and of this people. Unless we keep the barbarian virtues, gaining the civilized ones will be of little avail. I am particularly glad that you emphasize the probable selfishness of a milksop. My experience has been that weak and effeminate men are quite as apt to have undesirable qualities as strong and vigorous men. I thoroughly believe in cleanliness and decency, and I utterly disbelieve in brutality and cruelty, but I feel we cannot too strongly insist upon the need of the rough, manly virtues. A nation that cannot fight is not worth its salt, no matter how cultivated and refined it may be, and the very fact that it can fight often obviates the necessity of fighting. It is just so with a boy. Moreover when it comes to discipline, I cordially agree with you as to the need of physical punishment. It is not necessary often to have recourse to it, but it is absolutely necessary that the child should realize that at need it will be resorted to. With my own children (who I think I can say, are devoted to me, and who are close and intimate friends) I invariably have to punish them once physically so as to make them thoroughly understand that I will unhesitatingly resort to such punishment if they make it necessary. After that by treating them with justice, which implies firmness as well as mercy, I hardly ever have to proceed to extremities again.

Mrs. Roosevelt is as much pleased with what you say as I am.

With great regard, *Sincerely yours*

"THE EXPANSION OF GREAT NATIONS"

To Cecil Spring-Rice

Albany, December 2, 1899

Dear Cecil:

I was delighted to get your letter. But it is very tantalizing, for it makes me feel that there is so much to tell you, and so much that I should like to hear from you which cannot be satisfactorily put on paper. I wish you could be here during my brief moment of greatness; for it is certainly soon to pass, of course. What I should really most like to do would be to be Governor General of the Philippines; but I do not suppose I could leave New York, and in any event, it would not occur to the President to appoint me.

I have been absorbed in interest in the Boer War. The Boers are belated Cromwellians, with many fine traits. They deeply and earnestly believe in their cause, and they attract the sympathy which always goes to the small nation, even though the physical obstacles in the way may be such as to put the two contestants far more nearly on a par than at first sight seems to be the case. But it would be for the advantage of mankind to have English spoken south of the Zambesi just as in New York, and as I told one of my fellow knickerbockers the other day, as we let the Uitlanders of old in here, I do not see why the same rule is not good enough in the Transvaal. The Boers are marvellous fighters, and the change in the conditions of warfare during the past forty years has been such as to give peculiar play to their qualities. Mere pluck in advancing shoulder to shoulder no longer counts for as much as skill in open order fighting, in taking cover and in the use of the rifle, and as power of acting on individual initiative. A brave peasant, and still more, a brave man who has been bred in the garret of a tenement house, needs years of training before he can be put on a par with the big game hunter accustomed to life in the open. In our congested city life of today the military qualities cannot flourish as in a mounted pastoral population, where every male is accustomed to bearing arms, and, what is quite as important, is accustomed from his youth up to act under a rough but effective military organization. My regiment was composed of men much like the Boers, but who had not had their military organization; though this had been partially offset by the experience of many of them as deputy sheriffs and deputy marshals. Such a regiment was at the outset worth any three from our big cities, and even from our purely peaceful farming districts, although there was no difference of race. The same thing is true of the Boers; and the fighting will be hard and bloody beyond a doubt. But the end is inevitable. I am amused at the cordial hatred felt by France toward both England and America.

In the Philippines, where we have blundered for a year in a way that would have cost us dearly had we been matched against Boers instead of Tagals, we at last seem to have things pretty well in hand, and I guess there will be no trouble of any serious kind save in administering the islands hereafter.

My own business goes on fairly. At any rate, for this year I have had an absolutely honest administration from top to bottom in this State, and an absolutely efficient one too.

Today is the thirteenth anniversary of my marriage, and I have just given Mrs. Roosevelt a really handsome little watch. Having a good many children, and not being in any remunerative business, this is the first year when I felt that I really could afford to give her something handsome, and I grasped the opportunity!

What a wreck Genghis Khan and the Tartars made, from China to Muscovy, and south to the Persian Gulf. They were able to make the wreck because they struck people who could not fight as well as they could, and the feelings inspired in them by getting the upper hand made them irresistible. The idiot peace-at-any-price individuals, if they were capable of reasoning at all might learn something from this. The experience of the Greeks with the Turks, of the Italians with the Abyssinians, and of the Spaniards in Morocco proves perfectly clearly that if the northern races were not still fighting races, the Mahdists would have overrun the Mediterranean littoral as their lighter-skinned Arab kinsmen overran it twelve centuries ago. I believe in the expansion of great nations. India has done an incalculable amount for the English character. If we do our work well in the Philippines and the West Indies, it will do a great deal for our character. In the long run I suppose all nations pass away, and then the great thing is to have left the record of the nation that counts, — the record left by the Romans — the record that will be left by the English-speaking peoples. *Always yours*

"I HAD BETTER STAY WHERE I AM"

To Henry Cabot Lodge

Albany, December 11, 1899

Dear Cabot:

I have yours of the 7th inst. In the first place, do you not think that Beveridge would be a good man on the Committee on Foreign Affairs? He seems to be sound on those matters.

Now, about the Vice-Presidency. It seems to me that the chance of my being a presidential candidate is too small to warrant very serious consideration at present. To have been a good Colonel, a good Governor and a good Assistant Secretary of the Navy is not enough to last four years. If McKinley were to die tomorrow I would be one of the men seriously *considered* as his successor — I mean that and just no more. But four years hence the Spanish War will be in the very remote past and what I have done as Governor will not be very recent. Nobody can tell who will be up by that time. Of course, I should like to feel that I would still be in the running, but I do not regard it as sufficiently probable to be worth receiving very much weight.

There therefore remains the question of what each office is by itself. The Vice-Presidency is a most honorable office, but for a young man there is not much to do. It is infinitely better than many other positions, but it hardly seems to me as good as being Governor of this State, which is a pretty important State. Then while it is very unlikely that I could be President, there is a chance of my being something else — Governor General of the Philippines, or a Cabinet Officer, or perchance in the remote future, Senator. Mind you, I do not think that any of these things are likely, but at least there is sufficient chance to warrant my taking them seriously, while I do not think the chance for the presidency *is* sufficient to warrant our taking it seriously. If I am Vice-President I am "planted" for four years. Here I can turn around. Platt told me definitely that of course he was for me for a renomination — that everybody was — and though we shall have a good deal of friction from time to time, I do not believe it very likely that he will come to a definite break with me, because I like him personally, I always tell him the truth, and I genuinely endeavor to help him, if I can, with proper regard for the interest of the State and party.

The upshot of it is that it seems to me that I had better stay where I am. The great argument on the other side is, as I have said before, your judgment, which on the whole I have found better than my own. Some of the Western men are wild to have me go on to strengthen the ticket, but it scarcely seems to me that the ticket needs strengthening. Root would be an admirable man.

Give my best love to Nannie. *Ever yours*

"MY MEANS ARE VERY MODERATE"

To Henry Cabot Lodge

Albany, January 30, 1900

Dear Cabot:

I have just received your letter and it has given me much food for thought. I shall have to see Senator Platt before I can say anything. There is an amusing, new complication in the fact that Woodruff may have already gotten all the delegates from New York, so that Platt cannot get them away from him, in which case Platt will certainly not want me to stand. Moreover, if Woodruff is to be the Governor, that may again cause a grave question whether I ought to stand, as it is by no means certain that he could carry the State. Woodruff is a most goodhumored, friendly fellow, wild to have me nominate him for

Vice-President, which I suppose for my sins I might have to do (not if *I* can help it!), and he is amusingly and absolutely certain that nothing can prevent his nomination. He is a great worker, and he has had rather a remarkable success in getting nominations and handling the machine here, and he is absolutely confident that he can get the Vice-Presidency. He had a long and frank talk with me the other day, though I told him I could not speak as frankly in return. He explained that he did not want the Governorship; that he had seen Black cut his own throat from ear to ear, and seen me keep the machine from cutting its throat (and mine too) by main force, and at the constant peril of a break which would have been just as fatal and which could only be averted by the incessant exercise of resolution and sleepless judgment; and that he did not want the Governorship, while he did very much want the Vice-Presidency, chiefly because he had plenty of money and could entertain, and he knew he could act as Presiding Officer of the Senate. The money question is a serious one with me. As you know, my means are very moderate, and as my children have grown up and their education has become more and more a matter of pressing importance, I have felt a very keen regret that I did not have some money-making occupation, for I am never certain when it may be necessary for me to try to sell Sagamore and completely alter my whole style of life. As Governor, I am comparatively well paid, having not only a salary but a house which is practically kept up during the winter, and thanks to the fact that the idiots of the magazines now wish to pay me very large prices for writing, on account of my temporary notoriety, I was enabled to save handsomely last year and will be enabled to do so again this year. But great pressure would come upon me if I went in as Vice-President. I could only live simply. Of course, I could not begin to entertain as Morton and Hobart have; and even to live simply as a Vice-President would have to live would be a serious drain upon me, and would cause me, and especially would cause Edith, continual anxiety about money. If the place held out a chance of doing really good work, I should not mind this, for I must try to carry out my scheme of life, and as I am not to leave the children money, I am in honor bound to leave them a record of honorable achievement; but of course the chance for a Vice-President to do much of anything is infinitesimal. I suppose I should have leisure to take up my historical work again, but that is about all. If the Vice-Presidency led to the Governor Generalship of the Philippines, then the question would be entirely altered, but I have a very uncomfortable feeling that there will be a strong although entirely unreasonable feeling against my resigning. Of course, there should not be, as the succession is arranged in the Secretaryship of State.

I am extremely pleased at the conversation you report with the President. President Schurman had spoken to me about his intention to speak to the President concerning the Governor Generalship, but I had not thought over the matter one way or the other in connection with him and had not the slightest idea whether he had carried out his intention. It is quite needless to say that I absolutely agree with the theory that until the war is over, we want to have the military authority not merely supreme but alone. It would never do to have a divided authority, and it would not be worth while for a really good man to go out there with divided authority. In public life it seems to me the blue ribbon part is of very small value. The point is to get hold of some job really worth doing and then to do it well. The Governor Generalship of the Philippines, especially the first Governor Generalship, would be exactly such a piece of work. I should approach it with a very serious sense, not only of its importance, but of its difficulty; but as far as I can see among those who are likely to be considered as candidates, I would be quite as apt to do well as any.

As soon as I can I will see Senator Platt and then will let you know.

It would be idle for me to thank you, old man. As I have said before, if I began to thank you I should have to take up so much time that there would be very little time left for anything else. You are the only man whom, in all my life, I have met who has repeatedly and in every way done for me what I could not do for myself, and what nobody else could do, and done it in a way that merely makes me glad to be under the obligation to you. I have never been able to do, and never shall be able to do, anything in return, I suppose, but that is part of the irony of life in this world.

I am glad you like the canal report. I came to the conclusion that the position had to be taken boldly. I doubt if anything comes of it at the moment; but it will ultimately.

As for the Payn matter, seemingly I have won out; by dint
of combining inflexible determination with extreme good
nature, and resolutely refusing the advice of Godkin, Parkhurst and of the various small-fry Chapmans, Villards, etc.,
who wanted me to quarrel with the machine, in which case
I should have had about six votes out of the fifty in the
Senate. Of course, these gentlemen are not only unwise but
dishonest. Their opponents are too fond of calling them impracticable and omitting their dishonesty. Heaven knows they
are impracticable! but they are also eaten up by vanity, hypocrisy, mendacity and mean envy. In fact, they combine with
great nicety the qualities of the knave and the qualities of
the fool.

How I have gone over them! Whatever comes hereafter it
is a great pleasure to feel how I have trodden them down.

And on the other hand, I have made the machine act with
absolute decency and have never yielded one hair's breadth to
it on a question of morality or principle. I can say quite conscientiously that during my term the Governorship of New
York has been managed on as high a plane as the Governorship of Massachusetts!

What a terrible time the English are having! There is no
question that the Boers outfight them. I am heartily ashamed
of Mason, Hale and the other men of their stamp who show
the particularly mean attribute of jumping on England when
she is down. But of course those scoundrels who have been entirely against their own nation cannot be expected to have any
sense of propriety in dealing with another nation which was
friendly during the war with Spain when they were traitors.

With best love to Nannie. *Ever yours*

DESCRIBING THOMAS PAINE
To W. E. Warner

Albany, February 1, 1900

Dear sir:

Replying to yours of the 29th ult. permit me to say that the word "atheist" was used in the sense of the denial of the existence of the God of the Christians, and "filthy" described with scientific accuracy Paine's bodily habits and condition at the time alluded to. *Yours truly*

CORPORATE OPPONENTS
To Henry Cabot Lodge

Albany, February 3, 1900

Dear Cabot:

Now this letter is to be strictly secret.

I have found out one reason why Senator Platt wants me nominated for the Vice-Presidency. He is I am convinced, genuinely friendly, and indeed I think I may say really fond of me, and is personally satisfied with the way I have conducted politics; but the big-monied men with whom he is in close touch and whose campaign contributions have certainly been no inconsiderable factor in his strength, have been pressing him very strongly to get me put in the Vice-Presidency, so as to get me out of the State. It was the big insurance companies, possessing enormous wealth, that gave Payn his formidable strength, and they to a man want me out. The great corporations affected by the franchise tax have also been at the Senator. In fact, all the big-monied interests that make campaign contributions of large size and feel that they should have favors in return, are extremely anxious to get me out of the State. I find that they have been at Platt for the last two or three months and he has finally begun to yield to them and to take their view. Outside of that the feeling here is very strong indeed against my going. In fact, all of my friends in the State would feel that I was deserting them, and are simply unable to understand my considering it. I appreciate entirely the danger of this position, but after all I suppose there is no work without an attendant risk, and it does not seem to me that I am ready to leave a real piece of work for a position in which there is not any work at all and where I really do not think there is anything for me to do and no reputation to make.

I earnestly hope the Philippine business can wait a couple of years. *Ever yours*

OPPOSING AN INTERNATIONAL CANAL

To John Hay

Personal

Albany, February 18, 1900

I hesitated long before I said anything about the treaty through sheer dread of two moments — that in which I should receive your note, and that in which I should receive Cabot's. But I made up my mind that at least I wished to be on record; for to my mind this step is one backward, and it may be fraught with very great mischief. You have been the greatest Secretary of State I have seen in my time — Olney comes second — but at this moment I can not, try as I may, see that you are right. Understand me. When the treaty is adopted, as I suppose it will be, I shall put the best face possible on it, and shall back the Administration as heartily as ever; but oh how I wish you and the President would drop the treaty and push through a bill to build *and fortify* our own canal!

My objections are twofold. First, as to naval policy. If the proposed canal had been in existence in '98, the Oregon could have come more quickly through to the Atlantic; but this fact would have been far outweighed by the fact that Cervera's fleet would have had open to it the chance of itself going through the canal, and thence sailing to attack Dewy or to menace our stripped Pacific coast. If that canal is open to the war ships of an enemy it is a menace to us in time of war; it is an added burden, an additional strategic point to be guarded by our fleet. If fortified by us, it becomes one of the most potent sources of our possible sea strength. Unless so fortified it strengthens against us every nation whose fleet is larger than ours. One prime reason for fortifying our great seaports is to unfetter our fleet, to release it for offensive purposes; and the proposed canal would fetter it again, for our fleet would have to watch it, and therefore do the work which a fort should do; and which it could do much better.

Secondly, as to the Monroe Doctrine. If we invite foreign powers to a joint ownership, a joint guarantee, of what so vitally concerns us but a little way from our borders, how can we possibly object to similar joint action say in Southern Brazil or Argentina, where our interests are so much less evident? If Germany has the same right we have in the canal across Central America, why not in the partition of any part of Southern America? To my mind, we should consistently refuse to all European powers the right to control, in any shape, any territory in the western Hemisphere which they do not already hold.

As for existing treaties — I do not admit the "dead hand" of the treaty-making power in the past. A treaty can always be honorably abrogated — though it must never be abrogated in dishonest fashion. *Yours ever*

"I HAVE LIVED UP TO MY IDEALS"

To Josephine Shaw Lowell

Private and Confidential

Albany, February 20, 1900

My dear Mrs. Lowell:

I have received your two letters. Let me make one initial correction. You speak of the painful task I set you. You set the painful task yourself, but your first outline of it was so vague that I asked you what you meant.

Now my dear Mrs. Lowell, I am a little in a quandary how to answer you. You are an old friend and you have been very dear to me. I cannot answer you as I would answer a man — or rather refuse absolutely to answer you as I should in the case of almost anyone else writing me as you have written. Yet there is no good in my writing you at all unless I write you frankly, and I wish to state as kindly but as decidedly as possible that the only excuse for the beliefs that you seem to entertain as to my course is an ignorance of the facts which ought not to exist in one who criticizes. The duty of a critic is to be sure of the facts. If you were not sure of them, or wanted an explanation on any subject I would have given you any statement or any explanation at once. Before asking for such, however, you make your criticism.

In the first place, as to my having made mistakes. Surely, surely, you do not need to have recalled the old proverb that the man who has never made any mistakes has never made anything. I have not made anything like the number of mistakes that Cleveland made while he was Governor, for instance. I should indeed be ashamed of myself if I yielded to the politicians as Cleveland yielded when for eight months he declined to acquit or convict Sheriff Davidson, and then in order to save Davidson and at the same time to save his own reputation, turned the case over to Governor Hill, adding the sin of cowardice to the sin of failure to do his duty in an honest and straightforward fashion. I should indeed be ashamed if I acted ever in any one instance as Cleveland acted when he signed the reform bills affecting Tammany and the Republicans, which I, a republican, had put through the Legislature, but declined to sign the bill affecting the leader of the County Democracy, on the pretence that it contained a clause, *which clause had been put in at his special request*. There were a score of similar incidents.

I have taken Cleveland because I respect him in spite of certain of the things that he has done, because like all men of good sense I judge men by the *aggregate* of their deeds, knowing perfectly well that they will occasionally be guilty of shortcomings, and because I think Cleveland made an excellent Governor on the whole, although he yielded to political and personal considerations in a way that I have never yielded, and would never feel justified to yield.

Instead of taking a Governor for comparison, take one of

the two greatest of all Americans, Abraham Lincoln. Lincoln committed mistake after mistake. It would have been difficult to conceive of greater errors than the appointment of Simon Cameron in the War Department or of Burnside to command the Army of the Potomac, and in the former case it certainly was a mistake against the light.

I told you I thought it had been a mistake not to reappoint Mr. Backus, although I also told you I thought that Mr. Bradish Johnson would make a better man for the asylum. The reason I regard this as a mistake is not at all because of its effect on the Long Island State Hospital which I think will be benefited, but because as a matter of policy, since Dr. Backus was a sufficiently good man it was a mistake (merely from the standpoint of policy) to give to the malignant liars of the *Evening Post* and kindred papers the chance by their unscrupulous mendacity to mislead people like yourself. This answers by the way, what you have said in reference to attacks made upon me about Dr. Backus. The incident was of such trivial importance that it is difficult to have patience with those who treat it as of great consequence. I have to make many scores of these appointments on boards of managers of hospitals. When men are very good I reappoint them. When they are bad I do not reappoint them. When, as in the case of Dr. Backus, there are things in their favor and things against them, I am always in doubt whether to reappoint the man, or to try to get a man who will do better. Whichever I do there is always a possibility that the matter will turn out wrong; and this possibility means the absolute certainty that in a small percentage of the cases, were it Washington himself who had to act, either the retention or the change would be an error. The net result of the changes I have made has been enormously beneficial.

Now, about the factory inspectors. I told you I had made a mistake there. So I did, but there never was a mistake made which sprung from more honest sincerity of purpose. I have for years been intensely interested in trying to elevate the standard of the wageworker. I have wanted to work with him for his own benefit, not to try and approach him from above as if I were patronizing him, but to try to work with him hand in hand. I tried again and again to meet the views of the labor leaders. I went over with them what was to be done. I announced on the stump that I intended to appoint the best representatives I could find among the wageworkers themselves to try for the enforcement of the labor laws. I did this so as to try to satisfy the laboring men who are always extremely suspicious, of the absolute good faith with which the laws were being administered. I have long felt that if we could only get them into the frame of mind where they would accept the fact that public officials who desired good government were with equal honesty desirous of doing what was best for the wageworker, we would have taken a great stride forward towards actually achieving good government. I knew that unless wageworkers were appointed to administer the law, nothing would persuade them that the law was really being administered in their interests. What I did not foresee was that their intense jealousy of one another, their intense suspicion of one of their own number just as much as of an outsider, would largely nullify the advantages I hoped to gain from this course, and therefore would have the disadvantages with nothing to outweigh them. If I should run again I would state that in these offices I intended to appoint the men whom I thought could best administer them without regard to whether these men were wageworkers or not.

You say that I ought to remove the incompetent officials. Your saying this shows that complete ignorance of the law which renders it so difficult to deal with people who while of good intentions, do not take the trouble to find out the facts. In the first place, the charge has not been made against the Factory Inspector himself, but against one of his subordinates, O'Leary, whom only the Factory Inspector can remove. In the next place, were the charge against Williams I have no power whatever to remove him. Did you not follow the Lou Payn case? Did you not know that the trouble about getting his successor was that I had no power to remove him even after his term expired, much less before! I can remove no man excepting the Superintendent of Public Works, the Superintendent of Public Buildings and the Adjutant General, save by what are practically impeachment proceedings before the Senate; that is, by convicting him of misfeasance or malfeasance before the Senate and getting them to vote for his removal. This is a process which practically never takes place. It never has taken place in my day, and it would be sheer lunacy to attempt it where the charge would be that in my judgment Williams was wrong in disagreeing with certain outsiders as to the efficiency of one of his subordinates in a given case. The move for the appointment of unsalaried inspectors was made at the urgent request of Mr. James B. Reynolds and Mr. Jacob A. Riis, and no one who has studied the question doubts its wisdom. I will mention that when we thought that O'Leary would be put out, I was urged to appoint Mrs. Kelley in his place — all of the reformers joining in the request — but Mrs. Kelley has since committed errors of judgment distinctly more serious than any that have been committed by Mr. O'Leary.

The next point you mention is "the appointment of McRoberts a man with a dishonest past." Whoever told you this told you a deliberate falsehood. Twenty-five years ago when McRoberts was County Treasurer, in pursuance of a vote of the Board of Supervisors he deposited funds in a certain banking firm. After a while this banking firm failed and a loss of $25,000 to the county followed. McRoberts' bondsman then made good this loss and he in turn made it good to them, using every dollar he then had in the world. These charges sprung from crooked political rivals. They were made after his name had been sent in, his chief backer being Dr. Doty, the Health Officer, because of the way McRoberts had aided him in his difficult and responsible duties. When the charges were made I withdrew his nomination, went into the matter, satisfied myself that they were mere slanders and submitted his name again with a full explanation of the charges. Not a Senator, Republican or Democrat, voted against him, everything being made public in the papers at the time. Only a paper like the *Evening Post*, deliberately dishonest and deliberately purposeful by every kind of slander and mendacity to break down a man's character, would have dared to reiterate them. I may add that any person who accepts a single statement in the *Evening Post* as true without outside evidence, and acts upon it, must do so now with full and ample knowledge of the utter untrustworthiness of the authority, and therefore, to a certain extent, shares the culpability.

You then speak of the interference with the Bath Soldiers' Home affairs. Here to be perfectly frank, not only I do not know what you mean, but I do know that you yourself cannot possibly know what you mean. I have interfered to the extent of directing the proper officials to investigate charges against the Superintendent of drunkenness and against the trustees of dishonesty. What you or anyone else can see to object to in this "interference" I do not know. I first of all tried to get them to work together. That proved a failure. I then asked the trustees not to proceed against the Superintendent until the investigation by the State Board of Charities was ended. The request was not acceded to. It would be difficult for me to say for which side I had the most thorough contempt, — for those who have been defending those members of the Board of Trustees who have acted against the honest interests of the Home, or for those who have been defending the Superintendent when it became evident that through his unfortunate taste for liquor and his utter lack of management, his power of doing useful service in the Home was at an end.

Again when you come to the Civil Service Law and the State Civil Service rules, I am absolutely ignorant as to what you can possibly mean. The law and rules mark the greatest advance that has ever been made in the civil service reform movement. The only question is as to whether they go too far. I am inclined to think that they probably do, and that it would have been better if we could have allowed the appointing officer the choice of one of three men instead of making him take the man at the top of the list. There is no question whatever as to their not having gone far enough.

As to my statement about the canal inquiry at Hornellsville, it was unquestionably a mistake to make it, not because the statement itself was not true, (for it was) but because it was open to misconstruction by men who desired to misconstrue it. In any event, in my annual message I set out the facts with such absolute exactness that even my most malignant opponents failed to make a point against me about them.

Finally, there is what you say about my constant interviews with Senator Platt. More than to any one cause is it to these interviews that I owe my capacity to give a clean and efficient administration of this office; that I have been able, for instance, to substitute for Lou Payn the best man we ever had in the Insurance Department — an infinitely better man than

Grover Cleveland put in, by the way. If my virtue were of so frail a type that it could not stand seeing Senator Platt, I should indeed be unfit for public office. The man who does not face facts is a fool. For me to refrain from seeing Senator Platt would have been on a small scale exactly and precisely like Abraham Lincoln declining to see Simon Cameron or any other political leader of the day; in which case the Union would not now be a fact and Abraham Lincoln would have gone down to history as being a man as unfit as Wendell Phillips himself for serious leadership or responsible position. I have endeavored to see everyone with whom I could honestly and with self-respect work toward getting better government. There was no point in seeing my foes, whether they were men like Mr. Croker or men who for their own reasons temporarily acted as Mr. Croker's allies, like Mr. Godkin and Dr. Parkhurst; but with all men who were striving along the same lines, or whom I could get to go along the same lines, I wanted to be brought in contact. I have seen Senator Platt again and again. I have seen Congressman Lucius Littauer more often. I have seen Seth Low, Nicholas Murray Butler, Frederick W. Holls and the Rev. Mr. Slicer, for instance, quite as often as I have seen Senator Platt. Every man with whom I could work to some purpose I have seen and consulted. Senator Platt was the most influential of all of them. He could help me most and hinder me most. I have gotten on with him by the simple process of always telling him the truth, of always letting him know before anyone else when I was going to do something that I knew would be disagreeable to him; of scrupulously keeping faith; and of making it evident that where I disagreed with him it was not for the purpose of building up a machine of my own, but because I deemed the interests of the State to conflict with his views. There is no honest and intelligent man whom I should not be delighted to have hear every word I have said to Senator Platt or to see every line I have written to him or to anyone else. Unfortunately so many of the men who call themselves reformers are either so dull or so dishonest that they would (and do) distort the facts; but mind you I mean literally that all I should desire in anyone who was present at any conversation of mine with Senator Platt is that the person should have practical good sense, understanding of conditions, and an honest mind. No one possessing all these attributes can object for a moment, or do anything but laugh at the objections, to my seeing Senator Platt. I was aware, however, that my seeing him would cause some well-meaning people who are either misled or who do not think straight, to feel uneasy, and would give opportunity for slanderous criticism to men who purposely think crookedly. I could not have given efficient government for a month if I had heeded these men of foolish minds. But this was simply an evil which I had to accept.

Indeed the criticism about my meeting Senator Platt is so utterly absurd that it is difficult to discuss it seriously. Mind you that I announced long before I was elected that I should see him as often as I chose and should consult with him on all matters where I thought it proper, but that I should always act on my own best judgment. This I have done literally and exactly. I have dined with him. So in the past I have dined with Dr. Parkhurst and Mr. Godkin and Mr. Villard. Now, all three of these gentlemen have at times done things that were good. But on the whole all three of them during the period that I have been in politics, covering close on to twenty years, have done more damage to the community and less service than Senator Platt. Dr. Parkhurst's conduct has been so bad that I felt very much more uneasiness about having him at my house than I did about having any politician. Mr. Godkin's business profession has been the violation of the ninth commandment. He has made his livelihood by bearing false witness against his neighbor. He has written innumerable editorials so mendacious and slanderous, so wilfully and malignantly untruthful that they differed from perjury or subornation of perjury only in the fact that the one offense was purely against the moral law, while the other would have been against the statutory law.

As for Mr. Villard, the present editor of the *Post*, if Senator Platt had ever acted as Mr. Villard acted in connection with the Northern Pacific Railroad and in connection with his use of the *Evening Post* in stock jobbing operations where the Northern Pacific was concerned, Senator Platt would not now be in public life. If one comes down to degrees of offenses, I consider it a greater encouragement to viciousness in public

life to take the *Evening Post* or to support it in any way, than
to associate with any group of politicians with which I am ever
brought in contact.

You enclose a clipping from the *Evening Post* which you say
expresses your views. This clipping says that I have "succumbed to Platt and to (my) ambition for office." If you had
not said that these were your views I should simply have stated
that such an accusation was a falsehood pure and simple. I
have not "turned more and more" from the path I formerly
followed. I have trod exactly and precisely along the path I
started to tread years ago. I have lived up to my ideals here as
Governor, under infinitely greater difficulties, precisely as I
lived up to them when I was Police Commissioner. Then Platt
opposed me. Now he is supporting me. But I have remained
absolutely unchanged in one case as in the other. Looking
back at the fourteen months I have been in office I can state
with all sincerity that I can see no possible way in which any
man in my place could have accomplished more of the work
that I set out to do, and I am certain that I have done more
than any other Governor during the twenty years that I have
watched what has gone on here. Very possibly the machine
will cut my throat. One prime reason for their doing so will
undoubtedly be the fact that their belief in the insincerity of
the professional reformer has been amply justified by the professional reformer's conduct during these fourteen months.
He has deliberately striven to break me down to gratify his
own morbid vanity and mean jealousy, and he has shown
himself not one whit better than the worst machine politician.
His crimes are of a different kind, but they are just as black. I
feel toward him a feeling of contemptuous anger. I recognize
clearly his fundamental dishonesty of purpose and motive;
his fundamental incapacity to think straight and incapacity
really to live up to a high ideal, all this with the added evil of
hypocrisy.

The hope of this country lies in the men who are practical,
and yet are straight and decent and believe in reform. I can
never be sufficiently grateful to the men like Seth Low, like
Jacob Riis, like Reynolds, like Nicholas Murray Butler, like
Frederick W. Holls and the large number of others, for the
help they have given me and the way they have worked with

me to secure better results. But as for the other men whom I have mentioned above, and for their small understudies of the Jack Chapman type, I feel toward them an indignation that I feel only for the basest politicians. The diseased egotism which is the mainspring of their actions is of itself the type which ultimately produces a Booth or a Guiteau. No class of our people more richly deserve the contempt and abhorrence of decent men. *Very sincerely yours*

POLITICIANS AND REFORMERS

To James Coolidge Carter

                                        Albany, March 12, 1900
My dear Mr. Carter:
    I am in receipt of yours of the 9th inst.
    Such a letter as you write makes me feel very much less alone than before, and I am sure I need not say how I thank you for it. Moreover, I think it has done me good. But first, let me explain:
    I sought to, and I hoped I did, make it plain that I wanted to distinguish between bad politicians and good politicians, and between reformers who however mistaken were sincere and upright, and reformers who were seeking to gratify their own thirst for notoriety. Of course we need reformers and outside critics. The very fact, for instance, that I have to work for results which can be accomplished only by marshalling a dozen different forces, makes me exceedingly reluctant to alienate any one of the forces; whereas an outsider who is not striving to accomplish anything in the sense that I am, can and ought to criticize with entire freedom. But I have been deeply outraged by the attitude of many of the so-called reformers, — of the *Evening Post* people and Dr. Parkhurst, for instance — the *Evening Post* habitually and continually says of me what it knows to be untrue. When one of the editorial writers had put in a favorable comment upon something I had done, he informs me that Mr. Villard told him to strike it out,

as their policy was "to break down Roosevelt." When their correspondent in Albany gave them the facts in a certain case, he was rapped savagely over the knuckles in a letter which in effect told him that his reports were to be adverse to me. Of course, although I have been told these facts by both of the men in question, I cannot make them public for their sakes. Again, Jack Chapman and his crowd repeatedly tell what they deliberately know to be absolute untruths. All this I really mind less for myself than for the cause I am championing. At this very moment I have been exerting every ounce of resolution and tact combined to make the machine — Mr. Platt, Mr. Odell etc. — put through legislation which will stop the Ramapo job. I do not want merely to *denounce* the job. I want to put through legislation which will *stop* it, — a very different thing. I hope to succeed; yet Platt and Odell owe me for my course infinitely less than the reformers owe me, while they support me far more.

I appreciate entirely what you say about my not being too sensitive to criticism. I am glad you said it, and it will do me good. Believe me, however, I have been speaking less for myself than because I thought the cause I championed was jeopardized.

Then, about seeing Mr. Platt. You may be amused to know that at the meeting of the Republican State Committee the other day, the chief hostile comment was that I was altogether too free about consulting "visionary reformers," and always saw City Club men when I came to New York. This is true; because with all their irritating faults and shortcomings I recognize in these visionary reformers the vital spark which must be breathed into the machine body if it is to live to good purpose.

As for Mr. Platt, I do not have to tell you the object of my visits, because you understand. If I were willing to do his bidding it would not be necessary for me to see him; but I *have* to consult him if I am going to accomplish things which, with his enormous power in the party machinery, he is sure to oppose at the outset. If I am going to do anything that is disagreeable to him, I want him to know it from me first, and I want to keep showing him that the things I do of which he disapproves, are done because of a conception of duty on my part, and not either to build up a machine for myself or to humiliate him. I have always made a point of calling on him with absolute openness, and announced, as you know, before election, just what I was going to do. I do not have to tell you that there is no agreement or understanding, expressed or implied, in reference to any matter (even the smallest) which I have ever had with him, that I would not be delighted to put before you in its minutest details. *Faithfully yours*

PROSPECTS FOR RE-ELECTION

To Anna Roosevelt Cowles

Albany, April 30, 1900

Darling Bye:

You may have seen that when I was in Chicago I took the opportunity of saying that I would rather be in private life than to be vice-president. I thought that this was putting it as emphatically as I could put it, and much less offensively than to say that I would not accept the position even if nominated; because the latter is an attitude which a man in active politics, who is sincerely devoted to his party, ought to be very wary about taking.

The qualities that make Cabot invaluable as a friend and invaluable as a public servant also make him quite unchangeable when he has determined that a certain course is right. There is no possible use in trying to make him see the affair as I look at it, because our points of view are different. He regards me as a man with a political career. If I felt that I really had any great chance of such a career I might very possibly take his view. The reason I do not take his view is that I am thoroughly convinced that American politics in general, but above all New York State politics, are of such a kaleidoscopic character, that it is worse than useless for a man of my means and my methods in political life to think of politics as a career. This year we shall probably carry the Presidency, and because there is a presidential election, with Bryan against us, and only because of this, there is a chance of our carrying New York. Therefore, there is a chance of my being either vice-president or Governor. Personally, I regard the election of the republican candidate for the former position as more likely than for the latter. But there is nothing to do as vice-president and there is a great deal to do as Governor, and as I believe the swing of the pendulum will inevitably take me out of public life at the next election after the one this year, even if not at this one, it therefore seems to me wise to try for the position where I can really accomplish something; for the only point to my mind in holding a position is to accomplish something in it.

Cabot feels that I have a career. The dear old goose actually regards me as a presidential possibility of the future, which always makes me thoroughly exasperated, because sooner or later it will have the effect of making other people think that I so regard myself and that therefore I am a ridiculous personage. He thinks that at any rate I could legitimately aspire to some such position as a cabinet officer, or — the one position I should really like — that of Governor General of the Philippines. Now he realizes that when I come a cropper in New York, it means in all probability the end of any outside ambition, and he realizes that this cropper is perfectly certain to arrive sooner or later. There is at least an even chance of my being beaten for Governor this fall. Two years ago when I was in the first flush of my war honors I carried the State by less than 18,000 votes. This year a change of 9,000 votes would beat me. Now I have certainly alienated more than that number who voted for me, from the simple fact that with such a constituency as mine, and facing such difficulties as I have to face, I continually *have* to alienate men. The pharmacists want the regimental pharmacists to be made first lieutenants, which cannot be done without disorganizing all the grades; therefore, I have to alienate a number of good people who are generally for me. The labor unions want a certain course followed about the manufacture of school furniture; it is impossible to follow it without demoralizing the work in our prisons, and this costs me more votes. And so it goes with bill after bill. The wealthy corporations object to the franchise tax and are bitter against me in consequence. The federation of labor grows angry because I have out the militia with great promptness to prevent rioting in the strike at Croton Dam. The Machine men are with difficulty kept in line at all, and the more extreme among them mutter that they might as well have a democrat, because I show no mercy to incompetence and less than mercy to dishonesty; while on the other hand, the well-meaning impracticables get disgusted because I consult with the Machine at all. So it goes, all the time, and I continually alienate little interests, while so far as I can see there is no one who voted against me before whom I should have a right to expect would change his vote now. My chance of success therefore depends solely upon whether or not the feeling against Bryan is so strong that, among the democrats who will vote against him, there will be a sufficient number who will vote against the whole ticket, to offset any losses due to disaffection with me personally. Understand me. I think I am stronger probably than any other republican would be, but this is a democratic State, and we have against us the great sodden democratic mass and in addition scores of thousands of men who because they are goo-goos or mugwumps, or anti-expansionists, or mere impracticables at large, cannot be depended upon to back up a rational effort to do good work. The New York Democrats this year wish to win the Governorship at all hazards, because of the effect it will have for them in the councils of the party. They will put up the best candidate they can find and dropping the presidency will devote their whole attention to electing the Governor. I certainly think the chances are about even, if not in their favor.

This being so, Cabot from his standpoint is entirely right in not wishing to see me exposed to these chances. Moreover, he feels that if I am re-elected the same old trouble will begin of trying to keep the elements together, and that no matter how well I do, the mere swing of the pendulum will bring the democracy to the front two years hence; so that in the middle of McKinley's second term this State will be turned against me, or rather against the local republican organization; and this, even if I am able to avoid a split with the Machine or a smashup with the independents prior to that time.

I myself realize all these chances, but am not only willing, but anxious, to take them, as to my mind the final and conclusive consideration is that I do not want the vice-presidency and that I would like to be Governor again because of the work there is in it.

Of course, you will arrange so that I shall see a good deal of Cabot or rather you need not arrange it, because I shall make my morning and afternoon hours conform to his. I am particularly anxious to see Arthur Lee and go over some of the military problems of this Boer War. I cannot understand Long's choice of an Assistant Secretary.

With love to Will. *Ever yours*

HELPING A WOMAN IN DISTRESS

To Alice W. Beaudry

Albany, May 2, 1900

Dear Madam:

I have given most careful consideration to the application for the pardon of your husband, and regret exceedingly that I cannot consistently grant the same. He certainly deserved the punishment meted out to him. I am very sorry, however, that his imprisonment leaves you in such distressing circumstances, and would like to have you accept the inclosed check of fifty dollars. *Very truly yours*

DEATH PENALTY CASES

To William Allen White

Albany, June 12, 1900

My dear White:

Your letter of the 6th has given me a real pang, for I now feel as if I were hypersensitive and ought to have sent your first note on to Wood. You are awfully good to have taken in so fine a spirit what I very much feared might seem to you like churlishness. One of the most painful duties I have is in refusing requests made to me by intimate friends, and above all, in cases where criminals are concerned. With every death penalty I am certain to have distressing interviews which aggregate hours in length; for every man, however bad, has someone to whom he has shown a good side, and usually some poor creature, mother, wife or daughter, who perhaps has been ill-treated in the past, but who as the last awful moment approaches comes to me in terror and anguish, firm in the belief that just this once I will pardon the criminal no matter what he has done; for to them his awful fate is the one single fact in the entire universe.

Good-bye, old fellow, and good luck to you! *Faithfully yours*

ACCEPTING A NOMINATION

To William McKinley

Telegram

New York, June 21, 1900

I appreciate deeply your congratulations and am proud to be associated with you on the ticket.

"THE THING COULD NOT BE HELPED"

To Anna Roosevelt Cowles

Oyster Bay, June 25, 1900

Dear Bye:

The thing could not be helped. There were two entirely different forces at work. The first was the desire to get me out of New York, partly because the machine naturally prefers someone more pliable, but mainly because of the corporations' or rather the big speculative corporations' unhealthy attitude toward me. This desire was absolutely unoperative as regards results for I stood Mr. Platt and the machine on their heads when the trial of strength came and forced the entire New

York delegation to declare for someone else. It was the feeling of the great bulk of the Republicans that I would strengthen the National ticket and they wanted me on it at all hazards. Mr. Hanna was quite as much opposed to my going on as Mr. Platt was to my staying off, but both were absolutely and utterly powerless. While, of course, I should have preferred to stay where there was more work I would be both ungrateful and a fool not to be deeply touched by the way in which I was nominated. The vital thing in this election is to re-elect President McKinley and to this I shall bend all my energies. If we succeed, well and good, and as regards myself I shall try most earnestly, and I most humbly hope not to forfeit the respect and good will of the people who put me in as vice-president. If we are beaten, my own disappointment will not be a drop in the ocean to my bitter regret and alarm for the Nation.

Give my warm love to Will. I hope he is getting better.

THE NEW YORK MACHINE

To Seth Low

Oyster Bay, August 3, 1900

My dear Low:

I understand absolutely your feeling, and, as a matter of fact, in all essentials I sympathize with you. I will now write you in detail the whole trouble, but I must, of course, ask you to be very careful to see that no one gets hold of the letter. I should not have the slightest hesitation in saying it to Mr. Odell himself, and everything I write you is what I have told him, but it would obviously not do to have outsiders get hold of letters like this.

I have a very genuine and high regard, and I may say affection for Odell. He has been, as chairman of the state committee, the official head of the organization both at the time of my election and throughout my governorship, and I do not see how a governor could have pleasanter relations than mine have been with him. I have found him to be a man of strict integrity who scrupulously keeps faith. He has had the misfortune of being trained up in the Platt machine, in the school of politics which regards politics merely as a game. Mr. Platt, for instance, I believe looks upon New York politics much as Pillsbury looks upon a game of chess. He adheres scrupulously to what he believes to be the rules of the game. He wants success and he wants to see his own power secure against everyone within or without the party, and he wants to reward his adherents, and under such circumstances, he is apt to regard policies, not on their merit, but with the same indifference that Pillsbury would regard the red or white pawns. In developing the absolutely necessary essentials of party solidarity, the organization has gone to the exactly opposite extremes from our friends, the lunatic goo-goos, of the Godkin, Parkhurst, Villard and Chapman type, and have developed an entirely improper discipline, which always tends to make servility one of the qualities most prized by the organization in dealing with a public man. Odell has been trained in the school which accepts Platt's control unquestioningly, and demands that each of Platt's big subordinates should receive from his inferiors the same obedience he himself rendered to his superiors. One of my great efforts during the past two years has been to destroy this idea, and to try to produce the healthy feeling that on the one hand there must be organization and an earnest desire to come to an agreement and work together among the members of the party, each individual sacrificing many of his prejudices and individual beliefs, and that, on the other hand, no obedience of subordinates must be expected, which is not consistent with self-respect and good citizenship, so that the best men may be encouraged and not discouraged when there is any chance of their being put forward by the party, or taking control of party management. Far more than any one policy, about any one specific matter, such as the canal, or even the franchise tax, this general policy is what I have desired that my administration should stand for. My appointees have been of a higher grade than in any governor's whose administration I have seen, including Cleveland's, and my effort has been constant to put into active party management men like Frank Greene, to put into office men like Root, and to get high-minded and upright citizens who cannot take office or active control in political management and so keep in touch with the party leaders that they may be able to guide and strengthen them. Odell gradually has come round to these views. He has developed into a strong backer of men of the Greene type, and I really believe he has grown to have a hearty admiration for the ideals that have been set before him. He has entirely abandoned the theory that, if governor, Senator Platt and not he himself should have the final say. I believe he would make a good governor. I know he would make an honest one. But I don't think he has, as yet, shaken himself as entirely free as I would desire from machine influences, and, above all, I do not believe that the independent republicans, not to speak of the independents generally, would recognize that he was not merely Mr. Platt's candidate.

All this I have told him in detail, and substantially he agrees with me. He certainly does not want the governorship. He agrees with me that, as a man of large means, and with a genuine desire for party management, it would be better for him and for the party if he should strive for the position of Thurlow Weed rather than of Seward. If I had only him to deal with, I think I could without doubt get the organization united on some excellent upcountryman, like Sloane, if it appears impracticable to put Greene or yourself forward.

But Senator Platt offers an entirely different problem. I don't know whether you have realized how entirely during my administration I have had the kernel and Mr. Platt the husk. I have never sympathized with those diplomats whose object it has been to preserve their dignity by asserting their right to enter a room first, or to sit on a red instead of a green chair, instead of seeking to gain substantial benefits for their countrymen. Mr. Platt is very sensitive about his dignity and position. I am not in the slightest degree sensitive on these matters. I want results. I am only too glad to call on Mr. Platt, or to have him to dinner, or take breakfast with him, and to discuss with him first and at length all projects, provided, in the end, I have my way about these same projects. Throughout these two years in both legislation and administration I have carried my points nine times out of ten. Every appointment has been confirmed, and, while I have not been able to get affirmative action from the Legislature on certain points that I wished, I have been able to get a considerable share of legislation such as the franchise tax and the civil service law. There has been the great negative advantage of an entire absence of bad legislation. Not a scandal of any kind can be pointed out in connection with my administration, and the men who are administering the different departments are of a type higher than has before been known in New York politics.

All this has been, at the bottom, most exasperating to Senator Platt. He has put a good face on it publicly, for I have made every effort to enable him to do so, and he has been helped by the lunatics of the *Evening Post* and Parkhurst variety, who have been as anxious as he was, to show that I was subservient, but, as a matter of fact, he has realized thoroughly that my methods were the only practical methods by which boss rule can be successfully opposed; and the experience he had at Philadelphia, when in his own delegation I stood him on his head by a two to one vote, was not needed to make him understand what had happened. He does not want me. He does not want anyone like me.

But, unfortunately, I can not hand down to anyone the power that, partly by accident, has for the moment become mine in New York politics. Senator Platt could not have beaten me for renomination if I had not been nominated for vice-president at Philadelphia. But Platt retains a very great power, and the country districts, which were most devoted to me, and which gave me my greatest strength, are those where the republicans, while not inclined to submit to the dictates of Platt, have no sympathy with the anti-machine feeling of the independents in the big cities. These counties, such as St. Lawrence, Jefferson, Cattaraugus, Otsego, and the like, where the republicans would without hesitation have stood by me against Platt, are the same counties where the republicans have an entirely friendly feeling to Odell, and do not in the least object to his having been a machine man. In each county he would lose a proportion of the vote that I would have, but there is in those counties, among the overwhelming majority of the republicans a thoroughly friendly and kindly feeling for him, and they prefer what they call an organization man to an independent.

If Senator Platt had the wisdom to do as I think Odell

would genuinely like to have him do and throw his strength for such a man as Sloane, we could nominate Sloane, although we should have a struggle, but, if he merely sits still, the convention will not contain twenty per cent of men who realize that the independent republicans and independents generally form a factor which cannot wisely be neglected, and the alternative to Odell might be Woodruff or Nixon, or John Raines. Under such circumstances the only thing would be to take to Odell. George Ray, though an honorable man, would be less independent than Odell. Sereno Payne would, in my belief, be far more amenable to Platt's dictation than Odell, though an upright and high-minded man.

I absolutely agree with you that we should take no chances in this campaign, and should nominate a man for Governor who will help the entire ticket among the independents and especially the independent republicans, but I fear I am powerless to impress this view upon Senator Platt. I have seen him but once since I came back from Philadelphia. I don't think he cares to see me, and I don't suppose there is any reason he should care to, and, though he agrees with my statements in the abstract, he does not agree with the concrete deductions I draw from them. *Faithfully yours*

AN APPEAL TO DEMOCRATS

To John M. Palmer

Oyster Bay, August 9, 1900

My dear General Palmer:

I notice that in your recent very manly interview stating why you could not support the populistic democracy and the Kansas City platform and the nominees, that you allude to a statement, I was supposed to have made attacking the Democrats, in my St. Paul speech.

You have evidently seen a report which was not only garbled but falsified. I stand by this speech absolutely, and have nothing to explain in connection with it, but I do wish to point out that my remarks have been deliberately falsified, but that they did apply to the people who were smarting under the sting. I do not feel that this is in the least a merely party campaign. I feel that we have a right to appeal to all good citizens, whether in the past they have been Republicans or Democrats, no matter what their political affiliations have been, to stand with us now, as in '64 we had a right to make a similar appeal on behalf of Lincoln and against men like Vallandigham. We are warranted in making the appeal to all good Democrats just as we made the appeal to all good Democrats then because a crisis has arisen where the Democratic organization has taken such a position that it has lost its claim to the support of the best and truest men on its own party — just as in 1812–14 the Federalist party, when it declared itself to be the ally of a foreign foe and opposed the National interest at home became hopelessly discredited when it was abandoned by the best Federalists, or men of the John Quincy Adams type.

In my speech at St. Paul I began by saying: "We appeal not only to Republicans, but to all good citizens who are Americans in fact as well as in name, to help us in re-electing President McKinley." I ended by saying: "Study the Kansas City platform and you cannot help realizing that their policy (the policy of its makers and sponsors) is a policy of infamy, that their triumph would mean misery so widespread that it is almost unthinkable and a disgrace so lasting that more than a generation would have to pass before it could be wiped out. They stand for lawlessness and disorder, for dishonesty and dishonor, for license and disaster at home and cowardly shrinking from duty abroad. We ask the support of all Americans who have the welfare of the country at heart, no matter what their political affiliations may have been in the past. We ask the support of all sound-headed men who do not wish to see our material well-being swallowed up in an abyss of disaster. We appeal to all good men who believe in civic decency and shrink from the taint of financial dishonor, and we appeal to all brave men who are proud of the national name and reputation, and ask them to see to it that we are not humiliated before mankind, and that we do not abandon the position we have taken in the forefront of the great nations of the earth."

You will see that here I most explicitly draw the line between the men who support and ask support for the Kansas City platform, and all other citizens, whether in the past they have been Democrats or Republicans. I feel that, as a matter of fact, greater credit is due to men like you, my dear sir, and the other gold Democrats, who, four years ago, stood and now stand for National honor than is due to any other men.

I may mention that in my own administration as Governor of New York State, I have treated gold Democrats as I have treated Republicans both in appointments, and in counsel and advising with them as to the policies to follow. It is because the Kansas City platform itself stands for the policy of timid shrinking from duty abroad and of yielding to the foes of civic honesty and to the advocates of unsound finance and enemies of order at home, that I feel we have a right to appeal to the hundreds of thousands of brave honest Democrats to strike hands with us at this crisis of the Nation's history; for they have been betrayed in the house of their friends, and, if they are far-sighted, they must necessarily see that every principle of courage, of patriotism and of national self-respect demands that they repudiate the action of the populistic democracy by which they have been at this moment betrayed, just as under similar circumstances the Northern Democrats during the Civil War repudiated the principles of the men like Vallandigham, just as in 1812–14 the Northern Federalists repudiated their party under similar conditions.

In short, I feel that the Kansas City platform makers, and their followers, have forfeited the right to appeal to any Democrat who is keenly sensitive of the National honor.

They claim the late General Lawton was a Democrat. Doubtless he was such at one time, but the bitterest arraignment of the Kansas City platform is contained in the words Lawton wrote just before his death: "If I am shot by a Philippino bullet it might as well come from one of my own men, because I know from observation, confirmed by captured prisoners, that the continuance of fighting is chiefly due to reports that are sent out from America." *Very respectfully yours*

MEETING OKLAHOMA SUPPORTERS

To Henry Cabot Lodge

Oyster Bay, November 9, 1900

Dear Cabot:

Just a line to say how glad I was to get your telegram. I have any amount to tell you about the canvass. If political conditions were normal in the South, Bryanism would have received scarcely a score of votes in the electoral college. Well, I am delighted to have been on the national ticket in this great historic contest, for after McKinley and Hanna, I feel that I did as much as anyone in bringing about the result — though after all it was Bryan himself who did most.

Do tell Nannie that I have got to give her full information about certain of my ardent backers, the Mulhalls of Oklahoma Territory. The members of the family whom I know are Colonel Mulhall, his son and two daughters, one of whom is named Miss Bossie. There are also several gentlemen friends with sporting proclivities, occasional homicidal tastes and immense resourcefulness in every emergency. No ordinary novelist would venture to portray such types, because he would regard them as hopelessly exaggerated. They have a large and very prosperous ranch some sixty miles from Oklahoma City, and they all came in to see me at the regimental reunion last July, together with a dozen of the Mulhall cowboys. The Colonel is a solidly built person with chin whiskers and an iron jaw. One daughter drove the buckboard; the other rode a horse man fashion, the latter being Miss Bossie. She took her part with the cowboys in a steer-roping contest in the afternoon, and afterwards, together with the rest of her family, dined with me in evening dress, not particularly different from that of more conventional regions. They have many greyhounds and wanted me to come out for a wolf hunt, which I could not do, so Miss Bossie sent me a stuffed wolf as a mascot. During my campaign I came upon the entire family at St. Louis where they had come in to race some of their horses. They were democrats but were backing McKinley chiefly because I was on the ticket. I came upon the entire family including their gentlemen friends perfectly at home in the barroom of the Planters Hotel sitting around a table eating lunch and drinking whiskey in the shape known as "highballs." They were all very glad to see me, but especially the Colonel and Miss Bossie, both of whom had bet heavily upon me, Miss Bossie telling me that unless I won I must never venture to come near their ranch, as she had bet all her ponies and race horses on the result. She has written Edith to congratulate her and the Colonel has wired me. I assured Edith she would find Bossie a distinct addition to our social circle should she ever come here on a visit, but I regret to state that Edith has betrayed an unexpected narrow-mindedness and seems apprehensive as to exactly how the young lady would get on in the new environment.

I hope you noticed how I called down Croker, Van Wyck and Devery when there threatened to be trouble in New York. I was glad that Croker gave me the chance through his man Devery.

Harry Davis has written us such a characteristic note of congratulation upon our victory over what he calls the "combined idiocy and evil of the country." *Ever yours*

"I AM NOT NATURALLY . . . A FIGHTER"

To Edward Sanford Martin

Albany, November 26, 1900

Dear Dan:

I shall write to Bangs and thank him.

Now, about small Ted's fighting. I believe you will find that he is not quarrelsome, and that above all, he is not a bully. I think it has been in amicable wrestling and boxing bouts that in your boy's words he has "licked all the boys in his form." In a measure, I am responsible for some of his fighting proclivities, but most of them came naturally. For instance, my two youngest small boys are not in the least fighters like Ted, although I think I have succeeded in instilling into them the theory that they ought not to shirk any quarrel forced upon them.

Now, do you want to know the real underlying feeling which has made me fight myself and want Ted to fight? Well, I summed it up to Ted once or twice when I told him, apropos of lessons of virtue, that he could be just as virtuous as he wished *if only he was prepared to fight*. Fundamentally this has been my own theory. I am not naturally at all a fighter. So far as any man is capable of analyzing his own impulses and desires, mine incline me to amiable domesticity and the avoidance of effort and struggle and any kind of roughness and to the practice of home virtues. Now, I believe that these are good traits, not bad ones. But I also believe that if unsupported by something more virile, they may tend to evil rather than good. The man who merely possesses these traits, and in addition is timid and shirks effort, attracts and deserves a good deal of contempt. He attracts more, though he deserves less, contempt than the powerful, efficient man who is not at all virtuous but is merely a strong, selfish, self-indulgent brute; the latter being the type [   ] I was fortunate enough in having a father whom I have always been able to regard as an ideal man. It sounds a little like cant to say what I am going to say, but he really did combine the strength and courage and will and energy of the strongest man with the tenderness, cleanness and purity of a woman. I was a sickly and timid boy. He not only took great and loving care of me — some of my earliest remembrances are of nights when he would walk up and down with me for an hour at a time in his arms when I was a wretched mite suffering acutely with asthma — but he also most wisely refused to coddle me, and made me feel that I must force myself to hold my own with other boys and prepare to do the rough work of the world. I cannot say that he ever put it into words, but he certainly gave me the feeling that I was always to be both decent and manly, and that if I were manly nobody would long laugh at my being decent. In all my childhood he never laid hand on me but once, but I always knew perfectly well that in case it became necessary he would not have the slightest hesitancy to do so again, and alike from my love and respect, and in a certain sense, from my fear of him, I would have hated and dreaded beyond measure to have him know that I had been guilty of a lie, or of cruelty, or of bullying, or of uncleanness, or of cowardice. Gradually I grew to have the feeling on my own account, and not merely on his. There were many things I tried to do because he did them, which I found afterwards were not in my line. For instance, I taught Sunday school all through college, but afterwards gave it up, just as on experiment I could not do the charitable work which he had done. In doing my Sunday school work I was very much struck by the fact that the other men who did it only possessed one side of his character; [ ] My ordinary companions in college would I think have had a tendency to look down upon me for doing Sunday school work if I had not also been a corking boxer, a good runner, and a genial member of the Porcellian Club. I went in for boxing and wrestling a good deal, and I really think that while this was partly because I liked them as sports, it was even more because I intended to be a middling decent fellow, and I did not intend that anyone should laugh at me with impunity because I was decent. It is exactly the same thing with history. In most countries the "Bourgeoisie" — the moral, respectable, commercial, middle class — is looked upon with a certain contempt which is justified by their timidity and unwarlikeness. But the minute a middle class produces men like Hawkins and Frobisher on the seas, or men such as the average Union soldier in the civil war, it acquires the hearty respect of others which it merits.

Well, I have wanted to pass on to my boys some of what I got from my own father. I loathe cruelty and injustice. To see a boy or man torture something helpless whether in the shape of a small boy or little girl or dumb animal makes me rage. So far as I know my children have never been cruel, though I have had to check a certain amount of bullying. Ted is a little fellow, under the usual size, and wears spectacles, so that strange boys are rather inclined to jump on him at first. When in addition to this I have trained him so that he objects strongly to torturing cats or hurting little girls, you can see that there are chances for life to be unpleasant for him when among other boys. Now I have striven to make him feel that if he only fights hard enough he is perfectly certain to secure the respect of all his associates for his virtues. I do not believe he is quarrelsome. I do not think your little boy has found him so. I do not think he oppresses smaller boys, but he does hold his own. When his aunt goes to see him at school, he flings his arms around her neck and is overjoyed with her companionship and has the greatest difficulty to keep from crying when she goes away. Now there are certain of his companions who would be inclined to think him a mollycoddle for betraying such emotion over a female relative; but they won't think him a mollycoddle if he shows an instantaneous readiness to resent hostile criticism on the subject.

Of course, there are dangers in any such training. Every now and then Ted gets an attack of the big head and has to have it reduced, usually by his own associates, occasionally by his affectionate father. Moreover, I know perfectly well that all my training him will only amount to one element out of the many which will go to determine what he is in the future. As you say in your last article, the mother has much more to do than the father with the children's future.

By the way, Mrs. Roosevelt and I laughed all the way down in the cars the other day over that article. I suppose "Jonas" is Ted's school fellow. Your account of the father's function in sickness so exactly reproduced our experience that it made me feel guilty and Mrs. Roosevelt decorously exultant. So with my tendency to be a little late at meals, and the tuition of my wife towards the children on the subject.

There I have written you much longer than I had any idea I was going to. With hearty regards, *Faithfully yours*

P.S. I have just received your second note. I have rarely read a more touching letter than Mrs. Moore's. What a fine woman she must be and what a fine son she must have had! I return her letter herewith. If you think she would not mind it, I wish you would give her my most respectful and sincere sympathy.

DRAWING THE LINE

To William H. Llewellyn

Oyster Bay, December 24, 1900

My dear Major:

Our comrade who is in difficulties has written me already about the trivial incident you mention. His explanation was that though he had killed his sister-in-law, it was a pure accident such as might happen to any gent, because he was really shooting at his wife. I have a certain sympathy with your view that you wish he had killed the man. In fact, there were a good many men whose deaths would not arouse any overwrought feeling in my mind, at least under certain circumstances. But seriously, I do not feel much inclined to champion a man who shoots one woman while shooting at another. A good many of the boys recently have been up for homicide or attempted homicide. I have hitherto done whatever I could for each of them. But I think I have got to draw the line at woman shooting. *Faithfully yours*

HUNTING COUGARS

To Theodore Roosevelt Jr.

Keystone Ranch, Colorado,
January 14, 1901

Blessed Ted,

From the railroad we drove fifty miles to the little frontier town of Meeker. There we were met by the hunter Goff, a fine, quiet, hardy fellow, who knows his business thoroughly. Next morning we started on horseback, while our luggage went by wagon to Goff's ranch. We started soon after sunrise, and made our way, hunting as we went, across the high, exceedingly rugged hills, until sunset. We were hunting cougar and lynx or, as they are called out here, "lion" and "cat." The first cat we put up gave the dogs a two hours' chase, and got away among some high cliffs. In the afternoon we put up another, and had a very good hour's run, the dogs baying until the glens rang again to the echoes, as they worked hither and thither through the ravines. We walked our ponies up and down steep, rockstrewn, and tree-clad slopes, where it did not seem possible a horse could climb, and on the level places we got one or two smart gallops. At last the lynx went up a tree. Then I saw a really funny sight. Seven hounds had been doing the trailing, while a large brindled bloodhound and two half-breeds between collie and bull stayed behind Goff, running so close to his horse's heels that they continually bumped into them, which he accepted with philosophic composure. Then the dogs proceeded literally to *climb the tree*, which was a many-forked pinon; one of the half-breeds, named Tony, got up certainly sixteen feet, until the lynx, which looked like a huge and exceedingly malevolent pussy-cat, made vicious dabs at him. I shot the lynx low, so as not to hurt his skin.

Yesterday we were in the saddle for ten hours. The dogs ran one lynx down and killed it among the rocks after a vigorous scuffle. It was in a hole and only two of them could get at it.

This morning, soon after starting out, we struck the cold trail of a mountain lion. The hounds puzzled about for nearly two hours, going up and down the great gorges, until we sometimes absolutely lost even the sound of the baying. Then they struck the fresh trail, where the cougar had killed a deer overnight. In half an hour a clamorous yelling told us they had overtaken the quarry; for we had been riding up the slopes and along the crests, wherever it was possible for the horses to get footing. As we plunged and scrambled down towards the noise, one of my companions, Phil Stewart, stopped us while he took a kodak of a rabbit which sat unconcernedly right beside our path. Soon we saw the lion in a treetop, with two of the dogs so high up among the branches that he was striking at them. He was more afraid of us than of the dogs, and as soon as he saw us he took a great flying leap and was off, the pack close behind. In a few hundred yards they had him up another tree. Here I could have shot him (Tony climbed almost up to him, and then fell twenty feet out of the tree), but waited for Stewart to get a photo; and he jumped again. This time, after a couple of hundred yards, the dogs caught him, and a great fight followed. They could have killed him by themselves, but he bit or clawed four of them, and for fear he might kill one I ran in and stabbed him behind the shoulder, thrusting the knife you loaned me right into his heart. I have always wished to kill a cougar as I did this one, with dogs and the knife.

"I KILLED ONE OF THEM"

To William Carey Brown

Washington, March 12, 1901

My dear Major:

Your letter of Jany. 26th was very, very interesting. I have shown it and Bryan's picture to a number of our people here. I am delighted with your getting the bandit chief himself. But, my dear captain, if ever for your sins you should run for public office, the yellow press and some sentimental journals will unite in holding up their hands with horror at your blood-thirstiness in killing this murderer and plunderer. In the San Juan fighting I happened to get thrown into close quarters with a couple of Spaniards, both of whom shot at me and whom I shot at in return, just after they had done so. I killed one of them; and throughout last fall's campaign one of the favorite cries of my opponents was that I had "shot a man in the back." As it happened he was not shot in the back but in the left breast as he turned. However this detail in no way affected or disturbed my opponents.

You are one of the men whom I shall always remember. I have felt that not only by gallantry and energy, but by your thorough mastery of your profession, you were the kind of officer whom we wanted to push forward and develop. I do not know whether it will ever be in my power to be of the least assistance to you; but remember that if the time comes that I shall be most eager to render it, not in any way as a favor to you, but simply because I think the welfare of the army will be promoted thereby.

With high regard, my dear Major, believe me, *Faithfully yours*

LIFE AFTER POLITICS

To Leonard Wood

Oyster Bay, March 27, 1901

Dear Leonard:

The other day I had a few minutes' talk with John Kendrick Bangs who has become one of your great admirers. I have really no excuse for writing you at this moment except that I do wish you to understand how thoroughly everyone here whose opinion is worth having, appreciates the extraordinary work you have done under the most trying circumstances. For the last two years you have been one of the very few men who have had to do the great tasks of the world and who have done them well. Taft likewise has done a very great work. In your case, of course, you have had to combine military and civil work, and you have had to decide to a very large extent what the policy should be no less than to carry it out. It has been a hard task, but I do not pity you a bit, for it seems to me that in this life the best possible thing is to have a great task well worth doing, and to do it well. You have written your name indelibly on the record which tells how this country met one of the crises in its history. Through long years you prepared yourself to take advantage of your chance should it ever come, and when it came you grasped it, and made out of the Spanish war, with the problems which followed, a career which I think can be fairly called a great career. In view of Dewey's lamentable fall I think that from the personal standpoint it may be said that you made more than any other man in the Nation out of the Spanish war; and what is of more importance, you did this by rendering to the Nation a greater service than any other one man; for Taft came into the field later than you did, and Root's work, which is very great, has also covered much less time.

I have now, as one of Lodge's sons put it "taken the veil." I intend studying law with a view to seeing if I cannot go into practice as a lawyer when my term as Vice-President comes to an end. Of course, I may go on in public life, but equally of course it is unlikely, and what I have seen of the careers of public men has given me an absolute horror of the condition of the politician whose day has passed; who by some turn of the kaleidoscope is thrown into the background; and who then haunts the fields of his former activity as a pale shadow of what he once was; or else who finds himself adrift in the hopeless position of the man who says he can do anything but who therefore can do nothing. I have always thought I might end as a professor of history, but if possible I should prefer a more active life, and the next fifteen years will be the years of the greatest expense in bringing up and launching into life my children.

Give our love to Mrs. Wood. *Always yours*

"AN UTTERLY ANOMALOUS OFFICE"

To Leonard Wood

Private

Oyster Bay, April 17, 1901

My dear Leonard:

I have your letter of the 12th inst.

I would gladly go down to Cuba and look into the situation, if it would do any good. Now let me say in strictest confidence that I doubt whether the President would like me to do it. You know that the Vice-Presidency is an utterly anomalous office (one which I think ought to be abolished). The man who occupies it may at any moment be everything; but meanwhile he is practically nothing. I do not think that the President wants me to take any part in affairs or give him any advice, and if I am to be of any use in connection with him it must be by waiting until he does want me and then do as he requests. When he comes back from this western trip I shall probably see him and then I shall try to sound him and see whether he would care to have me go to Cuba or not. Of all things I do not want him to feel that on account of my old intimacy with you I am thrusting myself forward to do something concerning which he may have doubts.

As well as any outsider can, I appreciate to the full the infinite difficulties under which you have labored, and the infinite complexity and importance of the work you have done. The *Evening Post* correspondent in Havana has acted precisely as the *Evening Post* correspondent in Porto Rico has acted; that is, he has obeyed the behests of the paper. My experience with the paper both under the elder Godkin and Villard and under the present management has been that it is quite as dishonest and scandalously mendacious as the *Journal*, and though less blackguardly vulgar, it is on the whole less patriotic. Three times, twice at Albany and once at Washington, I have known them to turn down their correspondents because the correspondents gave accounts which though true were not, as the editors phrased it, in harmony with the policy of the paper. They got rid of Bishop, the best editor they had, because of a series of quarrels, one of which arose from his refusal deliberately to write lies about me — they explaining to him at the time that their policy was "to break down Roosevelt." In other words, they care no more for truth than they care for the well-being and honor of the country. Their correspondents are required to distort the facts so as to make them suit the views of the editors, and they are not only utterly reckless as to injuring personal reputations, but they actually take a malevolent pleasure in trying to hurt the nation. The present young Villard's mother, who was one of the Garrisons, was in Berlin at the time of the Spanish War and she went continually about saying that she earnestly hoped the Spaniards would win and she prayed for American defeat. The Villards, the Godkins and their like are simply unhung traitors, and are liars, slanderers and scandal-mongers to boot. It is bad enough when they exercise their traits in home matters, but when they deliberately try to nullify and undo work such as that you are doing, in which the national interests are vitally concerned, their conduct becomes absolutely infamous.

I see there is some talk of your coming up here. If so, I do hope you can get down here for a short while, and at any rate we must meet in New York. I hope Mrs. Wood and the children can pay us a little visit this summer. *Always yours*

P.S. I let the *Harper's Weekly* and *Commercial Advertiser* people see parts of your letter, because it gives them the chance to smash at the *Evening Post* and others with intelligence. Of course, you will not be quoted in any way.

GREEK AND BYZANTINE HISTORY

To Frederic Harrison

Oyster Bay, April 24, 1901

My dear Mr. Harrison:

I thank you very much for your Rede Lecture. I only wish you could elaborate it. By the way, I do not myself see much objection to the use of the word "Byzantine." No one word as descriptive of the empire on the Bosphorus, is free from objections; and when we employ Byzantine we fail to emphasize the continuity of the history, but it is on the whole a far better term than any other that has been proposed.

I am glad to see the way in which of recent years there has grown up an appreciation of the great part played by the Byzantine Empire from the time of its great rally against the Saracens about the beginning of the Eighth Century until in the Eleventh Century the disasters which befell it culminated in the onslaught of the Seljuk Turks. The attitude of historians about the Byzantine empire during these times has been disproportionate.

It has always seemed to me that on a much smaller scale there is similar wrong-headedness in the popular refusal on the part of scholars to give proper weight to the history of the larger Greek world from the days of Alexander to the close of the second Punic war. In the *Encyclopedia Britannica*, for instance, they solemnly break off Greek history with the death of Alexander, treating all up to that time as one epoch, and then considering as another epoch of mere degradation all from that time until the age of Constantine. Of course such a classification is utterly arbitrary and mischievous. Although cataclysms do occur in history, they are rare, and the particular date chosen in this instance as an arbitrary line of division, not only infringes against the law of continuity, but also has nothing to recommend it even from the cataclysmic stand-point. 1066 does mark a great gulf of division in English history. There is no such sharply defined break in one year in Greek history. There is of course no reason why we should merely treat of Greece proper, although this is really what Grote did; but if we do, then the reign of Philip and not of Philip's greater son marks the time in which Greece proper, Minor Greece, definitely lost her headship in the Grecian world. To stop short with Alexander's death and not to treat continuously the empires carved out of his conquests by his lieutenants and their successors is absurd. Moreover, it was nearly half a century after his death before Rome rose to such a place that the outside world regarded her as of the first rank. A half a century more went by before she began to exercise any appreciable influence upon the Hellenistic common-wealths; save that such influence as had previously been exercised from time to time by Samnites and Carthagenians. These post-Alexandrian Greek Empires had in them the seeds of decay just as the great empire of Napoleon had, and the rottenness grew rapidly after a short time exactly as in France in the days of the second Napoleonic empire. But though a corrupt, it was a very brilliant civilization. And it was to this later and not to the earlier Hellenic civilization that Roman art and literature owed most. The age of Pyrrhus, Demetrius Poliorcetes, Antigonus, the Ptolemys, Xantippus, Cleomenes and the statesmen and soldiers of the Achaian League; the age of Theocritus and later of Polybius, of the scientists of Alexandria, the architects of Rhodes and the sculptors of Pergamum — it is simply nonsense to ignore such an age as unworthy of serious study.

It was a very great pleasure to see you during your too-brief stay on this side. *Faithfully yours*

PLANS TO STUDY LAW

To Alton B. Parker

Oyster Bay, May 15, 1901

My dear Judge:

I have had a very discouraging time about my proposed law studies. May I trespass upon your good nature long enough to read the inclosed letter from Judge John Proctor Clarke, to whom I had written? Please return it to me.

Now, I do not intend to commit or procure the commission of perjury, and while I would honestly study in any office in which I entered and would guarantee to do more work than the average young student, yet of course while I am Vice-President I must be in Washington during the time the Senate is in session. Would it be possible to have service in a law office in Washington taken in lieu of service in an office in New York, inasmuch as by virtue of my official position I have to be out of the State? It does not seem to me that this would be improper. I was as you know one year in the Columbia Law School before I went to the legislature and was at that time also in the law office of my uncle Robert B. Roosevelt. I am very much afraid it would be out of the question for me to get admitted to the District of Columbia bar prior to the fourth of March next, and unless I do so I would not be able to practice there the three years necessary to entitle me to transfer to New York.

Give our warm regards to Mrs. Parker. *Sincerely yours*

PLANS TO ATTEND LAW SCHOOL

To Alton B. Parker

Oyster Bay, May 31, 1901

My dear Judge:

I am under great obligations to you. You have given me the very information I want. As soon as I get back to Washington

I shall begin to attend the law school there, and when I have completed my two years' course and feel myself fit I shall apply for the examination. In all probability I shall then take advantage of your very kind offer (which it is unnecessary to say I shall treat as strictly private), to get an examination by myself, as it does not seem to me it would be advisable to court the inevitable newspaper sensation which would be worked up by the yellow press, if I appeared in public. But I shall openly identify myself with the Washington law school.

Let me thank you again, my dear Judge. You are the first man of the two or three to whom I have applied who has given me the exact information I wanted.

With hearty regards, I am, *Faithfully yours*

NEW YORK SOCIETY

To Cecil Spring-Rice

Oyster Bay, July 3, 1901

Dear Cecil:

Your letter of the 15th ult. from Geneva received.

Somebody told me the other day that they had seen you looking fairly offensively plutocratic, and upon hearing the news we dolefully shook our heads and said that we did not believe you would now write us. So that we were very much pleased to get your letter. We were delighted to hear about the beloved Winty Chanlers and were both of us greatly interested in what you said as to social conditions at the top in England, and as to Russia and Germany.

I have a feeling of contempt and of anger for our socially leading people on this side, and our special apostles to culture irritate me almost as much. No more unhealthy developments can be imagined than the two which culminate in the New York four hundred and the New York *Evening Post*. But the classes represented here have no such leadership as they have with you, and so are not nearly as dangerous. The *Evening Post* stands for the bitter, sour, ineffective men who possess much refinement, culture, knowledge and scholarship of a wholly unproductive type. They always speak in the name of virtue, but they usually act against decency and almost invariably against manliness. They hate a good man who is strong so much, that they will even try to build up against him a bad man. They contribute nothing useful to our intellectual, civic or social life. At the best they stand aside. At the worst they get in the way, or help the forces of evil. As for the social people, — the four hundred, the men and women who at this moment find their most typical expression at Newport — they lead lives which vary from rotten frivolity to rotten vice. There are exceptions, of course, and plenty of them, but as a whole they are not serious people even when they are not immoral, and thanks to the yellow press, and indeed to the newspapers generally, they exercise a very unwholesome influence on the community at large by the false and unworthy standards which they set up.

Nevertheless, there is plenty of cause for hopefulness. Curiously enough, while the four hundred as a whole has rather grown worse. I believe that the colleges are constantly producing a rather better type. Harvard, Yale, Princeton and many others like them have grown tremendously during the last quarter of a century, and they not only turn out a far larger number of students, but they turn out better men. A cleaner, sturdier, more high-minded set than are these young fellows as a rule, it would be most difficult to find. Moreover, there is a very earnest set of men who do work at politics and civics [   ] in our great cities and who work exceedingly well. Finally, and what is far more important, although there are very uncomfortable and ugly developments in our people as a whole — notably in the diminishing birth rate — yet there is an immense amount of sturdy self-respect and manhood among them. I do not want to say anything that sounds cheap or demagogic, but I have much more trust in the man of moderate means, — in the mechanic, the [   ], the skilled handicraftsman, the farmer, — than I have in the big millionaire. Recently I joined the Masons, and in our lodge here in this village, for instance, I meet a set of men whom one can thoroughly and heartily respect, and with whom one can work with a clear conscience.

While there are very uncomfortable analogies between society now and Greek society in the period succeeding Alexander, and Roman society in the days of Augustus, and even to French society just before the Revolution, yet the analogy could readily be pushed too far. The women to whom you allude who are dowdy, but who live in the country, raise large families of healthy children, and with dull respectability fulfill their various duties, had but few representatives, comparatively speaking, in any of the societies above named. I earnestly wish there were more of them here.

I entirely agree with you about the very rich. Unfortunately, with me personally the lack of appreciation of riches has always taken too acute a form. I am so entirely satisfied with what I have got, and so thoroughly realize that I have had a thousand times as happy a life as any of the very rich men whom I know, that it has resulted in my following a career which will make my children do the drudgery from which I was free. I do not see very much of the big-moneyed men in New York, simply because very few of them possess the traits which would make them companionable to me, or would make me feel that it was worth while dealing with them. To spend the day with them at Newport, or on one of their yachts, or even to dine with them save under exceptional circumstances, fills me with frank horror. Money is undoubtedly one form of power and I appreciate this fact in them and acknowledge it; but I would rather have had the career of Dewey or of Tom Reed, though both ended in a failure (I say "a failure" and not "failure" for the latter would not be true) than the career of Pierpont Morgan. I have known a few men of wealth who use their wealth to full advantage. I have known plenty of men who are only able to do their work because they have inherited means. This is absolutely true of both Cabot and myself, for instance. Cabot is quite a rich man, but I am not; but each of us has been able to do what he has actually done because his father left him in such shape that he did not have to earn his own living. My own children will not be so left, and of course I regret the fact; but I shall try to bring them up — or to speak more accurately — I shall try to assist my wife to bring them up, so that they shall be fit to support themselves and to do good work as the occasion arises.

The more I have heard of the Kaiser the more my respect for him has grown, and though I do not think the Czar is as much of a man, still I think he is a good fellow in his way too. The German press at times makes me so angry that I feel a cordial desire to try a fall with Germany. But as a matter of fact I think it would be most unfortunate if Germany could not continue to get along well with both the United States and England. I have had a very interesting talk with the German Ambassador explaining to him in full my views on the Monroe Doctrine — a doctrine about which I feel so deeply that I should take my stand on it even without regard to the attitude of the administration.

By the way, that exceedingly pernicious idiot, Smalley, has simply infected the London *Times* and other English papers with the theory that when I speak of the Monroe doctrine I have especial reference to England. I should suppose that even Smalley's guinea-pig brain would take in the fact that as things are now the Monroe Doctrine does not touch England in any shape or way, and that the only power that needs to be reminded of its existence is Germany. I explained to the German Ambassador that I did not want to see America get a foot of territory at the expense of any one of the South American states, and that I did not want her to get a single commercial advantage over Germany or any other European power save as it was obtained by fair competition by the merchants or by the ordinary form of treaty; but that I most emphatically protested against either Germany or any other power getting new territory in America — just as I am certain England would object to seeing Delagoa Bay becoming German or French instead of Portuguese.

I have felt more and more melancholy over the South African business. A good many of the Boer leaders have called upon me, most of them with a certain dignified sorrow that though I was of Dutch blood, I seemed to have no sympathy with them when they so earnestly believed in the righteousness of their cause. As a matter of fact, I had and have the warmest personal sympathy with them, and yet I have always felt that by far the best possible result would be to have South Africa all united, with English as its common speech; and I believe that at present it cannot stand alone and that it can do infinitely better under Great Britain than under any other great power. I confess I am wholly puzzled by the duration of the war and the bitter and stubborn determination with which the Boers continue to fight. I have far too keen an appreciation of our own national shortcomings and blunders to feel the slightest inclination to criticize; but I do wish I knew the facts more accurately.

With love from all, *Ever yours*

READING FRANK NORRIS

To Owen Wister

Oyster Bay, July 20, 1901

Dear Dan:

I am immensely amused over the first part of your note of the 19th. If LL.D.'s were only to be granted to old men, well and good. But they are not only so granted. I took the greatest pleasure in voting one for Rhodes. He has won it. But he has not won it any more than Cabot Lodge. And yet Cabot has never been given it. However, I think the whole business is one of rather small vanity, and I only mentioned it because of the contrast between Yale, Columbia, and Princeton on the one hand and Harvard on the other. At Yale this year I understand that Seth Low, Whitelaw Reid, Bishop Potter and Archbishop Ireland are to be among my companions in getting the LL.D. Unless I mistake, it has been given by Harvard to Leonard Wood and also to General Miles — which last is preposterous. It was eminently proper to give it to Wood, although he is neither a scholar nor gray-haired.

Your coming here started me to re-reading your pieces. I want to reiterate my judgment that the "Pilgrim on the Gila," "Specimen Jones" and "The Second Missouri Compromise" are among the very best. I think they have a really very high value as historical documents which also possess an immense human interest. When you speak of the teachings of the Mormon bishop as having no resemblance to the Gospels but being right in the line of Deuteronomy, you set forth a great truth as to the whole Mormon Church. I shall always believe that Brigham Young was quite as big a man as Mahomet. But the age and the place were very unfavorable instead of highly favorable.

When I see Hitchcock I shall try to get you the insides of that Big Tree intrigue.

Now, about that book by Frank Norris, *The Octopus*. I read it with interest. He has a good idea and he has some power, but he left me with the impression that his overstatement was so utterly preposterous as to deprive his work of all value. A good part of it reads like the ravings which Altgeld and Bryan regard as denunciation of wrong. I do not know California at all, but I have seen a good deal of all the western States between the Mississippi and the western side of the Rocky Mountains. I know positively that as regards all those States — the Dakotas, Montana, Wyoming, Idaho, Colorado and New Mexico, the facts alleged in *The Octopus* are a wild travesty of the truth. It is just exactly as if in writing about the tyranny and corruption of Tammany Hall I should solemnly revive the stories of Mediaeval times and picture Mr. Croker as bathing in the blood of hundreds of babies taken from the tenement houses, or of having Jacob Schiff tortured in the Tombs until he handed over a couple of million dollars. The overstatement would be so preposterous that I would have rendered myself powerless to call attention to the real and gross iniquity.

Of course the conditions in California may have been wholly different from those in every other western State, but if so, Norris should have been most careful to show that what he wrote was absolutely limited by State lines and had no application to life in the west as a whole. What I am inclined to think is that conditions were worse in California than elsewhere, and that a writer of great power and vigor who was also gifted with self-restraint and with truthfulness could make out of them a great tragedy, which would not, like Norris's book, be contemptuously tossed aside by any serious man who knew western conditions, as so very hysterical and exaggerated as to be without any real value.

More and more I have grown to have a horror of the reformer who is half charlatan and half fanatic, and ruins his own cause by overstatement. If Norris's book is taken to apply to all the west, as it certainly would be taken by any ordinary man who reads it, then it stands on an exact level with some of the publications of the W.C.T.U. in which the Spanish War, our troubles in the Philippines, and civic dishonesty and social disorder, are all held to spring from the fact that sherry is drunk at the White House. *Faithfully yours*

THE SHOOTING OF McKINLEY

To Henry Cabot Lodge

Buffalo, September 9, 1901

Dear Cabot:

I answered your cable to Hotel Brighton, Paris, and hope it reached you. There is no use in telling you of the stunned amazement of the people over the attempted assassination of the President. You know all about it, because you know your own feelings. I was with Senator Proctor in Vermont at the time, and at first the news seemed literally incredible. You and I have lived too long, and have seen human nature from too many different sides to be astounded at ordinary folly or ordinary wickedness, but it did not seem possible that just at this time in just this country, and in the case of this particular President, any human being could be so infamous a scoundrel, so crazy a fool as to attempt to assassinate him. It was in the most naked way an assault not on power, not on wealth, but simply and solely upon free government, government by the common people, because it *was* government, and because though in the highest sense a free and representative government, it yet stood for order as well as for liberty. McKinley is a man hardly even of moderate means. He is about as well off say as a division superintendent of the New York Central railroad. He lives in a little house at Canton just as such a division superintendent who had retired would live in a little house in Auburn or some other small New York city or big country town. He comes from the typical hard-working farmer stock of our country. In every instinct and feeling he is closely in touch with and the absolute representative of the men who make up the immense bulk of our Nation — the small merchants, clerks, farmers and mechanics who formed the backbone of the patriotic party under Washington in the Revolution; of the Republican Party under Lincoln at the time of the Civil War. His one great anxiety while President has been to keep in touch with this body of people and to give expression to their desires and sentiments. He has been so successful that within a year he has been re-elected by an overwhelming majority, a majority including the bulk of the wage-workers and the very great bulk of the farmers. He has been to a high degree accessible to everyone. At his home in Canton anyone could see him just as easily as anyone else could be seen. All that was necessary was, if he was engaged, to wait until his engagement was over. More than almost any public man I have ever met, he has avoided exciting personal enmities. I have never heard him denounce or assail any man or any body of men. There is in the country at this time the most widespread confidence in and satisfaction with his policies. The occasion chosen by the assassin was one when the President was meeting great masses of his fellow-citizens in accordance with the old American idea of the relations between the President and the people. That there might be no measure of Judas-like infamy lacking, the dog approached him under pretense of shaking hands.

Under these conditions of National prosperity, of popular content, of democratic simplicity and of the absolutely representative character of the President, it does seem utterly impossible to fathom the mind of the man who would do such a deed. Moreover, the surgeons who have in all probability saved the President's life, have thereby saved the life of his assailant. If he is only indicted for assault with intent to kill, and behaves well while in jail, he will be a free man seven years hence, and this, after having committed a crime against free government, a thousand times worse than any murder of a private individual could be. Of course I feel as I always have felt, that we should war with relentless efficiency not only against anarchists, but against all active and passive sympathizers with anarchists. Moreover, every scoundrel like Hearst and his satellites who for whatever purposes appeals to and inflames evil human passion, has made himself accessory before the fact to every crime of this nature, and every soft fool who extends a maudlin sympathy to criminals has done likewise. Hearst and Altgeld, and to an only less degree, Tolstoi and the feeble apostles of Tolstoi, like Ernest Howard Crosby and William Dean Howells, who unite in petitions for the pardon of anarchists, have a heavy share in the burden of responsibility for crimes of this kind.

As soon as I heard the news I came straight to Buffalo. My position was of course most delicate, but I felt that the only course to follow was that which was natural, and that the natural thing was to come at once to Buffalo, where I might see how the President was getting on; and to stay here until he was on the highroad to recovery. As soon as I had seen and talked at length with the doctors, I cabled you. After my talk with them I became very confident of the President's recovery. I found that they would have felt this entire confidence if it had been an ordinary case of some stranger in a hospital, and that it was only the magnitude of the stake that caused their anxiety. Long before you receive this letter I believe the last particle of danger will have vanished; nor do I anticipate even a long convalescence. The President's splendid inherited strength, the temperate life he has led, and his singularly calm and equable temper of mind all count immensely in his favor.

Of course, I have stayed absolutely quiet here, seeing a great deal of Root, of whom I am very fond. We have had our own troubles during the past month. Curiously enough, Alice and Quentin at the same time had to be taken to the Roosevelt Hospital, although the trouble of neither was in any way connected with the trouble of the other. Alice was as brave and cheerful as possible. Quentin's trouble was in his ear and after the operation, during which he had been chloroformed, his ear had to be dressed every two hours for some days, and the poor little fellow suffered the most exquisite agony. I spent five or six days and nights at the hospital, and Edith was there steadily for a fortnight, and I was almost as glad for her sake as for the sake of the children when she was able to take them all, well and sick, up to the Adirondacks. I was about to join them when I was summoned to Buffalo.

I suppose you were as much astonished as we were at Austin Wadsworth's marriage, and of course you are as pleased as we are. I have always felt it very nearly a crime for Austin to leave no heirs for that beautiful Geneseo Valley estate.

In Vermont and just previously in Minnesota and Illinois I had a most interesting time. In each state I was received with wild enthusiasm, and the Governor of Illinois and Senator Knute Nelson in Minnesota and Senator Proctor in Vermont at the dinners to me proceeded to nominate me for President. I understand entirely that in the case of a promise where no consideration passes from the party on the other side, the promise is in no wise binding, and simply expresses present intentions. If I had been able I should have liked to defer the expression of feeling for some time to come, because in the next three years all may change utterly, and indeed probably will change; but just at present Illinois and Minnesota, like Vermont, are heartily for me, because there is a genuine popular sentiment for me. As yet, Odell has no hold whatever outside of New York. Fairbanks has gone to Illinois, Minnesota and Kansas, and in every place the leaders had told him they could not support him, because they were going to support me, as that was what the popular feeling demanded. All of this may absolutely change, and I do not want you to think that I attach any special importance to it; but I wanted you to know exactly how things stood. I am going to speak in the campaign both in Ohio and in Iowa. In New York Odell is absolutely in the saddle at the moment.

Give my warm love to Nannie and to all. *Ever yours*

PRESIDENT
1901–1909

"A DREADFUL THING"
To Henry Cabot Lodge

Washington, September 23, 1901

Dear Cabot:

I must just send you a line, hoping it will catch you before you leave, for naturally you have been in my thoughts almost every hour of the last fortnight. It is a dreadful thing to come into the Presidency this way; but it would be a far worse thing to be morbid about it. Here is the task, and I have got to do it to the best of my ability; and that is all there is about it. I believe you will approve of what I have done and of the way I have handled myself so far. It is only a beginning, but it is better to make a beginning good than bad.

I shall not try to give you even in barest outline the history of the last two weeks, and still less to talk of the policies that press for immediate consideration. I hope you can make it convenient to come and see me soon after your return.

I had a very nice talk with Murray Crane. Give my love to Nannie and all. *Ever yours*

A WARNING REGARDING LIQUOR
To Percival J. Werlich

Private

Washington, October 26, 1901

My dear Lieutenant Werlich:

After some thought I have approved of your promotion. I want now to send you this private and personal letter. It appears that you have sometimes taken too much liquor. After careful consideration I have decided to treat this as offset by your good conduct in action in the Philippines and the way in which you have won the approbation of your superior officers and on two occasions of General Lawton. But I wish to send you an emphatic word of warning. My experience has been that when a man finds himself tending to drink too much the only chance for him is to stop short and drink nothing. I make no condition in your promotion. I have not the right to, and if I had the right I would not exercise it. But for your own sake and for the sake of the service which is so dear to us both I wish greatly that you would write me pledging me your word as an officer and a gentleman that you would never again under any circumstances permit yourself to get under the influence of liquor; and indeed, I wish you would make up your mind to say that you would never again drink liquor.

This letter will not go on the official files, and no one will know that I have written to you. *Sincerely yours*

"DEALING WITH THE BLACK MAN"

To Albion W. Tourgée

Personal & Private

Washington, November 8, 1901

My dear Mr. Tourgée:

Your letter pleases and touches me. I too have been at my wits' ends in dealing with the black man. In this incident I deserve no particular credit. When I asked Booker T. Washington to dinner I did not devote very much thought to the matter one way or the other. I respect him greatly and believe in the work he has done. I have consulted so much with him it seemed to me that it was natural to ask him to dinner to talk over this work, and the very fact that I felt a moment's qualm on inviting him because of his color made me ashamed of myself and made me hasten to send the invitation. I did not think of its bearing one way or the other, either on my own future or on anything else. As things have turned out, I am very glad that I asked him, for the clamor aroused by the act makes me feel as if the act was necessary.

I have not been able to think out any solution of the terrible problem offered by the presence of the negro on this continent, but of one thing I am sure, and that is that inasmuch

as he is here and can neither be killed nor driven away, the only wise and honorable and Christian thing to do is to treat each black man and each white man strictly on his merits as a man, giving him no more and no less than he shows himself worthy to have. I say I am "sure" that this is the right solution. Of course I know that we see through a glass dimly, and, after all, it may be that I am wrong; but if I am, then all my thoughts and beliefs are wrong, and my whole way of looking at life is wrong. At any rate, while I am in public life, however short a time that may be, I am in honor bound to act up to my beliefs and convictions. I do not intend to offend the prejudices of anyone else, but neither do I intend to allow their prejudices to make me false to my principles.
Faithfully yours

"HE WILL GET BATTERED OUT"

To Endicott Peabody

Washington, January 4, 1902

Dear Cotty:

Pray do not think me grown timid in my old age until you read this note through. Ted would have a fit if he knew I were writing it, as I found that by having written you about his collarbone he was rendered very uncomfortable. In addition to Ted's collarbone, the dentist tells me that he has killed one front tooth in football, and that tooth will get black. Now I don't care a rap for either accident in itself; but Ted is only fourteen and I am afraid if he goes on like this he will get battered out before he can play in college. Last night a Groton graduate, one of the Harvard substitutes, told me of his own accord that he thought it had been a mistake for Ted to play against heavy boys so much this year. I do not know whether he knows anything about it or not; but De Saulles, the Yale quarterback, who was there, added that he thought it was a pity a young boy should get so battered up, if it came from playing larger ones, as it might interfere with other playing later. Now all this may be merely a rumor, and Ted may not have been playing against heavier boys, but I thought I would write you about it anyway.

I am very glad he got to be 2d in his class in studies. *Faithfully yours*

THE PHILIPPINES AND WOUNDED KNEE

To Elihu Root

Confidential

Washington, February 18, 1902

To the Secretary of War:

I send over for your personal information the enclosed note from General Miles with draft of an unsigned letter to you which he proposes to send.

General Miles came in yesterday morning in consequence of an appointment for which he had asked, and he then submitted an unsigned draft somewhat like that which is herewith enclosed, but containing a number of sentences which in effect recited alleged cruelties and brutalities committed by the United States Army on the Filipinos, and furthermore stated that in fighting with the Indians upon our own continent the United States Army had not been guilty of such cruelties and brutalities, and that he, General Miles, would see that any or all of such cruelties were stopped if he were sent over to the Philippines. I told him that as a matter of fact, as he could find out by inquiring of you or by reading the testimony of Judge Taft, the accusation that there had been anything resembling systematic or widespread cruelty by our troops was false; and I reminded him that when he was in command against the Sioux at the time of the Pine Ridge outbreak, a dozen years ago, the troops under his command had at Wounded Knee committed a massacre, as a sequel to a fight, in which massacre squaws, children, unarmed Indians, and armed Indians who had surrendered were killed, sometimes cold-bloodedly and with circumstances of marked brutality. I pointed out to him that this occurred in a comparatively easy and unimportant little campaign when he was in supreme command, and that in the Philippine Islands the task had been a thousand times more difficult and the provocation to our soldiers a hundred times greater, and yet that nothing had occurred as bad as this massacre which had taken place under him without any attempt being made to investigate the matter or punish the perpetrators. I pointed out further that the massacre had been seized upon at that time by those who wished ill to our government and who desired to discredit the army, and grossly distorted with these purposes in view; and that this was exactly what was being done now by the men whose baseless allegations he repeated in his letter, though these allegations, as infamous as they were false, were chiefly directed against the army of which he was head.

He stated that among the Filipinos whom he would like to bring back was Aguinaldo. I pointed out to him that at the time of the Pine Ridge outbreak the Aguinaldo of the period was Sitting Bull; that instead of bringing Sitting Bull here to Washington, the Indian police were sent out to arrest him and when he resisted he was killed. I pointed out that we had been far more merciful to the Filipinos than he and the troops associated with him in the old days had been toward the Indians of the plains, and that I did not intend to repeat the folly of which our people were sometimes guilty in those days when they petted the hostile Indians instead of standing by those who were friendly. I told him, furthermore, that the plan to bring a delegation of Filipinos here was foolish, and that the end he sought would be far better achieved by embodying Governor Taft's recommendation in law and having regular delegates elected or appointed from the Philippines to this government. Finally I told him that after a good deal of careful investigation I felt that Governor Taft and General Chaffee were accomplishing a remarkable work; that they were doing better work a great deal than he could do if he went out, and that his going out would merely hamper them and be productive of mischief.

WOODROW WILSON

To Cleveland Dodge

Washington, June 16, 1902

Dear Cleve:

Woodrow Wilson is a perfect trump. I am overjoyed at his election, and unless my arrangements render it absolutely impossible to get back in time I will attend his inauguration with the utmost pleasure. I do not dare to answer positively yet; but I am very sure I can come. *Faithfully yours*

OLIVER WENDELL HOLMES

To Henry Cabot Lodge

Personal

Oyster Bay, July 10, 1902

Dear Cabot:

I have received your letter. We were overjoyed by the arrival of your young namesake. I wrote to Bay that we were so glad to know that Bessie was doing well.

Now as to Holmes: If it becomes necessary you can show him this letter. First of all, I wish to go over the reasons why I am in his favor. He possesses the high character and the high reputation both of which should if possible attach to any man who is to go upon the highest court of the entire civilized world. His father's name entitles the son to honor; and if the father had been an utterly unknown man the son would nevertheless now have won the highest honor. The position of Chief Justice of Massachusetts is in itself a guarantee of the highest professional standing. Moreover, Judge Holmes has behind him the kind of career and possesses the kind of personality which make a good American proud of him as a representative of our country. He has been a most gallant soldier, a most able and upright public servant, and in public and private life alike a citizen whom we like to think of as typical of the American character at its best. The labor decisions which have been criticized by some of the big railroad men and other members of large corporations constitute to my mind a strong point in Judge Holmes' favor. The ablest lawyers and greatest judges are men whose past has naturally brought them into close relationship with the wealthiest and most powerful clients, and I am glad when I can find a judge who has been able to preserve his aloofness of mind so as to keep his broad humanity of feeling and his sympathy for the class from which he has not drawn his clients. I think it eminently desirable that our Supreme Court should show in unmistakable fashion their entire sympathy with all proper effort to secure the most favorable possible consideration for the men who most need that consideration.

Finally, Judge Holmes' whole mental attitude, as shown for instance by his great Phi Beta Kappa speech at Harvard is such that I should naturally expect him to be in favor of those principles in which I so earnestly believe.

Now a word as to the other side. It may seem to be, but it is not really, a small matter that his speech on Marshall should be unworthy of the subject, and above all should show a total incapacity to grasp what Marshall did. In the ordinary and low sense which we attach to the words "partisan" and "politician," a judge of the Supreme Court should be neither. But in the higher sense, in the proper sense, he is not in my judgment fitted for the position unless he is a party man, a constructive statesman, constantly keeping in mind his adherence to the principles and policies under which this nation has been built up and in accordance with which it must go on; and keeping in mind also his relations with his fellow statesmen who in other branches of the government are striving in cooperation with him to advance the ends of government. Marshall rendered such invaluable service because he was a statesman of the national type, like Adams who appointed him, like Washington whose mantle fell upon him. Taney was a curse to our national life because he belonged to the wrong party and faithfully carried out the criminal and foolish views of the party which stood for such a construction of the Constitution as would have rendered it impossible even to preserve the national life. The Supreme Court of the sixties was good exactly in so far as its members fitly represented the spirit of Lincoln.

This is true at the present day. The majority of the present Court who have, although without satisfactory unanimity, upheld the policies of President McKinley and the Republican party in Congress, have rendered a great service to mankind and to this nation. The minority — a minority so large as to lack but one vote of being a majority — have stood for such reactionary folly as would have hampered well-nigh hopelessly this people in doing efficient and honorable work for the national welfare, and for the welfare of the islands themselves, in Porto Rico and the Philippines. No doubt they have possessed excellent motives and without doubt they are men of excellent personal character; but this no more excuses them than the same conditions excused the various upright and honorable men who took part in the wicked folly of secession in 1860 and 1861.

Now I should like to know that Judge Holmes was in entire sympathy with our views, that is with your views and mine and Judge Gray's, for instance, just as we know that ex-Attorney General Knowlton is, before I would feel justified in appointing him. Judge Gray has been one of the most valuable members of the Court. I should hold myself as guilty of an irreparable wrong to the nation if I should put in his place any man who was not absolutely sane and sound on the great national policies for which we stand in public life. *Faithfully yours*

P.S. Judge Gray's letter of resignation to take effect upon the appointment of his successor, or as I may otherwise desire, has just come, so that I should know about Judge Holmes as soon as possible. How would it do, if he seems to be all right, to have him come down here and spend a night with me, and then I could make the announcement on the day that he left, after we have talked together?

ATROCITIES IN THE PHILIPPINES

To Hermann Speck von Sternberg

Private

Oyster Bay, July 19, 1902

Dear Speck:

If you and your wife get over here you must spend a night with us — at Oyster Bay if it is October, at the White House if it is November — as I have very much I want to say to you. I am greatly interested in all you say about the Indian Army. No people can amount to anything in any profession unless they take that profession seriously and work at it. Sport is an excellent thing as sport, but it is about the poorest business on the face of the globe. You and I have owed a good deal to our fondness for sport, for riding, shooting and walking; but we have made everything secondary to our respective works. It is an excellent thing for me to go on a mountain lion hunt and to ride a blooded hunter who can take me over fences; but it would be a very bad thing indeed if I treated either exercise as anything but a diversion and as a means of refreshing me for doing double work in serious governmental business. Of course I think that there is danger that the mere office man — the mere drudge who does not take part in rough game and rough play outside — will become a wretched routine creature, adept only in the pedantry of his profession and apt to come to an unexpected disaster.

Thanks to the kindness of the Emperor, I shall send three of my army officers, including General Wood, to see the German maneuvers this year. I am very anxious to start maneuvers on a small scale here, and I would like some of our men to see your army at work. Just at present I am busy trying to raise the target practice of our navy.

In the Philippines our men have done well, and on the whole have been exceedingly merciful; but there have been some blots on the record. Certain of the superior officers got to talking with loose and violent brutality, only about one-fourth meant, but which had a very bad effect upon their subordinates. The conditions were most exasperating. The enemy

were very treacherous, and it was well-nigh impossible to find
out who among all the pretended friends really had committed outrages; and in order to find out, not a few of the officers,
especially those of the native scouts, and not a few of the enlisted men, began to use the old Filipino method of mild torture, the water cure. Nobody was seriously damaged, whereas
the Filipinos had inflicted incredible tortures upon our own
people. Nevertheless, torture is not a thing that we can tolerate. I have bestowed rewards and praise liberally for all of the
good deeds that have been done there. But it was necessary to
call some of those who were guilty of shortcomings to sharp
account. Brigadier General Smith was an offender of high rank.
I had found out from many sources that he was habituated to
the use of violent and brutal language and that this had a very
bad effect upon his inferiors. For instance, Inspector General
Breckinridge happened to mention quite casually to me, with
no idea that he was saying anything in Smith's disfavor, that
when he met him and asked him what he was doing, he responded "shooting niggers." Breckinridge thought this a joke.
I did not. I found that the civil authorities were unwilling to
try to do anything in any province which Smith controlled because of the effect his language had on his subordinates. In
this very Samar expedition Major Waller, who is an exceedingly gallant man, when half crazed by the terrible privations
to which he had been exposed, ordered what I regard, or
pretty nearly what I regard, as an unjustifiable murder of ten
of his native bearers. These had doubtless been sullen and discontented, but I am not convinced that they were even treacherous, and their acts certainly fell very far short of warranting
the death penalty, which was imposed without any trial whatsoever. General Smith's language to his subordinates was not
much worse than that General Sherman used on one occasion
in reference to the Sioux Indians; but it was language to a subordinate in the form of a direction — that is, an order — and
it was of a kind that was habitual with him. I found that
Chaffee felt exactly as I did about both Smith and Waller,
except that he thought that Smith was somewhat insane, but
not enough so to warrant a court being held on the question
of his sanity. I have taken care that the army should understand that I thoroughly believe in severe measures when

necessary, and am not in the least sensitive about killing any number of men if there is adequate reason. But I do not like torture or needless brutality of any kind, and I do not believe in the officers of high rank continually using language which is certain to make the less intelligent or more brutal of their subordinates commit occasional outrages.

Ted now rides my hunter and has taken him over five feet of timber. He is a good shot; and has just finished Macaulay and Gibbon, taking elaborate notes on the latter. *Faithfully yours*

STUDYING ABRAHAM LINCOLN

To John Hay

Personal

Oyster Bay, July 22, 1902

Dear John:

What a wonderful address that was of Lincoln, after his re-election, to the District Republican Clubs! How he does loom up as one studies and reads him! He and Washington stand alone not only in our history but in the history of mankind during the periods covered by their respective lives — and I might say even more and still be moderate in the expression of truth.

In reading the great work of you and Nicolay this summer I have not only taken the keenest enjoyment but I really believe I have profited. At any rate, it has made me of set purpose to try to be good-natured and forbearing and to free myself from vindictiveness. It is just as Lincoln said, right in the throes of the mighty crisis; the men and the forces met with in each crisis — those against whom and through whom one has to do one's work — though they differ in degree from previous crises, are yet the same in their infinite variety of kind. In the little work, the easy work, of these days of peace and prosperity, I see on a small scale much what Lincoln saw in the supreme years of the nation's life struggle. Mrs.

Josephine Shaw Lowell is an utterly unimportant annoyance; and I doubt if Wendell Phillips was relatively much more of an annoyance to Lincoln. McClellan and Fremont were able to try to do great things for evil as well as to fail conspicuously. Miles and Schley have not had the chance to fail conspicuously or the chance to do very much for evil; although I am inclined to think that Miles would be a very bad man indeed if the opportunity came and his abilities were sufficient. The Missouri radicals and their fellows stood toward Lincoln with reference to his attitude on slavery in a position just as foolish and unreasonable as that of the ultra-reformers like Henry C. Lea, the Springfield *Republican* and *Evening Post* people, who solemnly desire me to destroy the Republican party by refusing to work with anybody whom they choose to call a "politician" or a "boss." Whenever there has been a sudden revolution of sporadic wrongdoing in the Philippines, or allegations of wrongdoing in connection with our foreign policy, a perfect crop of people has arisen whose attitude was as unreasonable as that of Horace Greeley himself. Every movement about trusts brings to the front analogies of Wade and Davis on the one hand and of Seymour on the other, and the ultra-protectionists are among the difficulties encountered by those who wish to keep a protective tariff.

What a wretched showing Chase and Sumner make! I never had much admiration for Sumner. Again, to compare big men with small men, Charles Francis Adams is now, in his infinitesimal way, adopting their attitude.

After reading your volumes I do congratulate myself that my father was a Republican and that I am a Republican. It seems to me it would be a dreadful thing to have to live down being descended from Vallandigham; and I should mortally hate to have had men like Seymour or McClellan for ancestors. *Ever yours*

As to Frye and the Callao consulship, I have told him that if I now try to right the matter, I must begin by dismissing Gottschalk! This will give him food for thought. Now, if the man *was* wrong — *is* wrong — or is simply unfit, all trouble would be stopped by Hill's simply saying so. Before he is appointed to any new position, I wish a report from Hill saying definitely whether he is a good or a poor official.

BROWNING AND LONGFELLOW

To Martha Baker Dunn

En route, Chattanooga, Tenn.,
September 6, 1902

My dear Miss Dunn:

Perhaps I should be writing to Mrs. Dunn; if so you must pardon me. Just before starting on this trip Mrs. Roosevelt handed me the *Atlantic Monthly*, saying that I must read your piece on Browning. I accepted the gift with rather a growl, for of recent years the *Atlantic's* view of life has not appealed to me — it has seemed rather anemic. But I have so thoroughly enjoyed your piece that I must take the liberty of writing to tell you so. There is a good deal of Browning which I am wholly unable to read, but he has just exactly the quality you attribute to him, and those poems which I can read appeal to me as very few poems indeed do. I don't care a rap what the inner meaning of "Childe Roland" is; What I care for is the lift, the thrill the poem gives; the look of the desolate country, the dauntless bearing of the Knight, and the strange thoughts and sights and the squat blind tower itself. I used to ranch in the Bad Lands, and I always thought of the hills which lay like giants at a hunting when I saw the great buttes grow shadowy and awful in the dusk. I am very fond of "Prospice" — what can a poet do better than sound the praises of a good fighter and a good lover? I wish you had quoted "Love among the Ruins." That has always been one of my favorites. Now I shall take up "Rabbi Ben Ezra," at which I have always shied hitherto. I should like to go on indefinitely with the catalogue of Browning's poems that appeal to me; but I shall spare you.

Just one word about Longfellow, however. Don't look down on him because he is so utterly different from Browning; so different that he might belong to another world. For all his gentleness he strikes the true ring of courage, the ballad-like ring of courage, in many pieces. The "Saga of King Olaf" is only a translation to be sure, but it seems to me that if a boy or girl likes it well enough to learn most of it by heart and feel the spirit of it, just as they ought to like Julia Ward Howe's battle hymn, they will always have in them something to which an appeal for brave action can be made. When Olaf strikes his sails and with his doom upon him makes ready to fight until the certain death overwhelms him, I think you can hear the clang of the weapons and the crash and splinter of the oars.

As for what you say about the Spanish War I should like to have it circulated as a tract among an immense multitude of philanthropists, Congressmen, newspaper editors, publicists, softheaded mothers and other people of sorts who think that life ought to consist of perpetual shrinking from effort, danger and pain.

With hearty thanks I am, *Sincerely yours*

MEDIATING THE COAL STRIKE

To Robert Bacon

Strictly Personal

Washington, October 5, 1902

Dear Bob:

Do you recollect when you wrote me a similar letter over four years ago just before the outbreak of the Spanish war? I have always prized that letter and now I shall prize this.

I send you a copy of a letter ex-President Cleveland has just sent me and my answer thereto. Of course these letters are not to be made public, but if you have any friends upon whose discretion you can entirely rely, to whom you think you would like to show them, why do it. The situation is bad, especially because it is possible it may grow infinitely worse. If when the severe weather comes on there is a coal famine I dread to think of the suffering, in parts of our great cities especially, and I fear there will be fuel riots of as bad a type as any bread riots we have ever seen. Of course once the rioting has begun, once there is a resort to mob violence, the only thing to do is to maintain order. It is a dreadful thing to be brought face to face with the necessity of taking measures, however unavoidable, which will mean the death of men who have been maddened by want and suffering. I feel that whatever I possibly can do to avert such a necessity I must do; and that I must not cease in my efforts while even the slightest chance to success remains.

At the conference between the miners and the coal operators in my presence John Mitchell towered above the six operators present. He was dignified and moderate and straightforward. He made no threats and resorted to no abuse. The proposition he made seemed to me eminently fair. The operators refused even to consider it; used insolent and abusive language about him; and in at least two cases assumed an attitude toward me which was one of insolence. This was not important. But it *was* important that they should absolutely decline to consider matters from the standpoint of the interests of the public in any way. One of them demanded outright and several of them hinted that they were going to demand, that I use the United States Army in their interests, being seemingly ignorant that I had no power whatever to send into the mines a single soldier, unless the Pennsylvania governmental authorities, being unable to preserve order, appealed to me to do so. They kept referring to Cleveland's course in the Debs' riots as offering a parallel, which was a course either ridiculous or dishonest on their part; and Cleveland's letter to me shows how entirely he sympathizes with my attitude in the matter. There is not the remotest resemblance between the situation in the coal fields as it now exists and the situation in Chicago when Cleveland interfered to protect national property. The operators forget that they have duties towards the public, as well as rights to be guarded by the public through its governmental agents. It is amazing folly on their part clamorously to demand by the public the exercise of the police powers, at no matter what expenditure of blood and money, and yet to resent any suggestion that they have duties toward the public of which its governmental representatives must take cognizance. Owing to the peculiar division of our powers under the constitution, while Boston and New York are as much interested as Philadelphia in the coal famine, only Pennsylvania has immediate power to deal with the situation. If the trouble comes through disorder by the miners who thereby prevent people who wish to go to work from going to work, then Pennsylvania should afford the fullest protection, by any exercise of the military power, to the miners, union or nonunion men, who may wish to work, and to the property of the mine owners. If the attitude of the mine operators on the other hand is insolent and improper then Pennsylvania through its legislature should take immediate action. I do not think I need assure you that in case I am called upon to act, through the inability of Pennsylvania to keep order and on the demand of her constitutional authorities, I will guarantee that order will be kept and life and property absolutely respected, and all men alike made to yield obedience to the law. But I wish to feel that I have done everything in my power to bring about a peaceful solution before any such dreadful alternative is forced upon me. The operators by their attitude have done all in their power to render such a peaceful solution impossible. But I have determined to inform Mitchell that if the miners will go back to work I will appoint a commission to investigate all the matters at issue and that I will do whatever I can to secure favorable action on their findings. I know nothing of the merits of the quarrel. Each side insists that it is wholly right. Commissioner Carroll D. Wright, in whom I have the utmost confidence has reported to me that while the issues are very complicated and while it is very hard to decide as to the rights and wrongs of the matter, there is certainly right and wrong on both sides. This finding alone in my opinion shows the impropriety of the operators' attitude in declining to submit to any arbitration; or to have matters adjusted by a commission or committee of conciliation.

At any rate, whatever, with my limited powers, I can do toward securing a peaceful settlement, if possible in the interests of both parties, at least in the interests of the general public, will be done; and if the worst comes to worst, no matter how dreadful any responsibility put upon me, I shall try to meet it faithfully and fearlessly. *Ever yours*

P.S. The Sun, in view of my attitude, seems inclined to go over to the Democracy; which in New York has just declared for national ownership of the coal mines! Apparently the Sun fails to understand that what I am doing offers the surest ground for hope of successful opposition to such ruinous plans as that of national mine ownership.

THE DANGER OF "RACE SUICIDE"

To Bessie Van Vorst

Private

Washington, October 18, 1902

My dear Mrs. Van Vorst:

I must write you a line to say how much I have appreciated your article, "The Woman Who Toils." But to me there is a most melancholy side to it, when you touch upon what is fundamentally infinitely more important than any other question in this country — that is, the question of race suicide, complete or partial, which must follow from the attitude of our people as a whole toward wifehood, motherhood, and fatherhood, if the feeling that you describe among the girls you met in the factory is typical of the class generally — for that is the numerically dominant class of our people.

In the same magazine there was an article on the unemployed rich. I do not think the writer appreciated what a dreadful type she was describing. Superficially the Newport girl there set forth and the girls who were your companions are very unlike, but in essentials they seem to me to be identical. An easy, good-natured kindliness, and a desire to be independent, that is, to live one's life purely according to one's own desires, are in no sense substitutes for the fundamental virtues, for the practice of the strong racial qualities without which there can be no strong races — the qualities of courage and resolution in both men and women, of scorn of what is mean, base, and selfish, of eager desire to work or fight or suffer as the case may be, provided the end to be gained is great enough, and the contemptuous putting aside of mere ease, mere vapid pleasure, mere avoidance of toil and worry. I do not know whether I most pity or most despise the foolish and selfish man or woman who does not understand that the only things really worth having in life are those the acquirement of which normally means cost and effort. If a man or woman, through no fault of his or hers, goes throughout life denied those highest of all joys which spring only from home life, from the having and bringing up of many healthy children, I feel for them deep and respectful sympathy; the sympathy one extends to the gallant fellow killed at the beginning of a campaign, or the man who toils hard and is brought to ruin by the fault of others. But the man or woman who deliberately avoids marriage and has a heart so cold as to know no passion and a brain so shallow and selfish as to dislike having children, is in effect a criminal against the race and should be an object of contemptuous abhorrence by all healthy people.

Of course no one quality makes a good citizen, and no one quality will save a nation. But there are certain great qualities for the lack of which no amount of intellectual brilliancy or of material prosperity or of easiness of life can atone, and which show decadence and corruption in the nation, just as much if they are produced by selfishness and coldness and ease-loving laziness among comparatively poor people as if they are produced by vicious or frivolous luxury in the rich. If the men of the nation are not anxious to work in many different ways, with all their might and strength, and ready and able to fight at need, and anxious to be fathers of families, and if the women do not recognize that the greatest thing for any woman is to be a good wife and mother, why, that nation has cause to be alarmed about its future.

There is no physical trouble among us Americans. The trouble with the situation you set forth is one of character, and therefore we can conquer it if we only will. *Very sincerely yours*

RACE AND GOVERNMENT APPOINTMENTS

To Robert Goodwyn Rhett

Personal

Washington, November 10, 1902

My dear Mr. Rhett:

I have read your letter carefully, together with that of Mr. Waring, and am concerned and pained by the position therein taken. How anyone could have gained the idea that I had said

I would not appoint reputable and upright colored men to office, when objection was made to them solely on account of their color, I confess I am wholly unable to understand. At the time of my visit to Charleston last year I had made, and since that time I have made, a number of such appointments, from almost every State in which there is any considerable colored population. For example, I made such an appointment in Mississippi, and another in Alabama shortly before my visit to Charleston. I have recently announced another such appointment for New Orleans, and have just made one from Pennsylvania. In short, in every State where there was any considerable colored population I have endeavored to make one or more such appointments. I am unable to see how I could legitimately be asked to make an exception for South Carolina. In Georgia I found the three most prominent offices held by colored men. I doubt whether as original appointments I should have appointed so many of the colored race in this one State; but after carefully going over the matter I came to the conclusion that I would not be justified in failing to reappoint all three, because they were men whose personal and official record was such that if white there would have been no opposition to their appointment; and under such conditions I felt that I would be untrue to my beliefs and principles if I failed to reappoint them merely because they were colored. In South Carolina to the four most important positions in the State I have appointed three men and continued in office the fourth, all of them white men — two of them, as I understand it, the sons of Confederate soldiers — three of them, as I am informed, originally gold Democrats. I have been informed by all of the citizens of Charleston whom I have met that these four men represent a high grade of public service. I do not intend to appoint any unfit man to office. If Mr. Crum is unfit I most certainly shall not appoint him, but as yet he has not even been charged with unfitness, so far as I am aware, or with any other offence save his color. So far as I legitimately can I shall always endeavor to pay regard to the likes and dislikes of the people of each locality, but I cannot consent by my action to take the position that the door of hope — the door of opportunity — is to be shut upon all men, no matter how worthy, purely upon the grounds of color. Such an attitude would according to my convictions be fundamentally wrong. The question of "negro domination" does not enter into the matter at all. You yourself know that the enormous majority of my appointments in South Carolina have been of white men, and so far as I know, of white men whose good character and uprightness were not questioned. The question simply is whether it is to be declared that under no circumstances shall any man of color, no matter how good a citizen, no matter how upright and honest, no matter how fair in his dealing with all his fellows, be permitted to hold any office under our government. I certainly cannot assume such an attitude, and you must permit me to say that in my view it is an attitude no one should assume, whether he looks at it from the standpoint of the true interest of the white men of the south or of the colored men of the south — not to speak of any other section in the Union. It seems to me that it is a good thing from every standpoint to let the colored man know that if he shows in marked degree the qualities of good citizenship — the qualities which in a white man we feel are entitled to reward — then he himself will not be cut off from all hope of similar reward. *Sincerely yours*

ENJOYING THE PRESIDENCY

To Maria Longworth Storer

Personal

Washington, December 8, 1902

Dear Maria:

Just at this time I could have received no other present which would have appealed to me so much as the picture by Encke, and I thank you for it with all my heart. I took an immense fancy to the picture. I cannot say that I think it looks particularly like me; but most emphatically it *does* look the way I should like to have my children and possibly grandchildren *think* that I looked! I have always wanted to have a picture taken in uniform, although I have felt shamefaced about sitting for such a picture in view of my very brief military career. So I wish you to feel that you have given me the very thing of all others I wanted.

Please tell Bellamy to give my most cordial regards to the King of the Belgians if or when he sees him. I was much interested in your description of your last meeting with him. I have always followed his career, especially after you had told me all about him, at close range, so to speak. What an extraordinary thing it has been, the way Belgium has played her part in the international development of Africa and to a certain extent of Asia. I have always felt that the Belgian experiment was one which through the coming centuries would assume the most far-reaching proportions and importance as a precedent no less than in itself.

Well, I have been President for a year and a quarter, and whatever the future may hold I think I may say that during that year and a quarter I have been as successful as I had any right to hope or expect. Of course political life in a position such as this is one long strain on the temper, one long acceptance of the second best, one long experiment of checking one's impulses with an iron hand and learning to subordinate one's own desires to what some hundreds of associates can be forced or cajoled or led into desiring. Every day, almost every hour, I have to decide very big as well as very little questions, and in almost each of them I must determine just how far it is safe to go in forcing others to accept my views and standards and just how far I must subordinate what I deem expedient, and indeed occasionally what I deem morally desirable, to what it is possible under the given conditions to achieve. Hay and Nicolay's *Life of Lincoln* has been to me a great comfort and aid. I have read it and profited by it, and often when dealing with some puzzling affair I find myself thinking what Lincoln would have done. It has been very wearing, but I have thoroughly enjoyed it, for it is fine to feel one's hand guiding great machinery, with at least the purpose, and I hope the effect, of guiding it for the best interests of the nation as a whole.

Edith has enjoyed it too. I do not think my eyes are blinded by affection when I say that she has combined to a degree I have never seen in any other woman the power of being the best of wives and mothers, the wisest manager of the household, and at the same time the ideal great lady and mistress of the White House.

The children are as well and happy as possible. Groton has been a great thing both for Ted and for Kermit; and Archie is doing excellently at the public school. The changes in the White House have transformed it from a shabby likeness to the ground floor of the Astor House into a simple and dignified dwelling for the head of a great republic. I am very much pleased with it.

With love to Bellamy, and renewed thanks, *Faithfully yours*

WILDLIFE IN YELLOWSTONE

To Clinton Hart Merriam

Yellowstone Park, Wyo., April 16, 1903

My dear Merriam:

I have had a most interesting trip and every opportunity of observing the game, which is certainly more plentiful than when I was last in the Park, twelve years ago. The elk far outnumber all the other animals.

Buffalo Jones has been a great hunter and frontiersman and has traveled far, and he has done admirable work with his buffalo and knows a great deal about trapping and about game generally. But he is not always an accurate observer, and his report on the elk was all wrong. The elk in the southern half of the Park winter outside of it to the south, chiefly in Jackson's Hole, and of them I know little; but those in the northern half of the Park winter within its borders and I have spent the last eight days among them. From very careful estimates, based for instance on actually counting the individuals in several different bands, I am convinced that there are at least fifteen thousand of these elk which stay permanently within the Park. In one day I saw between three and four thousand. But an insignificant number of them are killed by hunters, so as regards them there has been no killing off of the big bulls by sportsmen. There are rather too many for the winter feed, and so it is evident, from the carcasses I have seen, that a somewhat larger proportion than is normal dies, especially among the yearlings.

The cougars are their only enemies, and in many places these big cats, which are quite numerous, are at this season living purely on the elk, killing yearlings and an occasional cow; this does no damage; but around the hot springs the cougars are killing deer, antelope and sheep, and in this neighborhood they should certainly be exterminated.

Buffalo Jones' account of the bulls having been reduced to insignificant numbers is absolutely erroneous, and is due to his only going in the lower regions and seeing the big herds of cows and yearlings. He is wholly ignorant of the fact, which our traveling soon developed, namely, that the old bulls are now found by themselves in loose parties of from ten to fifty, for the most part high up the mountains. Of course an occasional big bull and more often a two-year-old or three-year-old is found with the great bands of cows and yearlings. Most of the elk we found dead had succumbed to the deep snow, cold, or starvation; two, a bull and a cow, had died from the scab; the others, yearlings with one or two cows, had been killed by cougars. Buffalo Jones also said that the cougars killed the yearling bulls only, but the first three yearlings I found which had been killed by cougars were all heifers.

Evidently the elk had spent the winter in the bottoms of the valleys, in great bands, browsing on the quaking asp, the willows, and the lower limbs of the conifers. They then rarely drank, eating snow instead. Where there was open water, however — as by beaver dams — they drank regularly. Sometimes they would leave the valleys and feed on the side hills nearby during the daytime. At present they have moved high up the mountain side, keeping for the most part above the line of the retreating snow. The bands evidently wander very little at this season, staying, as I myself saw, for days, and doubtless for weeks, within a radius of two or three miles. They sometimes sleep in the ravines; but some of them pass their entire time on the bare places. Others live chiefly in the snow, feeding on the patches of old grass, left bare as the snow melted. They lie out in the snow in the bleak wind, seeming not to feel the cold at all. At present they are grazing; they are weak and I had no difficulty in running into the herds on horseback — especially if I could make them go up hill. After a short run they open their mouths and pant heavily. They are more timid than the deer, but also more stupid. I saw a golden eagle threaten a band, driving them in their fright directly towards me. It separated a weak yearling from the herd and then hovered around his head — almost striking at it but evidently unable quite to make up its mind to the attack; finally it left and flew away. The coyotes wander about among the sleeping or feeding elk without attracting any attention whatever.

The antelope are quite shy. Their winter range is only the open country near Gardiner.

The deer — which except along the Gardiner are blacktail — are common and tame. They come on the parade ground in troops to pick up the hay. The blacktail is tamer than the whitetail.

Singularly enough the mountain sheep are the tamest of all the creatures. I saw but two bands — one of nineteen near the post, and another of seven in the Yellowstone Canyon. I seated myself within fifteen yards of the former as they grazed, and they paid hardly any heed to me. I walked up to within thirty yards of the latter, right in the open, before they ran. Their mountaineering feats down the cliffs of the Yellowstone Canyon were marvelous. *Yours truly*

Some of the bears have already come out; they are *not* feeding on the young green grass, for there isn't any, but on what they find under and in dead logs, and on carcases.

The water ousels have wintered here.

"GOOD HARD BODILY EXERCISE"

To Pierre de Coubertin

Washington, June 15, 1903

My dear Baron Coubertin:

I was much interested in your letter and the accompanying newspaper clipping. The idea you suggest is to me new, at least to the extent that you have for the first time formulated it. I agree with you entirely. If a growing boy, a young fellow up to the time that he attains manhood, achieves a certain degree of mastery in such exercises as those you enumerate — walking, running, riding, shooting, swimming, skating, etc. — I fully believe that he does, through what you so aptly describe as muscular memory, acquire the capacity to retain a large degree of his powers through their comparatively infrequent use.

There are just two suggestions, both of which you have doubtless developed in your book. The first is that it is impossible to put all boys and young men on the same Procrustean bed, whether of body or of mind; and the second is that so far as possible, if only for the effect on the mind, the boy's own tastes should be consulted as to the sports in which he is chiefly exercised.

For example, I have four boys. The youngest is five and therefore can be left out of account for our purpose. The next oldest is nine. He is a sweet-tempered little fellow, not at all combative. He runs, walks, and climbs well, and has learned to swim fairly well. He is most fond of his bicycle and his pony. The latter, like all of my boys when young, he rides with a small Mexican or "cow" saddle. This summer I intend to teach him to shoot with a small calibre rifle.

The next oldest, Kermit, is thirteen. He had water on the knee when young and it kept him back and has prevented his ever becoming really proficient in sports. He is not at all combative but seems to hold his own well with boys. I have been utterly unable to teach him to box, but he wrestles pretty well for his weight and age. He does not take to horseback riding at all but is very fond of his bicycle. In running he is no good at all for the sprints, but has a good deal of endurance and comes in well for the long distances. I am utterly unable to make him care for shooting. He skates rather poorly. At last I have got him so that he swims fairly.

The oldest, Ted, is fifteen. He is a regular bull terrier and though devoted to his mother and sisters, and although I don't believe he is quarrelsome among his friends he is everlastingly having sanguinary battles with outsiders. In most branches of sport he has already completely passed me by. He can outwalk and outrun me with ease, and perhaps could outswim me — although I think not yet; I am inclined to think him a better rider than I am, and owing to his weight he can certainly take my horses over jumps which I would not care to put them at unless there was necessity. On account of my weight I could probably still beat him at boxing and wrestling, but in another year he will have passed me in these. I do not shoot at all with the shotgun, whereas he has already become a good wing shot. I can still beat him with the rifle. He plays football well. In a game last year he broke his collar bone, but finished the game without letting anyone know what had happened. [   ]

Now with all these boys I have been able to do a certain amount in guiding them, but their own instincts have decided the very marked differences among them. Personally I have always felt that I might serve as an object lesson as to the benefit of good hard bodily exercise to the ordinary man. I never was a champion at anything. I have never fenced, although this winter I have done a good deal of broadsword and singlestick work with my friend, General Leonard Wood, and other Army officers. I was fond of boxing and fairly good at it. I was a fair rider, a fair rifle shot, and possessing the ordinary hardihood and endurance of an out-of-door man I have done a good deal of work in the wilderness after big game. Of late years, since I have been Governor of New York and afterwards President, my life has necessarily been very sedentary; but I have certain playmates among my friends here in Washington and with them I occasionally take long walks, or rather scrambles, through the woods and over the rocks.

Mrs. Roosevelt is very fond of riding and we ride a good deal together. In summer at my home on Long Island Sound I often take her for long rows. Like the average married man of domestic habits, my ability to take violent exercise has been much diminished by the fact that when I have leisure I like, so far as possible, to spend it in doing something in company with my wife or children. Of late years I have gone back very much in physical prowess, tending to grow both fat and stiff. I could not begin to walk or run for the length of time or at the speed of the old days, and I could not successfully ride the kind of horses I used to ride on my ranch, or in the hunting field across a country so stiff as to insure my having bad falls, for I should shake myself up too much. But I have kept up just exactly the kind of exercise you describe and with exactly the same effect. I can ride fifty miles on horseback or walk twenty on foot, if I am allowed to choose my own gait. I can enjoy a day's hunting as much as ever. I have had to abandon wrestling because I found that in such violent work I tended to lay myself up; and I do but little boxing because it seems rather absurd for a President to appear with a black eye or a swollen nose or a cut lip. Four times I have broken bones in falls with horses.

I think that you preach just the right form of the gospel of physical development. You are well aware of the mistake that so many of my English friends have made, that is of treating physical development as the be-all and the end-all — in other words as the serious business — of life. I have met English officers to whom polo and racing, football and baseball were far more absorbing than their professional duties. In such a case athleticism becomes a mere harmful disease. Nevertheless the fact remains that in our modern highly artificial, and on the whole congested, civilization, no boon to the race could be greater than the acquisition by the average man of that bodily habit which you describe — a habit based upon the having in youth possessed a thorough knowledge of such sports as those you outline, and then of keeping up a reasonable acquaintance with them in later years.

When are you coming over here? I would like you to pay me a visit here in Washington and we will take some walks and rides together. If you come when I am in the country we will row or chop trees or shoot at a target, as well as ride and swim. *Sincerely yours*

MOTHERS AND SOLDIERS

To Hamlin Garland

Oyster Bay, July 19, 1903

My dear Garland:

Accept my heartiest congratulations to you and especially to your wife.

The pangs of childbirth make all men the debtors of all women. One feels a little shy about talking of the deepest things, and therefore it is difficult for me to say all I feel about the attitude that should be taken by the husband to the wife, by the son to the mother. Brutality by a man to a woman, by a grown person to a little child, by anything strong toward anything good and helpless, makes my blood literally boil. But I hate most of all the crime of a man against a woman. Only less do I hate brutal indifference, the failure to estimate the debt due to the woman who has had a child, and must have in her a touch of a saint — that is, of course, if she has the right spirit in her at all. And she also has that claim to regard which we give to the soldier, or to anyone else who does a great and indispensable service which involves pain and discomfort, self-abnegation, and the incurring of risk of life. But you are all wrong about big families. Of course to any rule there are exceptions, and moreover any principle can be carried to a ridiculous and noxious extreme. I do not wish to see a woman worn down and perhaps killed by too much maternity; but my parallel of the soldier holds good. A race whose men will not work and will not fight ought to die out, and unless it will either work or fight it generally does die out. And of course if the women flinch from breeding the deserved death of the race takes place even quicker. I have highest regard and veneration for the woman who is the mother of many children, just as to a less degree I respect the soldier who has fought well, the man who has worked hard. While I respect all three if they do what they ought to, I because of this very fact despise and reprobate them if they refuse to do what they ought to. The woman who flinches from childbirth stands on a par with the soldier who drops his rifle and runs in battle. He may have many other excellent traits, but these are all counterbalanced by the one fearful shortcoming. Of course, it is physically impossible for certain women to become mothers, just as it is physically impossible for certain men to be soldiers, and these women and these men may do admirable work in other lines and deserve the respect of their countrymen; but as a general rule what I have said holds true.

In short, in this life I honor beyond measure those who do their full duty, but I do not pity them, I admire them — and all the more because the doing of duty generally means pain, hardship, self-mastery, self-denial, endurance of risk, of labor, of irksome monotony, wearing effort, steady perseverance under difficulty and discouragement. If on the other hand a man or a woman refuses to do his or her duty, why they are contemptible creatures and have no right to live in a wholesome community. *Faithfully yours*

LYNCHING

To Winfield Taylor Durbin

Oyster Bay, August 6, 1903

My dear Governor Durbin:

Permit me to thank you as an American citizen for the admirable way in which you have vindicated the majesty of the law by your recent action in reference to lynching. I feel, my dear sir, that you have made all men your debtors who believe, as all farseeing men must, that the well-being, indeed the very existence, of the Republic depends upon that spirit of orderly liberty under the law which is as incompatible with mob violence as with any form of despotism. Of course mob violence is simply one form of anarchy; and anarchy is now, as it always has been, the handmaiden and forerunner of tyranny.

I feel that you have not only reflected honor upon the state which for its good fortune has you as its Chief Executive, but upon the whole nation. It is incumbent upon every man throughout this country not only to hold up your hands in the course you have been following, but to show his realization that the matter is one which is of vital concern to us all.

All thoughtful men must feel the gravest alarm over the growth of lynching in this country, and especially over the peculiarly hideous forms so often taken by mob violence when colored men are the victims — on which occasions the mob seems to lay most weight, not on the crime but on the color of the criminal. In a certain proportion of these cases the man lynched has been guilty of a crime horrible beyond description; a crime so horrible that as far as he himself is concerned he has forfeited the right to any kind of sympathy whatsoever. The feeling of all good citizens that such a hideous crime shall not be hideously punished by mob violence is due not in the least to sympathy for the criminal, but to a very lively sense of the train of dreadful consequences which follow the course taken by the mob in exacting inhuman vengeance for an inhuman wrong. In such cases, moreover, it is well to remember that the criminal not merely sins against humanity in inexpiable and unpardonable fashion, but sins particularly against his own race, and does them a wrong far greater than any white man can possibly do them. Therefore, in such cases the colored people throughout the land should in every possible way show their belief that they, more than all others in the community, are horrified at the commission of such a crime and are peculiarly concerned in taking every possible measure to prevent its recurrence and to bring the criminal to immediate justice. The slightest lack of vigor either in denunciation of the crime or in bringing the criminal to justice is itself unpardonable.

Moreover, every effort should be made under the law to expedite the proceedings of justice in the case of such an awful crime. But it cannot be necessary in order to accomplish this to deprive any citizen of those fundamental rights to be heard in his own defense which are so dear to us all and which lie at the root of our liberty. It ought certainly to be possible by the proper administration of the laws to secure swift vengeance upon the criminal; and the best and immediate efforts of all legislators, judges, and citizens should be addressed to securing such reforms in our legal procedure as to leave no vestige of excuse for those misguided men who undertake to reap vengeance through violent methods.

Men who have been guilty of a crime like rape or murder should be visited with swift and certain punishment and the just effort made by the courts to protect them in their rights should under no circumstances be perverted into permitting any mere technicality to avert or delay their punishment. The substantial rights of the prisoner to a fair trial must of course be guaranteed, as you have so justly insisted that they should be; but, subject to this guarantee, the law must work swiftly and surely and all the agents of the law should realize the wrong they do when they permit justice to be delayed or thwarted for technical or insufficient reasons. We must show that the law is adequate to deal with crime by freeing it from every vestige of technicality and delay.

But the fullest recognition of the horror of the crime and the most complete lack of sympathy with the criminal cannot in the least diminish our horror at the way in which it has become customary to avenge these crimes and at the consequences that are already proceeding therefrom. It is of course inevitable that where vengeance is taken by a mob it should frequently light on innocent people; and the wrong done in such a case to the individual is one for which there is no remedy. But even where the real criminal is reached, the wrong done by the mob to the community itself is well-nigh as great. Especially is this true where the lynching is accompanied with torture. There are certain hideous sights which when once seen can never be wholly erased from the mental retina. The mere fact of having seen them implies degradation. This is a thousandfold stronger when instead of merely seeing the deed the man has participated in it. Whoever in any part of our country has ever taken part in lawlessly putting to death a criminal by the dreadful torture of fire must forever after have the awful spectacle of his own handiwork seared into his brain and soul. He can never again be the same man.

This matter of lynching would be a terrible thing even if it stopped with the lynching of men guilty of the inhuman and hideous crime of rape; but as a matter of fact, lawlessness of this type never does stop and never can stop in such fashion. Every violent man in the community is encouraged by every case of lynching in which the lynchers go unpunished to himself take the law into his own hands whenever it suits his own convenience. In the same way the use of torture by the mob in certain cases is sure to spread until it is applied more or less indiscriminately in other cases. The spirit of lawlessness grows with what it feeds on and when mobs with impunity lynch criminals for one cause, they are certain to begin to lynch real or alleged criminals for other causes. In the recent cases of lynching over three-fourths were not for rape at all, but for murder, attempted murder, and even less heinous offences. Moreover, the history of these recent cases shows the awful fact that when the minds of men are habituated to the use of torture by lawless bodies to avenge crimes of a peculiarly revolting description, other lawless bodies will use torture in order to punish crimes of an ordinary type. Surely no patriot can fail to see the fearful brutalization and debasement which the indulgence of such a spirit and such practices inevitably portends. Surely all public men, all writers for the daily press, all clergymen, all teachers, all who in any way have a right to address the public, should with every energy unite to denounce such crimes and to support those engaged in putting them down. As a people we claim the right to speak with peculiar emphasis for freedom and for fair treatment of all men without regard to differences of race, fortune, creed or color. We forfeit the right so to speak when we commit or condone such crimes as these of which I speak.

The nation, like the individual, cannot commit a crime with impunity. If we are guilty of lawlessness and brutal violence, whether our guilt consists in active participation therein or in mere connivance and encouragement, we shall assuredly suffer later on because of what we have done. The cornerstone of this republic, as of all free government, is respect for and obedience to the law. Where we permit the law to be defied or evaded, whether by rich man or poor man, by black man or white, we are by just so much weakening the bonds of our civilization and increasing the chances of its overthrow and of the substitution of a system in which there shall be violent alternations of anarchy and tyranny. *Sincerely yours*

A WESTERN TRIP

To John Hay

Oyster Bay, August 9, 1903

Dear John:

Now I shall sit down and endeavor to keep my promise to write you something of what happened on the western trip. But I do not believe I can put it down as with Moody's assistance I told it when we were dining at your house. You see there was much of it about which I would not have thought at all if Moody had not been along during most of the time that Seth Bullock, for instance, was with me. It was Moody's intense interest in what he called the "neighborhood gossip" between Seth Bullock and myself that first made me think that there really was an interesting side to this gossip — chiefly because of the side lights it cast on our ways and methods of life in the golden days when the men of the vanishing frontier still lived in the Viking age. I looked up my books the other day to see if I had written down any of these anecdotes, but I could not find them. At the time they seemed to me very much less important than my various feats of adventure and misadventure in the hunting field. So it is really to Moody that I owe having thought of the matter at all.

Of course my whole trip was interesting anyhow. Although politics is at present my business I cannot stand more than a certain amount of uninterrupted association with men who are nothing but politicians, contractors, financiers, etc. Unadulterated Congress, like unadulterated Wall Street, though very good for a change, would drive me quite crazy as a steady thing. And there are only a certain limited number of politicians who have other sides to them. So on this trip I showed sedulous forethought in preparing cases for myself in the shape both of traveling companions and of places to visit. I went to the Yellowstone Park with John Burroughs, and to the Yosemite with John Muir, and to the Canyon of the Colorado with an assorted collection of Rough Riders, most of them with homicidal pasts. I had President Nicholas Murray Butler of Columbia University with me for three weeks, President

Wheeler of the University of California for nearly a fortnight; Root was with me for a day or two and Moody for nearly a month. Stewart White, the author of *The Blazed Trail*, which among recent novels I like next to *The Virginian*, was also with me for a fortnight.

Much of the trip of course was of the conventional kind with which you are so well acquainted; and this part I shall skip through hurriedly. For four days after leaving Washington I was in the thick of civilization. I left on Wednesday. Thursday I spent in Chicago. I went to the University of Chicago and the Northwestern University; made such addresses as I would have made to college men anywhere and spoke that night in the Auditorium on the Monroe Doctrine — a speech calculated to avoid jarring even the sensitive nerves of Carter Harrison, who as Mayor had to greet me, and who was just in the final days of a contest for re-election in which I fondly and vainly hoped he would be beaten. The next day I struck Wisconsin and the day after Minnesota. In both States I was greeted with bellowing enthusiasm. Wherever I stopped at a small city or country town I was greeted by the usual shy, self-conscious, awkward body of local committeemen, and spoke to the usual audience of thoroughly good American citizens — a term I can use in a private letter to you without being thought demagogic! That is the audience consisted partly of the townspeople, but even more largely of rough-coated, hard-headed, gaunt, sinewy farmers and hired hands from all the neighborhood, who had driven in with their wives and daughters and often with their children, from ten or twenty or even thirty miles round about. For all the superficial differences between us, down at bottom these men and I think a good deal alike, or at least have the same ideals, and I am always sure of reaching them in speeches which many of my Harvard friends would think not only homely, but commonplace. There were two bodies which were always gathered to greet me — the veterans and the school children. The veterans felt that I had fought too, and they claimed a certain right of comradeship with me which really touched me deeply; and to them I could invariably appeal with the certainty of meeting an instant response. Whatever their faults and shortcomings, and however much in practice they had failed to come up to their ideal, yet they had this ideal, and they had fought for it in their youth of long ago, in the times when they knew "how good was life the mere living," and yet when they were willing lightly to hazard the loss of life itself for the sake of being true to the purposes, half hidden often from themselves, which spurred them onward to victory. I have trouble enough, heaven knows, with the unreasonable demands which the veterans make on me all the time — and it is quite possible that they will suddenly champion some scoundrel like Miles as their especial hero and representative — but after all it is because of what they did that I am President at all, or that we have a country at all; and whenever I see in an audience a grim-featured old fellow with a hickory shirt and no collar or cravat and only one gallus to keep up his trousers, but with a Grand Army button in his buttonhole, there is a man to whom, if I am only able to strike the right note, I can surely appeal in the name of something loftier and better than his mere material well-being or advantage. As for the school children, I found to my utter astonishment that my letter to those Van Vorst women about their excellent book had gone everywhere, and the population of each place invariably took the greatest pride in showing off the children. Children always interest me — I am very fond of my own! — I have always cherished the way in which yours, when little, treated me with hail-fellow comradeship, when I spent the night with you at Cleveland, and it touches me to see a hard-working father, evidently in his holiday best, carrying one child, also in its holiday best, with three or four others tagging after him to "see the President," while for the woman, who in most cases cannot go out at all unless she takes her entire brood with her I have the liveliest sympathy and respect. I hope you won't think it absurd, but it was a real satisfaction to me to feel that the hard-worked mother of a large family felt a glow of pride and comfort when she showed that family to the President and felt that he deemed her worthy of respect and thanks as having done her part well by the Republic. If only we can make the man or the woman who, in the home or out of the home, does well his or her hard duty, feel that at least there is a recognition of respect because of that duty being well performed, we shall be by just so much ahead as a nation.

In Milwaukee, in St. Paul and in Minneapolis the crowds were something extraordinary. In Milwaukee there was a distant touch of novelty in the reception at the Deutscher Club, whose inmates received me at first with somewhat formal courtesy, having a lively memory of the fact that I was steadily engaged in the business of teaching the Kaiser to "shinny on his own side of the line"; but as I was heartily glad to see them they soon began to believe, possibly mistakenly, that they were also glad to see me, and we enjoyed our meeting to the full, and ended singing "Hoch soll er leben" with much enthusiasm.

On Sunday I struck Sioux Falls and began to get into the real West, the Far West, the country where I had worked and played for many years, and with whose people I felt a bond of sympathy which could not be broken by very manifest shortcomings on either part. Senator Kittredge was on hand to receive me. Not being himself a church-going man he had naturally fallen helpless when faced with the church problem, and I found he had committed me to a morning and an evening service. But I enjoyed both, contrary to my expectations. The morning service was in a little German Lutheran church of very humble folk, where the women, in primitive fashion, sat on one side of the aisle and the men on the other. They had imported a first-class preacher, the head of a Lutheran seminary in Iowa, and so clearly did he speak, though in German, that I was able to follow without effort his admirable sermon. It was on the Faith, Hope and Charity text, and I am rather ashamed to say that it was owing to this German Lutheran sermon that I for the first time realized the real meaning — "love" — of the word that we in the authorized version have translated "charity." The Dutch Reformed service in the evening was more canonical but it interested me much because so many good homely people were there, many of them with their babies, and all feeling such a kindly interest in having the President at their church. Between services, by the way, I took an afternoon ride of twenty miles with Seth Bullock and Dr. Rixey, Seth having turned up to see me safe through to the Yellowstone Park. From this time on I was able to get good long rides each Sunday, and I am sure that they did much toward keeping me in good trim throughout the trip.

Next day I went north through South Dakota, stopping at place after place, sometimes speaking from the end of the train, sometimes going in solemn procession with the local notables to a stand specially erected for the occasion, the procession being headed by the town brass band, which usually played "Hail to the Chief" as a brilliant novelty when I stepped off the train. The following day I went west along the Northern Pacific through North Dakota. In the forenoon it was just as it had been in South Dakota, except that at Bismarck they had a barbecue which I had to attend; where, by the way, the ox, which had been roasted whole, tasted deliciously. At each stop there were the usual audiences of grizzled, bearded, elderly men; of smooth-faced, shy, hulking young men; of older women either faded and dragged or exceedingly brisk and capable; and of robust, healthy, high-spirited young girls. Most of these people habitually led rather gray lives, and they came in to see the President much as they would have come in to see a circus. It was something to talk over and remember and tell their children about. But I think that besides the mere curiosity there was a good feeling behind it all, a feeling that the President was their man and symbolized their government, and that they had a proprietary interest in him and wished to see him, and that they hoped he embodied their aspirations and their best thought.

As soon as I got west of the Missouri I came into my own former stamping ground. At every station there was somebody who remembered my riding in there when the Little Missouri roundup went down to the Indian reservation and then worked north across the Cannon Ball and up Knife and Green Rivers; or who had been an interested and possibly malevolent spectator when I had ridden east with other representatives of the cow men to hold a solemn council with the leading grangers on the vexed subject of mavericks; or who had been hired as a train hand when I had been taking a load of cattle to Chicago, and who remembered well how he and I at the stoppages had run frantically down the line of the cars and with our poles jabbed the unfortunate cattle who had lain down until they again stood up and thereby gave themselves a chance for their lives; and who remembered how when the train started we had to clamber hurriedly aboard and make our

way back to the caboose along the tops of the cattle cars. At
Mandan two of my old cow hands, Sylvane and Joe Ferris,
joined me. At Dickinson all of the older people had known
me and the whole town turned out with wild and not entirely
sober enthusiasm. It was difficult to make them much of a
speech as there were dozens of men each earnestly desirous of
recalling to my mind some special incident. One man, how he
helped me bring in my cattle to ship, and how a blue roan
steer broke away leading a bunch which it took him and me
three hours to round up and bring back; another, how seventeen years before I had come in a freight train from Medora
to deliver the Fourth of July oration; another, a gray-eyed
individual named Paddock, who during my early years at
Medora had shot and killed an equally objectionable individual named Livingstone, reminded me how just twenty years
before, when I was on my first buffalo hunt, he loaned me the
hammer off his Sharp's rifle to replace the broken hammer of
mine; another, recalled the time when he and I worked on the
roundup as partners, going with the Little Missouri outfit
from the head of the Box Alder to the mouth of the Big
Beaver, and then striking over to represent the Little Missouri
brands on the Yellowstone roundup; yet another recalled the
time when I as deputy sheriff of Billings County had brought
in three cattle thieves named Red Finnigan, Dutch Chris, and
the Half Breed to his keeping, he being then sheriff in Dickinson, etc., etc., etc. At Medora, which we reached after dark,
the entire population of the Bad Lands down to the smallest
baby had gathered to meet me. This was formerly my home
station. The older men and women I knew well; the younger
ones had been wild towheaded children when I lived and
worked along the Little Missouri. I had spent nights in their
ranches. I still remembered meals which the women had given
me when I had come from some hard expedition, half famished and sharpset as a wolf. I had killed buffalo and elk, deer
and antelope with some of the men. With others I had worked
on the trail, on the calf roundup, on the beef roundup. We
had been together on occasions which we still remembered
when some bold rider met his death in trying to stop a stam-
pede, in riding a mean horse, or in the quicksands of some
swollen river which he sought to swim. They all felt I was their

man, their old friend; and even if they had been hostile to me in the old days when we were divided by the sinister bickering and jealousies and hatreds of all frontier communities, they now firmly believed they had always been my staunch friends and admirers. They had all gathered in the town hall, which was draped for a dance — young children, babies, everybody being present. I shook hands with them all and almost each one had some memory of special association with me which he or she wished to discuss. I only regretted that I could not spend three hours with them. When I left them they were starting to finish the celebration by a dance.

Next day I reached the Yellowstone and went into it for a fortnight with John Burroughs.

When I got out I struck down by the Burlington across northwestern Wyoming, which I had known so well in the old days. Except for the railroad it seemed very little changed. The plains rivers, winding in thin streams through their broad sandy beds fringed with cottonwoods, the barren hills, and great sage brush plains, all looked just as they did when I had crossed them looking for lost horses, or hunting game, or driving the branded herds to market or to new pastures. Each little town, however, was in gala attire, the ranchmen having driven or ridden in clad in their rough coats, often of wolf skin; the chief citizens of the town always stiff and stern in their very best clothing; the little boys marshaled by their teachers without having any very clear idea why; and the little girls, each in her Sunday best, and most of them with some gift of wild flowers for me. Seth Bullock, with Alec Mackenzie, another former sheriff whom I had known in the old days, was along, and at Edgemont, where a contingent of Black Hills miners joined us, we had the orthodox cowboy sports.

When I reached the Yellowstone Park Major Pitcher said to me, "By the way, Mr. President, an old friend of yours named Bill Jones has been very anxious to see you, but I am sorry to say he has got so drunk that we had to take him out into the sage brush. I will try to have him meet you before we leave the Park." Sure enough when I was leaving the Park Bill Jones turned up. He had been sheriff of Billings County when I was on the ranch and I had been deputy under him. Our positions relatively to one another had criss-crossed in public and private life. As a private citizen I was the owner of the ranch and he was one of my hired hands, but in public position he was the sheriff and I his deputy. His real name was not Bill Jones, and there were in the county at that time two other Bill Joneses — the name in each case being assumed because the owner did not think it advisable to go under his rightful title. To distinguish the Sheriff from the other two Bill Joneses, one of whom was known as Texas Bill and the other as Three-Seven Bill, he (the sheriff) was always called Hell-Roaring Bill Jones. He was a very good official when sober, and a trustworthy, hard-working man while in my employ; but on his occasional sprees he got very drunk indeed and then he swore a great deal and shot occasionally. The first time I ever saw Seth Bullock I had gone south with a wagon from Medora to the Belle Fourche. Bill Jones was driving the wagon. Sylvane Ferris and I were riding. We looked pretty rough when we struck the Belle Fourche — as Bill Jones expressed it, we looked exactly like an outfit of tinhorn gamblers; and when somebody asked Seth Bullock to meet us he at first expressed disinclination. Then he was told that I was the Civil Service Commissioner, upon which he remarked genially, "Well, anything civil goes with me," and strolled over to be introduced.

On this trip down the casual conversation between Sylvane and Bill cast some sidelights on Bill's past career. Happening to learn that he had been a constable in Bismarck but had resigned, I asked him why, whereupon he answered, "Well, I beat the mayor over the head with my gun one day. The mayor he didn't mind it, but the superintendent of police he said he guessed I'd better resign" — his evident feeling being that the superintendent of police had shown himself a mere martinet.

There was also a good deal of talk about a lunatic, and some cross-questioning brought out a story which cast light on the frontier theory of care for the insane. Sylvane began — "Well, the way of it was this. That lunatic he was on the train and he up and he shot the newsboy, and at first they wasn't going to do anything to him because they just thought he had it in for the newsboy. But someone said 'Why, he's plumb crazy and is liable to shoot one of us' — and then they threw him off the train." It was at Medora where this incident occurred, and it appeared that on demand being made for some official to take charge of the murderer Sheriff Jones came forward. Here he took up the tale himself: "The more fool I! Why, that lunatic didn't have his right senses. At first he wouldn't eat, till me and Snyder got him down in the shavings and *made* him eat!" (Snyder was a huge, happy-go-lucky cowpuncher, at that time Bill Jones' deputy.) Jones continued: "You know Snyder, don't you? Well, he's plumb stuck on his running and he's soft-hearted, too. He'd think that lunatic looked peaked and he'd take him out on the prairie for an airing and the boys they'd josh him as to how much start he could give the lunatic and then catch him again." According to the size of the "josh" Snyder would give the lunatic a greater or less start and then run him down. I asked what would have happened if Snyder had failed to catch him. This was evidently a new idea to Bill who responded, "Well, he always did catch him." "But supposing he hadn't caught him," I insisted. "Well," said Bill Jones thoughtfully, "if Snyder hadn't ketched the lunatic I'd have whaled hell out of Snyder." Under the circumstances Snyder naturally ran his best and always got his game.

The temple of justice in Medora was a low building with two rooms in one of which Bill Jones slept and in the other the lunatic. Bill continued: "You know Bixby? Well, Bixby thinks he's funny (with deep disfavor). He used to come and wake that lunatic up when I had gone to bed and then I'd have to get up and soothe him. But I fixed Bixby! I rigged a rope to the door and the next time Bixby came there to wake the lunatic I let the lunatic out on him and he most bit his nose off. I learned Bixby!" With which specimen of rather full-bodied humor the story closed.

My next three days after leaving Wyoming were very hard and rather monotonous. I went through Nebraska, Iowa and northeastern Missouri. I spoke at dozens of prosperous towns, in each case to many thousands of most friendly and often enthusiastic citizens. I genuinely liked and respected them all. I admired the thrift and indeed the beauty both of the country and the towns — and I could not to save my neck differentiate one town from another or one crowd from another. Moreover, much though I liked them and glad though I was to see them, it was inevitable that I should begin repeating myself unless I wished to become merely fatuous; and I was glad on the evening of the 29th to get to St. Louis. The next day, April 30th, I solemnly opened the World's Fair. The city was filled with enormous crowds. Everybody was enthusiastic and friendly; and the arrangements at the Fair itself represented confusion worse confounded. The drive through the multitudes; the review of the procession; the scrambling, pushing, shoving lunch in a densely packed tent; the shouting address in the great hall to forty thousand people, at least twenty thousand of whom could not hear one word I said — all this was of a kind with which you are thoroughly familiar. The next two days in Kansas City, Missouri, and then westward through Kansas, were but repetitions of those in Nebraska and Iowa.

Sunday, May 2d, we spent in a little ranch town in the extreme western part of the Kansas plains. Like Medora it was a regular town of the cow country; but it rejoiced in a church, although not in a preacher. The lack was supplied by draining the country for a hundred miles east and producing a Presbyterian, a Methodist and a dear old German Lutheran. I think every ranch within a radius of forty or fifty miles sent its occupants to church that day, and the church was jammed. My own pew was the only one that did not bulge with occupants. There were two very nice little girls standing in the aisle beside me. I invited them in and we all three sang out of the same hymn book. They were in their Sunday best and their brown sunburned little arms and faces had been scrubbed till they almost shone. It was a very kindly, homely country congregation, all the people of a type I knew well and all of them looking well-to-do and prosperous in a way hardly warranted as it seemed to me by the eaten-off, wire-fence-enclosed, shortgrass ranges of the dry plains roundabout. When church was over I shook hands with the three preachers and all the congregation, whose buggies, ranch wagons, and dispirited-looking saddle ponies were tied to everything available in the village. I got a ride myself in the afternoon and on returning found that all the population that had not left was gathered solemnly around the train. Among the rest there was a little girl who asked me if I would like a baby badger which she said her brother Josiah had just caught. I said I would, and an hour or two later the badger turned up from the little girl's father's ranch some three miles out of town. The little girl had several other little girls with her, all in clean starched Sunday clothes and ribbon-tied pigtails. One of them was the sheriff's daughter, and I saw her nudging the sheriff, trying to get him to make some request, which he refused. So I asked what it was and found that the seven little girls were exceedingly anxious to see the inside of my car, and accordingly I took them all in. The interior arrangements struck them as being literally palatial — magnificent. The whole population of the plains now looks upon the Pullman sleepers and dining cars just as Mark Twain describes the people along the banks of the Mississippi as formerly looking at the Mississippi steamers, and for the same reasons. I liked the little girls so much that I regretted having nothing to give them but flowers; and they reciprocated my liking with warm western enthusiasm, for they hung about the car until it grew dark, either waving their hands to me or kissing their hands to me whenever I appeared at the window. The badger was christened Josiah, and became from that time an inmate of the train until my return home, when he received a somewhat stormy welcome from the children, and is now one of the household. The numerous gifts I received on the trip, by the way, included not only the badger but two bears, a lizard, a horned toad and a horse.

Next day we entered Colorado, and at the first stopping place (where the Governor joined me together with his Adjutant General, Sherman Bell, who had been one of the best men in my regiment) the riders of a roundup had come in to greet me, bringing the chuck wagon. They had kindled a fire and cooked breakfast in expectation of my arrival. It seemed absurd to get off and eat at the tail end of a chuck wagon in a top hat and a frock coat, but they were so heartbroken by my refusal that I finally did. The rest of the day was of the ordinary type. Denver, Colorado Springs and Pueblo showed the usual features — enormous crowds, processions, masses of school children, local Grand Army posts; sweating, bustling, self-conscious local committees; universal kindliness and friendliness; little girls dressed up as Goddesses of Liberty; misguided enthusiasts who nearly drove the horses mad by dumping huge baskets of flowers over them and us as we drove by favorable windows; other misguided enthusiasts who endeavored to head stampedes to shake my hand and felt deeply injured when repulsed by the secret service men and local policemen, etc., etc., etc. But in the evening when I reached Trinidad I struck into the wild country once more. Do you remember that letter from Captain Llewellyn, which ran as follows?

My dear Colonel:

I have the honor to report that comrade Ritchie late of Troop G is in jail at Trinidad, Colo. on a charge of murder. It seems that our comrade was out at a small town some twelve miles from Trinidad, Aguillar, when he became involved in a controversy and said controversy terminated in his killing his man. I have just received a long letter from our comrade giving his version of the little affair, and it appears from said version that the fellow he killed called him very bad names, even going as far as to cast reflections on the legitimacy of our comrade's birth. He killed the fellow instantly, shooting him in the heart.

Ritchie was one of the boys in Troop G and was a splendid soldier and I am going to see that he has a first-class defense.

Also have to report that comrade Webb late of Troop D has just killed two men at Bisbee, Ariz. Have not yet received the detail of our comrade's trouble in this instance, but understand that he was employed as a ranger in Arizona and that the killing occurred in a saloon and that he was entirely justified in the transaction.

This is about all the news regarding the comrades in this neck of the woods. Was out at the Penitentiary yesterday, and had a very pleasant visit with comrade Frank Brito whom you will remember was sent to the Penitentiary from Silver City for killing his sister-in-law and he is very anxious to get out. The sentiment in Grant County is very strongly in his favor. You will doubtless recall the fact that he was shooting at his wife at the time he killed his sister-in-law. Since he has been in the Penitentiary his wife has ran off with Comrade Coyne of Troop H, going to Mexico. This incident has tended to turn popular sentiment strongly in Brito's favor.

Well, two days later I was joined by the hero of the Arizona killing, who it appears had been doing his duty, and on this evening at Trinidad Ritchie joined me. He explained to me how he had happened to kill his man. It appears that Ritchie, who is a justice of the peace, had, as he expressed it, "sat into a poker game" with several friends and a stranger. The stranger had bad luck and grew very abusive. Ritchie appears to tend bar as well as to be a justice of the peace, and when the stranger became too abusive he got up and walked behind the bar to get his gun. His friends appreciated the situation and either got outside the room or lay down. But the stranger leaped after him, endeavoring to wrench his pistol from his hip pocket, with much foul language, and Ritchie shot him. "Had he drawn his gun, Ritchie?" said I. "He didn't have time, Colonel," answered Ritchie simply. Ritchie was acquitted.

Next day we spent in New Mexico, stopping at Santa Fe and Albuquerque. Of course scores of my former regiment joined me, headed by Captain Llewellyn. The excellent captain is a large, jovial, frontier Micawber kind of personage, with a varied past which includes considerable man-killing. He had four bullets in him when he joined my regiment, and after the war when we had to have him operated on in the hospital for something or other, the surgeons who conducted the operation incidentally ran across two of these bullets. He was up in the Black Hills at one time, where Seth Bullock knew him, and Seth did not wholly approve of him. Seth has killed a good many men himself, but is at bottom a very tender-hearted man; whereas Llewellyn, for all his geniality, and although in a tight place where desperate fighting was needed I would not trust him as I would Seth Bullock, or Pat Garrett, or Ben Daniels, nevertheless has a ruthless streak which the others lack. Seth had explained to me, apropos of one man whom Llewellyn had killed in the Black Hills, that he had had great difficulty in getting the jury to acquit Llewellyn, and added, "Under the circumstances, Colonel, I wouldn't have killed that man, and you wouldn't either, Colonel" — which I thought was very likely true. I was much amused to see Llewellyn's face change when he heard I had been with Seth Bullock; and he asked with nervous eagerness what Seth had said of him — a curiosity I did not gratify.

As for the rest of my men, most of them were busy, hard-working fellows. Three or four were engineers or brakemen, others were at work on ranches or in the mines, or in the little frontier towns. For the most part they were entirely orderly and had lived decent lives; but death by violence had entered into their scheme of existence in a matter-of-course way which would doubtless seem alien to the minds of Boston anti-imperialists. The conversation would continually come back to this man or the other man who had "up and killed a man down in El Paso," or who had "skipped the country because the sheriff wanted him for stealing horses," or who "got killed when he went up against a faro game at Phoenix."

Santa Fe interested me particularly. One of my men, of pure Mexican origin, Sergeant Amigo, had been blessed by the arrival of a baby shortly before I came to Santa Fe, and nothing would do but that I must stand sponsor for it. He was a Catholic, but the Bishop made no objections, and accordingly, lighted taper in hand, I stood solemnly behind the father and mother while the baby was christened in the old adobe mission cathedral. His ancestors and mine had doubtless fought in The Netherlands in the days of Alva and Parma, just about the time this mission was built and before a Dutch or English colonist had set foot on American soil.

That evening the train went through the waterless desert country of New Mexico, a desolate land but always attractive with its strange coloring and outline. Next day we spent at the Canyon of the Colorado, to me the most impressive piece of scenery I have ever looked at. I don't exactly know what words to use in describing it. It is beautiful and terrible and unearthly. It made me feel as if I were gazing at a sunset of strange and awful splendor. When I was not looking at the canyon I was riding some forty miles with assorted members of my regiment, from the Governor of Arizona down — including Ben Daniels, he whose ear was bitten off when he was marshal of Dodge City, and whose appointment as marshal of Arizona, a proper recognition for his excellent fighting record in my regiment, had been revoked because it turned out he had been three years in the penitentiary for robbery under arms.

The Pacific Coast trip I shall not try to describe. After we got out of the Mojave Desert, with its burning plains and waterless mountains, its cactus and fantastic yucca trees, we crossed the Cascades and came at once into that wonderful paradise of southern California — a veritable hotbed of fruits and flowers. The people were wildly enthusiastic of course, and I have literally never seen anything like the flowers. Wherever I went the roads were strewn with them, and generally a large proportion of the men, women and children were festooned with them. It is an interesting country and I think will produce a new type. I felt as if I was seeing Provence in the making — that is, Provence being changed by, and in its turn changing, a northern race. The missions interested me greatly, and of course the people most of all.

I was very greatly impressed by the two universities also. The University of California is the greatest, but Leland Stanford was singularly beautiful in architecture and surroundings and climate — in every way. What an influence these two great universities will have on the Pacific Slope of our own country, and perhaps on all the countries around the Pacific!

In San Francisco I was received with bellowing hospitality and passed three wild days. There was not much to distinguish it from a visit to any other of our big cities except the way in which here, and from this time on, I was given gifts — a gold goblet by the Board of Trade of San Francisco; a gold ash receiver from the Arctic Brotherhood at Seattle (a collection of exceedingly well-dressed men and women who had come down from the Klondike), a gold vase, silver and copper vases, and drinking cups, etc., etc.

After visiting the Yosemite I went northward to Oregon and Washington. Their coast regions, including a territory about as large as England, have the English climate. And here again I think the people in the end will be different — will in the end represent a new type on this continent. Puget Sound impressed me greatly. I suppose our children will see some city thereon, probably Seattle, containing a million inhabitants.

From Washington I turned eastward and when I struck northern Montana again came to my old stamping grounds and among my old friends. I met all kinds of queer characters with whom I had hunted and worked and slept and sometimes fought. From Helena I went southward to Butte, reaching that city in the afternoon of May 27th. By this time Seth Bullock had joined us, together with an old hunting friend, John Willis, — A Donatello of the Rocky Mountains — wholly lacking, however, the morbid self-consciousness which made Hawthorne's faun go out of his head because he had killed a man. Willis and I had been in Butte some seventeen years before at the end of a hunting trip in which we got dead broke, so that when we struck Butte we slept in an outhouse and breakfasted heartily in a two-bit Chinese restaurant. Since then I had gone through Butte in the campaign of 1900, the major part of the inhabitants receiving me with frank hostility and enthusiastic cheers for Bryan. However, Butte is mercurial and its feelings had changed. The wicked, wealthy, hospitable, full-blooded little city welcomed me with wild enthusiasm of the most disorderly kind.

The mayor, Pat Mullins, was a huge good-humored creature, wearing for the first time in his life a top hat and a frock coat, the better to do honor to the President. National party lines count very little in Butte, where the fight was Heinze and anti-Heinze, ex-Senator Carter and Senator Clark being in the opposition. Neither side was willing to let the other have anything to do with the celebration, and they drove me wild with their appeals until I settled that the afternoon parade and speech was to be managed by the Heinze people and the evening speech by the anti-Heinze people; and that the dinner should contain fifty of each faction and be presided over in his official capacity by the mayor. The ordinary procession in barouches was rather more exhilarating than usual and reduced the faithful secret service men very nearly to the condition of Bedlamites. The crowd was filled with whooping enthusiasm and every kind of whiskey, and in their desire to be sociable broke the lines and jammed right up to the carriage. There were a lot of the so-called "rednecks" or dynamiters, the men who had taken part in the murderous Coeur d'Alene strike, who had been indulging in threats as to what they would do to me, and of course the city is a hotbed of violent anarchy. Seth Bullock accordingly had gone down three days in advance and had organized for my personal protection a bodyguard composed of old friends of his on whom he could rely, for the most part tough citizens and all of them very quick with a gun. By occupation they were, as he casually mentioned, for the major part gamblers and "sure thing" men. But they had no sympathy whatever with anarchy in any form. They thoroughly believed in men of wealth, for they wished to prey on them. These men kept a close watch over all who approached me, and I was far less nervous about being

shot myself than about their shooting some exuberant enthusiast with peaceful intentions. Seth Bullock rode close beside
the rear wheel of the carriage, a splendid-looking fellow with
his size and supple strength, his strongly marked aquiline face
with its big mustache, and the broad brim of his soft hat drawn
down over his hawk eyes. However, nobody made a motion
to attack me. At one point the carriage was brought to a stop
while a dozen large burly men fought their way through the
crowd till they got to it. I stood up while a bull-throated man
with a red face and a foghorn voice bellowed an address of
welcome on behalf of the citizens of Anaconda, and presented
me from them a really handsome copper and silver vase. When
we reached one hotel I made an address to the entire population of Butte, which was gathered in the cross streets below;
and then the mayor presented me with a large silver loving
cup in behalf of the Butte people. Immediately afterwards I
was genuinely touched by a representative of the colored citizens of Butte giving me as a present from them a miniature
set of scales with a design of Justice holding them even.

My address was felt to be honor enough for one hotel, and
the dinner was given in the other. When the dinner was announced the mayor led me in — or to speak more accurately,
tucked me under one arm and lifted me partially off the
ground, so that I felt as if I looked like one of those limp dolls
with dangling legs carried around by small children, like Mary
Jane in "The Golliwoggs," for instance. As soon as we got in
the banquet hall and sat at the head of the table the mayor
hammered lustily with the handle of his knife and announced,
"Waiter, bring on the feed!" Then in a spirit of pure kindliness he added, "Waiter, pull up the curtains and let the people
see the President eat!" — but to this I objected. The dinner
was soon in full swing and it was interesting in many regards.
Besides my own party, including Seth Bullock and Willis,
there were fifty men from each of the Butte factions. In Butte
every prominent man is a millionaire, a professional gambler,
or a labor leader; and generally he has been all three. Of the
hundred men who were my hosts I suppose at least half had
killed their man in private war, or had striven to compass the
assassination of an enemy. They had fought one another with
reckless ferocity. They had been allies and enemies in every

kind of business scheme, and companions in brutal revelry. As they drank great goblets of wine the sweat glistened on their hard, strong, crafty faces. They looked as if they had come out of the pictures in Aubrey Beardslee's *Yellow Book*. The millionaires had been laboring men once; the labor leaders intended to be millionaires in their turn or else to pull down all who were. They had made money in mines; they had spent it on the races, in other mines, or in gambling and every form of vicious luxury. But they were strong men for all that. They had worked and striven and pushed and trampled, and had always been ready, and were ready now, to fight to the death in many different kinds of conflict. They had built up their part of the West. They were men with whom one had to reckon if thrown in contact with them. There was Senator Clark with his Iscariot face; goat-bearded Carter with his cold gray eyes; Heinze, heavy-jowled, his cheeks flushed, his eyes glittering — he regarded the dinner as a triumph for him because the mayor was his man, and in pure joy he had lost twenty thousand dollars in reckless betting on horse races that afternoon. In Butte proper at the moment he was the wealthiest and most powerful man. There were plenty of those at the table who would stop at no measure to injure him in fortune, in limb or in life; and as he looked at them he would lean over and tell me the evil things he intended in turn to do to them. But though most of them hated each other, they were accustomed to taking their pleasure when they could get it, and they took it fast and hard with the meats and wines.

Old Con Kohrs, a fine old boy and old friend of mine, a member of the Legislature, and an absolutely honest man, was there. He repeated stories of hunting and Indian fighting and prospecting in the early days, and then told the company how he and I some twenty years previously had worked on the cattle ranges together, and been fellow delegates at the stockmen's meetings in the roaring little cattle town of Miles City. This started Willis upon our feats when we had hunted bear and elk and caribou together in the great mountain forests; and many a man spoke up to recall some incident when he and I had met in the past on a roundup, or in the rush to a new mining town, or out hunting. To my horror I found that Seth Bullock had drunk too much. I wanted him to go back to the train and go to bed. This he felt was ignominious. But he took off his gun, a long forty-four, and solemnly handed it to Loeb as a compromise.

Before the dinner could get too far under way I left to attend my meeting held under the auspices of the labor unions. At ten o'clock when the train pulled out, I stood on the rear platform while numerous friends howled and fired their guns in the air. From the shouting and the popping of guns Butte evidently intended to continue the celebration through the night.

Next day we went through Idaho, and at Boise City as at Walla Walla and Spokane and so many other of these far western towns, I was struck by the growing beauty of the town, by the trees, the well-built public library, the good taste and refinement evident in the dress, the bearing, and the homes of so many of the men and women.

Utah was much like the other States, although the lunch at Senator Tom Kearns' had its points of merit. He had a Catholic bishop and an Episcopal bishop and a Mormon apostle all at the lunch, together with various men and women of prominence. Among the latter was one of the plural wives of the Mormon elder. Most of the women were just such as one would meet at Washington, and some of them just such as one would meet at Boston. We discussed *The Virginian*, and the Passion Play, and Wagner, and the flora of the Rocky Mountains, and John Burroughs' writings, and Senator Ankeny's fondness for Bacon's *Essays*; and there at the table were the two bishops and the apostle, the plural wife, one Gentile who had done battle with the Danites in the long past; and in short every combination of beliefs and systems of thought and civilizations that were ages apart. In many of the leading men in Utah I was particularly struck by a queer combination of the fanaticism of the ages of faith, with in nonreligious matters the shrewdest and most materialistic common sense.

All this while Moody was delighting in the conversations of Seth Bullock, especially when Seth happened to be touching upon incidents in the past in which he and I had both taken part. These would usually come from his dwelling upon some story which would in some way lead up to a mutual friend and that mutual friend's career. Often, however, it would merely

be Seth's way of looking at things. Thus he explained the reluctance he had felt as to certain features of his professional
duty, remarking, "You see, when I was sheriff first there was
a good deal of shooting, and right at the outset I had to kill
two men. Moody, I felt like getting out of politics!"

When we got into Wyoming we now and then came across
individuals whom he had arrested but who had now reformed,
or men for or against whom he had fought. Among them were
occasional people I had had some connection with. Thus he
suddenly asked me if I knew what had become of Lippy Slim,
a half-breed horse thief whom I had caught at one time and
handed over to Granville Stewart who was then acting on
behalf of the Montana cattle men (he was afterwards Cleveland's minister to the Argentine). I said "No," whereupon
he responded, "Well, Stewart he hung him." I had also arrested a rather well-meaning but worthless young fellow
named Calamity Joe who had become involved in horse stealing. I took him down to Mandan, and the night before the
trial he and I and the judge all slept in one room with two
beds; and as the judge felt it undignified to sleep with a horse
thief he slept with me instead. It proved afterwards that
Calamity was a nephew of Senator Dietrich.

Seth was telling of an Indian fight in which one of his companions was named — Bill Hamilton. I asked if this was the
father of the Bill Hamilton who under the name of Three-
Seven Bill Jones, had been foreman of a cow outfit in the Little
Missouri country. It proved that the latter was his son. I knew
the son well. He had on one occasion stopped a mail train by
shooting at the conductor's feet to make him dance. Two or
three days after, I had been over at Mingersville, and in the
wretched little hotel had been put in a room with two beds
and three other men, one of them Bill Jones. He and I had
slept in the same bed. In the middle of the night there was a
crash, the door was burst in, a lantern was flashed in my face,
and as I waked up I found a gun had been thrust in my face
too. But I was dropped at once, a man saying "He ain't the
man. Here — here he is. Now Bill, come along quietly." Bill
responded, "All right, don't sweat yourselves. I'm coming quietly"; and they walked out of the room. We lit a light. I tried
to find out from my companions the reason of what had hap-

pened, but they possessed the alkali etiquette in such matters, the chief features of which are silence, wooden impassiveness, and uncommunicativeness. So we blew out the light and went to sleep again.

In this same hotel, by the way, I had more than one odd experience. It was the place where I was shot at by the fellow who had been on a spree and had shot up the face of the clock. By watching my chance I was able to knock him down, his head hitting the corner of the bar as he went down, so that he was knocked senseless. Upon another occasion I had a small room with one bed to myself upstairs, and had sat up to read, for I usually carried a book in my saddle pocket. Everyone had gone to sleep; when a cowboy arrived very drunk, yelling and shooting as he galloped through the darkness. When the host finally opened the door in response to repeated thumps the sounds below told that he at first had cause to regret having done so. Evidently the puncher seized him, half in play and half in enmity, jammed his gun against him, and then started to waltz around the room with him. The agonized appeals of the host came upward. "Jim, don't! Don't, Jim! It'll go off! Jim, It'll go off!" Jim's response was not reassuring. "Yes, damn you, it'll go off. I'll learn you! Who in hell cares if it does go off? Oh, I'll learn you!" Finally the host reduced his guest to a condition of comparative quiet, which was announced by loud demands for a bed, which was promised immediately. Then I heard steps in the hall, a knock at the door, and when I opened it there stood the host announcing that he was sorry but that he had to put a man in with me for the night. I explained that he was not as sorry as I was — and that the man could not come in. He reiterated his regret and said that the man was drunk and on the shoot and *had* to come in. This description did not add to the attractiveness of the proposal and I explained that I should lock my door again, put out my light, and shoot any man who tried to break in. Where the puncher slept that night I do not know, but I was left free.

From Laramie to Cheyenne we took a sixty-five mile ride, going around by Van Tassel's ranch. We had five relays of horses and most of the time we went like the wind. Before getting on my first horse I had to make half an hour's talk at Laramie. When we got within three miles of Cheyenne I stopped to review the troops of the post, and in Cheyenne I got off my horse to ascend a stand and make a three-quarters of an hour speech under the auspices of the veterans, as it was Decoration Day. I had very good horses and thoroughly enjoyed the ride. The marshal was with me, an excellent fellow; also a deputy marshal whose name I wish I could remember. He was a gentle, kindly little fellow, a Texan who looked much like Alf in one of Stewart White's stories; very soft-spoken, and had killed a large number of men. He knew all about me, as one of his brothers had been in my regiment and another brother was foreman of the Hash-knife outfit and had worked on the Box Alder roundup with me in the spring of '85.

The following Monday we saw some first-class steer roping and riding of mean horses out at the Cheyenne fair grounds. After that the way home through Nebraska, Iowa, Illinois, and Indiana, though important and irksome, offered nothing of special interest in the telling. We stopped at many towns and little cities; were greeted by enormous crowds of thoroughly good people; were escorted by Senators and Congressmen, by Uncle Joe Cannon and Secretary Wilson; visited Lincoln's tomb at Springfield, dedicated a monument to Lincoln at Freeport, and a hall to the old soldiers somewhere else; and on Friday, the 6th, I reached Washington on the minute, having made the two months and over trip without a hitch — which I think speaks well for the railroads. *Faithfully yours*

AVOIDING OVERATHLETICISM

To Theodore Roosevelt Jr.

Washington, October 4, 1903

Dear Ted

In spite of the "Hurry! Hurry!" on the outside of your envelope, I did not like to act until I had consulted Mother and thought the matter over; and to be frank with you, old fellow, I am by no means sure that I am doing right now. If it were not that I feel you would be so bitterly disappointed, I would strongly advocate your acquiescing in the decision to leave you off the second squad this year. I am proud of your pluck, and I greatly admire football — though it was not a game I was ever able to play myself, my qualities resembling Kermit's rather than yours. But the very things that make it a good game make it a rough game, and there is always the chance of your being laid up. Now, I should not in the least object to your being laid up for a season if you were striving for something worth while, to get on the Groton school team, for instance, or on your class team when you entered Harvard — for of course I don't think you will have the weight to entitle you to try for the varsity. But I am by no means sure that it *is* worth your while to run the risk of being laid up for the sake of playing in the second squad when you are a fourth former, instead of when you are a fifth former. I do not know that the risk is balanced by the reward. However, I have told the Rector that as you feel so strongly about it, I think that the chance of your damaging yourself in body is outweighed by the possibility of bitterness of spirit if you could not play; and therefore that you are to play. Understand me; I should think mighty little of you if you permitted chagrin to make you bitter on some point where it was evidently right for you to suffer the chagrin. But in this case I am uncertain, and I shall give you the benefit of the doubt. If, however, the coaches at any time come to the conclusion that you ought not to be in the second squad, why you must come off without grumbling.

As I said, I am delighted to have you play football. I believe in rough, manly sports. But I do not believe in them if they degenerate into the sole end of anyone's existence. I don't want you to sacrifice standing well in your studies to any overathleticism; and above all, I need hardly tell you that character counts for a great deal more than either intellect or body in winning success in life. Athletic proficiency is a mighty good servant, and like so many other good servants, a mighty bad master. Did you ever read Pliny's letter to Trajan in which he speaks of its being advisable to keep the Greeks absorbed in athletics because it distracted their minds from all serious pursuits, including soldiering, and prevented their ever being dangerous to the Romans? I have not a doubt that the British officers in the Boer War had their efficiency gravely reduced because they had sacrificed their legitimate duties to an inordinate and ridiculous love of sports. A man must develop his physical prowess up to a certain point; but after he has reached that point there are other things that count more. In my regiment nine-tenths of the men were better horsemen than I was, and probably two-thirds of them better shots than I was, while on the average they were certainly hardier and more enduring. Yet after I had had them a very short while they all knew, and I knew too, that nobody else could command them as I could. I am glad you should play football; I am glad that you should box; I am glad that you should ride and shoot and walk and row as well as you do. I should be very sorry if you did not do these things and if you lacked the spirit you show in them. But don't ever get into the frame of mind which regards these things as constituting the end to which *all* your energies must be devoted, or even the major portion of your energies.

Yes, I am to speak at Groton on prize day. I felt that while I was President and while you and Kermit were at Groton I wanted to come up there and see you, and the Rector wished me to speak, and so I was very glad to accept.

By the way, I am working hard to get Renown accustomed to automobiles. He is such a handful now when he meets them that I seriously mind encountering them when Mother is along. Of course I do not care if I am alone, or with another man, but I am uneasy all the time when I am out with Mother. Yesterday I tried Bleistein over the hurdles at Chevy Chase. The first one was new, high and stiff, and the old rascal never rose six inches, going slap through it. I thought he would fall; but he stood up like a house. I took him at it again and he went over all right.

I am very busy now, facing the usual endless worry and discouragement, and trying to keep steadily in mind that I must not only be as resolute as Abraham Lincoln in seeking to achieve decent ends, but as patient, as uncomplaining and as even-tempered in dealing, not only with knaves, but with the well-meaning foolish people, educated and uneducated, who by their unwisdom give the knaves their chance; and that I must show the same spirit in painfully groping to find out the right course. Garfield is a great comfort to me. I see much of him and take him out to walk, and I also play tennis with him; although tennis is not very exciting to him as he is at least as good a player as George, and I do not average more than one game in a set. He is working very hard, and as it is a new department, he actually took no holiday this summer. I shall have to bundle him off for a fortnight to the North Woods, if I can make him go. He has such poise and sanity — he is so fearless, and yet possesses such common sense, that he is a real support to me. He tells me that his father, President Garfield, when he and his brother were at school and only 15 and 13 years of age, used to write them in full about his plans — why he went to the Senate instead of staying in the House, etc., etc. The man has the sound body, the sound mind, and above all the sound character, about which I tend to preach until I become prosy! *Your loving father*

PRESIDENTIAL READING

To Nicholas Murray Butler

Washington, November 4, 1903

Dear Murray:

Well, the dog has returned to its vomit, as far as New York is concerned. If you noticed the *Sun's* editorial on Low this morning and the fact that the Whitney, Ryan, Lamont and Rockefeller stocks went up as soon as Tammany's victory was assured, it will be unnecessary to waste time in explaining one of the causes of defeat. The wealthy capitalists who practice graft and who believe in graft alike in public and in private life, gave Tammany unlimited money just as they will give my opponent, whoever he may be next year, unlimited money. And their organs, like the *Sun*, do not forgive Low for what they style his improper consideration of labor. With these rich men, who ludicrously enough style themselves conservatives, stood shoulder to shoulder all the corrupt and violent classes — as was natural enough — for the criminal and violent poor and the criminal and corrupt rich are in the essentials of character alike. Of course, I do not mean to say that these capitalists represent the main element in Low's overwhelming defeat, but they represent a big element. The Democratic desire to see a straight Democratic ticket elected counted for more; and the treachery or indifference of certain Republican Machine men counted for something, although I believe not nearly as much as is alleged. The chief element was the fact that Tammany on the whole comes nearer than a reform administration could come to giving New York the kind of administration which, when it is not having a spasm of virtue, it likes.

Outside of New York City and of Maryland, we have every reason to be satisfied with the showing at the polls. And it must be remembered that both New York City and Maryland did better than either did in the election immediately preceding the Presidential campaign of 1900. Up the state the Republicans were victorious everywhere. Cleveland took no stand against Tammany or in favor of Low, but he did try to accomplish something for Rice, the Democratic candidate for Mayor in Albany, who was beaten overwhelmingly. The victories in Ohio and Pennsylvania were truly phenomenal. Iowa and Nebraska, Colorado and Massachusetts, went Republican by very large majorities — phenomenal majorities for an off year. With Massachusetts I am particularly pleased, because the Cleveland-Olney-Gaston crowd made a tremendous effort to win by reviving the old alliance of the mugwumps, the corporation people, and all shades of the Democrats, including those of socialistic leanings.

You remember speaking to me about reading and especially about the kind of books one ought to read. On my way back from Oyster Bay on Election day I tried to jot down the books I have been reading for the last two years, and they run as follows. Of course I have forgotten a great many, especially ephemeral novels which I have happened to take up; and I have also read much in the magazines. Moreover, more than half of the books are books which I have read before. These I did not read through, but simply took out the parts I liked. Thus, in *Waverley*, I omitted all the opening part; in *Pickwick* I skipped about, going through all my favorite scenes. In Macaulay I read simply the essays that appealed to me, while in Keats and Browning, although I read again and again many of the poems, I think that there must be at least 80 or 90 per cent of the old poetry of each, as far as bulk is concerned, which I have never succeeded in reading at all. The old books I read were not necessarily my favorites; it was largely a matter of chance. All the reading, of course, was purely for enjoyment and of most desultory character. With this preliminary explanation, here goes!

Parts of Herodotus; the first and seventh books of Thucydides; all of Polybius; a little of Plutarch; Aeschylus' Orestean Trilogy; Sophocles' *Seven Against Thebes*; Euripides' *Hippolytus* and *Bacchae*; and Aristophanes' *Frogs*. Parts of the *Politics* of Aristotle; (all of these were in translation); Ridgeway's *Early Age of Greece*; Wheeler's *Life of Alexander*; and some six volumes of Mahaffy's *Studies of the Greek World* — of which I only read chapters here and there; two of Maspero's volumes on the early Syrian, Chaldean and Egyptian Civilizations — these I read superficially. Several chapters of Froissart. The *Memoirs* of Marbot; Bain's *Life of Charles the Twelfth*; Mahan's *Types of Naval Officers*; some of Macaulay's *Essays*; three or four volumes of Gibbon and three or four chapters of Motley. The Life of Prince Eugene, of Admiral de Ruyter, of Turenne, and of Sobieski (all in French). The battles in Carlyle's *Frederick the Great*; Hay and Nicolay's *Lincoln*, and the two volumes of Lincoln's *Speeches and Writings* — these I have not only read through, but have read parts of them again and again; Bacon's *Essays* — curiously enough, I had never really read these until this year; Mrs. Roosevelt has a volume which belonged to her grandfather, which she always carries around with her, and I got started reading this. *Macbeth*; *Twelfth Night*; *Henry the Fourth*; *Henry the Fifth*; *Richard the Second*; the first two Cantos of *Paradise Lost*; some of Michael Drayton's *Poems* — there are only three or four I care for; portions of the *Nibelungenlied*; portions of Carlyle's prose translation of Dante's *Inferno*; Church's *Beowulf*; Morris' translation of the *Heimskringla*, and Dasent's translation of the sagas of Gisli and Burnt Njal; Lady Gregory's and Miss Hull's *Cuchulain Saga* together with *The Children of Lir*, *The Children of Turin*, the *Tale of Deirdre*, etc., *Les Précieuses Ridicules*, *Le Barbier de Séville*; most of Jusserand's books — of which I was most interested in his studies of the *Kingis Quhair*; Holmes' *Over the Teacups*; Lounsbury's *Shakespeare and Voltaire*; various numbers of the *Edinburgh Review* from 1803 to 1850; Tolstoi's *Sebastopol* and *The Cossacks*; Sienkiewicz's *Fire and Sword*, and parts of his other volumes; *Guy Mannering*; *The Antiquary*; *Rob Roy*; *Waverley*; *Quentin Durward*; parts of *Marmion* and the *Lay of the Last Minstrel*; Cooper's *Pilot*; some of the earlier stories and some of the poems of Bret Harte; Mark Twain's *Tom Sawyer*; *Pickwick Papers*; *Nicholas Nickleby*; *Vanity Fair*; *Pendennis*; *The Newcomes*; *Adventures of Philip*; Conan Doyle's *White Company*; Lever's *Charles O'Malley*; *Romances* of Brockden Brown (read when I was confined to my room with a game leg, from motives of curiosity and with no real enjoyment). An occasional half hour's reading in Keats, Browning, Poe, Tennyson, Longfellow, Kipling, Bliss Carmen; also in Poe's *Tales* and Lowell's *Essays*; some of Stevenson's stories, and of Allingham's *British Ballads*; Wagner's *Simple Life*. I have read aloud to the children, and often finished afterwards to myself, *The Rose and the Ring*; Hans Andersen; some of Grimm; some Norse Folk Tales; and stories by Howard Pyle; *Uncle Remus* and the rest of Joel Chandler Harris' stories (incidentally, I would be willing to rest all that I have done in the South as regards the negro on his story "Free Joe"); two or three books by Jacob Riis; also Mrs. Van Vorst's *Woman Who Toils*, and one or two similar volumes; the nonsense verses of Carolyn Wells, first to the children, and afterwards for Mrs. Roosevelt and myself; Kenneth Grahame's *Golden Age*; those two delightful books by Somerville and Ross, *All on the Irish Shore* and *Experiences of an Irish M.P.*; Townsend's *Europe and Asia*; Conrad's *Youth*; *Phoenixiana*; Artemus Ward; Octave Thanet's stories, which I always like, especially when they deal with labor problems; various books on the Boer War, of which I liked best Viljoen's, Stevens', and studies by the writer signing himself Linesman; Pike's *Through the Subarctic Forest*, and Peer's *Cross Country with Horse and Hound*, together with a number of books on big-game hunting, mostly in Africa; several volumes on American outdoor life and natural history, including the rereading of much of John Burroughs; Swettenham's *Real Malay*; David Gray's *Gallops*; Miss Stewart's *Napoleon Jackson*; Janvier's *Passing of*

Thomas and other stories; the *Benefactress*; the *People of the Whirlpool*; London's *Call of the Wild*; Fox's *Little Shepherd of Kingdom Come*; Hamlin Garland's *Captain of the Gray-horse Troop*; Tarkington's *Gentleman from Indiana*; Churchill's *Crisis*; Remington's *John Ermine of the Yellowstone*; Wister's *Virginian, Red Men and White, Philosophy Four, Lin McLean*; White's *Blazed Trail, Conjuror's House* and *Claim Jumpers*; Trevelyan's *American Revolution*. Often I would read one book by chance, and it would suggest another.

There! that is the catalogue; about as interesting as Homer's Catalogue of the Ships, and with about as much method in it as there seems in a superficial glance to be in an Irish stew. The great comfort, old man, is that you need not read it and that you need not answer this! *Yours ever*

PANAMA

To Kermit Roosevelt

Washington, November 4, 1903

Dear Kermit:

Tonight while I was preparing to dictate a message to Congress concerning the boiling caldron on the Isthmus of Panama, which has now begun to bubble over, up came one of the ushers with a telegram from you and Ted about the football match. Instantly I bolted into the next room to read it aloud to mother and sister, and we all cheered in unison when we came to the Rah! Rah! Rah! part of it. It was a great score. I wish I could have seen the game.

In spite of Tammany's victory in New York and Gorman's in Maryland, I am on the whole well pleased with the results of the elections.

Just at present I am attending to the Panama business. For half a century we have policed that Isthmus in the interest of the little wildcat republic of Colombia. Colombia has behaved infamously about the treaty for the building of the Panama Canal; and I do not intend in the police work that I will have to do in connection with the new insurrection any longer to do for her work which is not merely profitless but brings no gratitude. Any interference I undertake now will be in the interest of the United States and of the people of the Panama Isthmus themselves. There will be some lively times in carrying out this policy. Of course, I may encounter checks, but I think I shall put it through all right. *Ever your loving father*

DRAWBACKS OF A MILITARY CAREER

To Theodore Roosevelt Jr.

Washington, January 11, 1904

Dear Ted:

This will be a long business letter. I sent to you the examination papers for West Point and Annapolis. I have thought a great deal over the matter, and discussed it at great length with Mother. I feel on the one hand that I ought to give you my best advice, and yet on the other hand I do not wish to seem to constrain you against your wishes. If you have definitely made up your mind that you have an overmastering desire to be in the Navy or the Army, and that such a career is the one in which you will take a really heartfelt interest — far more so than any other — and that your greatest chance for happiness and usefulness will lie in doing this one work to which you feel yourself especially drawn, — why, under such circumstances, I have but little to say. But I am not satisfied that this is really your feeling. It seemed to me more as if you did not feel drawn in any other direction, and wondered what you were going to do in life or what kind of work you would turn your hand to, and wondered if you could make a success or not; and that you are therefore inclined to turn to the Navy or Army chiefly because you would then have a definite and settled career in life, and could hope to go on steadily without any great risk of failure. Now, if such is your thought I shall quote to you what Captain Mahan said of his son when asked why he did not send him to West Point or Annapolis.

"I have too much confidence in him to make me feel that it is desirable for him to enter either branch of the service."

I have great confidence in you. I believe you have the ability, and above all the energy, the perseverance and the common sense, to win out in civil life. That you will have some hard times and some discouraging times I have no question; but this is merely another way of saying that you will share the common lot. Though you will have to work in different ways from those in which I worked, you will not have to work any harder, nor to face periods of more discouragement. I trust in your ability, and especially your character, and I am confident you will win.

In the Army and the Navy the chance for a man to show great ability and rise above his fellows does not occur on the average more than once in a generation. When I was down at Santiago it was melancholy for me to see how fossilized and lacking in ambition, and generally useless, were most of the men of my age and over who had served their lives in the Army. The Navy for the last few years has been better, but for twenty years after the Civil War there was less chance in the Navy than in the Army to practice, and do, work of real consequence. I have actually known lieutenants in both the Army and the Navy who were grandfathers — men who had seen their children married before they themselves attained the grade of captain. Of course the chance may come at any time when the man of West Point or Annapolis who has stayed in the Army or Navy finds a great war on, and therefore has the opportunity to rise high. Under such circumstances I think that the man of such training who has actually left the Army or the Navy has even more chance of rising than the man who has remained in it. Moreover, often a man can do as I did in the Spanish war, even though not a West Pointer.

This last point raises the question about your going to West Point or Annapolis and leaving the Army or Navy after you have served the regulation four years (I think that is the number) after graduation from the academy. Under this plan you would have an excellent education and a grounding in discipline, and in some ways a testing of your capacity greater than I think you can get in any ordinary college. On the other hand, except for the profession of an engineer, you would have had nothing like special training; and you would be so ordered about, and arranged for, that you would have less independence of character than you would gain from Harvard. You would *have* had fewer temptations; but you would have had less chance to develop the qualities which overcome temptations and show that a man has individual initiative. Supposing you entered at seventeen, with the intention of following this course. The result would be that at twenty-five you would leave the Army or Navy without having gone through any law school or any special technical school of any kind, and would start your life work three or four years later than your school fellows of today, who go to work immediately after leaving college. Of course, under such circumstances, you might study law, for instance, during the four years after graduation; but my own feeling is that a man does good work chiefly when he is in something which he intends to make his permanent work, and in which he is deeply interested. Moreover, there will always be the chance that the number of officers in the Army or Navy will be deficient, and that you would have to stay in the service instead of getting out when you wished.

I want you to think over all these matters very seriously. It would be a great misfortune for you to start into the Army or Navy as a career, and find that you had mistaken your desires and had gone in without really weighing the matter. *Your loving father*

You ought not to enter unless you feel genuinely drawn to the life as a lifework. If so, go in; but not otherwise.

Mr. Loeb told me today that at 17 he tried for the army, but failed. The competitor who beat him is now a captain; Mr. Loeb has passed him by, although meanwhile a war has been fought. Mr. Loeb says he wished to enter the army because he did not know what to do, could not foresee whether he would succeed or fail in life, and felt the army would give him "a living and a career." Now if this is at bottom your feeling I should advise you not to go in; I should say yes to some boys, but not to you; I believe in you too much, and have too much confidence in you.

LUCRETIUS AND GLADSTONE

To John Morley

Personal

Washington, January 17, 1904

My dear Mr. Morley:

Come by all means in October, if that is your only time. But if you could put off your visit to December it would be better for several reasons. In the first place, during October we shall be closing the presidential canvass, and if I am nominated for President there will be a good deal of work on hand. In the next place, Congress does not meet until December, and I should particularly like you to meet representative men of the Senate and the House. I don't mean merely men who would be congenial to you, but the men who are leaders, who represent different bodies of opinion in the country, without regard to whether you would be apt to like them or not; for I should desire you to see the real forces at play in our political life. But if October is your only time, come then by all means, and I shall try to show you as much as possible. Mrs. Roosevelt and I will both enjoy having you at the White House.

As I said in my previous letter, it is a temptation to me to write you at inordinate length about your *Life of Gladstone*. Incidentally, you started me to rereading Lucretius and Finlay. Lucretius was an astounding man for pagan Rome to have produced just before the Empire. I should not myself have thought of comparing him with Virgil one way or the other. It would be too much like comparing say Herbert Spencer with Milton. Excepting that part dealing with death, in the end of the third book (if I remember aright), I am less struck with the work because of its own quality (as a finished product, so to speak) than I am with the fact that it was opening up a totally new trail — a trail which for very many centuries, indeed down to modern times, was not followed much farther. He had as truly a scientific mind as Darwin or Huxley, and the boldness of his truth-telling was astonishing. As for Finlay, I have always been fond of him. But I would not like to be understood as depreciating Gibbon. Personally I feel that with all their faults Gibbon and Macaulay are the two great English historians, and there could be no better testimonial to their greatness than the fact that scores of authors have each made a comfortable life reputation by refuting some single statement of one or the other.

Of course, in reading the *Gladstone* I was especially interested because of the ceaseless unconscious comparisons I was making with events in our own history, and with difficulties I myself every day encounter. A man who has grappled, or is grappling, with Cuba, Panama and the Philippines, has a lively appreciation of the difficulties inevitably attendant upon getting into Egypt in the first place, and then upon the impossibility of getting out of it, in the second. Perhaps I was interested most of all in your account of the closing years of Gladstone's career, in which "Home rule" was the most important question he had to face. I suppose I am one of a large multitude to whom your book for the first time gave a clear idea of what Gladstone's actual position was in the matter, and of the gross injustice of the assaults upon him. You make it clear, for instance, that from the standpoint of Gladstone's assailants even, there was far more to be said against the consistency and frankness of the leaders who opposed him and the leaders who deserted him than against his. To my mind you prove your case completely, — and I have always been inclined to criticize Gladstone on this point, although I have personally been a home ruler ever since reading Lecky's account of Ireland in the Eighteenth Century. On no position do I feel more cordial sympathy with Gladstone's attitude than as regards Turkey and the subjugated peoples of the Balkan Peninsula.

Looking forward to seeing you here next year, I am, *Sincerely yours*

ELECTION CHANCES

To Theodore Roosevelt Jr.

Washington, January 29, 1904

Dear Ted:

Indeed I do understand your interest in all things affecting me, old boy, and I shall write you at length about the political situation. I do not write you such letters all the time because I do not want you to feel that all my correspondence with you is of a stilted and Chesterfield's-letters-to-his-son style.

In politics, as in life generally, the strife is well-nigh unceasing and breathing spots are few. Even if the struggle results in a victory, it usually only opens the way for another struggle. I believe we shall win out in the Panama business as soon as we can get a vote, for I think we shall confirm the treaty by a three to one majority; but they are filibustering and talking every which way in the vain hope that something will turn up to help them. In the Wood controversy also I think we shall win out, although possibly there will be an ugly fight. The only legislative matter looming up concerning which I feel uncomfortable is the service pension bill, which I think is on the whole right, but which contains possibilities of mischief on account of the hostility with which it is regarded by many business people, and by lots of good young fellows who do not realize how much the soldiers did in the Civil War, and how much we owe them.

By the way, if I were you I would not discuss the labor-union question from the side that labor unions are harmful. I think they are beneficial if handled as they should be, and that the attack should be made, not upon the principle of association among working people, but upon the abuses in the manifestation of that principle.

As regards myself personally, Senator Hanna and the Wall Street crowd are causing me some worry, but not of a serious kind. I doubt if they can prevent my nomination. Senator Hanna has not kept his promise to me of last June, and has been intoxicated by the thought that perhaps he could either be nominated himself, or at least dictate the nomination, but he will be thwarted completely if he makes the effort, and I think he will grow sullenly conscious of this fact and refuse to make the effort. He has caused me a little worry, but not much. The Wall Street people of a certain stripe — that is, the rich men who do not desire to obey the law and who think that they are entitled to what I regard as improper consideration merely because of their wishes — will do their best to secure the nomination for him, or at least to use him to beat my nomination and secure that of a third person. I think they will fail; and that when they realize that failure is ahead of them they will turn in and support me. But some will try to elect a democrat. A good many of them who are very bitter against me now will come over to my side when the campaign is actually on. I doubt if they can do much against me as far as the nomination is concerned. The election is a different matter. Of course I may be utterly mistaken, but personally I think I have a good deal of strength in the country districts and indeed in the West generally; but in the big cities, and especially in the eastern big cities, the extreme labor-union people and every one of anarchistic or socialist tendencies on the one hand, and the arrogant men of wealth on the other, will probably both combine against me. If the democrats put up a strong candidate upon whom all their factions can unite, I shall have a hard tussle. Nobody can say whether I shall win or lose. In any event, I have done a good many things worth doing while I have been President, and I have had the public service administered with efficiency and integrity.

I am worked very hard at present, and it is only now and then that I can get off in the afternoon for a ride with Mother or a walk with some friend. When the social season is over I think I shall have a little more leeway. *Ever your loving father*

P.S. Be careful not to let any of these letters in which I speak of political subjects lie about where they can be seen by anyone.

"I HAVE GREAT CONFIDENCE IN YOU"

To Theodore Roosevelt Jr.

Washington, February 6, 1904

Dear Ted:

I was glad to hear that you were to be confirmed.

Secretary Root left on Monday and Governor Taft took his place. I have missed, and shall miss, Root dreadfully. He has been the ablest, most generous and most disinterested friend and adviser that any President could hope to have; and immediately after leaving he rendered me a great service by a speech at the Union League Club in which he said in most effective fashion the very things I should have liked him to say; and his words, moreover, carried weight as the words of no other man at this time addressing such an audience could have done. Taft is a splendid fellow and will be an aid and comfort in every way. But as mother says he is too much like me to be able to give me as good advice as Mr. Root was able to do because of the very differences of character between us.

If after fully thinking the matter over you remain firmly convinced that you want to go into the army well and good. I shall be rather sorry for your decision because I have great confidence in you and I believe that in civil life you could probably win in the end a greater prize than will be open to you if you go into the army — though of course a man can do well in the army. I know perfectly well that you will have hard times in civil life. Probably most young fellows when they have graduated from college, or from their postgraduate course, if they take any, feel pretty dismal for the first few years. In ordinary cases it at first seems as if their efforts were not leading anywhere, as if the pressure around the foot of the ladder was too great to permit of getting up to the top. But I have faith in your energy, your perseverance, your ability, and your power to force yourself to the front when you have once found out and taken your line. However, you and I and mother will talk the whole matter over when you come back here on Easter. *Your loving father*

SADDLE HORSES AND THE CARIBBEAN

To Theodore Roosevelt Jr.

Washington, February 10, 1904

Blessed Ted:

I loved your letter coaxing for one of the six Arabian stallions, and if they had actually come to me I would not have been able to resist keeping one for your use as long as I was in the White House. But alas, it was all a newspaper story! They really went to the St. Louis Exposition, and so you will not be able to disturb your parents by witching the world with feats of horsemanship. Just at the moment what I most earnestly hope is that I shall have any horse whatever for you to ride when you come home at Easter. All three of my saddle horses are absolutely gone in the wind so that I can't ride them at all; and Yagenka is also touched a little. I think it is undoubtedly due to our stable, and I have had them put in another. I hope soon one of mine will get well. Yagenka I think certainly will. So at present I can't ride. When I get any exercise it takes the form of a walk with one of my faithful bodyguard — Garfield, Pinchot, Cooley or Fortescue. I have been able to get very little exercise indeed this winter.

I think the opposition to Panama is pretty well over and I shall be surprised if within a week or so we do not have the treaty ratified. Of course, there will be many perplexing problems to face during the actual work of constructing the canal.

Santo Domingo is drifting into chaos, for after a hundred years of freedom it shows itself utterly incompetent for governmental work. Most reluctantly I have been obliged to take the initial step of interference there. I hope it will be a good while before I have to go further. But sooner or later it seems to me inevitable that the United States should assume an attitude of protection and regulation in regard to all these little states in the neighborhood of the Caribbean. I hope it will be deferred as long as possible, but I fear it is inevitable.

I am greatly interested in the Russian and Japanese war. It has certainly opened most disastrously for the Russians, and their supine carelessness is well-nigh incredible. For several years Russia has behaved very badly in the far East, her attitude toward all nations, including us, but especially toward Japan, being grossly overbearing. We had no sufficient cause for war with her. Yet I was apprehensive lest if she at the very outset whipped Japan on the sea she might assume a position well-nigh intolerable toward us. I thought Japan would probably whip her on the sea, but I could not be certain; and between ourselves — for you must not breathe it to anybody — I was thoroughly well pleased with the Japanese victory, for Japan is playing our game. *Always yours*

THE DEATH OF MARK HANNA

To Elihu Root

Personal

Washington, February 16, 1904

Dear Elihu:

I am delighted that the Union League Club is to publish your speech in full. I agree with every word you say as to the conditions then existing in New York. The evil had gone very deep and the effects were becoming noticeable far from the original center. It needed a great speech — a speech which was not only masterly in matter but in manner, and which came from someone whose name demanded attention — in order to produce the necessary effect. I fully believe that you produced that effect. Scores of men have written to me about it, none more enthusiastically, by the way, than our staunch friend, General Grenville M. Dodge. He has just told me that he wishes Hay would now make a speech on our foreign policy which could be put with yours, and Moody's speech at the Republican Club, and issued as a campaign document. I can conceive of no more effective document.

Hanna's death has been very sad. Did I tell you the last letter he wrote was one to me? As soon as he was seriously sick I called at the hotel, as a matter of course. For some inexplicable reason this affected him very much, appealing to the generous and large-hearted side of his nature, and he at once sent me a pencil note running as follows:

My dear Mr. President:

You touched a tender spot, old man, when you called personally to inquire after me this a.m. I may be worse before I can be better, but all the same such "drops" of kindness are good for a fellow.

Sincerely yours,

M. A. HANNA.

Friday p.m.

No man had larger traits than Hanna. He was a big man in every way and as forceful a personality as we have seen in public life in our generation. I think that not merely I myself, but the whole party and the whole country have reason to be very grateful to him for the way in which, after I came into office, under circumstances which were very hard for him, he resolutely declined to be drawn into the position which a smaller man of meaner cast would inevitably have taken; that is, the position of antagonizing public policies if I was identified with them. He could have caused the widest disaster to the country and the public if he had attacked and opposed the policies referring to Panama, the Philippines, Cuban reciprocity, army reform, the navy and the legislation for regulating corporations. But he stood by them just as loyally as if I had been McKinley.

Mrs. Hanna has been very much shattered; and it has all been very sad.

Panama is certainly going through, and I think they will vote about the 23d. We shall get nearly half the democrats, and I don't think we shall lose a single republican. Even Hoar, by a path so bewilderingly devious that I am really unable to follow the windings, has come around to the support of the treaty.

Yes, it was on the suggestion of "Bill the Kaiser" that we sent out the note on the neutrality of China. But the insertion of the word "entity" was ours. His suggestion originally was in untenable form; that is, he wanted us to guarantee the integrity of China south of the latitude of the Great Wall, which would have left Russia free to gobble up what she really wanted. We changed the proposal by striking out the limitation, and Germany cheerfully acceded! It is a good thing to give Germany all credit for making the suggestion. As a matter of fact, in this instance Germany behaved better than any other power, for in England Lansdowne drove us half crazy with thick-headed inquiries and requests about our making more specific exactly what it was highly inexpedient to make specific at all.

Indeed the Japs showed themselves past masters in the practical application of David Harum's famous gloss on the "Do unto others" injunction. They did it fust! Oh, if only our people would learn the need of preparedness, and of shaping things so that decision and action can alike be instantaneous. Mere bigness, if it is also mere flabbiness, means nothing but disgrace. Moody, by the way, is being harried by Hale in naval matters until he feels like crying. Still, we do make progress.

'I have been, on the whole, delighted with Upton's book, and I think you rendered a great service in publishing it. But it is a one-sided book. Take his account of the 1813 campaign. The serious invasions of Canada in that year were made by two old army officers, Wilkinson and Hampton, with two regular armies amply sufficient in size for the task. They would have succeeded if they had been under the two militia, or volunteer, officers Jacob Brown and Andrew Jackson. They failed because they were under two incompetents, who had seen long service in the army. In other words, Upton should have remembered to qualify continually what he said by remembering that mere length of service, that mere calling troops "regulars," amount to nothing whatever.

When are you coming on to Washington? Remember that you and Mrs. Root and Miss Edith are to stay with us whenever you are here. *Ever yours*

THE NEED FOR A STRONGER NAVY

To Theodore Elijah Burton

Personal

Washington, February 23, 1904

My dear Mr. Burton:

I respect your character and ability so highly and believe so in your power for good, and therefore, as a corollary, in your power for evil if it is misused; and I am so confident in your good judgment, that I write you a word in reference to your speech on the navy.

As you can imagine, this speech was a genuine shock to me. To have Mr. Gorman and Mr. Williams advocate policies which, if carried out, mean jeopardy to the nation's interest and honor, is what we must expect; but that you should take what seems to me such a course, is a matter of grave concern. Let me point out very briefly what I regard as the fundamental error in the position of those who now wish to stop our building up the navy, and who nevertheless belong to the republican party. The one unforgivable crime is to put one's self in a position in which strength and courage are needed, and then to show lack of strength and courage. This is precisely the crime committed by those who advocate or have acquiesced in the acquisition of the Philippines, the establishment of naval stations in Cuba, the negotiation of the treaty for building the Panama Canal, the taking of Porto Rico and Hawaii, and the assertion of the Monroe Doctrine, and who nevertheless decline to advocate the building of a navy such as will alone warrant our attitude in any one, not to say all, of these matters. It is perfectly allowable, although I think rather ignoble, to take the attitude that this country is to occupy a position in the New World analogous to that of China in the Old World, to stay entirely within her borders, not to endeavor to assert the Monroe Doctrine, incidentally to leave the Philippines, to abandon the care of the Panama Canal, to give up Hawaii and Porto Rico, etc., etc., and therefore to refuse to build up any navy. It is also allowable, and as I think, in the highest degree far-sighted and honorable, to insist that the attitude of the republican party in all these matters during the last eight years has been the wise and proper attitude, and to insist therefore that the navy shall be kept up and built up as required by the needs of such an attitude. But any attempt to combine the two attitudes is fraught with the certainty of hopeless and ignominious disaster to the Nation. To be rich, aggressive, and yet helpless in war, is to invite destruction. If everything that the republican party has done during the past eight years is all wrong; if we ought not to have annexed Hawaii, or taken the Philippines, or established a kind of protectorate over Cuba, or started to build the Panama Canal, then let us reverse these policies and give up building a navy; but to my mind it is to inflict a great wrong on the generations who come after us if we persevere in these policies and do not back them up by building a navy. Mr. Williams, for instance, is against the fortification of Subig Bay. He affects to regard the fortification of Subig Bay as a menace to the independence of the Philippines; with which it has nothing in the world to do. I do not know how much his attitude is due to sheer ignorance, or unwillingness or inability to think things out, or how much it is mere affectation. Of course, in any event, for him, coming from a State where his party supremacy and his own political success rest wholly and exclusively on the basis of governing the majority of his fellow citizens, who happen to have different colored skins, without their consent, it is hypocritical and base to make the false plea that he does for the Filipinos. An honest but misguided enthusiast can make such a plea and retain his self-respect, when it is known that at home he is equally sincere in insisting that all men, of whatever race, however incompetent, shall have equal chances to govern themselves. But for a man by his life and by every act which gratifies his own ambitions at home to prove the negation of what he asserts in reference to people abroad, is even more base than it is foolish. Without regard to this, however, Mr. Williams' attitude about Subig Bay is monstrous in view of what we have seen happen before our eyes to the Russians at Port Arthur because of their unpreparedness. If we are to have a naval station in the Philippines; if we are to have a fleet in Asiatic waters, or to exert the slightest influence in eastern Asia where our people hope to find a market, then it is of the highest importance that we have a naval station at Subig Bay. If we are not to have that station, and are not to have a navy, then we should be manly enough to say that we intend to abandon the Philippines at once; not to try to keep a naval station there; and not to try to exercise that influence in foreign affairs which comes only to the just man armed who wishes to keep the peace. China is now the sport and plaything of stronger powers because she has constantly acted on her belief in despising and making little of military strength afloat or ashore, and is therefore powerless to keep order within or repel aggression from without. The little powers of Europe, although in many cases they lead honorable and self-respecting national lives, are powerless to accomplish any great good in foreign affairs, simply and solely because they lack the element of force behind their good wishes. We on the contrary have been able to do so much for The Hague Tribunal and for the cause of international arbitration; we have been able to keep the peace in the waters south of us; to put an end to bloody misrule and bloody civil strife in Cuba, in the Philippines, and at Panama; and we are able to exercise a pacific influence in China, because, and only because, together with the purpose to be just and to keep the peace we possess a navy which makes it evident that we will not tamely submit to injustice, or tamely acquiesce in breaking the peace.

This letter is for you personally. I write it because I respect you and like you. *Faithfully yours*

OPPOSING AN ALL-WHITE PARTY

To Francis Bennett Williams

Personal

Washington, February 24, 1904

My dear Mr. Williams:

I take it for granted that there is no intention of making the Louisiana delegation all white. I think it would be a mistake for my friends to take any such attitude in any State where there is a considerable negro population. I think it is a great mistake from the standpoint of the whites; and in an organization composed of men whom I have especially favored it would put me in a false light. As you know, I feel as strongly as anyone can that there must be nothing like "negro domination." On the other hand, I feel equally strongly that the republicans must consistently favor those comparatively few colored people who by character and intelligence show themselves entitled to such favor. To put a premium upon the possession of such qualities among the blacks is not only to benefit them, but to benefit the whites among whom they live. I very earnestly hope that the Louisiana republicans whom I have so consistently favored will not by any action of theirs tend to put me in a false position in such a matter as this. With your entire approval I have appointed one or two colored men to office in Louisiana. There must certainly be an occasional colored man entitled by character and standing to go to the National Convention. *Sincerely yours*

JAPANESE WRESTLING

To Kermit Roosevelt

Washington, March 5, 1904

Dear Kermit:

It does not look as if Renown would ever be worth anything, and I am afraid that Wyoming is gone too. Bleistein probably, and Yagenka almost certainly, will come out all right. Allan is back here now and very cunning, so you will see him on your return.

I am wrestling with two Japanese wrestlers three times a week. I am not the age or the build, one would think, to be whirled lightly over an opponent's head and batted down on a mattress without damage; but they are so skillful that I have not been hurt at all. My throat is a little sore, because once when one of them had a strangle hold I also got hold of his windpipe and thought I could perhaps choke him off before he could choke me. However, he got ahead! *Your loving father*

To Lawrence Fraser Abbott

Personal

Washington, March 14, 1904

My dear Mr. Abbott:

Referring to your letter of the 12th instant to Mr. Loeb, I should be very glad to have you make public what the real facts are as to those expenses. Let me say also that I think it rather a tribute to my administration that they are obliged to come down to this kind of misstatement in order to make a point.

In the first place, about the stable. No appropriation has been made for a new stable. Without my knowledge the Superintendent of Public Buildings and Grounds reported, with entire propriety, that inasmuch as the present stable is on unhealthy ground and the Government horses become sick in it, a new one should be built. Moreover, the ground on which the present stable stands has been set apart for monumental purposes, and sooner or later the building will have to be removed. However, on learning that the recommendation had been made, I directed Colonel Symons to state to the Committee that I did not wish the appropriation made, though if I am defeated I shall certainly recommend that it be done for the benefit of my successor.

It is stated that my "private naval review" cost the people over $200,000. There was no private naval review, and the review that took place did not cost the people a cent. The fleet was in the North Atlantic, and it was deemed very important that the President should show his interest by going out to it and seeing it pass in review and maneuver. Accordingly, it came into Long Island Sound and I there reviewed it. The review took place, of course, in the presence of hundreds of craft, and was far less private than the ordinary reviews off the coast. Equally of course, it did not cost one penny more than any review off the coast when the Secretary of the Navy or the Admiral goes down to visit the fleet. This review was made solely because the naval officers felt it would be so good a thing to have the President show an interest in the fleet. I confess it never occurred to me that there could be any scoundrel so base as to misinterpret such an action.

Now, as to the President's yacht, with all the expensive furniture, etc. This probably refers to the *Mayflower*, as she is the only boat that has expensive fittings. Not a dollar was spent on the *Mayflower* for the President or his family in the way of furnishing or equipping her. She is ordinarily used for the Admiral or the Secretary of the Navy. For instance, she was used by Admiral Dewey when he was at the fleet maneuvers in the Caribbean. She was used by the Secretary of the Navy when he inspected the fleet. She has been on duty all winter with the squadron at Panama. She came down for me to review the fleet last summer in the Sound. On another occasion I was on her for the purpose of witnessing the target practice, because I wanted to impress upon the Navy the interest I take in the target practice. Here again it is wicked to allow partisanship to go to the extreme of desiring to interfere with the promotion of efficiency in the Navy, especially in such a matter as marksmanship. All told, since I have been President I have been on the *Mayflower* on some three occasions; the third time being when I went to review the National Guard of New Jersey at Sea Girt, a strictly official function. I have also been three or four times on the smaller vessel, the *Sylph* — as for instance, when I visited with Jake Riis the summer home for poor children of Westchester County last summer; and again when I went to visit the immigration station at Ellis Island. I think I was once or twice on a Government tug also. In short, all this statement is such absolute fatuous folly that it is hard to answer it. I have to move about, and where I can move about on sea it is obviously better than moving about on land, and all told I have on six or eight different occasions taken advantage of either the *Sylph* or the *Mayflower* or a tug being handy, and gone on such vessel. So little did I use these vessels that I have finally given up having any one of them in the neighborhood of Oyster Bay, because I found it was not used enough to make it worth while. Remember that even when they were at Oyster Bay it did not cost the Government a cent more. They had to lie somewhere. They never were sent to Oyster Bay when there was any other duty to perform. It is perfectly true that the children, being healthy children, boarded them with eagerness when they appeared, and made friends with the sailors. When I have had meals aboard these vessels they have been paid for by me. The Government has been to no extra expense in the matter whatever, save perhaps on the four or five occasions when there has been the expense of the coal used up on some visit to Ellis Island, or something of the kind, when otherwise the vessel would have been at anchor and would not have burned coal. Surely this is too trivial to be considered.

They speak of the entertainments in the White House. These are all paid for out of my private pocket. You have now and then taken meals at the White House, and also at Oyster Bay. You were just as much my guest at one place as the other. I am almost ashamed to mention this, but apparently people do not understand, or some people do not understand, that I pay the butcher, the baker and the grocer at Washington just as I do at Oyster Bay; and the protest is apparently against my having people whom I like lunch or dine with me at the White House, just as I have them lunch or dine with me out at Oyster Bay.

It is true that I have a tennis court in the White House grounds. The cost of it has been trivial — less than 400 dollars. It has been paid for exactly as the adjacent garden, for instance, is paid for. The cost is much less than the cost of the greenhouses under Presidents Grant, Harrison, Cleveland, etc. It surely cannot seriously be meant that there is objection to the President and his children playing tennis, and of course it is impossible for them to play tennis excepting in the White House grounds. The greenhouses now cost *less* than they did; less than for a dozen years back.

Finally, as to the enlargement of the White House. It is perfectly true that this has been done, and you can speak of your own knowledge as to the immense improvement. It was not done on my recommendation, for I made none whatever, and did not think of making one. It was done because in Congress democrats and republicans alike agreed that it was absolutely necessary it should be done; that the White House was unsafe, and that it was improper and undignified longer to leave it in the condition that it was. Senator Cockrell, of Missouri, and Congressman McRae, of Arkansas, were among the Senators and Congressmen who took the lead in having the changes made. The changes were carried through by McKim, Mead and White, the effort being to restore the White House to what it was originally planned and designed to be in the days of Washington and Jefferson. Every competent architect in the country will tell you that it was a genuinely patriotic service thus to restore it to its old simple and stately dignity. If you will turn to the *Century Magazine* for April, 1903, you will see the changes described there. I also enclose you a report from which you may gather some additional information. To complain of what has been done is to complain of the erection of buildings like the Congressional Library building, or the Washington Monument. Only a yahoo could have his taste offended; and excepting a yahoo, only a very base partisan politician would complain of it.

Cannot you see McKim in New York and find out from him just how the changes were made, and how it was done, and what architects think of it? I enclose you a copy of his statement.

This article in the Memphis *Appeal* is simply one of those which appeared after the Hearst papers had a full-page sensational article on the subject of White House extravagance. *Sincerely yours*

P.S. Will you please return the enclosed magazine when you are through with it?

To Bruseius Simons

Personal

Washington, March 19, 1904

My dear Mr. Simons:

Your letter pleased and interested me much. The first work I saw of yours was the "Seats of the Mighty," and it impressed me so powerfully that I have ever since eagerly sought out any of your pictures of which I heard. When I became President Mrs. Roosevelt and I made up our minds that while I was President we would indulge ourselves in the purchase of one really first-class piece of American art — for we are people whom the respective sizes of our family and our income have never warranted in making such a purchase while I was in private life! As soon as we saw "When Light and Shadow Meet," we made up our minds at once and without speaking to one another that at last we had seen the very thing we wanted.

Mrs. Roosevelt and I feel that in your letter you have expressed much which we have felt but not formulated. I agree absolutely with you that art, or at least the art for which I care, must present the ideal through the temperament and the interpretation of the painter. I do not greatly care for the reproduction of landscapes which in effect I see whenever I ride and walk. I wish "the light that never was on land or sea" in the pictures that I am to live with — and this light your paintings have. When I look at them I feel a lift in my soul; I feel my imagination stirred. And so, my dear Mr. Simons, I believe in you as an artist and I am proud of you as an American. *Sincerely yours*

PHILIPPINE INDEPENDENCE

To Charles William Eliot

Personal

Washington, April 4, 1904

My dear Mr. Eliot:

I have recently been reading Hadley's admirable volume on *Freedom and Responsibility*; and I have also recently seen the petition signed by a number of very high-minded citizens, including you, which I am informed it is the intention to present to the conventions of both parties next June; this petition being that the United States shall pledge itself to give political independence to the Philippines sometime in the future. Now it seems to me that if the signers of this petition, or rather those among them for whose opinions I had the real respect that I have for yours, either appreciated the common sense doctrines laid down by Hadley in the volume I have referred to, or knew by correspondence, (say with Taft or with Luke Wright — or with almost any other man who was really fit to speak on the subject) what the actual facts in the matter were, they would not sign such a petition. I do not believe the petition will have much effect; but so far as there is any effect at all it will be purely mischievous. The Republican convention will of course not consider it, for the Republican administration is practically endeavoring to better conditions in the Philippines and has met with great success in its efforts, and therefore, cannot afford to set back this particular work by doing something which would be worse than foolish. The Democrats may very possibly adopt the program, for they may think that they will get some votes by it; and they will be wholly indifferent to the damage done either to the Philippines or the United States, provided that damage does not unfavorably affect their chances in the election. To anyone not acquainted with the vagaries of human nature it would seem incredible that the southern Democrats in Congress, who include all the Democratic leaders, should be willing to prate about the doctrines contained in the Declaration of Independence, as applied to brown men in the Philippines, when they themselves own their political existence, their presence in Congress, their influence in the nation, solely to the fact that they embody a living negation of those doctrines so far as they concern the black man at home. It is perhaps even more singular that this incongruity of attitude never seems to strike the conscientious allies of these men in the north. Senator Hoar for instance is to a certain degree logical in demanding for the Filipino and for the negro alike what he does demand. But there is no southern Democrat of any prominence who at this time can keep his place in his party save by brutal insistence upon the evasion and violation of law, upon depriving the negro of the rights which he is constitutionally guaranteed; and there is no one of these southern Democrats who talks about the "consent of the governed" in the Philippines whose hypocrisy is not so apparent as to justly entitle him to the scorn and distrust of honest-minded men. I am not now discussing the attitude of the southerner to the negro; but his relative attitudes to the negro and Filipino. If your petition is favorably acted upon by the Democratic National Convention it will be, and can be, only because the southerners who determine the action of that convention believe that an attitude of cynical hypocrisy on their part in this matter may gain them the votes of certain people in the north.

It is, however, only of these people of the north that I intend to speak. It seems to me that very many men who sincerely feel that they are conscientious have in this matter of the Philippines acted much as those ancient anchorites and hermits acted, who left society, and ceased to try to do good to their fellow men, because they became absorbed in the essentially morbid and essentially selfish task of sacrificing all duty to others to the business of trying to save their own souls. The easy thing, the cheap thing, to do is to sign a petition or make a speech in favor of our abandoning a difficult and doubtful task, washing our hands of all responsibility in the matter, and leaving the Filipinos to the impossible task of working out their own salvation. The hard thing, the wise and brave thing, is to keep on doing the work which Taft and Luke Wright and their fellows have been doing with such astonishing success; that is the task of working for the actual betterment, moral, industrial, social, and political, of the Filipinos;

the task of laying the foundations of a growth which we believe will in the end fit them for independence. The task is in many respects like that of Cromer in Egypt; though it is greater. You may possibly remember that at one time Cromer suffered a very serious setback because it became widely spread about that the British intended to surrender the government of Egypt; and a period of utter demoralization among the natives followed. So it is now in the Philippines. When Bryan or General Miles or any other man, for political or sentimental reasons, excites false hopes of independence among the Filipinos, it invariably and immediately produces a certain amount of demoralization and gives a certain setback to the effort for their betterment; and just such demoralization, just such damage, to the Filipinos themselves, will be caused by the present effort of which I am speaking if it achieves prominence enough to be known in the islands at all. The natives will not and cannot be under the control of two sets of ideas at once. Either they will turn their attention to working by practical methods for their own betterment under existing conditions, or they will turn their attention to scheming and planning for what can be done when they are independent. They certainly will not be fit for independence in the next half dozen or dozen years, probably not in the next score or two score years. Further than this we cannot say. Therefore any promise of independence, any expression by us of our belief that they will ultimately get their independence (though personally this is my belief) means an expression on our part of the belief of what will happen in a future too remote to entitle it to any weight among those working to solve the problems of the actual present; therefore, any such expression as that which your petition calls for would be either misleading (for of course a promise of independence to the Filipinos means to them a promise of independence in a reasonably near future) or else would be a promise to do them the utmost damage we can do — for this is precisely and exactly what granting them their independence in the near future would mean. We are far more necessary to the Filipinos than the Filipinos are to us.

As Hadley has well said, freedom does not mean absence of all restraint. It merely means the substitution of self-restraint for external restraint, and therefore, it can be used only by people capable of self-restraint; and they alone can keep it, or are ethically entitled to it. It is not a matter to be determined by reading Rousseau in the closet, but by studying the needs in each individual case. There are nationalities and tribes wholly unfit for self-government; there are others singularly fitted for it; there are many between the two extremes. Cuba we believed to be fit for it, provided we threw certain safeguards around her, and gave her a short preliminary training. The event has admirably justified our belief. At the time many unwise people wished us to turn Cuba adrift at once, to her own irreparable damage. This we declined to do. We kept her for four years and then gave her independence under certain qualifications. She is now more prosperous than any other Spanish-American republic of approximately the same size. In Santo Domingo a hundred years of freedom, so far from teaching the Santo Domingans how to enjoy freedom and turn it to good account, has resulted so badly that society is on the point of dissolution; and I am now obliged to use every expedient to avert the necessity, or at least to stave off the necessity, of American interference in the island. If I acted purely in accordance with the spirit of altruistic humanitarian duty, I would grant the prayers of the best people of the island and take partial possession of it tomorrow. I do not do this, chiefly because if I did many honest people would misunderstand my purposes and motives; and so I feel obliged to put off the action until the necessity becomes so clear that even the blindest can see it — exactly as because of the shortsightedness of our people we had to put off turning Spain out of Cuba, although the delay meant the sacrifice of hundreds of thousands of lives and the creation of untold misery in the island, until at last the public sentiment became so aroused as to sustain a righteous war.

Now in the Philippines the questions we have to decide are not in the least theoretical. They are entirely practical, and can only be decided if there is knowledge of the facts. The Filipinos are not fit to govern themselves. They are better off in every way now than they ever have been before. They are being given a larger measure of self-government than they ever had before, or than any other Asiatic people except Japan now enjoys. They have immeasurably more individual freedom than they ever enjoyed under Spain, or than they ever could have under Aguinaldo or any other despot — for of course I suppose no one seriously believes that if the Filipinos were free at present their government would represent anything except a vibration between despotism and anarchy. They may, and I personally believe that they will, ultimately become fit for a measure of independence something like that of Cuba; but the surest way to prevent them from so fitting themselves would be to promise them this independence now. Such a promise would mean nothing to them unless it meant independence in a comparatively short time; it would be taken by them to mean this, and this only; and if they afterwards found that it meant something else they would become convinced that we were treacherous and had broken faith. Meanwhile, they would cease from all effort to build themselves up under existing conditions, and would restlessly plot as to what would happen in the future. The result would be somewhat as if a similar course were taken as regards India, Egypt, Algiers or Turkestan.

Don't you think you could come on and see Taft? A more high-minded and disinterested man does not live; and he represents as high-minded and disinterested, aye, and as successful, an effort to help a people as any recorded in history. To mar his work now would be a calamity. *Very sincerely yours*

"I ALMOST LOSE MY TEMPER"

To Kermit Roosevelt

Washington, April 9, 1904

Dear Kermit:

I was very glad to get your letter. David Gray, the author of *Gallops* has been here. Aunty Bye and Mr. Bob Fergy dined here tonight. Mother and I had a lovely ride together this afternoon. The bloodroot and hepaticas are out and spring has really come. Archie has celebrated his tenth birthday today. Mother gave him a tool chest, and at supper he was as cunning as possible with his ten-candle cake.

It is awfully hard work keeping one's temper in public life. Such infamous lies are told. The *World* and *Journal* try to get pictures of poor sister when she is at the races; and the *Army and Navy Journal*, which ought to be a reputable paper, has made as foul and dirty, and as false, an attack on Uncle Will as ever was made by any dog in human form. Continually I am goaded so that I almost lose my temper. But of course my one safety at present and for the next seven months is to refuse to be drawn into any personal controversy or betray any irritation, under no matter what provocation.

Today mother and I went to lunch on the *Mayflower* with good Captain Gleaves. Mother looked so young and pretty in her blue dress and I felt as proud of her as possible. Last night I had to spank Quentin for having taken something that did not belong to him and then not telling the truth about it. Ethel and Mother acted respectively as accuser and court of first resort, and then brought him solemnly in to me for sentence and punishment — both retiring much agitated when the final catastrophe became imminent. Today Quentin has been as cunning as possible. He perfectly understood that he had brought his fate on himself. *Your loving father*

P.S. Good Heavens! The news has just come about your having the mumps. Mother is just starting for Groton to be with you, for I am afraid we cannot get you down here. It was the most unexpected stroke imaginable. How I wish we had kept you!

"A SUM OF SUBSTANTIAL ACHIEVEMENT"

To George Otto Trevelyan

Personal

Washington, May 28, 1904

My dear Sir George:

My blunder in my last letter brought me a better reward than I deserved, because owing to it I have read your son's *Age of Wycliffe* with great pleasure. Pray congratulate him from me upon all that he is doing.

I find reading a great comfort. People often say to me that they do not see how I find time for it, to which I answer them (much more truthfully than they believe) that to me it is a dissipation, which I have sometimes to try to avoid, instead of an irksome duty. Of course I have been so busy for the last ten years, so absorbed in political work, that I have simply given up reading any book that I do not find interesting. But there are a great many books which ordinarily pass for "dry" which to me do possess much interest — notably history and anthropology; and these give me ease and relaxation that I can get in no other way, not even on horseback!

The Presidential campaign is now opening. Apparently I shall be nominated without opposition at the Republican Convention. Whom the Democrats will put up I do not know, and of course no one can forecast the results of the contest at this time. There is one point of inferiority in our system to yours which has been very little touched on, and that is the way in which the Presidential office tends to put a premium upon a man's keeping out of trouble rather than upon his accomplishing results. If a man has a very decided character, has a strongly accentuated career, it is normally the case of course that he makes ardent friends and bitter enemies; and unfortunately human nature is such that more enemies will leave their party because of enmity to its head than friends will come in from the opposite party because they think well of that same head. In consequence, the dark horse, the neutral-tinted individual, is very apt to win against the man of pronounced views and active life. The electorate is very apt to vote with its back to the future! Now all this does not apply to the same extent with your Prime Minister. It is not possible for the politicians to throw over the real party leader and put up a dummy or some gray-tinted person under your system; or at least, though perhaps it is possible, the opportunity and the temptation are much less.

In my own case, for instance, I believe that most of my policies have commanded the support of a great majority of my fellow-countrymen, but in each case I have made a certain number of determined foes. Thus, on Panama I had an overwhelming majority of the country with me; but whereas I am not at all sure that any Democrat will vote for me because of my attitude on Panama, there are a certain number of mug-wumps who will undoubtedly vote against me because of it. So as regards Cuban reciprocity. The country backed me up in the matter, but there is not a Democrat who will vote for me because I got Cuban reciprocity, while there are not a few beet sugar men who will vote against me because of it. In the same way the whole country breathed freer, and felt as if a nightmare had been lifted, when I settled the anthracite coal strike; but the number of votes I shall gain thereby will be small indeed, while the interests to which I gave mortal offense will make their weight felt as of real moment. Thus I could go on indefinitely. However, I certainly would not be willing to hold the Presidency at the cost of failing to do the things which make the real reason why I care to hold it at all. I had much rather be a real President for three years and a half than a figurehead for seven years and a half. I think I can truthfully say that I now have to my credit a sum of substantial achievement — and the rest must take care of itself.

With renewed regard, *Sincerely yours*

SPRINGTIME IN WASHINGTON

To Theodore Roosevelt Jr.

Washington, May 28, 1904

Dear Ted:

That was a first-class victory! I am extremely pleased that Groton won and I am very glad too that George did so well. It was a real pleasure to be at Groton, although I had not looked forward to it as such.

I am having a reasonable amount of work and rather more than a reasonable amount of worry. But after all life is lovely here. The country is beautiful and I do not think that any two people ever got more enjoyment out of the White House than Mother and I. We love the House itself without and within, for its associations, for its stateliness and its simplicity. We love the garden. And we like Washington. We almost always take our breakfast on the south portico now, Mother looking very pretty and dainty in her summer dresses. Then we stroll about the garden for fifteen or twenty minutes looking at the flowers and the fountain and admiring the trees. Then I work until between four and five, usually having some official people to lunch — now a couple of Senators, now a couple of Ambassadors, now a literary man, now a capitalist or a labor leader, or a scientist, or a big-game hunter. If Mother wants to ride, we then spend a couple of hours on horseback. We had a lovely ride up on the Virginia shore since I came back, and yesterday went up Rock Creek and swung back home by the roads where the locust trees were most numerous — for they are now white with blossoms. It is the last great burst of woodland bloom which we shall see this year except the laurels. But there are plenty of flowers in bloom or just coming out, the honeysuckles most conspicuously. The south portico is fragrant with them now. The jasmine will be out later. If we don't ride I walk or play tennis. But I am afraid Ted has gotten out of his father's class in tennis! *Ever yours*

THE RISE OF JAPAN

To Cecil Spring-Rice

Personal — Be very careful that no one gets a chance to see this.
                                  Washington, June 13, 1904
Dear Cecil:
    Like everyone else I, of course, continue to be immensely interested in the war in the East. Do you recollect some of the letters I have written you in the past about Russia? I never anticipated in the least such a rise as this of Japan's, but I have never been able to make myself afraid of Russia in the present. I like the Russian people and believe in them. I earnestly hope that after the fiery ordeal through which they are now passing they will come forth faced in the right way for doing well in the future. But I see nothing of permanent good that can come to Russia, either for herself or for the rest of the

world, until her people begin to tread the path of orderly free-dom, of civil liberty, and of a measure of self-government. Whatever may be the theoretical advantages of a despotism, they are incompatible with the growth of intelligence and in-dividuality in a civilized people. Either there must be stagna-tion in the Russian people, or there must be what I should hope would be a gradual, but a very real, growth of govern-mental institutions to meet the growth in, and the capacity and need for, liberty.

The other day the Japanese Minister here and Baron Kaneko, a Harvard graduate, lunched with me and we had a most in-teresting talk. I told them that I thought their chief danger was lest Japan might get the "big head" and enter into a general career of insolence and aggression; that such a career would undoubtedly be temporarily very unpleasant to the rest of the world, but that it would in the end be still more unpleasant for Japan. I added that though I felt there was a possibility of this happening, I did not think it probable, because I was a firm believer in the Japanese people, and that I most earnestly hoped as well as believed that Japan would simply take her place from now on among the great civilized nations, with, like each of these nations, something to teach others as well as something to learn from them; with, of course, a para-mount interest in what surrounds the Yellow Sea, just as the United States has a paramount interest in what surrounds the Caribbean, but with, I hoped, no more desire for conquest of the weak than we had shown ourselves to have in the case of Cuba, and no more desire for a truculent attitude toward the strong than we had shown with reference to the English and French West Indies. Both of them, I found, took exactly my view, excepting that they did not believe there was any danger of Japan's becoming intoxicated with the victory, because they were convinced that the upper and influential class would not let them, and would show the same caution and decision which has made them so formidable in this war. They then both proceeded to inveigh evidently with much feeling, against the talk about the Yellow Terror, explaining that in the 13th century they had had to dread the Yellow Terror of the Mongolians as much as Europe itself, and that as their aspi-rations were in every way to become part of the circle of civilized mankind, a place to which they were entitled by over two thousand years of civilization of their own, they did not see why they should be classed as barbarians. I told them that I entirely agreed with them; that without question some of my own ancestors in the 10th century had been part of the "white terror" of the Northmen, a terror to which we now look back with romantic satisfaction, but which represented everything hideous and abhorrent and unspeakably dreadful to the people of Ireland, England and France at that time; and that as we had outgrown the position of being a White Terror I thought that in similar fashion such a civilization as they had developed entitled them to laugh at the accusation of being part of the Yellow Terror. Of course they earnestly assured me that all talk of Japan's even thinking of the Philippines was nonsense. I told them that I was quite sure this was true; that I should certainly do all in my power to avoid giving Japan or any other nation an excuse for aggression; that if aggression come I believed we would be quite competent to defend ourselves. I then said that as far as I was concerned I hoped to see China kept together, and would gladly welcome any part played by Japan which would tend to bring China forward along the road which Japan trod, because I thought it for the interest of all the world that each part of the world should be prosperous and well policed; I added that unless everybody was mistaken in the Chinese character I thought they would have their hands full in mastering it — at which they grinned and said that they were quite aware of the difficulty they were going to have even in Korea and were satisfied with that job. They then began to discuss with me the outcome of the war if they were successful in taking Port Arthur and definitely establishing the upper hand in Manchuria over the Russians. They said that they were afraid the Russians would not keep any promises they made, in view of what I was obliged to admit, namely: the fact that the Russians have for the last three years been following out a consistent career of stupendous mendacity, not only with Japan but with ourselves, as regards Manchuria. It was evident from what the Minister said that their hope is to get the Russians completely out of Manchuria and to turn it over to the Chinese, but that he was not sure whether the Chinese would be strong enough to support themselves. I said that of course if we could get a Chinese Viceroy able to keep definite order under the guarantee of the Powers in Manchuria, that would be the best outcome; but that I did not know whether this was possible, or whether the powers would even consider such an idea. The Minister was evidently very anxious that there should be a general international agreement to guarantee the autonomy of China in Manchuria. Some of the things he said I do not wish to put down on paper — which may astonish you in view of what I fear diplomats would regard as the frankness of this letter anyhow.

Well, my troubles will be domestic I suppose for the next few months. By the end of this month I shall probably be nominated for President by the republican convention. How the election will come out I do not know, but in any event I shall feel that I have had a most enjoyable three years and a half in the White House, and that I have accomplished a certain amount of permanent work for the nation.

Give my love to the future Mrs. Spring Rice. Mrs. Roosevelt sends you hers. *Always yours*

P.S. Don't understand from the above that I was laying the ground for any kind of interference by this government in the Far East. The Japanese themselves spoke purely hypothetically as to whether circumstances would arise to warrant such interference, even to the extent of the offer of good services to both parties, and I explained that I could not say that so much as this offer could be made. I was immensely interested to find out the way in which their minds were working.

Of course, in many ways the civilization of the Japs is very alien to ours. I told Takahira and Kaneko that I thought we had to learn from them many things, especially as to the misery in our great cities, but that in return they had to learn from us the ideal of the proper way of treating womanhood. Both cordially agreed with me — whether from mere politeness or not I cannot say.

The Japs interest me and I like them. I am perfectly well aware that if they win out it may possibly mean a struggle between them and us in the future; but I hope not and believe not. At any rate, Russia's course during the past three years has made it evident that if she wins she will organize northern

China against us and rule us absolutely out of all the ground she can control. Therefore, on the score of mere national self-interest, we would not be justified in balancing the certainty of immediate damage against the possibility of future damage. However, this was merely an academic question anyhow, as there was nothing whatever to warrant us going to war on behalf of either side, or doing otherwise than observe a strict neutrality, which we have done. The good will of our people has been with the Japanese, but the government has been scrupulous in its impartiality between the combatants. As I have said before, I like the Russians; but I do not think they can ever take the place they should take until they gain a measure of civil liberty and self-government such as Occidental nations have. I am not much affected by the statement that the Japanese are of an utterly different race from ourselves and that the Russians are of the same race. I suppose we have all outgrown the belief that language and race have anything to do with one another; and the more I see of life the more I feel that while there are some peoples of a very low standard from whom nothing can be expected, yet that there are others, widely different one from the other, which, nevertheless, stand about on an equality in the proportions of bad and good which they contain — and a good man is a good man and a bad man a bad man wherever they are found. I know certain southern Frenchmen like Jusserand, for instance, (the Ambassador here) and certain Scandinavians like Nansen, or for the matter of that, certain Americans like Peary, who in physical habit of body are as far apart as either is from a Japanese gentleman. Yet they are good fellows, with all the essentials in common, because they have the same conscience and the same cultural creed. Of course, the modern Turks are not Mongolians at all. In the eyes of the physiologist they are just as much white people as the Balkan Christians, or as the Russians, and physiologically they do not differ any more from Danes, Englishmen, Swiss, or Italians, than the latter differ among themselves. But they are absolutely alien because of their creed, their culture, their historic associations, and inherited governmental and social tendencies. Therefore, they are a curse to Europe, and the curse is not mitigated in the least by the fact that by blood they do not differ any more from the European peoples who speak an Aryan tongue than do, for instance, those excellent members of the European body politic, the Magyars, Finns and Basques, all of whom likewise speak non-Aryan tongues. The Turks are ethnically closer to us than the Japanese, but they are impossible members of our international society, while I think the Japs may be desirable additions. That there are large classes of the Japanese who will sometimes go wrong, that Japan as a whole will sometimes go wrong, I do not doubt. The same is true of my own beloved country. I do not anticipate that Tokyo will show a superior morality to that which obtains in Berlin, Vienna and Paris, not to speak of London and Washington, or of St. Petersburg. But I see nothing ruinous to civilization in the advent of the Japanese to power among the great nations.

SOUTHERN REPRESENTATION

To Lyman Abbott

Personal

Oyster Bay, July 26, 1904

My dear Dr. Abbott:

I was much interested in that statement from the *Spectator*, quoted by you in your last number. The writer, whoever he was, has exactly got what I think is my mental attitude. Normally I disbelieve in the extreme view, the fanatical view. For instance I would not be willing to die for what I regard as the untrue abstract statement that all men are in all respects equal, and are all alike entitled to the same power; but I would be quite willing to die — or better still, to fight so effectively that I should live — for the proposition that each man has certain rights which no other man should be allowed to take away from him, and that in certain great and vital matters all men should be treated as equal before the law and before the bar of public opinion. In government generally I have a feeling of distaste and impatience for those who indulge in declamatory statements about an impossible righteousness; but I believe that a high standard of righteousness is eminently possible, and I should be entirely willing to face any defeat in fighting for such a standard.

Now, a word about another article in the same *Outlook*, that referring to the plank in the Republican platform about representation in Congress, which of course meant primarily representation from the Southern States. I knew nothing of this plank, and had I been consulted would have advised strongly against putting it in for the simple reason that I think there are too many people who feel just as the *Outlook* feels about it, and that where a wrong cannot be remedied it is not worth while to sputter about it; but while the verbiage of the plank is clumsy, I think its meaning is entirely moral, and the thing that astounds me is the queer dough-faced indifference with which the North submits on this matter. Take John Sharp Williams, for instance. He represents a district in which there are 48,000 whites and 143,000 blacks. That is, for every white man like John Sharp Williams there are three colored men. He and his fellow whites have suppressed this colored vote so absolutely by force, by fraud, by every species of iniquity (and I am not speaking at random; I am simply repeating what John Sharp Williams' leading constituents frankly told me when I was in Mississippi a couple of years ago), that it is not only not worth while for a colored man to vote, but it is not worth while for a white man to vote after the Democrats have nominated their candidate. At the last election Williams did not have a single vote against him, and but 1400 for him; and with what I feel is peculiarly repulsive hypocrisy, he whose very political existence is the negation of the Declaration of Independence, who could not stay one hour in politics if he did not refuse to take the consent of three-fourths of his constituents in governing themselves — if he did not in his own district treat the "consent of the governed" theory as the veriest nonsense — this man comes to Congress and declaims against our policy in the Philippines on the ground that it is a contravention of the Declaration of Independence and of the "consent of the governed" theory! Why, if he would head a movement to give the colored people of his own district but a fraction of the rights that we have already given the Philippine people, I should feel that the race question in the South was well on the way toward solution. But instead of this he stands at home as the representative of those who would deny to the negro, not only the right to vote, but the right to hold any office or do any work which a white man wants to hold or to do.

Now, there are two sides to this. In the first place there is the fact that John Sharp Williams' existence in Congress means the cynical violation of the Fifteenth Amendment. Mississippi has an entire right to establish any qualifications for its voters. If in Williams' district the three black men, whose votes he first suppresses, and then casts for them, are incompetent to vote; if they are too ignorant, or too thriftless, or too criminal, or too foolish to be able to exercise their responsibility aright, why of course let them be refused the right to vote; but let them be refused, not because of the color of their skins but because of their unfitness, and let us hold the same standard for black and for white alike. Is this not fair? Can we afford, as a people, permanently to occupy any other ground?

But more than this; aside from the question of the injustice done the black, is the injustice done the white man in the North or in such portions of the South as eastern Tennessee, western North Carolina, and western Virginia. Williams has the same right in law and in morals to have his vote count in every way that any man in the North has. His vote, no matter how foolishly he chooses to exercise it, must be counted as equal to that of any voter in Indiana or Massachusetts; but he has no right, either in law or in morals, to have his vote counted so as to equal the votes of four white men in Indiana or Massachusetts. Yet this is just precisely what now happens. Surely so gross a travesty on the rights and duties of man under a system of popular government cannot permanently obtain.

Now, I am well aware that there are plenty of things which are wrong, which nevertheless it may be impossible at the moment to change, and that we are bound in such cases to face facts as they are, to make the best of a bad business. But if the issue is forced upon me, I shall certainly not hesitate to meet it; and it seems to me that if one has to speak about it, there is but one way in which it is possible to speak of it.

I have written you thus frankly in the midst of a political

campaign, where I have nothing to gain and everything to lose by any agitation of the race question, because while I want to win out if I legitimately can, there are some great fundamental questions that interest me a great deal more than any possible success or defeat of mine. You will have noticed that in my speech of acceptance I did not touch upon this matter at all. If I can avoid touching upon it and retain my self-respect, I shall do so; but I have not the slightest question as to what the right of the matter is, or as to what should be done if it were possible. *Faithfully yours*

By the way, the assertion that McKinley brought up the friendly feeling of the South is fiction. In 1896 the South was more friendly to him than in 1900. The South was the only section in which McKinley's vote fell off and Bryan's increased in 1900.

HONORING UNION VETERANS

To Oliver Otis Howard

Washington, August 6, 1904

My dear General Howard:

It is a matter of keen regret to me that I am unable to be present at the annual encampment of the Grand Army in Boston this summer. I have already written the Commander in Chief of the Grand Army, General Black, and the Chairman of the Invitation Committee, General Blackmar, expressing my regret. To you, with whom I have been thrown into associations of affectionate respect, and with whom I have consulted in reference to so many of the governmental problems affecting our Nation, I wish to send a special note and I ask you to say to your comrades of the great days of '61 to '65 a word to tell them that I feel a sense of real and personal loss at my inability to be present and to see them pass in review and to wish them well. Ever since the days when, at the close of the War, the armies of Grant and of Sherman marched up the streets of the National Capital, the great march in review of the veterans of the Civil War at the national encampments where they have been gathered together has been something to thrill the blood of every younger man. The lessons that you and your comrades taught us, alike in peace and in war, lay down for us and the younger generation the lines along which we must steadfastly strive to do our work for the honor and the interest of the Nation. *Faithfully yours*

GOO-GOOS AND TAMMANY

To John Hay

Personal

Washington, August 12, 1904

Dear John:

Some of the developments of this campaign are too deliciously funny for anything. The professional goo-goo, the professionally and virtuous neurotic of the Carl Schurz–*Evening Post* stamp (for the New York *Times* type of individual combines professional virtue with practical venality, and therefore comes in a different but not much lower category) — some of these professionally virtuous impracticables are supporting Parker on the ground that he and the Democracy represent a higher type of morality than I and the Republican party represent. Of course their main hope in New York is Tammany, and in Indiana the Chairman of their National Committee, the genial Tom Taggart. Tom Taggart has always, and with cynical openness, stood as the embodied representative of corruption in politics; and he was made Chairman of the National Democratic Committee because it was believed that he might be able to buy up Indiana. As for Tammany, it always counts at least upon twenty thousand votes which it will obtain by colonization, ballot-box stuffing, bribery, violence, etc., etc. In Tammany, all these methods of obtaining votes are treated, not merely as legitimate, but as being the methods which are to be used by every adherent of the party who expects to be considered genuinely loyal to the party ticket. The *Evening*

Post and Carl Schurz are counting upon the loyalty of Tammany and Tom Taggart with the full knowledge that that loyalty finds its expression in corruption and fraud. It is Blifil sniveling in the sanctum of the *Nation*, while Black George crams the cheap lodging houses of the Bowery with repeaters.

A couple of deliciously unconscious portrayals of this state of things were recently furnished me, one by ex-Congressman Bynum, the Gold Democrat of Indiana, and the other by Mike Dady, the Republican sub-boss from Brooklyn. Bynum came to me, out of the kindness of his heart, to reassure me, and said in entire good faith, "Mr. President, Taggart is not nearly as formidable as those men think, for aside from the money he has obtained from his gambling houses, most of his fortune has come from moneys he has received for running campaigns which he has kept for his own purposes. He is a very expensive campaign manager, and always keeps for himself a large proportion of the funds placed in his hands. I think this will offset the fact that he will probably get much more money this year than the Democrats have obtained for a long time!"

Mike Dady called me aside, and in great secrecy told me as follows:

"On Monday night Tim Sullivan (Dry Dollar Sullivan, a Tammany leader who has always been fond of me, partly because of kindred tastes in the matter of prize fights) came to my house and said that I was to tell you, when I came to Washington, from him, that you need not be at all alarmed about New York, because he was going to do his best to see to it that Tammany men were instructed none of them to commit any offense which would expose them to being put in the penitentiary in the interest of Parker's success." Not only Sullivan but Dady regarded this as being symptomatic of a great breakdown in the Tammany vote, and as being equivalent on the part of Sullivan to practically bolting Tammany in my interest! *Ever yours*

BEARS AND TIN CANS
To John Burroughs

Washington, August 12, 1904

Dear Oom John:

I think that nothing is more amusing and interesting than the development of the changes made in wild beast character by the wholly unprecedented course of things in the Yellowstone Park. I have just had a letter from Buffalo Jones, describing his experiences in trying to get tin cans off the feet of the bears in the Yellowstone Park. There are lots of tin cans in the garbage heaps which the bears muss over, and it has now become fairly common for a bear to get his paw so caught in a tin can that he cannot get it off, and of course great pain and injury follow. Buffalo Jones was sent with another scout to capture, tie up and cure these bears. He roped two and got the can off of one, but the other tore himself loose, can and all, and escaped, owing, as Jones bitterly insists, to the failure of duty on the part of one of his brother scouts, whom he sneers at as "a foreigner." Think of the grizzly bear of the early Rocky Mountain hunters and explorers, and then think of the fact that part of the recognized duties of the scouts in the Yellowstone Park at this moment is to catch this same grizzly bear and remove tin cans from the bear's paws in the bear's interest!

The grounds of the White House are lovely now, and the most decorative birds in them are some redheaded woodpeckers.

Give my regards to Mrs. Burroughs. How I wish I could see you at Slabsides! But of course this summer there is no chance of that. *Always yours*

THE HYSTERIA OF TOLSTOI

To Robert Grant

Personal

Oyster Bay, September 1, 1904

Dear Bob:

I have received both your notes. I wish there was any such chance of rest ahead of me as a visit to you, but it is simply out of the question. I shall have to wait until you can come to Washington.

I am much amused over the indignation of both Sioux Falls and Sioux City. *Faithfully yours*

P.S. I send you a queer letter I have received, which I shall ask you to return after reading it. I did not answer the man, thinking it might have been a campaign trick, but I have half a mind after election sending him a short note, expressing in great plainness my view about him and the young lady and gentleman to whom he refers. The older I grow the more profound is my disbelief in the hysterical and morbid type of reformer; and these two are Tolstoi's attitudes on many subjects. He sees the evils of unjust war, and says what is of course true, that in any just war there are attendant evils. He could go further. You cannot build a railroad; you cannot clear or till a farm, without doing some incidental damage. To declaim against all war as immoral is in itself as fundamentally immoral as to declare against all industry because there is an immense amount of evil in most industrial enterprises and an immense amount of sordidness and selfishness inevitable to the average industrial life. So he declaims against marriage because there are hideous evils attendant upon unregulated or twisted passion. I have always regarded his books, *My Religion* and the *Kreutzer Sonata* as supplementary to one another. The man has a diseased mind. He is not wholesome. He is not sane; and therefore, being prone to hysterical excess of a wicked kind, he atones for it by hysterical assault on the good qualities which can be abused into being bad qualities.

CATHOLIC PRESIDENTS

To Eugene A. Philbin

Personal

Oyster Bay, September 10, 1904

My dear Mr. Philbin:

I think your advice most sound. Of course if people were reasonable they could understand, because they could not possibly misunderstand, my attitude, which is simply that I am not favoring Catholics any more than I am favoring Protestants; that I am simply acting as any decent man should by treating them exactly alike — just as I do in my social relations, for instance, where the fact that such good friends of mine as Grant La Farge and Gussie Montant are Catholics never enters my head from one year's end to another. But unfortunately there are bigots of my own faith who utterly fail to realize this simple fact. I have been rather amused at seeing how some very good and broad men shied off from the suggestion in my letter about Catholic Presidents. Now, I not only hope, but believe, that this country will last with substantially its present form of popular government for many centuries. If so, there will be many Catholic Presidents. I trust that if any one of these Catholic Presidents happens to know anything of me or my conduct, he will feel that I have acted along just the lines that he can afford to set. In 1884, by the way, I was engaged in a movement, which proved abortive, to see if we could not nominate Phil Sheridan for the Presidency.

Young Hammond has sent a very excellent letter to the papers about my removal of Asa Bird Gardiner, that amiable Colonial Dame, which I wish you would look at. *Faithfully yours*

THE INFAMY OF JEFFERSON DAVIS

To George McClellan Harvey

Personal and confidential

Oyster Bay, September 19, 1904

My dear Colonel Harvey:

I do not think it well to go into any controversy on that matter, and I shall ask you to treat this letter as for your own personal information merely and not in any way for publication. I certainly cannot be put in the attitude of in any way apologizing for or regretting anything I have said about Jefferson Davis; but as my views about him are not of active moment in the present campaign, I do not think it necessary to bring them in at all. So that what I am about to write is for your private information merely.

I have always drawn a sharp line between the men who intrigued for secession and the men who, like Lee, when the Civil War was on went with their section. If secession was not a crime, if it was not a black offense against humanity to strive to break up this great republic in the interest of the perpetuation of slavery, then it is impossible ever to commit any political crime, and there is no difference between good men and bad men in history. Jefferson Davis for many years had intrigued for secession — had intrigued for the destruction of this republic in the interest of slavery; and the evidence is overwhelming to my mind that in this course he was largely influenced by the eager desire to gratify his own ambition.

If you will turn to Scott's *Memoirs* you will see that he championed the repudiation of the Mississippi bonds. I never referred to his private financial conduct.

In a public utterance of mine some eighteen or twenty years ago, I grouped together Jefferson Davis and Benedict Arnold. As a matter of pure morals I think I was right. Jefferson Davis was an unhung traitor. He did not, like Benedict Arnold, receive money for his treachery, but he received office instead. The difference is one of degree, not of kind. The two men stand on an evil eminence of infamy in our history. They occupy the two foremost positions in the small group of Americans which also numbers the names of Aaron Burr, of Wilkinson, of Floyd. As a matter of exact historic accuracy I later came to the conclusion that Jefferson Davis did not divide the first position with Benedict Arnold, but that if one were to draw degrees of infamy, he should come second; that is, taking into account his prominence and his crime, he came behind Benedict Arnold and ahead of Aaron Burr and Wilkinson on the roll of dishonor. In my *Winning of the West* you will see that when I spoke of the different secessionists who had been prominent in our country, I coupled him with Aaron Burr.

Now, this is my personal belief. If it became necessary for me to give expression to this belief I should do so, but it is not necessary for me to say anything about it now and therefore I shall not.

If you will turn to what I said of Lee in my *Life of Thomas Hart Benton*, or to what I have said about southerners and ex-confederates in speech after speech in the volume of my speeches which I enclose to you, you will see that I have been generous in speaking of them. While as a public man I expect to preserve proper reticence in what I say, yet people may as well understand that I have not the slightest apology to offer for having, as a historian, told the truth as I saw it. It is not my business now to speak of secession any more than to speak of the alien and sedition acts; but when I, in my writings, touch on secession, I shall say about it what I really feel, and I shall speak of its leaders as I think they deserve.

Jefferson Davis wrote me a letter of violent protest after I had made the statement in question. I thought it most undignified of him to write me at all, and of course it would have been simply silly to have entered into an argument with him as to whether his conduct did or did not compare unfavorably with that of Benedict Arnold; and I wrote him back that I must decline to enter into any controversy with him of any kind, sort or description. I cannot at the moment give you more than the substance of my letter, though I think I somewhere have preserved both his letter and a copy of my answer thereto, and if I can find them will send you copies; but as I say, I do not think it proper to go into any public discussion of the matter whatsoever.

I venture to send you a copy of my *Rough Riders*, and ask

that you look at the last appendix, in view of the statements of some of the Democratic southern press that I was not at the battle of San Juan Hill at all, was not under fire, and did not see a Spaniard that day. You will notice that these letters were written by regular army officers, recommending me for a Congressional medal of honor. On the day in question my regiment suffered a greater percentage of loss than any one of the twenty-two out of the twenty-four regular regiments engaged; and a greater loss than all the other volunteer regiments put together. *Sincerely yours*

PIONEERS AND THE SECOND-RATE

To Oliver Wendell Holmes

Personal

Washington, October 21, 1904

My dear Judge:

I have read the Montesquieu pamphlet with the utmost interest, and return it herewith. I appreciate your having sent it to me. I think that an immense idea of yours, that in one sense it is only the second-rate that lasts, and that the greatest works of intellect soon lose all but their historic interest. In other words, the man who writes of what is deepest, about what goes below the surface, must be only a pioneer as regards those who come after him, no matter how much he may have profited by and improved upon the work of those who were ahead of him. Of course what you call, for convenience's sake, the second-class, may be very good indeed, and in its own way the first-class. Thus Macaulay and Sydney Smith may very possibly be read with interest and profit a couple of thousand years hence, if anybody then knows English, and if all our books have not vanished. But Darwin, who was one of the chief factors in working a tremendous intellectual revolution, will be read then just as we read Lucretius now; that is, because of the interest attaching to his position in history, in spite of the fact that his own work will have been superseded by the work of the very men to whom it pointed out the way.

As a side issue, don't you think Bagehot failed to see that George III was really much more of an executive than the Prime Minister of the day, and that the founders of our Constitution of course had the English King, as he actually was at the moment, in mind?

It was delightful seeing you last night. Remember to tell Mrs. Holmes what we said. *Faithfully yours*

THE PRESIDENTIAL CAMPAIGN

To Kermit Roosevelt

Washington, October 26, 1904

Blessed Kermit:

Mother read me your letter in which you want a "list of the doubtful states," so I am going to write you a letter about nothing but politics. I enclose you a check for $5.00, with which you can celebrate after election if we win, or console yourself if we lose.

In the first place, be sure not to leave this letter about where any janitor or anyone else could get a glimpse of it and make public the information. It wouldn't do to have our opponents get hold of it, because they would be sure to twist and garble it.

On the whole this has been an easy campaign for me, because my real campaign work has been done during the three years that I have been President; in other words, I am content to stand or fall on the record I have made in these three years, and the bulk of the voters will oppose or support me on that record and will be only secondarily influenced by what is done during the campaign proper. There remains, however, a sufficient mass of voters to decide the campaign overwhelmingly one way or the other, who have to be aroused from apathy and forced to vote or converted or kept from going over to the enemy, and it is to influence these voters that the active management of the campaign has been directed. In the campaign proper I made my letter and my speech which have, I think, formed the basis of our line of attack, and I have taken a hand in what I regarded as crises, as for instance, in getting Taft to have Luke Wright cable over denials of Parker's falsehoods about the Philippines, in furnishing Knox most of the statement, and getting him to make the remainder of the statement, which he delivered yesterday so effectively smashing Parker because of his attitude on the trust question, in getting the Treasury statement ready showing how Parker has misstated the facts about our expenditures, etc., etc. But, speaking generally, I have not had to do much actual work because of the campaign. As you know, while at Oyster Bay I was really freer and able to enjoy myself more than in previous summers. In a sense, however, this freedom from work has meant more worry, because I have felt as if I was lying still under shell fire just as on the afternoon of the first of July at Santiago. I have continually wished that I could be on the stump myself, and during the last week or ten days I have been fretted at my inability to hit back, and to take the offensive in person against Parker. He lays himself wide open and I could cut him into ribbons if I could get at him in the open. But of course a President can't go on the stump and can't indulge in personalities, and so I have to sit still and abide the result. I shall be heartily glad when the next two weeks are over and the election is decided one way or the other. I am the first Vice-President who became President by the death of his predecessor, who has ever been nominated for the Presidential office. This is no small triumph in itself. As the result of my being President I at least won the unquestioned headship in my own party, and I have to my credit a big sum of substantive achievement — the Panama Canal, the creation of the Department of Commerce and Labor with the Bureau of Corporations, the settlement of the Alaska boundary, the settlement of the Venezuela trouble through the Hague Commission, the success of my policy in Cuba, the success of my policy in the Philippines, the Anthracite Coal Strike, the success of such suits as that against the Northern Securities Company which gave a guaranty in this country that rich man and poor man alike were held equal before the law, and my action in the so-called Miller case which gave to trades-unions a lesson that had been taught corporations — that I favored them while they did right and was not in the least afraid of them when they did wrong.

Now as to the election chances: At present it looks as if the odds were in my favor, but I have no idea whether this appearance is deceptive or not. I am a very positive man and Parker is a very negative man, and in consequence I both attract supporters and make enemies that he does not in a way that he cannot. He can be painted any color to please any audience; but it is impossible to make two different pictures of any side of my character. I have done a great many things and said a great many things; and a great many people who like my general course dislike some particular thing I have said or done. Often people are against me for directly conflicting reasons. Thus, the *Evening Post* and Carl Schurz profess loud sympathy for my attitude toward the colored man of the South, but in spite of this oppose me because of my attitude toward the Filipinos. On the other hand, *Collier's Weekly* and a much larger body of men profess great sympathy with my attitude toward the Filipino, but attack me because of my attitude toward the colored man of the South. These two sets of people are therefore diametrically opposed to one another, and for diametrically opposite reasons unite on the one point of opposing me. As a matter of fact I am right both as regards the point upon which the *Evening Post* attacks me and as regards the point upon which *Collier's Weekly* attacks me! but the fact that I am right does not alter the further fact that because of my attitude on both points I lose a certain number of votes. In the same way the great capitalists who object to any restraint being exercised over the deeds of corporations oppose me, while the rather hysterical men who want to go to lengths against capital, and especially against corporate wealth which would bring ruin to this country also oppose me. So it is in many other matters.

There are thus many conflicting currents of feeling. I will have accessions of strength of unknown force, and I have repelled interests whose actual effect on election day we cannot now reckon. It is, therefore, utterly impossible to say what the outcome will be. The betting is in my favor, and our people are very confident that I will be elected. Some of our opponents are not so confident in Parker's success, but those at headquarters undoubtedly are. Moreover, in the next ten days there is always the possibility that something will happen that will upset all calculations. So what I am about to say you must remember is a guess only and I may be hopelessly wrong at that, but you shall have my guess in detail as to actual conditions.

We need 239 votes in the electoral college to give me a majority. Of these I think we are practically sure to have 200 from the following states: California 10, Illinois 27, Iowa 13, Kansas 10, Maine 6, Massachusetts 16, Michigan 14, Minnesota 11, Nebraska 8, New Hampshire 4, North Dakota 4, Ohio 23, Oregon 4, Pennsylvania 34, South Dakota 4, Vermont 4, Washington 5, Wyoming 3. Then in addition it looks now as though we should probably carry the states of Wisconsin 13, Utah 3, Connecticut 7, New Jersey 12, Idaho 3, which number 38 votes all told. This leaves us just one short of a majority, and we now come into the region of entire doubt. I should put the following states as doubtful: New York 39, Rhode Island 4, Delaware 3, Indiana 15, West Virginia 7, Colorado 5, Montana 3, Nevada 3, 79 votes. If we get all those I have enumerated as sure and as probably our way and also any one of these doubtful states we win. Then, in addition, there is a very small chance of carrying Nevada or Maryland, and an even smaller chance of carrying Missouri; but in all probability these three states will vote in company with the eleven ex-Confederate states, which are solidly Democratic because there is in reality no popular election in them and their Democratic majorities represent a mixture of force and fraud.

From the above you will see how difficult it is to make anything like a certain guess. In New York the revolt against what people call, without exactly understanding it, Odellism threatens defeat to the State ticket, although our nominee, Higgins, is a most admirable man. If it were not for this revolt I am very sure I should carry New York by a large majority; but it is perfectly possible that the revolt may bring me down in ruin as well as Higgins, although I hope the contrary will take place and that instead of the State ticket pulling me down to defeat I shall pull through the State ticket to victory. Indiana ought to go our way, but Bryan has made a most telling canvass there for Parker, while Cleveland has helped Parker in the East. You see the Democratic canvass is absolutely double-faced. In the East they are trying to get everybody to vote for them on the ground that if Parker and his people keep control of the Democratic organization it means the death of Bryanism. In the West they try to get votes by saying that the success of Parker really means the success of Bryanism and Bryan's ultimate mastery of the party which will control the country.

So, Kermit, we shall know nothing about the result until the votes are counted, and in the meanwhile must possess our souls in patience. If things go wrong remember that we are very, very fortunate to have had three years in the White House, and that I have had a chance to accomplish work such as comes to very, very few men in any generation; and that I have no business to feel downcast or querulous merely because when so much has been given me I have not had even more. *Your loving father*

CONGRESS AND APPOINTMENTS

To Augustus Peabody Gardner

Washington, October 28, 1904

My dear Congressman:

I have received your letter concerning the appointment of a postmaster at Haverhill, where Attorney General Moody, your predecessor, who has served in my Cabinet successively as Secretary of the Navy and now as Attorney General, has recommended that the present incumbent be reappointed; this present incumbent being a man admitted by everyone to have the character and capacity which fit him for the place, and being, from all I can find out, entirely satisfactory to the people of Haverhill. He was appointed by President McKinley, at the suggestion of the secretary, then congressman [   ]

You speak of your "privilege of naming the Haverhill postmaster." In your letter to Mr. Moody you say, "It is not a parallel case in Massachusetts to those other States where Senators select the postmasters. In Massachusetts it has been understood that a Congressman shall select the postmasters in the cities and towns in his own district." To clear up any possible misapprehension, I would like, at the outset, to say that the Senators do not select postmasters in any State while I am President. I consult them always, and in the vast majority of cases act on the recommendations they make; but the selection is mine and not theirs, and time and again during the three years I have been President I have positively refused to select individuals suggested to me for nomination as postmaster by various Senators. If I am not satisfied with the character and standing of the man whose name is suggested to me I never nominate him. I understand perfectly that under the first article of the Constitution the Senators are part of the appointing power, and that they have the same right to reject that I have to nominate, and that therefore the appointment must represent an agreement between them and me; and as the acquaintance of the Senator with his State is always much greater than the knowledge of the President can possibly be, it is the normal and natural thing that I should listen to his advice as to these appointments, and I generally do so. But I stop listening to it as soon as I realize that he is advising me wrongly. While it is impossible to avoid mistakes in nominating thousands of candidates to local offices on the advice of hundreds of different advisers, yet I never knowingly nominate a candidate whom I think unfit, or to whose candidacy I think there is good objection; and the question of unfitness I regard as one to be determined by my judgment and not that of the Senator. My practice during the last three years has been exactly that set forth in this statement; and I may add that repeatedly I have refused to nominate, at the request of some Senator, a man to succeed some public servant who I felt had peculiar claims to be renominated, or whom I regarded as markedly superior to his proposed successor.

So much as to my relations with my Constitutional advisers. But the relation of a Congressman to those appointments rests not upon law but purely upon custom. It has been found in the actual working of our Government that, as a rule, the Congressman is the best man to consult about the appointments which come under his special ken. Someone must be consulted, and as a rule the Congressman is the man whose advice is most apt to be that which can be followed with advantage to the community, and therefore to the party. But this is a mere custom, and I have never hesitated for a moment to deviate from it whenever circumstances arose that satisfied me it was wise and proper and in the interest of the community to do so. In scores of cases I have been obliged to disregard the recommendations of Congressmen for all kinds of reasons. Usually I have disregarded them because I have believed that the man recommended to me was unfit. Occasionally I have disregarded them because I felt that the man who was in office was so conspicuously fit that he ought to be retained.

Holding in mind that the recommendation of the Congressman is merely a matter of custom, I wish to point out to you that it is also the custom to pay heed to the wishes not only of Cabinet officers, but even of Senators of the opposite party, and occasionally to the wishes of Congressmen of the opposite party, in the case of nominations to office in their own towns. In such cases I have sometimes nominated the man requested by a Democratic Senator, for instance (always provided I regarded him as fit for the position), and even where I have not done this I have generally consulted him about the man whom I did appoint. That I should consult one of the members of my own Cabinet in reference to the postmaster of his own city ought to go without saying.

After carefully considering all the circumstances I feel that the wise and proper thing is to nominate Mr. Pinkham to succeed himself. I intend to nominate him because he is a thoroughly fit man, who has been an excellent postmaster, who is of good standing in the community, whose retention in office will undoubtedly be agreeable to the bulk of the patrons of the office, and whose reappointment is asked for by the Attorney General, himself a citizen of Haverhill, who, when in Congress as your predecessor, secured the appointment of this man to office by President McKinley.

I regret to have to take any action which will be displeasing to you; but I do not see how I can avoid doing so in this case. *Sincerely yours*

"I HAVE HAD A FIRST-CLASS RUN"

To Rudyard Kipling

Personal

Washington, November 1, 1904

Dear Kipling:

That was awfully good of you, and I never dreamed that you would have taken such trouble or I should not have spoken of the matter to Doubleday. I am greatly obliged for the stories. Do not think me altogether a prig if I say that I have been obliged to think so seriously of many things that I am apt to like to have a story contain a moral — provided always that the story has the prime quality of interest.

We are now closing the campaign, and the Lord only knows how it will go. I have done a good many things in the past three years, and the fact that I did them is doubtless due partly to accident and partly to temperament. Naturally, I think that I was right in doing them, for otherwise I would not have done them. It is equally natural that some people should have been alienated by each thing I did, and the aggregate of all that have been alienated may be more than sufficient to overthrow me. Thus, in dealing with the Philippines I have first the jack fools who seriously think that any group of pirates and head-hunters needs nothing but independence in order that it may be turned forthwith into a dark-hued New England town meeting; and then the entirely practical creatures who join with these extremists because I do not intend that the islands shall be exploited for corrupt purposes. So in Panama, I have to encounter the opposition of the vague individuals of serious mind and limited imagination, who think that a corrupt pithecoid community in which the President has obtained his position by the simple process of clapping the former President into a wooden cage and sending him on an ox cart over the mountains (this is literally what was done at Bogota) — is entitled to just the treatment that I would give, say, to Denmark or Switzerland. Then, in addition, I have the representatives of the transcontinental railways, who are under no delusions, but who do not want a competing canal. In the same way I have alienated some of the big representatives of what we call the trusts, and have had a muss with the trades-unions on the other side. So only a merciful providence can tell what the outcome will be. If elected I shall be very glad. If beaten I shall be sorry; but in any event I have had a first-class run for my money, and I have accomplished certain definite things. I would consider myself a hundred times over repaid if I had nothing more to my credit than Panama and the coaling stations in Cuba. So you see that my frame of mind is a good deal like that of your old Viceroy when he addressed the new Viceroy!

With regards to Mrs. Kipling, and renewed thanks, believe me, *Sincerely yours*

LABOR AND CAPITAL

To Philander Chase Knox

Personal

Washington, November 10, 1904

My dear Senator Knox:

Now that the fight is over I want to say one word about general policy. There seems to me to be nothing of better augury for the country than the fact that you and Murray Crane are in the Senate — and especially that *you* are in the Senate. I shall serve for four years in the White House, if I live. You, I trust, will serve for twenty or thirty years in the Senate; and I feel that with every additional year you will render better service, for the Senate is peculiarly a body in which length of service enables the man to do constantly better work. Now, you have done what no other man of our generation has done in grappling with the great problem of the day — or rather, the multitude of problems connected with the relations of organized labor and organized capital to each other as well as the general public, to unorganized labor and to unorganized capital. So far as organized capital is concerned, I have not even a suggestion to make to you. You know far too much for any hint of mine to be of any service to you. But I do most earnestly hope that you will make the problem of labor as thoroughly yours as you have made the problem of capital. More and more the labor movement in this country will become a factor of vital importance, not merely in our social but in our political development. If the attitude of the New York *Sun* toward labor, as toward the trusts, becomes the attitude of the Republican party, we shall some day go down before a radical and extreme democracy with a crash which will be disastrous to the Nation. We must not only do justice, but be able to show the wageworkers that we are doing justice. We must make it evident that while there is not any weakness in our attitude, while we unflinchingly demand good conduct from them, yet we are equally resolute in the effort to secure them all just and proper consideration. It would be a dreadful calamity if we saw this country divided into two parties, one containing the bulk of the property owners and conservative people, the other the bulk of the wageworkers and the less prosperous people generally; each party insisting upon demanding much that was wrong, and each party sullen and angered by real and fancied grievances. The friends of property, of order, of law, must never show weakness in the face of violence or wrong or injustice; but on the other hand they must realize that the surest way to provoke an explosion of wrong and injustice is to be shortsighted, narrow-minded, greedy and arrogant, and to fail to show in actual work that here in this republic it is peculiarly incumbent upon the man with whom things have prospered to be in a certain sense the keeper of his brother with whom life has gone hard.

Now, my dear Senator, I hope you won't mind my writing you in this way. I feel that you have definitely put your hand to the plow in political life, and that you neither can nor ought to draw back, and I know that all you care for in political life is to render service; and furthermore, I know that you have to an extraordinary degree not merely the desire to render service but the power to render it. You have the mind and the training; and you have an impatient contempt for the little prizes, and the little, sordid arts, methods and aims of the ordinary politician. Therefore you have the chance to do this great service.

I wish you could get into touch with some of the labor people. After getting in touch with them you might find that you had to go against most of what they wished; but I would like you to know what they desire to do — what their real feelings are.

When you and I first came together I found that the aspirations I had half formulated, the policies in which I earnestly believed but to which I could not myself give shape, were exactly those in which you most thoroughly believed; and that you had thought them all out and were able to give them shape in speech and in action in fashion which made them effective. Now I feel that you can do the same thing on an even larger scale during the years to come in the Senate, with reference not only to capital, but to labor. I feel that you can do infinitely more than under any circumstances I could have done.

With warm regards to you and yours, believe me, *Always yours*

P.S. What has apparently happened in Colorado illustrates what I mean. Peabody manfully did his duty in stopping disorder and in battling against a corrupt and murderous conspiracy among the Federation of Western Miners; but he let himself be put in the position of seeming to do this not in the interest merely of law and order, of evenhanded justice to wageworker and capitalist, but as the supporter and representative of the capitalist against the laborer. This has been the root of his trouble. I am sure that if he had acted as you would have acted in his place, he would have made it so evident that he was acting not as the representative of capital against labor, but as the representative of law, order and justice against all forces of disorder and corruption, that the State would have rallied to him by a great majority.

ELECTION NIGHT

To Kermit Roosevelt

Washington, November 10, 1904

Darling Kermit:

I am stunned by the overwhelming victory we have won. I had no conception that such a thing was possible. I thought it probable we should win, but was quite prepared to be defeated, and of course had not the slightest idea that there was such a tidal wave. If you will look back at my letter you will see that we carried not only all the States I put down as probably republican, but all those that I put down as doubtful, and all but one of those that I put down as probably democratic. The only States that went against me were those in which no free discussion is allowed and in which fraud and violence have rendered the voting a farce. I have the greatest popular majority and the greatest electoral majority ever given to a candidate for President.

On the evening of the election I got back from Oyster Bay, where I had voted, soon after half past six. At that time I knew nothing of the returns and did not expect to find out anything definite for two or three hours; and had been endeavoring not to think of the result, but to school myself to accept it as a man ought to, whichever way it went. But as soon as I got in the White House Ted met me with the news that Buffalo and Rochester had sent in their returns already and that they showed enormous gains for me. Within the next twenty minutes enough returns were received from precincts and districts in Chicago, Connecticut, New York and Massachusetts to make it evident that there was a tremendous drift my way, and by the time we sat down to dinner at half past seven my election was assured. Mrs. Cortelyou was with us at dinner, just as interested and excited as we were. Right after dinner members of the Cabinet and friends began to come in, and we had a celebration that would have been perfect if only you had been present. Archie, fairly plastered with badges, was acting as messenger between the telegraph operators and me, and bringing me continually telegram after telegram which I read aloud. I longed for you very much, as all of us did, for of course this was the day of greatest triumph I ever had had or ever could have, and I was very proud and happy. But I tell you, Kermit, it was a great comfort to feel, all during the last days when affairs looked doubtful, that no matter how things came out the really important thing was the lovely life I have with mother and with you children, and that compared to this home life everything else was of very small importance from the standpoint of happiness.

I have been reading Robinson's poems again and like them as much as ever. *Your loving father*

"NO MORE CONTEMPTIBLE IDEAL"

To Amelia Glover

Personal

Washington, November 10, 1904

Dear Madam:

Mrs. Roosevelt has handed me your letter. It is an impertinent letter, and the newspaper clipping you enclose is an indecent clipping. I never have heard of Miss or Mrs. Lula McClure Clark, of Edith, Colorado, whose open letter you enclose and thereby make your own. In what she says about me she says what is not the truth. But that is of small consequence. I am interested not in either your or her attitude toward me, but in your and her attitude toward womanhood. I wish that you and she would read a novel called *Unleavened Bread*, by Robert Grant. The character of the heroine, Selma, especially in her sexual relations, is exactly and precisely such a character as produced by the writings and efforts of the woman whose newspaper letter you enclose, and whom you follow. This Selma represents her and your ideal of womanhood; and in all the ages there has been no more contemptible ideal. *Yours truly*

ADVICE TO A SCULPTOR

To Frederick William MacMonnies

Washington, November 19, 1904
My dear Mr. MacMonnies:
I have just received your very kind note, and of course I shall be delighted to have you make the little statue or statuette that you desire, for, my dear sir, I think that any American President would be glad to have an American sculptor like you or Saint-Gaudens do such a piece of work. But before sending you over the things you would like I want to point out something. You say that you like that photograph of me jumping a fence, and apparently intend to use that as the model; but you ask me for my soldier suit. Now, of course I do not jump fences in my khaki and with sword and revolver in my belt — as a matter of fact I rarely wore my sword at all in the war — and if you want to make me jumping a fence I must send you my ordinary riding things. It seems to me it would be better to put me in khaki and not to have me jumping the fence. Horses I jump fences with have short tails. The horses I rode in the war had long tails; and, by the way, as soon as I got down to active work they looked much more like Remington's cavalry horses than like the traditional war steed of the story books.
Now, which way do you want to make that statuette? It seems to me it would be better in uniform.
With regard, *Sincerely yours*

ANGLOPHOBIA AND ANGLOMANIA

To Finley Peter Dunne

Personal

Washington, November 23, 1904
Dear Mr. Dunne:
Can you and Mrs. Dunne come down here and spend the night of December 8th? We have a small musical that evening,

and as you would rather not go out to anything big perhaps that evening will be about right.

Now, oh laughing philosopher, (because you are not only one who laughs, but also a genuine philosopher and because your philosophy has a real effect upon this country) I want to enter a strong protest against your very amusing and very wrong-headed article on "The 'Anglo-Saxon' Triumph." In this article, as in everything else you have written about me, you are as nice as possible as to me personally, and the fun about the feeling abroad, including England, is perfectly legitimate. If you have ever happened to see what I have written on the matter of the Anglo-Saxon business you may have noticed that I have always insisted that we are not Anglo-Saxons at all — even admitting for the sake of argument, which I do not, that there are any Anglo-Saxons — but a new and mixed race — a race drawing its blood from many different sources. In this particular election no Casey hunted me up. I hunted up Cortelyou as the manager of my campaign myself, and it was a pure accident that on his father's side he, like myself, was a Dutchman; so there is nothing particularly Anglo-Saxon about our triumph. I think that the way you describe the attitude of Judge Higgins to Casey after election expresses a great moral truth. My own view is, that if a man is good enough for me to profit by his services before election, he is good enough for me to do what I can for him after election; and I do not give a damn whether his name happens to be Casey, or Schwartzmeister, or Van Rensselaer, or Peabody. I think my whole public life has been an emphatic protest against the Peabodys and Van Rensselaers arrogating to themselves any superiority over the Caseys and Schwartzmeisters. But in return I will not, where I have anything to say about it, tolerate for one moment any assumption of superiority by the Caseys and Schwartzmeisters over the Peabodys and Van Rensselaers. I did not notice any difference between them as they fought in my regiment; and I had lots of representatives of all of them in it. If you will look at the nomenclature of the Yale, Harvard and Princeton teams this year, or any other year, and then at the feats performed by the men bearing the names, you will come to the conclusion, friend Dooley, that Peabody and Van Rensselaer and

Saltonstall and Witherspoon are pretty tough citizens to handle in a mixup and that they will be found quite as often at the top of the heap as at the bottom. There is nothing against which I protest more strongly, socially and politically, than any proscription of or looking down upon decent Americans because they are of Irish or German ancestry; but I protest just exactly as strongly against any similar discrimination against or sneering at men because they happen to be descended from people who came over here some three centuries ago, whether they landed at Plymouth, or at the mouth of the Hudson. I have fought beside and against Americans of Irish, of German, and of old Colonial stock in every political contest in which I have engaged; I have been a fairly good rough-and-tumble man myself; I have never asked any odds; and I have generally held my own. When you come down here you will see my oldest boy, Ted. He is of medium size; but out on the football field or in boxing he will hold his own with other boys of his weight and inches, just as I have held my own in the political field; and he will hold his own just as well against Hogan and Rafferty as against Peabody and Saltonstall. Sometime I shall take you up to Groton School and you will see that the Rev. Plantagenet Peabody is a good man with his hands and quick on his feet, and that there is as little of the snob about him as about any man I have ever met. Presidents Eliot and Hadley have their faults; but the Lord knows there is no snobbishness about them, or any idea of discriminating against anybody because of his parentage or descent.

There! You may think I have taken your article rather seriously, and so I have, because I think you are a force that counts and I do not want to see you count on the side of certain ugly and unpleasant tendencies in American life. Ted goes to Harvard next year. If he makes his Freshman eleven he will find other boys on it of every variety of parentage and descent. I should be heartily ashamed of him if he discriminated against any one of them because of either parentage or descent, or if he failed promptly to resent any similar effort to discriminate against him. I shall go over this more at length with you on the 8th, and I look forward to seeing Mrs. Dunne and you down on that day! *Faithfully yours*

P.S. I am sure you will agree with me that in our political life, very unlike what is the case in our social life, the temptation is toward Anglophobia, not toward Anglomania. The cheapest thing for any politician to do, the easiest, and too often politically one of the most remunerative, is to make some yell about England. One of the things I am most pleased with in the recent election is that while I got, I think, a greater proportion of the Americans of Irish birth or parentage and of the Catholic religion than any previous republican candidate, I got this proportion purely because they know I felt in sympathy with them and in touch with them, and that they and I had the same ideals and principles, and not by any demagogic appeals about creed or race, or by any demagogic attack upon England. I feel a sincere friendliness for England; but you may notice that I do not slop over about it, and that I do not in the least misunderstand England's attitude, or, for the matter of that, the attitude of any European nation, as regards us. We shall keep the respect of each of them just so long as we are thoroughly able to hold our own, and no longer. If we got into trouble, there is not one of them upon whose friendship we could count to get us out; what we shall need to count upon is the efficiency of our own fighting men and particularly of our navy. But, nevertheless, it is a mighty good thing to be on thoroughly friendly terms with all, just so far as our self-respect will let us; and these terms are those upon which I endeavor to keep our relations. But when it comes to a question like the Alaska boundary or the Venezuela business or anything of the kind you may notice that I see that America's end is well kept up!

There is one thing to which I should like to call your attention. If an Anglomaniac in social life goes into political life he usually becomes politically an Anglophobiac, and the occasional political Anglophobiac whose curious ambition it is to associate socially with "vacuity trimmed with lace," is equally sure to become an Anglomaniac in his new surroundings. Bourke Cockran beautifully illustrates what I mean. Of course, he has not a principle or conviction of any kind, sort or description, and under such circumstances it is natural that he should strive to rise politically by pandering to any prejudice and therefore that he should become a howling and raving Anglophobiac when on the stump; and it is quite in keeping with the rest of his character that he should be as he is in his social life — a hanger-on around any Englishman and especially any titled Englishman or Englishwoman of what he deems good social position whose acquaintance he can manage to scrape. In London and New York alike he is socially as unpleasant an example of the snob and Anglomaniac as I know; in public life I need perhaps say little more of him than he is a fit companion for Senator Carmack and John Sharp Williams.

"WE WON A GREAT TRIUMPH"

To George Otto Trevelyan

Personal

Washington, November 24, 1904

My dear Sir George:

It was a real pleasure to hear from you. I was saying the other day to John Morley how much I regretted that it did not seem likely that you could get over here. By the way, Morley spent three or four days with us, and I found him as delightful a companion as one could wish to have, and I quite understand the comfort he must have been to you when you sat beside him in the House. Incidentally, it is rather a relief to have you speak as you do about the tedious and trivial quality of most of the eloquence in the House. I am glad to find that it is characteristic of all parliamentary bodies, and not merely of those of my own country!

We won a great triumph at the elections. A candidate is so apt to hear nothing but the favorable side that I had kept my mind absolutely open to accept either defeat or victory. Most of my friends were very confident, but no one anticipated such an overwhelming triumph. Now I know that it is practically impossible to avoid the personal equation, and as I am naturally very proud and happy over the victory, and, equally naturally, very sure that on the whole my acts and the policies I stood for were right and therefore deserved approval by the people, it follows as a corollary that what I am about to say must be taken with a large and liberal measure of discount. But trying to look at the matter disinterestedly, it does seem to me that it was a good thing to have the people decide for the candidate and the party representing the positive side — the side of achievement in many different directions — instead of for the colorless candidate and the party whose position had become one of negation, criticism and obstruction merely. Moreover, while Mr. Parker was not at all a dangerous man for the country to put at the head of affairs, and while there was nothing of great menace to the country's immediate material interest in the success of his party under his leadership, it is also true that the Democratic canvass this year was on a thoroughly insincere and unworthy basis; and it is never wholesome to have the people vote "Yes" to a lie. From the outset Mr. Parker's attitude, and the attitude of the party behind him, were one of trickiness and double-dealing. All they wished for was success, and every principle and conviction was handled only from the standpoint of getting votes. I thoroughly believe in handling a campaign so as to get votes, but I do not believe in lying directly or indirectly for that purpose or any other, or in doing anything cowardly or base for that purpose. Mr. Parker and his supporters wished to be for the gold standard strongly enough to secure the gold vote, and yet not strongly enough to hurt the feelings of the silver people. They wished to be for free trade, and yet in the same breath to assure the protectionists that they had nothing whatever to fear as regards the tariff. They wished to use language about the Philippines which would convince the so-called anti-imperialists that they intended to give them up, while at the same time the promise could be construed so as to mean that they would not be given up for half a century or a century to come. They wished to be understood as being for the cutting down of the army and navy, and yet be able to give private assurances that in each case the action would be nominal. They endeavored to make the labor people feel that I was not radical enough in my action to suit them, and yet to make the big financial magnates understand that at bottom Parker was a conservative who could be trusted by them not to do the radical things I had done. In short, the canvass was one with which all students of history are familiar, for it occurs every now and then in every free country. To use the continental terminology, it was an effort to unite the extreme right and extreme left against the middle. It is rare indeed that the success of such an effort is a healthy sign for the body politic.

By the way, I venture to send you a volume of my speeches and addresses made since I was President. This volume really contains the platform upon which I stood in the last election; and to me one of the gratifying features of the canvass was that in my speech and letter of acceptance and subsequent statement, and in the speeches of my great supporters, Root, Knox, Hay, Taft and Moody, there was nothing said in which we did not believe with entire faith, and nothing promised whatever except that the Government would be continued along the lines followed in the last three years. We won on clean-cut issues, stated with absolute truthfulness, and with only the promise that our performance in the past could be taken as the measure of what our performance would be in the future.

Although the canvass naturally caused me at times a good deal of worry, I did not have to do much work. Each Nation has its conventions. Whereas a Prime Minister is expected to take the stump on his own behalf, with us it is regarded as improper for a President to do so. This is the kind of custom which could be disregarded in a great emergency, but which it is never wise or politic to disregard for insufficient reasons. In the same way it has become one of our customs, with even more than the conventional force, that no President is to have a third term; whereas in England the longer a Prime Minister serves, the more he is esteemed as having been true to his party. Naturally, an Englishman cannot understand the force that a custom like this has upon the American mind; and I see that the *Spectator* cannot understand, exactly as John Morley could not understand, my immediate announcement that I had no intention of accepting a third term. If it were not for the certainty of fools misunderstanding the terminology, and failing to see that a short-term elective King has nothing whatever in common with a hereditary King, I could best express to a foreigner the President's power by putting it in that form.

Of course a constitutional King reigns all his life and does not govern at all, while the President never reigns, but governs most actively for 4 or 8 years; and our President, in the actual exercise of his power, resembles the Prime Minister far more than he does a functionary like the French President. But his power is even greater, and therefore it is natural that the people should desire to hedge it about with certain restrictions, and above all to make it certain that it can only be of limited duration. I think the feeling healthy myself; and moreover I feel very strongly that, at least in our country, a public man's usefulness in the highest position becomes in the end impaired by the mere fact of too long continuance in that position. People get tired of the everlasting talk about Aristides; and moreover Aristides himself, after a certain number of years, finds that he has really delivered his message and that he has a tendency to repeat it over and over again. For example, suppose that there was no third-term tradition in our government, and none of the valid reasons (as I regard them) against a third term; it would yet be true that in 1908 it would be better to have some man like Taft or Root succeed me in the Presidency, at the head of the Republican party, than to have me succeed myself. In all the essentials of policy they look upon things as I do; but they have their own ways of thought and ways of expression, and what they did and said would have a freshness which what I did and said could not possibly have; and they would be free from the animosities and suspicions which I had accumulated, and would be able to take a new start and would have a much greater chance of achieving useful work. After eight years in the Presidency, not only is it unwise for other reasons to re-elect a man, but it is inadvisable because it is almost certain that someone can be found with the same principles, who, from the mere fact that he is someone else, can better succeed in putting those principles into practice.

This is a rambling digression. When I started out I merely meant to show why it was essential for me to have interpreters like Hay, Knox and the others, who could set forth on the stump what I had done and what I intended to do.

In my hours of leisure I did a good deal of reading. I reread your history of our Revolution and liked it more than ever, but came to the conclusion that you had painted us a little too favorably. I also reread both your *Macaulay* and your *Fox*, and then reread Macaulay's *History*. When I had finished it I felt a higher regard for him as a great writer, and as in the truest sense of the word a great philosophical historian, than I have ever felt before. It is a pretty good test of such a history to have a President, who is also a candidate for the Presidency, read it in the midst of a campaign, with the keenest appreciation of its wisdom and its knowledge of the motives and acts of men engaged in the difficult task of self-government, and with at the same time a great sense of relaxation and pure enjoyment. All the motives and tendencies for good and for evil of which Macaulay show working in the England of the end of the Seventeenth Century, were at work right around me in the America of the beginning of the Twentieth Century. Of course some were strong and some were weak now, as compared to what under the utterly different conditions they had been in another land two centuries before; but fundamentally they were all there, and the wise man who was neither a mere doctrinaire nor a vicious man, had to grapple with them and make the best of them now as then.

Do you recollect one of Abraham Lincoln's speeches, just after he was re-elected in 1864? It runs in part as follows:

*** The strife of the election is but human nature practically applied to the facts of the case. What has occurred in this case must ever occur in similar cases. Human nature will not change. In any future great national trial, compared with the men of this, we shall have as weak and as strong, as silly and as wise, as bad and as good. Let us, therefore, study the incidents of this as philosophy to learn wisdom from, and none of them as wrongs to be revenged. ***

*** now that the election is over, may not all having a common interest reunite in a common effort to save our common country? For my own part, I have striven and shall strive to avoid placing any obstacle in the way. So long as I have been here I have not willingly planted a thorn in any man's bosom. While I am deeply sensible to the high compliment of a re-election, and duly grateful, as I trust, to almighty God for having directed my countrymen to a right conclusion, as I think, for their own good, it adds nothing to my satisfaction that any other man may be disappointed or pained by the result.

May I ask those who have not differed with me to join with me in this same spirit toward those who have?

It seems to me that aside from its fine and noble quality, this has in it the real philosophy of statesmanship.

I read a number of other books during the campaign; Rhodes's excellent history, for instance; and a good deal of Dickens. In the American characters in *Martin Chuzzlewit*, Dickens made a mistake in generalizing and insisting that all Americans were represented by his figures, which of course is as nonsensical as to say that Pecksniff, Bill Sykes and Sir Mulberry Hawk, taken in the aggregate, typify all of English society. But all the same I would like to have *Martin Chuzzlewit* studied as a tract in America. Hearst and Pulitzer are Jefferson Brick and Colonel Diver, in a somewhat fuller stage of development, while Senator Carmack of Tennessee, Congressman John Sharp Williams of Mississippi and Governor Vardaman of Mississippi, not to speak of Senator Tillman of South Carolina, are Hannibal Chollop and Elijah Pogram over again. *Faithfully yours*

"THE OFFICE DOES GOOD TO HIM"

To William Emlen Roosevelt

Personal

Washington, November 29, 1904

Dear Emlen:

Between ourselves, Townsend represents one of my difficulties. He possess all the superficial requirements of the minister, and none that are of the slightest consequence when there is any real work to be done. He is a gentleman. He speaks foreign languages. He knows the minutiae of diplomacy, and he has a beautiful wife who, as a matter of fact, got him his present position and expects to keep him in it. All kinds of social and some political pressure is exercised on his behalf. But he is in the office not because he can do good to the service, but because the office does good to him, and he has no claim whatever on retention — which is equally true of four-fifths of our European ambassadors and ministers. I have not an idea what I shall do about him yet. The appointments, while not the most serious, make up the most harassing of my troubles.

Give my love to Christine and all your family. *Always yours*

CIVIL WAR AND RECONSTRUCTION

To James Ford Rhodes

Personal

Washington, November 29, 1904

My dear Rhodes:

I have just finished your fifth volume and am delighted with it. I do not know whether I told you that during the campaign I reread your first four. At the same time I read Macaulay's *History* and many of Lincoln's letters and speeches; and I got real help from all of them. It seems to me that, allowing for difference of epoch and nationality, you and Macaulay approach the great subject of self-government by a free people in much the same spirit and from much the same philosophical standpoint.

In this last volume I was immensely pleased with everything. Perhaps I should bar one sentence — that in which you say that in no quarrel is the right all on one side, and the wrong all on the other. As regards the actual act of secession, the actual opening of the Civil War, I think the right was exclusively with the Union people, and the wrong exclusively with the secessionists; and indeed I do not know of another struggle in history in which this sharp division between right and wrong can be made in quite so clear-cut a manner. I am half southern. My mother's kinsfolk fought on the Confederate side, and I am proud of them. I fully believe in and appreciate not only the valor of the South, but its lofty devotion to the right as it saw the right, and yet I think that on every ground — that is, on the question of the Union, on the question of slavery, on the question of State rights — it was wrong with a folly that amounted to madness, and with a perversity that amounted to wickedness.

Incidentally, I most cordially agree that our form of government is not one suitable for military exertions. That is one reason why I feel that at all hazards our navy should be made large and should be kept up to the highest point of efficiency. If we have a sufficiently large and sufficiently good navy, the chances are strong that we shall not have serious war; and it will offer us a chance of coming with honor out of any serious war if we do have one. In view of the interests we now have in the Pacific as well as the Atlantic, I feel that the building of the Panama Canal is of vital importance, because it will nearly double the efficiency of our Navy.

I am much interested in what you say as to Grant's superiority over Lee in the fortnight's operations ending at Appomattox which brought the Civil War to a close. For the previous year it seems to me that Lee had shown himself the superior, but during this fortnight Grant rose to his Vicksburg level. A mighty pair of generals they were!

I am immensely interested in your discussion of Reconstruction, and it seems to me you have handled the problem with equal ability and fairness. Reading your history brings out the essential greatness of Lincoln ever more and more. Perhaps, as you say, he and Washington do not come in the very limited class of men which includes Caesar, Alexander and Napoleon, but they are far better men for a nation to develop than any of these three giants; and, excepting only these three, I hardly see any greater figures loom up in the history of civilized nations. There have been other men as good — men like Timoleon and John Hampden; but no other good men have been as great.

The trouble I am having with the southern question — which, my dear sir, I beg you to believe I am painfully striving to meet, so far as in me lies, in the spirit of Abraham Lincoln — emphasizes the infinite damage done in reconstruction days by the unregenerate arrogance and shortsightedness of the southerners, and the doctrinaire folly of radicals like Sumner and Thaddeus Stevens. The more I study the Civil War and the time following it, the more I feel (as of course everyone feels) the towering greatness of Lincoln, which puts him before all other men of our time; while, on the other hand, I very strongly feel that Chase, Seward, Sumner and Stanton by no means come up to, say, Hay, Root, Knox and Taft. But I am not dead sure that just at the moment we have leaders in Congress quite up to the Trumbull or Fessenden level!

I am having my own troubles now. I feel sure that Congress ought to revise the tariff, not so much from any economical need as to meet the mental attitude of the people; but it is not an issue upon which I should have any business to break with my party or with Congress, and just how much I shall accomplish I cannot tell, for I shall have to feel them carefully in order to be sure that I go right up to the breaking point but not beyond it.

On the question of the corporations, I also have one or two things I want to do — notably in the matter of stopping rebates. Here I rather hope that Congress will follow me. The southern question is not of immediate menace, but it is one of perpetual discomfort. The southerners show a wrongheadedness and folly the same in kind, though of course not in degree, that they showed in the years you write of. Their problem is very difficult, and I should be only too glad to co-operate with them in any honest effort to make even a beginning toward its solution. But they not only refuse to make the effort, but deliberately try to make things worse, and they are of course helped by the present-day representatives of the old copperhead and dough-face vote in the North — from little solemn creatures like Norman Hapgood up to serious politicians of the stamp of Parker, Hill and Bryan. On the other hand the heirs of the Wendell Phillips and Lloyd Garrison people, the Oswald Villards, Rollo Ogdens, Carl Schurzes and Charles Francis Adamses, who do take a genuine interest in the welfare of the negro, have frittered away their influence until at this time they literally have not the slightest weight with either Democrats or Republicans; and moreover they are as irrational on this as on other subjects, so that no help whatever can be obtained from them. I wish I could agree with you that no one in the South wishes to re-establish slavery. In my judgment this is so far from the fact that in reality there are at this very moment not only active but partially successful movements for the reintroduction of slavery under the form of peonage in at least three Southern States. This peonage has been broken up, for the moment at least, in Alabama; and is being broken up, again at least temporarily, in Mississippi; and it has seemed to me that the only feasible way for me to help was by backing the southern men, such as Judge Jones, who have shown themselves willing to break it up. Indeed, as yet I see nothing to do in this southern business save to go on exactly as I have gone on during the past three years, and to back up the few good and brave men in the different Southern States who are striving to make the best out of conditions which are bad enough by nature, and have been made worse by the folly of the ruling class in the South during the last quarter of a century. There is a very strong movement in the North to reduce the representation of the South, and from the standpoint of abstract morality this movement is absolutely right; but as yet I do not see where it will do good.

However, I did not intend to burden you with my own troubles. I have already thanked you for your congratulations upon the victory. It was very gratifying, and I cared especially for carrying Missouri because that is partly a Southern State. I hope I have taken to heart Lincoln's life, at least sufficiently to make me feel that triumph gives less cause for elation than for a solemn realization of the responsibility it entails. There is one point in connection with the last election which has amused me. Owing to the peculiar methods of attack chosen by my antagonists they did me certain services which my friends could not have rendered. Parker at the close of the campaign succeeded in making my personal honesty an issue, and gave me a chance to put myself into the campaign in a way which would have been impossible under other conditions. Again, it would have been an absurdity for my supporters to say anything about my having been a military man, or having been a ranchman; for one appeal would have looked ridiculous in view of my having served only four months in a very small war, and the other would have looked demagogic. But the opposing papers, and especially the opposing caricaturists, invariably represented me in the rough rider uniform, or else riding a bucking broncho and roping a steer, or carrying a big stick and threatening foreign nations,

and thereby made to the younger among their own readers the very kind of *ad captandum* appeal on my behalf which it would have been undignified for my supporters to have made.
Faithfully yours

OBLIVION AND MEMORY

To Oliver Wendell Holmes

Washington, December 5, 1904

Dear Mr. Justice:

I am immensely pleased with President Eliot's little book, which you sent me, and I agree with you absolutely as to its worth. It is very unsafe to say of anything contemporary that it will be a classic, but I am inclined to venture the statement in this case. It seems to me pre-eminently worth while to have such a biography of a typical American. How I wish President Eliot could write in the same shape biographies of a brakeman or railroad locomotive engineer, of an ordinary western farmer, of a carpenter or blacksmith in one of our small towns, of a storekeeper in one of our big cities, of a miner — of half a dozen typical representatives of the forgotten millions who really make up American life. I am immensely pleased with the book, it is good wholesome reading for all our people.

I was rather struck at what President Eliot said about oblivion so speedily overtaking almost everyone. But after all, what does the fact amount to that here and there a man escapes oblivion longer than his fellows? Ozymandias in the Desert — when a like interval has gone by who will know more of any man of the present day than Shelley knew of him? I suppose it is only about ten thousand years since the last glacial epoch (at least that is, I understand, the newest uncertain guess of the geologists); and this covers more than the period in which there is anything that we can even regard as civilization. Of course, when we go back even half that time we get past the period when any man's memory, no matter how great the man, is more than a flickering shadow to us; yet this distance is too small to be measured when we look at the ages even at rather short range — not astronomically but geometrically. That queer creature Ware, my Pension Commissioner, who always uses the terminology of his Kansas environment, but who has much philosophy of his own, once wrote the following verses on this very question:

HISTORY.

Over the infinite prairie of level eternity,
    Flying as flies the deer,
Time is pursued by a pitiless, cruel oblivion,
    Following fast and near.

Ever and ever the famished coyote is following
    Patiently in the rear;
Trifling the interval, yet we are calling it "History" —
    Distance from wolf to deer.

Whether the distance between the wolf and the deer is a couple of inches or a quarter of a mile is not really of much consequence in the end. It is passed over mighty quickly in either event, and it makes small odds to any of us after we are dead whether the next generation forgets us, or whether a number of generations pass before our memory, steadily growing more and more dim, at last fades into nothing. On this point it seems to me that the only important thing is to be able to feel, when our time comes to go out into the blackness, that those survivors who care for us and to whom it will be a pleasure to think well of us when we are gone, shall have that pleasure. Save in a few wholly exceptional cases, cases of men such as are not alive at this particular time, it is only possible in any event that a comparatively few people can have this feeling for any length of time. But it is a good thing if as many as possible feel it even for a short time, and it is surely a good thing that those whom we love should feel it as long as they too live.

I should be quite unable to tell you why I think it would be pleasant to feel that one had lived manfully and honorably when the time comes after which all things are the same to every man; yet I am very sure that it is well so to feel, that it is well to have lived so that at the end it may be possible to know that on the whole one's duties have not been shirked, that there has been no flinching from foes, no lack of gentleness and loyalty to friends, and a reasonable measure of success in the effort to do the tasks allotted. This is just the kind of feeling that President Eliot's hero had the right to have; and a Justice of the Supreme Court or a President or a General or an Admiral, may be mighty thankful if at the end he has earned a similar right!

With love to Mrs. Holmes, *Faithfully yours*

A BOXING INJURY

To Michael Joseph Donovan

Personal

Washington, December 13, 1904

Dear Mike:

Luck is hard with me as regards boxing. A couple of days ago I spent a good afternoon with Ted and one of his football friends and a couple of young army officers sparring, playing singlestick, etc., and I am sorry to say I have wrenched my thigh again and succeeded in breaking a blood vessel in one eye, while Ted put his thumb out of joint. Accordingly we shall have to lay up until after the holidays. Then I will write you again, and if you are still able to come down will get you to do so. I want to have you in the White House and put on the gloves with you myself, and see Ted do so. *Your friend*

RELATIONS WITH RUSSIA

To George von Lengerke Meyer

Confidential

Washington, December 26, 1904

Dear George:

This letter is naturally to be treated as entirely confidential, as I wish to write you very freely. I desire to send you as Ambassador to St. Petersburg. My present intention is, as you know, only to keep you for a year as Ambassador, but there is nothing certain about this inasmuch as no man can tell what contingencies will arise in the future; but at present the position in which I need you is that of Ambassador at St. Petersburg. St. Petersburg is at this moment, and bids fair to continue to be for at least a year, the most important post in the diplomatic service, from the standpoint of work to be done; and in the category of public servants who desire to do public work, as distinguished from those whose desire is merely to occupy public place — a class for whom I have no particular respect. I wish in St. Petersburg a man who, while able to do all the social work, able to entertain and to meet the Russians and his fellow diplomats on equal terms, able to do all the necessary plush business — business which is indispensable — could in addition, the really vital and important things. I want a man who will be able to keep us closely informed, on his own initiative, of everything we ought to know; who will be, as an Ambassador ought to be, our chief source of information about Japan and the war — about the Russian feeling as to the continuance of the war, as to the relations between Russia and Germany and France, as to the real meaning of the movement for so-called internal reforms, as to the condition of the army, as to what force can and will be used in Manchuria next summer, and so forth and so forth. The trouble with our Ambassadors in stations of real importance is that they totally fail to give us real help and real information, and seem to think that the life work of an Ambassador is a kind of glorified pink tea party. Now, at St. Petersburg I want some work done, and you are the man to do it. It happens to be the only embassy at which I do want work done just at present. There is at St. Petersburg, in the English Embassy, an Englishman whose name I will not give you, but whom I shall ask to call on you and talk freely over the situation, alluding to what he has written me. I have gained the most valuable information from him — better information than I have ever gained from any of our own people abroad, save only Harry White. Our First Secretary, Spencer Eddy, has also written us continually and given us good information. With the exception of Harry White and John Riddle, he is the only secretary during my time of whom this can be said.

The situation in the far East is one which needs careful watching. I am not inclined to think that Tokyo will show itself a particle more altruistic than St. Petersburg, or for the matter of that, Berlin. I believe that the Japanese rulers recognize Russia as their most dangerous permanent enemy, but I am not at all sure that the Japanese people draw any distinctions between the Russians and other foreigners, including ourselves. I have no doubt that they include all white men as being people who, as a whole, they dislike, and whose past arrogance they resent; and doubtless they believe their own yellow civilization to be better. It is always possible, though I think improbable, that Russia and Japan will agree to make up their differences and assume an attitude of common hostility toward America or toward England, or toward both. Under such circumstances they might have Germany or France or both in with them. This country cannot count upon any ally to do its work. We must stand upon our feet and try to look into the future as clearly as may be. For years Russia has pursued a policy of consistent opposition to us in the East, and of literally fathomless mendacity. She has felt a profound contempt for England and Japan and the United States, all three, separately or together. It has been impossible to trust to any promise she has made. On the other hand, Japan's diplomatic statements have been made good. Yet Japan is an oriental nation, and the individual standard of truthfulness in Japan is low. No one can foretell her future attitude. We must, therefore, play our hand alone, or be ready to play it alone, so far as either of these two nations is concerned. Germany and France for their own reasons are anxious to propitiate Russia, and of course care nothing whatever for our interests. England is inclined to be friendly to us and is inclined to support Japan against Russia, but she is pretty flabby and I am afraid to trust either the farsightedness or the tenacity of purpose of her statesmen; or indeed of her people.

Our Navy is year by year becoming more efficient. I want to avoid any blustering or threatening, but I want to be able to act decidedly when any turn of affairs menaces our interests, and to be able to make our words good once they have been spoken; and therefore I need to know each phase of any new situation. *Sincerely yours*

To Richard Harding Davis

Confidential

Washington, January 3, 1905

My dear Davis:

I am glad to hear you think so well of the four men at Tokyo. They are the kind of men I intend to keep in the service, because they are in the service to do work for the Government. But there are a large number of well-meaning ambassadors and ministers, and even consuls and secretaries, who belong to what I call the pink-tea type, who merely reside in the service instead of working in the service, and these I intend to change whenever the need arises.

What follows is confidential, but will serve to illustrate what I mean. The minister to Belgium is a nice man with an even nicer wife. He has been eight years in the service. He is polite to people, gives nice little dinners, and so forth and so forth. During all that time it has never made one atom of real difference to the country whether he was in or out. He is in the service for his own advantage, not for the good of the service, although he does all the secondarily important work well; and in all probability I shall change him and promote some such man as Wilson, who during all that time has done really hard work in South America in a place where there was no pink-tea possibility. In Spain we have a gentleman, a novelist, who went to Spain, when John Hay wanted him to come here as Assistant Secretary of State; because he could not make a bargain for his own future promotion (I am putting it truthfully) he did not care to come here, where he was needed. When he tried to make conditions of this kind Hay abandoned the effort to get him and got Loomis to come in his stead. Loomis came, made no attempt at a bargain, and did first-class work. Now if the chance comes Loomis shall have a promotion, whereas I shall consider Hardy as having had all he is entitled to and shall put someone else in his place. He comes of that class which reflects no discredit on the country, but on the contrary is rather creditable; and which is in ornamental, and to some extent in nonornamental matters, useful to American people traveling abroad; but which gets far more than it gives, and which is therefore in no way entitled to permanency in place.

On the other hand, Griscom, whom we approached at the same time that we did Hardy, was anxious to go to Japan instead of to Europe because he knew there was work to be done there; and he shall have his reward, just as John Riddle and Harry White, who have also done good work, shall have their rewards.

In short, I shall not make a fetish of keeping a man in, but if the man is a *really* good man he will be kept in. A pink-tea man shall stay in or go out just as I find convenient. Of course most places at embassies and legations are pink-tea places. A few are not, and in these we need real men, and these real men shall be rewarded.

Do come on here as soon as possible and tell me about those men who are bad men. I particularly want to know, as I want to remove them when I make the changes on the 4th of March. Write about them if you cannot come on.

You know how deeply I sympathize with you in the death of your father. *Sincerely yours*

THE UNITED STATES AND COLOMBIA

To Rafael Reyes

Confidential

Washington, February 20, 1905

Mr. President:

I thank you for your confidential letter. Your quotation of me is substantially correct when you say that I addressed you as follows on the occasion of your visit to me as Colombia's agent in the Panama matter:

If you had been President of Colombia you would have saved Panama, because you would have known how to safeguard its rights and the interests of all and would have avoided the revolution which caused its secession from Colombia. In that case my Government could have helped Colombia to be one of the richest and most prosperous countries of South America.

Like you, I desire to draw a veil over the past, but my dear Mr. President, as you speak of your country as being deeply injured by my country do let me point out to you that in the words of my own quoted above I was endeavoring to show why I thought you would have saved Colombia from the trouble that befell her had you been her President. This country, so far from wronging Colombia, made every possible effort to persuade Colombia to allow herself to be benefited. I cannot seem by remaining quiet to countenance for one moment the idea that this country did anything but show a spirit not merely of justice but of generosity in its dealings with Colombia. Had you been President, I firmly believe that this spirit would have been met with a like spirit from Colombia, and that therefore Colombia, by the mere fact of ratifying the treaty agreed upon with the United States, would have prevented the revolution in Panama, and would have itself become rich and prosperous.

You say you are lacking at present the means of arranging in a decorous manner the pending questions between Colombia, the United States and Panama, and you ask me to do justice and thereby help you. Of course if I can help you in any way I will; but, my dear Mr. President, I do not quite understand what it is expected we shall do. If the people of Panama desire to take a plebiscite as to whether or not they shall resume connections with Colombia, most emphatically I have no objections and will be delighted so to inform them; but I cannot press them unless they desire to do it. So about their assumption of a portion of Colombia's debt. We have stated that in our judgment this should be done by Panama, and we were informed by their minister here, Mr. Bunau-Varilla, that they intended to do it; but we cannot force them to do it.

As for the purchase of the islands which I understand Colombia would like to sell to us, our Navy Department does not deem it to our interest to procure them, and I am very much afraid that a treaty for their purchase would not be approved by the Senate of the United States.

I have shown your letter to Mr. Hay. I wish I could write you in a manner that would be more agreeable.

With profound respect, I am, *Sincerely yours*

PRAISE FOR A POET

To Edwin Arlington Robinson

Washington, March 27, 1905

Dear Mr. Robinson:

I have enjoyed your poems especially "The Children of the Night" so much that I must write to tell you so. Will you permit me to ask what you are doing and how you are getting along? I wish I could see you. *Sincerely yours*

HELPING ROBINSON

To Richard Watson Gilder

Personal

Washington, March 31, 1905

My dear Gilder:

I thank you for your letter and am particularly interested about Robinson. Curiously enough I had just written him, but evidently had the wrong address. Now I should like to help him, but it seems to me that it is inadvisable for him to go to England. You know I believe that our literary men are always hurt by going abroad. If Bret Harte had stayed in the West, if he had not even come East, he might have gone on doing productive work. To go to England was the worst thing possible for him. In the same way, I think Joel Chandler Harris has continued to do good work because he has remained in Atlanta instead of going to New York. I wish you could find out for me how Robinson is getting along. Perhaps

I could give him some position in the Government service, just as Walt Whitman and John Burroughs were given Government positions. It seems to me inadvisable to send him abroad. *Faithfully yours*

THE KAISER

To Cecil Spring-Rice

Personal

Washington, May 13, 1905

Dear Cecil:

Of course in a way I suppose it is natural that my English friends generally, from the King down, should think I was under the influence of the Kaiser, but you ought to know better, old man. There is much that I admire about the Kaiser and there is more that I admire about the German people. But the German people are too completely under his rule for me to be able to disassociate them from him, and he himself is altogether too jumpy, too volatile in his policies, too lacking in the power of continuous and sustained thought and action for me to feel that he is in any way such a man as for instance Taft or Root. You might as well talk of my being under the influence of [   ] I very sincerely wish I could get England and Germany into friendly relations. While my business is to look primarily after the interests of my own country, I feel that I help this country instead of hurting it when I try to benefit other countries. I do not intend for a moment to be improperly meek about it. I have steadfastly preached a big navy, and I have with equal steadfastness seen that our navy is practiced until I have reason to believe that ship for ship it is as efficient as any. I do not believe that as things are now in the world any nation can rely upon inoffensiveness for safety. Neither do I believe that it can rely upon alliance with any other nation for safety. My object is to keep America in trim so that fighting her shall be too expensive and dangerous a task to likely be undertaken by anybody; and I shall try at the same time to make her act in a spirit of justice and good will toward others, as will prevent anyone taking such a risk lightly, and will, if possible, help a little toward a general attitude of peacefulness and righteousness in the world at large. I have tried to behave in this way toward England primarily, and also toward France and Germany and toward Japan. As for Russia, I like the Russian people and earnestly hope for their future welfare, but I agree with all you say as to the Russian system of government. I loathe it.

Now in treating with the Kaiser I have simply applied in his special case my general rules. In one of your last letters you speak of the German army as being a bulwark for civilization against disorder in view of the breakup in Russian affairs. I doubt if I really have as strong a feeling for Germany as this that you thus by implication express. I wish her well. I wish the Kaiser well. I should never dream of counting on his friendship for this country. He respects us because he thinks that for a sufficient object and on our own terms we would fight, and that we have a pretty good navy with which to fight. I shall hope that on these terms I can keep the respect not merely of Berlin, but of St. Petersburg and Tokyo both. I know that except on these terms the respect of any one of the three cannot be kept. But by combining a real friendliness of attitude with ability to hold our own in the event of trouble coming, I shall hope to keep on good terms with all, and to lend some assistance to Japan in the present war in which I think she is right. The Kaiser has so far acted with me in the far East. I do not for one moment believe that he has any long-settled and well-thought-out plans of attack upon England, such as Bismarck developed, first as regards Austria, and then as regards France. He is, and I think your people ought to be able to see it, altogether too jumpy and too erratic to think out and carry out any such policy. If England ever has trouble with Germany I think it will come from some unreasoning panic which will inspire each to attack the other for fear of being attacked itself. I get exasperated with the Kaiser because of his sudden vagaries like this Morocco policy, or like his speech about the yellow peril the other day, a speech worthy of any fool congressman; and I cannot of course follow or take too seriously a man whose policy is one of such violent and often wholly irrational zigzags. But I don't see why you should be afraid of him. You have told me that he would like to make a continental coalition against England. He may now and then have dreamed of such a coalition; and only last December your people were fully convinced he intended to make immediate war on them. But it is perfectly obvious that he had no such thought, or he would never have mortally insulted France by his attitude about Morocco. If the Kaiser ever causes trouble it will be from jumpiness and not because of long-thought-out and deliberate purpose. In other words he is much more apt to be exasperating and unpleasant than a dangerous neighbor. I have been reading de La Gorce's *Histoire du Second Empire*, and I can imagine no greater contrast than that offered by Bismarck's policy from '63 to '71, with that of the Kaiser during the last eight years, the only ones in which I have watched him closely.

To turn to matters of more immediate importance, I am of course watching to see what the Russian and Japanese fleets will do in eastern waters. France has obligingly given the Russians a base, but she may have to take it away from them. The Russian fleet is materially somewhat stronger than the Japanese. My own belief is that the Japanese superiority in morale and training will more than offset this. But I am not sure, and I wish that peace would come. Personally I wish that Japan had made peace on the conditions she originally thought of after Mukden was fought; as I pointed out to her Government, a few months' extra war would eat up all the indemnity she could possibly expect Russia to pay. Just at the moment Russia is riding a high horse and will not talk peace. However, by the time you receive this letter all of what I have said may be an old story. I hope you like Meyer.

Give my love to Mrs. Springy. *Ever yours*

INTELLIGENCE IN ANIMALS

To John Burroughs

Washington, May 29, 1905

Dear Oom John:

I have read your *Atlantic Monthly* article with much interest. I have nothing to suggest except a slight toning-down of your statement as to the effect from the protective standpoint of the mother bird's indistinct coloration. It is, as you point out, well-nigh impossible to say with our present knowledge exactly what effects such things have on the life of the species; yet I am strongly inclined to believe that the coloration of the mother in the case of certain ground-breeding birds, where this coloration blends with the dead leaves and soil, is of benefit. In some species the cock bird takes part in incubating. I wonder whether this is the case as often in cases where the bird is brightly colored as where he is dull colored?

Long, under the name of "Peter Rabbit," makes an attack upon you in *Harper's Monthly*. I am utterly at a loss to understand how reputable publications can encourage such a man. I do not think he is worth while your mentioning by name in your forthcoming volume. But do let me, at the risk of seeming offensive, repeat what I have once before written you about care in taking certain [   ] positions in matters that are at least open to argument. Long and his crew have been only too glad to divert attention from the issue, which was their untruthfulness in reporting what they purported to have seen, to the issue of how much intelligence animals display — as to whether they teach their young, and so forth. Some of the closest observers I know — men like Hart Merriam, for instance — feel that animals do teach their young in certain cases and among the higher forms; and feel very strongly that the higher mammals, such as dogs, monkeys, wolves, foxes, and so forth, have mental faculties which are really far more akin to those of man than they are to the very rudimentary faculties out of which they were developed in the lower forms of life. I am inclined to sympathize with both of these views myself. I think there has been preposterous exaggeration among those who speak of the conscious teaching by animals of their young; but I feel that the balance of proof certainly is in favor of this being at least occasionally true. I believe it would be very valuable if we could get observations to show its frequency, and the kind of animals in which it occurs. So it is with mental processes. Man, and the higher anthropoid apes, for instance, have developed from ancestors which in the immemorial past possessed only such mental attributes as a mollusk or crustacean of today possess. For reasons which we may never know, man, perhaps sometime in the Quaternary period — or sometime before — began to advance in extraordinary fashion. Yet wide and deep though the gulf is between even the lowest man and an anthropoid ape or some carnivore as intelligent as a dog, there are in both the latter animals and in a good many other higher animals intellectual traits and (if I may use the word loosely) moral traits, which represent embryonic or rudimentary forms of such intellectual and moral traits of our own, and perhaps prefigure them, just as the little skin-covered bony knobs or knoblike epidermal growths on the heads of the animals which, ages ago, were the ancestors of the deer, the antelope, the rhinoceros of today, prefigured the extraordinary horn and antler growth of the existing forms. Of course my comparison is not meant to be accurate. The distance traveled in our case has been immeasurably greater, and the make-believe out-of-door observers who read human emotions and thoughts into all kinds of birds and mammals deserve the most severe chastisement, and I feel that you rendered a really great service by what you did in reference to them; but all I mean is that I would be careful not to state my position in such extreme form as to let them shift the issue to one in which they will have very excellent observers on their side.

I am amused at your falling foul of Hudson, that Englishman who writes of South America. I happened to study what he said of the cougar, and became convinced that now and then his romances were as wild as those of Long himself. *Always yours*

THE RUSSO-JAPANESE WAR

To Cecil Spring-Rice

Confidential

Washington, June 16, 1905

Dear Springy:

Well, it seems to me that the Russian bubble has been pretty thoroughly pricked. I thought the Japanese would defeat Rojestvensky; but I had no conception, and no one else had any conception save possibly Admiral Evans and Lord Charles Beresford, that there would be a slaughter rather than a fight, and that the Russians would really make no adequate resistance whatever. I have never been able to persuade myself that Russia was going to conquer the world at any time [   ] justified in considering, and I suppose this particular fear is now at an end everywhere.

What wonderful people the Japanese are! They are quite as remarkable industrially as in warfare. In a dozen years the English, Americans and Germans, who now dread one another as rivals in the trade of the Pacific, will have each to dread the Japanese more than they do any other nation. In the middle of this war they have actually steadily increased their exports to China, and are proceeding in the establishment of new lines of steamers in new points of Japanese trade expansion throughout the Pacific. Their lines of steamers are not allowed to compete with one another, but each competes with some foreign line, and usually the competition is to the advantage of the Japanese. The industrial growth of the nation is as marvellous as its military growth. It is now a great power and will be a greater power. As I have always said, I cannot pretend to prophesy what the results, as they affect the United States, Australia, and the European powers with interests in the Pacific, will ultimately be. I believe that Japan will take its place as a great civilized power of a formidable type, and with motives and ways of thought which are not quite those of the powers of our race. My own policy is perfectly simple, though I have not the slightest idea whether I can get my country to follow it. I wish to see the United States treat the Japanese in a spirit of all possible courtesy, and with generosity and justice. At the same time I wish to see our navy constantly built up and each ship kept at the highest possible point of efficiency as a fighting unit. If we follow this course we shall have no trouble with the Japanese or anyone else. But if we bluster; if we behave rather badly to other nations; if we show that we regard the Japanese as an inferior and alien race, and try to treat them as we have treated the Chinese; and if at the same time we fail to keep our navy at the highest point of efficiency and size — then we shall invite disaster.

You of course have seen all that I have had on hand in the matter of the peace negotiations. It has been rather worse than getting a treaty through the United States Senate! Each side has been so suspicious, and often so unreasonable, and so foolish. I am bound to say that the Kaiser has behaved admirably and has really helped me. I hope that your people are sincerely desirous of peace and will use their influence at the proper time to prevent their asking impossible terms. In this particular case I think that peace will be in the interest of all mankind, including both combatants. If the war goes on for a year Japan will drive Russia out of East Asia. But in such a case she will get no indemnity; she will have the terrific strain of an extra year's loss of blood and money; and she will have acquired a territory which will be of no use to her. On the other hand, Russia will have been pushed out of East Asia and will have suffered a humiliating loss which a century could not repair. If they now make peace, Russia giving up Sakhalin and paying a reasonable indemnity — these being the two chief features of the peace, together with Japan retaining control of what she has already obtained — then we shall have Russia with the territory she possessed in East Asia a dozen years ago still practically intact, so that no unbearable humiliation and loss will have been inflicted upon her. Japan will have gained enormously by the war. At the same time each power will be in a sense the guarantor of the other's good conduct. As I told you, I do not need any such guarantee as far as the United States is concerned. In the first place, I do not believe that Japan would menace the United States in any military way; and in the next place, if the menace comes I believe we could be saved only by our own efforts and not by an alliance with anyone else. And I believe that the peace I am trying to get will not be only a good thing temporarily, but will be a good thing permanently. I earnestly hope that your people take the same view, and that they will not permit any feeling that they would like to see both combatants exhausted to prevent them doing all they can to bring about peace. Germany and France should make their influence felt by making Russia willing to yield what she ought to yield; and England should make her influence felt in making the Japanese terms not so severe that Russia, instead of granting them, would prefer to continue the war.

Give my love to Mrs. Springy. *Ever yours*

THE DEATH OF JOHN HAY

To Henry Cabot Lodge

Confidential

Oyster Bay, July 11, 1905

Dear Cabot:

John Hay's death was very sudden and removes from American public life a man whose position was literally unique. The country was the better because he had lived, for it was a fine thing to have set before our young men the example of success contained in the career of a man who had held so many and such important public positions, while there was not in his nature the slightest touch of the demagogue, and who in addition to his great career in political life had also left a deep mark in literature. His *Life of Lincoln* is a monument, and of its kind his *Castilian Days* is perfect. This is all very sad for Mrs. Hay. Personally his loss is very great to me because I was very fond of him, and as you know always stopped at his house after church on Sunday to have an hour's talk with him. From the standpoint of the public business — not from the standpoint of the loss to the public of such a figure — the case is different. Of course, what I am about to say I can only say to a close friend, for it seems almost ungenerous. But for two years his health has been such that he could do very little work of importance. His name, his reputation, his staunch loyalty, all made him a real asset of the administration. But in actual work I had to do the big things myself, and the other things I always feared would be badly done or not done at all. He had grown to hate the Kaiser so that I could not trust him in dealing with Germany. When, for instance, the Kaiser made the excellent proposition about the integrity of China, Hay wished to refuse and pointed out where the Kaiser's proposition as originally made contained what was inadvisable. I took hold of it myself, accepted the Kaiser's offer, but at the same time blandly changed it so as to wholly remove the objectionable feature (that is, I accepted it as applying to all of China outside of Manchuria, whereas he had proposed in effect that we should allow Russia to work her sweet will in all northern China) and had Hay publish it in this form. Even before this time in the British Panama canal negotiations I got the treaty in right shape only by securing the correction of all of the original faults. But all this is only for you and me to talk over together, for it is not of the slightest consequence now, and what is of consequence is that America should be the richer by John Hay's high and fine reputation.

I hesitated a little between Root and Taft, for Taft as you know is very close to me. But as soon as I began seriously to think it over I saw there was really no room for doubt whatever, because it was not a choice as far as the Cabinet was concerned between Root and Taft, but a choice of having both instead of one. I was not at all sure that Root would take it, although from various hints I had received I thought the chances at least even. To my great pleasure he accepted at once and was evidently glad to accept and to be back in public life and in the Cabinet in such a position. He will be a tower of strength to us all. I not only hope but believe that he will get on well with the Senate, and he will at once take a great burden off my mind in connection with various subjects, such as Santo Domingo and Venezuela. For a number of months now I have had to be my own Secretary of State, and while I am very glad to be it so far as the broad outlines of the work are concerned, I of course ought not to have to attend to the details.

At Russia's request I asked Japan for an armistice, but I did not expect that Japan would grant it, although I of course put the request as strongly as possible. Indeed I cannot say that I really blame Japan for not granting it, for she is naturally afraid that magnanimity on her part would be misinterpreted and turned to bad account against her. The Japanese envoys have sailed and the Russians I am informed will be here by August first. I think then they can get an armistice. I received a message of thanks from the German Government for my part in securing a conference between Germany and France with the other Powers on the Morocco question. This is a dead secret. Not a word of it has gotten out into the papers; but I became the intermediary between Germany and France when they seemed to have gotten into an impasse; and have already been cordially thanked by the French Government through Jusserand. I suggested the final terms by which they could come together. Speck acted merely of course as the mouthpiece of the Emperor; but with Jusserand I was able to go over the whole matter, and we finally worked out a conclusion which I think was entirely satisfactory. Do not let anyone, excepting of course Nannie, know of this. Even Whitelaw Reid does not know it. I had told Taft but not Hay. I shall tell Root.

Taft is a great big fellow. He urged me to bring Root into the Cabinet. Of course the papers with their usual hysteria have for the moment completely dropped Taft, whom they were all booming violently up to three weeks ago, and are now occupied with their new toy, Root. They are sure that he has come into the Cabinet for the purpose of making himself President, and the more picturesque among them take the view that he stipulated this before he accepted and that I in effect pledged him the Presidency — omitting the trifling detail that even if I had been idiot enough to feel that way, he would not have been idiot enough to think that I had any power in the matter. As a matter of fact I am inclined to think that Taft's being from the west, together with his attitude on corporations, would for the moment make him the more available man. Of course no one can tell what will be the outcome three years hence.

Will you tell Nannie that I have sent her at Nahant one of

the Saint-Gaudens inauguration medals. I am very glad we got Saint-Gaudens to do this work. Edith makes believe that she thinks it is a good likeness of me, which I regard as most wifely on her part. But of the eagle on the reverse I do approve and also of the Latin rendering for "a square deal."
Ever yours

P.S. About the Morocco business I received the following cablegram from Ambassador Tower:

The German Minister for Foreign Affairs announces to me that the agreement between Germany and France in regard to Morocco was signed in Paris last Saturday. He asked me to communicate the information to you and say that the Government of Germany recognizes the interest which the President has taken in that subject, and greatly appreciates what he has done to bring about a speedy and peaceful solution of the questions at issue.

and also the following from Ambassador Jusserand:

I leave greatly comforted by the news concerning Morocco, the agreement arrived at is in substance the one we had considered and the acceptation of which you did so very much to secure. Letters just received by me from Paris show that your beneficent influence at this grave juncture is deeply and gratefully felt. They confirm also what I guessed was the case, that is that there was a point where more yielding would have been impossible; everybody in France felt it, and people braced up silently in view of the possible greatest events.

I consider it rather extraordinary that my suggestions should apparently have gratefully been received by both sides as well as acted on. A still more extraordinary thing is that the Emperor should have sent through Speck a statement that he should instruct his delegate to vote as the United States delegate does on any point where I consider it desirable. This is a point, however, about which I shall be very wary of availing myself of.

COUGARS AND LEOPARDS

To Frank Charles Bostock

Oyster Bay, July 18, 1905

My dear Mr. Bostock:

In connection with your book on the training of wild animals, in which I was greatly interested, I would like to ask whether you find that the puma or cougar shows a different kind of temper from the leopard or old world panther, and from the jaguar? I ask this because in hunting it I have found it to be compared to the big bear, a cowardly animal, and if what I read of the danger of hunting the Indian and African leopard is true, then the puma is not nearly as formidable as the leopard or the jaguar — in short is not nearly so formidable as the big spotted cats, though it is as big and as formidably armed. Have you noticed any difference in your work among these species taking the average of one and comparing it as to temper, ferocity, etc., with the average of the other? Of course there are wide individual differences; but that is not what I am after at present. I notice that you say there is little or no difference between the tiger, lion, leopard or jaguar.

With regard, *Sincerely yours*

HELPING AMERICAN LETTERS

To James Hulme Canfield

Personal

Oyster Bay, August 16, 1905

My dear Canfield:

I am much obliged to you for your letter and for the volume, *Captain Craig*.

You may be interested in knowing that it was my son Kermit who first called my attention to Robinson's poems. He took a great fancy to them and gave a copy to his mother and another copy to me. Then he found out that Robinson was having a hard time and was at work on the subway in New York, and Kermit and John Lodge (Senator Lodge's son) both began to press me to do something for him. And finally — tell it not in civil-service-reform Gath, nor whisper it in the streets of merit-system Askelon — I hunted him up, found he was having a very hard time, and put him in the Treasury Department. I think he will do his work all right, but I am free to say that he was put in less with a view to the good of the government service than with a view to helping American letters.

Sincerely yours

URGING JAPAN TO MAKE PEACE

To Kentaro Kaneko

Confidential

Oyster Bay, August 23, 1905

My dear Baron Kaneko:

In supplement to what I wrote you yesterday, for the consideration of His Majesty the Japanese Emperor's envoys, let me add this:

It seems to me that it is to the interest of the great empire of Nippon now to make peace, for two reasons: 1, self-interest; 2, the interest of the world, to which she owes a certain duty. Remember, I do not speak of continuing the war rather than give up Sakhalin, which I think would be right; but of continuing the war in order to get a great sum of money from Russia, which I think would be wrong. Of course you may succeed in getting it; but in my judgment even this success would be too dearly paid for; and if you failed to get the money, no additional humiliations and losses inflicted on Russia would repay Japan for the additional expenditure in blood, in money, in national exhaustion.

1. It is Japan's interest now to close the war. She has won the control of Korea and Manchuria; she has doubled her own fleet in destroying that of Russia; she has Port Arthur, Dalny, the Manchurian railroad, she has Sakhalin. It is not worth her

while to continue the war for money, when so to continue it would probably eat up more money than she could at the end get back from Russia. She will be wise now to close the war in triumph, and to take her seat as a leading member at the council table of the nations.

2. Ethically it seems to me that Japan owes a duty to the world at this crisis. The civilized world looks to her to make peace; the nations believe in her; let her show her leadership in matters ethical no less than in matters military. The appeal is made to her in the name of all that is lofty and noble; and to this appeal I hope she will not be deaf.

With profound regard, *Sincerely yours*

A MESSAGE FOR THE CZAR

To George von Lengerke Meyer

Telegram

Oyster Bay, August 25, 1905

My second cable was forwarded after the arrival of your first. Japan has now on deposit in United States about fifty million dollars of the last war loan. I do not know whether she has more. Please tell His Majesty that I dislike intruding any advice on him again, but for fear of misapprehension I venture again to have these statements made to him. I of course would not have him act against his conscience, but I earnestly hope his conscience will guide him so as to prevent the continuance of a war when this continuance may involve Russia in a greater calamity than has ever befallen it since it first rose to power in both Europe and Asia. I see it publicly announced today by Count Lamsdorff that Russia will neither pay money nor surrender territory. I beg His Majesty to consider that such an announcement means absolutely nothing when Sakhalin is already in the hands of the Japanese. If on such a theory the war is persevered in no one can foretell the result, but the military representatives of the Powers most friendly to Russia assure me that the continuance of the war will probably mean the loss not merely of Sakhalin but of eastern Siberia, and if after a year of struggle this proves true then any peace which came could only come on terms which would indicate a real calamity. Most certainly I think it will be a bad thing for Japan to go on with the war, but I think it will be a far worse thing for Russia. There is now a fair chance of getting peace on honorable terms, and it seems to me that it will be a dreadful thing for Russia and for all the civilized world if the chance is thrown away. My advices are that the plenipotentiaries at Portsmouth have come to a substantial agreement on every point except the money question and the question of Sakhalin. Let it now be announced that as regards these two points peace shall be made on the basis of the retrocession of the northern half of Sakhalin to Russia on payment of a sum of redemption money by Russia, the amount of this redemption money and the amount to be paid for the Russian prisoners to be settled by further negotiations. This does not commit the Russian Government as to what sum shall be paid, leaving it open to further negotiation. If it is impossible for Russia and Japan to come to an agreement on this sum they might possibly call in the advice of say some high French or German official appointed by or with the consent of Russia and some English official appointed by or with the consent of Japan and have these men then report to the negotiators their advice, which might or might not be binding upon the negotiators. This it seems to me would be an entirely honorable way of settling the difficulty. I cannot of course guarantee that Japan will agree to this proposal, but if His Majesty agrees to it I will endeavor to get the Japanese Government to do so likewise. I earnestly hope that this cable of mine can receive His Majesty's attention before the envoys meet tomorrow, and I cannot too strongly say that I feel that peace now may prevent untold calamities in the future. Let me repeat that in this proposal I suggest that neither Russia nor Japan do anything but face accomplished facts and that I do not specify or attempt to specify what amount should be paid, leaving the whole question of the amount to be paid in redemption money for the northern half of Sakhalin to be settled by further negotiation. I fear that if these terms are rejected it may be possible that Japan will give up any idea of making peace or of ever getting money and that she will decide to take and to keep Vladivostok and Harbin and the whole Manchurian railway and this of course would mean that she would take east Siberia. Such a loss to Russia would in my judgment be a disaster of portentous size, and I earnestly desire to save Russia from such a risk. If peace is made on the terms I have mentioned Russia is left at the end of this war substantially unharmed, the national honor and interest saved, and the results of what Russians have done in Asia since the days of Ivan the Terrible unimpaired. But if peace is now rejected and if Japan decides that she will give up any idea of obtaining any redemption money or any other sum no matter how small the military situation is such that there is at least a good chance and in the estimate of most outside observers a strong probability that though Japan will have to make heavy sacrifices she will yet take Harbin, Vladivostok and east Siberia, and if this is once done the probabilities are overwhelming that she could never be dislodged. I cannot too strongly state my conviction that while peace in accordance with the suggestions above outlined is earnestly to be desired from the standpoint of the whole world and from the standpoints of both combatants, yet that far above all it is chiefly to Russia's interest and perhaps to her vital interest that it should come in this way and at this time.

SUBMARINES

To Charles Joseph Bonaparte

Personal

Oyster Bay, August 28, 1905

My dear Bonaparte:

I am not in the least surprised at what you tell me about Commander Young. I have grown to feel that he is not very much of a fellow. He gets intoxicated quite often and on one occasion came into my office in that condition while I was President.

Now may I first of all make one suggestion about politics and then one about the Navy Department?

First, about politics. It is stated that you are going to speak in the municipal campaign at Philadelphia. I hope this is not so. I heartily sympathize with the Mayor, and if I were a private citizen I should be actively supporting him, as I take it for granted you would. But you and I have all we can well attend to in national affairs, and I do not think that the amount of good that you could do by speaking in Philadelphia would compensate for the bitter fight you would probably cause between the administration and certainly one, and probably both, of the United States Senators from Pennsylvania. Moreover, it would mean that we should be asked to interfere in every similar case in the union. For instance, I am inclined to think that here in New York this fall if Jerome were nominated I should support him though there is much about him I dislike and disapprove of. But it might well be that the contact will take such shape that for me to support him would force a break with both the New York Senators. Yet if you took part in the Philadelphia campaign, which would of course be accepted as the administration taking part, it would be almost impossible for the administration to refuse to take part also in the New York campaign. So it would be in many other cities. Probably the rumor that you are to take part in the Philadelphia campaign has no foundation in fact.

As to the second matter, I have become greatly interested in submarine boats. They are in no sense substitutes for above-water torpedo boats, not to speak of battleships, cruisers, and the like, but they may on certain occasions supplement other craft, and they should be developed. Now there are excellent old-style naval officers of the kind who drift into positions at Washington who absolutely decline to recognize this fact and who hamper the development of the submarine boat in every way. One of the ways they have done it has been by the absurd and worse than absurd ruling that the officers and men engaged in the very hazardous, delicate, difficult and responsible work of experimenting with these submarine boats are not to be considered as on sea duty. I felt positively indignant when I found that the men on the *Plunger*, who incur a certain risk every time they go down in her and who have to be trained to the highest point as well as to show iron nerve in order to be of any use in their positions, are penalized for being on the *Plunger* instead of being in some much less responsible and much less dangerous position on a cruise in a big ship. I find that the officers, for instance, have no quarters on board and yet none on shore, and the Auditor for the Navy Department has refused to allow commutation for such quarters while the Navy Department has refused to allow the men such quarters, servants or mess outfits. Of course this is monstrous. There should be a cook, steward and mess outfit allowed for each submarine vessel, and where possible — in almost every case it would be possible — quarters should be allowed for the officers. The regulations should provide that the services of officers attached to submarines should be considered as service on ships on the cruise. The case of the enlisted men, in whom I am even more interested, should be met by the embodiment in the regulations of certain changes as follows:

Ratings for Submarine Men

(a) That enlisted men serving on submarines under acting appointments as Chief Petty Officers, having finished their one-year probation and having been found professionally, mentally and morally qualified by a proper board of officers from ships other than those on which they are serving, shall receive permanent appointments in their ratings irrespective of service on cruising vessels.

(b) Enlisted men serving in submarines may be advanced in rating without regard to the compliment of the vessel.

Pay for Submarine Men

(a) That enlisted men regularly detailed for instruction in submarine boats but not having qualified shall receive five dollars per month in addition to the pay of their rating.

(b) Enlisted men serving with submarine boats and having been reported by their commanding officers to the Navy Department as qualified for submarine torpedo-boat work, shall receive ten dollars per month in addition to the pay of their rating.

(c) Enlisted men serving with submarine torpedo boats having been reported by their commanding officers to the Navy Department as qualified for submarine torpedo-boat work shall receive one dollar in addition to their pay for each day during any part of which they shall have been submerged in a submarine boat while underway.

Another matter I shall call your attention to, and that is the delay in repairing vessels, such delay being caused usually by delay in furnishing material. How would it do to have a report made on the cases of the following: *Iris, Glacier, Buffalo, Uncas, Yankee, Indiana, Luzon, Cuba* and the torpedo boats at Norfolk? *Sincerely yours*

Remember that whenever you can conveniently come here for a night I am anxious to have you.

"A JUST WAR MAY BE THE HIGHEST DUTY"

To Carl Schurz

Personal

Oyster Bay, September 8, 1905

My dear Mr. Schurz:

I thank you for your congratulations. As to what you say about disarmament — which I suppose is the rough equivalent of "the gradual diminution of the oppressive burdens imposed upon the world by armed peace" — I am not clear either what can be done or what ought to be done. If I had been known as one of the conventional type of peace advocates I could have done nothing whatever in bringing about peace now, I would be powerless in the future to accomplish anything, and I would not have been able to help confer the boons upon Cuba, the Philippines, Porto Rico and Panama, brought about by our action therein. If the Japanese had not armed during the last twenty years, this would indeed be a sorrowful century for Japan. If this country had not fought the Spanish War; if we had failed to take the action we did about Panama; all mankind would have been the loser. While the Turks were butchering the Armenians the European powers kept the peace and thereby added a burden of infamy to the Nineteenth Century, for in keeping that peace a greater number of lives were lost than in any European war since the days of Napoleon, and these lives were those of women and children as well as of men; while the moral degradation, the brutality inflicted and endured, the aggregate of hideous wrong done, surpassed that of any war of which we have record in modern times. Until people get it firmly fixed in their minds that peace is valuable chiefly as a means to righteousness, and that it can only be considered as an end when it also coincides with righteousness, we can do only a limited amount to advance its coming on this earth. There is of course no analogy at present between international law and private or municipal law, because there is no sanction of force for the former while there is for the latter. Inside our own nation the law-abiding man does not have to arm himself against the lawless simply because there is some armed force — the police, the sheriff's posse, the national guard, the regulars — which can be called out to enforce the laws. At present there is no similar international force to call on, and I do not as yet see how it could at present be created. Hitherto peace has often come only because some strong and on the whole just power has by armed force, or the threat of armed force, put a stop to disorder. In a very interesting French book the other day I was reading of how the Mediterranean was freed from pirates only by the "pax Britannica," established by England's naval force. The hopeless and hideous bloodshed and wickedness of Algiers and Turkestan were stopped, and only could be stopped, when civilized nations in the shape of Russia and France took possession of them. The same was true of Burma and the Malay states, as well as Egypt, with regard to England. Peace has come only as the sequel to the armed interference of a civilized power which, relatively to its opponent, was a just and beneficent power. If England had disarmed to the point of being unable to conquer the Sudan and protect Egypt, so that the Mahdists had established their supremacy in northeastern Africa, the result would have been a horrible and bloody calamity to mankind. It was only the growth of the European powers in military efficiency that freed eastern Europe from the dreadful scourge of the Tartar and partially freed it from the dreadful scourge of the Turk. Unjust war is dreadful; a just war may be the highest duty. To have the best nations, the free and civilized nations, disarm and leave the despotisms and barbarisms with great military force, would be a calamity compared to which the calamities caused by all the wars of the

Nineteenth Century would be trivial. Yet it is not easy to see how we can by international agreement state exactly which power ceases to be free and civilized and which comes near the line of barbarism or despotism. For example, I suppose it would be very difficult to get Russia and Japan to come to a common agreement on this point; and there are at least some citizens of other nations, not to speak of their governments, whom it would also be hard to get together.

This does not in the least mean that it is hopeless to make the effort. It may be that some scheme will be developed. America, fortunately, can cordially assist in such an effort, for no one in his senses would suggest our disarmament; and though we should continue to perfect our small navy and our minute army, I do not think it necessary to increase the number of our ships — at any rate as things look now — nor the number of our soldiers. Of course our navy must be kept up to the highest point of efficiency, and the replacing of old and worthless vessels by first-class new ones may involve an increase in the personnel; but not enough to interfere with our action along the lines you have suggested. But before I would know how to advocate such action, save in some such way as commending it to the attention of The Hague Tribunal, I would have to have a feasible and rational plan of action presented. *Sincerely yours*

It seems to me that a general stop in the increase of the war navies of the world *might* be a good thing; but I would not like to speak too positively offhand. Of course it is only in continental Europe that the armies are too large; and before advocating action as regards them I should have to weigh matters carefully — including by the way such a matter as the Turkish army. At any rate nothing useful can be done unless with the clear recognition that we put peace second to righteousness.

THE PORTSMOUTH TREATY

To Whitelaw Reid

Personal

Oyster Bay, September 11, 1905

My dear Reid:

I thank you for your very interesting letter. I think you were right in not giving out that interview. I have had just the same difficulty myself. I wanted to speak in the strongest terms of how well the Japanese had behaved, and yet was hampered by my unwillingness to offend the Russians.

The Kaiser stood by me like a trump. I did not get much direct assistance from the English government, but I did get indirect assistance for I learned that they forwarded to Japan my note to Durand, and I think that the signing of the Anglo-Japanese treaty made Japan feel comparatively safe as to the future. While it was even more to Russia's interest than to Japan's to make peace, yet it was also absolutely to Japan's interest. For her to continue the war for an indemnity, with the practical certainty of spending two dollars to get one and a likelihood of not even getting the one, would have been even greater folly than wickedness.

I was amused at what you told me as to the British Ambassador to Paris, Sir Francis Bertie, saying that the terms were very hard on Japan and would not be very well received there, and would tend to make the United States and me very unpopular in Japan, and would have commercial and political results, and so forth. Some of the English officials as well as some influential British merchants in the East have taken this tone and have encouraged the Japanese to demand the impossible. I do not know whether an attitude like that of Sir Francis is due to downright stupidity or desire to see Russia worried and exhausted, no matter how great the damage to Japan. At any rate it was a shortsighted view, alike from the standpoint of Japan and from the standpoint of England. The Japanese government — that is the group of so-called "elder statesmen" as well as the Mikado — are sincerely grateful to me, and as you know, every step I took was only after previous consultation with them; and that I all along told them that they could not possibly get an indemnity unless Russia was sufficiently panic-stricken to give it. That the people may visit upon me and upon America some portion of the discontent which ought to be visited upon themselves and upon their own leaders for misleading them as to what they might obtain, is possible. In international matters I am no great believer in the long-continued effects of gratitude. The United States must rely in the last resort upon their own preparedness and resolution, and not upon the good will of any outside nation. I think England has a more sincere feeling of friendliness for us than has any other power; but even this English friendliness would be a broken reed if we leaned on it, unless we were entirely able in addition to fight for our own hand. No matter how great our strength, we could of course make trouble for ourselves if we behaved wrongly. But merely to be harmless would not save us from aggression. If we keep our navy at a high standard of efficiency and at the same time are just and courteous in our dealings with foreign nations, we will be able to remain on good terms with Japan, with Germany, with all foreign powers. As for Tokyo, I have no right to expect that in the long run its policy will be on a higher level than the policy of St. Petersburg, of Paris or of London.

I read the little skit you sent. Of course it is the kind of thing that has often been done. Nevertheless, the man is right in painting some of the dangers which threaten not merely the empire of Great Britain but all occidental civilization. There are some unpleasant resemblances between the occidental civilization of the present day — that is the civilization of America and Australia no less than of the European nations west of Russia — and the Hellenistic civilization of the centuries succeeding the death of Alexander, no less than the civilization of the Roman world during the first century or two of the empire. There are great differences also, however; and moreover, the evils pointed out in the pamphlet as bearing sway in Great Britain and Australia flourish to an even greater extent in France, to an only less extent in Germany and Scandinavia, and to quite as great an extent here, although here they are hardly as bad in their effects because we have a whole continent to work on and draw an immense mass of immigrants from abroad. The decline in the birth rate I should put as the chief cause as well as the chief symptom of what is evil in the nations I have mentioned; but we must not forget that it has not declined in Italy and but little if at all in Spain, and yet the conditions are quite as unsatisfactory in the former and much more so in the latter country. The general softening of fibre, the selfishness, the luxury, the relaxation of standards, the growth of a spirit such as that of the anti-imperialists — all these are among the unpleasant symptoms which cannot but give us concern for the future. But there are plenty of good symptoms too; and after all none of us can read the future, and our duty is simple. Let us stand valiantly for what is decent and right; let us strive hard, and take with unshaken front whatever comes, whether it be good or ill. Then the fates must decide what the outcome shall be.

Give my warm regards to Mrs. Reid. *Sincerely yours*

P.S. Do you remember writing me as to the rather impertinent and offensive remarks made to you about our administration of the Philippines by an Englishman who was a Governor of a Malay Province, a man named Swettingham, or something like that, who had written a clever book called *The Real Malay*? Well, the other day Leonard Wood was out here and I had a very satisfactory time with him. He told me of what had been done in the last three years under him in the Moro country. As a matter of fact during those three years we have had more difficult work to do than the English have had to do in the Malay Settlements, and it has been done better. It is quite true, as the English say, that we ought to have examined what they have done in Egypt, India and Malay Straits in connection with our own work in the Philippines. But they fail to understand that such an examination would have been useless if it had not been conducted with quite as great care to find out what we should not copy as what we should. In the Moro Provinces we have had substantially the same problems that the English have had in dealing with the Malays and perhaps the Burmese, and we have done our work at least as well as they have theirs, while none of their men in Burma or the Straits Settlements have come up to, for instance, Wood's record. In the rest of the Philippines our problem was entirely different from the British problem, and while we have made some mistakes they are not as a rule the mistakes which the English think we have made; and I may add that they are never mistakes which the anti-imperialists think we have made.

CORPORATE CAMPAIGN CONTRIBUTIONS

To Lincoln Steffens

Personal and confidential

Oyster Bay, September 25, 1905

My dear Steffens:

In your letter you say that the papers report me as wishing that I "could give back the money contributed to the Republican campaign fund by the insurance and other corporations seeking national legislation." The report is absolutely erroneous. I have never said anything of the kind and never thought anything of the kind. You also advise me to pay back the money by asking contributions from "the people who didn't want anything out of the government except general laws and an administration of justice and fair play," and suggest that I should return the money given by "the men who wanted special legislation," and to say that I would like to have it made up by those who asked no favors. In such case you offer to contribute one or five dollars, and you add that if I did what you suggest I "would make the millions feel that it is their government," and that I and my "administration were beholden to the many and not the few." Most emphatically at the present time I feel beholden to the many more than to the few; and I feel beholden both to the many and to the few only in the sense that it is my duty to do my level best both for the many and for the few. I shall certainly not sacrifice the interests of the many to the few; and on the other hand, no matter how few any group of persons may be I shall studiously protect these few people from wrongdoing from the multitude. Do you not heartily approve of both of these positions?

You wish me to search the hidden domain of motive as regards each contributor. I do not suppose you draw the line at the amount contributed. Indeed, it would be impossible to draw such a line. Last year there were thousands of people who contributed one dollar, five dollars, ten dollars, twenty-five dollars or fifty dollars to my campaign fund — not office-holders at all, but plain people of small means. Scores of such subscriptions came to Mr. Loeb and some to me personally. These were the only subscriptions of which I had any personal knowledge, or could have any such knowledge. I know, however from hearing, that when I ran for Governor several friends of mine or believers in me gave sums of from five hundred to two thousand dollars, and a close friend, a kinsman, when I ran for President subscribed ten thousand dollars; while I believe, although I do not know, that a very wealthy man whom I do not know very well but whom I heartily respect and who for some reason admires me, gave over fifty thousand dollars. In all these cases the contributors had no earthly interest, whether they contributed much or contributed little, except in seeing "good laws and an administration of justice and fair play." I would certainly not know where to draw the line in receiving their contributions. I think that some of the men who contributed five dollars to me contributed, relatively to their fortunes, just as much as the men who contributed most to me. I suppose I can discard the idea that you would have me draw the line at any specific amount in contributions.

We therefore come to the question of motive. You say that you would advise my returning the money "given by men who wanted special legislation," and you speak of the insurance and other corporations who contributed "because they wished national legislation." I do not know of a single corporation which contributed last year and which now desires legislation, and I do know that some of those who contributed heavily, or at least whose officers contributed heavily, object very much to the legislation I have been endeavoring to secure. Most certainly, if at the time I had had any information that any man or corporation contributed because they wanted special legislation, or wanted executive or legislative favors of any kind, I should have directed that corporation's money to be returned. But when the money has been received and spent it is out of the question to return it. For instance, I am informed that certain corporations which I am having prosecuted for violation of the law complain that they are being prosecuted and that this is very unjust in view of the fact that they contributed to my campaign fund. I did not know that they had contributed. But if they contributed under the impression that thereby they would secure any improper favor, or immunity for wrongdoing, all I can say is that they entirely misread me, and if I had known what their motives were and that they had contributed I should have had their contributions returned. But inasmuch as this is impossible, it is nonsense for me to express any regret, for the fault is purely theirs and not mine. Excepting this hearsay statement as to certain corporations (which, as a matter of fact, have not been mentioned so far as I know in the press as having contributed to me) I have no information whatever of any man or corporation having contributed for the purpose of obtaining special legislation. For instance, take the case of two men whose testimony has caused all the present talk — Messrs. McCall and Perkins. I knew these two men were supporting me and rather took it for granted that they had contributed to the campaign fund, although I did not know the amount and had no idea that they had contributed as officers of a corporation, and not in their individual capacity. But they certainly do not want national legislation. Mr. McCall has never directly or indirectly, so far as I know, asked or accepted anything out of me in any shape or way, and does not desire anything now, while on the only occasion when I took any action that affected Mr. Perkins' interests the action affected him adversely in the shape of the Northern Securities suit. As yet there has not been a suggestion to me, excepting as above mentioned, that any corporation contributed for improper purposes. Still less has there been a suggestion that any corporation or individual was approached in an improper way by any man connected with my campaign. I know that Mr. Cortelyou informed me just before the close of the campaign and again just after it was over that I could feel absolute certainty as to his actions, and that no man having any authority to speak for me had committed me in any shape or way to do more than fair and square justice to every interest and every individual. I should suppose that you would know that if any fool or scoundrel made any promise on my behalf they would be made without my authority; and that no one, not even a scoundrel unless he was also a fool, would believe that there was any authority lying behind such a promise. Ten months have passed since my election. You surely must know that during that time we have gone ahead without deviating a hair's breadth from the line of policy marked out by me during the six preceding years while I was Governor and President. As a matter of fact, of the people who contributed to my campaign fund, so far as I know, but four have made any kind of a request for favors from me. Three of them were requests for signed photographs, which I granted. At the same time I granted hundreds of similar requests to people who had not contributed. The fourth was a request which I could not grant, and those making it did not put it upon the ground that they had contributed to the campaign fund.

In short, my dear Steffens, I think that if you will reflect a little you will come to the conclusion that in the first place your premises are wrong, and that in the next place for me to follow such a line as you indicate would be simply silly. Last year I urged upon Congress the need for providing for the publicity of contributions and expenditures by both national parties. Whether corporations should be permitted to contribute or not is doubtful. They always have been allowed to contribute, sometimes to one fund and sometimes to another, often by the authority of the stockholders. If the stockholders do not give the authority to the officers to contribute, the latter should be held responsible, for those who receive the contributions cannot possibly know that they did not have such authority.

When the money has once been expended it is nonsense to speak of the people being reimbursed. Last year, as I happen to know personally, we refused several big contributions because they were offered by corporations concerning which the government was about to take some action — a case in point being Mr. Cortelyou's refusal to receive any money from either the Tobacco Trust or independent tobacco people, in view of my having at that time to decide the tobacco stamp controversy. But ever since I was a boy campaigns have had to be managed by the considerable expenditure of money. My campaign cost a good deal of money. It did not cost as much as either of McKinley's, or as Cleveland's '92 campaign. I doubt if it cost more than Parker's, but it probably cost more than Bryan's or than Harrison's '92 campaign. That an occasional man contributed for an improper motive, that some of the money was improperly used, is doubtless true as regards the campaign of every candidate who was up for the Presidency in any election. My belief was that no campaign was managed on a cleaner basis than my campaign was last year; that in no campaign was the money expended in a cleaner fashion than by the Republican campaign committee of which Mr. Cortelyou was chairman and Mr. Cornelius Bliss treasurer; and that in no campaign was there less pressure of any kind, direct or indirect, to secure contributions from any source; and that in no campaign were the contributions given with less expectation of receiving any favor whatever in return, whether by special legislation or otherwise. I think that an immense proportion of whatever was given, was given simply with the idea that I and the forces I represented stood for the good of the country; that I would give a square deal to every man; that I would protect the poor man in his rights and the man of means in his (and do not forget that the protection is as much needed for the latter as for the former); and that in short it was to the interest of the country, and therefore to the interest of both the man of large means and the man of small means that I should be continued as President. *Yours truly*

P.S. Remember that the wrong lies not in receiving the contribution, large or small, but in exercising, directly or indirectly, any improper pressure to get it, or in making any promise, express or implied, as to any consideration being given for it; by the action or inaction of any government official.

INACCURATE WILDLIFE STORIES

To George Herbert Locke

Private

Oyster Bay, September 27, 1905

My dear Sir:

What I am about to say to you I wish to have treated as for private use only (for yourself and Mr. Long) and not in any way for publication, for I of course could not go into any public discussion.

I thank you for Mr. Long's book. I enjoyed it and am reading it to the children; but I have told them that it is to be judged just as we judge Kipling's *Jungle Books*, and I regret that it is not explicitly stated that it is of this order, although of course with a generally closer fidelity to fact than was possible for Kipling under his scheme. Take the first, and to my mind the most interesting story — that of the great white wolf. There is much in this that is undoubtedly true, just as in the *Song of Roland* there is much light cast on the history of the times of Charlemagne and of the times immediately succeeding. But there are many statements which, if true, are so new and seem so improbable that they should under no circumstances be set forth as accurate (or, as the preface claims, "every incident being minutely true to fact") without the most careful and detailed setting forth of all the authorities for them and of exactly what was observed in each case, exactly by whom and when and where. There are other statements made in the story which from my own knowledge of animals I am confident are utterly inaccurate. To anyone who knows the relative prowess of a single big wolf and of a lynx, or has seen the ease with which a good fighting dog who knows his business will kill a lynx without himself getting harmed, the whole account of the way two wolves kill a lynx is absurd. Then again, take the account of the killing of the caribou by the white wolf, by a "quick snap where the heart lay." This whole account is full of inaccuracies which it is hard to understand in any observer who knows anything about wolves or deer. For instance, after the above injury had been given, Mr. Long describes the big wolf as "holding himself, with tremendous will power, from rushing in headlong, from driving the game, which might run for miles if hard pressed." Now this is sheer nonsense and must come from a complete misunderstanding of how game acts when hurt. A gut-shot or broken-legged caribou will, if hard pressed, go for miles; whereas if not hard pressed it will lie down and the wound stiffen, and it can more easily be approached. But if an animal is hurt in the heart or around the heart, as here described, it makes not the slightest difference whether it is hard pressed or not, any more than it would make if it were hurt in the brain or spine. Such a heart-struck animal will usually make a short, rapid dash, but it is a physical impossibility for it to continue that dash. Whether the wolf had followed it close up or far off would not make twenty yards difference in its run. Personally I greatly doubt the wolf's holding himself in at all under such circumstances, or at least from any such motive as is alleged. But this is not all. If the place of attack on the deer specified by Mr. Long is ever chosen by a wolf, it must be very, very rarely. Mr. Long describes in detail two caribou being killed; and in one case he states that one quick snap of the old wolf's teeth just behind the forelegs "pierced the heart more surely than a hunter's bullet"; exact words used in describing the death of the other caribou I have already quoted. Now not only is this not the usual way in which a wolf kills, but it is so very unusual that I am tempted to doubt if it is a normal way at all, it certainly cannot happen normally as described. Of course, in a sudden scurry of confusion a wolf might seize anywhere; but in the scores and perhaps hundreds of kills by wolves which I have examined — kills of deer, sheep, and young and old cattle — I have never known of one instance in which the heart was the point of the wolf's attack. A moment's reflection will show anyone how unlikely it is that the heart should be so attacked. In a fawn it might occur, under altogether exceptional circumstances, but in a bull caribou I am inclined to think it a physical impossibility. The heart is protected by the ribs, and the wolf's jaws simply could not bite through the ribs into the heart from the side. The gape of a wolf's jaw would not permit this. Apparently Mr. Long means that the wolf bites through from underneath the caribou, taking the whole caribou's chest into his mouth, the dogteeth being supposed to pierce the heart. Now the attitude necessary to make such a bite would be a very unhandy one, and in the case of the full grown caribou a very dangerous one, for the wolf. It is possible, although most unprobable, that under exceptional circumstances a wolf might kill a fawn in this very clumsy way, but I am inclined to think that with an old caribou it would be a physical impossibility. If a caribou were standing or running the wolf would have to turn almost upside down, like a shark, in order to deliver such a bite. Wolves normally kill any large animal by biting at the flanks or haunches. Occasionally, but much more rarely, they seize by the throat. I have known them in the hurly-burly of the fight to seize in many different ways, but never under any circumstances have I known them to seize in the way described by Mr. Long. It cannot possibly be their regular method of seizure, and if it is ever resorted to it must be under such extraordinary circumstances, and in itself it is so extraordinary in nature, that the most minute account of exactly what was done should be given in order that the matter may be authenticated.

I have mentioned offhand a couple of things as I think they would strike any observing hunter who read the book. I could mention scores of others, but it is of course not worth while. I speak of these at all only to emphasize my regret that the book was not put out frankly as an animal romance, founded on fact but not professing to come too close to the facts — such a book as London's *Call of the Wild* or Kipling's *Jungle Books. Sincerely yours*

Let me mention one more typical inaccuracy. The last anecdote in the account of the big wolf, the story of it's acting as the friendly and super-humanly intelligent guide of the children, is of course pure fable. It ranks with the adventures of Mowgli with Kaa and Bagheera. I am using very mild language when I say that it is a mistake for Mr. Long to assert of such fables that "every incident is minutely true to fact."

"THESE CURSED NEWSPAPERS"

To Theodore Roosevelt Jr.

Washington, October 2, 1905

Blessed old Ted:

You have been having an infernal time through these cursed newspapers. I was so indignant that I wrote to President Eliot about it, and I felt positively warlike. I have been talking it over with Gifford Pinchot and some other college fellows, and we are all agreed that it is just one of the occasions where the big bear cannot help the small bear at all, though he sympathizes awfully with him. The thing to do is to go on just as you have evidently been doing, attract as little attention as possible, do not make a fuss about the newspapermen, camera creatures, and idiots generally, letting it be seen that you do not like them and avoid them, but not letting them betray you into any excessive irritation. I believe they will soon drop you, and it is just an unpleasant thing that you will have to live down. Ted, I have had an enormous number of unpleasant things that I have had to live down in my life at different times, and you have begun to have them now. I saw that you were not out on the football field on Saturday and was rather glad of it, as evidently these infernal idiots were eagerly waiting for you; but whenever you do go you will have to make up your mind that they will make it exceedingly unpleasant for you for once or twice, and you will just have to bear it; for you can never in the world afford to let them drive you away from anything you intend to do, whether it is football or anything else, and by going about your own business quietly and pleasantly, doing just what you would do if they were not there, gradually they will get tired of it, and the boys themselves will see that it is not your fault and will feel, if anything, rather a sympathy for you. Meanwhile I want you to know that we are all thinking of you and sympathizing with you the whole time; and it is a great comfort to me to have such confidence in you and to know that though these creatures can cause you a little trouble and make you feel a little downcast, they cannot drive you one way or the other, or make you alter the course you have set out for yourself.

We were all of us, I am almost ashamed to say, rather blue at getting back in the White House, simply because we missed Sagamore Hill so much. But it is very beautiful and we feel very ungrateful at having even a temporary fit of blueness, and we are enjoying it to the full now. I have just seen Archie dragging some fifty foot of hose pipe across the tennis court to play in the sand box. I have been playing tennis with Mr. Pinchot, who beat me three sets to one, the only deuce set being the one I won. *Your loving father*

This is just an occasion to show the stuff there is in you. Do'n't let these newspaper creatures and kindred idiots drive you one hairsbreadth from the line you had marked out, in football or anything else; & avoid any fuss, if possible.

WRONGS BY THE POOR AND BY THE RICH

To S. S. McClure

Personal

Washington, October 4, 1905

My dear Mr. McClure:

I return you the letter to Mr. Colton and Mr. Colton's to you. It seems to me that in the rough Dr. Colton has a great deal of justice in his position. As I said to you and Steffens today, I think Steffens ought to put more sky in his landscape. I do not have to say to you that a man may say what is absolutely true and yet give an impression so one-sided as not to represent the whole truth. It is an unfortunate thing to encourage people to believe that all crimes are connected with business, and that the crime of graft is the only crime. I wish very much that you could have articles showing up the hideous iniquity of which mobs are guilty, the wrongs of violence by the poor as well as the wrongs of corruption by the rich. I feel that very great good is done by a crusade against corruption such as you have carried on, provided only it is clearly shown that we must *not* confine our hostility to the wealthy, nor feel indignant only at corruption. There are other classes just as guilty, and other crimes as bad. At the time of the French Revolution most of what was said about the op- pression of the people was true; but inasmuch as the reform- ers dwelt only on the wrongs done by the noble and wealthy classes, and upon the wrongs suffered by the poorer people, their conduct led up to the hideous calamity of the Terror, which put back the cause of liberty for over a generation. Put sky in the landscape, and show, not incidentally but of set pur- pose, that you stand as much against anarchic violence and crimes of brutality as against corruption and crimes of greed; as much against demagogic assaults on the well off, as against crimes by the well off.

It was a great pleasure to see you both today. *Sincerely yours*

TAINTED MONEY

To Isaac Wayne MacVeagh

Personal

Washington, October 8, 1905

My dear Mr. MacVeagh:

The more I have thought over that the more unwise it seems to me to vary in my attitude as to the federal control of life insurance. I am sure it is a wise thing to have. I am doubtful whether I can get it. Senator Bulkeley is against it, as Senator Dryden is for it. I have been asked to favor it because one man is against it, and to oppose it because the other man is for it. It does not seem to me that I can pay heed to the position of either.

You may be amused to know that Mr. Andrew Carnegie has offered to give the *last* $50,000 (thereby showing his canni- ness) if we return *all* the contributions — which, for some reason, in the clipping he enclosed were assumed to be $480,000 — supposed to be tainted money. Remembering your remark to me that Mr. Carnegie had obtained most of his money by simple theft I felt that if the suggestion was adopted for our returning this money we would probably need a jury of experts to pass upon the comparative motives of the donors in both cases and the comparative amounts of taintedness of the different sums of money. Of course the whole agitation about giving back the money is nine-tenths mere hysteria and one-tenth dishonesty. *Sincerely yours*

LIES ABOUT THE GOVERNMENT

To Lyman Abbott

Personal

Washington, October 14, 1905

My dear Dr. Abbott:

You know I swear by the *Outlook* and feel it renders an incalculable service in the cause of decent government. Therefore I feel a real regret when the *Outlook* publishes such an article as Clifford Howard's "Spirit of Graft." I never heard of Mr. Howard and of course would never dream of entering into a controversy with him, but you are quite welcome to show him this letter, for his statements derive importance when they appear in your publication. The whole article is the kind that almost more than any other helps dishonest people, for it tends to confuse the minds of honest people as to the real issues. To speak of the fact that clerks use pencils and government stationery as being in principle as bad as theft is, of course, simply nonsense, and wicked nonsense, too. The law rule *de minimis* applies. Such a statement as that "The spirit of graft finds universal expression throughout the government service" can be truthfully stigmatized in but one way. It is a lie and a wicked lie, and Mr. Howard having been guilty of it occupies a position in my judgment not one whit better than the real grafter, and infinitely below the very worst of the men whom he accuses; for most of the latter are not guilty of any shortcomings whatever. There are *small* abuses here and there in the Government service; we correct them where possible; but to speak as if they were criminal "graft" is a harmful absurdity.

But this is not all. Mr. Howard speaks of the story of a widow being appointed to office as a reward for returning a valuable gold watch which had been lost by an influential official. This story was published about the Secretary to the President, Mr. Loeb. It was immediately contradicted and it had no foundation whatever of any kind or sort. Yet this baseless slander is repeated by Mr. Howard. The New York *Times* used this story as the basis of an editorial, but on the facts being made public apologized for having done so.

Again Mr. Howard speaks, as another instance of the improper emoluments of higher office, of that afforded by the private use of horses and carriages provided for official purposes. He is apparently ignorant or else he wilfully conceals the fact that the law at present specifically provides for exactly this use, designating the officials by title who are authorized to have carriages for their "personal and official" use. By immemorial custom this privilege had obtained, most wisely, for various officials. But when Congress took it up and, as I think, quite improperly cut down the number of carriages used by officials most of whom are very much underpaid, it specifically provided that the carriages which were appropriated for should be for the personal as well as official use of the officials concerned. If Mr. Howard had any knowledge of conditions in Washington, or any honesty in describing them, he would know that when these equipages are, as he puts it, "at the service of wives and daughters for calling" — they are really being used for official purposes quite as much as when used to drive to and from the Departments. The same thing is true of what he says as to the use of messengers. There may be a few cases such as he describes; but in all the cases I know of the men are paid by their superiors for outside service. As a general and broad statement it is a falsehood. Again Mr. Howard says that the head of a large bureau in Washington not long ago had three servants regularly installed in his household who appeared on the rolls of the government as clerks or laborers; that in reality one was a seamstress and the other two were a coachman and a butler. I suppose this relates to the *Herald* story about Willis Moore, the Chief of the Weather Bureau.

Mr. Moore denied it as false. If Mr. Howard has any proof of the matter I shall take it up at once.

In short, my dear Doctor Abbott, I feel that the same condemnation that we mete out to a thief in the government service should be meted out to a liar who slanders the government servant, for the liar is the man who does most to produce the thief and to make it easy for him to be a thief by confusing the mind of the public between honesty and dishonesty. *Sincerely yours*

I also enclose you copy of a letter I have just sent to George Kennan.

P.S. I enclose you a newspaper clipping and a memorandum by Dr. Stokes, about Dr. Seaman. I think I told you that I got Dr. Seaman down here, thinking he might have something of value to say; but after a full interview with him I found that there was literally not one thing to be gained from him, not a fact that he had to tell which we did not already know, and not an intelligent remedy to propose. It is possible that he has done some good by calling to the attention of the public the fact that there are needs in the army which ought to be met by an increase in our medical force; but it would be impossible to accept him as an ally, because no one could afford to be responsible for his utterly reckless statements.

"THE REAL SPIRIT OF POETRY"

To Kermit Roosevelt

Washington, November 6, 1905

Dear Kermit:

Just a line, for I really have nothing to say this week. I have caught up with my work. One day we had a rather forlorn little poet, Madison Cawein and his nice wife in at lunch. They made me feel quite badly by being so grateful at my having mentioned him in what I fear was a very patronizing, and indeed almost supercilious way, as having written an occasional good poem — that was in my review of Robinson. I am much struck by Robinson's two poems which you sent

Mother. What a queer, mystical creature he is! I did not understand one of them — that about the gardens — and I do not know that I like either of them quite as much as some of those in *The Children of the Night*. But he certainly has the real spirit of poetry in him. Whether he can make it come out, I am not quite sure.

Prince Louis of Battenberg has been here and I have been very much pleased with him. He is a really good admiral, and in addition he is a well-read and cultivated man and it was charming to talk with him. We had him and his nephew, Prince Alexander, a midshipman, to lunch alone with us, and we really enjoyed having them. At the state dinner he sat between me and Bonaparte, and I could not help smiling to myself and thinking that here was this British Admiral seated beside the American Secretary of the Navy — the American Secretary of the Navy being the grandnephew of Napoleon and the grandson of Jerome, King of Westphalia; while the British Admiral was the grandson of a Hessian General who was the subject of King Jerome and served under Napoleon, and then, by no means creditably, deserted him in the middle of the battle of Leipzig.

I am off to vote tonight. *Ever yours*

REFUSING AN INTERVIEW

To Henry Melville Whitney

Washington, November 18, 1905

Sir:

I have your letter of the 17th instant. In view of my previous experience with you I am obliged to state, with regret, that it is out of the question for me to grant you another interview. In this letter of November 17th, in which you make this request, you furnish additional evidence of the wisdom of my refusing to communicate further with you, my refusal being based upon your evident inability to understand, or determination to misrepresent, what I say. In this letter you state that you "regret more than anything else in connection with this matter that the righteous cause of reciprocity with neighboring countries, of so much value to our people, and to the whole of the human race, is not to have the endorsement of your (my) great name, and the benefit of your (my) potent aid."

Nothing that I have said at any time has given you the slightest warrant for making this assertion; and when, in the very letter asking for an interview and denying that you ever willfully misrepresented my previous remarks, you incorporate another deliberate misstatement, you can hardly wonder that I decline to see you; nor would there in any event be the slightest point in such an interview. In your speeches you pretended to quote from memory certain statements made in the course of a long conversation occurring nearly a year previous. You quoted portions of what I said; even as to these portions, your language was inaccurate; and all the context was suppressed. As a result you have completely misrepresented me, as in the sentence of your present letter which I quote above. It matters little whether this was due to a deliberate purpose of deception; or to a lack, in both your companions and yourself, of a nice sense of propriety and of the power of exact thinking and of correct apprehension and repetition of what was said. In either event I feel that it would serve no useful purpose again to see you or further to correspond with you.

You are at liberty to make this correspondence public if you choose. *Yours truly*

CONTRIBUTIONS AND SPECIAL FAVORS

To Nevada Northrop Stranahan

Confidential

Washington, November 23, 1905

Dear Stranahan:

I have seen a number of people from New York and they all take exactly the view expressed by Governor Higgins. I shuddered when I read Senator Platt's testimony today in which he said that he recognized it as a moral obligation to take care of the interests of the corporations that contributed to the campaigns. Neither Cortelyou nor Bliss nor anyone else connected directly or indirectly with raising subscriptions for the national campaign has ever approached me about any matter connected with the interests of those who gave the money, always telling me, what from outside sources I know to be the fact, that they had explained to any man who contributed that the contribution must be given simply from the sense of the interest of the donor in the prosperity and welfare of the country and in the principles of the Republican party, and that no special favor of any kind would be either given or withheld because of giving or failure to contribute. Only on such terms were the contributions accepted. It is a lamentable thing to realize the attitude in which the Republican leadership of New York is put by the testimony brought out before the committee.

I have asked both Mr. Willcox and Mr. Henry W. Taft to see you. *Faithfully yours*

I enclose my letter to Senator Platt. Without giving the name of the man to whom the letter is addressed you are welcome to give the substance — practically verbatim — to all who call on you to find out my attitude.

RAILROAD REGULATION

To Ray Stannard Baker

Personal   Washington, November 28, 1905
My dear Mr. Baker:

Indeed it is a pleasure to hear from you or to see you. I shall see you at any time that you come on. I now answer your note of the 25th.

In the first place, my dear Mr. Baker, let me take up your last paragraph, in which you say that last year the whole country was with me, whereas now the railway men will be against me, and "also a very large number of people whose distresses will not be relieved by any maximum rate law." Last winter I did not attempt to define the legislation with precision; but beginning with my Colorado speech last May, I, and Taft in his speeches and Moody in his opinions, have tried to define our position absolutely, so that this is no new position of ours. It is the position which we took as soon as we were requested to prepare formatively measures which we hoped would at least to a considerable extent remedy the evils, and which would stand the test of the courts. As you know, the one thing I do not want to do is to enact a sham — that is, to enact a law which, when it goes before the courts, will prove to be valueless. In the next place, while I will try to relieve people whose position is a distressing one whenever it is possible, I can no more afford to back a bill because I shall have a universal popular sentiment behind me than I can afford to back it because the great railroads are behind it, unless in each case I am convinced the bill is right and proper, will work justice, and will stand the test of the courts. Surely you must agree with me in this. Remember that I abhor a demagogue as much as I abhor a corruptionist.

You say "that the power to fix the maximum rate would be a step in the right direction. * * * It seems to me that it will not touch the real seat of greatest distress. It may probably relieve cases of discrimination between individuals, but it seems to me that it will not touch those much more difficult problems of discrimination between localities and between commodities." I am inclined to believe that it will accomplish more than you think as regards commodities; but as regards discrimination between localities, I freely admit that it will not do nearly as much. But whereas I am perfectly clear as to our duty in the matter of discrimination between individuals, and within certain limits as regards commodities (comparing a commodity like dressed beef with a commodity like live cattle, for instance), I am not at all clear that a satisfactory result can be achieved as regards localities. But I shall try to formulate some plan which, in a separate section of the bill, shall allow the imposition of a minimum rate to prevent improper differentials between commodities, and between localities on the same railroad where the conditions are alike — where one has no advantage in water competition, for instance. I want the section in such form that if the courts kill it, it shall not kill the bill. This is for two reasons. In the first place, it is much more difficult to say what ought to be done in any given case as regards localities, and in the second place a tribunal is under much greater temptation to yield to pressure, which will bring about improper decisions. As to the first point, it is sufficient to point out that all kinds of complicated elements enter into the decision. The question as to which community is accessible by water is vital, because then water competition introduces an entirely new element in the problem. On the other hand, each community is sure to claim that it is unjustly treated, and there will be pulling and hauling by rival communities to influence the Commission, and each side will be able to make a more or less specious case. No such case can be made out if the discrimination is against an individual; but it is the easiest thing in the world to make a showing which will convince each of two rival communities that there is discrimination against it, whatever is done. Actual experience in Germany has shown that there is normally apt to be very gross injustice done as between localities when the Government fixes the rate. I know of no proof that such injustice normally follows where the Government fixes the rate as between individuals.

In short, I do not want to do anything blindly. I do not want to do anything that the courts will probably declare to be worthless. I am sure about the maximum rate. It may be that we can provide that the minimum rate can be applied under safeguards in certain cases. I am sure that we ought to stop discrimination between individuals. I think we can do it as regards commodities. I am not at all sure how far we can with safety go as between localities. Whatever I do, I want to do something real and I do not want to make any mistake. I cannot afford to yield to a popular demand on the one hand any more than I can afford to yield to the frantic expostulations of the railway men and the big men of property on the other, unless in one case as in the other I am convinced that we are on the right track.

In social and economic, as in political, reforms, the violent revolutionary extremist is the worst friend of liberty, just as the arrogant and intense reactionary is the worst friend of order. It was Lincoln, not Wendell Phillips and the fanatical abolitionists, who was the effective champion of union and

freedom; it was Washington, and not the leaders of the "liberty mobs" who did the real work in securing us national independence and then the national unity and order without
which that independence would have been a curse and not a
blessing. *Sincerely yours*

APPOINTING A REFORMED ROBBER

To Clarence Don Clark

Washington, December 8, 1905
My dear Senator Clark:
I have sent to the Senate the name of Benjamin Franklin
Daniels, now serving under a recess appointment as Marshal
of Arizona. This name I presume will go before your committee and I would like through you to put before the committee certain facts about Mr. Daniels. He was born and
brought up in the West when it was a very wild West indeed,
and his early life was passed in conditions which have now as
completely vanished from this country as the age of the
Vikings has vanished from Europe; and Daniels and the men
like him, who were the only ones who could grapple effectively with those conditions, bore no small resemblance in
both their virtues and their faults to these same Vikings. By
the time he was eighteen Daniels was a frontier scout and
ranger, and had been in fight after fight with the Indians as
well as with white desperadoes; and for ten years afterwards
he led a turbulent life on the remote frontier of civilization.
He repeatedly rendered staunch service to the courts of justice, serving with distinction in the dangerous position of one
carrying out the behests of the court, even while living this
wild, reckless life; but he finally got in with a set of men of
bad character and took part in the robbery under arms of a
band of horses or mules from a Government agency. The
older criminals escaped; the younger man was captured, tried
and convicted and served a term in the penitentiary. Since
coming out he has served in many important positions with
great credit; and both before and after the commission of the

crime he displayed signal heroism in supporting the cause of law and order at the peril of his life. He was a deputy marshal under Bat Masterson in Dodge City when Dodge City was the toughest town on this continent, and when only the gamest kind of man could do good work in such a position. Mr. Masterson, who is now himself a deputy marshal in New York City, testifies in the warmest terms to Daniels' efficiency, courage and honesty. He has many other testimonials of the highest kind. The then Governor of Arizona, Alexander O. Brodie, writes me as follows:

Washington, D.C., March 8, 1905.

My dear Mr. President:

While Governor of Arizona, it gave me unqualified pleasure to appoint Mr. B. F. Daniels, formerly a member of the 1st U.S. Vol. Cavalry as Superintendent of the Territorial Prison at Yuma on a vacancy occurring by the resignation of Superintendent Griffith, and I am addressing this letter to you in order that you may be acquainted with the valuable service he rendered the Territory and me while holding this position. I found him honest, honorable, sober, reliable and fearless in this place of trust and responsibility; humane in his care of those in his charge, impartial in his administration and at all times absolutely in command of the situation and in charge. As a matter of fact, I had such trust in his wisdom in the management of affairs that I did not deem it necessary to make frequent trips to the institution, knowing that I could absolutely rely upon his reports. I consider him a man of the true American type, patriotic, home loving, honest and honorable and at all times to be relied upon. He has shown himself always to be a man of dignity, whether in success or adversity.

Daniels' services to his country in the Spanish-American War as a member of the 1st U.S. Vol. Cavalry you are acquainted with as well as I, but I have felt that I should like you to know of the service he has rendered the Territory of Arizona and me as Governor.

With expressions of high regard,

Yours sincerely,
ALEXANDER O. BRODIE.

I also received the following two letters:

San Antonio, Texas, Dec. 18, 1901.

Dear Sir:

I am in receipt of information that Mr. Ben Daniels is an applicant for the position of U.S. Marshal for the territory of Arizona. It affords me pleasure to be able to recommend Mr. Daniels to any position of that character. I have known Mr. Daniels for quite a number of years. He was in the employ of Wells Fargo & Company, and a greater part of the time under my direct employment. I never have found him wanting in any respect, and if my recommendation can in any way advance his cause, I would certainly be very much pleased if you would give the matter the consideration that is due to the man.

I remain,

Very respectfully,

F. J. DODGE,

Special Officer, Wells Fargo & Company.

Washington, D.C., December 14, 1901.

To Whom It May Concern:

This is to certify that I have known Ben Daniels since 1878. Most of the time I have known him he has been an officer. First he was Assistant Marshal of Dodge City, Kansas, and afterwards Marshal of Guthrie. He is a man of good ability and good nerve. When a paper is put in his hands to be served, anyone who knows him knows that he will serve it. I consider him entirely fearless. He is not afraid of anybody. At the same time he is a gentleman and I would be pleased to recommend him for any office that the President of the United States should deem him worthy to fill. Very respectfully,

H. P. MYTON.

Four years ago I nominated him for this position. He was confirmed and I commissioned him, but then found out that he had been in the penitentiary and canceled the appointment because he had not frankly told me the facts. But I think that he has now atoned for his fault. Since I thus canceled his appointment, he has served under the Territorial Government as Warden of the Penitentiary and has done well. The Governor of the Territory and the Chief Justice wire me as follows about him:

Phoenix, Arizona, December 8, 1905.

The President.

Ben Daniels' administration as superintendent of the territorial prison was an excellent one, both as disclosed by the record and by comment of those who know. I have had no opportunity to know of his administration of the office of United States Marshal during his short incumbency, but the fact that I hear no complaints signifies that it is good.

JOSEPH H. KIBBEY,

Governor.

Phoenix, Arizona, December 8, 1905.
The President.

Daniels' record as warden of penitentiary was very good, as marshal he has been satisfactory to the court in the performance of his duties. As you know he is fearless and energetic. He has a great desire to acquit himself well in his responsible position and I believe he will do so.

EDWARD KENT,
Chief Justice.

My own acquaintance with him dates from 1898, when he joined my regiment. I was in close touch with him all through the Santiago campaign because I speedily found that he was one of the men in whom I could place entire trust and whom I could use in the most hazardous and responsible service. A more gallant, more loyal and more trustworthy soldier never wore the United States uniform. Not only was he absolutely indifferent to personal danger of any kind, but he showed excellent judgment, was a strong steadying influence in the regiment in every way, and was as useful in camp as in battle. He was as devoted to his comrades in sickness as he was indifferent to his own life in battle. He nursed his comrades when down with the fever with assiduous care, at the very time that he himself was so sick with the fever that he came right to death's door. In battle I repeatedly entrusted him with the performance of hazardous duty. For example, I entrusted him with the leadership of the sharpshooters who were to lie all day in the jungle between the Spanish lines and ours so as to keep down their fire on our trenches. He was always at the front in any emergency, and his coolness was absolutely unshaken either by day or by night; and when the fighting was over, and the fatigue had been so great as to exhaust all but the very strongest, I would employ him, although himself a sick man, in conducting on foot the carts containing the fever-struck men whom we had to send to the fever hospitals in the rear, being certain that he would care in every way for those in his charge. I would now trust him absolutely in anything connected with my own interests, and I am not willing that the United States should lose the value of his proved courage and efficiency. Still less am I willing to admit that even a grave offense in a man's youth cannot be wiped out by a record such as I have given above. *Sincerely yours*

REFUSING AN "ASTOUNDING" PROPOSAL

To Maria Longworth Storer

Washington, December 11, 1905

My dear Mrs. Storer:

Secretary Taft has just shown me your letter of November 26th, this letter evidently being intended for me as much as for him. On inquiry of Mrs. Roosevelt I find that she had received from you a letter to me, which is probably the one to which you refer in your letter to Mr. Taft; but she tells me she treated this letter as she sometimes has treated other letters that you have sent her to deliver to me, when she has known that the receipt of them would merely make me indignant, and puzzle me as to what action I ought to take about Bellamy's remaining in the service; that is, she did not give it to me. Your direct or implied complaints of and reflections upon my own personal conduct give me no concern; but I am very gravely concerned at the mischievous effect your letters must have in misrepresenting the position of the United States Government, and by the far-reaching governmental scandal your indiscretion may at any time cause. I have now seen your letter to me sent through Mrs. Roosevelt. In it you actually propose that I (as in your letter to Taft you propose that he) should authorize you to go to Rome to take part in what I must call an ecclesiastical intrigue, and to drag the United States Government into it. Such a proposal is simply astounding. You say that Cardinal Merry del Val has stated that I have "requested that two Archbishops," one Farley, be made Cardinals. All you had to say was that such a statement was a deliberate untruth, because you knew that I had refused to make such a request even for Ireland. You say in your letter to me, "You can trust me really." How can you say this, when you write to Taft a letter which if by accident published would absolutely misrepresent, in the most mischievous manner, both me and the American Government? You have no more right to meddle in these matters than Mrs. Reid would have to meddle in the Ritualist controversy, or Mrs. Tower to try to take charge of the relations of Germany to the American Lutherans.

Your letter to Mr. Taft and the letters to Cardinal Merry del Val and Archbishop Keane (of the answers to which you enclose copies), and your letter to the Princess Alexandrine (of the answer to which you also enclose a copy), are all letters which it is utterly improper for you to have written, in your position as the wife of an American Ambassador, and show a continued course of conduct on your part which is intolerable if your husband is to remain in the diplomatic service. In the first place, I wish it to be explicitly understood that though since I have been President I have been approached at different times by prelates of your Church and even by laymen in your Church with requests that I ask of the Vatican, or express a preference for, the appointment of some person as Cardinal, I have always positively and unequivocally refused directly or indirectly thus to ask for the appointment of any man as Cardinal; and it would have been a gross impropriety for me to have made any such request, while it is an outrage to represent me as having, in any shape, made it. To Archbishop Keane, to Mgr. O'Connell and to other men who have approached me on behalf of Archbishop Ireland, I have said that I had a very high regard for the Archbishop, and that I should be delighted to see him made a Cardinal, but that I could no more try to exercise pressure to have him made a Cardinal than pressure to get the Archbishop of Canterbury to establish an Archbishopric in America. Other persons have spoken to me, saying that Ireland could not be made a Cardinal, unless another Cardinal was made in the eastern states, and that they hoped that two American Cardinals (usually mentioning Ireland and Farley) would be appointed, one in the East and one in the West. I always answered that I had a great regard for both men and would be delighted to see them made Cardinals, just as there were Episcopal clergymen and Methodist clergymen whom I would be delighted to see made Bishops; but that I would no more interfere in one case than I would in the other. It is a matter of settled and traditional policy of this Government not to interfere, as you desire me to interfere, and as you have yourself been trying to interfere, under any possible circumstances. Your letters not only convey a totally wrong impression of my attitude; but they are such as you have no business whatever to write, in view of the position of your husband in the diplomatic service. The letter of Cardinal Merry del Val to you of November 23rd is a rebuke to you, expressing plainly his belief that you have been unwarrantably officious in matters with which you have properly no concern. It should of itself be enough to show to you how exceedingly unwise and improper your action in writing to him was. I am indignant that the wife of an Ambassador in the United States service should have written such a letter, should have given the impression undoubtedly conveyed by that letter, and should have incurred such a rebuke. You do not seem to realize that it is out of the question for me knowingly to permit the wife of one of our diplomats to engage in ecclesiastical intrigues to influence the Vatican. For the last couple of years I have continually been hearing of your having written one man or the other about such matters. I find that you are alluded to by foreign members of the diplomatic body in Washington, Paris and Berlin as the "American Ambassadress to Rome." I was unofficially informed on behalf both of Berlin and of Paris that because of these actions of yours it would not be agreeable to them to have Bellamy come as Ambassador to either place. Information of this kind has been repeatedly brought to Secretary Root. I have consulted him and Secretary Bonaparte, who is a member of your Church, as to this last letter of yours. Root's feeling about the case is stronger than I care to put into words; Bonaparte's feeling is exactly my own. Suffice it to say that in any event it will probably be impossible to send Bellamy as Special Ambassador to Spain, having in view what you have done. But I must go a little further than this. You and Bellamy must understand that so long as Bellamy continues in the diplomatic service of the United States you must refrain from writing or speaking in the way you have been doing on any of these matters, affecting what are simply the personal politics of church policy, to anyone, and above all to anyone connected with the Vatican. If you cannot make up your mind absolutely to alter your conduct in this regard, while your husband is in the diplomatic service, to refrain absolutely from taking any further part in any matter of ecclesiastical politics at the Vatican, and to refuse to write or speak to anyone (whether laymen or ecclesiastics, at home or abroad) as you have been writing and speaking in this Cardinal's hat matter, then Bellamy cannot with propriety continue to remain Ambassador of the United States. I must ask you to give me this positive promise in writing, if Bellamy is to continue in the service; and if you even unintentionally violate it I shall have to ask for Bellamy's resignation; for I can no longer afford to have the chance of scandal being brought on the entire American diplomatic service, and on the American Government itself, by such indiscreet and ill-advised action as yours has been. *Yours very truly*

P.S. Since writing the above I have looked up my correspondence with you and Bellamy and I find that I have expressed myself not merely once but again and again about this matter in terms which it was simply impossible for you to misunderstand. For instance, on December 19, 1903, I wrote to Bellamy saying that Mgr. O'Connell asked me to write something on behalf of Archbishop Ireland, and continuing:

> I told him of course that I could not interfere in such a matter, as it was none of my business who was made Cardinal; that personally I had a very strong friendship and admiration for the Archbishop, and that individually it would please me greatly to see him made Cardinal, just as it pleased me when Dr. Satterlee was made Bishop of Washington; but that I could no more interfere in one case than in the other — in short, that my feeling for the Archbishop was due to my respect for him as a useful and honorable man — just such a feeling I had had for Phillips Brooks and for many other clergymen of various denominations; but that I could not as President in any way try to help any clergyman of any denomination to high rank in that denomination.

On December 27, 1903, I again wrote to Bellamy enclosing an article which showed that he had been talking about my interest in Archbishop Ireland, and stating that such conduct on his part had been mischievous, and I continued as follows:

> I have the heartiest admiration for Archbishop Ireland. I should be delighted to see him made Cardinal, just as I was delighted to see Lawrence made the Episcopal Bishop of Massachusetts; just as I have been delighted at various Methodist friends of mine who have been made Bishop. But as President, it is none of my business to interfere for or against the advancement of any man in any church; and as it is impossible to differentiate what I say in my individual capacity

from what I say as President — at least in the popular mind, and apparently also in the Roman mind — I must request you not to quote me in any way or shape hereafter.

On December 30th, by which time I had found out that Bellamy had written what I considered an entirely improper letter to Senator Hanna about the dismissal of Hurst, I again wrote him and this time included the following paragraphs:

I know, my dear Bellamy, that you have not intended to do anything disloyal or improper, but surely on thinking over the matter you will see that there would be but one possible construction to be put upon such a letter from you. Think of the effect if your letter were made public!

Let me repeat to you that, in reference to matters affecting the Catholic church, events have conclusively shown that while you are Ambassador you must keep absolutely clear of any deed or word in Rome or elsewhere which would seem to differentiate your position from that of other Ambassadors. The mere fact of the report in the newspapers about your calling at the Vatican has had a very unfortunate effect. I dare say you did not call; you may merely have seen some Cardinal privately; but the unpleasant talk over the affair emphasizes the need of extreme circumspection while you are in your present position. While I am President and you are Ambassador neither of us in his public relations is to act as Catholic or Protestant, Jew or Gentile; and we have to be careful, not merely to do what is right, but so to carry ourselves as to show that we are doing what is right. I shall ask you not to quote me to any person in any shape or way in connection with any affair of the Catholic church, and yourself not to take action of any kind which will give ground for the belief that you as an American Ambassador are striving to interfere in the affairs of the church.

Surely these three letters of mine should have been enough warning to both Bellamy and you. Apparently you have quoted isolated sentences from my letters to convince some people that I am doing just exactly what I again and again in writing stated explicitly that I would not and could not do. This being so, I must ask you to return to me all of my letters in which I have spoken on any of these ecclesiastical subjects. If I were in a private position I should not have the least objection to your keeping them. But as I have apparently been totally unable, even by the language I have quoted above as used in my letters to Bellamy two years ago, to make you understand my position as President in these matters, I feel that my letters should be returned to me. *Again sincerely yours*

THE JEWS OF RUSSIA

To Jacob Henry Schiff

Washington, December 14, 1905

My dear Mr. Schiff:

I sent your previous letter to Secretary Root. I did not answer it because, my dear Mr. Schiff, I must frankly say that it would be difficult to answer it without hurting your feelings. You made a request for action on my part which if I took it would make the United States Government ridiculous, and so far from helping the condition of the Jews would have hurt them in Russia and would have tended to hurt them here. It is simply nonsense to suppose that when Russia is in the condition that she now is any kind of action on my part would accomplish anything. When the governmental authorities in Russia are wholly unable to protect themselves — when there is revolt in every quarter of the empire among every class of the people — and the bonds of social order everywhere are relaxed, it is idle to suppose that anything can be done by diplomatic representation. The idea of a European coalition in which we should join is of course wholly chimerical. What would such a coalition do: enforce liberty or order — restore the autocracy or install a republic? Therefore it is evident we could do nothing, and where we can do nothing I have a horror of saying anything. We never have taken — and while I am President we never will take — any action which we cannot make good. Why, my dear Mr. Schiff, the case was much simpler as regards the Armenians a few years ago. There the Turkish Government was responsible and was able to enforce whatever was desired. The outrages on the Armenians were exactly the same as those perpetrated upon the Jews of Russia both in character and in extent. But we did not go to war with Turkey. Inasmuch as it was certain that our people would not go into such a war, at least with the determination for the lavish outlay of blood and money necessary to make it effective, it would have been worse than foolish to have threatened it, and not the slightest good would have been or was gained by any agitation which it was known would not be backed up by arms. I shall take no action until I know that any action I take will do good instead of harm, and I shall announce no position which I may have to abandon at the cost of putting the United States Government in a humiliating and ridiculous attitude. I thoroughly believe that in national affairs we should act in accordance with the plains adage when I was in the ranch business: "Never to draw unless you mean to shoot." *Sincerely yours*

P.S. I sympathize thoroughly with your feelings, wrought up as they are and ought to be by the dreadful outrages committed on the Jews in Russia; anything I can do I will do; but I will not threaten aimlessly and thereby do harm.

AFRICAN BIG GAME

To Frederick Courtney Selous

Washington, December 18, 1905

My dear Mr. Selous:

I have been delighted with all the pieces you sent me and have read and reread them all. Do go on with your lion article. I earnestly wish you would now write a book describing the natural history of big game. You are the only man alive, so far as I know, who could do it. Take Swayne's book, for instance, which you sent me. It is an excellent book in its way, but really it is only a kind of a guide book. The sole contribution to natural history which it contains is that about the wolves and the big sheep. But you have the most extraordinary power of seeing things with minute accuracy of detail, and then the equally necessary power to describe vividly and accurately what you have seen. I read Swayne's book and I have not the slightest idea how the sheep or the ibex or the deer look; but after reading your articles I can see the lions, not snarling but growling, with their lips covering their teeth, looking from side to side as one of them seeks to find what had hurt it, or throwing up its tail stiff in the air as it comes galloping forward in the charge. I can see the actual struggle as the lion kills a big ox or cow buffalo. I can see the buffalo bulls trotting forward, stupid and fierce looking but not dangerous unless molested, while they gaze from under their brow armor of horn at the first white man they have ever seen. I can see wild hounds, with their ears pricked forward, leaping up above the grass to see what had shot at the buffalo they were chasing.

I was immensely interested in your description of these same wild hounds. And what a lesson you incidentally give as to the wisdom of refraining from dogmatizing about things that observers see differently. That experience of yours about running into the pack of wild hounds, which nevertheless, as you point out, often run down antelopes that no horse can run down, is most extraordinary. I am equally struck by what you say as to the men who have run down cheetahs on horseback. Judging from what Sir Samuel Baker saw, for instance, cheetahs must be able to go at least two feet to a horse's one for half a mile or so. I wonder if it is not possible that the men who succeeded in running them down were able to get a clear chase of two or three miles so as to wind them. If different observers had recorded the two sets of facts you give as to the speed of the wild hounds under different conditions, a great many people would have jumped to the conclusion that one of the two observers, whose stories seemed mutually contradictory, must have been telling what was not so.

Let me thank you again for the real pleasure you have given me by sending me these articles. Now do go on and write that book. Buxton and I and a great many other men can write ordinary books of trips in which we kill a few sheep or goat or bear or elk or deer; but nobody can write the natural history of big game as you can. *Faithfully yours*

A PRICELESS ART COLLECTION

To Melville Weston Fuller

Washington, December 19, 1905

Sir:

I herewith enclose a copy of a letter sent to me by Mr. Charles L. Freer offering to bequeath his art collections to the Smithsonian Institution or the United States Government, together with $500,000 in money to construct a suitable building; or if it is deemed preferable, to make a present conveyance of the title to such Institution or the Government and a bequest of the sum of $500,000 for the building. The offer is made upon certain terms and conditions which in my judgment are proper and reasonable.

It is impossible to speak in too high terms of the munificence shown by Mr. Freer in this offer; and it is one which the Government of the United States should at once close with as a matter of course. Mr. Freer's collection is literally priceless; it includes hundreds of the most remarkable pictures by the best known old masters of China and Japan. It also includes hundreds of pictures, studies and etchings by certain notable American artists; those by Whistler alone being such as would make the whole collection of unique value — although the pictures by the Chinese and Japanese artists are of even greater worth and consequence. There are other art pieces which I need not mention. Any competent critic can testify to the extraordinary value of the collection. I should suggest that either Dr. Sturgis Bigelow or Mr. John LaFarge be sent to Detroit to examine the collection, if there is any question about it; although I assume that every member of the Board of Regents is familiar with its worth. The conditions which Mr. Freer imposes are in effect that nothing shall be added to or taken from the collection after his death, and that the collection shall be exhibited by itself in the building to be constructed for it without charge to the public; furthermore, that he shall have the right to make such additions to the collection as he may deem advisable, but not to take anything away from it after April next, the collections remaining in the possession of Mr. Freer until his death and then in the possession of his executors until the completion of the building. These conditions are of course eminently proper.

All that is asked of the Government or the Regents of the Smithsonian now is that they shall accept this magnificently generous offer. Nothing whatever else is demanded at present. When Mr. Freer's death occurs land will of course have to be allotted for the erection of the building — a building which will itself be a gift of great beauty to the Government — and when the building is completed and the collection installed therein, and not before, Congress will have to take some steps to provide the comparatively small sum necessary to take care of what will be a national asset of great value.

I need hardly say that there are any number of communities and of institutions which would be only too glad themselves to promise to erect such a building as that which Mr. Freer is going to erect, for the sake of getting this collection. The offer is one of the most generous that ever has been made to this Government, and the gift is literally beyond price. All that is now asked is that we shall agree to accept on behalf of the Nation the great benefit thus to be bestowed upon the Nation.

I hope that the Regents of the Smithsonian will feel warranted to close with the offer; for they are the national guardians of such a collection. If in their wisdom they do not see their way to accept the gift I shall then be obliged to take some other method of endeavoring to prevent the loss to the United States Government, and therefore to the people of the United States, of one of the most valuable collections which any private individual has ever given to any people. *Sincerely yours*

To James Wolcott Wadsworth Jr.

Personal

Washington, January 3, 1906

My dear Mr. Speaker:

Just a word of hearty congratulations. I believe that you possess to a marked degree the three qualities essential to a public servant if he is to be of use — courage, honesty and common sense. You will need all three. I cannot give you specific advice because I am not acquainted with the situation closely enough. I know you will encounter great difficulties. I have entire faith that you will overcome them.

I wonder if you will mind an older man, who has a great belief in you, giving you two bits of general advice which will probably sound platitudinous? At any rate I shall venture to do so. Remember that in the long run, for a man of your instincts and of your ambitions, which are always strictly honorable, the only way in which he can help himself is by trying to make the party useful to the public and the State; and in order to do this he has got to try to act in accordance with high ideals, and yet by the aid of practical methods. In the second place, my own experience has been that both my pleasure and my usefulness in any office depended absolutely upon my refusal to let myself get to thinking about my own future political advancement; for I have always found that such thought merely tended to hamper me and impair my usefulness, without giving me the miserable offset of a continuance in place. I very early, while myself in the Legislature, became convinced that if I wished to have a good time in public life and to keep my self-respect by doing good service, it paid me to think only of the work that was actually up, to do it as well as I knew how, and to let the future absolutely take care of itself. I believe that you have a future before you, and this future will come not through scheming on your part but by giving first-class service through your party, to the State. The Odell type of politician can advance himself by scheming and by practices which to you and me are impossible. We could not win by such methods, because we should practice them too clumsily, and if we could win, we would find the prize not worth having on such terms, while to fail would mean hideous disaster. Go ahead just as you have begun — fearlessly, honorably, and trying to show both your good judgment and good temper, neither flinching nor showing petty vindictiveness. I think you will win out, and even if you do not you will have nothing to regret, and you will have already achieved something substantial for the credit of your name. *Sincerely yours*

P.S. It seems to me that both Rogers and Moreland have behaved very squarely with you and that so far as you can it would be well to show your appreciation to them. It was very hard upon Rogers, and I think he showed a really first-class spirit in coming out and doing yeoman's work for you. He got into line in good shape when the end came; and of course Moreland acted squarely from the beginning. I am also anxious to see if you think you can get down here during the course of this week. I want to talk over the State Chairmanship and other matters with you. If you like you can show this letter or any part of it to the Governor, or tell him that I have asked you to come down and the purpose for which I have asked it. My dear fellow, you cannot imagine what a comfort it is to have you Speaker.

JAPAN AND THE PHILIPPINES

To Leonard Wood

Washington, January 22, 1906

Dear Leonard:

I regarded your letter as not merely very interesting but very able. I entirely agree with you about fortifying the Sandwich Islands; and wish you had a little experience in the difficulties of getting Congress to agree with me in such matters! Moreover, I entirely agree with you that we can retain the Philippines only so long as we have a first-class fighting navy, superior to the navy of any possible opponent. I do not for a moment agree, however, that Japan has any immediate intention of moving against us in the Philippines. Her eyes for some time to come will be directed toward Korea and southern Manchuria. If she attacked us and met disaster, she would lose everything she has gained in the war with Russia; and if she attacked us and won, she would make this republic her envenomed and resolute foe for all time, and would without question speedily lose the alliance with Great Britain and see a coalition between Russia, the United States, and very possibly Germany and France to destroy her in the Far East. No man can prophesy about the future, but I see not the slightest chance of Japan attacking us in the Philippines for a decade or two, or until the present conditions of international politics change.

I entirely agree with you in what you say about the Chinese situation. Under no circumstances would I ever approve any legislation admitting any form of Chinese labor into the United States; and I agree entirely with your criticism upon the English colonies.

As for what you say about the legislation for the Philippine Islands, I agree with most of it, but I am amused at your falling into the common mistake of thinking that the United States shipping laws apply to the islands. They do not have any application to the Philippine Islands at all. The shipping regulations of the islands are subject to the Commission, and the American coastwise shipping laws as yet have never been applied to the islands. I am trying to prevent their being applied, and I am also trying to secure the abolition of the Philippine tariff.

With love to Mrs. Wood, believe me, *Faithfully yours*

THE COMFORT OF LIKING BOOKS

To George Otto Trevelyan

Washington, January 22, 1906

My dear Sir George:

Yes, Mrs. Roosevelt and I are both as fond as you are of the immortal Soapy Sponge; but I shall be very grateful if you will send me that copy, because the only copy we have in the house is one Mrs. Roosevelt inherited from her father. It is a rather cheap American edition, though with the Cruikshank pictures, and we have read it until it has practically tumbled to pieces. So you see I am greedily closing with your offer!

You may be amused at an expression of opinion on literary matters the other day by a man over here to whom I have taken a great liking. He is Stevens, whom I have appointed as the Chief Engineer to build the Panama Canal — as responsible an appointment as I have in my gift. He was originally a backwoods boy from Maine, who married on a salary of sixty dollars a month, and has done an immense amount of hard railroad engineering work in the West. I never supposed he had any particular literary tastes, but I happened to find out that he read a great deal and that he has the same trick that I have of reading over and over again books for which he really cares. His favorite books are, all of Macaulay, all of Scott, the poetry of Edgar Allan Poe (this I regard as astounding); and as individual books, Mark Twain's *Huckleberry Finn*, which he reads continually, *Lorna Doone*, and Whyte Melville's *Gladiators*. The last two I like myself; but the others, including *Huckleberry Finn*, I regard as classics.

Just at present I am having a rough-and-tumble time with Congress, and have been enjoying the experience of keeping my temper resolutely under every kind of provocation. I have four or five measures I am anxious to get through, namely, first and foremost, the appropriations for the Panama Canal; second, the railway rate legislation; third, the Philippine tariff; fourth, the Santo Domingo treaty; and fifth, joint statehood for the territories, or at least for Oklahoma and Indian Territory. I think I shall get the first three all right (and they are the most important) and there is a chance of my getting the last two. To succeed in getting measures like these through one has to be a rough-and-tumble man oneself; and I find it a great comfort to like all kinds of books, and to be able to get half an hour or an hour's complete rest and complete detachment from the fighting of the moment, by plunging into the genius and misdeeds of Marlborough, or the wicked perversity of James II, or the brilliant battle for human freedom fought by Fox — or in short, anything that Macaulay wrote

or that you have written, or any one of most of the novels of
Scott and of some of the novels of Thackeray and Dickens; or
to turn to Hawthorne or Poe; or to Longfellow, who I think
has been under estimated of late years, by the way.

With many thanks, *Sincerely yours*

"THE STERN AND HARDY VIRTUES"

To Ian Hamilton

Personal

Washington, January 24, 1906

My dear General Hamilton:

I think your *Staff Officer's Scrap-book* much the best thing
that has appeared about the Japanese war. Didn't you see more
fighting? I should give a good deal to get your criticisms upon
the great battles which closed at Mukden. I trust you will go
on and publish another volume.

By the way, I want to express the most cordial agreement
with the sentiments you express as to the need of encouraging the fighting qualities, morally and physically, in the average individual soldier, and therefore in the average individual
citizen; and with what you say as to the preposterous ignorance of all our people in the matter of the relative superiority of at least certain forms of barbarian over the hypercivilized
man of the great industrial centers, and especially of the cities.
In the small military experience which I have had and in the
study that I have been forced officially and practically to make
of the fighting in the Philippines I was immensely struck by
the superiority of the man who had been bred in the open or
was accustomed to the open, who knew how to take cover and
to handle horse and rifle, over the ordinary clerk or mechanic
or similar individual from the great industrial centers. I reck-
oned that on the average the former was just about three times
as good as the latter. Of course there were exceptions and
plenty of them, for the moral is more than the physical; and
a city-bred man with the right ambitions, the right standards,

who has taken advantage of his opportunities to do something as regards horsemanship and marksmanship and is eager to learn, can speedily turn himself into a thoroughly good soldier. But speaking roughly what I have said is true. Moreover, it is disheartening to see the way the materialists of this day and generation come to think of absolutely nothing but money and the most vacuous kind of soft, material luxury; while the idealists in at least too many cases construct an ideal which is not only fantastic but excessively undesirable, and in the horror of war — which they profess and inculcate, tend to produce a habit of mind under the effect of which the military or warlike virtues tend to atrophy. I do not however share your disbelief in Hague conferences and similar meetings. I think they can do a great deal if they are managed in a spirit of sanity; and the Japanese army itself has certainly shown that the most reckless indifference to death and the most formidable fighting capacity can be combined with a scrupulous compliance with all the modern ideas as regards proper treatment of prisoners, proper care of the wounded, abstention from plunder, and so forth, and so forth. But nothing should interfere with our cultivation of the stern and hardy virtues. *Sincerely yours*

JUDO AT THE NAVAL ACADEMY

To Charles Joseph Bonaparte

Washington, February 17, 1906

My dear Mr. Secretary:

I forgot to bring up one thing with you and Admiral Sands yesterday. I am not satisfied about the giving up of the judo or jujitsu at the Naval Academy. It is not physical exercise so much as it is an extraordinarily successful means of self-defense and training in dexterity and decision. Naturally, elderly men of a routine habit of mind who have known nothing whatever of it are against it; but I know enough of boxing, wrestling, rough-and-tumble fighting, and of the very art in question to be absolutely certain that it is of real and on occasions may be of great use to any man whose duties are such as a naval officer's may at any time become. I should like to have it continued next year at the Naval Academy.

With great regard, *Sincerely yours*

"THEY ARE PAID TO LIE"

To John Albert Sleicher

Personal

Washington, February 25, 1906

My dear Mr. Sleicher:

Don't you think that the result of the action of the Senate Committee saves me from any necessity of saying anything as to these lies in the New York *Times* and similar papers? I do not care a snap of my finger what they say. Moreover, I cannot help their saying that I am "undecided and vacillating," for the simple reason that papers like the New York *Times*, both in their editorials and in their correspondence, lie in response to the demands of the big corporations that the editors and correspondents shall lie; and lie these editors and correspondents like those of the New York *Times* do, because they make their bread and butter by so doing. They do not lie because they believe it, but because they are paid to lie. I never see the *Times* excepting when you or some other friend calls my attention to it, and really I do not think it has any effect; certainly I pay no more heed to its assaults than I would to its praise. The representatives of the railroad interests have for a month been beseeching me to keep an "open mind," and of course I have been doing it; and because I thus did as they asked they try to represent me as "vacillating"; but, my dear sir, the accusations are bubbles that hardly last long enough even to go downstream.

With many thanks for your writing me, *Sincerely yours*

MODERN GERMANY

To Oscar Solomon Straus

Personal

Washington, February 27, 1906

My dear Mr. Straus:

Of course that would be a most satisfactory disposition of the Morocco matter, from my standpoint, but I do not know that either France or Germany would consent to it. Carl Schurz's advice is absolutely worthless, for he does not know anything about existing facts, and in addition, his judgment is wretchedly poor. He is not an American and he is not a present-day German. He is a left-over German of 1848, of the amiable, visionary, impractical, revolutionary type, now soured by his own constant wrong behavior for many years. He knows nothing whatever of modern Germany. He has not the slightest influence there, and he has not the slightest influence here. And what is much more important, he cannot suggest anything that will do good either there or here. Modern Germany is alert, aggressive, military and industrial. It thinks it is a match for England and France combined in war, and would probably be less reluctant to fight both those powers together than they would be together to fight it. It despises the Hague Conference and the whole Hague idea. It respects the United States only in so far as it believes that our navy is efficient and that if sufficiently wronged or insulted we would fight. Now I like and respect Germany, but I am not blind to the fact that Germany does not reciprocate the feeling. I want us to do everything we can to stay on good terms with Germany, but I would be a fool if I were blind to the fact that Germany will not stay in with us if we betray weakness. As for this particular case, when I see you next I shall tell you all that I have done and you will see that I have been using my very best efforts for peace. *Sincerely yours*

DINNER WITH THE LODGES
To Anna Cabot Mills Lodge

Washington, March 11, 1906

Dear Nannie:

I write to you because I feel more confidence in my ability to exert a favorable response from you than from Cabot. Can you have me to dinner either Wednesday or Friday? Would you be willing to have Bay and Bessie also? Then we could discuss the Hittite empire, the Pithecanthropus, and Magyar love songs, and the exact relations of the Atli of the *Volsunga Saga* to the Etzel of the *Nibelungenlied*, and of both to Attila — with interludes by Cabot about the rate bill, Beveridge, and other matters of more vivid contemporary interest. *Ever yours*

SOCIALISM AND STARVATION
To Upton Sinclair

Personal

Washington, March 15, 1906

My dear Mr. Sinclair:

I have your letter of the 13th instant. I have now read, if not all, yet a good deal of your book, and if you can come down here during the first week in April I shall be particularly glad to see you.

I do not think very much of your ecclesiastical correspondent. A quarter of a century's hard work over what I may call politico-sociological problems has made me distrust men of hysterical temperament. I think the preacher furnishes his measure when he compares you to Tolstoy, Zola and Gorki, intending thereby to praise you. The abortiveness of the late revolution in Russia sprang precisely from the fact that too much of the leadership was of the Gorki type and therefore the kind of leadership which can never lead anybody anywhere save into a Serbonian bog. Of course the net result of Zola's writings has been evil. Where one man has gained from them a shuddering horror at existing wrong which has impelled him to try to right that wrong, a hundred have simply had the lascivious, the beast side of their natures strengthened and intensified by them. Oliver Wendell Holmes has an excellent paragraph on this in his *Over the Teacups*. As for Tolstoy, his novels are good, but his so-called religious and reformatory writings constitute one of the age-forces which tell seriously for bad. His *Kreutzer Sonata* could only have been written by a man of diseased moral nature, a man in whose person the devotee and debauchee alternately obtain sway, as they sometimes do in successive generations of decadent families or in whole communities of unhealthy social conditions. In the end of your book, among the various characters who preach socialism, almost all betray the pathetic belief that the individual capacity which is unable to raise itself even in the comparatively simple work of directing the individual how to earn his own livelihood, will, when it becomes the banded incapacity of all the people, succeed in doing admirably a form of government work infinitely more complex, infinitely more difficult than any which the most intelligent and highly developed people has ever yet successfully tried. Personally I think that one of the chief early effects of such attempt to put socialism of the kind there preached into practice, would be the elimination by starvation, and the diseases, moral and physical, attendant upon starvation, of that same portion of the community on whose behalf socialism would be invoked. Of course you have read Wyckoff's account of his experiences as an unskilled laborer of the lowest class. Probably you know him. He was a Princeton man wholly without the physique to do manual labor as well as the ordinary manual laborer can do it, yet in going across the continent his experience was that in every place, sooner or later, and in most places very soon indeed, a man not very strong physically and working at trades that did not need intelligence, could raise himself to a position where he had steady work and where he could save and lead a self-respecting life. There are doubtless communities where such self-raising is very hard for the time being; there are unquestionably men who are crippled by accident (as by being old and having large families dependent on them); there are many, many men who lack any intelligence or character and who therefore cannot thus raise themselves. But while I agree with you that energetic, and, as I believe, in the long run radical, action must be taken to do away with the effects of arrogant and selfish greed on the part of the capitalist, yet I am more than ever convinced that the real factor in the elevation of any man or any mass of men must be the development within his or their hearts and heads of the qualities which alone can make either the individual, the class or the nation permanently useful to themselves and to others. *Sincerely yours*

But all this has nothing to do with the fact that the specific evils you point out shall, if their existence be proved, and if I have power, be eradicated.

TAFT'S POLITICAL FUTURE

To William Howard Taft

Confidential

Washington, March 15, 1906

Dear Will:

I received your letter and afterwards had a half-hour's talk with your dear wife.

Judging from one phrase of your letter I think I have been in error as to your feeling. You say that it is your decided personal preference to continue your present work. This I had not understood. On the contrary I gathered that what you really wanted to do was to go on the bench, and that my urging was in the line of your inclination, but in a matter in which you were in doubt as to your duty.

What you say in your letter and what your dear wife says alter the case. My dear Will, it is pre-eminently a matter in which no other man can take the responsibility of deciding for you what it is right and best for you to do. Nobody could decide for me whether I should go to the war or stay as Assistant Secretary of the Navy. Nobody could decide for me whether I should accept the Vice-Presidency, or try to continue as Governor. Nobody could decide for Garfield whether he should go on as Commissioner of Corporations or become a District Judge; or for Root, whether he should decline the Governorship, or the following year accept the Secretaryship of State. In each case it is the man himself who is to lead his life after having decided one way or the other. No one can lead that life for him; and neither he nor anyone else can afford to have anyone else make the decision for him; because the vital factor in the decision must be the equation of the man himself.

As far as I am personally concerned I could not put myself in your place because I am not a lawyer and would under no circumstances, even if I had been trained for a lawyer, have any leaning toward the bench; so in your case I should as a matter of course accept the three years' of service in the War Department, dealing with the Panama and Philippine question, and then abide the fall of the dice as to whether I became President, or continued in public life in some less conspicuous position, or went back to the practice of the law — but mind you I would not for a moment contemplate leaving Ohio, for after fifty a man does not as a rule do well if he leaves his native State, at least for an older State. But I appreciate as every thoughtful man must the immense importance of the part to be played by the Supreme Court in the next twenty-five years. I do not at all like the social conditions at present. The dull, purblind folly of the very rich men; their greed and arrogance, and the way in which they have unduly prospered by the help of the ablest lawyers, and too often through the weakness or shortsightedness of the judges or by their unfortunate possession of meticulous minds; these facts, and the corruption in business and politics, have tended to produce a very unhealthy condition of excitement and irritation in the popular mind, which shows itself in part in the enormous increase in the socialistic propaganda. Nothing effective, because nothing at once honest and intelligent, is being done to combat the great amount of evil which, mixed with a little good, a little truth, is contained in the outpourings of the *Cosmopolitan*, of *McClure's*, of *Collier's*, of Tom Lawson, of David Graham Phillips, of Upton Sinclair. Some of these are socialists; some of them merely lurid sensationalists; but they are all building up a revolutionary feeling which will most probably take the form of a political campaign. Then we may have to do, too late or almost too late, what had to be done in the silver campaign when in one summer we had to convince a great many good people that what they had been laboriously taught for several years previous was untrue. In the free silver campaign one most unhealthy feature of the situation was that in their panic the conservative forces selected as their real champion Hanna, a man with many good qualities, but who embodied in himself more than any other big man, all the forces of coarse corruption that had been so prominent in our industrial and political life; and the respectable people either gave to him or approved of the giving to him of a colossal bribery fund. As it happens, I think that in that campaign for the most part the funds were honestly used as a means of convincing people; but the obligations Hanna incurred and the way in which the fund was raised were most unfortunate. I earnestly hope that if any similar contest of a more important kind has to be waged in the future that the friends of conservatism and order will make their fight under different kinds of leaders and by different methods.

Under such circumstances you would be the best possible leader, and with your leadership we could rest assured that only good methods would prevail. In such contest you could do very much if you were on the bench; you could do very much if you were in active political life outside. I think you could do most as President; but you could do very much as Chief Justice; and you could do less, but still very much, either as Senator or as Associate Justice. Where you can fight best I cannot say, for you know what your soul turns to better than I can.

As I see the situation it is this. There are strong arguments against your taking this justiceship. In the first place my belief is that of all the men that have appeared so far you are the man who is most likely to receive the Republican Presidential nomination and who is, I think, the best man to receive it; and under whom we would have most chance to succeed. It may well be that Root would be at least as good a President as either you or I; but he does not touch the people at as many points as you and I touch them. He would probably not be as good a candidate as I was, or as you would be. It is not a light thing to cast aside the chance of the Presidency; even though of course it is a chance, however good a one. It would be a very foolish thing for you to get it into your thoughts, so that your sweet and fine nature would be warped and you would become bitter and sour as Henry Clay and Tom Reed became; and thank Heaven this is absolutely impossible. But it is well to remember that the shadow of the Presidency falls on no man twice, save in the most exceptional circumstances. The good you could do in four or eight years as the head of the Nation would be incalculable. Furthermore, casting aside the question of the Presidency, if you do not go on the bench you have three years of vital, important service in connection with the Panama canal and the Philippines, not to speak of the regular army itself, and the certainty, if not on the bench, that in the future you will be one of the great leaders for right in the tremendous contests that are sure to arise through the play of the half hidden forces now in blind revolt, against not only what is bad but against much that is good, and against much that is inevitable, in the present industrial system. Finally, there is a chance that you might well take a position on the bench sometime during the next three years through a vacancy occurring; although I do not think very much of this argument, because the reasons which I consider weighty as against your taking the present vacancy would obtain just as much at any time within the next two years; and after the Presidential nomination, if you were not nominated, though they would not obtain to the same degree they would still obtain partially, when of course your chance of being put upon the bench might be much smaller. Moreover, the chance of your obtaining the Chief Justiceship would of course be lessened, for it might be, although it probably would not be, the case, that I might find some big man like Root or Knox who would consent to take the present vacancy if he knew that the Chief Justiceship was open but who would not take it if he knew that the appointment was foreclosed; and under such circumstances I would not feel that I had the right to foreclose it. I do not regard this argument as important because I do not believe that the big men I have in mind would now go on the bench in any event; but it is an argument that must be considered. In other words the fact must be faced that it is possible, although improbable, that not to go on the bench now means your definitely keeping off it; although I do not myself have any serious doubt that even if the opportunity did not come for me to put you on the bench it would come under some subsequent President.

The chief arguments in favor of your accepting the position are: first and infinitely foremost, the fact that it does give you, humanly speaking, the opportunity for a quarter of a century to do a great work as Justice of the greatest court in Christendom (a court which now sadly needs great men) on questions which seem likely vitally and fundamentally to affect the social, industrial and political structure of our commonwealth. A small secondary point is that it would increase your chance of being Chief Justice, making it certain that you would be such if the vacancy occurred during my term. But as I have said, I do not attach any importance to this point because it might be if you did not go on now that if the vacancy did occur in my term could appoint you anyhow (and indeed probably would, save in such an event as I speak of above); while I feel that the probabilities would also favor any Republican successor of mine appointing you to the position if he got the chance.

Now, my dear Will, there is the situation as I see it. It is a hard choice to make, and you yourself have to make it. You have two alternatives before you, each with uncertain possibilities, and you cannot be sure that whichever you take you will not afterwards feel that it would have been better if you had taken the other. But whichever you take I know that you will render great and durable service to the Nation for many years to come, and I feel that you should decide in accordance with the promptings of your own liking, of your own belief as to where you can render the service which most appeals to you, as well as that which you feel is most beneficial to the Nation. No one can with wisdom advise you. *Sincerely yours*

PRAISE FOR AN AMBASSADOR

To Jean Jules Jusserand

Personal

Washington, April 25, 1906

My dear Mr. Ambassador:

During the past year our relations have been those of peculiar intimacy in dealing with more than one great problem, and particularly in connection with the Morocco conference, and there are certain things which I think I ought to say to you.

It is the simple and literal truth to say that in my judgment we owe it to you more than to any other one man that the year which has closed has not seen a war between France and Germany, which, had it begun, would probably have extended to take in a considerable portion of the world. In last May and June the relations between the two countries were so strained that such a war was imminent. Probably the only way it could have been avoided was by an international conference, and such a conference could only have been held on terms compatible with France's honor and dignity. You were the man most instrumental in having just this kind of conference arranged for. I came into the matter at all most unwillingly, and I could not have come into it at all if I had not possessed entire confidence alike in your unfailing soundness of judgment and in your high integrity of personal conduct. Thanks to the fact that these are the two dominant notes in your personality my relationship with you has been such as I think has very, very rarely obtained between any ambassador at any time and the head of the government to which that ambassador was accredited; and certainly no ambassador and no head of a government could ever stand to one another on a footing at once more pleasant and more advantageous to their respective countries than has been the case with you and me. If, in these delicate Morocco negotiations, I had not been able to treat you with the absolute frankness and confidence that I did, no good result could possibly have been obtained; and this frankness and confidence were rendered possible only because of the certainty that you would do and advise what was wisest to be done and advised, and that you would treat all that was said and done between us two as a gentleman of the highest honor treats what is said and done in the intimate personal relations of life. If you had been capable of adopting one line of conduct as a private individual and another as a public man I should have been wholly unable to assume any such relations with you; nor, on the other hand, however high your standard of honor, could I have assumed them had I not felt complete confidence in the soundness and quickness of your judgment. The service you rendered was primarily one to France, but it was also a service to the world at large; and in rendering it you bore yourself as the ideal public servant should bear himself; for such a public servant should with trained intelligence know how to render the most effective service to his own country while yet never deviating by so much as a hand's breadth from the code of mutual good faith and scrupulous regard for the rights of others, which should obtain between nations no less than between gentlemen. I do not suppose that you will ever gain any personal advantage, and perhaps not even any personal recognition, because of what you have done in the past year; but I desire that you should at least know my appreciation of it.

With hearty respect and good will, believe me, *Very faithfully yours*

THE SOUTH AND THE NORTH

To Owen Wister

Personal

Washington, April 27, 1906

Dear Dan:

That I have read *Lady Baltimore* with interest and that I think it a very considerable book the length of this letter will show. If my wife were to write the letter it would be one of almost undiluted praise, because she looked at it simply as a work of art, simply as a story, and from either standpoint it is entitled to nothing but admiration. The description of the people and of their surroundings will always live in my memory, and will make me continually turn back to read bits of the book here and there. Moreover, (to a man of my possibly priggish way of looking at novels), the general tone of the book is admirable, and to one who does not look at it in any way as a tract of the times it leaves the right impression of sturdy protest against what is sordid, against what is mere spangle-covered baseness, against brutal greed and sensuality and vacuity; it teaches admiration of manliness and womanliness, as both terms must always be understood by those capable of holding a high ideal.

But I am afraid the book cannot but be considered save as in part a tract of the times, and from this standpoint, in spite of my hearty sympathy with your denunciation of the very things that you denounce and your admiration of the very things that you admire, I cannot but think that at the best you will fail to do good, and that at the worst you may do harm, by overstating your case. The longer I have been in public life, and the more zealous I have grown in movements of true reform, the greater the horror I have come to feel for the exaggeration which so often defeats its own object. It is needless to say to you that the exaggeration can be just as surely shown as in any other way by merely omitting or slurring over certain important facts. In your remarkable little sketch of Grant, by reciting with entire truth certain facts of Grant's life and passing over with insufficient notice the remainder you could have drawn a picture of him as a drunken, brutal and corrupt incapable, a picture in which almost every detail in the framework would have been true in itself, but in which the summing up and general effect would have been quite as false as if the whole had been a mere invention. Now, of course, I don't mean that this is true of *Lady Baltimore*. You call attention to some mighty ugly facts and tendencies in our modern American civilization, and it is because I so earnestly wish to see the most effective kind of warfare waged against exactly what you denounce that I regret you did not put your denunciation in a way which would accomplish more good. In the first place, though it may have been all right from the standpoint of the story, from the standpoint of the tract it was a capital error to make your swine-devils practically all northerners and your angels practically all southerners. You speak so sweepingly, moreover, that you clearly leave the impression of intending the swine-devils to be representative not of a small section of the well-to-do North, but of the overwhelming majority of the well-to-do North; indeed, of the North which leads. Now, as a matter of fact (remember I am speaking from the standpoint of the tract) the contrast could have been made with much more real truth between northerners and northerners, for then there would not have been a strong tendency to divert the attention from the difference of quality to the difference of locality, and to confound this difference of quality with difference of locality.

In the next place, I do not regard your sweeping indictment of the northern people as warranted. That there is an immense amount of swinish greed in northern business circles and of vulgarity and vice and vacuity and extravagance in the social life of the North, I freely admit. But I am not prepared to say that these are the dominant notes in either the business life or the social life of the North. I know they are not the only notes. I am struck, whenever I visit a college, whenever I have a chance to meet the people of any city or town, with the number of good, straight, decent people with whom I am brought in contact, with the number of earnest young fellows with high purpose whom I meet, with the sweet young girls whom I see. The men I get together to settle the Anthracite Coal Strike, the men I see when there is a scientific gathering in Washington, the artists like Saint-Gaudens and French and MacMonnies, the writers like Crothers and Hyde, the men of the army whom I meet, the young fellows with whom I am brought in contact in doing political work, the families with whom I am intimate, yours, the Grant La Farges, the Gilders, my cousins, the Bacons, and so I could go on indefinitely — all these go to show that the outlook is in no shape or way one of unrelieved gloom. There is plenty of gloom in it, but there is plenty of light also, and if it is painted as all gloomy, I am afraid the chief effect will be to tend to make people believe that either it is all black or else it is all white; and in its effect one view is just as bad as the other. Smash vacuous, divorce-ridden Newport; but don't forget Saunderstown and Oyster Bay!

You also continually speak as if we have fallen steadily away from the high standard of our past. Now I am unable to say exactly what the proportions of good and evil are in the present, but I have not the slightest doubt that they are quite favorable as in the past. I have studied history a good deal and it is a matter of rather grim amusement to me to listen to the praise bestowed on our national past at the expense of our national present. Have you ever read Lecky's account of the Revolutionary war? It is perhaps a trifle too unfavorable to us, but is more nearly accurate than any other I have seen. Beyond all question we ought to have fought that war; and it was very creditable to Washington and some of his followers and to a goodly portion of the Continental troops; but I cannot say that it was very creditable to the nation as a whole. There were two and a half millions of us then, just ten times as many as there were of the Boers in South Africa, and Great Britain was not a fourth as strong as she was in the Boer war, and yet on the whole I think the Boers made a good deal better showing than we did. My forefathers, northerners and southerners alike, fought in the Revolutionary army and served in the Continental Congress, and one of them was the first Revolutionary governor of Georgia, so that I am not prejudiced against our Revolutionary people. But while they had many excellent qualities I think they were lacking as a whole in just the traits in which we are lacking today; and I do not think they were as fine, on the whole, as we are now. The second greatest Revolutionary figure, Franklin, to my mind embodied just precisely the faults which are most distrusted in the average American of the North today. Coning down to after the Revolution, we have never seen a more pitiful exhibition of weakness at home or a greater mixture of blustering insolence and incapacity in reference to affairs abroad than was shown under Jefferson and Madison. So I could go on indefinitely. But let me take only what I have myself seen; where I can speak as a witness and participator. Thirty years ago politics in this country were distinctly more corrupt than they are now, and I believe that the general tone was a little more sordid and that there was a little less of realizable idealism. The social life in New York was not one bit better than it is now. Gould Sage, Daniel Drew, the elder Vanderbilt, Jim Fisk and the other financiers of the day of that type were at the very least as bad as the corresponding men of today. No financier at present would dare perpetrate the outrages that Huntington was perpetrating some thirty years ago. Nothing so bad has been done in the insurance companies as was done in the *Chapter of Erie*. The Newport set is wealthier and more conspicuous now, and I think the divorce business is more loathsome, but I would certainly hesitate to say that things were worse now than then, taking it as a whole. The Porcellian Club of the last ten years, for instance, averages at least as well as the Porcellian Club for the ten years before I went into it. Among my own friends and in the little circle in which I live at Oyster Bay I don't see that there is any difference of an essential kind as compared with my father's friends and with the circle in which he lived. In the Civil War our people — a mere democracy — were better than in the Revolution, when they formed in part a provincial aristocracy.

When you come to the South and imply or express comparison between the South and the North, I again think you have overstated it. I am half southerner myself. I am as proud of the South as I am of the North. The South has retained some barbaric virtues which we have tended to lose in the North, partly owning to a mistaken pseudo-humanitarianism among our ethical creatures, partly owing to persistence in and perhaps the development of those business traits which, however, distinguished New York, New England and Pennsylvania a century ago just as they do today. On the other hand the southerners have developed traits of a very unhealthy kind. They are not as dishonest as, they do not repudiate their debts as frequently as their predecessors did in the good old times from which you think we have deteriorated; but they do not send as valuable men into the national councils as the northerners. They are not on the whole as efficient, and they exaggerate the common American tendency of using bombastic language which is not made good by performance. Your particular heroes, the Charleston aristocrats, offer as melancholy an example as I know of people whose whole life for generations has been warped by their own willful perversity. In the early part of South Carolina's history there was a small federalist party and later a small and dwindling union party within the State, of which I cannot speak too highly. But the South Carolina aristocrats, the Charleston aristocrats and their kinsfolk in the upcountry (let me repeat that I am of their blood, that my ancestors before they came to Georgia were members of these very South Carolina families of whom you write) have never made good their pretentions. They were no more to blame than the rest of the country for the slave trade of colonial days, but when the rest of the country woke up they shut their eyes tight to the horrors, they insisted that the slave trade should be kept, and succeeded in keeping it for a quarter of a century after the Revolutionary war closed, they went into secession partly to reopen it. They drank and dueled and made speeches, but they contributed very, very little toward anything of which we as Americans are now proud. Their life was not as ignoble as that of the Newport people whom you rightly condemn, yet I think it was in reality an ignoble life. South Carolina and Mississippi were very much alike. Their two great men of the deified past were Calhoun and Jefferson Davis, and I confess, I am unable to see wherein any conscienceless financier of the present day is worse than these two slave owners who spent their years in trying to feed their thirst for personal power by leading their followers to the destruction of the Union. Remember that the Charleston aristocrats (under Yancey) wished to reopen the slave trade at the time of the outbreak of the Civil War. Reconstruction was a mistake as it was actually carried out, and there is very much to reprobate in what was done by Sumner and Seward and their followers. But the blame attaching to them is as nothing compared to the blame attaching to the southerners for forty years preceding the war, and for the years immediately succeeding it. There never was another war, so far as I know, where it can be honestly and truthfully said as of this war that the right was wholly on one side, and the wrong wholly on the other. Even the courage and prowess of those South Carolina aristocrats were shown only at the expense of their own country, and only in the effort to tear in sunder their country's flag. In the Revolutionary war, in that remote past which you idealize, as compared to the present, the South Carolinians made as against the British a fight which can only be called respectable. There was little heroism; and Marion and Sumter, in their fight against Tarleton and the other British commanders, show at a striking disadvantage when compared with De Wet and De La Rey and the other Boer leaders. In the war of 1812 South Carolina did nothing. She reserved her strength until she could strike for slavery and against the Union. Her people have good stuff in them, but I do not think they are entitled to overpraise as compared to the North. As for the days of reconstruction, they brought their punishment absolutely on themselves, and are, in my judgment, entitled to not one particle of sympathy. The North blundered, but its blunders were in trying to do right in the impossible circumstances which the South had itself created, and for which the South was solely responsible.

Now as to the Negroes! I entirely agree with you that as a race and in the mass they are altogether inferior to the whites. Your small German scientific friend had probably not heard of the latest scientific theory — doubtless itself to be superseded by others — which is that the Negro and the white man as shown by their skulls, are closely akin, and taken together, differ widely from the round skulled Mongolian. But admitting all that can be truthfully said against the Negro, it also remains true that a great deal that is untrue is said against him; and that much more is untruthfully said in favor of the white man who lives beside and upon him. Your views of the Negro are those expressed by all of your type of Charlestonians. You must forgive my saying that they are only expressed in their entirety to those who don't know the facts. Are you aware that these white men of the South who say that the Negro is unfit to cast a vote, and who by fraud or force prevent his voting, are equally clamorous in insisting that his votes must be counted as cast when it comes to comparing their own representation with the representation of the white men of the North? The present leader of the Democrats in the House of Representatives is John Sharp Williams, a typical southerner of the type you mention. In his district three out of every four men are Negroes; the fourth man, a white man, does not allow any of these Negroes to vote, but insists upon counting their votes, so that his one vote offsets the votes of four white men in New York, Massachusetts or Pennsylvania. During my term as President bills have been introduced to cut down the southern representation so as to have it based in effect only on the white vote. With absolute unanimity the southerners have declared that to deprive them of the right of the extra representation which as white men they get by the fraudulent or violent suppression of the black vote is an outrage. With their usual absurd misuse of nomenclature they inveigh against the effort to prevent them crediting themselves with the votes of which they deprive others as "waving the bloody shirt," or being a plea for "negro domination." Your Charleston friends lead this outcry and are among the chief beneficiaries, politically, of the fraud and violence which they triumphantly defend. The North takes absolutely no interest in any such measure, and so far from having any feeling against the South or giving any justification for the South's statement that it wants to interfere with the South's concerns, it is really altogether too indifferent to what is done in the South.

Now remember, Dan, what I am saying has nothing to do with the right of the Negro to vote, or of his unfitness generally to exercise that right. It has to do simply with the consistent dishonesty championed and gloried in by your special southern friends who will not allow the Negro to vote and will not allow the nation to take notice of the fact that he is not voting; and insist upon his vote counted so as to enable them to overcome the honest white vote. I may add that my own personal belief is that the talk about the Negro having become worse since the Civil war is the veriest nonsense. He has on the whole become better. Among the Negroes of the South when slavery was abolished there was not one who stood as in any shape or way comparable with Booker Washington. Incidentally I may add that I do not know a white man of the South who is as as good a man as Booker Washington today. You say you would not like to take orders from a Negro yourself. If you had played football in Harvard at any time during the last fifteen years you would have had to do so, and you would not have minded it in the least; for during that time Lewis has been field captain and a coach. When I was in Charleston at the exposition the very Charlestonians who had hysterics afterward over Crum's appointment as collector of the port, assured me that Crum was one of the best citizens of Charleston, a very admirable man in every way, and while they protested that Negroes ought not to be appointed as postmasters they said there was no such objection to appointing them in other places, and specifically mentioned the then colored collector of customs in Savannah as a case in point. You cannot be more keenly aware than I am of the fact that our effort to deal with the Negro has not been successful. Whatever I have done with him I have found has often worked badly; but when I have tried to fall in with the views of the very southern people, which in this volume you seem to be upholding, the results have been worse than in any other way. These very people whose views you endorse are those who have tried to reintroduce slavery by the infamous system of peonage; which, however, I think in the last three years we have pretty well broken up. I am not satisfied that I acted wisely in either the Booker Washington dinner or the Crum appointment, though each was absolutely justified from every proper standpoint save that of expediency. But the anger against me was just as great in the communities where I acted exactly as the Charlestonians said I ought to act. I know no people in the North so slavishly conventional, so slavishly afraid of expressing any opinion hostile to or different from that held by their neighbors, as is true of the southerners, and most especially of the Charleston aristocrats, on all vital questions. They shriek in public about miscegenation, but they leer as they talk to me privately of the colored mistresses and colored children of white men whom they know. Twice southern senators who in the Senate yell about the purity of the white blood, deceived me into appointing postmasters whom I found had colored mistresses and colored children. Are you acquainted with the case of the Indianola post office in Mississippi? I found in office there a colored woman as postmaster. She and her husband were well to-do, and were quite heavy taxpayers. She was a very kindly, humble and respectable colored woman. The best people of the town liked her. The two bankers of the town, one of them the Democratic State senator, were on her bond. I reappointed her, and the Senators from Mississippi moved her confirmation. Afterwards the low whites in the town happened to get stirred up by the arrival of an educated colored doctor. His practice was of course exclusively among the Negroes. He was one of those men who are painfully educating themselves, and whose cases are more pitiful than the cases of any other people in our country, for they not only find it exceedingly difficult to secure a livelihood but are followed with hatred by the very whites who ought to wish them well. Too many southern people and too many northern people, repeat like parrots the statement that these "educated darkies" are "a deal worse than the old darkies." As a matter of fact almost all the Tuskegee students do well. This particular Negro doctor took away the Negro patients from the lowest white doctors of the town. They instigated the mob which held the mass meeting and notified the Negro doctor to leave town at once, which to save his life he did that very night. Not satisfied with this the mob then notified the colored postmistress that she must at once resign her office. The "best citizens" of the town did what throughout the South the "best citizens" of the type you praise almost always do in such emergencies, what your Charleston friends have invariably and at all times done in such emergencies; that is they "deprecated" the conduct of the mob and said it was "not representative of the real southern feeling"; and then added that to save trouble the woman must go! She went. The mayor and the sheriff notified her and me that they could not protect her if she came back. I shut up the office for the remainder of her term. It was all I could do and the least I could do. Now Dan, so far from there being any reprobation of this infamy the entire South, led by your friends in Charleston, screamed for months over the outrage of depriving the citizens of Indianola of their mail simply because they let a mob chase away by threats of murder a worthy, refined, educated and hard-working colored woman whom every reputable citizen of that town had endorsed for the position! This is at present the typical southern attitude toward the best type of colored men or colored women; and absolutely all I have been doing is to ask, not that the average Negro be allowed to vote, not that ninety-five per cent of the Negroes be allowed to vote, not that there be Negro domination in any shape or form, but that these occasionally good, well-educated, intelligent and honest colored men and women be given the pitiful chance to have a little reward, a little respect, a little regard, if they can by earnest useful work succeed in winning it. The best people in the South I firmly believe are with me in what I have done. In Trinity College in North Carolina, in Roanoke College, Virginia, here and there elsewhere, they have stood up manfully for *just what I have done*. The bishops of the Episcopal church have for the most part stood up for it. The best southern judges have stood up for it. In so standing up all of these college professors and students, bishops and occasional businessmen have had to face the violent and angry assaults of the majority; and in *Lady Baltimore* you give what strength you can to those denouncing and opposing the men who are doing their best to bring a little nearer the era of right conduct in the South.

Now Dan, I have written to you as I should only write to a dear friend whose book is a power, and who has written about things as to which I think I know a good deal, and as to which I hold convictions down to the very bottom of my heart.

Can't you get on here soon and spend a night or two? I will get Root and Bob Bacon and Taft to come to dinner and perhaps Moody, and I will tell you in full detail some of the various facts about the North and South on which I base my beliefs.

With love to Mrs. Wister, *Ever yours*

P.S. Have you read *Democracy*, a novel published nearly thirty years ago? Of course you have read *Martin Chuzzlewit*, published over sixty years ago. Each deals mainly with the society of the North; each makes any number of statements which are true as isolated facts; and each would go to show worse conditions than those you set forth. I think poorly of the author of *Democracy*, whoever he or she may have been; but Dickens was a great writer, and the American characters in *Martin Chuzzlewit* are types that are true as well as amusing, and the book itself is valuable as a tract even today; yet as a picture of the social life of the United States at the time which you are tempted to idealize, it is false because it suppresses or slurs over so much of the truth. Now in each of these books, as in yours, I eagerly welcome the assault on what is evil; but I think that it hinders instead of helping the effort to secure something like a moral regeneration if we get the picture completely out of perspective by slurring over some facts and overemphasizing others.

David Graham Phillips has written a book called *The Plum Tree*. I only read the first half. In it he portrays all politics as sordid, base and corrupt. Sinclair, the socialist, has written a book called *The Jungle*, about the labor world in Chicago. He portrays the results of the present capitalistic system in Chicago as on one uniform level of hideous horror. Now there is very much which needs merciless attack both in our politics and in our industrial and social life. There is much need for reform; but I do not think the two books in question, though they have been very widely read and are very popular and have produced a great effect, have really produced a healthy effect, simply because, while they set forth many facts which are true, they convey an entirely false impression when they imply that these are the only facts that are true and that the whole life is such as they represent it. Of course *Lady Baltimore* is the work of a master and so cannot be compared with either of these two books; but as a tract on the social life of the North as compared with the North's past and the South's present, it really seems to me to be about as inaccurate as they are; and what is more, it produces the very feeling which makes men followers of David Graham Phillips, the Hearst writer, and of Sinclair, the socialist, and which makes them feel that there is no use of trying to reform anything because everything is so rotten that the whole social structure should either be let alone or destroyed.

IDENTIFYING A WARBLER

To John Burroughs

Washington, May 5, 1906

Dear Oom John:

That warbler I wrote you about yesterday was the Cape May warbler. As soon as I got hold of an ornithological book I identified it. I do not think I ever saw one before, for it is rather a rare bird — at least on Long Island, where most of my bird knowledge was picked up. It was a male, in the brilliant spring plumage; and the orange-brown cheeks, the brilliant yellow sides of the neck just behind the cheeks, and the brilliant yellow under parts with thick black streaks on the breast, made the bird unmistakable. It was in a little pine, and I examined it very closely with the glasses but could not see much of its back. Have you found it a common bird? *Ever yours*

DISCIPLINING QUENTIN

To Virginia J. Arnold

Washington, May 10, 1906

Dear Miss Arnold:

I thank you for your note about Quentin. Don't you think it would be well to subject him to stricter discipline — that is, to punish him yourself, or send him to Mr. Murch for punishment that you are not able to give? Mrs. Roosevelt and I have no scruples whatever against corporal punishment. We will stand behind you entirely in doing whatever you decide is necessary. I do not think I ought to be called in merely for such offences as dancing when coming into the classroom, for singing higher than the other boys, or for failure to work as he should work at his examples, or for drawing pictures instead of doing his sums. My own belief is that he is a docile child, although one that needs a firmness that borders on severity. We refused to let him take his Indian suit to school, as he said the other boys were going to do with their suits, because we told him he had not been good enough. If you find him defying your authority or committing any serious misdeed, then let me know and I will whip him; but it hardly seems wise to me to start in whipping him every day for offenses which in point of seriousness look as if they could be met by discipline in school and not by extreme measures taken at home. *Sincerely yours*

If he brings play toys to school, confiscate them & keep them

"A TOTALLY FALSE PICTURE" OF POLITICS

To George Horace Lorimer

Personal and private

Washington, May 12, 1906

My dear Lorimer:

After our conversation I read *The Plum Tree* completely through, and am glad I did so. As you know, I had felt so disgusted before that I threw the book aside after having gotten halfway through it.

In the last chapter the idealist shows himself — perhaps especially in the last sentence. I so firmly believe myself that all other success, once the means of actual subsistence have been secured, counts for nothing compared to the success of the man in winning the one woman who is all the world to him, that Phillips' being right on this point reconciles me to a good deal in which he is hopelessly wrong. I have always felt an utter contempt for the sordid souls who regard themselves as practical and hardheaded because they have not the capacity to understand what love is; to understand that no other kind of success can in any shape or way compensate for the lack of that success which on the one hand means the enjoyment of the purple splendor of youth, and on the other hand means the pride and content and comfort of a middle age and old age passed together by the two people each of whom stands first in the thought of the other, with their children growing up around them. It is, if I remember aright, the last line of Browning's "Love Among the Ruins," which sums up the whole matter.

But of course no man is worthy of the highest happiness to be found within the home if he has not got in him the stuff that makes him do a man's work outside of the home. The best and highest work is of course to be done in time of just war, for the nation's welfare. But just wars are rare; and next to just wars I am inclined to put, both in point of interest and in point of importance, the constructive work of the public servant in time of peace — or at any rate, the work of the statesman ranks with that of the masters of art, literature and science, for I include genuine philanthropy as a part of public service. Now the very fact that I wish to see unceasing and merciless warfare waged upon corruption, cruelty and treachery and all kindred forms of evil in public life, makes me resent the overstatement which must surely defeat its own ends. It is just this overstatement of which, in my judgment, Phillips is guilty in *The Plum Tree*. Like others who do not measure the terms in which they denounce the evil of the present, he is inclined by contrast to deify the past. He speaks of the bygone generations, especially the generation just before the Civil War, as dwelling in a period before the rise of commercialism in politics, which commercialism he holds as the real root of all our evils. If he will go back twenty-five or thirty years and read a bright, sinister little novel called *Democracy*, he will see what the cultivated cynics of that period thought of public men and public opinion then. The writer of *Democracy* felt as bitter contempt for the American democracy and its servants during the seventies as Mr. Phillips feels for the same people at the beginning of the twentieth century. The former writer did not treat commercialism as the chief factor, or indeed as a considerable factor, in debauching national life. In his (or her) view the corruption was that inevitably attendant upon unregulated mob rule. The men he hated were, not the conscienceless millionaire and the politician who combines politics and business (the two people whom Mr. Phillips hates), but the skillful, tricky, conscienceless machine politician, and the raw, crude democrat. Now, as a matter of fact, all are thoroughly unhealthy characters, all of them exist, and against all we should make war. But Mr. Phillips' perspective is as mistaken as that of the author of *Democracy*. As for the people before the war, let Mr. Phillips read *Martin Chuzzlewit*. Jefferson Brick and Elijah Pogram and Hannibal Chollop and Scadder and Diver and all the rest are the creations of a master mind. Each is a substantially accurate representation of an American type. The error lay in Dickens' assumption that taken all together they constituted practically all that there was of American public life — a life even less attractive than that of the descendants of these people some sixty years later, as portrayed by Mr. Phillips. Now Mr. Phillips has fallen into just the same error in treating his characters as constituting practically all that there is in public life; for Scarborough is painted so that we could hardly recognize him as being real, and he no more offsets the disagreeable features of the book than Zola's unreal hero and heroine in his *Rêve* offset the hideous human swine in his other books.

I have been active in politics almost from the moment I left Harvard twenty-five years ago. I possessed a very moderate income. I could not have gone into politics at all if the expenses of election had at any time come anywhere near the salaries I have received in the different positions I have held; and except from these salaries, I of course never made a cent out of politics — I could no more do it than I could cheat at cards. I have always occupied working positions. I have seen New York State politics from the inside as a member of the Legislature, and New York City politics from the inside as Police Commissioner. I have carried my ward and lost it; have been delegate to county and state and national conventions; have stumped year in year out, and served on committees, before and after elections, which determined much of what the inside policy was to be. I have had on occasions to fight bosses and rings and machines; and have had to get along as best I could with bosses and rings and machines when the conditions were different. I have seen reform movements that failed and reform movements that succeeded and have taken part in both, and have also taken part in opposing fool reform movements which it would be a misfortune to have succeed. In particular, I have been so placed as to see very much of the inside of the administrations of three Presidents in addition to my own — that is, of Harrison, Cleveland and McKinley.

Now, I feel that almost each individual fact brought forward by Phillips is true by itself, and yet that these facts are so grouped as to produced a totally false impression. Of course there are some things that he alleges that I never have seen or heard of. I do not believe that ever, under any circumstances, the "Wall Street crowd" made to any man any advance even remotely resembling that he describes as made to Scarborough. I do not for a moment believe that there is or has been any powerful senatorial boss who in our time has been influential in handling at the same moment the nominations of the two parties. In fact, I do not for a moment believe that in our time any boss in one party has had any effect upon the presidential nomination of the other. I know that there are many wealthy men who have changed parties at different elections, and supported, for instance, Cleveland first and then McKinley. To my somewhat grim amusement, the chief representatives of this class, or at least the majority, went into a futile conspiracy against me of which they sought to make Mr. Hanna the head; and at that time they expected that if they could not nominate Mr. Hanna or someone who would be agreeable to Mr. Hanna, they would nominate Mr. Parker on the Democratic ticket and turn in and elect him. But their plan miscarried at every point, and it was merely a purely rich men's conspiracy, not a politicians' at all. If you will look at the list of the Cabinet Ministers and Ambassadors under my predecessors in office, I think you will see that it could only have been in very exceptional cases that any one of them owed his position to money alone, whether money contributed by himself or by outsiders. There were several, Mr. Whitney being perhaps the most prominent example, who were very big moneyed men of the identical unpleasant type portrayed by Mr. Phillips. But these were also men of great political power and activity within their own party, and men who held strong convictions on certain points entirely disconnected with wealth. There were many others, like Mr. Olney and like Mr. Griggs, who undoubtedly in the points which were closest to the hearts of the big corporation men held just the views these big corporation men did, but who, I am sure, held them with entire sincerity, just as hundreds of thousands of small outsiders in no way connected with the big corporations now hold these same views with entire sincerity and quite honestly look askance even at the very moderate amount of radicalism which they believe that I embody.

Again, Mr. Phillips errs in making his big politicians think only of that which is directly to their own pecuniary interests. For example, Hale and Foraker both violently opposed me this year on the rate matter no less than on other matters. They have stood for the forces that I am combating. But to me the most exasperating fact has been that I do not question their entire sincerity in standing against me. How Hale, having no earthly interest at stake, can nevertheless be so rabid against the upbuilding of the navy, and the Philippine tariff, I do not know. But I do know that he is entirely disinterested, and that the rich men have no control over him. Foraker, again, while violently against me on corporation matters, is as enthusiastic for the Philippine tariff bill and for the navy and for Panama and a proper foreign policy generally as any human being can be, and this without the slightest personal interest in any of the matters.

As for my own appointees; the members of my Cabinet, the judges I have appointed; the ambassadors and ministers I have appointed, the assistant secretaries and heads of bureaus around me — I really believe that we have never before had a finer grade of men, men more capable, more zealous, fearless and disinterested. I am as proud of them and have the same feeling about them as if they were my old regiment and we were down at Santiago. Scarborough is made by Mr. Phillips to feel hopeless about getting the right type of men. My experience shows that there was not the slightest need of any such fear on his part!

But to my mind the worst mistake that Phillips fell into — a mistake which has naturally resulted in his since enlisting under the banner of Hearst — was the mistake of painting all evil as due to corrupt commercialism, and all rich men as influenced only by what was base. There are plenty of rich men exactly such as he describes, just as there are Senators and Congressmen such as he describes, and bosses, state and city, such as he describes. But so there are plenty of labor leaders, plenty of men engaged in the effort to persuade poor people to organize for their own betterment, who are murderers, incendiaries, corruptionists, blackmailers, bribe takers and brutal scoundrels generally. Sam Parks in New York, and the leaders of the Western Federation of Miners in Idaho and Colorado, were and are figures more sinister and more full of menace to this country than even the worst of the big moneyed men — the C. P. Huntingtons and Jay Goulds of a former period, who were far more brutal and defiant than any of the big corporation men today. But it would be all nonsense to write a novel in which Sam Parks and Debs and Moyer and Haywood and Dennis Kearney appeared over and over again as the only types of labor leader. So it is wrong to portray all men of capital as Mr. Phillips portrays them. In the Senate the chief opponents of what is decent and right during the last few years have been men like Tillman. I have had to ride roughshod now and then over the men who accept Mr. Aldrich as their leader, but it has not been anything like as often as I have found it necessary in the interest of the country, in the interest of justice and decency, to ride roughshod over the men like Tillman. Tillman has sometimes been right; but not nearly as often as Aldrich.

It is with these rich men as with the bosses and corrupt politicians. In New York State and New York City I have seen at times things as bad done by the machines and the bosses, and the people they represent, as Mr. Phillips describes; and I have no question that the same is true of other States with which I am less familiar. But there are lights in the pictures as well as shadows! No other Governor of New York ever handled the big men of Wall Street as I did; as see my Franchise Tax bill; it cost me violent enmity; but plenty of rich men stood by me!

As for these rich men, I can speak quite disinterestedly. They are not my friends and never have been. My tastes, unfortunately, were wholly alien from those which I hope my sons will possess in sufficient quantity to make them able to do their part in the industrial world. The money-maker pure and simple not merely has no attraction for me, but is so antipathetic that if I am to get on well with him it is best that we should see each other as little as possible. The men and women who have been intimate with me since I have been in the White House are the same as those who were intimate with me before I came to the White House. They include artists and architects and writers, philanthropists of the genuine kind, politicians who possess ideals, and hard workers in the business world who, nevertheless, do take a proper interest in politics or in philanthropy (to use a word I hate) as well as in business; they include men I met in the mountains and the backwoods and on the ranches and the plains. If you were able to see my various guests at the White House (as you have seen some of them) you would find that taken in the aggregate they seem rather an incongruous lot, including Jacob Riis and Jim Reynolds, Mark Twain, Alfred Henry Lewis, Bat Masterson, Ben Daniels, Saint-Gaudens, John La Farge, Howells, Henry Adams, Seth Bullock, Llewellyn, Octave Thanet, Laura Richards, Merrifield and Sewall (who were on the ranches with me), Willis (with whom I hunted bear and caribou and white goat), Buffalo Bill (who was a genuine plainsman and scout long before he was a showman) and many, many others, including quite as many leaders of labor unions as heads of great corporations — John Mitchell has been to see me quite as often as Pierpont Morgan; Harvard and Yale men; and quite as often men of the scantiest schooling.

Now, I only mention these to show that I am disinterested in what I am about to say. I have never had these rich men ask favors from me save as I have had the leaders of labor organizations ask favors, or as I have had representatives of almost any body of citizens ask me — as, for instance, the Grand Army, or a bar association, or a medical association, or philanthropic or religious bodies, or temperance people. For what Mr. Phillips says about the corruption funds to be used in great campaigns there is some justification, but not very much. One of the most disinterested men I have ever met in politics is Cornelius Bliss, the great merchant and manufacturer, who was treasurer of the Republican National Campaign Committee when McKinley and I were elected in 1900, and when I and Fairbanks were elected in 1904. He is an old man who not only wishes no reward but would refuse to accept any reward. He undertook in each year the inconceivably harassing, arduous and difficult task without a thought of any kind save of doing what he believed ought to be done. He has never asked me for a favor of any kind or description, and indeed has hardly communicated with me save three or four times to write a statement as to the qualifications of some man who he knew was an an applicant for some unimportant position, and to speak to me on several occasions when I have myself requested him to come and consult with me. I think he has felt that I was going a good deal too far in my program about the so-called trusts, about railway rate legislation and the like; but he has differed from me simply as one friend differs from another — simply as Root has at times differed from me, both when within and when without the Cabinet. Cortelyou was the chairman of our National Committee. Not only has he never made me a request of any kind based upon the fact of any man or corporation having contributed; he tells me that no such request has been made of him.

Now I do not pretend to say that these conditions which obtain in regard to my own administration and election can be accepted as altogether normal; but I am confident they are a great deal nearer the normal than those which Mr. Phillips sets forth in *The Plum Tree*. *Sincerely yours*

May 23, 1906.

P.S. The above letter got laid aside and I have only just come across it. I want to add another thing, not bearing upon *The Plum Tree*, but upon Phillips' recent articles on the Senate. Here again is an instance in which Phillips takes certain facts that are true in themselves, and by ignoring utterly a very much larger mass of facts that are just as true and just as important, and by some downright perversion of truth both in the way of misstatement and of omission, succeeds in giving a totally false picture. You say that Phillips himself is an absolutely straight and honest man, with entire sincerity of conviction. I shall not question this, but I can only avoid questioning it by unstintedly condemning his judgment and his diligence. You doubtless know that many entirely honest people firmly believe that Mr. Phillips, in accepting the money of Mr. Hearst to attack the public servants of the United States, was actuated merely by a desire to achieve notoriety and at the same time to make money out of the slanders by which he achieves notoriety. I accept your statement that this is not the fact; but the appearances are more against him than the appearances are against any of the men he condemns. To be in the employ of Mr. Hearst and engaged in such work as Mr. Phillips is engaged in, from the point of view of ethics is not one particle better than to be a public man engaged in the practices he rightly condemns. He certainly makes no serious effort to find out the facts. In these articles he in two or three places touches upon things of which I know personally, and in each such place he is guilty of reckless untruth, the untruth invariably taking the form of slander. There may be some truth in some of the things that he says about some of the men, but it is so mixed up with falsehood, that I, for instance, would not venture to accept a single unsupported statement he makes as true, simply because of the way he misrepresents the facts with which I am acquainted. Some of the senators whom he has incidentally attacked I happen to know well, and they are high-minded, honest men; while there is an element of pure comedy in some of the praise he bestows, when it is considered that it comes from a man who professes to be holding aloft such an exalted standard of public morality. Apparently he thinks that to be a foul-mouthed coarse blackguard is a guarantee of honesty. He either ought not to be or is not aware of the fact that in practically every State legislature there are from ten to one hundred times as many blackmailing schemes, as many strike bills, introduced to blackmail corporations, as there are bills introduced corruptly to favor corporations, or good bills which are killed by corporations through improper methods. He either is or ought to be well aware of the fact that the average congressman, the average legislator, the average man in public life, is a great deal more afraid of the labor vote than of corporations, and that it is easier to get injustice done in the interest of a labor organization than injustice done in the interest of a corporation. He is or ought to be well aware of the fact that together with the gross and hideous wrong done by certain wealthy men should be placed the gross and hideous wrong done by certain labor unions and labor leaders. He should condemn both alike, and should condemn the wrongdoing in each case in a way that shall neither lead him into general assaults upon men of property nor into general assaults upon labor leaders. In other words he should tell the truth, and try to do justice as between the bad man, whether rich or poor, and the good man, whether rich or poor.

I do not believe that the articles that Mr. Phillips has written, and notably these articles on the Senate, do anything but harm. They contain so much more falsehood than truth that they give no accurate guide for those who are really anxious to war against corruption, and they do excite a hysterical and ignorant feeling against everything existing, good or bad; the kind of hysteria which led to the "red fool fury of the Seine,"

the kind of hysteria which renders it so difficult for the genuine reformers in Russia to secure reform in the teeth of those
who mix up reform and destruction.

INVESTIGATING MEAT PACKING

To Upton Sinclair

Personal

Washington, May 29, 1906

My dear Mr. Sinclair:

I have received your letter of the 26th instant together with
your telegram of the 27th, and I have now seen your articles
in the New York *Times* of May 28th and 29th. You have of
course committed no discourtesy in the interview you have
given. You are not bound to me by any agreement or understanding not to make public anything you see fit. I must add
that you do not seem to feel bound to avoid making and repeating utterly reckless statements which you have failed to
back up by proof. But my own duty is entirely different. I am
bound to see that nothing but the truth appears; that this
truth does in its entirety appear; and that it appears in such
shape that practical results for good will follow. The results
of the investigation are not yet in final form, nor is the investigation itself finished. Until these investigations are
finished and until the results are in final form, I should most
emphatically object to having them made public unless it
should become necessary to make a preliminary and un-
finished portion of them public in order to secure the passage
of some measure substantially like the Beveridge amendment.
Such hasty and premature action could only be justified if it
became necessary in order to secure a remedy for the evils.
What I am after is this remedy. The time when publicity is to
be given to the report is not in itself a vital matter. The vital
matter is to remedy the evils with the least possible damage
to innocent people. The premature publication that you request would doubtless cause great pecuniary loss not merely
to the beef packers and to all those responsible for so much

of the conditions as are bad, but also to scores of thousands of stock growers, ranchers, hired men, cowboys, farmers and farm hands all over this country, who have been guilty of no misconduct whatever. Some of the men thus hurt would be wealthy men. Most of them would be poor men. If it is necessary ultimately to hurt them in order that the reform shall be accomplished, then they must be hurt; but I shall certainly not hurt them needlessly nor wantonly. My object is to remedy the evils. The facts shall be made public in due time, but I shall give no preliminary report to the public unless it becomes necessary in order to bring about the result aimed at.

I think I ought to make two comments upon your interview in this morning's paper. In the first place it is to my mind an absurdity to have advocated any investigation by the Federal Government at all if the Federal Government has not power to take action. You say in effect that the Beveridge amendment, and, indeed, any legislative act of the kind, must be inoperative. Of course if I supposed you were right in this it would have been hardly worth while to go into the investigation. To "give the people the facts," as you put it, without pointing out how to better the conditions, would chiefly be of service to the apostles of sensationalism and would work little or no permanent betterment in the conditions. Now what I intend to bring about is just precisely this permanent betterment, and what is more I intend to bring it about by the establishment of a Government body which shall not only insist upon decent conditions, but which shall at any and all times keep the public informed when the conditions are not what they should be in any given instance.

In the second place, I ought to tell you that for many of your more startling statements there is not as yet any justification whatever in the way of proof; there are many things that you have asserted which should under no conceivable circumstances have been asserted unless you were prepared to back them up with testimony which would satisfy an honest man of reasonable intelligence; and hitherto in these cases no such testimony has been forthcoming. On other points you have furnished facts which enabled us to test what you have said. On some of these points we have already tested the accuracy of your statements by investigation. On

other points we intend so to test them; but as yet the examination is not finished and is not in shape to be made public.
Sincerely yours

SCIENCE AND LITERATURE

To Henry Bryant Bigelow

Personal

Washington, May 29, 1906

My dear Mr. Bigelow:

Dr. Bigelow has just handed me not only your pamphlets but the extremely interesting typewritten sketch "Summer on the Labrador Coast." I am so much pleased with what you have written that I want to send you a personal word. We are producing thousands — I may almost say tens of thousands — of good, honest, hard-working, small scientific observers, each of whom, in the world of science, corresponds to a good ordinary bricklayer in the world of mechanical industry. I have a hearty respect for such a scientific worker, just as I have a hearty respect for a good, honest bricklayer; but just as ten thousand bricklayers do not make up for the failure to produce one first-class architect, so ten thousand small scientific observers will not atone for the failure to produce a great faunal naturalist; while if we can only bring forth in this country one man who, in addition to the power of accurate observation and of painstaking research, possesses also the power of vivid description, we shall have made a great permanent contribution alike to science and to letters. We have innumerable so-called nature writers who write more or less well and more or less interestingly, but who have no idea of observing or recording truthfully — the chief example being John Luther Long. Now of course it is better that a book be so dull as to be unreadable than that it should not be worth reading and yet readable; and therefore the driest list of birds or mammals from any given locality, provided it be truthful, is better than any of Mr. Long's books. But the real combination to be devoutly hoped for is a book which shall contain the facts from the industrious and truthful small scientist and yet be really literary. Such a book must have mass, and, in addition, must have charm. To have written hundreds of little pamphlets does not in any way or shape make the writer stand on an equality with a great faunal naturalist like Audubon, simply because the latter wrote a big, coherent work, and wrote as a nature lover as well as a scientific observer.

One of the most foolish of modern attitudes is the attitude of the dry-as-dust person who says that history must henceforth be treated as science and not as literature; whereas of course the only great historians are also great literary men, and any historian who is not such is merely the gatherer of bricks and stones which may some day be used by the master architect. Such a man does a good work and is entitled to praise, but he in no shape or way comes in the class with Gibbon and Macaulay, Tacitus and Thucydides, and it is in this last class that the great historian of the future — the really great historian — must come.

So it is in scientific matters. We need that the greatest scientific book shall be one which scientific laymen can read, understand and appreciate. The greatest scientific book will be a part of literature; as Darwin and Lucretius are.

Now all this leads up to what I want to say, which is that it looks to me as if you had it in you to do just this work. Your Labrador sketches are fine. There is only one false note in them, to my mind, and that is where you speak of wondering what the caribou, lemming and wolf think of the Northern Lights — which was a little sentimental as they doubtless do not think of them at all. That piece of yours ought to be published. You should send it to one of the magazines; but for Heaven's sake do not rest content with sending it to the magazines. Do not become a mere magazine writer. You might just as well merely write unsigned articles in the daily press or even in the Sunday newspapers. You have it in you to write a great nature book, in which you shall set forth the facts and in which you shall vividly portray the results of most painstaking and careful investigations; in which you shall record many things that are new and of importance; and in which you shall, in addition, give the vividness and charm that these facts in their own surroundings should present to the beholder. It would be everything if we could see such a totally new departure as would be implied by a great book on our mammals and birds — a great faunal natural history which should enable us to see the different animals and different groups of animals in their surroundings, just as you have enabled me to see the Labrador coast. I earnestly hope that you will work steadily with some such end in view. *Sincerely yours*

LABOR CONFLICT IN THE WEST

To Calvin Cobb

Confidential

Washington, June 16, 1906

My dear Mr. Cobb:

I trust that Governor Gooding understands my hearty and deep sympathy with, and appreciation of, the work he is doing in striving to bring to trial the men charged with the murder of ex-Governor Steunenberg. I appreciate that he is doing this literally at the peril of his life. For a dozen years there has been in parts of the Rocky Mountain regions a reign of terror in which officers and leading members of the Western Federation of Miners have been foremost, and these men and their allies have again and again by assassination removed from their path men who were or had been valiant in opposing their criminal misconduct. Ex-Governor Steunenberg was their most noted victim. They will, if they are given the chance, and unless they are cowed, certainly endeavor to make Governor Gooding another victim. I wish you to assure Governor Gooding that every honorable and decent man, whether wageworker or capitalist, who has taken the trouble to find out what the facts are, is his hearty supporter. I cannot express the keen indignation I feel with certain men of good position who, because they have not taken the trouble to find out the facts, have been lukewarm in supporting him or even hostile to him. I had made a thorough investigation of his conduct in connection with procuring from Colorado the men accused of this murder, by an Assistant Attorney General, and he reports that the Governor's conduct has been in all respects exactly what it should be. At the proper time, if necessary, this report will be made public. I have been outraged at the attitude of certain labor organizations in extending their sympathy to the men accused of this crime, Moyer, Haywood and their allies. It is conduct precisely on a par with, but even worse than, the action of the Chicago Board of Trade in championing the beef packers at this moment. In one case as in the other there is a complete willingness to sacrifice justice and condone or approve infamous wrongdoing, provided only the man of one's own class, capitalist in the one case and labor man in the other, can be saved from suffering the penalty of the law. Moyer and Haywood are entitled to an absolutely fair trial and if innocent of this crime, to an acquittal in spite of their black record of wrongdoing in the past. But this black record of wrongdoing should be enough to warn any man to extend no sympathy to them and to see to it that they simply get the justice to which any accused man is entitled. If the Governor or the court fail to give them this justice, I would be myself the first to protest, just as I should protest against any injustice to any monopolist in the land no matter what that monopolist's record in the past had been.

In confidence, I wish you would tell the Governor that I do hope he will most carefully guard against falling into the grave errors that the Governor of Colorado fell into in 1903 and 1904. If I had been in Governor Peabody's place I would have cinched the Western Federation of Miners until it looked like an hourglass, but I would have cinched the big corporations on the other side just as tight. For instance, the failure to insist that the legislature should obey the will of the people and pass the eight-hour law, and if it did not do so to keep it in session every day of the whole time for which it was elected, was in my judgment unpardonable. In the same way the failure to exact the quickest justice for the looting of the miners' co-operative store was in my judgment unpardonable. There are plenty of unscrupulous and lawless corporations of great wealth, and some of those in the Rocky Mountain States are as unscrupulous and lawless as any I have ever known. I should handle them without mercy where they do wrong, but where the Western Federation of Miners does wrong, on the other side, I should handle it equally without mercy. I cannot express my contempt and indignation for the men like Norman Hapgood who, sitting in their editorial sanctums, wholly without any experience with the rough and dangerous side of life, and with to their account the minimum credit of manly work, yet condemn, explicitly or implicitly, men like the Governor, who is doing the work of civilization on the dangerous frontier of our social life.

I enclose you copies for your own private information of my letter to the Department of Justice requesting the investigation by Assistant Attorney General Robb and of Assistant Attorney General Robb's report. *Sincerely yours*

TRAVELING EXPENSES

To James Albertus Tawney

Washington, June 17, 1906

My dear Mr. Tawney:

I thank you for your letter of the 15th instant. If Mr. Williams should make his protest again, as far as I am concerned I should be entirely willing to have a provision put in that none of the $25,000 appropriated should be for the President's own railroad ticket, his own food, and his own accommodations on the train. In other words, if the House feels that the President should pay for his own traveling expenses I would be more than delighted to do so. Then the entire $25,000 will be paid for the traveling expenses of the clerks, stenographers and other governmental employees who are obliged to go with me, for the newspapermen, including the photographers, who are also on the train, and for the Governors, Senators, Congressmen, and occasional private citizens who in each state join me on the train. If I travel as I intend to next year my own ticket, food, and so forth, will not cost a thousand dollars, and at least $24,000 will go for the other people. The extra cost of the private train comes, not because of my ticket, but because of the other people who go upon it, and because I have to suit my movements to the institutions, the bodies of citizens, and so forth, before whom I appear, and therefore cannot use the regular trains. A President traveling on a regular train would completely interrupt the traffic, and the railroads would in most cases be not only unwilling but unable to have him do so.

Mr. Jefferson is said to have on one occasion traveled on horseback. Personally, I should always rather travel on horseback than on a special train — but I would not cover as much ground. Jefferson was not, however, required to furnish fifty additional horses for the government employees, newspapermen, Governors, Senators, Congressmen and outsiders who went along with him, nor did he have to furnish accommodations for all of them throughout the trip. *Sincerely yours*

LUXURY AND FOOTBALL AT COLLEGE

To Arthur Twining Hadley

Personal

Oyster Bay, August 1, 1906

My dear President Hadley:

It is a great comfort to have, among the two or three leading college presidents, one who can always be relied upon to say what is wise and sane as well as fearless. I thank you for your admirable article on the growth of luxury in the American college, and I wish that the foolish people who desire to abolish football and minimize athletics would pay heed to what you show to be one of the best reasons for their maintenance. *Faithfully yours*

THE HAGUE PEACE CONFERENCE

To Andrew Carnegie

Personal and private

Oyster Bay, August 6, 1906

My dear Mr. Carnegie:

Your letter is most interesting. Do you know, I sometimes wish that we did not have the ironclad custom which forbids a President ever to go abroad. If I could meet the Kaiser and the responsible authorities of France and England, I think I could be of help in this Hague Conference business; which is now utterly impossible, and as facts are unadvisable. In any such matter the violent extremists who favor the matter are to be dreaded almost or quite as much as the Bourbon reactionaries who are against it. This is as true of the cause of international peace as it is of the cause of economic equity as between labor and capital at home. I do not know whether in the French Revolution I have most contempt and abhorrence for the Marat, Hébert, Robespierre and Danton type of revolutionists, or for the aristocratic, bureaucratic and despotic rulers of the old regime; for the former did no good in the revolution, but at the best simply nullified the good that others did and produced a reaction which re-enthroned despotism; while they made the name of liberty a word of shuddering horror for the time being.

I hope to see real progress made at the next Hague Conference. If it is possible in some way to bring about a stop, complete or partial, to the race in adding to armaments, I shall be glad; but I do not yet see my way clear as regards the details of such a plan. We must always remember that it would be a fatal thing for the great free peoples to reduce themselves to impotence and leave the despotisms and barbarisms armed. It would be safe to do so if there was some system of international police; but there is now no such system; if there were, Turkey for instance would be abolished forthwith unless it showed itself capable of working real reform. As things are now it is for the advantage of peace and order that Russia should be in Turkestan, that France should have Algiers, and that England should have Egypt and the Sudan. It would be an advantage to justice if we were able in some way effectively to interfere in the Congo Free State to secure a more righteous government; if we were able effectively to interfere for the Armenians in Turkey, and for the Jews in Russia. But at present I do not see how we can interfere in any of these three matters, and the one thing I won't do is to bluff when I cannot make good; to bluster and threaten and then fail to take the action if my words need to be backed up.

I have always felt that our special peace champions in the United States were guilty of criminal folly in their failure to give me effective support in my contest with the Senate over the arbitration treaties. In this contest I had the support of certain Senators, headed by the very best man in the Senate — O. H. Platt of Connecticut. But the Senate, which has undoubtedly shown itself at certain points not merely an inefficient but often a dangerous body as regards its dealings with foreign affairs, so amended the treaties as to make them absolutely worthless. Yet there were some people — including, for instance, a man named Love or Dove, who is the head of the peace conference that meets at Lake Mohonk — who in their anxiety to get anything, no matter how great a sham, and in their ignorance of the fact that foreign powers would undoubtedly have refused to ratify the amended treaties, declined entirely to give me any support and thereby committed a very serious wrong against the cause of arbitration.

You have doubtless seen how well the Pan-American Conference has gone off. Root's going there was a great stroke. Gradually we are coming to a condition which will insure permanent peace in the Western Hemisphere. If only the Senate will ratify the Santo Domingo treaty, we shall have taken another stride in this direction. At The Hague I hope we can work hand in hand with France and England; but all three nations must be extremely careful not to get led off into vagaries, and not to acquiesce in some propositions such as those I am sorry to say Russia has more than once made in the past — propositions in the name of peace which were really designed to favor military despotisms at the expense of their free neighbors. I believe in peace, but I believe that as things are at present, the cause not only of peace but of what is greater than peace, justice, is favored by having those nations which really stand at the head of civilization show, not merely by words but by action, that they ask peace in the name of justice and not from any weakness.

With warm regards to Mrs. Carnegie, believe me, *Faithfully yours*

SUMMER AT OYSTER BAY

To Henry Cabot Lodge

Oyster Bay, August 6, 1906

Dear Cabot:

I have sent your and Gussie's letters to Bacon, asking that the action Gussie requests be taken unless there is good reason to the contrary of which I am not informed.

I have been having a real rest this summer, and incidentally have grown to realize that I have reached that time of life when too violent physical exercise does not rest a man when he has had an exhausting mental career. Roswell has behaved excellently ever since that one day when he reared so badly, and I think he will be all right in the end.

Have you read the Life of Hamilton by that Englishman, Oliver? I like it.

I shall do what I can to help out the Congressional Committee this fall, but there are mighty ugly propositions to be faced in several different States. The Republicans of Ohio, for instance, want to down both Dick and Foraker, just as the Republicans of Pennsylvania want to down Penrose, while Platt and Odell between them have absolutely deviled the situation here in New York. Their alliance has broken down, though. Hearst in New York has completely run away with the Democracy. It may be that he will be elected; if so I think he will prove a thorn in Bryan's side. As for Bryan, though he has many kindly and amiable traits, what a shallow demagogue he is! I do not believe he is a bit worse than Thomas Jefferson, and I do not think that if elected President he will be a worse

President. The country would survive, but it would suffer just as the country suffered for at least two generations because of its folly in following Jefferson's lead.

We have been having a delightful summer. The secret-service men are a very small but very necessary thorn in the flesh. Of course they would not be in the least use in preventing any assault upon my life. I do not believe there is any danger of such an assault, and if there were it would be simple nonsense to try to prevent it, for as Lincoln said, though it would be safer for a President to live in a cage, it would interfere with his business. But it is only the secret-service men who render life endurable, as you would realize if you saw the procession of carriages that pass through the place, the procession of people on foot who try to get into the place, not to speak of the multitude of cranks and others who are stopped in the village. I have ridden and rowed and chopped and played tennis. We are about to have an evening picnic in the boats. I always especially welcome anything in the boats, because it gives me a chance to row Edith, so I get some exercise without having her tired out.

Archie is off for a week's cruise with Captain Joshua Slocum — that man who takes his little boat, without any crew but himself, all around the world.

Give my love to Nannie. *Ever yours*

HAMILTON AND JEFFERSON

To Frederick Scott Oliver

Personal

Oyster Bay, August 9, 1906

My dear Mr. Oliver:

I have so thoroughly enjoyed your book on Hamilton that you must allow me the privilege of writing to tell you so. I have just sent a copy to Lodge. There are naturally one or two points on which you and I would not quite agree; but they are very few, and it is really remarkable that you, an English man of letters, and I, an American politician largely of non-English descent, should be in such entire accord as regards the essentials. I shall inflict upon you a rather cruel punishment for having written the book; for I am sending you a volume of mine. As it deals with New York City most of it will be of no interest whatever to you; but it is possible that pages 104 to 158, in which I touch on some of the very questions you deal with, both as regards the Revolutionary War, the adoption of the Constitution, and Hamilton himself, will appeal to you, because it seems to me that the ideas are substantially like those which you develop.

Thank Heaven, I have never hesitated to criticize Jefferson; he was infinitely below Hamilton; I think the worship of Jefferson a discredit to my country; and I have as small use for the ordinary Jeffersonian as for the ordinary defender of the house of Stuart — and I am delighted to notice that you share this last prejudice with me. I think Jefferson *on the whole* did harm in public life. At the same time, there are two [   ] Jefferson stood at [   ] advantage compared to his Federalist opponents (always excepting Washington). He did thoroughly believe in the people, just as Abraham Lincoln did, just as Chatham and Pitt believed in England; and though this did not blind Lincoln to popular faults and failings any more than it blinded the elder and the younger Pitts to English failings, it was in each case a prerequisite to doing the work well. In the second place, Jefferson believed in the West and in the expansion of our people westward, whereas the northeastern Federalists allowed themselves to get into a position of utter hostility to western expansion. Finally, Jefferson was a politician and Hamilton was not. Hamilton's admirers are apt to speak as if this was really to his credit; but such a position is all nonsense. A politician may be and often is a very base creature, and if he cares only for party success, if he panders to what is evil in the people, and still more if he cares only for his own success, his special abilities merely render him a curse. But among free peoples, and especially among the free peoples who speak English, it is only in very exceptional circumstances that a statesman can be efficient, can be of use to the country, unless he is also (not as a substitute, but in addition) a politician. This is a very rough-and-tumble, workaday world, and the persons, such as our "anti-imperialist" critics over here, who sit in comfortable libraries and construct theories, or even the people who like to do splendid and spectacular feats in public office without undergoing all the necessary preliminary outside drudgery, are and deserve to be at a disadvantage compared to the man who takes the trouble, who takes the pains, to organize victory. Lincoln — who, as you finely put it, unconsciously carried out the Hamiltonian tradition — was superior to Hamilton just because he was a politician and was a genuine democrat and therefore suited to lead a genuine democracy. He was infinitely superior to Jefferson of course; for Jefferson led the people wrong, and followed them when they went wrong; and though he had plenty of imagination and of sentimental aspiration, he had neither courage nor farsighted common sense, where the interests of the nation were at stake.

I have not much sympathy with Hamilton's distrust of the democracy. Nobody knows better than I that a democracy may go very wrong indeed, and I loathe the kind of demagogy which finds expression in such statements as "the voice of the people is the voice of God"; but in my own experience it has certainly been true, and if I read history aright it was true both before and at the time of the Civil War, that the highly cultivated classes, who tend to become either cynically worldly-wise or to develop along the lines of the Eighteenth Century philosophers, and the moneyed classes, especially those of large fortune, whose ideal tends to be mere money, are not fitted for any predominant guidance in a really great nation. I do not dislike, but I certainly have no special respect or admiration for and no trust in, the typical big moneyed men of my country. I do not regard them as furnishing sound opinion as regards either foreign or domestic policies. Quite as little do I regard as furnishing such opinion the men who especially pride themselves on their cultivation — the men like many of those who graduate from my own college of Harvard, and who find their organs in the New York *Evening Post* and *Nation*. These papers are written especially for cultivated gentlefolk. They have many minor virtues, moral and intellectual; and yet during my twenty-five years in public life I have found them much more often wrong than right on the great and vital public issues. In England they would be howling little Englanders, would be raving against the expense of the navy, and eager to find out something to criticize in Lord Cromer's management of Egypt, not to speak of perpetually insisting upon abandoning the Sudan. Sumner, whose life of Hamilton you quote, is an exact representative of this type. He is a college professor, a cold-blooded creature of a good deal of intellect, but lacking the fighting virtues and all wide patriotism, who has an idea that he can teach statesmen and politicians their duty. Three times out of four he goes as wrong on public questions as any Tammany alderman possibly could go; and he would be quite unable even to understand the lofty ambition which, for instance, makes you desire to treat the tariff as something neither good nor bad in itself, but to be handled in whatever way best contributes to solidifying the British Empire and making it a compact and coherent union.

You speak of your lack of direct familiarity with American politics. Do come over to this side next winter and spend a night or two with me at the White House. I shall have Lodge and various others in to see you, and I think you would enjoy meeting them. By the way, I shall, under those circumstances, try to have you meet one of Hamilton's many descendants, Miss Louisa Lee Schuyler of whom I am very fond; she is a dear, — almost an elderly lady now; whenever she comes to dine at the White House she wears a brooch with Hamilton's hair. I shall also have you meet my Commissioner of Corporations, Garfield, — his father, the President, was the first of our Presidents who publicly put Hamilton in the high place where he belongs. By the way, the inkstand I am using was given me by the Hamilton Club of Chicago when I was inaugurated Governor of New York.

With regard, *Sincerely yours*

"AN IDEAL PRESIDENT"

To William Allen White

Personal

Oyster Bay, August 11, 1906

My dear White:

I have your letter of the 8th. Personally I wish very much that you would write exactly that article. For me to say what I think, which is that it is an insult to the people to suppose that we have not got men who can carry on my work, might look a little like what our southern friends call "biggity." You have exactly expressed my ideas. Of course I am not going to try to nominate any man. Personally you know how highly I think of Secretary Taft, but I am not going to take a hand in his nomination, for it is none of my business. I am sure Kansas will like him. He would be an ideal President. He is the kind of broad-gauge American that Kansas ought to like. But I do not believe that for any consideration he would consent to be "mighty keerful"! It is not his style. I think he and Kansas speak the same language — the American language — the language which perhaps is spoken best in some districts of the West, but which is familiar to all good Americans in every part of our country.

No, don't send me any more of those Leavenworth *Times* articles. I am delighted to have you send anything to me that you think worth while that attacks me, but it makes me red-hot to see how people persecute Wood. I enclose Taft's letter on the subject.

Get on to see me at Washington in October. *Faithfully yours*

SIMPLIFIED SPELLING

To Charles Arthur Stillings

Oyster Bay, August 27, 1906
My dear Mr. Stillings:
I enclose herewith copies of certain circulars of the Simplified Spelling Board, which can be obtained free from the Board at No. 1 Madison Avenue, New York City. Please hereafter direct that in all Government publications of the executive departments the three hundred words enumerated in Circular No. 5 shall be spelled as therein set forth. If anyone asks the reason for the action, refer him to Circulars 3, 4 and 6 as issued by the Simplified Spelling Board. Most of the criticism of the proposed step is evidently made in entire ignorance of what the step is, no less than in entire ignorance of the very moderate and common-sense views as to the purposes to be achieved, which views are so excellently set forth in the circulars to which I have referred. There is not the slightest intention to do anything revolutionary or initiate any far-reaching policy. The purpose simply is for the Government, instead of lagging behind popular sentiment, to advance abreast of it and at the same time abreast of the views of the ablest and most practical educators of our time as well as the most profound scholars — men of the stamp of Professor Lounsbury. If the slight changes in the spelling of the three hundred words proposed wholly or partially meet popular approval, then the changes will become permanent without any reference to what public officials or individual private citizens may feel; if they do not ultimately meet with popular approval they will be dropt, and that is all there is about it. They represent nothing in the world but a very slight extension of the unconscious movement which has made agricultural implement makers and farmers write "plow" instead of "plough"; which has made most Americans write "honor" without the somewhat absurd, superfluous "u"; and which is even now making people write "program" without the "me" — just as all people who speak English now write "bat," "set," "dim," "sum," and "fish," instead of the Elizabethan "batte," "sette," "dimme," "summe,"

and "fysshe"; which makes us write "public," "almanac," "era," "fantasy," and "wagon," instead of the "publick," "almanack," "aera," "phantasy," and "waggon" of our great-grandfathers. It is not an attack on the language of Shakespeare and Milton, because it is in some instances a going back to the forms they used, and in others merely the extension of changes which, as regards other words, have taken place since their time. It is not an attempt to do anything far-reaching or sudden or violent; or indeed anything very great at all. It is merely an attempt to cast what slight weight can properly be cast on the side of the popular forces which are endeavoring to make our spelling a little less foolish and fantastic. *Sincerely yours*

READING EURIPIDES

To Florence La Farge

Oyster Bay, September 5, 1906

Dear Florence:

I return herewith the *Electra*. It seems to me that Murray has rendered the play admirably. The first twenty lines are particularly good.

What extraordinary people the Greeks were! I do not know whether most to admire the wonderful power and artistic beauty of the play, or to shrink from the revolting nature of the theme. I have never been able to see that there was the slightest warrant for resenting the death of Agamemnon on the part of his son and daughter, inasmuch as that worthy gentleman had previously slain another daughter, to whose loss the brother and sister never even allude; not to mention the fact that he obtained possession of the daughter, in order to slay her, by treachery, and that he brought Cassandra home with him as his mistress. I think Clytemnestra's sin mild indeed compared with Agamemnon's. If it is said that the Greek judgment was influenced by the very different culpabilities to be attached to a man and a woman, then why should no punishment whatever be awarded to Electra for her part in the murder of her mother, in which she was really the determining factor? Whereas Orestes was haunted by the Furies, Electra was promptly married "to an earl who kept his carriage."

It was delightful having you here. *Ever yours*

WINSTON CHURCHILL

To Henry Cabot Lodge

Oyster Bay, September 12, 1906

Dear Cabot:

I agree absolutely with what you say. I want on the bench a follower of Hamilton and Marshall and not a follower of Jefferson and Calhoun; and what is more I do not want any man who from frivolity, or disinclination to think, or ignorance, or indifference to popular moods, goes wrong on great questions. I am going to see Taft and Day together as soon as I return to Washington and go over most carefully with them the whole Lurton business.

In view of the fact that the question of liquor or temperance always works to our harm, and that the liquor men and temperance people invariably subordinate all greater issues to the one in which they are immediately interested, I think we came out very well in Maine. Littlefield was the easiest mark the labor men could have tackled, and it was very hard saving him because he has in times past essayed to rise by trampling down others. That is, he has done in a modified way the McCall act of trying to appear great by criticizing his associates in the House, the President, and all others. It is the cheapest way that I know of striving to get a reputation for independence, and is never resorted to by a really fine man. But of course the issue came in a way that rendered it more important to save Littlefield than almost anyone else who was up for Congress.

I had sent you the Hapgood correspondence before receiving your letter. It is only rarely that one can get at a conceited and insincere jack of the advanced mugwump type, because usually it doesn't pay to shoot at him; but this particular time I did take solid satisfaction out of hanging even so small a hide on the fence.

I have been over Winston Churchill's life of his father. I dislike the father and dislike the son, so I may be prejudiced. Still, I feel that, while the biographer and his subject possess some real farsightedness, especially in their appreciation of the shortcomings of that "Society" which had so long been dominant in English politics, and which produces in this country the missionary and the mugwump; yet they both possess or possest such levity, lack of sobriety, lack of permanent principle, and an inordinate thirst for that cheap form of admiration which is given to notoriety, as to make them poor public servants. *Ever yours*

P.S. I have asked Shaw to stop all proceedings in reference to appraiser's store site until after I have an opportunity to go over the matter with you after my return to Washington.

THE CORPORATION MEN

To Henry Cabot Lodge

Washington, October 8, 1906

Dear Cabot:

Your speech was excellent, and I do wish you would tell Mr. Bates how much I liked his speech. Surely he knows the regard and respect I have for him.

Perhaps you are right about its having been proper for me to bear down harder upon Hearst and Moran, or upon their type, in my Harrisburg speech. But of course it was a speech that I hoped would do good to the party, and I did not know how far it was wise to go in denouncing our opponents by name. Moreover, I have been more shocked than I can say by the attitude of some of the corporation men within the last two or three weeks. Last week Jim Sherman called upon E. H. Harriman to ask for a contribution. Harriman declined flatly to give anything. He said he had no interest in the Republican party and that in view of my action toward the corporations he preferred the other side to win. Sherman told him that the other side was infinitely more hostile to corporations than we were; that all we were doing was to be perfectly honest with them, decline to give them improper favors, and so on, and that Harriman would have to fear, as other capitalists would have to fear, the other side more than us. To this Harriman answered that he was not in the least afraid, that whenever it was necessary he could buy a sufficient number of Senators and Congressmen or State legislators to protect his interests, and when necessary he could buy the Judiciary. These were his exact words. He did not say this under any injunction of secrecy to Sherman, and showed a perfectly cynical spirit of defiance thruout, his tone being that he greatly preferred to have in demagogs rather than honest men who treated them fairly, because when he needed he could purchase favors from the former. At the same time the Standard Oil people informed Penrose that they intend to support the Democratic party unless I call a halt in the suits begun against the Standard Oil people, notably a suit which Moody is inclined to recommend; and they gave the same reasons as Harriman, namely that rather than have an administration such as the present they would prefer to have an administration of Bryans or Hearsts, because they could make arrangements with them — they did not use the naked brutality of language which Harriman used, but they did state in substance that they could buy what favors they needed.

In New York this year, in securing the election of Parsons over Quigg, and the triumph in Brooklyn of the anti-Odell forces, the chief dangers we encountered were caused by the lavish use of Harriman and Ryan money by Quigg and Odell, and many of the Wall Street financiers quite openly say they would just as leave have Hearst as Hughes, their attitude being that they object as much to the discovery of rascality and the suppression of bribery and theft as they do to blackmail & robbery. Do you wonder that I feel pretty hot with them? Of course I could not feel hotter with them than I do with the Hearsts and Morans; and in this same speech you may have noticed that I spoke of demagogs and agitators just as I did of reactionaries. *Always yours*

WILLIAM RANDOLPH HEARST

To John St. Loe Strachey

Personal & Private

Washington, October 25, 1906

My dear Strachey:

I am always delighted to tell you anything I can. Of course it is a little difficult for me to give you an exact historic judgment about a man whom I so thoroly dislike and despise as I do Hearst. I think that he is a man without any real principle; that tho he is posing as a radical, he is in reality no more a radical than he is a conservative. But when I have said this, after all, I am not at all sure that I am saying much more of Hearst than could probably be said — or which would contain a large element of truth if said — about both Winston Churchill and his father, Lord Randolph. Hearst's private life has been disreputable. He is now married, and as far as I know, entirely respectable. His wife was a chorus girl or something like that on the stage, and it is of course neither necessary nor advisable, in my judgment, to make any allusion to any of the reports about either of them before their marriage. It is not the kind of a family which people who believe that sound home relations form the basis of national citizenship would be glad to see in the Executive Mansion in Albany, and still less in the White House. But I think that only harm comes from any public discussion of, or even allusion to, such a matter.

Hearst has edited a large number of the very worst type of sensational, scandal-mongering newspapers. They have been edited with great ability and with entire unscrupulousness. The editorials are well written, and often appeal for high morality in the abstract. Moreover, being a fearless man, and shrewd and farsighted, Hearst has often been of real use in attacking abuses which benefited great corporations, and in attacking individuals of great wealth who have done what was wrong. In these matters he has often led the way, and honest men who are overconservative have been shocked and surprised to find that they had to follow him. He will never attack any abuse, any wickedness, any corruption, not even if it takes the most horrible form, unless he is satisfied that no votes are to be lost by doing it. He preaches the gospel of envy, hatred and unrest. His actions so far go to show that he is entirely willing to sanction any mob violence if he thinks that for the moment votes are to be gained by so doing. He of course cares nothing whatever as to the results to the nation, in the long run, of embroiling it with any foreign power, if for the moment he can gain any applause for so doing. He cares nothing for the nation, nor for any citizens in it.

Mr. Bryan I regard as being a man of the Thomas Jefferson type, altho of course not as able. I would greatly regret his election and think it detrimental to the nation, just as I think Thomas Jefferson's election meant that the American people were not developed to the standard necessary for the appreciation of Washington, Marshall and Hamilton — a standard which they did not reach until Lincoln came to the front sixty years later; for Lincoln had, in addition to the good qualities of Hamilton and Marshall, also those good qualities which they lacked and which Jefferson possest. So much for Bryan. Hearst, I should think, would represent a distinctly lower level than we have ever sunk to as President. As Governor of New York I should think he would be more dangerous, but perhaps not intrinsically worse, than one or two others we have had.

But all this is the judgment of a man who is himself in the thick of the fight; who knows that we have in Hughes an ideal candidate; who does not see how decent citizens can hesitate between Hughes and Hearst; but who thoroly appreciates the gross iniquity, corruption and selfishness of men in high financial and political places which have given Hearst the chance to take advantage of the reaction; and who also appreciates how seared the conscience of the public has sometimes seemed in the presence of great wrong, and how necessary it is that the conscience should be forcefully awakened. If the circumstances were ripe in America, which they are not, I should think that Hearst would aspire to play the part of some of the least worthy creatures of the French Revolution. As it is, he would, if successful, merely do on a larger scale what was done by some of the men who became populist Governors in the Western States. Those States have now recovered, or partially recovered and are conducting themselves in decent fashion. But the damage done, morally and physically, was real and lasting. So it would be with Hearst. He is the most potent single influence for evil we have in our life.

I should not think that it was advisable for you to make more than very brief comments on the situation. In your place I should show a good deal of self-restraint in handling Hearst, but I should certainly not be led into anything that would even impliedly seem to be praise of him. *Faithfully yours*

RELATIONS WITH JAPAN

To Eugene Hale

Private

Washington, October 27, 1906

My dear Senator Hale:

This letter is of course strictly private. I write you because of your position in the Senate, where I *know* you to be one of the two or three men of most influence, and where I *believe* you to be the man of most influence.

You have doubtless seen the trouble we are having in connection with the Japanese in California. This is not due to the possession of the Philippines, for our clash with Japan has come purely from the Japanese in Hawaii and on the Pacific Slope (save in connection with the Japanese seal poachers last summer). Under the lead of the trades unions the San Francisco people, and apparently also the people in certain other California cities, have been indulging in boycotts against Japanese restaurant keepers; have excluded the Japanese children from the public schools, and have in other ways threatened, sometimes by law and sometimes by the action of mobs, the rights secured to Japanese in this country by our solemn treaty engagements with Japan. I am doing everything in my power to secure the righting of these wrongs. Thru the Department of Justice we are seeking such aid as the courts will grant. I have sent Secretary Metcalf out to California to confer with the authorities and with the labor union people, and to point out the grave risk they are forcing the whole country to incur. Probably Root will have to communicate formally with the Governor of California. Exactly how much further I shall go I do not know. It is possible I may have to use the army in connection with boycotting or the suppression of mob violence.

If these troubles merely affected our internal arrangements, I should not bother you with them; but of course they may possibly bring about war with Japan. I do not think that they will bring it about at the moment, but even as to this I am not certain, for the Japanese are proud, sensitive, warlike, are flushed with the glory of their recent triumph, and are in my opinion bent upon establishing themselves as the leading power in the Pacific. As I told you at the time, while my main motive in striving to bring about peace between Japan and Russia was the disinterested one of putting an end to the bloodshed, I was also influenced by the desirability of preventing Japan from driving Russia completely out of East Asia. This object was achieved, and Russia stands face to face with Japan in Manchuria. But the internal condition of Russia is now such that she is no longer in any way a menace to or restraint upon Japan, and probably will not be for a number of years to come. I do not pretend to have the least idea as to Japan's policy or real feeling, whether toward us or toward anyone else. I do not think that she wishes war as such, and I doubt if she will go to war now; but I am very sure that if sufficiently irritated and humiliated by us she will get to accept us instead of Russia as the national enemy whom she will ultimately have to fight; and under such circumstances her concentration and continuity of purpose, and the exceedingly formidable character of her army and navy, make it necessary to reckon very seriously with her. It seems to me that all of this necessitates our having a definite policy with regard to her; a policy of behaving with absolute good faith, courtesy and justice to her on the one hand, and on the other, of keeping our navy in such shape as to make it a risky thing for Japan to go into war with us. The first part of the policy I shall carry out as well as I am able; but our federal form of government, with all its advantages, has very great disadvantages when we come to carrying out a foreign policy, and it would be a most difficult thing to prevent mobs and demagogs in certain parts of the country from doing a succession of acts which will tend to embroil us with the Japanese. This being the case, I most earnestly feel that we cannot afford to let our navy fall behind. The Cuban business this year was managed admirably, alike by the navy and the army; and as a matter of practical experience I am now able to say that the general staff of the army and the general board of the navy were among the most efficient causes in bringing about this result. The improvement in both army and navy over things as they were at the beginning of the Spanish War is marvelous. I do not think we can afford to let the army go back, and I think we must keep building the navy up. I have made a very careful study of the Japanese-Russian War last year, and I am convinced that the advantages of size and speed in battleships, the advantages of having battleships carrying say eight twelve-inch guns, are very, very great. I would be delighted if the Hague Conference would agree that hereafter all battleships should be limited in size; but after sounding France, Germany, England and Italy in the matter, I see no hope of accomplishing this result. In view of this I feel that we ought to go ahead with the steady progress of building this year the ship authorized last year and the ship to be authorized this — that is, two ships the equal of any laid down by any nation.

I very earnestly hope that you will consider this matter especially from the standpoint of our possibly having trouble with Japan because of the peculiar circumstances of our relations.

With great regard, believe me, *Sincerely yours*

THE BROWNSVILLE INCIDENT

To Curtis Guild Jr.

Telegram

                              Washington, November 7, 1906

Your telegram received. The order in question will under no circumstances be rescinded or modified. The action was precisely such as I should have taken had the soldiers guilty of the misconduct been white men instead of colored men. I can hardly believe that those who requested you to communicate with me were aware of the extreme gravity of the offense committed. Certainly only ignorance of the facts could justify such an appeal to me. As for the concluding paragraph of your telegram in which you state that the men in question do not desire to make any political capital by public attacks on me, I can only say that I feel the most profound indifference to any possible attack which can be made on me in this matter. When the discipline and honor of the American Army are at stake I shall never under any circumstances consider the political bearing of upholding that discipline and that honor, and no graver misfortune could happen to the American Army than failure to punish in the most signal way such conduct as that which I have punished in the manner of which you complain. There has been the fullest and most exhaustive investigation of the case. To show you how little the question of color enters into the matter, I need only point out that when a white officer was alleged to be guilty in speaking of the incident of commenting unfavorably on the black troops generally, I directed an immediate investigation into his words and suitable proceedings against him should he prove to have been correctly quoted.

SAILING TO PANAMA

To Kermit Roosevelt

On Board U.S.S. *Louisiana*, November, 1906

Dear Kermit:

So far the trip has been a great success, and I think Mother has really enjoyed it. As for me I of course feel a little bored as I always do on shipboard, but I have brought on a great variety of books, and am at this moment reading Milton's prose works, Tacitus and a German novel called *Jörn Uhl*. Mother and I walk briskly up and down the deck together or else sit aft under the awning or in the aftercabin, with the gun ports open and read; and I also spend a good deal of time on the forward bridge and sometimes on the aft bridge, and of course have gone over the ship to inspect it with the Captain. It is a splendid thing to see one of these men-of-war, and it does really make one proud of one's country. Both the officers and the enlisted men are as fine a set as one could wish to see.

It is a beautiful sight, these three great war vessels steaming southward in close column, and almost as beautiful at night when we see not only the lights but the loom through the darkness of the ships astern. We are now in the tropics and I have thought a good deal of the time over eight years ago when I was sailing to Santiago in the fleet of warships and transports. It seems a strange thing to think of my now being President, going to visit the work of the Panama Canal which I have made possible.

Mother, very pretty and dainty in white summer clothes, came up on Sunday morning to see inspection and review, or whatever they call it, of the men. I usually spend half an hour on deck before Mother is dressed. Then we breakfast together alone; have also taken lunch alone, but at dinner have two or three officers to dine with us. Doctor Rixey is along and is a perfect dear as always.

November 14th.

The fourth day out was in some respects the most interesting. All the forenoon we had Cuba on our right and most of the forenoon and part of the afternoon Haiti on our left; and in each case green, jungly shores and bold mountains — two great, beautiful, venomous tropic islands. These are historic seas and Mother and I have kept thinking of all that has happened in them since Columbus landed at San Salvador, (which we also saw), the Spanish explorers, the buccaneers, the English and Dutch seadogs and adventurers, the great English and French fleets, the desperate fighting, the triumphs, the pestilences, all the turbulence, the splendor and the wickedness, and the hot, evil, riotous life of the old planters and slave-owners, Spanish, French, English and Dutch; their extermination of the Indians and bringing in of negro slaves, the decay of most of the islands, the turning of Haiti into a land of savage negroes, who have reverted to voodooism and cannibalism; the effort we are now making to bring Cuba and Porto Rico forward.

Today is calm and beautiful as all the days have been on
our trip. We have just sighted the highest land of Panama
ahead of us, and we shall be at anchor by two o'clock this afternoon; just a little less than six days from the time we left
Washington. *Your loving father*

INSPECTING THE CANAL

To Kermit Roosevelt

U.S.S. *Louisiana*, At Sea, November 20, 1906
Dear Kermit:
  Our visit to Panama was most successful as well as most interesting. We were there three days and we worked from
morning till night. The second day I was up at a quarter to six
and got to bed at a quarter of twelve, and I do not believe that
in the intervening time, save when I was dressing, there were
ten consecutive minutes when I was not busily at work in some
shape or form. For two days there uninterrupted tropic rains
without a glimpse of the sun, and the Chagres River rose in a
flood higher than any for fifteen years; so that we saw the climate at its worst. It was just what I desired to do.
  It certainly adds to one's pleasure to have read history and
to appreciate the picturesque. When on Wednesday we approached the coast and the jungle-covered mountains loomed
clearer and clearer until we could see the surf beating on the
shores, while there was hardly a sign of human habitation, I
kept thinking of the four centuries of wild and bloody romance, mixed with object squalor and suffering, which made
up the history of the Isthmus until three years ago. I could
see Balboa crossing at Darien, and the wars between the
Spaniards and the Indians, and the settlement and the building up of the quaint walled Spanish towns; and the trade,
across the seas by galleon, and over land by pack train and river
canoe, in gold and silver, in precious stones; and then the
advent of the buccaneers, and of the English seamen, of Drake
and Frobisher and Morgan, and many, many others, and the

wild destruction they wrought. Then I thought of the rebellion against the Spanish dominion, and the uninterrupted and bloody civil wars that followed, the last occurring when I became President; wars, the victorious heroes of which have their pictures frescoed on the quaint rooms of the palace at Panama city, and in similar palaces in all the other capitals of these strange, turbulent little half-caste civilizations. Meanwhile the Panama railroad had been built by Americans over a half a century ago, with appalling loss of life, so that it is said, of course with exaggeration, that every sleeper laid represented the death of a man. Then the French canal company started work, and for two or three years did a good deal until it became evident that the task far exceeded its powers; and then to miscalculation and inefficiency was added the hideous greed of adventurers, trying each to save something from the general wreck, and the company closed with infamy and scandal.

Now we have taken hold of the job. We have difficulties with our own people, of course, I haven't a doubt that it will take a little longer and cost a little more than men now appreciate, but I believe that the work is being done with a very high degree both of efficiency and honesty; and I am immensely struck by the character of American employees who are engaged not merely in superintending the work, but in doing all the jobs that need skill and intelligence. The steam shovels, the dirt trains, the machine shops, and the like are all filled with American engineers, conductors, machinists, boilermakers, carpenters. From the top to the bottom these men are so hardy, so efficient, so energetic, that it is a real pleasure to look at them. Stevens, the head engineer is a big fellow, a man of daring and good sense, and burly power. All of these men are quite as formidable, and would if it were necessary do quite as much in battle as the crews of Drake and Morgan; but as it is they are doing a work of infinitely more lasting consequence. Nothing whatever remains to show what Drake and Morgan did. They produced no real effect down here. But Stevens and his men are changing the face of the continent, are doing the greatest engineering feat of the ages, and the effect of their work will be felt while our civilization lasts. I went over everything that I could possibly go over in the time at my disposal. I examined the quarters of married men and single men, white men and negroes. I went over the ground of the Gatun and La Boca dams; went through Panama and Colón, and spent a day in the Culebra cut, where the great work is being done. There the huge steam shovels are hard at it; scooping huge masses of rock and gravel and dirt previously loosened by the drillers and dynamite blasters, loading it on trains which take it away to some dump, either in the jungle or where the dams are to be built. They are eating steadily into the mountain cutting it down and down. Little tracks are laid on the side hills, rocks blasted out, and the great ninety-five ton steam shovels work up like mountain howitzers until they come to where they can with advantage begin their work of eating into and destroying the mountainside. With intense energy men and machines do their task, the white men supervising matters and handling the machines, while the tens of thousands of black men do the rough manual labor where it is not worth while to have machines do it. It is an epic feat, and one of immense significance.

The deluge of rain meant that many of the villages were knee-deep in water, while the flooded rivers tore through the tropic forests. It is a real tropic forest, palms and bananas, breadfruit trees, bamboos, lofty ceibas, and gorgeous butterflies and brilliant colored birds fluttering among the orchids. There are beautiful flowers, too. All my old enthusiasm for natural history seemed to revive, and I would have given a good deal to have stayed and tried to collect specimens. It would be a good hunting country too; deer and now and then jaguars and tapir, and great birds that they call wild turkeys; there are alligators in the rivers. One of the trained nurses from a hospital went to bathe in a pool last August and an alligator grabbed him by the legs and was making off with him, but was fortunately scared away, leaving the man badly injured.

I tramped everywhere through the mud. Mother did not do this roughest work, and had time to see more of the really picturesque and beautiful side of the life, and really enjoyed herself. *Your loving father*

P.S. The Gatun dam will make a lake miles long, and the railroad now goes at what will be the bottom of this lake, and it was curious to think that in a few years great ships would be floating in water 100 feet above where we were.

To Silas McBee

Personal

Washington, November 27, 1906

My dear Mr. McBee:

Of course I liked your letter. I have been amazed and indignant at the attitude of the negroes and of shortsighted white sentimentalists as to my action. It has been shown conclusively that some of these troops made a midnight murderous and entirely unprovoked assault upon the citizens of Brownsville — for the fact that some of their number had been slighted by some of the citizens of Brownsville, the warranting criticism upon Brownsville, is not to be considered for a moment as provocation for such a murderous assault. All of the men of the companies concerned, including their veteran noncommissioned officers, instantly banded together to shield the criminals. In other words they took action which cannot be tolerated in any soldiers, black or white, in any policeman, black or white, and which, if taken generally in the army, would mean not merely that the usefulness of the army was at an end but that it had better be disbanded in its entirety at once. Under no conceivable circumstances would I submit to such a condition of things. There has been great pressure not only by sentimentalists but by the northern politicians who wish to keep the negro vote. As you know I believe in practical politics, and, where possible, I always weigh well any action which may cost votes before I consent to take it; but in a case like this, where the issue is not merely one of naked right and wrong but one of vital concern to the whole country, I will not for one moment consider the political effect.

There is another side to this also. In that part of my message about lynching, which you have read, I speak of the grave and evil fact that the negroes too often band together to shelter their own criminals, which action had an undoubted effect in helping to precipitate the hideous Atlanta race riots. I condemn such attitude strongly, for I feel that it is fraught with the gravest danger to both races. Here, where I have power to deal with it, I find this identical attitude displayed among the negro troops. I should be recreant to my duty if I failed by deeds as well as words to emphasize with the utmost severity my disapproval of it. *Sincerely yours*

DOING GOOD SERVICE

To William Allen White

Personal

Washington, November 28, 1906

My dear White:

I have your letter of the 24th instant. Do write me at once about Judge Dickerson and also about Judge Townsend. I am rather concerned at what you say about Judge Townsend, for my impression is that I have heard very well of him. Do let me know as fully and as soon as possible about them.

I have been reading the advance sheets of your article about me, and I need hardly say that I very sincerely appreciate what you have written. Whether I deserve what you say or not, I am at any rate very glad that a man whom I respect and admire as much as I do you should think I deserve it. There is one thing which I did not like, and that is your even by implication assuming that I or my friends could think of my position as being in any shape or way akin to that of Washington or Lincoln or Franklin — the men of the great crises, the men who I think we can truthfully say are great figures in the history of the world. Down at bottom I think you and I feel much alike as to this question of a man's place in history, his place in literature. I am not in the least concerned as to whether I will have any place in history, and, indeed, I do not remember ever thinking about it. Without being able clearly to formulate the reasons for my philosophy, I am perfectly clear as to the philosophy itself: I want to be a straight and decent man and do good service; and just as the officers and crew of a big battleship feel, each of them, if they are worth their salt, that it is quite enough reward to be one of the men actively engaged in doing the work aboard that battleship, so I feel it is in itself an ample reward to have been engaged with Root and Taft and Moody and Garfield and all the honest, brave, decent fellows who are trying in practical fashion to realize ideals of good government. I want to feel, when I leave two years hence, that I have played my part honestly and well. While I live it will be a great satisfaction if I can feel this, and I should like my descendants to know it; and I should like to feel that those who know me and care for me, and whom I value, will also feel it. But aside from this it does not seem to me that after a man is dead it matters very much whether it is a little longer or a little shorter before the inevitable oblivion, steadily flooding the sands of time, effaces the scratches on the sand which we call history. As the ages roll by in the life of this globe, small indeed does the difference seem between the few weeks' remembrance of the average hard-working, clean-living citizen, and the few years, or few hundreds of years, or few thousands of years, before the memory of the mighty fades into the dim gray of time and then vanishes in the blackness of eternity.

Give my love to the family — Mrs. White and both babies.
Faithfully yours

NOBEL PRIZE MONEY

To Kermit Roosevelt

Washington, December 5, 1906

Dear Kermit:

I have written Mr. Fergie. I enclose the program of the entertainment and also the menu of the dinner given us by the Chief Petty Officers' Mess.

As Mother is away, I have been doing what little I could for Archie and Quentin. It has chiefly taken the shape of reading to them in the evening what the absurd little geese call "I" stories. Being translated this term includes all hunting stories I read them, which are naturally told in the first person; the little boys evidently have a vague feeling that being thus told in the first person they all somehow represent the deeds of the same individual. My reading for the last two evenings to them has been a most satisfactorily lurid Man-eating Lion story. After breakfast this morning Ethel started to school in high spirits driving Mollie, her high spirits being due to the fact that she anticipated that Mollie would balk, and thereby furnish excitement.

I have been a little puzzled over the Nobel prize. It appears that there is a large sum of money — they say about $40,000 — that goes with it. Now, I hate to do anything foolish or quixotic and above all I hate to do anything that means the refusal of money which would ultimately come to you children. But Mother and I talked it over and came to the conclusion that while I was President at any rate, and perhaps anyhow, I could not accept money given to me for making peace between two nations, especially when I was able to make peace simply because I was President. To receive money for making peace would in any event be a little too much like being given money for rescuing a man from drowning, or for performing a daring feat in war. Of course there was the additional fact that what I did I was able to do because I was President. Altogether Mother and I felt that there was no alternative and that I would have to apply the money to some public purpose. But I hated to have to come to the decision, because I very much wisht for the extra money to leave all you children.

Yes, I saw Robinson's poem, which you had already shown me, and I like it. He certainly has a touch of genius in him. *Your loving father*

"A SMALL ADMINISTRATION JOKE"

To Kermit Roosevelt

Washington, January 19, 1907

Dear Kermit:

Mr. Loeb sent you the matter about the Brownsville incident for your debate, didn't he? It is really not any of the Senate's business; but they have had a terrific fight over it and now they are nearly to the crisis. I do not know how it will come out. I hope those that support me will win; but if they do not, it will not make the slightest difference in my attitude.

The other night an amusing thing happened. Nice Mrs. Bonaparte has had a great number of rather dreary people whom she has brought around to the various receptions and entertainments at The White House. We have rather wondered at her choice of friends; but the mystery was solved the other day thru her announcing with great satisfaction and in a fine philanthropic spirit that she was so glad that she was able to give pleasure to people who led gray and humdrum lives by taking them around to The White House! I wish you could have seen Mother laugh when she heard it and realized that her entertainments were thus being used as hospitals for social incapables. Of course Mrs. Bonaparte, who is just as kind and nice as she can be, is really only trying to be friendly — but it is rather at the expense of The White House. I need not say you must not breathe a word of this to anyone; but Mother and I felt you were discreet enough to be trusted with a small administration joke.

People here are not the only offenders. The Emperor of Austria's daughter, an Imperial Archduchess of exalted standing, has just sent me a note introducing a Countess with a remarkable German name, with the exprest hope that I would in turn introduce her into the society of "influential Americans" — whatever that may mean. I had in the Ambassador and told him that he must succeed in getting full information about the lady and about exactly what it was the Archduchess wisht, before I could commit myself one way or the other on the subject.

This week it has rained, sleeted or snowed every day. I have been so busy that the utmost I have been able to do was to get out for a half an hour or so in the evening after dark just to take a walk or else a trot so slow that *you* would not call it a trot at all.

Archie and his guinea pigs remind me so much of you and Ted and Ethel when you were little. The guinea pigs, who rejoice in the names of Mr. and Mrs. Longworth, have had two small guinea pigs — the very cunningest things you ever saw.
Your loving father

THE AMERICAN DEMOCRATIC IDEAL

To William Crary Brownell

Personal

Washington, January 29, 1907

My dear Mr. Brownell:

Every now and then one suddenly comes across a sentence which exactly phrases a thought which there has long seemed to be need of formulating, but as to which the words to express it have been lacking. In your article on Lowell, which of course I liked all thru (except that I would put parts of *The Biglow Papers* higher with reference to the "Commemoration Ode" than you do), I particularly like your phrase "the American democratic ideal is Brahminism in manners and tastes, not in sympathies and ideas." Abraham Lincoln's democracy was so essential and virile that it would not have lost in any way if he had had the manners and tastes of Lowell. One can like to see the White House restored by McKim, and our gold coinage modeled by Saint-Gaudens, without the least abatement of the feeling of being one of Abraham Lincoln's plain people and of keenest sympathy with, admiration for, and desire to represent, them.

With great regard, *Sincerely yours*

WOMAN'S DUTIES

To E. H. Merrell

Washington, January 31, 1907

My dear Mrs. Merrell:

Mrs. Roosevelt has shown me your letter of the 27th. I hardly know how to advise you, and can do little more than to wish you all success in your work. Mrs. Roosevelt and I feel, as you know, that there is not any association more deserving of our sympathy and support than yours.

For one of your topics, how would it do to speak of the place of the father in the home? Now and then people forget that exactly as the mother must help the breadwinner by being a good housewife, so the father in his turn, if he is worth his salt, must in every way back up the mother in helping bring up the children. After all, the prime duties are elemental, and no amount of cultivation, no amount of business force and sagacity, will make the average man a good citizen unless that average man is a good husband and father, and unless he is a successful breadwinner, is tender and considerate with his wife, and both loving and wise (for to be loving and weak and foolish is utterly ruinous) in dealing with the children. I think it a crime for the woman to shirk her primary duties, to shrink from being a good wife and mother. Of course, the woman should have the same right as the man to train her mind, to better herself; and occasionally a woman can, and ought to, follow some especial vocation in addition to (never in substitution for) her home work. But just as the highest work for the normal man is work for his wife and children, so the highest work for the normal woman is the work of the home — where, Heaven knows, the work is ample enough. But I also feel she can do the best work in her home if she has healthy outside interests and occupations in addition; and I most firmly believe that she cannot do her full duty by her husband if she occupies a merely servile attitude toward him or submits to ill-treatment, and that she is quite as bad a mother if weak and foolish as if hard and unloving. *Sincerely yours*

RAILROAD LEGISLATION

To Henry Lee Higginson

Personal

Washington, February 11, 1907

My dear Colonel Higginson:

You touch on a most difficult subject. I wish you would look at the opening paragraphs in the last *Review of Reviews* and I think you will see what the average sensible outsider feels in regard to the railroads. The present unsatisfactory condition in railroad affairs is due ninety-five per cent to the misconduct, the shortsightedness, and the folly of the big railroad men themselves. Unquestionably there is loose demagogic attack upon them in some of the States, but not one particle of harm has come to them by Federal action; on the contrary, merely good. I wish very much that our laws could be strengthened, and I think that the worst thing that could be done for the railroads would be an announcement that for two or three years the Federal Government would keep its hands off of them. It would result in a tidal wave of violent State action against them thruout three-fourths of this country. I am astonished at the curious shortsightedness of the railroad people; a shortsightedness which, thanks to their own action, extends to would-be investors. Legislation such as I have proposed, or whatever legislation in the future I shall propose, will be in the interest of honest investors and to protect the public and the investors against dishonest action.

I may incidentally say that I think that no possible action on railroads would have as disturbing effect upon business as action on the tariff at this time. I earnestly and cordially agree with you on the need of currency legislation, and have been doing all I can for it; but the big financial men of the country, instead of trying to get sound currency legislation, seem to pass their time in lamenting, as Wall Street laments, our action about the railroads.

My dear Colonel, I do not like to disagree with you, but when you speak of the analogy of our dealings with the Southern States and express your approval of Rhodes' last two volumes, I must say that these two volumes of his, in sharp contrast with his earlier volumes, are exceedingly foolish and completely distort the facts. The policy of "trusting the South" at that time, which you say ought to have been tried, was tried by Andrew Johnson. It produced peonage clauses in the constitutions and laws of the Southern States. It produced the rejection of the Fourteenth Amendment by these States. If persisted in it would have produced the reintroduction of slavery, under a slightly modified form, in the South. The North erred in its reconstruction action; but the prime error was that of the South. The analogy is fairly good with the railroad situation — except as to the aftereffects.

I wish I could have the chance of seeing you in person. *Sincerely yours*

THE AMERICAN BIRTH RATE

To Albert Shaw

Washington, April 3, 1907

My dear Dr. Shaw:

You know how sincerely I believe that your magazine generally stands for moral betterment all around. I was really shocked to see in it the last paragraph but one by Dr. Cronin in his article on "The Doctor in the Public School." Dr. Cronin may not be consciously immoral; but if so, it is an unwarranted compliment to speak of his intellect as half-baked. He is not to be excused for writing in a great periodical in such fashion. The ordinary individual thinks so little on these questions that it is pardonable for him to think in confused fashion even on such an elemental proposition as this; but the man who affects to instruct others in matters of moral and hygienic reform must be expected to exhibit at least the rudimentary intelligence and morality necessary to prevent his saying what the Doctor has here said. He states clearly that it is an erroneous idea to assume that the average American family should have a larger number of healthy children than the present birth rate shows. If he were fit to write on any such subject he would, before making such a statement, have studied the vital statistics of, for instance, a State like Massachusetts, which show that there the average native American family of native American descent has so few children that the birth rate has fallen below the death rate. This of course means race suicide; and even Dr. Cronin ought to understand that if, after a while, there are no children to go to school, the question of their health in school would not be even academic. His statement that "physical defects go hand in hand with a large number of children, both in the rich and in the poor," is simply not true, as he could tell at a glance by looking up, for instance, the fact that athletes are most apt to be found in fair-sized families. I am not speaking now of families of inordinate size (tho even as to such, the high standard of health and strength among the French Canadians, for instance, is astonishing), but of those of half a dozen children or thereabouts. Let him look up any serious statistics, or study any author worthy of reading on the subject at all, including Benjamin Franklin, and he will see that in the ordinary family of but one or two children there is apt to be lower vitality than in a family of four or five or more. All he has to do if he doubts this is to study the effects of the marriages with heiresses by the British nobility. He advocates "a little study of sociology" in others. He needs himself a little study of the most primary and elementary kind; and in the beginning he needs to learn a little arithmetic. The question at issue is not between having "a few perfect children" and "a dozen unkempt degenerates"; it is between having in the average family a number of children so small that the race diminishes, while, curiously enough, the physique in such case likewise tends to fall off, and the reasonable growth which comes when the average family is large enough to make up for the men and women who do not marry and for those that do and have no children, or but one or two. He quotes the statistics for Berlin. Let him study them a little more; let him study other statistics as well; let him turn to any book dealing with the subject, if written by a man capable of touching on it at all (as, for instance, let him turn to page 162 of Finot's *Race Prejudice* which I happen at the moment to be reading) and he will see that in cities like Berlin the upper classes, the wealthier classes, tend to die out, precisely because of the low birth rate to which he points with such fatuous approval. The greatest problem of civilization is to be found in the fact that the well-to-do families tend to die out; there results, in consequence, a tendency to the elimination instead of the survival of the fittest; and the moral attitude which helps on this tendency is of course strengthened when it is apologized for and praised in a magazine like yours. It is not the very poor, it is not the people with large families, who tend to read articles by Dr. Cronin in magazines like the *Review of Reviews*; it is the upper-class people, who already tend to have too few children, who are reached and corrupted by such teachings.

I have spoken strongly because I feel strongly. Our people could still exist under all kinds of iniquities in Government; under free silver, under official corruption, under the rule of a socialistic proletariat or a wealthy oligarchy. All these things would be bad for us, but the country could still exist. But it could not continue to exist if it paid heed to the exprest or implied teachings of such articles as this of Dr. Cronin's. These teachings give a moral justification to every woman who practices abortion; they furnish excuses for every unnatural prevention of child-bearing, for every form of gross and shallow selfishness of the kind that is really the deepest reflection on, the deepest discredit to, American social life. There are countries which, and people in all countries who, need to be warned against a rabbit-like indifference to consequences in raising families. The ordinary American, whether of the old native stock or the self-respecting son or daughter of immigrants, needs no such warning. He or she needs to have imprest upon his or her mind the vital lesson that all schemes about having "doctors in public schools," about kindergartens, civic associations, women's clubs, and training families up in this way or that, are preposterous nonsense if there are to be no families to train; and that it is a simple mathematical proposition that where the average family that has children at all has only three, the race at once diminishes in numbers, and if the tendency is not checked, will vanish completely — in other words, there will be race suicide. Not only the healthiest but the highest relations in life are those of the man and the woman united on a basis of full and mutually respecting partnership and wise companionship in loving and permanent wedlock. If thru no fault of theirs they have no children, they are entitled to our deepest sympathy. If they refuse to have children sufficient in number to mean that the race goes forward and not back,* if they refuse to bring them up healthy in body and mind, then they are criminals; and Dr. Cronin's article is an incitement to such criminality. *Sincerely yours*

*This must mean on an average four among the families which are not from natural causes childless or limited to a less number than four.

CAMPAIGN CONTRIBUTIONS IN 1904

To Thomas McDonald Patterson

Personal

Washington, April 8, 1907

My dear Senator:

That is a very nice article of yours and I thank you sincerely for it. It seems to me that the letters of mine to Mr. Harriman in the fall of 1904, all of which were at once made public upon the publication of the Webster letter, leave the case pretty clear. On October 14th I wrote Harriman, explicitly stating that there was no need of his coming down here because what I had to say would keep until after election. Of course this is incompatible with the supposition that what I wanted him to do was to subscribe funds for the election. As you point out, there was no lack of money whatever during the last two weeks of the campaign. As a matter of fact, Harriman, who lies about private conversations just as he swindles in railway transactions, came to see me simply to ask me to secure money and other assistance for the State ticket in New York. He stated that he had subscribed a hundred thousand dollars to it himself, but that he did not feel that all of this should be permanently his own loss. He urged us to have Cortelyou and Bliss turn over all the money possible to Odell, and urged Depew's appointment because certain financiers whom he named would subscribe heavily if Depew were to be taken care of, and, as he explained, Odell had decided that Depew could not be re-elected Senator. I told him I would of course be very glad to do all I could for the State campaign, tho I did not think I could appoint either Depew or Hyde, and explained that I was being approached, as he was approaching me, from very many different States on behalf of the several State campaigns, but that I would communicate with Cortelyou and Bliss and request them to give all the aid they could to the New York State campaign. My memory is that I communicated only with Cortelyou; as I do not think I communicated with Bliss directly at all except as to one contribution, which I insisted should be returned — the history of which I shall give you in full on some occasion when I see you.

In what I said and in what Mr. Cortelyou said we were both of us scrupulously careful *not* to say that no money contributions had been made to the campaign fund by corporations. At that time it was legal for corporations to contribute. They had contributed in 1892, in 1896 and in 1900. They had contributed chiefly to the Democratic campaign fund in 1892, chiefly to the Republican campaign fund in 1896 and 1900. They contributed to both funds in 1904. The subsequent revelations convinced me that corporations should not be allowed to contribute, and this was why I advocated the law which you were instrumental in passing thru Congress forbidding it being done. In my answer to Mr. Parker you will remember that I explicitly stated that such contributions had been made to both campaign funds, and Mr. Cortelyou specified that the amount contributed to the campaign fund (from individuals and corporations together) was about half of that contributed in 1896. Mr. Parker's allegations did not refer merely to contributions; contributions were of course freely made to the extent of hundreds of thousands of dollars to his own campaign fund. His assertion was that these contributions to the Republican campaign fund were extorted by threat or by promise of some consideration on our part. This was a lie; and it seems to me that even the most rudimentary intelligence would prove to any man who has followed the legislative and the executive action of the past two and a half years in reference to the Standard Oil, the Harriman people, the sugar trust, the tobacco trust, and so forth, and so forth, that no human being and no corporation had gained immunity of any kind in the matter of wrongdoing, so far as this administration is concerned. I am quite content to be judged by the adage "By their fruits shall ye know them."

The real trouble with Harriman and his associates is that they have found themselves absolutely powerless to control any action by the national government. There is no form of mendacity or bribery or corruption that they will not resort to in the effort to take vengeance. The Harriman–Standard Oil combination and the other owners of predatory wealth hate me far more than they do those who make a profession of denouncing them, because they have learned that while I do not attack them in words as reckless as those often used against them, I do try to make my words bear fruit in deeds. They have never before been obliged really to reckon with the federal government. They have never before seen practical legislation such as the rate bill, the beef inspection bill and the like become laws. They have never before had to face the probability of adverse action by the courts and the possibility of being put in stripes. Such being the case, and inasmuch as they have no moral scruple of any kind whatsoever, it is not to be wondered at that they should be willing to go to any length in the effort to reverse the movement against them. By reading the New York *Sun* and similar papers we can get a clear idea of the extent to which they will go in that portion of the press which they control.

With great regard, *Sincerely yours*

MAKING TAFT PRESIDENT

To William Allen White

Personal

Oyster Bay, July 30, 1907

My dear White:

First, about the Taft business. I have been puzzled by precisely the experiences you have met with. Of course there are men who will say just what you state Senator Curtis said. In Kansas, however, rather curiously, my experience with Curtis, Long, and all the others of both sides have led me to understand that the State was going to be all right; was going to be straight out for Taft; and that the same was true of Nebraska. As for Taft, you know exactly my feeling. I am well aware that the American people does its own thinking, and even if it likes a man has not the slightest intention of permitting that man to transfer the liking to someone else. I am well aware that nothing would more certainly ruin Taft's chances than to have it supposed that I was trying to dictate his nomination. On the other hand, it is preposterously absurd to say that I have not the right to have my choice as regards the candidates for the Presidency, and that it is not my duty to try to exercise that choice in favor of the man who will carry out the governmental principles in which I believe with all my heart and soul. I am quite sincere when I say that I am not trying to dictate the choice of anyone, and that I stand for the kind of man rather than any particular man. But it is also true that of the men available for President it would seem to me that Taft comes nearer than anyone else to being just the man who ought to be President. There are some good reasons which could be advanced to show that Root would be a better President than Taft, or me, anyone else I know. I could not express too highly my feeling for him. But at present it does not seem to me that there would be much chance of nominating or electing him, and therefore I do not consider him in the running. On the other hand, Taft, in point of courage, sagacity, inflexible uprightness and disinterestedness, and wide acquaintance with governmental problems, seems to me to stand above any other man who has yet been named. Take Governor Hughes, for instance. Hughes has been a good Governor. I think he would make a good President. But he does not begin to compare with Taft, either morally, intellectually, or in knowledge of public problems. The reactionaries, the big capitalists, for whom the *Sun* and *Harper's Weekly* and the *Evening Post* speak, and who in curious ways control such a nominally populistic paper as the New York *Press*, would all prefer Hughes because they would hope that his unfamiliarity with the needs of the country as a whole, and his lawyer-like conservatism, would make him a President like Cleveland instead of a President like me. And of course Cleveland, because of his defects no less than for his good qualities, represents to the Wall Street type of men almost the ideal President. Moreover, the difference between Hughes and Taft was illustrated by a remark Hughes made to a New York official the other day, when he said that his great ambition was to get thru the Governorship without being under obligations to anyone. Taft's great ambition when in office is to do the job in the best way it can possibly be done, and he simply never thinks as to whether he is under obligations to anyone or whether anyone is under obligations to him. He will help Root or me, or get Root or me to help him; or appeal to Lodge or Long or Kittredge for help, without the slightest thought excepting for the work he is on. In other words, one man's chief concern is himself, and the other man's chief concern is to do well the job at which he is working.

The same reasons that influence me for Taft against Hughes, both being good men, apply with the necessary changes and with varying force in any comparison between Taft and anyone else who has been put up. Under such circumstances it seems to me, as things stand at this moment, that Taft is the best man to nominate. But while I can write this to you purely confidentially and not to be shown to anyone else, I cannot make it public. While I have a right to have my choice, my chief business is not to nominate the President but to try to do my own work as President for the next eighteen months, and this is a big enough job by itself. I do not want to get into a row with any of the other candidates if I can legitimately keep out of it. I have again and again and again repeated what I said the night after election. It may be that I shall have to repeat it again, but it does not seem to me that the present moment is opportune. For instance, Taft's friends in the West say to me that they wish I would repeat my statement, because it would make men come out for Taft who still cling to me. But Taft's friends in New York believe that if I repeated that statement too often, the result would be that we should have a New York delegation solidly anti-Taft — probably for Hughes, possibly for Knox. In the Southern States many of the Taft people have told me that they wanted me to keep clear for the moment because any further repetition of what I had said might result in the delegations being captured definitely away from Taft. All of this, let me repeat, is for your own eye only; but I should like to go over it with you at length here in person.

Now for the next, and far more important, part of your letter. You puzzle me more than I can say. I should like to consult the Attorney General before giving you a definite answer. I can say now that I will see you with Bonaparte at once if you come on. I am very doubtful whether Borah ought to come on. As you know, I have incurred the bitterest attacks, not merely from the socialist and anarchist crowd, but from those men of predatory wealth who prefer socialists and anarchists to my style of conservatism; and I have incurred these attacks because of what I did in trying to back up the party of law and order, of elementary civilization, in Idaho, against the thugs and murderers who have found their typical representation in Moyers and Haywoods, in Pettibones and Debs. I sent Taft out to speak for Gooding last year. I took the first opportunity to range myself definitely publicly on behalf of the action that Borah was taking. Now, as regards Borah's own guilt, you already know what the Attorney General thinks. I have been consulting him recently about the procedure. We have on our own motion put over the case until next winter, against the protest of Ruick. It seems to me, with my present knowledge, and subject of course to changing my mind if new facts are brought before me, that it would be a bad thing from every standpoint not to let the case be tried. Moreover, it seems to me that to have Borah come on here in person to meet the Attorney General and myself would create a most undesirable impression and would give an opportunity to the newspapers wholly to misrepresent the actual condition of affairs. I am therefore inclined to think that if you could come on yourself, with some good lawyer competent to speak for Borah — and there must be plenty such in Idaho — the object we have in view would be obtained. I have accordingly wired you to know if you could not bring on such lawyer to meet me here at Oyster Bay with Bonaparte on August 9th. Bonaparte and I will go over the whole matter with you and with him.

Give my warm regards to Mrs. White and to both babies.

I particularly want you to come on so that I can see you and go over both of the above things together. Could not you get Connolly to come on? *Faithfully yours*

THE GREAT WHITE FLEET

To Lawrence Fraser Abbott

Personal

Oyster Bay, September 13, 1907

My dear Abbott:

The two letters and two telegrams about the Standard Oil Company were sent to you for your own information merely, but looking over them they appear to be pretty good stuff, not alone with reference to this specific thing, but as to my general attitude. Of course make no reference of any kind to these letters or telegrams.

Now, as to your questions:

(1) The fleet will be composed of sixteen battleships, which will be joined by two others now on the Pacific coast. It will be met at San Francisco by eight armored cruisers. Six torpedo-boat destroyers will also go to San Francisco from the Atlantic coast, altho not at the same time.

(2) The torpedo vessels will leave about the 1st of December; the battleships shortly afterwards. The armored cruisers are on their way now.

(3) The battleships will stop to coal at three or four places in South America, and somewhere for thirty days' target practice. They will make no special hurry. I cannot give the exact date of their arrival in San Francisco.

(4) The battleships will contain some twelve thousand officers and men; the armored cruisers half as many more.

(5) Cruisers and the like will be left in the Atlantic, but the only battleships will be four that are being repaired and cannot leave at this moment.

(6) If this enterprise is carried out it will represent a far longer cruise than has ever been made in modern times by a battleship fleet of even half the strength.

(7) It is a cardinal point of my policy that the battleship fleet, the backbone of the fighting force of the navy, shall always be kept as a unit, whether in Atlantic or Pacific waters. If it is in the Atlantic when a war breaks out with a Pacific power, it would have to go to the Pacific. If it is in the Pacific,

it will have to go to the Atlantic. It will in neither ocean, however, be used to protect the shipping and the ports save by striking at the enemy's fleet. We have, unfortunately, very little shipping, save in the coast trade, and of course it would be an utter absurdity to use battleships to protect fleets of coasting schooners. Ports must be protected by fortifications, mines, torpedoes, torpedo boats etc. The object of forts is to leave the fleet foot-lose, and normally it represents literally the destruction of the navy to try to use it to protect ports. It means that it would be scattered piecemeal along the coast, to be picked up in detail by any respectable-sized opponent. I doubt if I would say much about this seventh question of yours, for it may give an alarmist tone to the article. Our relations with all European powers are so good that it seems in the highest degree unlikely that trouble will occur, pending the absence of the fleet; and it might well be that if it did occur, the fleet could get into the Atlantic for action almost as quickly as if it were in home waters. I could not send it to the Pacific at a better time; and as it must either be in the Pacific or the Atlantic — both, remember, home waters — wherever it is there is always the *chance* that war may break out on the other ocean. That chance exists now as regards the Pacific; when the fleet is in the Pacific it will exist (as it does now) as regards the Atlantic. But it is a mighty small chance. *Faithfully yours*

FAMILY NEWS

To Anna Cabot Mills Lodge

Oyster Bay, September 10, 1907

Dear Nannie:

Quentin is devoted to his little Canadian governess, who has been in Quebec this summer, and he writes her frequently in French — that is, in what, by an elastic construction of the word, can be called French. His letters are purely off his own bat and neither instigated nor supervised by anybody. The other day he brought me one to address and post, and without his knowledge I made a copy of it which I enclose. Will you send it back after you have read it?

Edith is now putting up the house, and we feel a little melancholy, as we always do when the summer is over. I suppose I shall have an awful time with Congress this winter. But the summer has been very pleasant and satisfactory for all the children. Ted has circulated somewhat irrelevantly from Beverly to northern Minnesota. He will try to get thru college in three years so that next summer he can go to work, just before he is twenty-one. I shall be glad if he can do this, for I do not see that there is anything more that he can get out of college. He has had a very good time, as I of course wish him to have, and he is mature enough to settle down to earning his own living. He is a very vigorous, hardy boy, able to get on with all kinds of people; and I am sincerely glad to say that he combines much natural prowess in field sports with much indifference to them. That is, he is a good shot, and especially a good rider, but he does not really care for hunting or for horses. He will take out one of my hunters if somebody is here who will ride the other, and then will jump over every fence there is nearby. Once this summer he got a slight concussion of the brain thru his horse coming down with him while he was larking it over a very stiff fence nearly five feet high, on our own place. But he does not really care for horses, and he will not miss them very greatly when the future comes and he cannot have them. He is fond of reading and fond of writing poetry; but he will not bother with trying to polish his poems, having what I think is the very wise feeling that he could not do enough as a poet to justify himself in doing nothing else, and that if he does anything else it is a positive disadvantage to him to be known to write poetry. I should like to have him go out to northern Minnesota in the iron country, under John Greenway, and buckle down to the roughest work. But I shall not force him to do anything which he does not really wish to undertake, and very possibly something else will turn up which he will think will be better.

Kermit is very different. He has none of Ted's natural prowess. With horses, for instance, he took a long time in learning how to ride them. But he has become a good rider, and cares far more for it than Ted does. This year he spent a few days at the Wadsworths' at Geneseo at the time of the sports, taking part in the sports and riding all the young hunters, many of them not yet trained. He got bucked off of them now and then and had falls with them at different fences, but he thoroly enjoyed himself. Then he went up for a week to take charge of the Groton camp for poor boys sent out there by different societies from Boston. He did this work well, and I was extremely glad to have him do it, for I hope the children will grow up with the feeling that they must not be selfish and must do a certain amount for others. Then he went for three weeks to the West — first, for a week marching with the Thirteenth Cavalry in company with Fitz Lee, and then on a prairie-chicken shoot to Dakota, topping off with a deer hunt in Wisconsin. The cavalrymen said he did very well on the march with them, and he made a good bag of prairie chickens and ducks and one deer. He has more genuine literary taste than any other of the children, being much like Edith in this way. What he will do in after life, I do not know. If he enters college, it will be next fall. If he developed any strong taste for any particular kind of work, I should not try to send him to college.

Archie passed the happiest summer he has ever passed, because he found out the thing of which he was most fond, namely, sailing. He has a dory, and is president of the local Dory Club. He has won half a dozen silver, bronze and pewter cups in races, sometimes taking as crew Captain Norman, the pilot, sometimes Seaman, our hired man, who is an ex-oysterman, and sometimes a sailor from the *Sylph*. He also knows definitely what he wants to do in life. He wants to enter the navy, and if I can get him an appointment to Annapolis and he is able to pass the entrance examinations, his career will be settled. Tho he has any amount of character, he is not at all a bright little boy and I do not know whether he will be able to pass the entrance examinations even if I can get him the appointment. Anything connected with the water he delights in. Small tho he is, he dove twenty-two feet to bottom from the *Sylph* this summer, only two or three of the *Sylph's* men being able to make the dive. He had a heart-breaking experience just before he left for Groton, for Skip was run over and killed by an automobile. Skip was never out of his company day or night, and even sailed all of his races with him, and you can imagine Archie's grief — and indeed, for the matter of that, the grief of the rest of us. So poor little black Skip was buried under the stone that bears the names of the dogs for which we have cared the most; and next morning Archie and Kermit started for Groton together — Archie's first experience away from home.

Quentin is a roly-poly, happy-go-lucky personage, the brightest of any of the children, but with a strong tendency to pass a very happy life in doing absolutely nothing except swim or loaf about with other little boys. However, Edith has made him ride a good deal, and yesterday he took his pony over — or, to be more accurate, he went over in more or less close connection with his pony — a three-foot fence. He went over it five times, and the last time sat very well.

Ethel is a dear. She is sixteen now and well-grown, and she and Ted have house parties and go off very occasionally to other house parties. She teaches a Sunday school class and helps Edith in the house, and leads just about such a life as Edith herself led at her age; and altho she has a tendency to be too nervous and excitable and to do too much, she is a very satisfactory child, on the whole.

Edith is well. But of course there is always a good deal of bother for her. I shall be away for over three weeks in October, first on a speech-making trip and then for a two weeks' bear hunt in the Louisiana canebrakes. Edith intends to occupy those three weeks in as unmixt rest as can possibly be obtained. She does not want to go anywhere. I have been trying to find some place that she would like to go on a trip by herself or with some friend, but there isn't any such place. Of course while I am President no trip with me would be anything save wearisome exertion.

As for me, I have worked every day this summer for three or four hours, but I have had plenty of holiday, too, and am in fine shape. I have played tennis; I have taken Edith rowing and riding; I have chopped industriously; and now and then have shot at a mark with the rifle. There is plenty of work ahead. I do want to leave certain things to my successor in such shape that the work I have done won't be undone. The Panama Canal is getting along very well. I hope to get it so started that my successor will not be tempted to change the type or do something of the kind, as he is certain to be advised to do by various people, and as he will be tempted to do in order not to appear to be merely carrying out my policy. So with the navy. I want to put the navy on such a basis that it cannot be shaken from it. I am very well pleased with the personnel of the officers up to and including the grade of lieutenant commander; but beyond that the percentage of good men diminishes very rapidly. They come to command rank too old. They lack initiative and training; they are inert and unable to bear responsibilities. I am exceedingly sorry that Harry has retired, for I should like to feel that he was second in command on this Pacific trip and able to take Evans' place should the need arise.

As for my internal policies, the last few years have convinced me more than ever that it is to the ordinary plain people that we must look for the future welfare of the Republic, and not either to the overeducated parlor doctrinaires, nor to the people of the plutocracy, the people who amass great wealth or who spend it, and who lose their souls alike in one process and the other.

Love to Cabot. His letters are a continual pleasure and strength to me. *Ever yours*

JEFFERSON AND THE FEDERALISTS

To William Henry Moody

Personal

Oyster Bay, September 21, 1907

My dear Moody:

I hope you will like *your* speech at St. Louis! You will agree with most of it, I guess, for the excellent reason that most of it is taken from your letter to me — of course I mean the part in reference to the subject matter of your letter. You will have to pardon one statement in praise of Judge Amidon. I have recently been glancing thru Jefferson's works. In 1823 he writes, anent Marshall — the measure of whose services to the country may be gauged by Jefferson's hatred of him — that there was no danger which he (Jefferson) considered so great as the strengthening of the Government "by the noiseless and therefore unalarming instrumentality of the Supreme Court." Does not this really mean that Jefferson felt that during the twenty-three years since the Federalists had gone out of power, but while Marshall had directed the Supreme Court, that the Supreme Court had done active constructive work in reference to the Constitution? Isn't it really a matter of unimportance from the largest standpoint whether we say that this was done on the principle of broad construction, or whether we say that a wise court will recognize that the Constitution cannot be made a straight jacket; that the process of formal amendment can very rarely be resorted to, and that there must be a process of growth and adjustment by the decisions of the court itself? It seems to me that the difference between the two views is chiefly one of terminology; and as I know that terminology has a profound effect upon people, I am delighted to use whatever terminology will excite the least friction and suspicion, provided the end is obtained. That is why it seems to me that Judge Amidon's speech was fundamentally sound, even tho he could with advantage have couched certain of his statements in other language. I wish you would look at it carefully.

I am continually brought in contact with very wealthy people. They are socially the friends of my family, and if not friends, at least acquaintances of mine, and they were friends of my father's. I think they mean well on the whole, but the more I see of them the more profoundly convinced I am of their entire unfitness to govern the country, and of the lasting damage they do by much of what they are inclined to think are the legitimate big business operations of the day. They are as blind to some of the tendencies of the time, as the French noblesse was before the French Revolution; and they possess the same curious mixture of impotency to deal with movements that should be put down and of rancorous stupidity in declining to abandon the kind of reaction in policy which can do nothing but harm. Moreover, usually entirely without meaning it, they are singularly callous to the needs, sufferings, and feelings of the great mass of the people who work with their hands. They show this in their attitude toward such a matter as the employers' liability bill. They are simply unable to understand what it means to a working man's family to have the breadwinner killed or crippled. They are not able to grasp the unmerited and dreadful suffering thus brought on so many different people. Heaven knows how cordially I despise Jefferson, but he did have one great virtue which his Federalist opponents lacked — he stood for the plain people, for the same people whom Abraham Lincoln afterwards represented.

By the way, speaking of Jefferson, isn't it humiliating to realize that Jefferson — who I think was, not even excepting Buchanan, the most incompetent chief executive we ever had, and whose well-nigh solitary service as President to his country, the acquisition of Louisiana, was rendered by adopting the Federalist principles which he had most fiercely denounced — isn't it humiliating to think that he should have been, as President, rather more popular than Washington himself at the very close of his administration, and that almost all of the State legislatures, excluding Massachusetts but including Rhode Island and Vermont, should have petitioned him to serve for another term and should have sent him formal messages of grateful thanks for his services after his term was over? We lived thru Jefferson's administration, tho he did us much damage; and we could live thru Bryan or a reactionary; but I do not want to see the experiment tried. *Ever yours*

CHEAPENING "IN GOD WE TRUST"

To Roland C. Dryer

Washington, November 11, 1907

Dear Sir:

When the question of the new coinage came up we lookt into the law and found there was no warrant therein for putting "IN GOD WE TRUST" on the coins. As the custom, altho without legal warrant, had grown up, however, I might have felt at liberty to keep the inscription had I approved of its being on the coinage. But as I did not approve of it, I did not direct that it should again be put on. Of course the matter of the law is absolutely in the hands of Congress, and any direction of Congress in the matter will be immediately obeyed. At present, as I have said, there is no warrant in law for the inscription.

My own feeling in the matter is due to my very firm conviction that to put such a motto on coins, or to use it in any kindred manner, not only does no good but does positive harm, and is in effect irreverence which comes dangerously close to sacrilege. A beautiful and solemn sentence such as the one in question should be treated and uttered only with that fine reverence which necessarily implies a certain exaltation of spirit. Any use which tends to cheapen it, and, above all, any use which tends to secure its being treated in a spirit of levity, is from every standpoint profoundly to be regretted. It is a motto which it is indeed well to have inscribed on our great national monuments, in our temples of justice, in our legislative halls, and in buildings such as those at West Point and Annapolis — in short, wherever it will tend to arouse and inspire a lofty emotion in those who look thereon. But it seems to me eminently unwise to cheapen such a motto by use on coins, just as it would be to cheapen it by use on postage stamps, or in advertisements. As regards its use on the coinage we have actual experience by which to go. In all my life I have never heard any human being speak reverently of this motto on the coins or show any sign of its having appealed to any high emotion in him. But I have literally hundreds of times heard it used as an occasion of, and incitement to, the sneering ridicule which it is above all things undesirable that so beautiful and exalted a phrase should excite. For example, thruout the long contest, extending over several decades, on the free coinage question, the existence of this motto on the coins was a constant source of jest and ridicule; and this was unavoidable. Everyone must remember the innumerable cartoons and articles based on phrases like "In God we trust for the other eight cents"; "In God we trust for the short weight"; "In God we trust for the thirty-seven cents we do not pay";

and so forth and so forth. Surely I am well within bounds when I say that a use of the phrase which invites constant levity of this type is most undesirable. If Congress alters the law and directs me to replace on the coins the sentence in question the direction will be immediately put into effect; but I very earnestly trust that the religious sentiment of the country, the spirit of reverence in the country, will prevent any such action being taken. *Sincerely yours*

DISINTERESTEDNESS AND SINCERITY

To Frederic Harrison

Washington, December 18, 1907

My dear Mr. Harrison:

I am sure that any President would be pleased to receive such a letter as you have written, coming from so distinguished a man of letters who is also a man of the moralities — to use a sentence that seems about a century and a quarter out of date. My dear sir, you touch upon something that has puzzled me not a little. On the one hand I freely confess that I hate for personal reasons to get out of the fight here and that I have the uncomfortable feeling that I may possibly be shirking a duty. On the other hand, it is the business of every practical statesman to reckon with the temper of the people to whom he owes his position, and he can accomplish nothing worth accomplishing if he does not retain their confidence in his integrity and disinterestedness. Now there are some peoples who have grown, by training, to accept the position that the longer a man remains at the head of public affairs the more useful he is, and who do not feel the fear — very possibly the vain fear — that he will intrench himself in power against their wishes as a sequence to staying in power in accordance with their wishes. But there are other peoples who do not accept this point of view; who fear lest a President too long kept in power might do as has been done in more than one Spanish-American Republic, as was done in France at the close of the second Republic, and gradually establish what is in fact a dictatorship under the form of popular government. No matter whether these fears are just or not, no matter whether the beliefs of these peoples on this point are with or without warrant, a man who tries to serve them can do so only by frankly reckoning with this mental attitude.

Moreover, in my case remember that I had embarked on a course of action which has peculiar attractions for the demagog, for the man who hopes to raise himself to high political position by posing as the incorruptible foe of the great and the wealthy. The man who in public life consciously or unconsciously panders to the great and the wealthy when they are wrong receives his reward in ways wholly alien to popular favor, and this man is under no temptations to follow a course such as I followed. But the demagog — and by demagog I mean not demagog in the old Greek sense, but in the modern and sinister sense, the man who panders to the prejudices of, and excites what is base and evil in, the people, just as the typical courtier does in dealing with a monarch — foregoes all possible advantage to be obtained by the first type of evil public servant and counts for his reward for the evil which he does on popular favor and the offices which result from popular favor. Now, I believe that if I have rendered or can render any service at all to the American people it is because of their belief in my disinterestedness and sincerity. This sounds as if I were talking like a prig, or at least with an unpleasantly priggish self-consciousness; and perhaps I am; but I do not know how else to express my meaning, which is that whatever of value in the way of service I can render my country is conditioned upon their believing that it is not rendered with an eye to my personal well-being. I think that to show them that they are justified in this belief as to my character is probably as important a service as I can render; in other words, whether or not I think that I have certain peculiar advantages of position and temperament which would enable me to continue to render service to the people, it yet remains true that taking into account their inherited mental attitude on the subject of the long continuance of a President in place, I can render them the best service by showing that in what I have done I have been actuated, not by self-interest, but by devotion to a high ideal together with the firm purpose to try measurably to realize that ideal in practical fashion.

Do you recollect my once speaking to you about the Mongol conquest of eastern Europe, anent your essay on the 13th century? I wish you would look at Curtin's book on the Mongols which is just out. I know your studies have dealt chiefly with Latin Europe; but that world outburst of the Mongols was so phenomenal that it is worth your while glancing at the first readable book in English which has told the story.

Again thanking you, my dear sir, I am, *Sincerely yours*

P.S. One of the chief things I have tried to preach to the American politician, and the American businessman, is not to grasp at money, place, power, or enjoyment in any form, simply because he can probably get it, without regard to considerations of morality and national interest — which means the interest of the neighbor, for the nation is simply all of our neighbors combined. Now, when I am preaching this and striving to lead the forces of decency in a sane but resolute effort to put a stop to greed, selfishness, arrogance and hatred, I am bound in honor so to conduct myself as not to give good people cause to doubt whether I am not myself actuated by the same kind of self-interested motives and disregard of the higher and finer ethical considerations which I denounce in others.

THE UNCERTAIN FUTURE

To Cecil Spring-Rice

Washington, December 21, 1907

Dear Cecil:

As usual Mrs. Roosevelt and I were equally pleased and interested with your letter. You speak as if you were to have a little holiday from official life. Cannot you take advantage of it to bring your wife over and spend a few days with us at The White House? Not so very much time remains now, and I do wish we could see you both here. Do not leave the diplomatic service unless you have to. You have worked thru the years of mere drudgery. You have made your reputation. You are at the very time of life when your training and experience will enable you to do your best; and even if the harness galls a little, you will be happier doing steady trace-and-collar work. If you have to get out, well and good. You have done honorably; you have won your spurs, and it is all right. But if you can go on, by all means go on. My own case is peculiar, for I am not very clear that there will be anything possible for me to do after a year from the next fourth of March. But we are all on the knees of the Gods and must await events; tho when the opportunity comes we can improve it, and, indeed, can to a certain extent make it.

I do very much wish to talk with you over some of the questions which you raise which I can hardly discuss at length in a letter. Fundamentally my philosophy is yours, tho not so pessimistic. I do not think we know enough about the future to be able to say with certainty how great any given danger is. The things we dread do not occur, and evils which no human being had foreseen or could have foreseen loom portentous. We may have a race conflict such as you dread in the Pacific, but I hope not; and therefore I hope that the ten-year limit that you set is altogether too short. I very much wish that Australia would either encourage European immigration or would see a higher birth rate among its own citizens. It is not pleasant to realize how slowly the scanty population of that island continent increases. But as long as Great Britain retains her naval superiority and Australia is part of the British Empire Australia is safe. On our own Pacific coast British Columbia feels exactly as our Pacific Coast States feel. Both the United States and Canada are increasing so much in population that it is hard to imagine an ethnic conquest by a yellow race here on the mainland; but of course national folly on the part of the United States, both in permitting outrages against the Japanese and in declining to keep the navy up to the highest point of efficiency, might result in a bitterly humiliating and disastrous war which would turn over not only the Philippines but Hawaii to Japan. I do not anticipate any such war, and I think I am taking the best possible measures to prevent it and to get the two races or nations on a footing which will permit a policy of permanent friendliness or at least mutual toleration. Here again all we can say is that the future is dim before our eyes. With the voyages of Columbus and Vasco da Gama, the invention of printing, and the Reformation, began the great modern movement of spreading European civilization and its influences over the whole world, just as at one time the Greek civilization spread so largely over the Mediterranean world. Tho checked here and there, and while one European race after another has fallen back, the movement as a whole has gone on for four centuries, with as one side of it the spread of the European peoples and their influence over Asia, Africa, America and Australia, with as the other side, the development within their own limits of a highly complex, highly efficient, but luxurious and in some respects enervating and demoralizing, industrial civilization. There is as yet no sign of the movement as a whole being arrested. Industrial inventiveness of all kinds and the exploitation of the world's resources go on with increasing rapidity. Our children and our children's children will see the mechanical agents of this civilization working with an ever increasing strength and effectiveness. Gyroscope trains may cross these continents in a day; we may see airships; we may see all kinds of things; on the other hand the century that has opened may in all probability see something like a timber famine and also the approaching exhaustion of the iron fields. Even the coal itself cannot last for many centuries. What will come after? Will substitutes be found? Will a simpler and saner civilization, really better, succeed our own; or will it be overwhelmed by barbarism from within or without? No one can tell. It matters very little whether we are optimists or pessimists. Our duty is to do our work well and abide the event.

As regards myself, I am at the moment having rather more than my usual share of difficulties. The panic is bad and it has produced great depression in business, with, as a consequence, laborers thrown out of employment, farmers suffering, and an unhealthy stagnation everywhere. Inevitably and naturally ignorant good men, under the lead of men who are neither ignorant nor good, tend to hold me responsible for this condition. As a matter of fact, it is in part the kind of reaction that comes under any circumstances; it is in part due to unhealthy and dishonest methods in the field of speculative high finance;

and my own share is limited to having exposed abuses and therefore to bringing on the crisis a little quicker than it otherwise would have come, but making it less severe. In large part, however, the movement is world-wide. You have with great acuteness stated in your letter the exact fact about the newspapers and any movement on behalf of the fundamental rights of the people as a whole, such as that in which I think I may fairly say I have taken a considerable part. The movement itself will in the end succeed, but the man who leads it must necessarily fail or seem to fail for the time being. All I am fighting for, in the last analysis, is honest methods in business and in politics, and justice alike for (and on to) capitalist and working man. I have never hesitated to oppose labor unions when I thought them wrong, any more than to oppose corporations when I thought them wrong. I am certain that if our Republic is to endure on a healthy basis, it must proceed along the course I have outlined. But the thing that astonishes me is not that I should now be attacked, but that I should have been triumphant for so long a period, for I have awakened the bitter antagonism of very powerful men and very powerful interests whose memory is as long as the memory of the public at large is short, and their attacks on me thru the papers which they subsidize (and these are the big papers of the biggest industrial centers) never cease for a moment. They misrepresent everything I say or do; the wonder is that anyone should have any belief in me at all. But it is all in the day's work. I have had an uncommonly good run for my money; I have been treated mighty well and favored by fortune above my deserts; and whatever comes in the future, I am ahead of the game.

It certainly is curious how the great racial questions are looming up. I was glad to see your agreement with Russia; but of course we are all perfectly ignorant of what Russia's future will be. As for the governing class in England having no real foreign policy, of course our people tend to have even less, and the melancholy fact is that the capitalist and educated classes are those least to be trusted in this matter. It is, as you say, a melancholy fact that the countries which are most humanitarian, which are most interested in internal improvement, tend to grow weaker compared with the other countries which possess a less altruistic civilization. The great countries with strong central government and military instincts do tend to be the dominant ones; and I have fought, not very successfully, to make our people understand that unless freedom shows itself compatible with military strength, with national efficiency, it will ultimately have to go to the wall. For your sins I send you a copy of my message and ask you to look at what I say about the army and navy, pages 45 to 55. It is astounding to see how shortsighted many people in your country and mine and even in France are where war is concerned. Carnegie represents the most objectionable class of these peace advocates. He represents those people who in crude and foolish fashion have imbibed Tolstoi's foolish theory that good men should never make war because, forsooth, when bad men are stronger than good men they make war in evil fashion, and who add a peculiar baseness to this view by championing an industrialism which wrecks far more lives than any ordinary war. The country that loses the capacity to hold its own in actual warfare with other nations, will ultimately show that it has lost everything. I abhor and despise that pseudo-humanitarianism which treats advance in civilization as necessarily and rightfully implying a weakening of the fighting spirit and which therefore invites destruction of the advanced civilization by some less-advanced type.

Good-by, Springy; and do bring Mrs. Springy over to see us sometime this year. *Ever yours*

A CHRISTMAS PRESENT

To Charles Edward Magoon

Washington, December 23, 1907

My dear Governor:

I feel like an awful reprobate to grab what was to have been your Christmas present to Mrs. Roosevelt! But the fact is, my dear Governor, that the pitcher and basin are so very beautiful that I simply cannot bear not to give them to her myself;

and after all, altho I shall have to make you permit me to pay for them (so please send me the amount I owe you), the major part of the gift, that is, the trouble in finding it and the taste in choosing it, cannot but be yours, and so you have simply put us *both* under an obligation. If I had not written you first I should not have the heart to take this course; but as I did write you first, and felt very proud of myself for having found out something that Mrs. Roosevelt really wanted, I shall ask you to let it remain on this basis. Remember that our obligation is as great to you as if I had followed the other course.

I thank you heartily for the cigars.

Wishing you a merry Christmas and many happy New Years, I am, *Faithfully yours*

MOB RULE AND PLUTOCRACY

To Arthur Hamilton Lee

Washington, December 26, 1907

My dear Lee:

It was a great pleasure to receive your long and interesting letter, but I do wish you could come over here and give me a glimpse of you in person.

I do not need a rest and do not want one, and there is nothing I should like so well as to stay in the fight; but every public man if he is to do good work must understand the temper and convictions of the people for whom he works. Our people feel very strongly about a third term, and in dealing with them my chief asset of value is their belief in my disinterestedness and honesty. I would not for anything give them cause to alter this belief. Here in the United States, and I suppose in many other countries as well, there are always the twin opposite dangers to be feared — the Scylla of mob rule, and the Charybdis of subjection to a plutocracy. It does not help one to have avoided the reef on the right if shipwreck follows from striking on the reef to the left. Again and again in my public career I have had to make head against mob spirit, against the tendency of poor, ignorant and turbulent people who feel a rancorous jealousy and hatred of those who are better off. But during the last few years it has been the wealthy corruptionists of enormous fortune, and of enormous influence thru their agents of the press, pulpit, colleges and public life, with whom I have had to wage bitter war. In consequence, I find myself on many points at one with some of the demagogs, and I feel it all the more important that I should make it evident that I am not following this course, so congenial to the demagogic temperament, from any unworthy motives. But as I say, I have to get out of the fight, and I am fully awake to the fact that there is always something very real to be said against the leader who, from whatever motives, does leave the fight before it is finished. In this case I am certain that the arguments on one side are far outweighed by the arguments in favor of the course I have followed, however.

That the course which I have taken in dealing with the big corporations is the only course compatible with the real welfare of the Republic, I am certain. It has not caused the panic, but it may have brought it on a little sooner than otherwise and have accentuated it for the moment; but it was simply impossible to permit such wild speculation and gross corruption as existed to go on unchecked. At the worst it was an operation for appendicitis. The patient's life may depend upon the surgeon acting at once, but it is certain that the patient will have to stay in bed a few days no matter how successful the operation is. The *Sun, Harper's Weekly, Times, Evening Post,* and so forth, are owned or controlled by Wall Street. I do most seriously feel that this reactionary crowd may succeed in convincing the plain people that they had better go to Hearst or Bryan as long as the businessmen won't accept me or a man like me. To use the terminology of Continental politics, I am trying to keep the left center together.

I like the correspondents of the London *Times.* Of course if Taft succeeds me our foreign policy will go on absolutely unchanged. Indeed, I think this will be the case with almost any Republican. I do not think there will be any real outburst against Great Britain, even under a Democrat. Then the danger would be with Japan, and would come from the possibility of some foolish doctrinaire declining to control mob action against the Japanese, and at the same time declining to keep the navy in such shape that we could resist if attacked. In the Japanese matter our Pacific States and Australia and British Columbia feel exactly alike, and fundamentally their attitude is proper; but its manifestations are often exceedingly improper.

I am greatly interested in what you say of your own politics.

Now about your friend the great Hungarian portrait painter, Laszló. It seems very churlish for me not to say "yes" out of hand, but you have no conception of the pressure there is upon me to have my picture painted and of the small amount of time at my disposal. Nevertheless, my dear fellow, I am very much touched at your wanting my picture for yourself and at your wanting to have it painted by a real genius. Will you let me see Laszló when he comes and find out just how long he will need? Give him a note of introduction to me.

With warm regards to Mrs. Lee, believe me, *Always your friend*

THE WAR OF INDEPENDENCE

To George Otto Trevelyan

Washington, January 1, 1908

Dear Sir George:

The loving cup has at last gone and I hope will reach you. It represents, my dear sir, a very genuine affection and admiration in three of your many American friends.

I look forward eagerly to your next volume. With one of the smaller fights with which you will have to deal, that of King's Mountain, I am fairly well acquainted. I made rather a study of it, as well as of the western campaigns of George Rogers Clark during the Revolution, in a book I wrote called *The Winning of the West*. I look forward to seeing what you say of Tarleton. My admiration for that dashing, even tho somewhat ruthless, cavalryman has steadily grown. In my library his volume stands side by side with the memoirs of

Lighthorse Harry Lee — where it belongs. As you so well say, men are very apt to consider as cruel any form of killing to which they are unaccustomed. The British thought the sharpshooters who picked off their officers were nothing short of murderers; and the Americans stigmatized as a massacre any fight that was won by unsparing use of saber or bayonet, whether under Tarleton or Grey. It seems to me you have been eminently just to Burgoyne, Howe and Clinton. It is nonsense to attack them as so many British historians, and with still less excuse so many American historians, have done. They were not military men of the first rank; but very few such are produced in any war; and many far less deserving men to whom the fates were kind now hold respectable positions as victors in the histories of commonplace campaigns against mediocrities. I shall be interested in seeing what you say of Rawdon. His name always possesses for me an attraction which I suppose is due to a subconscious feeling that he *must* be connected in some way with his namesake, that fundamentally good fellow, Captain Crawley. I look forward especially to your account of Cornwallis. Green and Cornwallis were the two commanders who stood next to Washington; Wayne got his growth after the Revolutionary War had ended. It seems to me that there has never been a more satisfactory summing up of Washington as a soldier than is contained in your pages 284 to 286. How well you have done Benedict Arnold! How will you deal with his fall; with the money-paid treason of the rider of the war storm? What a base web was shot thru the woof of his wild daring! He was at heart a Lucifer, that child of thunder and lover of the battle's hottest heat; and dreadful it is to think that when he fell his fall should have been, not that of the lightning-blasted Son of the Morning, but that of a mere Mammon or Belial. Your etching of Morgan's riflemen is fine. The victors of King's Mountain were just such men, but without a Morgan to train them. Now, for a bit of brag. My Rough Riders, hunters of the mountains and horsemen of the plains, could not, taken as a whole, have walked quite as well as Morgan's men, nor yet have starved as well, tho they were good enough at both. But they rode without thought horses that Morgan's men would not have ventured so much as to try to get on, and I firmly believe that they were fully as formidable in battle. Mine was a volunteer regiment, and at least half of the officers at the outset were very bad, so that in a long campaign I should have had to make a complete change among them — a change that was already well begun when the regiment was disbanded. But as compared with any volunteer regiment of the Revolution or the Civil War during a like short period of service — four months — I think its record stood well. It was raised, drilled — so far as it was drilled — armed and equipped, kept two weeks on transports, and put thru two victorious aggressive (not defensive) fights, in which it lost over a third of its officers and nearly a fourth of its men, and this within sixty days. The men already knew how to ride, shoot, and live in the open; and they had the fighting edge.

You speak of the Indians just as they should be spoken of; altho I am not sure that from your account men will realize what formidable and terrible foes they usually were on their own ground.

I was especially delighted with your account of Franklin abroad, and of the unfortunate diplomats whom Congress first sent to Europe. You have, it seems to me, done justice as regards the civilian agents of the Revolution.

Now, poor André! His tragedy was like that of Nathan Hale; and the tragedy was the same in the case of the brilliant young patrician, gallant, fearless, devoted, and the plain, straightforward yeoman who just as bravely gave up his life in performing the same kind of duty. It was not a pleasant kind of duty; and the penalty was rightly the same in each case; and the countrymen of each man are also right to hold him in honor and to commemorate his memory by a monument. Among our monstrosities in the statue line in New York we have one really beautiful statue by a master; it is Nathan Hale's. By the way, it is one of the sad ironies of history that a difference in the outcome of a war should necessarily in so many cases utterly change the way the descendants of the two sides look at one another's heroes. In Canada, for instance, Wolfe and Montcalm are equally national heroes, now, because the English conquered the French and yet live in the country on terms of absolute equality with them; so that of necessity, if they are to have a common national tie, they must have as common heroes for both peoples the heroes of each people. So in a very striking fashion it is with us and the memories of the Civil War. My father's people were all Union men. My mother's brothers fought in the Confederate navy, one being an admiral therein, and the other firing the last gun fired by the *Alabama* before she sank. When I recently visited Vicksburg in Mississippi, the state of Jefferson Davis, I was greeted with just as much enthusiasm as if it had been Massachusetts or Ohio. I went out to the national park which commemorates the battle and siege and was shown around it by Stephen Lee, the present head of the Confederate veterans' organization, and had as a guard of honor both ex-Confederate and ex-Union soldiers. After for many years talking about the fact that the deeds of valor shown by the men in gray and the men in blue are now the common heritage of all our people, those who talked and those who listened have now gradually grown, first to believe with their minds, and then to feel with their hearts, the truth of what they have spoken. But where such results flow from battles as flowed from Bannockburn and Yorktown, centuries must pass before the wound not only scars over but becomes completely forgotten, and the memory becomes a bond of union and not a cause of division. It is our business to shorten the time as much as possible; and no one has done better work toward this end than you yourself.

This Christmas I was given an original proclamation issued in 1776 by my great-great-grandfather, the first governor (or, as he was called, President) of the Revolutionary State of Georgia. Two among my forbears were soldiers who fought under Marion and Sumter, one was in the Continental army of the North, and one a member of the Continental Congress. They were plain people, farmers or merchants, for the most part, tho I suppose one or two would have been ranked among the gentry. In 1693 one of them was "Landgrave" of South Carolina under Locke's absurd constitution.

I should like to write you of my troubles here, but I forbear. I am engaged in the difficult business of trying to keep together the men who are equally bent on reform and resolute not to go into anything vindictive or visionary. A government like ours must equally dread the Scylla of mob rule and the Charybdis of the reign of a mere plutocracy. I have often had to take measures against the mob spirit in its various forms; but during the last six years my chief fight has been to prevent the upgrowth in this country of the least attractive and most sordid of all aristocracies, as unattractive now as in the days of Carthage, a plutocracy, a caste which regards power as exprest only in its basest and most brutal form, that of mere money. The typical American multimillionaire is an unlovely being, and scant is his share of heirship in Washington and Lincoln, in the deeds of the men who in successive generations founded this Government, conquered this continent, and fought to a finish the great war for union and for liberty. *Faithfully yours*

P.S. This morning I shook hands with six thousand people at the White House reception. This afternoon I took a two hours good hard ride with four of my children and a dozen of their cousins and friends; jumping fences, scrambling over the wooded hills, gallopping on the level; and it was the kind of fun to fit a public man for work.

CONTROVERSIES IN THE NAVY

To Victor Howard Metcalf

Washington, January 2, 1908

To the Secretary of the Navy:

In accordance with our conversation of today, Captain Pillsbury will be appointed Chief of the Bureau of Navigation.

The action of the late chief of the Bureau, Admiral Brownson, in tendering his resignation because he did not agree with the President and the Department regarding an order, issued before he came into the Bureau, by the Secretary of the Navy, as to the control of the hospital ships, was unseemly and improper, and, coupled with the various controversies among the officers of the navy and their adherents as to details of naval construction and methods of training, has undoubtedly been prejudicial to the interests of the navy and may seriously impair the confidence in the navy which is essential to securing the legislation so sorely needed by the navy. The way in which these controversies have been carried out is highly injurious to the service, whether the communications are made openly over the signatures of the naval officers, or by civilians who have evidently gained their information from naval officers. There always are and always will be defects to correct both in the construction of ships and in the organization of the Department and in the actual drill of the fleet. It is well that these defects should be pointed out, but it is also well that they should be pointed out without hysterical exaggeration or malicious untruthfulness; while it is of course reprehensible in the highest degree to exploit them in grossly exaggerated form in the fancied interest of an individual or clique of individuals, or for the sake of supplying sensational material to some service or non-service newspaper. The officers of the navy who are guilty of such conduct deserve grave rebuke. They cast discredit upon the service and their conduct is deeply mortifying to every American who believes in the navy and is anxious to uphold its interest and honor. There has been so much misrepresentation and exaggeration that I desire you to make me a statement as to the exact facts concerning which there has been dispute. In particular I desire you to get the opinion of Admiral Converse, who, until last spring, was Chief of the Bureau of Navigation, and whose high professional standard of conduct and duty, and high professional knowledge and attainments, render him peculiarly fit to give judgment.

I would willingly pass over the conduct of Admiral Brownson because of his fine service in the past if it were not that at a time when a new chief is chosen to succeed him it becomes imperative to stamp with disapproval the behavior which, if followed thruout the navy generally, would literally ruin the navy's efficiency. The question as to which Admiral Brownson took issue with the Department I will deal with in a separate letter. It is one as to which there can be entirely legitimate differences of opinion, altho in my judgment the considerations in favor of the course decided upon are overwhelming. But there is no room for difference of opinion as to the gross impropriety of the Admiral's conduct in resigning sooner than carry out the orders of his superior officers in such a matter.

The officers of the navy must remember that it is not merely childish but in the highest degree reprehensible to permit either personal pique, wounded vanity, or factional feeling on behalf of some particular bureau or organization, to render them disloyal to the interests of the navy and therefore of the country as a whole. The question whether one officer or another shall command a ship is of little consequence compared with the weakening of all command and discipline which would result if officers were to refuse to serve whenever their tempers are ruffled by adverse decisions on the part of their superiors. Their sole concern should be the good of the service, and save only courage in actual warfare, obedience and loyalty are the most essential qualities in keeping the service up to the highest standard. The different bureaus of the Department, the different branches of the service, must act in coordination, and the questions that arise between them must be settled by the authority of the Secretary of the Navy and of the President, under and in accordance with the law enacted by Congress; and the first duty of every officer, whether of the line, of the pay department, of the medical department, or of the construction department, whether in one bureau or in another, is to give immediate and loyal obedience to every lawful command of a superior, and of course above all to the law itself. This duty is incumbent upon all, but it is most incumbent upon those highest in rank, whose example may be of far-reaching effect.

"THE SOUND OF TRUMPET AND HORN"

To George Meredith

Washington, January 9, 1908

My dear Mr. Meredith:

Will you permit a stranger to join in very hearty greetings to you on your eightieth birthday? After a writer's work reaches a certain height, he can no longer be claimed only by the people of his own nation; and there are now as many in

America as in England who owe you a debt of honorable obligation. I hardly venture to suppose that you will come to America; if you could, your greeting would be warm; and not the least warm from those of us who do not put your poems second to your prose writings. It is good to hear the sound of trumpet and horn, whether in verse or prose; in Attila or Brann, or when the Goshawk fights the marauder Baron; and as each man necessarily thinks especially of the problems of his own trade, it is natural for me to feel that what was written to Colonel Charles should appeal to the public men of every free country.

With high regard and all good wishes, believe me, *Sincerely yours*

THE LAW AND PRIMITIVE JUSTICE

To Melville Davisson Post

Private

Washington, January 17, 1908

My dear Mr. Post:

Apropos of Madame Versäy, you may possibly be amused to know my experience in connection with the decision of the United States Supreme Court that Confederate notes were not counterfeit. While Knox was Attorney General there came before me the case of two criminals who had passed these notes. The lower court held that the notes were counterfeit and both men were imprisoned. One of the men took an appeal and the other did not. After some time the superior court declared that Confederate notes were not counterfeits and thereupon the man was released. Knox then brought around to me a formal order for the release of the other. This I promptly refused to issue, and Knox and I then had an argument, he standing for the law and I for rude and primitive justice. The argument reminded me a little of the famous discussion between the King, the Queen and the Headsman in *Alice in Wonderland*. Knox's position was that as the act committed by the man had been declared by the court not to be criminal, I could not keep him in prison. My position was that as he was undoubtedly a scoundrel and a swindler and morally a criminal, I certainly would not let him out of prison; and that as for saying that I could not keep him in, why, he *was* in, and that was all there was about it. I think Knox had the best of the argument as regards the law, but I had the final say-so as to the facts and the man stayed in for nearly a year longer. I was sorry I could not punish both scoundrels, but at least I was able to punish one. *Sincerely yours*

TAFT AND HUGHES

To Kermit Roosevelt

Washington, January 27, 1908

Dear Kermit:

The campaign for Taft seems to be getting along well. Of course the statements that I am trying to dictate his nomination are ludicrous falsehoods, and the statements that I am using the offices to force his nomination are wicked falsehoods. But I believe with all my soul that Taft, far more than any other public man of prominence, represents the principles for which I stand; and, furthermore, I believe in these principles with all my soul; and I should hold myself false to my duty if I sat supine and let the men who have taken such joy in my refusal to run again select some candidate whose success would mean the undoing of what I have sought to achieve. The men most hostile to me show a tendency to gather around Hughes. Hughes is a fairly good man (but not a big man) and an inordinately conceited one. He is therefore jealous of me, and the men who are backing him believe that they could count upon his jealousy of me to make him take action which would amount in effect to undoing what I had done, altho that might not be Hughes' conscious purpose. Hughes is not knee-high to Taft in any way, but he has the kind of quality which is apt to win out in conventions as against a man of bold, generous type like Taft, who looks out too little for his own interests. But this year I believe we shall be able to awaken people to what the real situation is. I am confident that if the convention was held at once Taft would be nominated. It is always unsafe to prophesy in politics, and all that can be said is that if we can hold things as they are we shall be all right. Whether we can so hold them I cannot tell, and nobody can.

We are at the height of the social season, and as formal social entertainments are rather a nightmare to me, I look forward eagerly to its ending. I am worked up to my limit, having just been carefully preparing a message to Congress in which I intend to draw the issue as sharply as I well can between the men of predatory wealth and the administration. As I also try to get some exercise riding or walking every day this means that going to entertainments in the evening makes a serious tax upon me. *Your loving father*

JANE ADDAMS AND PACIFISM

To Florence La Farge

Washington, February 13, 1908

Dear Florence:

I have read Miss Addams' book and I am greatly disappointed in it. Hull House has done admirable work which means that Miss Addams has done admirable work; just as Dr. Rainsford in his parish did admirable work which I am not sure was not even better in its ultimate results upon the people affected. But evidently Miss Addams is one of those confused thinkers whose thought cannot be accepted for the guidance of others. In certain of the chapters of her book she states facts and conditions that are interesting and once or twice develops theories which have in them an element of good. But there is always in what she says an element both of the fantastic and of the obscure; and this is absolutely inevitable when the book is written with an *idée fixe* — the theory that antimilitarism is the solvent for all troubles. Of course she might just as well say that vegetarianism or antivaccination would solve our industrial problems as to say that militarism has anything of the kind, sort or description to do with any of either the social or industrial troubles with which this country is confronted. Her idea on militarism is itself preposterous; but granting that it were right the fact would remain that militarism has no more to do with the crisis of American society than, say, eating horseflesh in honor of Thor. The benefits and abuses of militarism are very real in the social and industrial life of the nations of continental Europe; but militarism has been a practically imponderable element in producing the social and industrial conditions of England during the last ninety years, and has not been any element at all in the United States for the past forty years.

The trouble evidently is that Miss Addams is a striking example of the mischievous effect produced by the teachings of a man like Tolstoi upon a mind without the strength, training and natural ability to withstand them. Tolstoi is a great novelist, and his novels like *Anna Karenina, War and Peace, The Cossacks,* and *Sevustopol* can be read with advantage if we read them just as we read the novels of medieval Poland by Sienkiewicz; but the minute that Tolstoi is accepted as a moral teacher he can benefit only the very small fraction of mankind which can differentiate the good he teaches from the mass of fantastic and unhealthy absurdity in which it is embodied. As it happens, I have never yet met any human being who had been morally benefited by Tolstoi; but I have met hundreds of well-meaning, crude creatures who have been seriously damaged by him. He preaches against war, for instance, just as he preaches against marriage. His *Kreutzer Sonata* is treated by his admirers as if it were a melancholy and unnatural production of his. It is melancholy, but it is not unnatural in the least. The same law of action and reaction which tended under the old regime in France to make the debauchee and the devotee alternate in the same family and sometimes in the same individual, makes it natural that a filthy and repulsive book like the *Kreutzer Sonata* should be written by a man in whom a fantastic theory of race annihilation by abstention from marriage is fitly and inevitably supplemented by gross and criminal aberrations of the sexual passion. No really good

pure-minded and healthy man or woman could have written
or approved of the *Kreutzer Sonata;* and just as little would
any such man or woman be capable of approving either the
unnatural asceticism which Tolstoi preaches or the gross and
unnatural debauchery which such asceticism in its turn inevitably breeds.

Now all this applies in principle just as much to his assault
on all war — which foolish Jane Addams, like still more foolish Justice Brewer, enthusiastically applauds. Of course Tolstoi himself is logical in his folly. He is against all industrialism
just as he is against all war; and he wants the whole race to
die out immediately. Industrialism under any circumstances
means the loss of thousands of lives. Industrialism in the
United States has to its credit probably a hundred times the
number of men and women killed and crippled that have been
killed and crippled since the foundation of the Republic in all
our wars. We must make every effort to lighten the suffering
that this killing and crippling entails; but to declare that because lives are lost in mines, on railways and in factories, we
should abandon all work in or on them, would be not one bit
better and not one bit worse than declaring that righteous
people must not be prepared to defend their rights because
scoundrels often do wrong by violence. There is no possible
theory by which the existence of a policeman can be justified
that does not also justify the existence of a soldier. Russia, Tolstoi's own country, suffers primarily because for two centuries
and a half she was under the hideous Tartar yoke, and she endured this slavery because her people could not fight successfully. If the Russians of the 13th, 14th and 15th centuries had
been able to fight as the Swiss fought at the same period, I
very firmly believe that Russia would today be as prosperous
and progressive as Switzerland. There is misery and suffering
in Switzerland, but nothing like what there is in Russia. The
doctrine of nonresistance is old, and its results have always
been evil. The same fantastic morality on this point which Tolstoi now develops was rife in the later ages of Byzantium, and
that decadent people disbelieved in militarism as heartily as
Miss Jane Addams. Up to the very last, with the Turk at their
gates, there were plenty of priests and laymen in Constantinople who declared it unlawful to shed blood, even that of

an enemy; and such an attitude had no small part in producing the condition which has subjected southwestern Europe for four centuries to the unspeakable horror of Turkish rule. In our own country the most sordid political corruption has, as Owen Wister recently pointed out, existed in the regions where the English and German nonresistant and antimilitary sects had supreme control. What the distant future holds in store, no man can tell; but today it is just as wicked to preach unrighteous peace as to preach unrighteous war, and it is even more foolish.

With love to Grant, *Ever yours*

READING DICKENS

To Kermit Roosevelt

Washington, February 23, 1908

Dearest Kermit:

I quite agree with you about Tom Pinch. He is a despicable kind of character; just the kind of character that Dickens liked, because he had himself a thick streak of maudlin sentimentality of the kind that, as somebody phrased it, "made him wallow naked in the pathetic." It always interests me about Dickens to think how much first-class work he did and how almost all of it was mixt up with every form of cheap, second-rate matter. I am very fond of him. There are innumerable characters that he has created which symbolize vices, virtues, follies and the like almost as well as the characters in Bunyan; and therefore I think the wise thing to do is simply to skip the bosh and twaddle and vulgarity and untruth and get the benefit out of the rest. Of course one fundamental difference between Thackeray and Dickens is that Thackeray was a gentleman and Dickens was not. But a man may do some mighty good work and not be a gentleman in any sense.

Yes, it was Phil Roosevelt who wrote that poem. I do not wonder that you were astonished at it. His own family have been quite as much surprised; I saw Cousin Emlen and Christine at lunch yesterday with the Frank Lowells. I really think the poem is very good; and, as Ted pointed out, the simile of the sagebrush and the puma is not only excellent but altogether new. How in the world Phil did it I do not know. They say that he has shown remarkable ability as a debater, and I should not wonder if he was cut out for a lawyer.

Last night I dined with the Jusserands, the only other guest being Justice Moody, and we had a thoroly enjoyable evening. You and I, if we get the chance, must surely call on him and look at his books the next time you are here. *Your loving father*

"FAIR DEALING BETWEEN MAN AND MAN"

To Grafton Dulany Cushing

Washington, February 27, 1908

Dear Cushing:

With the exception of one letter, from Samuel Crothers, I am tempted to say that of all the letters that have been written me, yours is the one that has touched me most; and without exception, yours is the letter that most clearly sets forth just what I have felt and have tried to do — with what failure to achieve complete success I am only too well aware.

I feel just exactly as you do. Most of the men of our little world do not see beyond their own circle. They know nothing of the lives and desires of their fellow countrymen. They do not realize the fervor of intensity with which these countrymen are demanding a change in the old order of things in politics and in the world of great business. The evils against which they rise in revolt are very real, and moreover are very base; and if the men in revolt are not well led, and if a substantial measure of victory is not achieved under sane and moderate leadership, there is danger that we shall embark on that evil course of oscillation between extremes that permanently lowered the French character during the years between 1789 and 1871. The abuses of the old regime, the folly of the reactionaries, and the folly of the demagogs, combined to bring about the Red Terror. The reaction against the Red

Terror brought about Napoleonism. Then came the White Terror, and the reaction against this also found vent in revolution. The July monarchy really marked the victory of the moderates; but partly thru their own fault and partly thru the folly and wickedness of the extremists on both sides, the legitimists and the radicals, this monarchy was overthrown. The Second Republic came in under the nominal lead of the moderates; but the extreme radicals, the men who would correspond to some of the Bryanites and some of the Debsites of today, got control and adopted every kind of impossible policy, including the famous national workshops for the unemployed; and the moderates and radicals grew so distrustful of one another, the moderates showed such inefficiency and the radicals such wicked folly, while the extreme reactionaries conspired against both and welcomed disaster provided only that it hurt their foes for the moment, that in the end Louis Napoleon's pinchbeck empire of intrigue was the inevitable result. This could exist only when based on force, corruption and repression. When it fell the Red Commune rose on its ruins.

Now, what we ought all to strive for here is a steady and orderly development along the lines of fair dealing between man and man, and of honesty demanded from all men in business and politics alike. Ours must neither be a movement of the rich nor of the poor. If it can be kept, as I believe it can and will be kept, along these lines, the future of the nation is secure; and such an issue is well worth fighting for in spite of any temporary discouragement. Of course, both the foolish and sinister radical and the foolish and sinister reactionary will take advantage, as it was inevitable that they would take advantage, of this year of depression, and temporarily the outcome may be bad in one direction or the other; but I think we have made substantial gain, lookt at from the larger viewpoint, and that some of the gain will be permanent.

I wish you could get down here this spring to visit us for a day or two. Is this possible? If you can, I will have you meet a number of the men who are really carrying out the policies of this administration. *Faithfully yours*

P.S. As you so well put it, our aim must be the supremacy of justice, a more satisfactory distribution of wealth — so far as this is attainable — with a view to a more real equality of opportunity, and in sum a higher social system. In international affairs we have in the past six years measurably realized our ideal; we have shown our ability to hold our own against the strong; while no nation has ever behaved towards the weak with quite the disinterestedness and sanity combined which we have shown as regards Cuba and the Philippines.

"SPECULATIVE HISTORY"

To Arthur James Balfour

Washington, March 5, 1908

My dear Mr. Balfour:

Thru Arthur Lee I have just received the copy of *Decadence*, and thank you for it. I confess I began to read it with some apprehension lest it might have something to do with some phase of French literary thought. Naturally, therefore, I was glad when the first few lines showed that my fears were groundless.

It seems to me that you are eminently right in seeing that it is good to give a name to something of vital consequence, even tho in a sense the name only expresses our ignorance. It is a curious thing in mankind, but undoubtedly true, that if we do not give such a name to our ignorance, most of us gradually feel that there is nothing to be ignorant about. Most emphatically there is such a thing as "decadence" of a nation, a race, a type; and it is no less true that we cannot give any adequate explanation of the phenomenon. Of course there are many partial explanations, and in some cases, as with the decay of the Mongol or Turkish monarchies, the sum of these partial explanations may represent the whole. But there are other cases, notably of course that of Rome in the ancient world, and, as I believe, that of Spain in the modern world, on a much smaller scale, where the sum of all the explanations is that they do not wholly explain. Something seems to have gone out of the people or peoples affected, and what it is no one can say. In the case of Rome, one can say that the stocks were completely changed, tho I do not believe that this in the least represents even the major part of the truth. But in the case of Spain, the people remain the same. The expulsion of Moor and heretic, the loss of the anarchistic and much-misused individual liberties of the provinces and towns, the economic and social changes wrought by the inflow of American gold — all of them put together do not explain the military decadence of the Spaniard; do not explain why he grew so rigid that, at first on sea and then on land, he could not adapt himself to new tactics; and above all, what subtle transformation it was that came over the fighting edge of the soldiers themselves. For nearly a century and a half following the beginning of Gonsalvo's campaigns, the Spanish infantry showed itself superior in sheer fighting ability to any other infantry of Europe. Toward the end of the sixteenth century, neither the Hollanders, fighting with despair for their own firesides, nor the Scotch and English volunteers, actuated by love of fighting and zeal for their faith, were able on anything like equal terms to hold their own against the Spanish armies, who walked at will to and fro thru the Netherlands, save where strong city walls or burst dikes held them at bay. Yet the Hollander, the Englishman and the Scotchman were trained soldiers, and they were spurred by every hope and feeling which we ordinarily accept as making men formidable in fight. A century passed; and these same Spaniards had become contemptible creatures in war compared with the Dutch and Scotch, the English and French, whom they had once surpassed. Many partial explanations can be given for the change, but none that wholly or mainly explains it.

What is true of military prowess is even more true of national life as a whole. I do not see how any thinking man can fail to feel now and then ugly doubts as to what may befall our modern civilization — the civilization of the white races, who have spread their influence over the entire world — and the culture they have inherited or acquired in extreme western Asia and in Europe during the last three or four thousand years. There are unpleasant analogies between the twentieth century and Hellenistic antiquity in the first period of the post-Alexandrian monarchies; and of course the resemblance is even closer with the orderly, peace-loving, cultivated Roman world from Trajan to Marcus Aurelius. The resemblances are in the way of analogy rather than homology it is true, and there are deep fundamental differences. But the resemblances are there. Why the creative literary spirit should practically have vanished from Roman lands after the time of Trajan, we do not know. We can see better why the citizens lost the traits which make good individual soldiers; but we cannot see why the very time of the astounding urban growth of North Africa, Gaul and Spain should have been coincident with the growth of utter inability to organize on a sufficiently large scale either in peace or war, until everything grew to depend upon the ability of one or two men on top. Much of the fall of the Roman Republic we can account for. For one thing, I do not think historians have ever laid sufficient emphasis on the fact that the widening of the franchise in Italy and the provinces meant so little from the governmental standpoint because citizens could only vote in one city, Rome; I should hate at this day to see the United States governed by votes cast in the city of New York, even tho Texas, Oregon and Maine could in theory send their people thither to vote if they chose. But the reasons for the change in military and governmental ability under the empire between, say, the days of Hadrian and of Valens are hardly even to be guessed at.

I have always been greatly interested in what you point out as to the inability of the people of that strip of Western Asia which is geographically North Africa ever to recover themselves after the downfall of the Roman Empire. It is a rather irritating delusion — the delusion that somehow or other we are all necessarily going to move forward in the long run no matter what the temporary checks may be. I have a very firm faith in this general forward movement, considering only men of our own race for the past score or two centuries, and I hope and believe that the movement will continue for an indefinite period to come; but no one can be sure; there is certainly nothing inevitable or necessary about the movement. For a thousand years, from the days of Alexander to the days of Mahomet, in spite of fluctuations, the civilization of Asia west of the Euphrates was that of Greeks and of Asiatics profoundly affected by Greek influences. Then it disappeared from the land; just as the extraordinary Roman civilization disappeared from North Africa, and left not a vestige behind save the ruins of cities and the masonry around the springs that have dried up under the destructive impotence of the rule that succeeded it.

It is hopeful of course to think how peoples do revive now and then; peoples doubtless partly the same in blood as those that fell, and at least with the ancestral inheritance of language, of culture. You have pointed out the greatest instance of this in Italy. A totally different and much smaller example is furnished by modern Switzerland.

The intrusion of an alien race into another civilization, its growth and supremacy and dying away, is of course curiously paralleled by what we see in the animal world, and the parallel is complete in at least one point — that is, in the fact that in each case the causes may be shrouded in absolute darkness. South America, until the middle of the Tertiary period, had a mammalian fauna almost as unique as that of Australia, composed chiefly of small marsupials, and of what we loosely call edentates, also of small size. Then there occurred physical union with the great arctogeal continent by the Isthmus of Panama. There followed an inrush of northern fauna and an extraordinarily powerful and abundant faunal life sprang up. The dominant forms were those of the intruders — saber-tooth tigers, bear, deer, elephants, swine, camels, tapirs, horses, all of great abundance in species, and many of the species of giant size. Under the pressure most of the old forms disappeared; but some of the so-called edentates developed into ground sloths and giant armadillos as large as elephants; and some of these forms when thus developed proved not only able to hold their own in South America, but gradually in their turn made their way north across the Isthmus and spread into North America in the teeth of the competition of the descendants of the forms that had anciently overrun South America. Thus there grew up in South America a faunal life as gigantic, as fierce, as varied, as that of Central Africa at this moment, and on the whole more like that of Central Africa than like the life of South America today, and infinitely more so than like the old eocene life of South America. Then there came a change, we know not why. In North America the glacial period may have had much to do with it, but surely this cannot have been true of South America; yet all of these huge formidable creatures died out, alike the monsters of alien type from the North, and the monsters developed from ancient autochthonous types. A few weak representatives were left, of both types; but the old magnificent fauna completely vanished; and why we cannot say, any more than we can explain why the Roman so completely failed permanently to leave North Africa to his descendants.

Of course there is a small side trouble, due to our terminology. All species of animals of course ultimately disappear, some because their kind entirely dies out, and some because the species is transformed into a wholly different species, degenerate or not; but in our nomenclature we make no distinction between the two utterly different kinds of "disappearance." So it is, of course, with nations. I really believe that people sometimes think of "new" nations as being suddenly created out of nothing; they certainly speak as if they were not aware that the newest and the oldest nations and races must of course have identically the same length of racial pedigree. They talk, moreover, of the "destruction" of the inhabitants of Mexico, and of the "destruction" of the inhabitants of Tasmania, as if the processes were alike. In Tasmania the people were absolutely destroyed; none of their blood is left. But the bulk of the blood of Mexico, and a part of the blood of the governing classes of Mexico (including Diaz), is that of the Mexicans whom Cortez and his successors conquered. In the same way Australia and Canada and the United States are "new" commonwealths only in the sense that Syracuse and Cyrene were new compared with Athens and Corinth.

Another thing that makes one feel irritated is the way that people insist on speaking as if what has occurred during the last three or four hundred years represented part of the immutable law of nature. The military supremacy of the whites is an instance in point. From the rise of the Empire of Genghis Khan to the days of Selim, the Mongol and Turkish tribes were unquestionably the military superiors of the peoples of the Occident, and when they came into conflict it was the former who almost always appeared as invaders and usually as victors. Yet people speak of the Japanese victories over the Russians as if they had been without precedent thruout the ages.

One practical problem of statesmanship, by the way, must be to keep on good terms with these same Japanese and their kinsmen on the mainland of Asia, and yet to keep the white man in America and Australia out of home contact with them. It is equally to the interest of the British Empire and of the United States that there should be no immigration in mass from Asia to Australia or to North America. It can be prevented, and an entirely friendly feeling between Japan and the English-speaking peoples preserved, if we act with sufficient courtesy and at the same time with sufficient resolution. But this is leaving speculative history for present politics.

With regard, *Sincerely yours*

GREAT WEALTH

To Cecil Spring-Rice

Washington, April 11, 1908

Dear Cecil:

I was delighted with the Mazzini, and with no part of it quite so much as with the poem on the title page. How I wish that you and Mrs. Springy were to be here! There is such an infinity of things to talk over and I cannot begin to write about them all. Mrs. Roosevelt and I were thinking just the other day, in connection with the recent fuss over the American Ambassador to Berlin, about a remark in your last letter in which you spoke of the growing materialism of the Germans. The ambassadorial incident emphasized this. Tower is a good fellow of great wealth, & of rather cultivated tastes. Hill is a somewhat better man — in fact I think a decidedly better man — but without the wealth. In consequence, to my surprise, I found that not only the American sojourners abroad who belong to the class of the vulgar rich, but all of the vulgar rich in Berlin, and especially those who are connected with the court circle, were violently against the change.

Not a few both in the court circle and among the traveling Americans stated with obvious sincerity that under Tower the American Embassy stood easily foremost in Berlin as compared with all the other Embassies, and it evidently never entered their heads that in the question of standing foremost there was anything to be considered save wealth combined with social aptitude. As a matter of fact I am anxious to have it understood that it is not necessary to be a multimillionaire in order to reach the highest positions in the American diplomatic service. The trouble was entirely unexpected to me. I am simply unable to understand the value placed by so many people upon great wealth. I very thoroly understand the need of sufficient means to enable the man or woman to be comfortable; I also entirely understand the pleasure of having enough more than this so as to add certain luxuries, and above all, that greatest of all luxuries, the escape from the need of considering at every turn whether it is possible to spend a dollar or two extra; but when the last limit has been reached, then increase in wealth means but little, certainly as compared with all kinds of other things. In consequence, I am simply unable to make myself take the attitude of respect toward the very wealthy men which such an enormous multitude of people evidently really feel. I am delighted to show any courtesy to Pierpont Morgan or Andrew Carnegie or James J. Hill; but as for regarding any one of them as, for instance, I regard Professor Bury, or Peary, the Arctic explorer, or Admiral Evans, or Rhodes, the historian, or Selous, the big game hunter (to mention at random guests who have been at the White House not long ago) — why, I could not force myself to do it even if I wanted to, which I do not. The very luxurious, grossly material life of the average multimillionaire whom I know, does not appeal to me in the least, and nothing would hire me to lead it. It is an exceedingly nice thing to have enough money to be able to take a hunting trip in Africa after big game (if you are not able to make it pay for itself in some other way). It is an exceedingly nice thing, if you are young, to have one or two good jumping horses and to be able to occasionally hunt — altho Heaven forfend that anyone for whom I care should treat riding to hounds as the serious business of life! It is an exceedingly nice thing to have a good house and to be able to purchase good books and good pictures, and especially to have that house isolated from others. But I wholly fail to see where any real enjoyment comes from a dozen automobiles, a couple of hundred horses, and a good many different homes luxuriously upholstered. From the standpoint of real pleasure I should selfishly prefer my old-time ranch on the Little Missouri to anything in Newport.

There! I did not intend to go into a statement of my own views. I merely got interested in trying to explain why it is that I have been quite unable either to get on with the typical multimillionaire, or to understand the attitude of admiration toward him assumed by a good many different persons, from sovereigns down.

Give my love to Mrs. Springy. *Faithfully yours*

MISCHIEF IN THE WHITE HOUSE

To Archibald Roosevelt

Washington, April 11, 1908

Dearest Archie:

Ethel has bought on trial an eight-months' bulldog pup. He is very cunning, very friendly, and wriggles all over in a frantic desire to be petted.

Quentin really seems to be getting on pretty well with his baseball. In each of the last two games he made a base hit and a run. I have just had to give him and three of his associates a dressing down — one of the three being Charlie Taft. Yesterday afternoon was rainy, and the four of them played five hours inside the White House. They were very boisterous and were all the time on the verge of mischief, and finally they made spitballs and deliberately put them on the portraits. I did not discover it until after dinner, and then pulled Quentin out of bed and had him take them all off the portraits, and this morning required him to bring in the three other culprits before me. I explained to them that they had acted like boors; that it would have been a disgrace to have behaved so in any gentleman's house, but that it was a double disgrace in the house of the Nation; that Quentin could have no friend to see him, and the other three could not come inside the White House until I felt that a sufficient time had elapsed to serve as a punishment. They were four very sheepish small boys when I got thru with them! *Your loving father*

THE NEED FOR MILITARY PREPARATIONS

To Elihu Root

Washington, April 17, 1908

Dear Elihu:

These enclosures from Speck are most interesting. Note the divergence of view in the report of the German Consul and the German Military Attaché. Also note the matter-of-course way in which the Japanese accept the view that in the event of war they will obtain the naval supremacy of the Pacific. The views of their military men offer a bitter commentary on the folly of the lower House of Congress yesterday in refusing to vote for the four battleships. Indeed, it is the kind of folly which can only be called wicked. You will also see that this statement of the German Military Attaché corroborates the information we have had both through the Austrian Embassy at Tokyo and the French Embassy at St. Petersburg, to the effect that many of the Japanese generals and of the military party generally accept as a matter of course the view that they would land a strong army on the Pacific Slope; and you may remember that this was the view that Mackenzie King found to obtain among some of the Japanese in British Columbia. You will also see that the German Consul takes exactly your view, that the Japanese can restrict immigration hither if they wish to. It is an act of the most one-sided folly for this country not to make the military preparations, and especially naval preparations, sufficient to put a stop to all thoughts of an aggressive war on the part of Japan. I think that the probabilities are that war will not take place; but there is a sufficient likelihood to make it inexcusable for us not to take such measures as will surely prevent it. If we have adequate coast defenses and a really large navy, the war cannot take place. *Ever yours*

CONGRESS AND THE NAVY

To Kermit Roosevelt

Washington, April 19, 1908

Dearest Kermit:

Ted turned up Thursday morning with a very sore throat, the doctor having sent him home. Being home with Mother and Ethel, and the rest and good food, speedily set him all right, and by Friday afternoon he was able to play tennis with great vigor, and Saturday he and Fitz went out riding. Mother and I also rode, going up the new bridle trail beside Rock Creek just beyond the other end of the Park. It is in low ground, and the flowers were too beautiful for anything, especially the Virginia cowslips and the dogtooth violets.

I made a hard fight to get Congress to give me four battleships, but they wouldn't do it. Most of them mean well enough, but do not know much, and the leaders are narrow-minded and selfish, and some of them, like Senator Hale, profoundly unpatriotic, and others, like McCall and Burton, if not unpatriotic, at least utterly indifferent to the honor and interest of the country when compared with their own advancement. I cannot give in public my reasons for being apprehensive about Japan, for of course to do so might bring on grave trouble; but I said enough to put Congress thoroly on its guard, if it cared to be on its guard. I do not believe there will be war with Japan, but I do believe that there is enough chance of war to make it eminently wise to insure against it by building such a navy as to forbid Japan's hoping for success. I happen to know that the Japanese military party is inclined for war with us and is not only confident of success, but confident that they could land a large expeditionary force in California and conquer all of the United States west of the

Rockies. I fully believe that they would in the end pay dearly for this, but meantime we would have been set back at least a generation by the loss of life, the humiliation, and the material damage. *Your loving father*

I enclose another poem of Phil's; good, but not as good, or as original, as the first.

LEGISLATIVE AND EXECUTIVE POWER

To John Wolcott Stewart

Washington, May 7, 1908

My dear Senator:

Judging from your question yesterday I do not think you entirely appreciate my position as to my rights and duties in the army. The proposal of Senator Foraker is that Congress shall take away from the President the power of discipline and control over the army, and shall itself exercise the appointing power without regard to the President. At the same time Senator Rayner intimates that Congress may take away the power of the President to deal with worthless and inefficient officers by depriving them of command and saying where they shall or shall not be assigned to duty. My position is that Congress wholly lacks the power to take either motion. I enclose you copies of letters I have sent to Senator Rayner and Senator William Alden Smith. I will no more entertain the proposition as regards enlisted men who are black than I will as to the colonel who is white. Not only do I feel that both in the case of Colonel Stewart and of the colored troops at Brownsville I am absolutely right; but I feel even more intensely that the proposed action by Congress in each case would be ineffective, because absolutely without warrant under the Constitution (as well as, to the last degree pernicious). We might literally as well disband the army as permit it to be commanded by some [   ] of Congress as Senator Foraker proposes; that is, permit murderers to be reinstated, under fancied party exigencies or to gratify political and personal spite; or on the other hand, to permit a colonel unfit for command to be restored to command partly because he has influential social backing which appeals particularly to the Senators from Maryland, and partly because this also offers an opportunity for attack upon the Administration. Of course in each case the large class of maudlin sentimentalists gathers around the wrongdoers, exactly as similar people always petition for the pardon of murderers and other criminals — as, for instance, they championed the cause of Thaw. Moreover, a few excellent men sincerely believe that Colonel Stewart or the colored soldiers did no wrong; just as General Gordon for instance, who was an able man, believed that by consulting the Prophet Isaiah he could get practical advice in dealing with the political exigencies of today; just as otherwise well-behaved, tho humble, fellow citizens of ours believe in the efficacy of the left hind foot of a graveyard rabbit. There is nothing so foolish that some otherwise intelligent men cannot be found to believe in it. But the great point to consider is that under the Constitution the President alone has power to appoint, just as the Legislature alone has power to pass laws and appropriate money. The Legislature may think that the Executive ought to make a particular appointment, just as the Executive may think that the Legislature ought to pass a particular law; but neither side can make the other perform the act which that other is alone competent to perform, without a complete, and I may add, an exceedingly inadvisable, change in the Constitution. I am often accused of violating the Constitution (the accusation being usually made with especial vehemence when I am carrying on a lawsuit, which the courts themselves decide); but no action of which I have been even accused is so clearly a violation of the Constitution as the attempted usurpation by one branch of the Government of the power of another branch of the Government; such would be the effort (and, I may add, the futile effort) to deprive me of my power of appointment. *Sincerely yours*

AMERICANS AND MONARCHY

To Whitelaw Reid

Washington, May 25, 1908

My dear Mr. Ambassador:

First let me extend my very earnest good wishes for Miss Jean. Mrs. Roosevelt found an old book dealing with New York which we hoped that she, as a New Yorker, might accept as a trifling token of our regard for her, no less than for you and Mrs. Reid.

I was immensely amused and somewhat irritated at the recital of your experiences with that Virginia young lady as to whom I wrote you in connection with a presentation at court. I was fairly caught in the matter, for it was asked for by her aunt, a dear old Virginia gentlewoman, with of course not the slightest idea of what she was asking, who showed us certain courtesies and upon whom we were calling while at Pine Knot. But since then I have adopted the plan of never under any circumstances making a request that anyone be presented at court or presented to a sovereign unless on urgent public business. I am exceedingly glad that you failed to find the foolish young lady in question, and that owing to her own fault she has missed the presentation; and now I ask that you be careful not to present her if she should again turn up. I have grown to have a constantly increasing horror of the Americans who go abroad desiring to be presented at court or to meet sovereigns. In very young people it is excusable folly; in older people it is mere snobbishness. I am exceedingly sorry I ever asked you to present the Shontses; but officially he was entitled to it, and until I made my present rule of never asking a presentation, his was just a case which it was impossible to refuse. I cannot be too sincerely grateful that when Mrs. Roosevelt and I were abroad before I was President, we refused to be presented. I have a hearty respect for the right kind of a king and for the right kind of aristocracy, and for the right kind of Englishman who wishes to be presented or have his wife or daughter presented; but it is the business of an American to be a Republican, a Democrat, to behave in a simple and straightforward manner, and, without anything cheap or blatant about it, to be just what he is, and that is, a plain citizen of the American Republic, an intensely Democratic Republic; and he is thoroly out of place, loses his dignity in the eyes of others, and loses his own self-respect, when he tries to play a role for which he is not suited, and which personally I think is less exalted than his own natural role. I have been immensely amused, and not a little astonished, to find how many people, some of them pretty good people, believe that when I am thru here I shall visit the courts of Europe. It would take ten strong yoke of oxen to drag me thither; and my present intention is not to go to Europe at all until the memory of my Presidency has faded, so as not to make the wretched sovereigns and statesmen feel obliged to see me or entertain me. Then, if I can go just as I went before I was President, sometime I should like to take Mrs. Roosevelt; to see the picture galleries, the quaint cities, the scenery; but not otherwise. When I stop being President I stop being President. I become an ordinary citizen, entirely contented to be such; and as I am not a man of large means I neither wish myself to be put into the position of the earthen pot driven downstream with the brazen pots, nor to see my children so placed. If, for instance, I could meet the German Emperor now, when each is head of a big State and there are plenty of things on which we could naturally talk from an equal standpoint, why, I should be delighted to do so. But I haven't the slightest desire to meet him when my hand is no longer on the lever. I hope to get a holiday next spring and go for nine months or a year to Africa, to see the big game, and shoot a very moderate number of head, taking my second boy, Kermit, with me; and if the British and German officers of the territories in which I go will then show me whatever consideration they show to other fairly well-known people of good character who behave themselves — why, that is all I shall ask, and quite as much as I have any right to expect.

Congress is ending, by no means in a blaze of glory. The leaders in the house and Senate felt a relief that they did not try to conceal at the fact that I was not to remain as President, and need not be too implicitly followed; and they forgot that the discipline they have been able to keep for the last six years over their followers was primarily due to the fact that we had a compact and aggressive organization, kept together by my leadership, due to my hold, and the hold the policies I championed had, upon the people. Accordingly they have seen their own power crumble away under their hands and both the House and Senate are now in chaos. All opposition to Taft has died down and he will be nominated easily. But in electing him we shall have no help from the record of the present Congress. The election must be won upon his own personality; upon the general Republican achievement of the past twelve years; and, by no means least, upon the rather absurd attitude of the Democracy.

I hope you have seen Laszló's picture and like it. *Faithfully yours*

"THE FEW AND THE MANY"

To Ray Stannard Baker

Personal

Washington, June 3, 1908

Dear Baker:

I have your letter of the 5th instant. I read your article with interest, but on some points with much less agreement than I have felt with most of your articles. I have been obliged to study the careers of Tillman, Vardaman, and Jefferson Davis of Arkansas, simply in connection with my work. I am satisfied that they have had a deeply debasing effect upon our young men. I have no question that Tillman has some good points — the other two may have good points because they are human beings, but I have not discovered them. They have trained all the young men who have come under their influence to believe that yelling, foul-mouthed vulgarity; coarse abuse in the most violent terms of all opponents; crass and brutal class selfishness, equally hostile to the class above or the class below; blatant contempt for the ordinary decencies of civilization, including common courtesy and physical cleanliness; and readiness violently to champion everything from murder down if the slightest political advantage is to be gained therefrom — they have taught the young men that to indulge in all this is the way to achieve success. It seems to me a great pity that you and the *American Magazine* should in the name of reform and civic betterment add to this impression. Yet I think that this is precisely the impression that you strengthened; for from what I have seen the deepest mark left on the average man from the South who does not consider well is that you are standing by Tillman and Vardaman and Jefferson Davis. Of course those who read carefully will see far more in your article, but there are a great multitude who do not read carefully.

Personally I think you lay altogether too much stress, or rather a twisted stress, upon your theory that everywhere and at all times political thought divides itself into two opposing forces, two great parties or points of view "representing the fundamental social conflict between the few and the many." I think the facts of history directly disprove your statement that slavery in the South was abolished, as an incident to this struggle, "because it was undemocratic." On the contrary the mob of the North, and most of the politicians who howlingly demanded the rule of mere numbers, were violently pro-slavery. This was as true in the country districts of Indiana as in the crowded city of New York. The restriction of slavery was due to the growth of the ethical resentment against it. Its abolition was due to the firm belief which finally grew up in the minds of men that it was inconsistent with national union. A greater proportion of the Few than of the Many went into the final movement for its destruction. Tillman, Jefferson Davis, and Vardaman do not represent in the least championship for the Many on principle; but championship either of the Many or of the Few by accident. There are in every community some men who are natural champions of privilege; and others, of the Lincoln type, who are natural opponents of privilege and champions of equal rights. There are in addition a great many men of good instincts who do not think clearly on the subject; and finally there are a considerable number of men who are actuated by their self-interest or by the accidents of their position. The coarsest and most violent demagogs are often at bottom of precisely the same nature and actuated by the same motives as the coarsest and most violent despots. The man is either despot or demagog as the accidents of his position determine. The three men you mention exactly illustrate what I mean. It has been to their interest to champion the cause of the poor white, the ignorant white, who lives in poverty, as against the white man who has more money and has enjoyed greater advantages. To the superficial view, therefore, they appear as the representatives of the great principle of democracy as against aristocracy. How ridiculous this view is, is shown by the fact that each man stands, not passively or moderately, but with a fury which amounts to mania and frequently turns into homicidal mania, against the majority where the majority happens to be black. This is partly because neither of the men is a genuine democrat at all but is simply an intolerant advocate of privilege for his own caste — for the poor whites as against the well-to-do whites, for the poor whites as against the blacks. It is even more an expression of a fundamental fact far deeper than that which you think is fundamental; the fact of the conflict between race and race, which, with the average man, goes immeasurably farther down in his soul than any conflict between the Few and the Many. If you treat the trouble that we have with the Negro, the trouble as regards misconduct on the part of the white man and misconduct on the part of the black man, as merely an incident to a democratic struggle, you will fall into the most far-reaching error. The question is one of race. This is not a matter of theory at all. All you have to do is to study the history of Haiti when it yielded to the influence of the French Revolution, and see what became of the Jacobite or ultrademocratic movement after it had been tried for a year or two in that island. The condition of Haiti today and the condition of Liberia today is something with which I am obliged practically to deal as President; just as I have to deal now and then with race prejudice both in the South and in the North. To say that any trouble or any conflict in connection with the fearful deterioration of either Haiti or Liberia has anything whatever to do with the conflict between the Few and the Many is, my dear Mr. Baker, pure nonsense. In exactly the same way no progress whatever will be made toward solving the Negro problem if we apply to it a wholly inapplicable simile.

I have so greatly enjoyed your articles and have profited so much from them that I am really sorry to see you show symptoms of being misled by this prevalent habit of hasty and exceedingly unwise generalization. Here in America, taken as a whole our salvation lies in applying the democracy of Abraham Lincoln. I have a thoro and hearty distrust, a distrust which has grown steadily ever since I left college and took part in the practical affairs of men, both of the very well-to-do people who would like to give our Government and our social system a plutocratic caste, and of the other people, who find their chief exponents in papers like the New York *Nation* and New York *Evening Post*, who believe that an arid and cloistered culture produces a class worthy of special consideration; I am a democrat of the democrats; my friends and supporters, the people in whom I believe, are the plain people who work with their hands, on the farm, in the factory, on the railroads. But I no more believe in a mob than I believe in a plutocracy; and I am no more to be misled by a foolish appeal on behalf of the Many than by a foolish appeal on behalf of the Few. As regards many races, and as regards some populations of the remaining races, notably some European populations, the whole effort to translate the terms of the real struggle for righteousness into the terms of a fanciful struggle between the Many and the Few is an effort which does not represent real facts and which can only result in confusion and damage. Most of our fighting for betterment has to do not at all with a conflict between the Few and the Many, but with the improvement of the man as a man, whether he comes in one category or the other. At the moment I am engaged in a savage fight with the big financier caste, the big Wall Street crowd, because I am fighting privilege; but I have fought the Western Federation of Miners, the whole mob spirit, just as hard; and I believe with all my soul that irreparable harm is done by teaching men to substitute hatred of evil in one class only for hatred of all evil as it shows itself in any man in any class. Marat and Robespierre did not improve on the morality of the worst nobles of the Old Regime; they merely damaged freedom as their predecessors had damaged order. I fight against privilege; I fight for the control of great wealth; I fight against mob rule; I fight for equal opportunities for all; but more ardently still I desire to see the growth of a morality which will make each man self-respecting, will make him ashamed of either supporting or opposing another because that one belongs to either the Few or the Many, or to any other artificial aggregation of human beings, will make him just as intolerant of little graft as of big graft (otherwise both will flourish), will make him judge his neighbor, rich or poor, on that neighbor's worth, will make him try to be hardworking, energetic, thrifty, a good husband and father, a man concerned with his rights but concerned still more with his duties.

As for what you say about the colored man I have profited much by it; but I should like to put before you some considerations you have not emphasized.

If you can come on here I will explain what I mean more at length. *Sincerely yours*

ROBERT LA FOLLETTE

To Lincoln Steffens

Private and Personal

Washington, June 5, 1908

My dear Steffens:

In view of Mr. Cosgrave's statement that I had read the proof of your very interesting article, I think I ought to leave it on record that I had not read the proof. I do this simply because the ordinary man would gather the impression — which I fear Cosgrave intended to convey — that as I had read the proof I endorsed all that you say. Now, as regards myself I am often interested in what you say; I sometimes agree with it and sometimes not; but I am always a hundred times more interested in some idea that you develop in the course of what you say about me than I am in what you thus say about me. You have an entire right to your opinion; and while I may or may not be interested in this opinion, I am a hundred-fold more interested in some idea which you apparently consider as incidental. Indeed, often I have been so wholly uninterested in your view of me, and so genuinely interested in your view of something else which you have developed in connection with the former, that I have simply forgot that you were expressing any view of me, and concentrated my attention on the other matter. It is a little difficult for me to express myself clearly without seeming to be slightly uncomplimentary. I know you will acquit me of any such intention. I merely wish to make it clear that I am not to be held as acquiescing in what you say because I do not express dissent from it. To me, for instance, it seems simply nonsense — a nonsense not much above the average spiritualistic seance type, or, to use another simile, not much above the average long-haired and wild-eyed violent socialist type, or the silly, self-advertising parlor socialist of the Robert Hunter type, — to say that I am not interested in fighting *the* Evil or do not see the great underlying cause of it; whereas others, by which I suppose you mean La Follette, do see it. When you express this view either in conversation or writing I do not contradict you or comment upon it because it seems to me a mere foolish vagary on your part, and I pass it by to deal with the points where you really do express needed truths that have not been exprest as well. For instance, in this article, if I gather aright what you mean, you contend that Taft and I are good people of limited vision who fight against specific evils with no idea of fighting against the fundamental evil; whereas La Follette is engaged in a fight against *the* "fundamental" evil. Now, I am really flattered by your having as good an opinion of me as you have. I am pleased at it; and it would never enter my head to point out where I think it is erroneous, if it were not that apparently I am considered as having endorsed your views. Not only I do not endorse them, but I think them on this point childish. Your attitude is to my mind precisely the attitude of the man who patronizes a good country doctor because the latter admits that he cannot cure *all* diseases nor give a specific remedy against all "Disease"; whereas when you prefer La Follette as a type, I feel just as if you held up as better than this country doctor the man who blazons out that he has a particular kind of vegetable pill which will cure old age, consumption, broken legs, and every other ill to which flesh is heir. You can say quite truthfully that the country doctor is fighting evils, not *"the Evil"*; you can also say that the other individual is showing real "leadership" and is going to put a stop not only to "evils" but to *all* "Evil"; but if you said this you would be saying something that was foolish. The same is absolutely as true of political life as of medical life. It is only the quack who will tell you that he has a cure for everything, whether in the world of medicine and surgery, in the world of politics, or in the world of social and industrial endeavor. For instance, you speak of La Follette as standing for the great principle of really representative government, and you seem to imply that the application of this principle would put a stop to all evils. It will do nothing of the kind, and if you proceed upon the assumption that it will, you will yourself work far-reaching harm and will work it in a foolish manner. I have made a pretty careful study of communities in which the initiative and referendum exist, as compared with communities which live under representative institutions, and the difference between them in point of average welfare is so small that I am unable to get up any special enthusiasm for one side or the other. The system of direct primaries under the law works a *slight* betterment over existing conditions. That is, it works, I think, on the whole a very slight improvement over the other system, but it is very slight and consists, on the whole, of a preponderance of slight betterments over slight hurts. An absolutely representative government in the Yazoo would bring about the condition of Haiti. You must have a pretty robust faith in names and theories if you think the conditions of Haiti satisfactory. Absolutely representative government in the city of New York would mean the very most trifling improvement over present conditions unless with it went hand in hand the uplifting of the conscience of the average man. I am trying, however feebly, to make men better, as well as to get better laws, better administration of the laws; and the first is by far the most important. Graft obtains in little things as well as in big; the little grafter is morally as bad as, and no worse than, the big grafter; and I wish to fight against graft as such, and not let the issue be twisted into an attack on a class, which attack can never result in any real betterment. I am fighting evil in the mass, in the only way in which it is possible to fight it, when I fight different evils in the concrete. When you speak of "the system" you use a word that has a certain convenience and that appeals more or less to the imagination; but when you begin practically to speak of fighting "the system," as if it meant anything else than doing a man's duty according to the old standards, you simply lapse back into the condition of those religious enthusiasts of the days of Cromwell who announced that they wisht to fight "principalities and powers" and that they were for the "fifth monarchy, the monarchy of Jesus," and that it was useless to try to improve humanity unless by a radical change and the installation of the "fifth monarchy." This kind of talk did not indicate advanced morality nearly as much as it indicated an unsound mind, and the same statement applies exactly to those who use large phrases to cover up utter vagueness of thought when they come to deal with the political and social evils of today. La Follette has been three years in the Senate. His "plan" which you quote in the article referred to consists so far as it is good of a string of platitudes, and, practically, to adopt it wouldn't mean anything. He talks about the railroads; but as far as action goes, he has not helped at all, since he came to the Senate, in the great work we have actually done towards getting control over the railroads. He has rather hindered this work. Like Tillman he has made great personal gains by what he has done as Senator, because he has advertised himself so that both he and Tillman are very popular in chautauquas, where the people listen to them both, sometimes getting ideas that are right, more often getting ideas that are wrong, and on the whole not getting any ideas at all and simply feeling the kind of pleasurable excitement that they would at the sight of a two-headed calf, or of a trick performed on a spotted circus horse. I tried faithfully to work with La Follette, just as I tried faithfully to work with Aldrich. Neither has been of much use in public life during the last three years, each has often worked detriment. Now and then I have been able to work a little with one, and now and then to work with the other; but the deification of one is just as absurd as the deification of the other — I might add just as absurd as the diabolization of one or the other. The men who have done good in the twenty-five years I have been in politics are those who have had ideals but who have tried to realize them in plain, practical fashion, and who have tried to do each his duty as the day came, and to fight each evil as they found it arise without bothering their heads as to the "ultimate" evil. I believe in the men who take the next step; not those who theorize about the 200th step. Again my experience has been that mighty little good comes from the individual who is fighting "the system" in the abstract; just as mighty little good comes from the church member who is fighting Beelzebub in the abstract. I care nothing either for the reformer or the church member who does not try to do good in the concrete, and who is not ashamed to cover his deficiencies in particular concrete cases by vague mouthings about general abstract principles which are as nebulous in his mind as in the minds of others. It was Lincoln and Oliver P. Morton and the men like them who really saved the Union and abolished slavery, and relatively thereto the part was insignificant which was played by the Wendell Phillips and the Garrisons and the others who liked to think of themselves as "leaders," and to construct an imaginary plan for the perfection of everything which could not even be defined, and which could not have worked in one smallest part if there had been any attempt to realize it.

If you will come down to see me I will go over all this more at length with you, and for once, instead of passing by or brushing aside what you say about me or about anyone else with which I disagree, I will tell you just what I *do* disagree with. *Sincerely yours*

"DIXIE" AND THE "BATTLE HYMN"

To Joel Chandler Harris

Washington, June 15, 1908

Dear Uncle Remus:

Here is something in which I would like to get the assistance of Mr. Billy Sanders, the sage of Shady Dale, and of all the readers of the *Home Magazine* and of all who think as the editors of the *Home Magazine* evidently do think.

Last Saturday, in the late afternoon, when it had grown a little cool, I was riding with two of my aides, Captain Fitzhugh Lee, and Captain Archie Butt of your own State and my Mother's State of Georgia. The mare I was on by the way was named Georgia, and a good mare she is, too, well-behaved, and a good jumper. We were taking our horses out to exercise them over some jumps. We had just been listening to the really superb singing of the men's chorus of the Arion Singing Society, an organization of citizens of German birth or parentage, who were about to go abroad to appear at certain courts and elsewhere in Europe, and who had wisht to sing in the White House as a farewell before starting on their foreign journey. Among other things they had, at my request, sung "Dixie" (as well as the Old Kentucky Home and the Suwanee River). While riding we were talking over the fact that "Dixie" was far and away the best tune (and the best military tune, that we knew, not even excepting Garry Owen), and that it had won its way until it was the tune which would bring everybody to his feet with a yell in any audience in any part of the country; and we were bemoaning the fact that there never had been any words which were in any way adequate to the tune, and dwelling on the further fact that it was such a fine battle tune — the best battle tune of our army. Captain Butt then added that just as "Dixie" stood alone among tunes, so we had in Julia Ward Howe's great "Battle Hymn of the Republic" the very finest and noblest battle hymn possest by any Nation of the world, a hymn that in loftiness of thought and expression, in both words and tune, lent itself to choral singing as no other battle hymn did in any country; and he added that there was not a sectional line in the hymn, not a word that could awaken a single unpleasant thought in the mind of any American, no matter where he lived and no matter on which side he or his father had fought in the great war. I told him I entirely agreed with him, and that, just as "Dixie" was becoming the tune which when played excited most enthusiasm among Americans everywhere, so I hoped that sooner or later all Americans would grow to realize that in this "Battle Hymn of the Republic" we had what really ought to be a great National treasure, something that all Americans would grow to know intimately, so that in any audience anywhere in the land when the tune was started most of the audience should be able to join in singing the words.

We then grew to wondering if this good result would ever be achieved, and we thought it would be worth while to write to you. We know that any such movement can come, if at all, only because of a genuine popular feeling, and with small regard to the opinion of any one man or any particular set of men; and it can only come slowly in any event; but we thought it might be helped on a little if what we had to say was published in your magazine. I append a copy of the Battle Hymn. *Faithfully yours*

LORD NELSON AND HANNIBAL

To French Ensor Chadwick

Oyster Bay, July 8, 1908

My dear Admiral:

I have your letter of the 6th instant. I think you have defined the Spaniards in capital shape. The Spaniards — and, for the matter of that, the southern Italians — are much more like the Berbers than like the tall, long-headed, blond races of North Europe, or the round-headed, comparatively tall, and comparatively blond people of Middle Europe. I am bound to say however that I think that the Spaniards on shore have showed themselves formidable fighters for the century and a half following Gonsalvo, the Great Captain. It certainly seems to me that thruout the Sixteenth Century the French, Germans, English, Scotch and Dutch were as a rule greatly inferior to the Spanish infantry on stricken fields. But taking their history thruout, I agree with you absolutely that their courage is primarily that of passive endurance, not of active and aggressive daring. Moreover, I am delighted at what you say about Nelson at Trafalgar and the English navy at the period of its greatest glory. It is a curious commentary upon the inability of mankind to appreciate the achievement at its true worth that everyone, even Mahan himself, should ignore the fact that the English navy at that great culminating period of its achievement and glory should have won its tremendous victories

against foes of utter military inefficiency. At Copenhagen the
Danes had only hulks. They had not been engaged in a war
for eighty years, and the hulks were manned for the most part
by volunteers. The Russian fleet in the Baltic, as had been
shown in its previous conflict with the Swedes, was manned
by landsmen and could barely maneuver. The Spanish warships were such in name only; it was physically impossible for
them to win against an antagonist who could fight at all. The
Dutch navy suffered from precisely the trouble of the French,
as it was a revolutionary navy, disorganized by a revolution
which also in part took the form of a foreign invasion. The
French navy, the chief foe, was during the earlier years of
the republic officered and manned in a fashion which made it
ludicrous to think of its opposing any respectable opponent,
and it was saved from utter annihilation only because of the
wooden formalism of the elderly officers who commanded the
English fleets of that period, and of the further fact that, as
always then after a peace, the English navy had itself been allowed to sink into a condition of great inefficiency. Then these
initial successes of the English put the French at such a disadvantage that they were never able to dispute the English supremacy with anything like equal chances. Trafalgar and the
Nile were great victories; but in according to the great sea captain who won them all the praise to which he is entitled, it yet
remains true that his opponents were of so poor an order as
to offer him every possible advantage and to make his victory
as nearly certain as such a thing can be. Contrast all this with
the fears of that greatest of all soldiers, Hannibal, who led a
mercenary army upon an expedition as daring as that of
Alexander, into the heart of the most formidable fighting
nation of antiquity, and with his Sepoys again and again defeated the superior numbers of the most formidable troops
that the world then held. Nelson won crushing and decisive
victories over a foe whom all his fellow admirals also invariably, tho much less decisively, beat. But Hannibal defeated a
foe against whom no army not commanded by himself could
make head, and for a space nearly equaling the lifetime of half
a generation, marched to and fro at will thru that foe's own
country.

With regard, believe me, *Sincerely yours*

To Charles William Eliot

Oyster Bay, July 10, 1908

My dear President Eliot:

I had of course no idea that the telegram Bacon and I sent you would be made public. But in view of its publication, together with your response, I feel I ought to write you so that if the matter should come up in the future there can be no chance to misunderstand my position. I telegraphed freely because I took it for granted that the matter would be kept confidential; and therefore put in none of the qualifications and explanations that I would have put in had I supposed the correspondence would be made public, with the accompanying certainty of wilful misconstruction by certain outsiders. The telegram we sent ran as follows:

> Is it not possible, and would it not be more fitting and just, to substitute another punishment for Fish and Morgan, if, as is stated, they merely took away a book which they were permitted to use in the library? It seems to us, and we feel sure to the great body of graduates, it is unfair and unnecessary to make all of us suffer for an offense of this kind for which some other punishment might surely be found.

I take the above from what has appeared in print in the newspapers, which is substantially correct. The newspapers, as by the attached, put on, falsely, an Oyster Bay date. I have no copy of the telegram, and never have had one. It was written by Bacon, who submitted it to me. I approved and signed it, and he took it away with him. It is therefore absolutely impossible that this telegram could have gotten out from my office. Bacon says that when he sent it he gave the original to his private secretary, and that it is absolutely impossible it could have gotten out from his office. I do not know who in your office had access to it; but if it did not get out from there, it must have been taken from the files of the telegraph company, which I should regard as well-nigh impossible. Whoever put on, or procured the putting on, of the Oyster Bay date and headline, committed a hundredfold worse offense than that of Fish and Morgan.

Your telegram in answer read as follows:

Each man did a dishonorable thing. One violated in his private interest and in a crooked way a rule made in the common interest. The other gave a false name and did not take a subsequent opportunity to give his own. The least possible punishment was put on probation, but even that drops from the crews. A keen and sure sense of honor being the finest result of college life, I think the college and the graduates should condemn effectively dishonorable conduct. The college should also teach that one must not do scurvy things in the supposed interest or for the pleasure of others.

There then followed the telegrams between Mr. Greene and Mr. Loeb:

Cambridge, Mass., June 23, 1908.
Wm. Loeb, Jr.,
 Oyster Bay.
President Eliot is much concerned at publication of telegrams in New York paper with Boston date. Careful inquiry has excluded possibility of their having come from his office.

J. D. Greene.

Oyster Bay, N.Y., June 24, 1908.
J. D. Greene,
 Harvard University,
  Cambridge, Mass.
Your telegram received. The telegrams were certainly not published from this office. As a matter of fact we have no copy of message sent by the President and Mr. Bacon, which was sent by Mr. Bacon from Washington after having been submitted to the President and approved by him. In view of their publication the President is making certain inquiries and will write President Eliot himself.

Wm. Loeb, Jr., Secretary.

The publication of the telegrams of course left the impression that you regarded what Bacon and I did as an effort to secure the pardoning of "dishonorable" and "scurvy" conduct. Now, one reason why I regretted the publication was because I did condemn the conduct of the two boys. I think it deserved punishment of some kind, and I do not wish the boys to feel that such conduct should not be condemned. But I must also add that I think the punishment was ill-judged, and so excessive that I am convinced the effect has been the exact reverse of what you believe, and of what you and the faculty undoubtedly sought to obtain. The publication of your telegram, stigmatizing the conduct as "crooked," "scurvy," and "dishonorable," was an added punishment; a severe, and as I believe, an unwarranted and improper punishment. Other publications in the press, seemingly emanating from the college, have denounced the act as a "theft." To speak of the act as a "theft," in any but a purely technical sense, is nonsense. Morgan's act had nothing whatever in common with that of the student or graduate who some years ago did actually steal certain books and keep them for months in his room, removing the college bookplate, etc. Fish and Morgan, on the two crews, were emphatically engaged in doing work that was of benefit to the whole college, and according to my view, it would be eminently desirable to make them feel that they were doing work for the benefit of the whole college. They had to go down to Red Top just about the time of the examinations, and the college authorities, as a matter of honorable obligation, should have endeavored to give them every facility to study at Red Top to just as much advantage as if they were not at Red Top. There was a book in the library in question which Morgan needed to study in connection with his thesis. He was entitled to study it. It is unfortunate if the rules are such that under these circumstances he was unable to take it with him to Red Top; but apparently they are such, and therefore by obeying the rule he would be put at a disadvantage compared with his fellow students, who were not rowing, and who were therefore, according to my way of looking at it, not entitled to quite the consideration that he was entitled to. From conversation with a number of Harvard undergraduates during the last fortnight, I find that taking these books out has been by no means an uncommon thing, and that in several instances where men have been discovered, the man discovering them has simply given them a sharp dressing down, or has prohibited them from using the library for a month. The action of the faculty has convinced the students that it was because a member of the crew committed the misdeed that the punishment was made heavy. Morgan took out a book intending to read it on the way down in the train to Red Top, and then to send it back. There is no suggestion that he intended to keep it, and he was getting no unfair advantage over any fellow student. He of course had no business to take the book, as it was forbidden, and he deserved punishment; but in my view his offense was venial compared with the offense of the college authorities in the method and therefore degree of punishment they allotted. Fish's offense had both a less serious and a more serious side. He had no interest whatever in the book, was simply trying to help his rowing mate, and therefore received it when it was passed out of the window. He had nothing to gain at all from the transaction. But when caught and asked his name, he gave a false name. Immediately afterwards, when his interlocutor lookt up the name, found that there was a Harvard student of that name, and asked him if he was the man, he responded that he was not; I do not know whether he merely said he was not the Harvard student of that name, altho he admitted that he was a Harvard student, or that he said that it was not his name — not a difference which I regard as very important, as it is perfectly clear that he was admitted to be a Harvard student, that he gave a false name, and that as soon as it was found that there was another and only one other man in the college who bore that name, he promptly repudiated it. He had on his crew hat ribbon; his offense was on the order of, altho more serious than, the offense of the man who is caught driving an automobile beyond the speed limit and gives a false name when paying his fine. I reprobate the action in each case; but in neither case does the action really amount to a lie; there is no real intent to deceive; it is simply an improper way of refusing to give the man's real name. I think that Fish was much to blame and should have been punished; but I do not think that the punishment should have taken such form as to take him off the crew. People tell me that no other form of punishment could be provided; my answer must be that when it comes to purely administrative acts, it is almost always possible to avoid serious injustice.

My concern was somewhat for the crew, because, like most sane and healthy Harvard graduates, I am always anxious to see the eleven, or the nine, or the crew, or the track team, win. I abhor dishonorable conduct. But I reprobate also the false perspective and confusion of ideas which are implied in improperly heavy punishment for an offense which should be condemned and punished, but which it is absurd to treat as a crime. However, I am far more concerned with the effect upon the college morals than upon the crew; for I entirely agree with you that the matter of first importance is to have the proper standard of character, the proper standard of morality, for the college. Now, I have spoken to scores of undergraduates, and to a number of graduates, since this matter occurred, and without exception the former, and almost without exception the latter, condemned unstintedly the action of the faculty, and felt so much more indignant at the faculty than at the two offenders that they were in the very dangerous attitude of not regarding the latter as having been guilty of misconduct at all. I cordially agree with what you say as to the need of the college inculcating a keen and sure standard of honor. But I also sincerely believe that by the action taken in this case you have tended, not to preserve, but to blunt that sense of honor. Yesterday at lunch there were present certain Harvard graduates and undergraduates, and three or four editors of leading periodicals, and I was interested to find that they all of them attributed the action of the faculty, attributed your action, simply to your hostility to athletics; that is, they all accepted as a matter of course the view that no such disproportionate punishment would have been inflicted, excepting for the fact that this gave an opportunity for the Harvard College authorities to strike a blow at Harvard athletics. I of course am sure that their view was wrong, and told them so; but it is in my judgment exceedingly unfortunate to have taken action which makes such a view accepted as natural and proper, and most certainly such action defeats its own end if the end is to establish a higher sense of honor among the students. The general expression among the undergraduates was, "Well, this year we have been able to beat both Yale and the faculty. Whether we can do it another year or not, we don't know." And those who thought much on the matter — which, I am bound to say, most of them did not — evidently simply felt that the action showed that the faculty was thoroly out of sympathy with the students and with their purposes and ambitions, and that their own attitude in the future must be to prevent any chance of the faculty's being able to strike another blow at the crew or at athletics. They have not profited by "raising their standard of honor"; they feel that the use of such words as "scurvy" and the like was worse than the original offense; and what might have been their condemnation of this original offense has been diverted by the unfortunate action of the faculty into mere bitter resentment against the faculty. I believe the crew themselves, if properly approached, would have joined with the faculty in taking steps which really would have made it a matter of honor never to permit the repetition of such an offense.

I may add that the only thorogoing defense of the faculty's position which I happen to have heard was from a very large trust magnate, of the kind who thinks that the refusal to have wine on his table offsets sharp practice in business on the largest scale; and I thought it eminently natural that this particular man should take such a purely technical view of the offense, and decline to look at the offense and punishment combined in their larger aspect.

If the telegrams had not been made public, and had been kept purely private, with the rest of the correspondence unknown to the boys, I should not have felt it necessary to write you; but as things are, it may come up in the future, and if so I want my position to be perfectly clear. I do not want to be misunderstood as failing to condemn the conduct of the two boys, or as failing to see that it should be punished; but I do wish it to be understood that I think the punishment was so ill-judged and excessive as to turn the current of sympathy toward the offenders, and to make many undergraduates, and many graduates and outsiders, believe that the faculty was influenced not so much by the desire to punish wrongdoing as by the desire to interfere with athletics; and that the net result of the unfortunate incident has been to do harm rather than good from the standpoint of the inculcation of a proper sense of honor. Perhaps I can make the last point clearer when I say that without exception every man I have spoken to has felt that the conduct of these two boys did not really show that they lacked a fine sense of honor, or would be unfit to trust in business or profession, in private life or in public life; and that at any rate their offense was venial as compared to the offense of their punishment. I believe that many good people, who have little knowledge of college boys of the more vigorous type, approve your action; but I believe it has on the whole done damage to the college boys themselves. I believe the faculty could with much advantage read *Verdant Green*; in that book — not an immoral or criminal book — (and indeed in much higher books, like *Tom Brown at Oxford*) they would find the hero and his friends doing deeds much like those of Fish and Morgan, and yet the author would treat with healthy amusement the idea that the doers were really "scurvy," "dishonorable," and "crooked." Such deeds should be punished; but the punishment defeats its own end if it is of a character that ought to be reserved for offenses that really do show the man to be "scurvy" and "dishonorable." I am continually being confronted with acts of all degrees of wrongdoing; I see, and condemn, and have to punish acts of homicide, of protection of criminals, of theft, of betrayal of trust, and I also have brought before me numbers of offenses about on a level with driving an auto beyond the speed limit and then giving a false name when arrested. I condemn and punish the latter type of offense; but if I punished it, or extravagantly denounced it, as if it came in the former class, I should merely tend to blunt the fine sense of honor so necessary in our life, because such punishment or extravagance of denunciation is itself an offense against the nicest sense of honor — as any man who deals with either army or navy would speedily find out.

Several of the boys have made mention to me of an incident which occurred a few years ago. A Harvard professor — a professor I think of ethics and a doctor of divinity who had formerly been a member of The Pudding, had on The Pudding files a poem or something of the kind, written while he was an undergraduate, and which as a Harvard professor and doctor of divinity he wished he had not written. The Pudding records were kept in a safe deposit company, and they were of course the property of The Pudding. The professor in question obtained access to the records in the safe deposit company and cut out or destroyed the poem or writing in question. Immediately afterwards he went abroad. Now, this was not a defensible act, and in my judgment it was a more serious offense than the action for which Fish and Morgan

have been held up before the country in terms of oppro-
brium, which would not have been much more severe if they
had been boodle aldermen or wreckers of an insurance company. Yet, as far as I am aware, no public action whatever was
taken by the Harvard authorities in this case. I doubt very
much whether it called for any action; certainly, if the professor's course had been publicly stigmatized as "dishonorable,"
"crooked," and "scurvy," or as "theft," then whatever technical justification there might have been for the terms, and however much men of meticulous minds and other thoroly good
men who in this particular matter had lost their sense of proportion, might have applauded the action, I should have
strongly censured it, and should have felt that the original
wrong was far more than offset by the action taken; especially
if the punishment had been so inflicted as to bring into disre-
pute the whole body of professors, and for the time being at
least to remove the professor in question in spite of his otherwise excellent character and record from all connection with
the college. As a matter of justice a similar course should have
been pursued in one case as that pursued in the other, and the
same reasons which have made me feel that it would have been
unjust and improper to go to extremes in denouncing and
punishing the improper act of the Harvard professor makes
me feel that it is unjust, unwise, improper, and harmful to the
student body to have gone to extremes in denouncing and
punishing the admittedly improper act of the two Harvard
students. *Very sincerely yours*

JACK LONDON AND "NATURE FAKERS"

To Mark Sullivan

Personal and Private

Oyster Bay, September 9, 1908

My dear Sullivan:

I have been looking over the last number of *Collier's*, and
sometime or other I wish you and Hapgood could either come
out here to lunch or take lunch with me at the White House,

for I would like to say one or two things in connection with Hapgood's political articles in that number. But in the present letter I want to discuss the article you published by Jack London, and especially the headlines of the article — my position being that of the South Carolina lawyer who, in the dark days shortly after the Civil War, finally protested to a reconstruction judge that he could live under bad law but that he could not live under bad Latin. In the headlines (to this article by Jack London) for which I suppose *Collier's* itself is responsible, he is described as "locating the President in the Ananias Club." Now neither you nor I regard falsehood as a jest, and therefore we neither of us regard an accusation of falsehood as a jest. If that headline were correct, *Collier's* would not be justified in making the effort it did to get me to write for it. Moreover, there is, as far as I am able to see, in Jack London's article not a line in which London says anything on which such a headline could be based. If there is I should be glad to have you point it out to me.

Now as for Jack London himself; and here again I want to speak to *Collier's* rather than to Jack London, altho of course you are perfectly welcome to show him this letter, with the distinct understanding, however, that I am not entering into a controversy with him but with *Collier's*; and that of a purely private, not public, nature. In my Presidential speeches and messages which Collier published, in Volume VI on pages 1333 to 1345, you will find what I said on nature faking and nature fakers, including London, and my concluding words were that my quarrel was not with these nature fakers "but with those who give them their chance" — "who, holding a position which entitles them to respect, yet condone and encourage such untruth." In the first place, read thru this article of mine and anything else that I have written and you will see at once that when London says that I state that animals do not reason, that all animals below man are automatons and perform actions only of two sorts, mechanical and reflex, and that in such actions no reasoning enters at all, and that man is the only animal that is capable of reasoning or ever does reason — when London says this he deliberately invents statements which I have never made and in which I do not believe. As a matter of fact, on this point I disagree with John Burroughs, my points of agreement with John Burroughs being my admiration for his accuracy of observation, and the way he can report his observations, and for his abhorrence of untruth. As a matter of fact, I believe that the higher mammals and birds have reasoning powers, which differ in degree rather than in kind from the lower reasoning powers of, for instance, the lower savages. London's statement as to my attitude on this point — a statement to which you give currency — is wholly without basis; and he cannot find, and nobody else can find, anything that I have written which forms a basis for it.

But this is not his only invention or misstatement. In my article I stated and proved (see page 1325) that London knew nothing whatever about wolves or lynxes; that his story *White Fang* would be excellent if it was avowedly put forth as a fable, but as realism it was nonsense, and mischievous nonsense to boot. I attributed his making misstatements simply to ignorance; but in this article in *Collier's* his misstatements are deliberate. They are not due to ignorance at all. Get his book *White Fang* to which I am about to refer, and open it at the pages I shall mention, comparing them with my article on the page I have given you, and with his article in *Collier's*. In the first place he says that I tried and condemned him because a big fighting bulldog whipped a wolf dog. I did not. I condemned him because his wolf (for the amount of dog in it, or indeed in its mother, is so small that Jack London continually alludes to both as wolves and not wolf dogs) and his bulldog fought in impossible fashion. He describes this huge wolf which kills all other wolves against which it is pitted and all other dogs — a wolf that can hamstring a horse or gut a steer — as ripping and slashing with long tearing strokes a score of times a bulldog a third its size without inflicting any serious injury upon the bulldog. Now this is simply nonsense. Two or three such bites would mean the death of the bulldog. I will make a comparison which will bring it home. It is possible, altho very improbable, that a featherweight professional boxer, or say the champion heavyweight amateur boxer of a college or a theological institute, could knock out Jim Jeffries or John L. Sullivan when they were in full training. But it is not possible that the knockout could take place after Jeffries or Sullivan had a score of times knocked down said featherweight, or amateur heavyweight from a college or theological seminary, with blows striking them full on the point of the chin or over the heart. Such a description of a prize fight would be a purely fake description.

But this is small compared to Mr. London's second offense. He says that I claimed he was guilty of allowing a lynx to kill a wolf dog in a pitched battle, and that this was not true; that he never made such a statement in his story. Now turn to what I wrote on page 1325. What I say is that "London describes a great dog wolf being torn in pieces by a lucivee, a northern lynx." London denies this. Now turn to his book *White Fang*, page 83. He describes the she-wolf following a day-old trail of her mate, the great dog wolf. He goes on — "And she found him, or what remained of him, at the end of the trail. There were many signs of the battle that had been fought, and of the lynx's withdrawal to her lair after having won the victory." Mr. London should take the trouble to read what he himself has written before he again makes a denial of this type. A real nature observer, not a nature faker, James Sheldon, has just passed the winter in northern Alaska, and he caught or shot and weighed various lynxes, practically from the region London is supposed to discuss. The female lynx up there weighs barely twenty pounds; and London describes such an animal as tearing to pieces the huge fighting wolf six or seven times its weight. As a matter of fact, any capable fighting bull terrier would be an overmatch for such a lynx. I do not wonder that London did not like to admit having made such a statement, but I am rather surprised at his having the effrontery to make such a denial in *Collier's*.

Now mind you, I have not the slightest intention of entering into any controversy on this subject with London. I would as soon think of discussing seriously with him any social or political reform. But it does seem to me that *Collier's* should be rather careful about admitting such an article into its columns, and of giving it such a headline as that I have above quoted. *Sincerely yours*

WOMAN SUFFRAGE

To Harriet Taylor Upton

Private

Washington, November 10, 1908

My dear Madam:

I have your letter of the 9th instant. I will give you exactly my feeling about your request that I speak a word for woman suffrage in my annual message. I do not think it would be wise to do so; not in the least because of any consideration about myself, but because I think that it is not in any shape or way a live issue at this time, and because I do not see what good would come of my mentioning it.

Personally I believe in woman's suffrage, but I am not an enthusiastic advocate of it because I do not regard it as a very important matter. I am unable to see that there has been any special improvement in the position of women in those States in the West that have adopted woman suffrage, as compared with those States adjoining them that have not adopted it. I do not think that giving the women suffrage will produce any marked improvement in the condition of women. I do not believe that it will produce any of the evils feared, and I am very certain that when women as a whole take any special interest in the matter they will have the suffrage if they desire it. But at present I think most of them are lukewarm; I find some actively for it, and some actively against it. My two sisters are strongly against it; my wife favors it, but not very strongly. I am, for the reasons above given, rather what you would regard as lukewarm or tepid in my support of it because, while I believe in it, I do not regard it as of very much importance. I believe that man and woman should stand on an equality of right, but I do not believe that equality of right means identity of function; and I am more and more convinced that the great field, the indispensable field, for the usefulness of woman is as the mother of the family. It is her work in the household, in the home, her work in bearing and rearing the children, which is more important than any man's work, and it is that work which should be normally the woman's special work, just as normally the man's work should be that of the bread-winner, the supporter of the home, and if necessary the soldier who will fight for the home. There are exceptions as regards both man and woman; but the full and perfect life, the life of highest happiness and of highest usefulness to the State, is the life of the man and the woman who are husband and wife, who live in the partnership of love and duty, the one earning enough to keep the home, the other managing the home and the children.

I do not desire to go into a public discussion of this matter, so I will be obliged if you will treat this letter as private. *Sincerely yours*

"THESE CREATURES OF THE GUTTER"

To Henry Stimson

Washington, December 9, 1908

My dear Stimson:

I do not know anything about the law of criminal libel, but I should dearly like to have it invoked about Pulitzer, of the *World*. Usually, papers in making charges do not ascribe improper motives of financial interest, but the *World* made the mistake of doing it in this instance. Pulitzer is one of these creatures of the gutter of such unspeakable degradation that to him even eminence on a dunghill seems enviable, and he evidently hopes I will place him there beside Laffan and Delavan Smith. Heaven knows that they occupy a sufficiently low stratum of infamy, but Pulitzer has plumbed depths even lower and I do not wish to put him beside them unless it is necessary; this aside from the fact that when I was Police Commissioner I once for all summed him up by quoting the close of Macaulay's article about Barère as applying to him. But if he can be reached by a proceeding on the part of the Government for criminal libel in connection with his assertions about the Panama Canal, I should like to do it. Would you have his various utterances for the last three or four months on this subject lookt up, and let me know? *Faithfully yours*

To Kaiser William II

Washington, December 26, 1908

My dear Emperor William:

A Happy New Year to Your Majesty! and may prosperity be yours, and your peoples'.

This is merely a letter of good will; now that I am about to leave office, I wish to assure you how much I have appreciated the unvarying friendship you have shown this country during the years that I have been President. The combination of your personality and your position render you the most influential and powerful of living men; and your hearty good will to America has been of real moment to my fellow countrymen.

Well, I should like to have continued as President, if I had felt it right, and in accordance with the best spirit of our traditions, so to do; and, had I wished it, I think I could have continued. But I shall leave the White House with entire satisfaction; for I have achieved more than a fair proportion of the things I set out to achieve; and I have many interests. I am looking forward with eagerness to my year in Africa; if I have fair luck it will be a great adventure. I shall spend a few weeks in Europe on my way back to America, in the spring of 1910. While in Africa I hope to cross the border into German East Africa; but I shall not make definite plans until I am actually on the ground, and can learn at first hand about the game, the character of the season, and the like.

It is very unlikely that I shall ever hold office again. But if — what I most earnestly hope may never occur — there should be a big war in which the United States was engaged, while I am still in bodily vigor, I should endeavor to get permission to raise a division of mounted rifles — cavalry, in our use of the word; that is, nine regiments such as the one I commanded in the war with Spain. I hope the chance may never come, however.

I mourned the death of Speck von Sternberg; you had no more loyal and devoted man under you. I have done what I could to make things easier for the poor Baroness. He and she made the German Embassy, in every relation, social and political, of the first importance, in Washington, and therefore in the whole country.

With all good wishes, and profound regard, I am, *Very faithfully yours*

JOHN HAY AS SECRETARY OF STATE

To Henry Cabot Lodge

Personal

Washington, January 28, 1909

Dear Cabot:

I have been reading the letters of John Hay. There are three or four of the statements he makes which I think will be so understood as to cause a serious misapprehension of the facts, and therefore I write you about them.

Hay was a man of remarkable ability. I think he was the most delightful man to talk to I ever met, for in his conversation he continually made out of hand those delightful epigrammatic remarks which we would all like to make, and which in books many people appear as making, but which in actual life hardly anyone ever does more than think about when it is too late to say them. He was moreover, I think without exception, the best letter-writer of his age; altho the present volume does not give this impression, as it is atrociously edited. His dignity, his remarkable literary ability, his personal charm, and the respect his high character and long service commanded thruout the country, together with his wide acquaintance with foreign statesmen and foreign capitals, made him one of the public servants of real value to the United States. But he was not a great Secretary of State. For instance, he was not to be mentioned in the same breath with Root. He was no administrator. He had a very ease-loving nature and a moral timidity which made him shrink from all that was rough in life, and therefore from practical affairs. He was at his best at a dinner table or in a drawing room, and in neither place have I ever seen anyone's best that was better than his; but his temptation was to associate as far as possible only with men of refined and cultivated tastes, who lived apart from the world of affairs, and who, if Americans, were wholly lacking in robustness of fiber. His close intimacy with Henry James and Henry Adams — charming men, but exceedingly undesirable companions for any man not of strong nature — and the tone of satirical cynicism which they admired, and which he always affected in writing them, marked that phase of his character which so impaired his usefulness as a public man. In public life during the time he was Secretary of State under me he accomplished little. I was personally extremely fond of him. I had a great admiration for his fastidious literary skill, and liked to listen to him; I saw much of him, and found his company a relaxation; but in the Department of State his usefulness to me was almost exclusively the usefulness of a fine figurehead. He never initiated a policy or was of real assistance in carrying thru a policy; but he sometimes phrased what I desired said in a way that was of real service; and the general respect for him was such that his presence in the Cabinet was a strength to the administration. He was always afraid of Senators and Congressmen who possest any power or robustness, this fear being due in part to timidity and nervousness, and in part to a sheer fastidiousness which made him unwilling to face the rather intimate association which is implied in a fight. Accordingly, in actual practice he hardly ever opposed a Senator or Congressman, especially in the matter of patronage, and almost always did, especially in the matter of appointment or promotion, whatever any one of them, even the worst, asked, no matter how bad it might be. The result was thoroly bad for the Department and the service, and it had the further and rather unexpected effect of making Hay himself talk against Senators and Congressmen with extraordinary violence, the Senators being the especial object of his wrath. The very fact that in action in the presence of a Senator he was always feeble, made him try to atone to his own self-respect by being very forcible about him afterwards in speech. He would urge me to make any kind of improper appointment which a Senator desired, and then would relieve his feelings by railing in very bitter and very amusing and well-chosen language against the Senator and all his colleagues; and later still, to outsiders, would wail over, and lament, the appointment, if it happened that I had been misled by him into making it. Of course, much of his attack on the Senate was simply foolish. When he became Secretary of State the Senate contained among its leaders Republicans like Cushman K. Davis, Orville H. Platt, Allison, and Hoar, and Democrats like Cockrell. In character and intellect, these men stood at least level with all but the foremost of the men who have held the Presidency. Cockrell was a Missouri ex-Confederate, entirely fearless, as straight as a string, and a man of single-minded devotion for the public good; he and Allison rendered unwearied and invaluable service in the actual, and indispensable, working out of legislative business. Hoar was a scholar of the loftiest ideals, and ignorant of the meaning of the word fear. Davis was one of the most brilliantly able men I have ever met in public life, and the embodiment of courage and farsighted patriotism; old Orville H. Platt was not as brilliant a man, but he was of fine ability, of entire fearlessness, and of a transparently upright and honorable nature; we should have been fortunate to have either one as President or as Secretary of State. I saw much of all these men. It was a pleasure to work with them, and my association with them always left me with a higher sense of duty and a stronger feeling about my obligations as a public servant. Only the best Presidents, the best Cabinet officers, the highest judges, could be compared with them from the standpoint of service rendered to the public, and of credit and honor conferred by such service upon our public life. To villify in unmeasured terms, utterly without discrimination, a Senate which held these men and which acknowledged them as standing among its leaders, was to occupy a position both foolish and mischievous.

It is distressing to read the letters in which Hay harps on how tired he is of the "sordid wrangles" he lives among; they are not the letters of a strong or brave man. He was dealing with great affairs, he was backed by me in every way. In the Panama business, after the revolution, he did good work, but not as good as Knox and Root. The vital work, getting Panama as an independent Republic, on which all else hinged, was done by me without the aid or advice of anyone, save in so far as they carried out my instructions; and without the knowledge of anyone. But, when once it was done, Hay and Root were invaluable in finishing the business, and Knox also, tho at first he was a little sulky at not having known anything.

I think the most notable error into which an outsider would be led by these letters is concerning the Alaskan Treaty. Hay speaks of this as being in effect purely his own thought and his own work, and claims the result as his. As a matter of fact he had nothing to do with the treaty in any vital matter, his function being simply to phrase the statements which he was told to make; every original proposal he made as regards the treaty was rejected by me, and he in turn made futile objections, which I disregarded, to those things the doing of which brought about the actual result. His original proposal to me was for an arbitration treaty of the usual sort, one or more arbitrators being chosen by each country, and there being an outsider with a casting vote. To this I would not consent; and if I had consented, it would not have obtained a half-dozen votes in the Senate. There was not the slightest justification for the Canadian position, which England had been reluctantly and against her real convictions driven to champion. No American worthy of respect would for one moment have entertained the thought of giving up the territory which the Canadians claimed as being in dispute. To Sir Julian Pauncefote and to Michael Herbert I explained this repeatedly, when they pressed me to go into a treaty in the matter, saying to them not once but again and again that our position was impregnable and that we would no more consent to arbitrate (using the word "arbitrate" in the ordinary accepted sense) than the English would consent to arbitrate the possession of the Orkneys or the Hebrides, and that the utmost I would do would be to agree that representatives of both sides should come together and see if they could not themselves agree on the boundary line. I added that before doing this they must understand how serious the result would be if there was a failure among the men thus appointed to agree, because it would render it necessary for me to reduce to possession the territory in dispute; and as the time for making the agreement approached I actually moved troops up into Alaska so as to be able immediately to take possession of the important disputed points and hold them against small bodies of Canadians in the event that the effort to come to an agreement resulted in nothing. At first Pauncefote and Herbert said that in view of my statement they did not see how we could enter on negotiations. I was much hampered by the fact that Hay had previously and wholly without warrant consented to a *modus vivendi* with Great Britain under which American territory, afterwards admitted to be American territory and at this present moment held as such, was temporarily and improperly put under the British flag. After I had definitely told Hay that there would be no arbitration but simply an agreement of the kind indicated, he at first said, as did the two British Ambassadors, that there was no possibility of getting England to go into such an agreement. Afterwards he came to me and told me that he believed England would consent after all, as she was extremely anxious to have the matter settled. I told him at once to go ahead, and to be sure that Choate, who was then Ambassador, understood my attitude, and realized fully, and made the English realize, that I was simply going into the arrangement so as to let them have an easy way out of an otherwise impossible position, that the men I appointed would never consent to abandon American territory, and that if no agreement were reached I should have to reduce the territory to possession and would under no circumstances consent to an arbitration. When Choate came over in the spring I found that Hay had never made any such statement to him, and, when sitting with me and Hay on the rear portico of the White House, he solemnly told me that in case the two parties failed to agree there would have to be an arbitration. I answered him that he had evidently failed to receive or understand my directions; that he was now to understand absolutely that there would be no arbitration under any circumstances, &c., &c., as I have above stated. Choate immediately veered around, and said he clearly understood my position and would act accordingly. The Senate was extremely reluctant to ratify any treaty which even seemed to admit that there was anything to arbitrate in connection with the Alaskan boundary. The one chance of getting it thru the Senate was to convince the Senators that the men I appointed were men who would at all costs sustain the American contention; while nevertheless it was absolutely necessary to have these men of such high character that their actions could not be doubted nor their motives misconstrued. After a good deal of thought I announced that I should name Root, with you (a Republican Senator), and Turner (a Democratic Senator). The Senate would not have passed the treaty had I not let my intentions be known, or had I not intended to put on you and Turner. Hay strongly objected to both you and Turner, and at first was not satisfied with Root, altho he afterwards became so.

Thus up to this point there was nothing whatever which tended to make the negotiations successful for which he had been responsible. After this point he did nothing at all. The whole work was done by the three commissioners, save that I not only kept Choate up to the mark but also, as you know, wrote to Judge Holmes and to Harry White letters to be shown Chamberlain and Balfour — and which were shown to them — which I think were instrumental in making the British understand that there had to be an agreement with us, that I was not bluffing, and that the consequences would be very serious for them if there was a failure to adopt what was practically our position — for by no possibility could any just judge take any other position. Hay's part in the Alaskan boundary dispute from beginning to end was of far less consequence than that of Root, you and Turner. The letters to Holmes and White run as follows:

Oyster Bay, N.Y.,
July 25, 1903.

My dear Judge Holmes:

I thank you very much for your letter, which I thoroughly enjoyed. There is one point on which I think I ought to give you full information, in view of Chamberlain's remark to you. This is about the Alaska Boundary matter and if you happen to meet Chamberlain again you are entirely at liberty to tell him what I say, although of course it must be privately and unofficially. Nothing but my very earnest desire to get on well with England and my reluctance to come to a break made me consent to the appointment of a Joint Commission in this case; for I regard the attitude of Canada, which England has backed, as having the scantest possible warrant in justice. However, there were but two alternatives. Either I could appoint a commission and give a chance for agreement; or I could do as I shall of course do in case this commission fails, and request Congress to make an appropriation which will enable me to run the boundary on my own hook. As regards most of Great Britain's claim, there is not, in my judgment, enough to warrant so much as a consideration by the United States; and if it were not that there are two or three lesser points on which there is doubt, I could not, even for the object I have mentioned, have consented to appoint a commission. The claim of the Canadians for access to deep water along any part of the Canadian coast is just exactly as indefensible as if they should now suddenly claim the island of Nantucket. There is not a man fit to go on the commission in all the United States who would treat this claim any more respectfully than he would treat a claim to Nantucket. In the same way the preposterous claim once advanced, but I think now abandoned by the Canadians, that the Portland Channel was not the Portland Channel but something else unknown, is no more worth discussing than the claim that the 49th Parallel meant the 50th Parallel or else the 48th.

But there are points which the commission can genuinely consider. There is room for argument about the islands in the mouth of the Portland Channel. I think on this the American case much the stronger of the two. Still, the British have a case. Again, it may well be that there are places in which there is room for doubt as to whether there actually is a chain of mountains parallel to the coast within the ten-league limit. Here again there is a chance for honest difference and honest final agreement. I believe that no three men in the United States could be found who would be more anxious than our own delegates to do justice to the British claim on all points where there is even a color of right on the British side. But the objection raised by certain Canadian authorities to Lodge, Root and Turner, and especially to Lodge and Root, was that they had committed themselves on the general proposition. No man in public life in any position of prominence could have possibly avoided committing himself on the proposition, any more than Mr. Chamberlain could avoid committing himself on the question of the ownership of the Orkneys if some Scandinavian country suddenly claimed them. If this claim embodied other points as to which there was legitimate doubt, I believe Mr. Chamberlain would act fairly and squarely in deciding the matter; but if he appointed a commission to settle up all these questions, I certainly should not expect him to appoint three men, if he could find them, who believed that as to the Orkneys the question was an open one. Similarly, I wish to repeat that no three men fit for the position could be found in all the United States who would not already have come to some conclusion as to certain features of the Canadian claim — not as to all of them.

Let me add that I earnestly hope the English understand my purpose. I wish to make one last effort to bring about an agreement through the commission, which will enable the people of both countries to say that the result represents the feeling of the representatives of both countries. But if there is a disagreement I wish it distinctly understood, not only that there will be no arbitration of the matter, but that in my message to Congress I shall take a position which will prevent any possibility of arbitration hereafter; a position, I am inclined to believe, which will render it necessary for Congress to give me the authority to run the line as we claim it, by our own people, without any further regard to the attitude of England and Canada. If I paid attention to mere abstract right, that is the position I ought to take anyhow. I have not taken it because I wish to exhaust every effort to have the affair settled peacefully and with due regard to England's dignity.

Faithfully yours,

THEODORE ROOSEVELT.

Hon. O. W. Holmes,
   Care J. S. Morgan & Co.,
      London, England.

Oyster Bay, N.Y., September 26, 1903.

My dear White:

Many thanks for your very interesting letter. I was particularly delighted with what you say about the Alaska business. I most earnestly hope that your forecast is true. The Canadians have had some very ugly articles published, which I was afraid might influence English opinion. This would be unfortunate. It would be a bad thing for us if there was a deadlock in the present Commission; but it would be a very much worse thing for the Canadians and English; because it would leave me no alternative but to declare as courteously, but as strongly, as possible that the effort to reach an agreement having failed, I should be obliged to treat the territory as ours, as being for the most part in our possession, and the remainder to be reduced to possession as soon as in our judgment it was advisable — and to declare furthermore that no additional negotiations of any kind would be entered into.

*   *   *   *

Faithfully yours,

THEODORE ROOSEVELT.

Mr. Henry White,
   6 Whitehall Gardens, S.W.,
      London, England.

So in what Hay says of appointments to office. He is continually howling and moaning and complaining about bad men being forced upon him by the Senators, and continually saying that he cannot help himself, that these appointments are made in spite of him. On page 234, writing on October 1, 1901, about an interview with me, he says: "It is also evident I shall have no voice in appointments. The sordid 'necessities of the situation' will control as heretofore. H(errick) is to have R(ome) when M(eyer) resigns. S(torer) is to go to P(aris), if P(orter) gives up." The inference is that these appointments were unfit appointments of the old style. This is not ingenuous on his part, for at the time I explained to him at length what, as a matter of fact, I found he already knew, that I was simply carrying out McKinley's explicit promises in these two cases. Hanna told me when I came in that there were two or three promises that McKinley had made which he must ask me to carry out because McKinley's honor and his were involved in keeping them. They included the promise to Thompson that he should go as Ambassador to Brazil or Mexico, and to Herrick that he should go to Rome (altho Herrick in the end declined the office); and I had also personally promised, on behalf of McKinley and at his explicit direction, both Archbishop Ireland and Storer that Storer should have an embassy as soon as possible, this promise having been made by McKinley, in writing, thru me a few months previously while I was Vice-President. In these matters I simply carried out in good faith McKinley's positive pledges. I never said a word to Hay that would warrant his sneer about the "sordid necessities of the situation." On the contrary, I again and again, and always in vain, asked him to tell me of the fitness or unfitness of any men, for that I would not on any account appoint or retain an unfit man. But he was continually complaining of the bad character of the men put in, and at the same time positively and unequivocally declining, in response to my requests, to put in writing anything against them which would warrant my turning them out. Not only this, but he always deprecated, and strove to prevent my making any move to turn anyone out, no matter how unfit, or refusing to appoint any man, no matter how bad, if backed by strong influence. Here again the trouble was fundamental.

Hay would never stand up against any strong man, whether Senator or other politician. No matter how bad a man was, he would appoint or retain him if a big politician, coarse, robust and powerful, insisted upon it. He would then revenge himself to himself by violently denouncing the Senator and the appointee in private. As I have always endeavored to translate words into action, this conduct on his part very nearly got me into serious scrapes, for again and again, acting on what he said, I would either attack a given Senator or start to turn out a given man, only to find that Hay would not stand to what he said when the pressure came, so that I would be left without justification for my action. I suppose fifty times, when I heard that something was wrong in the consular service, I asked him if certain men were bad; and he always replied that they were. I would then propose to turn them out and he would at once positively refuse to make any complaint against them, leaving me, of course, unable to act, for he was the immediate head, who alone could speak with authority. In excuse, he used always to say that just as bad men would be appointed in their places. I would answer that if so it would be his own fault, as I should absolutely follow his advice. But nothing could be done with him; he would never venture to attack any abuse. Finally I took the matter into my own hands. The situation in China grew intolerable, and as Hay would not act I acted over his head. I sent out Peirce to China, and, paying no heed whatever to Hay, after investigation I removed Williams, McWade and Goodnow, three thoroly bad men who had brought great discredit upon the service, who were backed respectively by the entire Republican organization of New York, Pennsylvania and Minnesota. There was a yell which frightened Hay white. After a short while it died out. I put first-class men in the places of the delinquents, and then proceeded to try to clean out the rest of the service. It would have been quite impossible for me to have done this in really thorogoing and satisfactory fashion while Hay was in, because it was so exceedingly cumbersome to be running the office over his head — which I had to do not only as regards the consular service, but as regards everything else during the last year and a half of his incumbency. But I made a first-class beginning, by curing the evil where it was worst, and at the same time most difficult to cure. As soon as Root came in the situation changed as if by magic. All friction with the Senate ceased, and yet Root never yielded to the improper demands of any Senator, whereas Hay almost always did. Root proceeded immediately to reorganize the consular service, and by a system of investigations, and by securing some legislation and where he could not secure legislation supplying its lack by executive action, in the shape of regulations, he completely eliminated all questions of politics in the appointment of consuls to any but the very lowest grades, and in these grades strictly subordinated favoritism to merit; while in the higher grades nothing but merit was or is considered. I never saw a more remarkable instance of a strong man working a great reform in the presence of the need of which a weaker man had been wholly helpless.

It is pathetic to read Hay's ceaseless jeremiads about the way Senators forced bad appointments, and then to realize that under the same President and the same Senate all the difficulties ceased as soon as Root took charge. As I have said, the abuses became so very bad that before Root took charge I had been myself obliged to go over Hay's head, take the situation in the Far East into my own hands, and weed out the worst offenders.

It is curious also to read what Hay says about certain of the treaties. The first canal treaty was a simple atrocity as he drew it up. It prevented our fortifying the Isthmus, gave us no real control over it, and actually invited the powers of continental Europe to interfere in the matter. The Senate acted with the highest wisdom and patriotism in amending this treaty. The British Government rejected the treaty on account of the amendments. But when I came in the new treaty was promptly ratified by both Governments, and was practically and essentially, altho not altogether in form, what the old treaty had been after the Senate amendments had been adopted.

The fact was that Hay could not be trusted where England was concerned. His letter to Balfour on page 254 shows this. He had been the intimate companion of Lincoln. He was at the time Secretary of State, and had held that position under two President; yet he wrote to Balfour congratulating him

upon having become Prime Minister in a letter in which he stated that the position of Prime Minister was "the most important official post known to modern history." If he really thought the position of Prime Minister more important than that of President, he was foolish; but to give expression to the thought in writing to the English Prime Minister while he was the American Secretary of State was worse than foolish. On the other hand, he was foolishly distrustful of the Germans. Comparatively early in the Russian-Japanese war the Kaiser wrote us proposing a declaration by the powers in favor of the neutrality and integrity of China. This declaration we were extremely anxious to have made. The Kaiser's proposal was in poor form; it was drawn so as to interfere with any possible action by England or France, but not with action by Russia. The obvious thing was to put it in right form and agree to it. Hay actually proposed to reject it, and brought me around a draft of a note rejecting it. I told him that of course we could never justify ourselves in such a position, but on the contrary we must accept the proposal at once, and in our acceptance ignore the limitations the Kaiser set and announce our cordial adherence to his proposal in words that would commit him to a guarantee of the neutrality and integrity of the entire Chinese Empire. This was accordingly done, and the result was of far-reaching importance. Poor Hay was a sick man, however, by the time the Russian-Japanese war began, and I had ceased being able to pass matters to him. I did not consult him at all in any of the movements that led to the peace of Portsmouth; everything about this was concluded between the time that Hay died and that Root took office; while Taft was in the Philippines. In most matters I have always consulted Root and Taft if I could get at them; rarely did I consult Hay. The biggest matters however, such as the Portsmouth peace, the acquisition of Panama, and sending the fleet round the world, I managed without consultation with anyone; for when a matter is of capital importance, it is well to have it handled by one man only. In dealing with the Japanese situation at every stage I outlined and directed what was to be done; Root however rendered me thruout literally invaluable service, of a kind Hay would have been utterly helpless to render.
Ever yours

FORMER PRESIDENT
1909–1919

To Anna Roosevelt Cowles

Juja Farm, May 19, 1909

Darling Bye:

Here I am absolutely contented, except, of course, that I am dreadfully homesick for Edie; and I hardly know a thing which is going on in the outer world. The hunt has been very successful, so far. Our joint bag includes Lion, Leopard, Hyena, Rhino, Hippo, Giraffe, Eland, Zebra, Waterhog, and various kinds of Antelope. The three Naturalists are splendid fellows; we are really fond of them and they are doing great work. We have been in the settled country, and have had no hardships. Indeed, so far, African traveling has proved rather luxurious than otherwise, for I go on horseback, having two horses; each with its syce; and there are two tent boys who represent an even nearer approach to a valet than good Mary at home. We stayed some time at the ranch of Sir Alfred Pease, who is a perfect trump, and now, we are staying at the really beautiful and comfortable farm of Mr. and Mrs. McMillan: you know all their McMillan cousins, well. They are more than kind and hospitable and our lives are fairly luxurious. What queer contrasts the life affords! After returning from hunting today, I am sitting on the cool veranda of a very nice house with a beautiful garden around it. The three native gardeners working in it are savages, their ears slit and stretched in such fantastic shapes that they can put all kinds of bright objects in the lobes, and one of them, actually, at this moment, is carrying a tin can thrust through his ear lobe: they have blankets, but as they wear nothing else whatever, excepting brass bracelets, and frequently put their blankets around their necks or heads, where they are but a slight addition to decorum.

I have been as well as possible, and so has Kermit. Tell Will that I am really proud of Kermit. He is not a good shot but he is an excellent horseman and walker, and is exceedingly cool and daring. Two days ago he killed a Leopard which charged him twice, but he stopped it each time: it got, and mauled, one of our beaters. I am not a good shot either, but I have bagged a good deal of game during the past two weeks, far more than I had any idea, on coming out, of there being any possibility of getting. Give my love to Sheffield and to old Will. *Your Loving Brother*

"PUSHING DARING INTO RECKLESSNESS"
To Corinne Roosevelt Robinson

On Safari, June 21, 1909

Darling Corinne,

Gradually Kermit's and my rifles have tended to get ahead of the taxed resources of the naturalists. Finally three rhinoceroses, together with half a dozen buck of sorts, in three days, proved too much for them; and today we are not shoot anything (having tried in vain this morning for a lion which at dawn roared quarter of a mile from camp). So I take advantage of the unusual leisure to write home; ordinarily I have to put in any time I have for writing with my Scribner's articles. — of course excepting the letters to Edie. I have had plenty to write about for Scribner's, but it is not always easy to write in the field, and I do'n't know how I have done. Sometimes, when I come in early from a hunt, I just point blank refuse to write atall, and spend an hour or two reading a book from the "pigskin library," which has been the utmost possible comfort and pleasure. Fond tho I am of hunting and of wilderness life I could not thoroly enjoy either if I were not able from time to time to turn to my books.

I have no idea where you and Douglas are; I hope on your trip round the world. I am anxiously looking forward to news about Helen, and the baby-that-is-to-be.

Kermit is a great pleasure to me, and of course often a cause of much concern. Do you remember how timid he used to be? Well, my trouble with him now is that he is altogether too bold, pushing daring into recklessness. He is an excellent rider, and very enduring; but he is not yet a good shot (altho rapidly improving) and he has little *strength*, as distinguished from hardihood. He killed a big lion the other day, under circumstances that might well have entailed an accident. Yesterday he and I walked up to a large rhino, on a plain as bare as a billiard table, and killed it when fifty yards off; he was as cool as if it had been a rabbit, and shot well. But this kind of shooting necessarily entails some danger, and it is very difficult to make him realize this, in spite of the graves we see of the men who have been killed by lions, rhinos, &c, and the living men we meet who have been maimed, or crippled for life.

Darling Corinne, I hope that time will lighten your heavy burden of sorrow. Give my warmest love to dear old Douglas. *Ever your devoted brother*

DISAPPOINTMENT WITH TAFT

To Henry White

Lake Naivasha, July 21, 1909

Dear White:

This letter must be personal, for the last thing I must do is in any way to criticize my successor. But if as I hear to be the case you are to be displaced, I wish you to know that everything I could do was done on your behalf, not because of my affection for you, great though that is, but because as I told Taft I regard you as without exception the very best man in our diplomatic service. I told Taft that I had no personal request whatever to make of him, but there were certain men whose qualifications for the public service were of so high an order that I felt I ought to dwell on them, and that conspicuous among these was yourself. To me as well as to Cabot Lodge he said without any qualification that he intended to keep you. It was, of course, not a promise any more than my statement that I would not run again for President was a promise. But it was an expression of intention which I was at entire liberty to repeat. I feel that your loss will be very greatly felt, and I am sure that you will come back into the diplomatic service in the end.

Give my love to Mrs. White, and tell Jack how pleased I am whenever I think of the way he has gone to work. Remember me warmly to your daughter. I know you will be glad to hear that Kermit has really done very well, and we have had a most successful trip. *Always yours*

"A COLLECTION OF LARGE MAMMALS"

To Charles Doolittle Walcott

Lake Naivasha, July 23, 1909

My dear Dr. Walcott:

Your telegram about the deposit of the ten thousand dollars came as a great relief. We can now go on till the first of October. By the first of October we ought to have all the money, twenty thousand dollars, deposited in the bank, as it is out of the question to prepare for the Uganda and Enclave trip without at least six weeks' warning, and it is possible we may wish to start by November 15th. But now I am happy to say that if you found you could give no more money, the results of the trip would still be satisfactory. Mearns and Loring have collected thousands of birds and small mammals, reptiles and so forth, not to speak of plants; and by October 1st, they will have thoroughly worked the Kenya region. Meanwhile, Heller has secured for you, and by August will have shipped to you, a collection of large mammals such as has never been obtained for any other museum in the world on a single trip. We have for instance a group of thirteen lions, which possibly may be reduced to ten because, as I told you, I may want one or two trophies for myself. We have a group of six giraffe, one of three or four buffalo, five rhinoceros in addition to skeletons, four hippos in addition to skulls and skeletons, and similar groups of Zebra, wildebeest, spotted hyena, striped hyena, cheetah, leopard, wart hog, hartebeest, topi, impala, waterbuck, Singsing waterbuck (single individual), Grant's gazelle including the variety Robert's Gazelle, Thompson's gazelle, reedbuck, steinbuck, duyker, diddik, clipspringer, baboon, and so forth. In the next two months, I shall try for elephant, but I am not very hopeful of getting them until we reach Uganda. If we do, however, get them prior to October 1st, then even if you find no more money can be sent, the trip will be a thorough success from the National Museum standpoint. But the great prize of the trip from the zoological standpoint, will be the white rhinoceros from the Lado Enclave country, and I earnestly hope that if nothing else could be done, you would arrange enough money to have Heller go with me. This would give you the elephant and white rhino groups, always provided that we have luck. However, I do hope that you will be able to arrange to continue the trip to Khartoum, for Loring and Mearns would do literally invaluable work in Uganda and the Enclave, and down the Nile Valley.

I shall give Mearns all the bills of Newland, Tarlton & Co., and the Safari generally, so that they can be submitted to you and to Mr. Carnegie, if Mr. Carnegie is furnishing the added funds. This is necessarily an expensive trip, but I believe that so far it has also been a trip unique in its scope and its success. *Sincerely yours*

MACAULAY AND CARLYLE

To George Otto Trevelyan

Mount Kenya, September 10, 1909

My dear Trevelyan:

No ex-President, and no ex-Prime Minister, for that matter, ever enjoyed six months as I have enjoyed the six months now ending. We have had great sport with the noblest game in all the world; the country is fascinating; and it is most interesting to see, and admire, your government officials at work — while your settlers, especially those from South Africa or Australia, are in all essentials just like my own beloved westerners.

I always take in my saddle pocket some volume (I am too old now to be satisfied merely with a hunter's life), and among the most worn are the volumes of Macaulay. Upon my word, the more often I read him, whether the History or the Essays, the greater my admiration becomes. I read him primarily for pleasure, as I do all books; but I get any amount of profit from him, incidentally. Of all the authors I know I believe I should first choose him as the man whose writings will most help a man of action who desires to be both efficient and decent, to keep straight and yet be of some account in the world. I have also been reading Carlyle; and the more I read him the more hearty grows my contempt for his profound untruthfulness and for his shrieking deification of shams. What a contrast he offers to that real and great historian, your uncle! If only Carlyle were alive how I would like to review his Frederick the Great with the same freedom of epithet which he practised! and with all the sincerity and truthfulness to which he paid such lip worship, and in the practice of which he so wholly failed. Some of his writing is really fine; his battles for instance; but a far more truthful idea of the real Frederick can be gained from Macaulay's concise and brilliant essay, than from Carlyle's five long, brilliant and utterly disingenuous volumes. What I can't stand is his hypocrisy; his everlasting praise of veracity, accompanying the constant practise of every species of mendacity in order to give a false color to history and a false twist to ethics. He actually reprobates, with sanctimonious piety, the French for doing wrong much less than that which he imputes to Frederick for righteousness. When he speaks of his hero — indeed of any of his heroes — he always uses morality as a synonym for ruthless efficiency, and sincerity as a synonym for shameless lack of scruple; but in dealing with people who he does not like, the words at once revert to their ordinary uses, and he himself appears as the sternest rebuker of evil and treachery; whereas your uncle was a great teacher of uprightness and sound principle joined with that common sense the lack of which makes morality a mere balloon on the winds of chance.

The porters are just bringing in to camp the skin and tusks of a bull elephant I killed three days ago, and Kermit got another yesterday. We have killed 17 lions between us.

GRIEF

To Anna Roosevelt Cowles

En route Nairobi, October 17, 1909

Darling Bye,

I have just received a month's mail, including two letters from you. I was of course inexpressibly shocked and grieved by Bay's death. Poor Nannie and Cabot! I wish I were at least on the same side of the water with them; I would be a little comfort to Cabot, and I would just refuse to let Nannie be forced to see me. As for darling Corinne, it is a perpetual heartbreak. She wrote me a dear letter; but evidently she is still unable to face or overcome her grief. I hardly knew how to write her in return; nothing I could say would *comfort* her; and as yet it hardly seemed that the time had come when anything I could say would *strengthen* her. If I were about to die, I should be sorry not to feel that those I loved would mourn me; but I should be still more sorry to feel that they would be broken and beaten down by grief, and would not in every way strive to enjoy, and make the most of, life. Cherish tenderly the memories of the dead; but all that can be done for anyone must be done while he or she is living; grief in no way helps the dead; and tho one never gets over such grief, yet at least we can recognize that overindulgence in it is wrong. In Corinne's case her extraordinary unselfishness and constant thought for others have borne her through the bitter months when she simply *could* not for her own sake conquer her sorrow; now I hope that the voyage, and time, and all her many interests, will help her. But, normally, we may as well make up our minds that as we grow old blows will fall upon us; in their last years, this is the lot of all but a very few; and while it is foolish to pretend not to mind the blows, it is best to bear them bravely.

Our trip continues to be successful. Kermit has been off by himself with Tarlton for practically two months; he is now a better hunter than I am, for Twenty is hardier and more active and endowed with better eyes than Fifty One. I hope that in my articles I have been able measurably to reproduce what we have seen, and the wonder and charm of the life. In mid-December we leave East Africa, for Uganda and the Nile, and then our time of discomfort and trouble begins.

Give my love to blessed Quentin. I am always interested to hear what Will is doing. *Your loving brother*

That Peary reached the pole I am sure; whether or not Cook did I can't say, for Cook, though a capable man, is a fake.

"THIS CAULDRON OF POLITICS"

To Henry Cabot Lodge

Christiania, May 5, 1910

Dear Cabot:

With your note yesterday came the enclosed from Ward. In the sea of foolish correspondence I get, it struck me that this letter contained some sound common sense. I agree with you that the outlook is black.

As for your affairs, I am confident that we can pull the thing through all right. Massachusetts is a very sound State. Of course you will have to contend with the entirely preposterous tendency in a part of the public mind to identify you with the leaders in Congress whom, sometimes justly and sometimes unjustly, they dislike and hold accountable for what has gone wrong. But I think we can get the matter into proper shape. I am very glad you are to be at Oyster Bay immediately after my arrival in America. I wish to avoid making any public statement at all for two months after reaching America. I want to find just what the situation is, what I can accomplish, and how I had best set about accomplishing it. It seems to me that Taft, Cannon, Aldrich and the others have totally misestimated the character of the movement which we now have to face in American life. I am not at the moment striving to apportion praise or blame, either among the leaders or as between the leaders and the people, but it does seem to me that the fact itself must be faced, whatever explanations we can give, or remedies we can advance. For a year after Taft took office, for a year and a quarter after he had been elected, I would not let myself think ill of anything he did. I finally had to admit that he had gone wrong on certain points; and I then also had to admit to myself that deep down underneath I had all along known he was wrong, on points as to which I had tried to deceive myself, by loudly proclaiming to myself, that he was right. I went out of the country and gave him the fullest possible chance to work out his own salvation. On the other hand, remember that there are a great multitude of men inclined to hold me to sharp account for Taft's nomination, who are willing to forgive me on the ground that I was deceived, as they were, but who would not forgive me if I now went ahead, as they would regard it, to continue the deception. By the way, Hughes' nomination is excellent, and I think he will make a fine judge. I only hope that he has awakened to the fact that unless we are content to face disaster to the judiciary in the future, there must be a very radical change in the attitude of our judges to public questions. I verily believe that the conduct of the bench, in failing to move with the times, and in continually sticking on minor points of the law rather than turning to broad principles of justice and equity, is one of the chief elements in producing the present popular discontent. I do hope Hughes will realize this.

Ugh! I do dread getting back to America, and having to plunge into this cauldron of politics. Our own party leaders did not realize that I was able to hold the Republican party in power only because I insisted on a steady advance, and dragged them along with me. Now the advance has been stopped, and whether we blame the people on the one side, or the leaders on the other, the fact remains that we are in a very uncomfortable position. I do not attach any real importance to the seeming popularity which I for the moment enjoy. I don't see how it can work out for permanent good, and, as you know, I care nothing whatever for popularity, excepting as a means to an end. Of course I like to have the good-will and respect of those for whom I care, but wide popular acclaim, it seems to me, counts for almost nothing unless it can be turned to good tangible account, in the way of getting substantial advance along the lines of clean and wise government. I have never cared in the least for the kind of popularity which Lafayette so thoroughly enjoyed, and which Jefferson enjoyed, popularity which the popular man basks in for and of itself, without reference to transmuting it into any positive achievement. I want to accomplish things. Now I don't for a moment believe that popularity of the kind that at the moment I seem to enjoy will avail when there is a tide of bitter popular feeling against a party or an organization. I may be mistaken, but this is my present view.

I have no time to tell you of the really extraordinary reception that has been given me here. I have been somewhat puzzled by it. The various sovereigns have vied with one another in entertaining us. When we reached Denmark we stayed at the Palace; we are staying at the Palace here in Christiania; and shall do the same in Stockholm and Berlin. The popular reception, however, has been even more remarkable. I drive through dense throngs of people cheering and calling, exactly as if I were President and visiting cities at home where there was great enthusiasm for me. As I say, I have been much puzzled by it. It is largely because, and perhaps almost exclusively because I am a former President of the American Republic, which stands to the average European as a queer attractive dream, being sometimes regarded as a golden Utopia partially realized, and sometimes as a field for wild adventure of a by no means necessarily moral type — in fact a kind of mixture of Bacon's Utopia and Raleigh's Spanish Main. In addition, there is, I think, a certain amount to be credited to me personally, as a man who has appealed to their imaginations, who is accepted by them as a leader, but as a leader whom they suppose to represent democracy, liberty, honesty and justice. The diplomats are perfectly paralyzed, both at the enormous popular demonstrations, and at our being asked to stay in the royal palaces, something hitherto unheard of in the case of any but actual sovereigns. It is all interesting, and at times amusing, but it is very fatiguing and irksome, and much though I dread having to get into the confusion of American politics again, I long inexpressibly to be back at Sagamore Hill, in my own house, with my own books, and among my own friends.

I shall have any amount to tell you and Nannie. *Ever yours*

AN ASSESSMENT OF TAFT

To Gifford Pinchot

Cambridge, June 28, 1910

Dear Gifford:

It is very fortunate that we declined to let the Roosevelt Club do more than furnish a bodyguard. You probably saw the trouble that Halbert caused at the Republican Convention, and as so often happens in the case of an indiscreet and officious friend, he did damage by putting the Convention, much against its will, in such a position that outsiders who dislike me could say that it had been hostile to me, instead of merely being hostile to Halbert.

I read your speech carefully. I agree with you that it was chiefly Halbert's indiscretion that caused the speech itself to be here and there misconstrued. Yet, my dear Gifford, I also feel that in the remarkable, indeed unique, position that you have, it is wise to husband your influence, to speak with the utmost caution, and not to say anything that can even be twisted into something in the nature of a factional attack. Your enemies are hoping and praying for anything in the nature of an indiscretion on your part, and I want you to disappoint them. Moreover, Gifford, while I very keenly share your disappointment in Taft, and in a way perhaps feel it even more deeply than you do, because it was I who made him President, yet it behooves us to realize that it is not only possible, but probable, that two years hence circumstances will be such as make it necessary to renominate Taft, and eminently desirable to re-elect him over anyone whom there is the least likelihood of the Democrats naming. Such being the case, I do hope you won't take any position which would render it impossible, or even merely exceedingly difficult, for you to support him if necessary. He has not proved a good leader, in spite of his having been a good first lieutenant; but neither you nor I can allow any personal disappointment or any chagrin at the failure of our hopes to lead us to take any position save that which we regard as demanded by the interests of the country. You and I and Jim must all three do only, and at all costs, what we feel will satisfy the country's need. Now again and again in the past, all of us have had to support Presidents, Governors and other candidates for high office, not because we thought them ideally the best men for the positions, or anywhere near what they ought to have been, but merely because as circumstances actually were, they were the only men who could be nominated, and it was better for the country to have them elected than to see their opponents succeed. As you know, my judgment is that in all probability Taft has passed his nadir. He is evidently a man who takes color from his surroundings. He was an excellent man under me, and close to me. For eighteen months after his election he was a rather pitiful failure, because he had no real strong man on whom to lean, and yielded to the advice of his wife, his brother Charley, the different corporation lawyers who had his ear, and various similar men. But the signs now are that these advisers have themselves awakened up to the fact that they have almost ruined him. He has been given by them a first-class private secretary, and apparently Wickersham, and some at least of his friends, are bent upon his trying to redeem the past. I think that he will take his color from them as readily when they try to make him go right, as he did when they tried to make him go wrong. Moreover, I think that he has learned some bitter lessons, and that independently of outside pressure he will try to act with greater firmness, and to look at things more from the standpoint of the interests of the people, and less from the standpoint of a technical lawyer, whose interests outside of technical law are chiefly vapid ease and vapid amusement. If what I thus forecast comes to pass, he may and probably will turn out a perfectly respectable President, whose achievements will be disheartening compared with what we had expected, but who nevertheless will have done well enough to justify us in renominating him — for you must remember that not to renominate him would be a very serious thing, only to be justified by really strong reasons. If such should be the case, we will have to turn in and do all we can to try to re-elect him, simply because it will be on the whole the best thing for the country.

Incidentally I may add that from my own standpoint this is eminently desirable, as otherwise I could see very ugly times ahead for me, as I should certainly not be nominated unless everybody believed that the ship was sinking and thought it a good thing to have me aboard her when she went down. However, I am not asking you to consider my personal preferences, but the probable interests of the people as a whole; for this is far too important a matter for us to be in any way influenced by personal feeling. If you care to, you can show this letter to Jim, but of course to no one else. *Ever yours*

"WORDS WITH ME ARE INSTRUMENTS"

To Sydney Brooks

New York, October 17, 1910

Dear Mr. Brooks:

I don't know when I laughed more than over your description of my unintentionally puzzling the good Buckle by what I said about Johnson and Jeffries. Well, it is a needed lesson, but surely I ought to have known better than to try to jest in my own mental vernacular with a stranger from another land. However, I am extremely glad that you told me about it.

Now about your article. I liked it. There is, however, one mistake which I think furnishes a clue to some of your misunderstanding as to the Insurgents and Taft. The legislation put through at the end of the session represented for the most part bills which bore the titles of those recommended by the President, but which the Insurgents had succeeded in amending so that they were directly the reverse of those which were recommended by him in some most important particulars. These amendments were secured in spite of his opposition, an opposition which on the part of members of his cabinet was so bitter as to take the form of threats against the Insurgents who tried to amend them, and who succeeded in amending them. Under such circumstances, the Insurgents feel no real gratitude to Taft. The trouble has been that in this formative period the majority of the Republicans have wished to go forward, and the large minority to hang back. They would have followed a leadership that went moderately forward, but they came to the belief that Mr. Taft really wished to go backward; and as always happens in such a case, the men who desired to go forward, finding they were without any leader, went forward in every direction, some too far, some not far enough, some to one side and some to another.

Moreover, you utterly misestimate and misunderstand my position. If I had come out squarely for the tariff and the Administration, I should have done very little good to Mr. Taft, and I should have utterly ruined my power for use with the people. They would have thought I was either insincere, or else had turned a complete somersault, from wholly inexplicable motives. Every man's influence is within certain limits, and outside of these limits he has little or none. In the case of some men, the limits are much further apart than in the case of others; but they are always there. Lincoln had tremendous influence with the American people, but if he had tried to abolish slavery in 1861, or if he had been against its abolition in 1864, he would have utterly lost all hold upon the people. He would only work within the limits allotted.

Another thing. As to my platitudes: remember that most of these platitudes are not really words, but deeds, for they deal with specific cases. For instance, what I said about mob violence and being against poor men when they were wrong, and upon the need for order being imperative — all this was said to an audience composed in large part of the mob I was denouncing, and in answer to appeals to me to befriend the poor man, and not support an iniquitous corporation in a strike. For two months there had been a reign of terror in Columbus. The Governor and the Mayor had failed to act as they should have acted. I went there. I made an address filled with platitudes of the most direct *ad hominem* type, pointing at the leaders of the strike and their counsel, who were but thirty feet away from me; and my platitudes resulted in the restoration of order and the stoppage of violence within twenty-four hours.

So with what I said about corporations. I was dealing with the case of big corporations who were trying to get control of the water powers in Colorado, for instance, and by the platitudes I put an instant stop to the proceeding. In other words, my dear Brooks, words with me are instruments. I wish to impress upon the people to whom I talk the fact that I am sincere, that I mean exactly what I say, and that I stand for the things that are elemental in civilization. In order to succeed, I must use arguments that appeal to plain rugged men, who are not subtle and who would simply be puzzled and repelled by what would strike our friends of the London *Nation* as "originality" and "distinction." When I was in Cuba with my regiment, I over and over again in the fighting told the men to aim low, to be cool, to shoot straight, to remember to press and not pull their triggers, to think what distance the sight should be put up to etc., — all of these are platitudes from the rifleman's standpoint but in that fighting, and at that time, it was necessary to utter them. I am not trying to be subtle or original; I am trying to make the plain everyday citizen here in America stand for the things which I regard as essential to good government.

We are in an awful fight. Of course I would not say this in public, but privately, in New York, I think we shall be beaten, because the general drift is against us, and the animosity of Wall Street has become a positive mania, so that we are now witnessing a revival of the always frequent alliance between Blifil and Black George. Wall Street has struck hands with Tammany Hall, and is heartily supporting the Tammany Hall ticket. Meanwhile, my Western progressives think I am too conservative, and have not gone far enough, while Wall Street regards me as an Anarchist. The New York papers describe me as a Socialist, and the Socialist mayor of Milwaukee refuses to meet me because he says he has been deeply hurt by the tone of my articles on Socialism. *Faithfully yours*

CRITICIZING A JUDICIAL DECISION

To Simeon Eben Baldwin

Baltimore, Maryland, November 2, 1910

Dear Sir:

I have received your letter of October 31st. As I told you in my first letter, the sentence of mine to which you refer was not correctly reported, consisting of two sentences which have been put into one. The first sentence, namely, "The Democratic Party of Connecticut has nominated for Governor a man who, while judge, occupied the most retrogressive possible position on this question of workmen's compensation," is substantially correct. The next sentence is not given as I said it, nor was it said as part of the first sentence; indeed, as you first quoted it, it was nearer right, to the extent of having in it the word "grind," which was part of the phrase I had used "by grinding need," a phrase which is totally absent from the sentence you quote. But the sentence is wholly incomplete and inaccurate. The sentence as I actually said it opened with the use of the word "Progressives" or "Progressive" as an antithesis to "retrogressive," and contained a statement of our emphatic dissent from the position which I described in somewhat the language quoted, but not in the language quoted.

But my criticisms of you are set forth clearly in my second letter. In your answer to my letter, you entirely miss the point of the criticisms. I am not interested in your opinion as a law writer. I am interested in your opinion as a judge. My criticism of you as a reactionary was based, not upon what you may have said as a law writer, but upon what you did as a judge. Your long citations from decisions in courts of Connecticut are entirely irrelevant and beside the point. I know, as every layman knows, that it is not a function of a judge to make new laws. When there is no statute enacted by the lawmaking bodies of the people, the courts are no doubt bound to follow precedent. The question between us does not involve any such principle. In the Hoxie case you had before you a definite statute enacted by the Congress of the United States, declaring the responsibility of railroads to their employees for negligence. Section 5 of that act provided "That any contract, rule, regulation or device whatsoever, the purpose or intent of which shall be to enable any common carrier to exempt itself from any liability created by this act, shall to that extent be void." In that act, Congress declared that railway employees should have certain new legal rights of compensation for injuries occasioned by the negligence of the railroad itself. In placing this clause which I have quoted in the act, Congress was no doubt influenced by the well-known fact that in England an Employers' Liability Act enacted many years ago was

made a dead letter by employers insisting that their employees should sign contracts agreeing to waive the benefits of the statute and go without the legal rights which the statute proposed to give them. Congress doubtless intended that the beneficial value of this Federal Employers' Liability Act should not be destroyed by any such process. In the case decided by you which I have criticized, Hoxie *V*. N.H. Road, you declared that this clause was unconstitutional as being "in violation of the Fifth Amendment of the Constitution of the United States as tending to deprive the parties to such a contract of liberty and property without due process of law." You say specifically as to railway employees: "It denies them, one and all, that liberty of contract which the Constitution of the United States secures to every person within its jurisdiction."
Your declaration speaks for itself: in substance it amounts to stating that the employees' right to *give up* their rights under the law is a thing to be protected and not their right to *receive* those benefits, that the right to contract to get killed is "property" of which they cannot be deprived, that the right to get killed comes under the head of "life, liberty, and property" which the 5th Amendment to the United States Constitution says cannot be taken away without due process of law. Congress aimed at giving the railroad employee a substance. You construed the act as giving him a shadow by solemnly declaring that to give him the substance is to take away his property in the shadow.

I criticized your decision because it is to me an incredible perversion of the Constitution of the United States. I criticized it because it is not only reactionary but revolutionary. I criticized it because I am against Socialism, and this decision and every decision like it makes for Socialism, or something worse. Every strained construction of the Constitution which declares that the nation is powerless to remedy industrial conditions which cry for law gives aid to these enemies of our American system of government who wish to furnish in its place some new, vague and foolish substitute.

The result which you attempted to accomplish in this decision would produce, I am told, a strange anomaly. The United States Supreme Court has held that public policy *will not permit* a railroad company to make contracts with shippers of freight, that the railroad company shall not be responsible for its own negligence in transporting that freight. You say that the railroad *cannot be forbidden* to contract with its employees that it shall not be responsible for maiming or killing them by negligence. I protest that there is no public policy which makes freight more important than human lives and I criticized your decision, because you say that the Constitution will not permit protection of the lives of railway employees to the same extent to which, without a statute, freight is in the United States Courts protected now. My criticism is not as some of your supporters endeavor to have the people believe, a criticism of the judiciary in general. It is simply and solely a criticism of you for having given an extraordinary and unprecedented construction to the Fifth Amendment of the Constitution of the United States, so as to pervert its purpose and by so doing to nullify and destroy an essential part of a most important federal statute.

The platform on which you are seeking election for Governor in Connecticut promises an Employers' Liability Act. How can there be an Employers' Liability Act in Connecticut which will be of value to the employee if he can be compelled to contract to waive the benefits of that act through his necessities? Your answer to this need not be made to me. It is an explanation to which the working people of Connecticut are entitled. By your decision as judge you have declared the powerlessness of the State to enact an effective law on a subject which requires effective law. I regard your decision as reactionary in a matter of vital concern to all laboring men. I do not think it possible for you to explain how, as Governor, you would obviate the effect of your decision as judge.

You say you are running upon a platform favoring compensation legislation. The objections made by you in the Hoxie case would obviously nullify, as to a very large number of working people, any such compensation legislation. If your opinion in the Hoxie case is good law, no compensation law for those who need it most is possible, because there would still remain the freedom of contract of the employer to establish the terms and conditions by private bargaining as a constitutional right which you say cannot be invaded by legislation, a freedom which would enable him to contract with employees

constrained by their necessities to accept his terms and give
up the benefit of the statute to gain employment — a freedom
which the just employer does not ask and which the unjust
employer should not have. Either the Hoxie case is not good
law, or a false hope is being held out by the platform on which
you are a candidate.

You have further declared in this decision that the Connecticut courts have the right to refuse to recognize or enforce
a federal statute creating rights in favor of crippled railway employees. On this question I have nothing to say. I refer you,
however, to the decision of the Supreme Court of Iowa, filed
only a week ago, in the case of Bradbury v. Chicago Rock
Island and Pacific Railway Company. This explicitly cites the
Hoxie case and explicitly disagrees with it, pointing out that
even the comity which is granted by our courts generally to
courts of foreign nations, has in the Hoxie case been refused
to the laws of the United States in the courts of Connecticut.
You would doubtless urge that you had been bound by precedent in reaching your conclusion in this regard. I am confining myself, and have confined myself, in my criticism of you
to matters which involve no question of judicial precedent,
but to an unprecedented and extraordinary construction by
you of the Constitution of the United States.

It seems to me clear, from the language you used in the
Hoxie case, that you regarded the whole compensation theory
as enacted by Congress in the interests of workingmen as
being unjust. At any rate, I do not know what other construction can be placed upon your denying workingmen the
right to recover under the federal law, denying this right,
among other reasons, upon the expressed ground that the federal statute "would also compel courts established by a sovereign power, and maintained at its expense for the enforcement
of what it deemed justice, *to enforce what it deemed injustice.*"
In this opinion of yours, the importance of the maintenance
and permanence of rules of practice and procedure was enlarged upon. The property right of the carrier was given its
due importance. But not a line appears which can be distorted
into the slightest recognition of the right to life and limb of
the employee, into the slightest recognition of the grave perils
of the men engaged in railway work; not a word appears in

the whole opinion as to the grave importance of the question from the point of view of the thousands of railroad men annually killed, and hundreds of thousands annually injured in their dangerous calling. *Yours truly*

PROTECTIVE COLORATION

To Charles Atwood Kofoid

New York, February 2, 1911

My dear Mr. Kofoid:

I have read Mr. Tracy's pamphlet with great interest. He seems to me to have made his case very clear. (I am not certain about "sky pattern." My experience is that colors show almost as conspicuously against the sky as against any other background. A white gull or pigeon is quite visible against the sky.) There is one point, however, which I would like to suggest to you and to him. This is where he speaks of the dark colors of the crows, saying that such coloration "can exist largely because of their size and aggressiveness and therefore of their immunity from raptatorial birds," and added that seed-eating birds of delicate flesh and harmless disposition could not have developed black plumage like that of the raven, because they would have become extinct for lack of protective coloration. Now it seems to me that this is negatived by the fact that cow buntings are numerous. Indeed, I might go further and say that the abundance of purple and rusty grackles, yellow-headed grackles and red-winged blackbirds, not to speak of bobolinks, is proof to the contrary. With some of these birds, the black plumage only exists in the male during the breeding season; but the grackles are always quite as conspicuous except in point of size as are ravens, and the cow buntings which are very plentiful are almost as conspicuous — the cocks quite as much, and the hens not *much* less. From my piazza here in the Summer I can watch close by both grasshopper sparrows and cow buntings. The grasshopper sparrows behave just as Mr. Tracy describes. They try to hide, and I have not a doubt that their coloration has a concealing or protective value both when they crouch and when they skulk through the grass. But the cow buntings, as they stalk over the grass, make not the slightest effort to hide, and they are just as conspicuous as little crows or ravens would be. Their coloration has not the smallest protective or concealing quality. They are not big; they are not aggressive; their flesh is delicate; and yet they are very common, and are striking examples of an instance where the concealing coloration theory completely breaks down.

In my criticisms of Mr. Thayer's article, I have been very careful not to criticize the general theory of concealing or protective coloration. That it applies in multitudes of cases, I have no question. There are multitudes of other cases where I do not think that, as yet, we are able to say with definiteness one way or the other as to its application. There remain very large numbers of cases where his theory is certainly without even the smallest foundation of fact. (In the immense class of humming birds there is not one species in a score to which his theory, as he states it, can apply. See what Hudson says about them. It does not apply to swallows; the brilliantly colored species, wholly without concealing coloration are infinitely more numerous than those to which the theory could by any possibility apply — the bank swallows (& swifts).) The comparison I made with Agassiz and some of the other ultra-glacialists is applicable. In the Northern continents the discovery of the effects of glacial action was of enormous importance, but it was a simple absurdity to try to explain phenomena in South America, and in Africa — in the Amazon Valley, for instance — on the theory that the land had been subjected to glacial action. It is similarly a wild absurdity for Mr. Thayer to make such sweeping announcements as he does where he says, in speaking of the nuptial dress of birds, that even this dress is protective. But we can go much further than this. There are unquestionably large numbers of species of both mammals and birds as to which Mr. Thayer's theory has not the smallest particle of justification. Indeed merely reading his own book shows such a fantastic quality of mind on his part that it is a matter of very real surprise to me that any scientific observer, in commenting on the book, no matter how much credit he may give to Mr. Thayer for certain discoveries and theories, should fail to enter the most emphatic protest against the utter looseness and wildness of his theorizing. Think of being required seriously to consider the theory that flamingos are colored red so that fishes (or oysters for that matter — there is no absurdity of which Mr. Thayer could not be capable) would mistake them for the sunset! This is only an extreme example of the literally countless follies of which Mr. Thayer is guilty. I think that serious scientific men, when they come to discuss Mr. Thayer, should first of all and in the most emphatic way repudiate the ludicrous part of his theory, the part in which he pushes it to extremes. (To discuss the effects of glacial action, for instance, would be absurd without the statement that it was potent only in boreal realms or at high elevations.) There then will remain much matter for serious discussion. But there can be no serious discussion of the theory as a whole until such eliminations have been made. Our first business is to see whether, as he says, the law is one of universal and practically inclusive potency, or whether it is one of many laws, all of which are limited by others, and act with various effects. Of course you are familiar with Allen's pamphlet on *The Influence of Physical Conditions in the Genesis of Species*, and also of course you are familiar with Nelson's very interesting discussion on Directive Coloration in the Southern Jack Rabbit Group.

What I would like to get is a serious study by a competent scientific man who will first of all try to distinguish between cases where the coloration is concealing, or protective, and the cases where it is not. At this moment here on the Sound there are two kinds of ducks found in far greater abundance than any others. These are the surf ducks or scoters, and the long-tailed ducks or old squaws. The former are black, or in the case of young birds so dark a brown that the effect at a distance is the same. They are as conspicuous as ravens. They can be seen on the water as far as it is possible to see anything. Their coloration is not only not concealing or protective, but it is in the highest degree advertising. The old squaws have a broken pattern of coloration, and while they are conspicuous birds they are very much less conspicuous in coloration than the scoters; but they are the most noisy and restless of any ducks. They can be heard long before they are seen, and they are almost always moving. I do not believe that they ever escape observation from any possible foe, owing to their color. Now as to these ducks — the most numerous ducks around here, the most successful in other words — Mr. Thayer's theory certainly does not apply. It is just the same with land birds. The soaring hen hawks and the bigger true falcons alike are always conspicuous even to human eyes. It simply is not possible, as far as I can see, that they are helped by their coloration in catching prey. If they are, the fact must certainly be shown by a totally different series of experiments from anything that Mr. Thayer has even attempted.

So with a number of our smaller birds. Bluebirds, Baltimore orioles, scarlet tanagers, red-winged blackbirds, grackles, swallows, indigo buntings, towhees, and many many others are either all the time, or at certain important seasons, colored in a manner most calculated to strike the attention. (This is true of thousands of kinds of large birds (like all the white egrets and glossy or dark ibises, pied storks, coots, water hens &c) as of brilliantly colored birds in the tropics.) Even as regards warblers, I think that the nuptial coloration of certain species must have an advertising rather than a concealing value; and with some I should say that this would apply at other seasons also. The mourning warbler, the Kentucky warbler, the Maryland yellowthroat, the Blackburnian, the black-throated green, the blue-winged yellow — I might almost indefinitely extend the list — are colored so that at certain seasons, or at all seasons, they attract the eye under normal conditions. The only reason that they do not attract the eye here is that their size and the leafy cover in which they dwell offset the effect of their brilliant and highly nonprotective nonconcealing special coloration.

The utter breakdown of the theory as regards most big game I have elsewhere discussed. Giraffes, zebras, buffalos, oryx, gnu, hartebeests owe nothing whatever to concealing coloration; they have none. Moreover, where a number of different species utterly differently colored exist with equal success, two things are sure; first, that if one of them is protectively colored, the others are not; and second, that this protective coloration must be of very small consequence compared with other features in enabling the animal to thrive. If a chipmunk's stripes are concealing, then the uniform tint of a weasel or a red squirrel is not concealing; or vice versa. In fact, as regards a great multitude of mammals, large and small, I think there is need of far more thorough examination than has yet been made before we can say just how far countershading, for instance, is of real protective value. It is an interesting discovery about color; but its value in effecting concealment as regards many mammals, snakes, birds &c, is enormously exaggerated.

I look forward to seeing your museum. As you know, I have presented it an elephant. *Sincerely yours*

In Egypt, on the edge of the desert, there are sand chats which are protectively colored above and which try to escape notice by crowding; and there are black and white chats, whose coloration is advertising; they never try to escape notice, and are as conspicuous as if they were little crows.

SUFFRAGE AND WOMEN'S DUTIES

To Mary Ella Lyon Swift

Oyster Bay, March 7, 1911

My dear Mrs. Swift:

I am interested in those letters about the suffrage that you have written. I am rather in favor of the suffrage, but very tepidly. Women do not really need the suffrage although I do not think they would do any harm with it. Their needs are along entirely different lines, and their duties are along entirely different lines. Indeed, the longer I stay in politics the more I realize for men quite as much as for women, while there are very grave duties connected with politics there are even greater and more important duties either outside of them altogether or only indirectly connected with them. *Faithfully yours*

RAISING A DIVISION

To William Howard Taft

Personal and private

En route El Paso, Texas, March 14, 1911

Dear Mr. President:

I don't suppose that there is anything in this war talk, and I most earnestly hope that we will not have to intervene even to do temporary police duty in Mexico. But just because there is, I suppose, one chance in a thousand of serious trouble such as would occur if Japan or some other big power were to back Mexico, I write. Of course I would not wish to take any part in a mere war with Mexico — it would not be my business to do peculiarly irksome and disagreeable and profitless police duty of the kind any occupation of Mexico would entail. But if by any remote chance — and I know how remote it is — there should be a serious war, a war in which Mexico was backed by Japan or some other big power, then I would wish immediately to apply for permission to raise a division of cavalry, such as the regiment I commanded in Cuba. The division would consist of three brigades of three regiments each. If given a free hand, I could render it, I am certain, as formidable a body of horse riflemen, that is, of soldiers such as those of Sheridan, Forrest and Stuart, as has ever been seen. In order to make it efficient and formidable, and to prepare it in the shortest possible time, I would need to choose my own officers. To follow any other course would be to risk losing half, or possibly all, of the efficiency of the force. I have my brigade commanders, colonels, and in many cases majors and captains already in mind, and they would be men under whom organization could be pushed to very rapid completion, while the ranks would be immediately filled to overflowing with men, every one of whom would be already a good horseman and rifleman, able to live in the open and take care of himself. My brigade commanders would be Howze and Boughton of the regular army, and Cecil Lyon of Texas. My nine colonels would include men like Fitzhugh Lee and Gordon Johnston of the regular army, and among others John Greenway,

Seth Bullock, Harry Stimson and John McIlhenny. I need not bother you with the names of the majors and captains whom I have already picked out because I understand that I am writing in view of an exceedingly remote possibility. Nevertheless I would like you to know what my intention is. To let volunteer regiments as the rule elect their own officers is to insure very many of the regiments being utterly incompetent. There were three rough rider regiments in the Spanish War, but you have never heard of more than one, simply because the other two, although composed of just as good material, did not have at the head of either a man in any way comparable to Wood. If I am allowed to raise a cavalry division, choosing my own upper officers as above outlined, and many or most of the lower officers, the organization will proceed with the utmost speed, and I will guarantee the efficiency of the division. I ask, Sir, that instead of treating this as a boast, you will remember that in the war with Spain our regiment was raised, armed, equipped, mounted, dismounted, drilled, kept two weeks on transports, and put through two victorious aggressive fights in which it lost nearly a quarter of the men engaged, and over one third of the officers, a loss greater than that suffered by any but two of the twenty-four regular regiments in the same army corps; and all this within sixty days. Each regiment would consist of from 1,200 to 1,400 men all told, the division being 10,000 to 12,000 strong. I know just where I would raise these men, some of them coming from the East, most from the West and South. *Very respectfully yours*

GENUINE DEMOCRACY

To Charles Dwight Willard

New York, April 28, 1911

My dear Mr. Willard:

Not only is your letter very interesting, but I am touched by its sincerity and kindly frankness. I do not think you need be told how genuine my admiration for you is, nor what it means to me to have the chance of hearing from and working with one whose motives and purposes are so transparently high and fine, and who has done and is doing and will be doing such a quantity of invaluable work for the State.

Now I want to make one thing a little clearer than I did. I judge by your letter that you think I am putting my chief stress upon the question as to how far it is "politic" and expedient for me to go in my advocacy of what you call "democratic principles and popular rule legislation" in view of the tremendous disapproval in the East. In the first place I ought to have made it more evident than I apparently did make it, that I was using the words "politic" and "expedient" only in the sense that I would use them in discussing Abraham Lincoln's attitude toward slavery or Washington's attitude toward liberty and independence. When a very young man in the Illinois Legislature Lincoln fearlessly put himself on record as against slavery; but he resolutely declined to join the antislavery parties in '44 and '48 on the ground that the movements were so inexpedient that they did harm and not good to the cause; and in '56, '58, '60, and even well on into '62, he also resolutely declined to join the abolitionists, and to head a crusade for the total destruction of slavery, confining himself to opposition to the extension of slavery into new territory, until the time became ripe to move for its total abolition. I do not agree with you in your description of his statement in 1858 that the Union could not permanently endure half slave and half free. He again and again sought to modify what he had said by words and phrases, and for over a year after the civil war had begun, in '61 and '62, when he was President, in his letter to Horace Greeley, in his answer to the deputation of ministers, and on many other occasions, including his first inaugural, he explicitly stated that his effort was to preserve the Union with or without slavery, and that if it could best be preserved by keeping slavery undisturbed in the Southern States, then he believed in keeping slavery — that is, he believed in the effort to keep the Union just as he said it could not permanently be kept. This, however, is a historic question merely, and with no real bearing upon what I wish to say to you; except that I do wish you to understand that according to my lights, however dim they may be, I am endeavoring to work in the spirit in which Abraham Lincoln worked. I believe his success was due to the fact that he refused to be swerved out of the path of cautious and moderate advance by the denunciations of the fiery and sincere enthusiasts like Wendell Phillips, who, as you will remember, denounced him as "the slave-hound of Illinois." I do not think that these extremists were purer and better men than Lincoln, the head of the moderates, was; I think they were merely more foolish men, and that if they had had their way, instead of bringing about a better condition of affairs, they would have wrecked the Union and destroyed the antislavery cause. Just in the same way I believe that the French revolutionists, when, not content with what they had gained in 1789, they pushed forward into the four years of red anarchy that culminated in the terror, did more to damage democracy, more to put back the cause of popular government, than any despot or oligarchy from that time to this. Remember that these were the men who made a "religion" of democracy, who typified "liberty" as a goddess; and who prattled words like these while their hearts were black with murder committed in such names. Do read Acton's *Lectures on the French Revolution*.

Now do not think I believe that to be moderate and to show wisdom and common sense means ever to be halfhearted, or means that the "root and branch" policy is not sometimes the wisest and indeed the only wise policy. Lincoln was not halfhearted. His zeal was just as intense, his purpose as inflexible, as the zeal and the purpose of the extremists who denounced him. And his policy of moderation did not mean weakness; on the contrary, when the time was ripe he struck with iron determination, and he saw the time when compromise would be fatal just as he saw the time when insistence upon no compromise would be fatal.

My dear fellow, I absolutely agree with what you say as to the new conditions under which I am speaking. The only point on which I disagree with you is as to the importance of the new role. I do not believe that I have a very great role to play as adviser, but I do want to feel that, however little the effect I may have, yet that that effect shall be for good. I do want to be useful, and I thank you for seeing and saying that I want to be useful.

Now all of this is preliminary to what you have said, and to what I wish to say, as to what you call the concrete issue; as you put it, "your attitude toward democracy, and your method of expression in presenting the case to the public." Now I deeply err about my own attitude if it is not that of a genuine democrat, and if my democracy does not represent not only reasoned conviction but intense sympathy, and, as I believe, deep understanding. I have always kept a cartoon that appeared about me while I was President. This cartoon was called "His Favorite Author." It represented a barely furnished room, and before a small fire, seated in a shabby old rocking chair, shabbily dressed, was an old fellow, apparently a farmer, with furrowed chin and whiskered face. It was the picture of a man who worked hard, for whom life was not too easy, who had had no unfair advantages in life — the face of a kindly, good, hard-working man — and the "Favorite Author's" work which he was reading was one of my Presidential messages. The cartoon represented very much to me. That is the man I have tried to represent. That is the man with whom I deeply sympathize, whose welfare and beliefs and convictions I have ever before me, and with whom I feel absolute community of thought in the essential things of life. Our views of war and peace, of family life and business, of politics, of justice and morality, of all the really essential things are fundamentally the same. I am very fond of books and of study, of pictures and of bronzes, just as I am fond of the woods and of watching wild birds and beasts, and I like to talk with scholars and literary men, and leaders of thought of all kinds. But the men with whom I feel genuine sympathy are not big business men, big corporation lawyers, big contractors of the ordinary type; the men of whom I am always thinking, and whose emotions and convictions I understand and represent, are men like those whom I meet at railway employees' conventions, or out on ranches, or down at the lodge, where I come in contact with the bayman, the oyster-sloop captain, the express agent, the brakeman, the farmer, the small store-keeper, the man who is my cousin's gardener, my own chauffeur, and others like them. They are the men beside whom I have fought in battle, beside whom I struggle in politics, with whose business and domestic ideals I sympathize. But, my dear Mr. Willard, I think the very fact that I am a genuine democrat, and that I feel that these are men like me and that I am like them, prevents my falling into what I feel is the dangerous frame of mind that has been so fatally attractive to the French and most of the Latin peoples in the past, the tendency to speak of democracy, for instance, as if it were a goddess, as if the mere name had a fetishistic or superstitious value. I think you yourself in your letter unconsciously used "democracy" with two or three different significations, now, for instance, as a method of government, now, for instance, as expressing a social ideal.

Take the first use for a moment, the use of the word "democracy" to mean a method of government. You speak as if the initiative, referendum and recall meant more genuine rule by the people than is obtained through representative government. Now this may or may not be so. If you tried to push matters to an extreme in this way, you would destroy all popular rule. If, for instance, you abolished the Legislature, and had all the laws enacted by popular vote, you would as a matter of actual practice deprive ninety-nine per cent of the people of all real control over legislation; just as New York City if you, in the name of popular rule, attempted to elect by the people all the forty-five thousand employees of the city, it would merely result in depriving the people absolutely of all power over their representatives. I say this because I am one of the people, and I am reasoning about the rest of the people from my own experience. Where I have to hire and work with only four or five men, I of course hire them myself and work with them myself. But when I was Colonel, I had to delegate the business of enlisting men into the regiment to a number of subordinates, and then I could carry on the business of the regiment only by dealing primarily not with each individual but with the various heads of various groups of individuals. So in civic life. As I am not a professional bread-and-butter politician, I find it enormously to my interest to choose some man whom I believe to be honest and competent, and to delegate to him the task of appointing governmental agents, or of passing the great majority of the laws that ought to be passed. This delegation of authority, so far from meaning the surrender of authority, is merely a method of making authority more efficient; and the question as to how far the delegation shall go is one of pure expediency, and the only way it can be tested is by its results. I was immensely impressed with the Wisconsin people, when I stopped at Madison on my return journey, just because they were not approaching the question of the initiative, referendum and recall in a fetishistic spirit, but in entirely practical fashion, with the belief that it was an advantage rationally to apply the principles in governmental work, and that it would be a very great disadvantage if they were not applied under such conditions as made good result from them. In certain places in Switzerland, for instance, the initiative has had the unexpected result of giving a small and alert minority an altogether improper advantage over the majority, enabling them ceaselessly to worry the majority, and sometimes, when they caught the majority napping, to do them real damage. Under such conditions, the majority is bound in the end to protect itself without much regard to theory by facing facts as they are. Governor Bass of New Hampshire was here last evening, and I took the liberty of reading him part of your letter. He is as sincere a progressive as Governor Johnson, but he has not endeavored to press the initiative, referendum and recall in New Hampshire any more than Governor Johnson has deemed it necessary to try to introduce the town meeting style of government into Los Angeles. The town meeting represents much more genuine democracy in the sense that you in part of your letter use the word "democracy" than the initiative and referendum, and I think it is the best possible government for the best type of small community; but I think it would be a complete failure in a big city as was proved by the experience of Boston. If the New Hampshire Legislature does not prove responsive to the popular will, then New Hampshire will have to secure more direct governmental control by the people as a whole; but at present the people take no interest in such direct legislation, simply because they feel that their representatives are representing them. In Vermont, methods of legislation which I should like to see adopted in some other States are not necessary, simply because Vermont representatives do represent the people. Any trouble in Vermont is due to causes operating among the people themselves, not among their representatives. Here in New York, while I think that much good could be accomplished by introducing certain features of the initiative, referendum and recall (and in New York State, curiously enough, I think the need for the recall as applied to the judiciary is far greater than in most States, although no greater than in California), yet the fundamental need is to have the people take the right view on public questions. Last year, for instance, the issue was perfectly clean-cut here in New York. Decent people and decent principles were on one side; the bosses of both parties, and the whole system of alliance between big business and big politics, and all else that was bad from the civic and social standpoints, were represented on the other side. The people of New York went by sixty thousand the wrong way. No initiative or referendum, or anything else, would have been of use in preventing them going wrong; and no good that the initiative, or the referendum, or the recall, or any other device, could have accomplished last year or this year could in any way compensate for the amount of damage the people did to themselves by trusting in and following bad leadership at the last election. In other words, as I have so often insisted, while the government machinery is important, it is the spirit of the people behind the machinery that counts most. In our government the question of the rights of the people is not nearly as important as the question of the duties of the people. Here the people is sovereign. Let the sovereign beware of flatterers! If your son is to do well in any occupation it will be because you have instilled into him, or at least because he acts on, the belief that he needs to think of his duty ten times where he needs to think of his rights once; and what is true of each of us individually is true of all of us collectively, that is of the people.

So much for democracy where you use the word as implying a preference for one system of popular government over another. Now for what you say about democracy in its larger aspect. My dear fellow, you say "To us it seems the one thing in the whole scheme of human affairs that we can believe in without limitation and without reservation, that the people should rule." If you literally applied this without qualification and explanation in California, it would of course mean that the Chinese and Japanese should come in in unlimited quantities, and should rule you. Now you don't mean this, any more than the Texan and Mississippian who use the same phraseology mean that the negroes of the black belt should rule. There is to me always something both pathetic and grimly ironic in the Socialistic propaganda when coupled with the fact that as a working theory no Socialist party in this country could endure for twenty-four hours if, not as a matter of theory, but as a matter of practice, it applied its doctrines to black men and yellow men. Every real democrat in this country, every democrat who tries to put his democracy into practice, and does not treat it either as a theory to be used for his selfish benefit, or as an agreeable abstraction not to be applied in real life; every such democrat acts and always must act on the perfectly sound (altho unacknowledged, and often hotly contested) belief that only certain people are fit for democracy. When face to face with facts no democrat would really contend that Aruwimi dwarfs or digger Indians are fit for democracy — that is, no democrat who lives among them, would so contend. You say that you would rather have bad government with democracy than good government without it, because "government itself is only a means to an end to give a man a chance to be happy, and to develop the best that is in him. And that is just what democracy does at firsthand, directly. Its function as a maker of men is almost Godlike." If you take a people, a race, that stand high enough, this is true; but if you seek to apply this doctrine to all men everywhere, it is lamentably and ludicrously false. Remember that a lie is just as much a lie if designed to bolster up a beautiful theory as under any other circumstances. As Emerson says, in the long run the most unpleasant truth is a safer traveling companion than the pleasantest falsehood. In Haiti, absolute democracy has been at work for over a century; and really, my dear Mr. Willard, it is sad to think of your sentence of the function of democracy being "Godlike as a maker of men," and then to think of what democracy has done in Haiti. It would be far truer to say that its functions there had been "devil-like" than that its function there had been "Godlike." I firmly believe that the American people is so advanced that on the whole they can do better for themselves than any man or men are able to for any other people, because the best and highest government must necessarily be democracy, for the very reason that only the best and highest people can fully realize democracy. But those who expect the impossible from the adoption of democratic forms prepare for themselves the most bitter disappointment, and may do dreadful harm to the cause of popular freedom, to the cause of the elevation of the race. I believe that as a governmental expedient the rule of the majority is the only safe rule for us in America to adopt. But I hold that insistence that the majority is always right may be just as slavish and vicious as insistence upon the doctrine that the king can do no wrong. I suppose that no one now seriously contends that during reconstruction days the negro majority in Mississippi and South Carolina acted wisely, or that it was possible to continue the government in the hands of that majority. On the other hand, the whites of Mississippi and South Carolina, not merely by a majority but with substantial unanimity, decided in 1861 to leave the Union, decided to plunge the country into four years of dreadful war and to ruin their own States, with the purpose of breaking up the one great free republic on the face of the earth, and of enthroning slavery in perpetuity. The views of the majority of those two States, and the aims of those two States at that time, were those of the Devil and not those of God; and that man deserved best of his fellows who fearlessly withstood the popular will. When a State votes to repudiate its debts, it does not mean that it is right that the debts should be repudiated, it means that the majority is acting badly. Three centuries ago the rule of the majority in Scotland meant savage oppression of Catholic and Episcopalian and frightful cruelty to witches and freethinkers; and at the same time the rule of the majority in Spain meant infinitely more hideous persecution of Protestant, Jew and Moslem. In both cases the rule of the majority, of the people, meant the negation of liberty; in Spain it meant the destruction of everything that makes life worth living, and ultimately the destruction of the Spanish people. At present the rule of the majority in Morocco means every variety of hideous cruelty, injustice and social and governmental abomination. It would be enormously to the benefit of the people of Morocco if the French took hold of them and did for them what they have done in Algiers. When the people of the Sudan ruled themselves, they were guilty of conduct which not figuratively but literally meant that it would be better that they should all die than thus continue to rule themselves; as a matter of fact, two thirds of them did die, and justice and liberty came only when the rule of an alien supplanted the rule which, by the action or with the acquiescence of the majority, had been established. All of this seems to me so elemental as to be trite. The rule of the majority is good only if the majority has the will and the morality and the intelligence to do right; and the majority of the peoples of mankind are not yet in such shape that they can prosper under the very kind of rule which it is essential for us here in America to have, and under which alone *we* can prosper and bring ourselves to the highest point of developed usefulness.

My dear Mr. Willard, read what Lincoln said in his answer to Douglas as to the real meaning of the Declaration of Independence, and in the comparison he makes in speaking of equality between himself and a negro, and you will get exactly the idea of what I regard as the proper temper in which to approach these subjects. I do not think that the most fervent zeal, the utmost earnestness, and the most resolute determination to help forward the cause of the people, ought to be permitted to mean that we are afraid to look facts in the face. I too am a dreamer of dreams; I hold the man worthless who is not a dreamer, who does not see visions; but I also hold him worthless unless in practical fashion he endeavors to shape his actions so that these dreams and visions can be partially realized, and shall not remain mere dreams and visions, or, what is worse still, shall not be turned into will-o'-the-wisps to lead struggling mankind to destruction. Robespierre and Marat, and Danton and Barère, and the other dreadful miscreants of the Terror used all the fine phrases known to lovers of mankind at the very time that they worked to France a damage almost as great as that which had been wrought by Louis XV and his predecessors and ministers and associates; a damage from which France has never recovered, and which largely offset even the tremendous good accomplished by overthrowing the iniquity of the Old Regime. I shall be sorry indeed if I ever unwittingly use words which shall dampen the zeal and dim the burning vision of those who fight for the right and struggle toward it; but I shall be equally sorry if I ever use words which shall deceive good men for whom life is not easy into following wrong paths, or into preparing bitter disappointments for themselves, by trusting in promise which cannot be fulfilled.

Are you ever coming to this side of the continent? I should like to see you when we can talk over these matters face to face for a whole evening. *Faithfully yours*

P.S. You say that I can never be admitted into your lodge by the use of words such as I have used. Friend, friend, in my lodge the masters of the past are Washington and Lincoln, and admission to it is not by words, or fine, futile phrases, but by service and achievement; and it is only by membership in this lodge that good can really be done by the lovers of mankind.

DISSOLVING STANDARD OIL

To Arthur B. Farquhar

Oyster Bay, August 11, 1911

My dear Mr. Farquhar:

Your letter gives me real pleasure, not merely because of what you say about my attitude in this particular matter, but because I so thoroughly agree with your general view of the trust question. I do not myself see what good can come from dissolving the Standard Oil Company into forty separate companies, all of which will still remain really under the same control. What we should have is a much stricter governmental supervision of these great companies, but accompanying this supervision should be a recognition of the fact that great combinations have come to stay and that we must do them scrupulous justice just as we exact scrupulous justice from them.

I am so pleased that you are taking such an interest in the social and industrial affairs of the open country. *Sincerely yours*

AN ARGUMENT FOR WOMAN SUFFRAGE

To Florence Kelley

New York, January 9, 1912

My dear Miss Kelley:

I have read that book, but I shall reread it. All that is necessary to make me the most ferociously intense believer in woman suffrage instead of its moderate supporter as at present, is to convince me that women will take an effective stand against sexual viciousness, which of course means especially against male sexual viciousness. They did take such a stand in Seattle. They have helped Lindsey in Denver, but I do not think they have done as much as I had hoped in Denver.

I hope you like what I wrote about the judges. *Faithfully yours*

ADVANCING BIOLOGICAL SCIENCE

To Francis Hobart Herrick

Oyster Bay, January 15, 1912

Dear Professor Herrick:

I thank you for your very interesting pamphlet on nests and nest building. It seems to me to represent just the kind of work that it is necessary to do if we are further to develop our knowledge of the underlying problems of biology — and this aside from the fact that I personally take a pleasure in studying habits for the simple pleasure of studying them. Darwin and the great scientific men of his day forced science to take an enormous stride in advance in the decades succeeding the publication of *The Origin of Species*, but for nearly fifty years now we have tended to make the same mistake that the schoolmen of the Middle Ages made about Aristotle. The rediscovery of the works of Aristotle produced an immense forward movement in knowledge. Then there came a period of fossilization, when everybody accepted Aristotle as having summed up all possible knowledge, and when in consequence he became a positive obstacle to advance. It has been somewhat so with Darwin and the Darwinians. Instead of new research, new investigation, and sane speculation based on such research and investigation, too many Darwinians, including I am sorry to say Mr. Wallace himself, have of recent years done little except build up closet theories on such subjects as protective coloration, recognition and warning marks, nesting habits and the like. I doubt if we have ever seen anything less scientific than the extreme dogmatism of men like Haeckel, and the solemn acceptance as facts of Weismann's extreme theories. *Sincerely yours*

PUBLICLY CHALLENGING TAFT

To Elihu Root

Private & Confidential

New York, February 14, 1912

Dear Elihu:

I thank you for your long letter, and I genuinely appreciate it. In the month that has passed since I wrote my letter to Munsey, things have moved fast. I do not believe it is possible for me now to refrain from speaking publicly. I cannot treat the request of nine Governors as I have treated mere private requests. Moreover, the action of the supporters of the President, including both his real supporters and the supporters who wish him nominated with every intention of trying to beat him when nominated, is I think at last beginning to produce in the public mind the belief that there is a certain furtiveness in my position. I am inclined to think, therefore, that the time has come when I must speak, and simply say in public very briefly what I have already said in private. I appreciate the force of all your arguments, and you yourself cannot feel as strongly as I do the disadvantages of my position from my own personal standpoint. But the arguments on the other side are even stronger. As far as I am able to judge of my motives, I am looking at this purely from the standpoint of the interests of the people as a whole, from the standpoint of those who believe in the causes which I champion, which three years ago I had every reason to believe the President ardently championed, and which most reluctantly I have come to believe he either does not understand at all, or else is hostile to.

Give my love to Mrs. Root, *Ever yours*

SEEKING THE NOMINATION

To William Glasscock et al.

New York, February 24, 1912

Gentlemen:

I deeply appreciate your letter, and I realize to the full the heavy responsibility it puts upon me, expressing as it does the carefully considered convictions of the men elected by popular vote to stand as the heads of government in their several States.

I absolutely agree with you that this matter is not one to be decided with any reference to the personal preferences or interests of any man, but purely from the standpoint of the interests of the people as a whole. I will accept the nomination for President if it is tendered to me, and I will adhere to this decision until the convention has expressed its preference.

One of the chief principles for which I have stood, and for which I now stand, and which I have always endeavored and always shall endeavor to reduce to action, is the genuine rule of the people, and therefore I hope that so far as possible the people may be given the chance, through direct primaries, to express their preference as to who shall be the nominee of the Republican Presidential Convention. *Very truly yours*

"MY WARM PERSONAL AFFECTION FOR YOU"

To Henry Cabot Lodge

New York, March 1, 1912

Dear Cabot:

I don't know whether to be most touched by your letter or most inclined to laugh over it. My dear fellow, you could not do anything that would make me lose my warm personal affection for you. For a couple of years I have felt that you and I were heading opposite ways as regards internal politics. I shan't try to justify my viewpoint because it would seem as if I were attacking yours. As regards my Columbus speech, every single point has appeared in editorials in *The Outlook* and what I said about the judges was said in my Cooper Union speech last October and recapitulated at length in *The Outlook* about two months ago. Of course, you will stand by your convictions.

Now, don't you ever think of this matter again. Tell Nannie how delighted I was to see John and Mary — and I took a real fancy to Mary. She was not only pretty but refined. She is a little shy but entirely natural and anyone can see that she is an innate lady. I look forward to having her and John visit us at Sagamore. I don't think I have ever seen John so happy. *Ever affectionately*

OPPOSING AN "INFAMOUS CAMPAIGN"

To Albert Cross

New York, June 4, 1912

Dear Mr. Cross:

Your letter really pleased me very much. Do let me see you if you come down to New York.

In this contest I have felt that we are fighting for a very high ideal. In fact, with the sole exception of the fight in the early days of the Republican Party, there has been no such contest as this. Since the adoption of the Constitution, there has been no other contest that appealed as does this contest to all men who believe in our principles of government and all men who believe in the root ideas of public right.

I am particularly glad to hear from you because the one feature of this contest that has excited not only my indignation, but also my concern for the country, has been the attitude of so many educated persons, including college presidents, literary men, professors and the like. To support Mr. Taft and his allies in this contest now is precisely like standing for Buchanan, Franklin, Breckenridge, the slave Democrats and the Cotton Whigs and Copperheads in 1860 in the Civil War. I have always thoroughly understood the attitude of the Southerners who, like my mother's people, stood with their own section in the line. In the same way I can understand, although I do not sympathize with, the attitude of the big business men — men like Pierpont Morgan or Jim Hill — whose interests blind them to the needs of the present day. I can also understand the attitude of the ordinary good citizen who gets his information from newspapers and does not know that his sources of information are poisoned, because the press is subsidized or controlled. But there is no excuse for the man who is supposed to guide others, whether men or boys, in their judgment. If he does not know the facts, then it is his fault and he cannot ask pardon because of his ignorance. The cause of our opponents has now become naked — the cause of the political bosses and of special privilege in the business world. It is the cause of corruption and of bad government, and there has never been a more infamous campaign than the campaign waged by and on behalf of Mr. Taft during the last six weeks. Under such circumstances it is lamentable to see any man who claims to be a man of honor supporting Taft, and if, in addition, the man now pretends, or has ever pretended, to preach my ideas, his action is not merely lamentable, but it makes him an object of derision.

Yet it is too true that the large majority of the college presidents, the professors and the like have in this contest sided with the powers of evil. It is the fashionable side today; it is the side taken by the children of this world and probably will bring material rewards to those who take it. But to take it is to do damage of the gravest kind to the cause of public morality and of sound, clean, decent politics. Therefore, I feel that men like you who resist the pressure and stand for a high ideal, for what is sound and decent, make all your debtors.

As I said, I grow concerned and indignant over the attitude of too many of our friends in this crisis. Yet, after all, one must not put too much stress upon it. One of the commonest things in life is to see men pay homage to principles in the past which they indignantly repudiate in the present. For instance, I know plenty of people who solemnly pay heed to Decoration Day and encourage boys being marched to decorate the graves and who, nevertheless, opposed the Spanish War, opposed the taking of the Panama Canal, opposed even the voyage of the battle fleet around the world. My tendency is to feel that these people are hypocrites, but I suppose that really the fault lies in their heads and not in their hearts; they are not hypocrites, they are simply foolish and rather weak souls who praise heroism that is dead because that is evidently safe, but who shrink with foolish terror from the doing of those deeds today which, if done fifty years ago, they could not too much admire.

With all good wishes, *Sincerely yours*

"IT IS A FORLORN HOPE"

To Paul A. Ewert

Oyster Bay, July 5, 1912

Dear Mr. Ewert:

First as to the accusations about myself. No suggestion was ever made to me that the roll would be purged and the Taft men then join in the nomination of Hadley. I was told that intimations had come to Hadley from the Taft men that they might turn to him, but without purging the roll. I was also told that at that identical moment the same intimations had been made by the Taft men to Senator Cummins and even to Senator La Follette. A definite proposition was made to me that the Roosevelt delegates from Washington (not California or Texas) might be admitted by the votes of the Taft men added to our own if that would make me consent to stay in the Convention. The implication was that I would thus get the nomination myself. I answered that I was not in the least concerned about getting the nomination myself, but that I demanded a thorough purging of the roll not only as regards Washington, but as regards California and Texas and the other places, and I stated that I would then ask my forces to continue to stay in the Convention and see that the roll was purged and if that were done I would gladly work and support the man whom the Convention chose to nominate, and if he were not Mr. Taft that I would gladly support his nomination. This of course applied to Governor Hadley and Senator Cummins. The reason I excepted Taft was that by that time he had made it perfectly clear that he insisted on his representatives stealing the nomination for him, and under such circumstances I could not support him.

Is this sufficient explanation? Senator Dixon knows all the circumstances and will corroborate the above statements if you write to him. The trouble of denying such statements as those to which you refer is that unless they are made from some responsible source my denial merely gives tenfold circulation to the original statement.

Now for the second charge. I wish you would ask the man who made this statement to you to bring before you either of his informants, and to let that informant give his name and have his statement forwarded to me. If he is a man of sufficient substance, I will at once proceed against him for criminal libel. On the day I spoke at Osawatomie I did not touch a drop of anything stronger than coffee or tea; I know this because on those trips I do not drink at all. On the Mississippi trip it is possible, although not probable, that if they had white wine at dinner on the boat, I may have taken a glass or a couple of glasses. I never drink beer; I never touch whisky; I have never drunk a highball or a cocktail in my life. I never, at St. Louis or anywhere else, drank any whisky unless it was on a prescription by a doctor — and it has been certainly ten or fifteen years and perhaps longer since I even drank a prescription of a doctor. At St. Louis, at a great public dinner, I publicly rose and drank a glass of champagne, chiefly because I had been warned I must not do so by men who were much excited by the Fairbanks cocktail incident. I usually have sherry or Madeira or white wine at my table if there are guests, just as I would have if you were to visit me, for instance. And I always have it when Methodist bishops visit me, just because I don't want anyone to think that I am hypocritical. But the amount I drink in any given year is confined to a few glasses of Madeira or in Summer white wine with apollinaris and occasionally a glass of champagne. I do not touch a dozen teaspoonfuls of brandy a year and I never touch whisky at all. When I was in the White House we had a mint julep party every Spring when I suppose I would drink three or four mint juleps. We have not any mint here so I have not had any since I left the White House. The only other way which I even touch brandy is in a milk punch, and I doubt if I average half a dozen milk punches a year. Even those half dozen are only taken when for some reason I have had an extraordinarily exhausting day and when I am just about to go to bed. Nine times out of ten when in such condition I take nothing but a glass of either milk or a cup of tea.

There! I don't know how I could make that point any straighter.

Now, my dear Mr. Ewert, let me tell you how much I appreciate your attitude and what you are doing. It very deeply touches me. But, my dear Mr. Ewert, I don't want you to get into trouble with your superiors. I have directly or indirectly received statements from you, Frankfurter, Herbert Knox Smith, Valentine and Lawrence Murray. I suppose you know all of them in Washington. I should be very glad if you cared to get them together and read this letter to them, especially what I am now about to say, but I must ask you to treat this as confidential except so far as they are concerned.

Nothing has touched me more than the willingness of men in whom I earnestly believe to leave their official positions and come out in this fight. But in such a case I feel that the sacrifice ought not to be made unless the good that will be done outweighs the damage that will also be done. It is a good deal now as it was when I went to the war — I refused to take into my regiment any married man who was depending upon his own exertions for the livelihood of his wife and children, although I gladly took in married men who had an independent fortune so that his family would not suffer if he were killed. I did not feel that the emergency justified the sacrifice of the man's family. In the same way, just at present I do not feel that our cause is sufficiently bright to warrant me to have men like you and those I have named come out for me. Moreover, I am inclined to think that at present you can do better work for the public in office than you can by coming out for the cause. Events shaped themselves so that I had no alternative except to lead, but I am under no illusion about it. It is a forlorn hope. The probabilities are against success. I have been careful to try to bring with me only the men of the crusading temperament and I have discouraged men from joining me if I felt that the damage done to their families, or to the public service was more than counterbalanced by the gain that would come to the cause. Probably all the men who are with me in this fight will suffer more or less because they are with me and will gain nothing. Thank Heaven! I think I can conscientiously say that I myself will suffer most, and gain least — otherwise I should be profoundly uncomfortable. Now it is necessary that the fight should be made and of course there is some small chance of victory; but not enough for us to take into account. Under such circumstances a parallel of what I did in my regiment is complete! The men who come with me should be men who have little or nothing to lose and unless can render very great essential service to the cause by coming out for me they ought not to do so at the cost of impairing their usefulness to the community in other positions. Personally I hate to write this to you for I should like to have you and Frankfurter, and Smith and Murray and Valentine as my associates and counselors in this great cause for which I am fighting. But at present my honest judgment is that you would not do enough good to the cause to counterbalance the damage you would do by leaving your present position. If you desire, I shall write you frankly if the situation changes so that I think you ought to come out. But the above is my personal feeling. Of course do not let it get beyond the men I have mentioned for even in a forlorn hope it does not do to let your soldiers think that their commander won't lead them to victory — although there are occasions when it is his highest duty to fight no matter how great the risk of defeat.

Again most heartily thanking you, I am, *Your friend*

To Julian La Rose Harris

Oyster Bay, August 1, 1912

My dear Mr. Harris:

In pursuance of our conversation I write you this letter. There is a peculiar fitness in writing it to the son of the man whose work made all Americans his debtors. Your father possessed genius; and moreover he possessed that gentleness of soul, that broad and tender sympathy with his fellows, for the lack of which genius cannot atone. His life and his work tended to bring his fellow countrymen, North and South, into ever closer relations of good will and understanding; and surely it should be needless to say that the author of *Uncle Remus* and of "Free Joe and the Rest of the World" felt a deep and most kindly interest in the welfare of the negro.

Many letters dealing with the subject of which you spoke to me have been sent to me within the last few days. These letters, from equally worthy citizens, take diametrically opposite positions. Those written by men living in the North usually ask me to insist that we get from the South colored Delegates to the National Progressive Convention. Those written by citizens of the South ask that I declare that the new party shall be a white man's party. I am not able to agree to either proposal.

In this country we cannot permanently succeed except upon the basis of treating each man on his worth as a man. We can fulfill our high mission among the nations of the earth, we can do lasting good to ourselves and to all mankind, only if we so act that the humblest among us, so long as he behaves in straight and decent fashion, has guaranteed to him under the law his right to life, to liberty, to protection from injustice, his right to enjoy the fruits of his own honest labor, and his right of the pursuit of happiness in his own way, so long as he does not trespass on the rights of others. Our only safe motto is "All men up" and not "Some men down." For us to oppress any class of our fellow citizens is not only wrong to others but hurtful to ourselves; for in the long run such action is no more detrimental to the oppressed than to those who think that they temporarily benefit by the oppression. Surely no man can quarrel with these principles. Exactly as they should be applied among white men without regard to their difference of creed, or birthplace, or social station, without regard to whether they are rich men or poor men, men who work with their hands or men who work with their brains; so they should be applied among all men without regard to the color of their skins.

These are the principles to which I think our countrymen should adhere, the objects which I think they should have steadily in mind. There is need not merely of all our high purpose, but of all our wisdom and patience in striving to realize them. Above all, it is essential that we should not in such a way as to make believe that we are achieving these objects, and yet by our actions indefinitely postpone the time when it will become even measurably possible to achieve them. For this reason I cannot adopt either of the two diametrically opposite suggestions made to me in the letters of which I have spoken.

I believe that the Progressive Movement should be made from the beginning one in the interest of every honest, industrious, law-abiding colored man, just as it is in the interest of every honest, industrious, law-abiding white man. I further believe that the surest way to render the movement impotent to help either the white man or the colored man in those regions of the South where the colored man is most numerous, would be to try to repeat the course that has been followed by the Republican Party in those districts for so many years, or to endeavor in the States in question to build up a Progressive Party by the same methods which in those States have resulted in making the Republican Party worse than impotent.

Henry Ward Beecher once said that the worst enemy of the colored man was the man who stirred up enmity between the white and colored men who have to live as neighbors. In the South the Democratic machine has sought to keep itself paramount by encouraging the hatred of the white man for the black; the Republican machine has sought to perpetuate itself by stirring up the black man against the white; and surely the time has come when we should understand the mischief in both courses, and should abandon both.

We have made the Progressive issue a moral, not a racial issue. I believe that wherever the racial issue is permitted to become dominant in our politics, it always works harm to both races, but immeasurably most harm to the weaker race. I believe that in this movement only damage will come if we either abandon our ideals on the one hand, or, on the other, fail resolutely to look facts in the face, however unpleasant these facts may be. Therefore I feel that we have to adapt our actions to the actual conditions and actual needs and feelings of each community; not abandoning our principles, but not in one community endeavoring to realize them in ways which will simply cause disaster in that community, although they may work well in another community. Our object must be the same everywhere, but the methods by which we strive to attain it must be adapted to the needs of the several states, or it will never be attained at all.

In many of the States of the Union where there is a considerable colored population we are able in very fact and at the present moment to bring the best colored men into the movement on the same terms as the white man. In Rhode Island and Maryland, in New York and Indiana, in Ohio and Illinois, in New Jersey and Pennsylvania, to speak only of States of which I have personal knowledge, this is now being done, and from some or all of these states colored delegates will be sent to the National Progressive Convention in Chicago. Let me point out that the Progressive Party is already, at its very birth, endeavoring in these States, in its own home, to act with fuller recognition of the rights of the colored man than ever the Republican party did. Until I was President the white Republicans of the North, although they had loudly insisted that the colored man should have office with even greater firmness insisted that he should have office only in the South, or at any rate, not in the North. When, for instance, I tried to appoint a colored man to office in Ohio I was wholly unable to get the necessary assent from the white Republican leaders of Ohio, and had to appoint the man in Washington; and in appointing a colored man to a high position in New York I was obliged to do it by main force and against the wish of the entire party organization. In the Republican National Conventions the colored members have been almost exclusively from the South, and the great majority of them have been men of such character that their political activities were merely a source of harm, and of very grave harm, to their own race. We, on the contrary, are hoping to see in the National Progressive Convention colored delegates from the very places where we expect to develop our greatest strength, and we hope to see these men of such character that their activities shall be of benefit not only to the people at large but especially to their own race. So much for the course we are able to follow in these States; and the citizens of these States can best help the negro race by doing justice to these negroes who are their own neighbors. In many Northern States there have been lynchings and race riots with sad and revolting accompaniments; in many of these States there has been failure to punish such outrageous conduct and what is even more important, failure to deal in advance wisely and firmly with the evil conditions, among both black man and the white, which has caused the outrages.

There are other States, including the majority of the Southern States, where the conditions are wholly different. Much is to be said for the men who forty-five years ago, with motives which were for the most part and among most of their number of a lofty and disinterested type, attempted a course of action in those States which in actual practice has lamentably failed to justify itself and I make no attempt at this time to strive to apportion the blame for the failure. It is unwise to revive bitterness by dwelling on the errors and shortcomings of the past. Let us profit by them, but reproach no man because of them. We are now starting a new movement for the betterment of our people, a movement for social and industrial justice which shall be nationwide, a movement which is to strive to accomplish actual results and not to accept high-sounding phrases as a substitute for deeds. Therefore we are not to be pardoned if at the outset, with the knowledge gained by forty-five years' experience of failure, we repeat the course that has led to such failure, and abandon the effort to make the movement for social and industrial justice really nationwide.

For forty-five years the Republican Party has striven to build up in the Southern States in question a party based on the theory that the pyramid will unsupported stand permanently on its apex instead of on its base. For forty-five years the Republican Party has endeavored in these States to build up a party in which the negro should be dominant, a party consisting almost exclusively of negroes. Those who took the lead in this experiment were actuated by high motives, and no one should now blame them because of what, with the knowledge they then had and under the then existing circumstances, they strove to do. But in actual practice the result has been lamentable from every standpoint. It has been productive of evil to the colored men themselves; it has been productive only of evil to the white men of the South; and it has worked the gravest injury to, and finally the disruption and destruction of, the great Republican Party itself. In the States in question where the negro predominates in numbers, and in the sections of other states in which he predominates in numbers, the Republican Party has in actual fact become practically non-existent in so far as votes at the polls are concerned. The number of votes cast in these states and districts for the Republican ticket on Election Day has become negligible. It has long been recognized that these states will never give a Republican electoral vote; that these states or districts will never send a Republican or a colored man to Congress. The number of colored men in them who hold any elective office of the slightest importance is negligible. In these states and districts the Republican Party, in actual practice, and disregarding individual exceptions, exists only to serve the purposes of a small group of politicians, for the most part white, but including some colored men, who have not the slightest interest in elections, and whose political activities are confined to securing offices by sending to National Conventions delegations which are controlled by the promise of office or by means even more questionable. Once in four years they send to the National Conventions delegates who represent absolutely nothing in the way of voting strength, and in consideration of the votes of the delegates thus delivered they endeavor to secure their local offices from any National Republican Administration.

The progress that has been made among the negroes of the South during these forty-five years has not been made as a result of political effort of the kind I have mentioned. It has been made as the result of effort along industrial and educational lines. Again allowing for the inevitable exception, it remains true, as one of the wisest leaders of the colored race has himself said, that the only white man who in the long run, can effectively help the colored man is that colored man's neighbor. There are innumerable white men in the South sincerely desirous of doing justice to the colored man, of helping him upward on his difficult path, of securing him just treatment before the law; white men who set their faces sternly against lynch law and mob violence, who attack all such abuses as peonage, who fight to keep the school funds equitably divided between white and colored schools, who endeavor to help the colored man to become a self-supporting and useful member of the community. The white men who live elsewhere can best help the colored man in the South by upholding the hands of those white men of the South who are thus endeavoring to benefit and to act honestly by the colored men with whom they dwell in community neighborhood and with whose children their children will continue to dwell in community neighborhood. Actual experience for nearly half a century has shown that it is futile to endeavor to substitute for such action by the white man to his colored neighbor, action by outside white men, action which painful experience has shown to be impotent to help the colored man, but which does irritate the white man whom nevertheless it cannot control. We are not facing theories, we are facing actual facts, and it is well for us to remember Emerson's statement that in the long run the most unpleasant truth is a safer traveling companion than the pleasantest falsehood.

The action of the Republican machine in the South, then, in endeavoring to keep alive a party based only on negro votes, where, with few exceptions, the white leaders are in it only to gain reward for themselves by trafficking in negro votes, has been bad for the white men of the South, whom it has kept solidified in an unhealthy and unnatural political bond, to their great detriment and to the detriment of the whole Union; and it has been bad for the colored men of the South. The effect on the Republican Party has long been disastrous, and has finally proved fatal. There has in the past been much venality in Republican National Conventions in which there was an active contest for the nomination for President, and this venality has been almost exclusively among the rotten-borough delegates, and for the most part among the negro delegates from these Southern States in which there was no real Republican Party. Finally, in the Convention at Chicago last June, the breakup of the Republican Party was forced by those rotten-borough delegates from the South. In the Primary States of the North the colored men in most places voted substantially as their white neighbors voted. But in the Southern States, where there was no real Republican Party, and where colored men, or whites selected purely by colored men, were sent to the convention, representing nothing but their own greed for money or office the majority was overwhelmingly antiprogressive. Seven eighths of the colored men from these rotten-borough districts upheld by their votes the fraudulent actions of the men who in that Convention defied and betrayed the will of the mass of the plain people of the party. In spite of the hand-picked delegates chosen by the bosses in certain northern states, in spite of the scores of delegates deliberately stolen from the rank and file of the party by the corrupt political machine which dominated the National Committee and the Convention itself, there would yet have been no hope of reversing in the National Convention the action demanded by the overwhelming majority of the Republicans who had a chance to speak for themselves in their primaries, had it not been for the two hundred and fifty votes or thereabouts sent from the states in which there is no Republican Party. For forty-five years everything has been sacrificed to the effort to build up in these states a Republican Party which should be predominantly and overwhelmingly negro, and now those for whom the effort has been made turned and betrayed that party itself. It would be not merely foolish but criminal to disregard the teachings of such a lesson. The disruption and destruction of the Republican Party, and the fact that it has been rendered absolutely impotent as an instrument for anything but mischief in the country at large has been brought about in large part by the effort to pretend that in the Southern States a sham is a fact, by the insistence upon treating the ghost party in the Southern States as a real party, by refusing to face the truth, which is that under existing conditions there is not and cannot be in the Southern States a party based primarily upon the negro vote and under negro leadership or the leadership of white men who derive their power solely from negroes. With these forty-five years of failure of this policy in the South before our eyes, and with catastrophe thereby caused to a great National Party not yet six weeks distant from us, it would be criminal for the Progressives to repeat the course of action responsible for such disaster, such failure, such catastrophe. The loss of instant representation by southern colored delegates is due to the fact that the sentiment of the Southern negro collectively has been prostituted by dishonest professional politicians both white and black, and the machinery does not exist (and can never be created as long as present political conditions are continued) which can secure what a future of real justice will undoubtedly develop, namely, the right of political expression by the negro who shows that he possesses the intelligence integrity and self-respect which justify such right of political expression in his white neighbor.

We face certain actual facts, sad and unpleasant facts, but facts which must be faced if we are to dwell in the world of realities and not of shams, and if we are to try to make things better by deeds and not merely to delude ourselves by empty words. It would be much worse than useless to try to build up the Progressive Party in these Southern States where there is no real Republican Party, by appealing to the negroes or to the men who in the past have derived their sole standing from leading and manipulating the negroes. As a matter of fact and not of theory all that could possibly result from such action would be to create another impotent little corrupt faction of would-be officeholders, of delegates whose expenses to conventions had to be paid, and whose votes sometimes had to be bought. No real good could come from such action to any man, black or white; the negro would be hurt and not helped throughout the Union; the white man would be hurt in the South, the Progressive Party would be damaged irreparably at the beginning. I earnestly believe that by appealing to the best white men in the South, the men of justice and of vision as well as of strength and leadership, and by frankly putting the movement in their hands from the outset we shall create a situation by which the colored men of the South will ultimately get justice as it is not possible for them to get justice if we are to continue and perpetuate the present conditions. The men to whom we appeal are the men who have stood for securing the colored man in his rights before the law, and they can do for him what neither the Northern white man nor the colored men themselves can do. Our only wise course from the standpoint of the colored man himself is to follow the course that we are following toward him in the North and to follow the course we are following toward him in the South. *Very truly yours*

"I AM IN GREAT SHAPE"

To Anna Roosevelt Cowles

Chicago, October 19, 1912

Dearest Bye:

I am dictating this in bed, and it will have to be signed for me by Edith. It is just a line to tell you I am in great shape. Really the time in the hospital, with Edith and the children on here, has been a positive spree, and I have enjoyed it. Of course, I would like to have been in the campaign, but it can't be helped and there is no use in crying over what can't be helped! Do tell Joe Alsop and Herbert Knox Smith from me how immensely I appreciate the wonderful work they have done. I hate not being in Connecticut to speak for them. Joe especially has been a tower of strength throughout all this contest. I love Will's letter, and I am very proud of the praise he gave me, for I know no man who is gamer and cooler than Will in time of danger, or shows to better advantage in a crisis. *Your loving brother*

SPEAKING AFTER BEING SHOT

To Edward Grey

Oyster Bay, November 15, 1912

My dear Grey:

I greatly appreciate your letter. I am glad you sometimes think of our bird walk, because it was one of the incidents I shall always remember. I cannot help hoping that sometime I shall have the chance to get you over here and repay in kind.

I regret that you think your government may soon come to an end. As for the political fight here, I did not believe we would win, and I can say quite honestly that I have little or no personal regret in the outcome. But I do feel sorry from the broader standpoint. Nine tenths of wisdom is being wise in time, and if a country lets the time for wise action pass, it may bitterly repent when a generation later it strives under disheartening difficulties to do what could have been done so easily if attempted at the right moment. We Progressives were fighting for elementary social and industrial justice, and we had with us the great majority of the practical idealists of the country. But we had against us both the old political organizations, and ninety-nine per cent at the very least of the corporate wealth of the country, and therefore the great majority of the newspapers. Moreover we were not able to reach the hearts of the materialists, or to stir the imagination of the well-meaning somewhat sodden men who lack vision and prefer to travel in a groove. We were fought by the Socialists as bitterly as by the representatives of the two old parties, and this for the very reason that we stand equally against government by a plutocracy and government by a mob. There is something to be said for government by a great aristocracy which has furnished leaders to the nation in peace and war for generations; even a democrat like myself must admit this. But there is absolutely nothing to be said for government by a plutocracy, for government by men very powerful in certain lines and gifted with the "money touch," but with ideals which in their essence are merely those of so many glorified pawnbrokers.

I am a little amused, my dear fellow, at your saying that the account of the shooting stirred you with a curiosity to know whether, if the experience had been yours, you would "have had the nerve to make the speech," and whether your "body would have proved as healthy." I can answer both questions with absolute certainty. Your nerve would not have been affected in the least, you would have made the speech as a matter of course; and your body would have proved *more* healthy. You would have shown the absolute coolness and courage and lack of thought of self that your brother showed when mauled by the lion. Modern civilization is undoubtedly somewhat soft, and the average political orator or party leader, the average broker or banker or factory owner, at least when he is past middle age, is apt to be soft — I mean both mentally and physically — and such a man accepts being shot as a frightful and unheard-of calamity, and feels very sorry for himself and thinks only of himself and not of the work on which he is engaged or of his duty to others, or indeed of his real self-respect. But a good soldier or sailor, or for the matter of that even a civilian accustomed to hard and hazardous pursuits, a deep-sea fisherman, or railwayman, or cowboy, or lumberjack, or miner, would normally act as I acted without thinking anything about it. I believe half the men in my regiment at the least would have acted just as I acted. Think how many Bulgars during the last month have acted in just the same fashion and never even had their names mentioned in bulletins! Recently John Murray sent me The Life of Sir Harry Smith, and I was reading his experiences in the Peninsular War, and his account of the many officers who continued to perform their duties with bullets in them, it being often many hours before a surgeon could attend to them. Why! even in our little San Juan fight there were thirteen men of my regiment who after being shot continued in the fight. Now I wish to rank myself with such men as Harry Smith and his comrades in the Peninsular War, and with the men in my regiment, and I expect to be judged by their standards and not by the standards of that particular kind of money-maker whose soul has grown hard while his body has grown soft; that is, who is morally ruthless to others and physically timid about himself.

I doubt if any man has had a greater volume of obloquy

poured upon him than I have had during the past nine months, and I have been assailed with an injustice so gross as to be fairly humorous. But there is a good deal in Emerson's law of compensation, and to offset this I have been praised in connection with the shooting with quite as extravagant a disregard of my deserts. The bullet passed through the manuscript of my speech and my iron spectacle case, and only went three or four inches into the chest, breaking a rib and lodging against it. I never saw my assailant as it was dark and he was mixed with the dense crowd beside the automobile, and as I was standing unsteadily I half fell back for a second. As I stood up I coughed and at once put my hand to my lips to see if there was any blood. There was none, so that as the bullet was in the chest I felt the chances were twenty to one that it was not fatal. I would not have objected to the man's being killed at the very instant, but I did not deem it wise or proper that he should be killed before my eyes if I was going to recover, so I immediately stopped the men who had begun to worry him, and had him brought to me so that I might see if I recognized him; but I did not. There was then a perfectly obvious duty, which was to go on and make my speech. In the very unlikely event of the wound being mortal I wished to die with my boots on, so to speak. It has always seemed to me that the best way to die would be in doing something that ought to be done, whether leading a regiment or doing anything else. Moreover, I felt that under such circumstances it would be very difficult for people to disbelieve in my sincerity, and that therefore they would be apt to accept at its face value the speech I wished to make, and which represented my deepest and earnest convictions. If, on the other hand, as I deemed overwhelmingly probable, the wound should turn out to be slight, it was still likely that I would have little further chance to speak during the campaign, and therefore it behooved me to go on while I had the chance, and make a speech to which under the circumstances it was at least possible that the country would pay some heed. This is all there was to the incident.

I am sorry Bryce is going. I am glad Cecil Spring Rice is to succeed him. I had a delightful letter from Trevelyan the other day.

With all good wishes, *Faithfully yours*

To Cecil Spring-Rice

New York, December 31, 1912

Dear Springy:

Just a line to say how glad I am to get your letter. I do hope your children will be here with you. It is very hard that you should have been separated from them so long, and surely in this country you can find places that will be healthy for them at any and every season.

I am as well as possible. I did not care a rap for being shot. It is a trade risk, which every prominent public man ought to accept as a matter of course. For eleven years I have been prepared any day to be shot; and if any one of the officers of my regiment had abandoned the battle merely because he received a wound that did nothing worse than break a rib, I should never have trusted that officer again. I would have expected him to keep on in the fight as long as he could stand; and what I expect lieutenants to do I expect, a fortiori, a leader to do.

I hope you come here soon. The Panama question of course should be arbitrated. I am strongly against making promises that ought not to be kept, and therefore I am utterly against agreements to arbitrate questions of vital National interest and honor. But I emphatically believe in the Nation, like the individual, keeping its promise, and our promise to arbitrate applies to just such questions as this of the canal tolls. I think we are right in our position. Moreover, I think that almost all nations have a hostile interest to us and that therefore, in spite of our being right, an arbitral tribunal will probably decide against us. But all of this we should have considered when we made the arbitration treaties. I was lukewarm about those treaties. I only went into them because the general feeling of the country demanded it. But so far as possible I intend to see that the country after lightheartedly entering into them shall now proceed to live up to them.

With love to dear Lady Springy. *Ever yours*

To Michael A. Schaap

Oyster Bay, January 24, 1913

My dear Assemblyman Schaap:

It seems to me that in the interest of the people of New York it is now imperatively necessary that the Legislature of the State should undertake a thorough investigation into the labor conditions of the special industries severally designated as white goods, wrapper and kimono. In the dress and waist industry an investigation has already been arranged for within the industry itself by the joint action of the employers and the union.

No such joint action has been arranged concerning the white goods, wrapper and kimono industry, and it cannot be arranged until the employers in those industries recognize the fundamental need that the employees shall have the right to combine into unions recognized by the employers. This investigation should embrace all the conditions affecting the men and women in that industry, having especial regard to the wages, the earnings, the hours and conditions of work, drawing a sharp distinction between actual earnings and wage scales, and including contracting, subcontracting and minor subcontracting. I submit herewith a copy of a statement of Mr. Harry A. Gordon, the counsel of the employers in the white goods industry. Mr. Gordon claims that as regards the greater number of the establishments in the industry the conditions are good, and he courts investigation of them. He specifically admits that in some cases there is need of shorter hours of employment, of improved sanitation, and of a rise in wages — on all of which points all my other informants entirely agree with him. It is not my province, nor is it within my power, to pass judgment on conflicting claims as to the extent to which improperly low wages, unsanitary conditions and excessive hours prevail in this industry; there is no question that there are some factories in which the conditions are excellent, and in which the employers are fully alive to their duties towards their employees; there is also no question that in other factories the conditions are bad from every standpoint.

I emphatically dissent from the position taken by Mr. Gordon as representative of the manufacturers in their attitude towards trade unionism. This position is in effect that taken a number of years ago by a certain gentleman in the anthracite coal trade, and has since been known as the "Vicegerent of God" position, the position that the employer ought to treat his employees well and humanely, but should be held responsible only to God and his own conscience for his actions — a position taken throughout history not only by absolute monarchs who were good, but by absolute monarchs who were bad. The manufacturers represented by Mr. Gordon express their emphatic opposition to the protocol or memorandum of agreement in the cloak, suit and skirt industry between the manufacturers and the union, signed September 2nd 1910. As I am submitting this attack by Mr. Gordon on the protocol in question I must also add that his allegations of fact are challenged by such persons as Miss Wald, Mr. Henry Moskowitz, Mr. William J. Schieffelin, Mr. Julius Henry Cohen and others whose names can be given. The persons named are working continuously under the protocol and know whereof they speak. Moreover Mr. Gordon states that his organization will not deal with or recognize the union. To my mind this is the critical point of difference. No man can inquire in the most cursory manner into the situation as it actually exists among these kimono and white goods workers without realizing that these young girls are absolutely helpless if they are obliged to bargain for their rights individually. They must possess the right of collective bargaining, and they must be able to establish for themselves relations with kindred organizations which will support them when they are wrongfully treated. Moreover, in my judgment, there must be a government body, like the United States Department of Labor, whose business it shall be to oversee the actual workings of the industry under these different agreements. Already this Department has made an investigation of the workings of the protocol in the cloak industry. I send you herewith a copy of its report. Objection is often made that individual unions misbehave themselves. I have not the slightest question that this is the fact. It is well to bear in mind Abraham Lincoln's homely phrase that "There is a deal of human nature in mankind." There are, and will be, individuals and organizations that misbehave themselves among labor unions exactly as among employers' associations. One of the prime needs of our present social situation is that the genuine believer in trades unionism, the genuine believer in the rights of the working men and women of this country — including especially their right to combine and to speak collectively to their collective employers — shall fearlessly point out and reprobate the act of the union that is wrong, including specifically any attempt to prevent the discharge of incompetent workers, or the just and fair maintenance of shop discipline. For the employer to discharge a good man as "incompetent," when the real reason is that the man has stood for the rights of himself and his fellows, is an outrage; and it is equally an outrage for the union to support the kind of workingmen whose actions within and without the shop represent applied anarchy.

I visited bodies of girl strikers in Henry Street and in St. Mark's Place, and choosing at random listened to the stories of the different girls. In Henry Street the girls were mostly recent immigrants from Southern Spain and from the Turkish Empire. Those from the Turkish empire could not speak English, and although they were of Jewish faith they could not speak Yiddish, so that they were peculiarly helpless under our conditions here. Some of the girls were fourteen and fifteen years old, others sixteen, seventeen and eighteen. The wages were in one or two cases as low as $3 a week, and up to $5.50, $6, and $8 a week. I was informed that there were girls who worked for $2.50 a week, and there was one I saw who worked for $3.31 a week, and two or three who worked for $3 a week. One girl of fifteen earned $5 a week, but had to pay $30 for a machine on which she worked. Another, who had to pay $32 for a machine, worked from 8 a.m. to 8 p.m. and mentioned that in Summer she was charged 10 cents a week for ice water. Another girl who was earning $5 a week had a father in the hospital, and out of the $5 a week was supporting two young children, her brother and sister, in addition to herself. These young girls from Turkey represented the lowest and poorest paid workers that we saw; their fathers and brothers being ignorant of English find it difficult to get employment, and the girls often support the whole family on their scanty sweatshop earnings. Some of the girls out of the miserable pittance paid them have themselves to pay for repairs to machines and for thread and needles.

In St. Mark's Place the girls looked healthier and as if their lives were lived under better conditions — better conditions of course being a purely relative term, for the conditions as to many of the girls were very bad also. They spoke English. Many of these girls did not live at their homes, and in such cases the owner of the house in which they lived, whom they generally spoke of as the "missus," charged them $3 a month for lodging, this lodging sometimes consisting of one bed and sometimes of a place in a bed with other girls. I was informed that often three or four girls slept in one bed. One such girl, for instance, was earning $4.50 a week, $18 a month. Out of this she paid $3 for lodging, $2 a week or $9.50 a month, for breakfast and supper; leaving $6 a month for dinner or the midday meal, for carfare, for clothing, for medicine when sick, for dentist, for oculist, as well as for recreation if there was any. I mention the oculist particularly because the conditions of work are such that the eyes of many of the girls are affected.

Now here were young girls, many of them undeveloped children, toiling excessive hours each day, often (as Mr. George M. Price of the New York State Factory Investigating Commission informs me) in dark unsanitary shops, without any adequate fire protection, sometimes under grossly unsanitary conditions, generally for low wages, diminished in many cases by charges for machines, electric power, for needles and even for drinking water. These girls are to be the future mothers of part of our American citizenship of the next generation. Aside even from the feeling of deep sympathy for them personally, which must be aroused in any man who investigates their conditions, there is the larger question of the social good of the whole race. I do not think that either the National Government or the State Government can afford to ignore this question. We cannot as a community sit in apathy and permit these young girls to fight in the streets for a living wage and for hours and conditions of labor which shall not threaten their very lives. I very earnestly urge that a State Investigating Committee be appointed to inquire into the conditions of work in the wrapper, kimono and white goods trades (the shirtwaist and dressmakers' investigation being proceeded with under their own protocol).

This protocol just adopted in the dress and waist industry is a document for which I especially ask your earnest consideration. I enclose a copy. I especially ask your attention to the language used by Mr. Julius Henry Cohen on the inside of the first page of that document as follows:

> The protocol in the dress and waist industry — signed after deliberation — will bring peace and economic order out of anarchy and chaos. Let employers generally take notice. If they will but sit down and reason in conference with the rational representatives of organized labor, Dynamite and Sabotage will pass out of this land, and diplomacy and Voluntary Courts of Arbitration will take their place. Which is preferable? There is a crisis in our nation's industrial life. Let us meet it as statesmen, not as anarchists. The reactionaries in both camps — Capital and Labor — are the real enemies of society. Let us crowd them out. They have no place in an American Democracy.

Surely this represents the ideal towards which we should strive, with the purpose of realizing it in each industry as rapidly as the conditions will permit. Our aim should be to establish hearty co-operation between employer and employed, individually and collectively, each side temperately insisting on its own rights, freely recognizing the rights of the other side, and both sides recognizing the larger right of interest of the community as a whole.

I ask for the investigation not merely for the purpose of publicity, but as a means for bringing about necessary legislation. Under the protocol of which I send you a copy, minimum wage boards are established by the industry itself through co-operation between the manufacturers and the workers. I ask that the State not only further this idea but follow it by State action creating such boards in industries where they have not been created freely by the action of those in the industry itself. The Legislative Committee of the Progressive Party will present to the Legislature carefully prepared minimum wage bills, and the investigation for which I ask will furnish additional grounds for demanding the passage of such bills.

CONGRATULATIONS ON AN APPOINTMENT

To Franklin Delano Roosevelt

Oyster Bay, March 18, 1913

Dear Franklin:

I was very much pleased that you were appointed as Assistant Secretary of the Navy. It is interesting to see that you are in another place which I myself once held. I am sure you will enjoy yourself to the full as Assistant Secretary of the Navy and that you will do capital work. When I see Eleanor I shall say to her that I do hope she will be particularly nice to the naval officers' wives. They have a pretty hard time, with very little money to get along on, and yet a position to keep up, and everything that can properly be done to make things pleasant for them should be done. When I see you and Eleanor I will speak to you more at length about this. *Yours aff.*

WELCOME AND UNWELCOME GUESTS

To Winthrop Chanler

Oyster Bay, April 1, 1913

Dear Winty:

Why don't you take this letter and show it to George Meyer? He is an old goose! Show it to Cabot too if Cabot betrays any similar feelings. I very much wish to see both Cabot and George on here. Of course I don't know whether the meeting will embarrass *them*, but assure either or both of them from me that it won't embarrass *me*! I understood absolutely the attitude of both. I feel very strongly against Root, because Root took part in as downright a bit of theft and swindling as ever was perpetrated by any Tammany ballot box stuffer, and I shall never forgive the men who were the leaders in that swindling. But with Cabot and George it was wholly different. They had the absolute right to do each exactly as he did, and I never expected either of them to follow me. They have been among my best and most valued friends, Cabot most of course, but George very much so also. I am greatly attached to them, and I most certainly hope they will be on at the wedding. Use your own judgment about showing this to either of them. I don't suppose there is any need of showing it to Cabot, but if you think that George Meyer would really like to come to the wedding, and is staying away for any such reason as you indicate, why by all means let him see just what I have written and then bring him on yourself. We sent the invitations to both of them because we hoped they would come. We did not send invitations to Root or Taft or Nicholas Murray Butler or Cushing because they would have been just as unwelcome guests as Barnes or Penrose or Guggenheim.

I look eagerly forward to seeing you and Hester, who is a delightful replica of her delightful mother. *Always yours*

KEEPING THE FLEET UNDIVIDED

To Franklin Delano Roosevelt

Oyster Bay, May 10, 1913

Dear Franklin:

It is not my place to advise, but there is one matter so vital that I want to call your attention to it. I do not anticipate trouble with Japan, but it may come, and if it does it will come suddenly. In that case we shall be in an unpardonable position if we permit ourselves to be caught with our fleet separated. There ought not to be a battleship or any formidable fighting craft in the Pacific unless our entire fleet is in the Pacific. Russia's fate ought to be a warning for all time as to the criminal folly of dividing the fleet if there is even the remotest chance of war.

Give my love to Eleanor. I have written poor Hall. *Always yours*

EXPLORING THE MATO GROSSO

To Lauro Müller

Telegram

Manaus, April 30, 1914

My dear General Lauro Müller:

I wish first to express my profound acknowledgements to you personally and to the other members of the Brazilian Government whose generous courtesy alone rendered possible the Expedição Scientifica Roosevelt-Rondon. I wish also to express my high admiration and regard for Colonel Rondon and his associates who have been my colleagues in this work of exploration. In the third place I wish to point out that what we have just done was rendered possible only by the hard and perilous labor of the Brazilian Telegraphic Commission in the unexplored western Wilderness of Mato Grosso during the last seven years. We have merely put the cap on the pyramid of which they had previously laid deep and broad the foundations. We have had a hard and somewhat dangerous but very successful trip. No less than six weeks were spent in slowly and with peril and exhausting labor forcing our way down through what seemed a literally endless succession of rapids and cataracts. For forty-eight days we saw no human being. In passing these rapids we lost five of the seven canoes with which we started and had to build others. One of our best men lost his life in the rapids. Under the strain one of the men went completely bad, shirked all his work, stole his comrades' food and when punished by the sergeant he with cold-blooded deliberation murdered the sergeant and fled into the wilderness. Col. Rondon's dog, running ahead of him while hunting, was shot by two Indians; by his death he in all probability saved the life of his master. We have put on the map a river about 1500 kilometers in length running from just south of the 13th degree to north of the 5th degree and the biggest affluent of the Madeira. Until now its upper course has been utterly unknown to everyone, and its lower course altho known for years to the rubber-men utterly unknown to all cartographers. Its source is between the 12th and 13th parallels of latitude South, and between longitude 59° and longitude 60° west from Greenwich. We embarked on it about at latitude 12° 1′ south and longitude 60° 18′ west. After that its entire course was between the 60° and 61st degrees of longitude, approaching the latter most closely about in latitude 8° 15′. The first rapids were at Navaité in 11° 44′, and after that they were continuous and very difficult and dangerous until the rapids named after the murdered sergeant Paishon in 11° 12′. At 11° 23′ it received the Rio Kermit from the left. At 11° 22′ the Marciano Carlo entered it from the right. At 11° 18′ the Taunay entered from the left. At 10° 58′ the Cardozo entered from the right. At 10° 24′ we encountered the first rubber-men. The Rio Branco entered from the left at 9° 38′. We camped at 8° 49′ on approximately the boundary line between Mato Grosso and Amazonas. The confluence with the Amazonas, which entered from the left was in 7° 34′. The mouth, where it entered the Madeira was in 5° 30′. The stream we have followed down is that which rises farthest away from the mouth, and its general course is almost due north.

My dear Sir, I thank you from my heart for the chance to take part in this great work of exploration.

With high regard and respect, believe me, *very sincerely yours*

THE OUTBREAK OF WAR

To Arthur Hamilton Lee

Oyster Bay, August 22, 1914

Dear Arthur:

I cannot forbear writing you just a word of affectionate sympathy in the very hard time you are having in England. Thank Heaven! at least you do not have to suffer what the continental nations are suffering. I thought England behaved exactly as she ought to behave, and with very great dignity. It was a fine thing. In this country the feeling is overwhelmingly anti-German. It is emphatically in favor of England, France and Belgium; yet curiously enough it is very lukewarm as regards

Russia and Serbia. They feel that Germany's course on her Western frontier is a menace to civilization, whereas they are very doubtful when it comes to an issue between the Slav and the German. Our own preposterous little fools have thought this a happy time to pass universal arbitration treaties. In international affairs Wilson is almost as much of a prize jackass as Bryan. The arbitration treaties won't do us any serious harm, because they would be contemptuously disregarded if it was ever proposed to apply them in a way that would damage us in face of Germany or Japan, the only two nations from whom we have to fear aggression in the New World, at least so far as we can see now. But they do do us a certain amount of damage, and it seems incredible that at the moment when the experience of Luxembourg and Belgium shows the utter worthlessness of treaties of this kind, our sapient jacks should officially proclaim to the world their belief in the un-limited power of bits of paper with names put on them.

Belle and Kermit are in the house. Belle has recovered from her typhoid fever, as it was only a slight attack. My own parochial affairs are of no earthly consequence at a time like this, and so I do not write you about them. I hope you are entirely over your sickness. One good result of the war, so far as England is concerned, seems to be the absolute sweeping away of danger from the Home Rule question.

With dearest love to Ruth, *Ever yours*

P.S. After dictating the above, and when it was brought up for my signature, I received your welcome letter. It was most thoughtful to send it to me. By the time this reaches you I believe you will have practically regained your health and will be doing all you can in this grave crisis. I read your letter aloud at the table, and it gave the utmost satisfaction to all of us. I have never liked Winston Churchill, but in view of what you tell me as to his admirable conduct and nerve in mobilizing the fleet, I do wish that if it comes in your way you would extend to him my congratulations on his action. It must be strictly confidential, of course. It seems to me that Edward Grey behaved very well. All that you say about the conduct of England is true. I doubt if she has ever shown to more advantage. The great seriousness of the crisis seems to have brought out everything that is best in the national character.

I am bound to say substantially the same thing about both France and Belgium. As for the Germans, I have a very real and sincere liking and respect for them individually. In all essentials they are like ourselves — indeed so far as Americans are concerned they are largely ourselves, for we have an immense German strain in our blood, and I for instance number among my ancestors Germans as well as Englishmen, although they are outnumbered by my Dutch and Scotch ancestors. I can honestly say that I have not one particle of feeling except of respect and kindly regard for the German people as such. But the Government of Prussianized Germany for the last forty-three years has behaved in such fashion as inevitably to make almost every nation with which it came in contact its foe, because it has convinced everybody except Austria that it has no regard for anything except its own interest, and that it will enter instantly on any career of aggression with cynical brutality and bad faith if it thinks its interest requires such action. I do not know whether I would be acting right if I were President or not, but it seems to me that if I were President I should register a very emphatic protest, a protest that would mean something, against the levy of the huge war contributions on Belgium. As regards Belgium, there is not even room for an argument. The Germans, to suit their own purposes, trampled on their solemn obligations to Belgium and on Belgium's rights. The Belgians have fought for their hearthstones and homes and for the elemental rights without which it is not worth while to exist. To visit them with grinding punishment because of such action is proof positive that any power which now or hereafter may be put at the mercy of Germany will suffer in similar shape — and this whether the power were the United States, or England, or France, or Russia. I agree with you that if Germany is beaten, England will in self-defense be obliged utterly to destroy her colonial empire, and to take the sharpest measures in restriction of her navy. There is no alternative. For the last forty-three years Germany has spread out everywhere, and has menaced every nation where she thought it was to her advantage to do so. Her share in doing injury to Japan has now been promptly avenged by that nation, which has bided its time for nineteen years with quiet politeness, and struck at once when it was safe to do so. Of course Japan was not influenced in the least by any loyalty to England in thus striking; she simply took the opportunity when she could with safety deliver a smash at Germany, just as she would deliver a smash at us if ever she thought it safe and easy to do so. With the Japanese in the Pacific we can avoid war permanently only if we keep our navy at the highest state of efficiency. Without an efficient navy we would be as helpless before Japan as you would be before Germany if you had a useless navy. Italy has really been quite as much menaced by her ally Germany as by France, and I should not be a bit surprised to see her throw her forces into the scale against the two Germanic powers.

You are a little more ready to prophesy than I am, although the action of the Germans in Belgium has from a military standpoint exactly borne out the beliefs you gained from what occurred at the German maneuvers. It does, however, seem to me an impossibility that Germany can conquer in any complete sense. She will certainly lose all she has beyond the seas. At any time now I should expect to hear that the Australians had taken possession of the German islands and ports in the Pacific, and that the African possessions of Germany had gone; while of course Japan will gobble up what she has in Asia. Even from the standpoint of brutal self-interest, I think Germany's invasion of Belgium was a mistake. The Germans, as I happen to know, counted confidently upon being mobilized within ten days, and at the end of that time having an army which had marched through Belgium break up the French before their mobilization was complete. As it is, three weeks have gone by and no German troops are yet on French soil, while great loss has been experienced by the Germans in forcing their way into Southern Belgium, and hitherto they have not succeeded in taking the most important forts that the Belgians hold. If the Franco-British armies hold their own against the Germans, whether they win a victory or whether the result is a draw, it is in my judgment all up with Germany. Even if the Germans win against the Franco-British armies, my belief is that they cannot win sufficiently soon or in such crushing manner as to enable them to complete the conquest of France and the driving of the British Army from the continent before with enfeebled forces they turn to meet the tremendous advance of the Russian armies. Evidently Montenegro and Serbia now hold in check the Austrian armies which Austria is obliged to keep on her Southern frontiers instead of using them against either France or Russia. If Germany is mastered, she will be reduced to international impotence. If she wins, which I regard as possible but improbable, she will not be able to reduce Russia to impotence, she will not materially have harmed England, but will have turned it into a great military power, and in all probability will have excited in the United States a feeling of active hostility. Our people have never forgotten the attitude taken by Germany in the Spanish War, and since then threatened by Germany in South America. It was decades before we got over the remembrance of England's attitude during the Civil War, but England's friendliness for the last few decades, and Germany's hostile attitude for the last fifteen or twenty years, have worked an extraordinary change in public sentiment here.

At the same time I do not agree with you when you speak of this as being the last war for civilization. I see no reason for believing that Russia is more advanced than Germany as regards international ethics, and Japan with all her politeness and her veneer of western civilization is at heart delighted to attack any and every western nation whenever the chance comes and there is an opportunity for Japan to gain what she desires with reasonable safety. If Germany is smashed it is perfectly possible that later she will have to be supported as a bulwark against the Slav by the nations of Western Europe, and while as regards the United States there can be little chance of hostility between us and Russia, there is always the chance of hostility between us and Japan, or Oriental Asia under the lead of Japan.

It seems to me that the attitude of the Irish in this business has been fine, and of good omen to the British Empire; and I am also immensely impressed with the fine attitude of the warlike peoples of India.

You may remember that after my visit to Germany four years ago I told you that I was impressed that Germany might very possibly — whether probably or not I could not say — strike at England if she thought the chance favorable. You say you think that for ten years the Emperor and his advisers have been leading a pipe-dream type of existence. I should make it forty years. When Germany took Alsace and Lorraine from France she of course made France forever her bitter foe. It may be that at the time Germany was right in feeling that the course she took was the only one possible. But if so she should then have made up her mind that France would always be her foe, and that she must do everything in her power to isolate that foe and convince the other nations that Germany was no menace to them. She should not have tried for a colonial empire, or in any way have made England a foe, and should have made it evident to England that she was bent upon safeguarding the independence of both Holland and Belgium. She should have avoided giving mortal offense to Japan, and making the United States feel that she was antagonistic. She should have grappled Italy as well as Austria to her with hoops of steel and have exhausted every expedient to prevent that Austrian attitude which rendered a clash with Russia inevitable. Surely the directors of German policy must by this time realize the damage they have done.

Give my dearest love to Ruth. I am very glad at what you are doing around Chequers, and at what you propose to do with Chequers itself. Edith sends her love to both of you.

Of course this letter is only for you and Ruth. I am an ex-President; and my public attitude must be one of entire impartiality — and above all no verbal or paper "on to Berlin" business.

PROTECTING BELGIAN NEUTRALITY

To Cecil Spring-Rice

Oyster Bay, October 3, 1914

Dear Cecil:

I have received your letters. I am glad you liked the *Outlook* article and the others. I see the Cologne *Gazette* has attacked me. With this I am pleased, because, while I wished to be scrupulously fair and not in the least bitter toward Germany,

I yet wished to make my position as clear as a bell. As a matter of fact, it has been very hard for me to keep myself in. If I had been President, I should have acted on the thirtieth or thirty-first of July, as head of a signatory power of the Hague treaties, calling attention to the guaranty of Belgium's neutrality and saying that I accepted the treaties as imposing a serious obligation which I expected not only the United States but all other neutral nations to join in enforcing. Of course I would not have made such a statement unless I was willing to back it up. I believe that if I had been President the American people would have followed me. But whether I am mistaken or not as regards this, I am certain that the majority are now following Wilson. Only a limited number of people could or ought to be expected to make up their minds for themselves in a crisis like this; and they tend, and ought to tend, to support the President in such a crisis. It would be worse than folly for me to clamor now about what ought to be done or ought to have been done, when it would be mere clamor and nothing else.

The above is only for yourself. It is a freer expression of opinion than I have permitted myself in any letter hitherto.

Of course, I only acted in the Japanese-Russian affair when I had received explicit assurances, verbally from the Russians and in writing from the Japanese, that my action would be welcome; and three or four months of talk and negotiation had preceded this action on my part.

As for the people who clamor for peace now, I shall take the opportunity of reminding them that there were in the northern United States in 1864 several hundred thousand men who in the loudest terms declared their extreme devotion to peace and that these to a man voted against Abraham Lincoln; and if in that year England and France had joined, as certain of their public men wished them to join, in offering mediation so as to bring about "peace," we should have treated it as an unfriendly act.

I believe that you will put the war through. I am glad the opinion of our country is on your side. It is perfectly possible that Russia may in its turn become a great military danger in the future, but it is also possible that this war may see the dawn of the reaction against militarism and that Russia may tend to grow more civilized and more liberal. At any rate there is no question as to where the interests of civilization lie at this moment. *Faithfully yours*

GERMANY AND BELGIUM

To Hugo Münsterberg

Personal

Oyster Bay, October 3, 1914

My dear Professor Münsterberg:

I have received your very interesting book and it impresses me very much. But, my dear Münsterberg, there are two or three points that you leave out of calculation. The first and most essential is that when a nation faces immediate death or humiliation because of the deed of another nation, it cannot look to the future with lofty philosophy, see the possible resulting good of its own ruin, and disregard the moral question of the moment. I firmly believe that in 1812 it was an essential thing to overthrow Napoleonic France. I feel that the German movement against France and the English resistance to France represented the struggle for light. (Let me remind you that Russia, that Asia, as you call it, was then on the side of Germany and that Germany could have done nothing without Russia and would have acted inexcusably if she had remained under France's yoke because it could be truthfully said that France represented far more enlightenment than Russia.) At that time the United States made war on England and by just so much gave comfort and strength to the Napoleonic side in the European struggle. Yet the action of the United States was absolutely necessary. My criticism of the United States in 1812 is heavy but it is not because she went to war with England; it is because she did not prepare effectively in advance for the war and wage it effectively; and indeed, as far as I am concerned, I think she ought to have declared war on both France and England.

Now, this is the exact case with Belgium today. The more

I have studied the case, the more keenly I have felt that there can be no satisfactory peace until Belgium's wrongs are redressed and until there is some kind of effective guaranty against the repetition of them as against her and others. I do not for a moment believe that the predominant German motive in this war was aggression. I regard the talk about the Kaiser "wishing a blood-bath" as preposterous. I am sure that nine tenths of the German people have acted primarily from fear — from an honorable fear, just as you phrase it, that German civilization would be wiped out if they did not strike their foes. But, my dear Münsterberg, there was a ten per cent remainder, including the bulk of the men high up, who have for fifty years cultivated a theory in international matters quite as aggressive, quite as regardless of the rights of others and of all questions of international morality, as that which the French and to an only less extent the English had cultivated in the preceding seventy years. This country was strongly anti-English for a generation after the Civil War, because of the attitude of England and (also France) during the Civil War. But you probably do not realize the deep impression made upon this country by the attitude of Germany toward us in the Spanish War, especially in connection with Admiral Diederichs at Manila, and also by the attitude of Germany in South America.

Now, not for publication, but frankly between ourselves, do you not believe that if Germany won in this war, smashed the English Fleet and destroyed the British Empire, within a year or two she would insist upon taking the dominant position in South and Central America and upon treating the United States precisely as she treated Japan when she joined with Russia and France against Japan twenty years ago and took Kiaochow as her share? I believe so. Indeed I know so. For the great Germans with whom I have talked, when once we could talk intimately, accepted this view with a frankness that bordered on the cynical; just exactly as the big Russians with whom I have talked took the view that international morality had no place where Russian interests were concerned.

I am under no illusions as to any friendship for the United States that England or France may entertain. It would be worthless to us in any crisis unless it was greatly to the interest of France and England to support us. But it does seem to me that England had to act as she did when Belgium was invaded; and that as regards Belgium there are no two sides to the question.

I am not much interested in trying to get at the truth about the alleged outrages on individuals. The unquestioned fact is that Belgium has been ruined, that wonderful and beautiful old cities have been destroyed, that millions of entirely unoffending plain people have been reduced to the last pitch of misery, because Germany deemed it to its interest to inflict upon Belgium the greatest wrong one nation can inflict upon another. I grant you that Germany sincerely believed that this was necessary to her own existence; but surely we are not to be excused if we do not try to prevent the possibility of the recurrence of such incidents.

What the outcome of this war may be no human being can tell. At the moment it looks as if both sides might hammer themselves into a state of absolute exhaustion. If the allies should win and should then wish to dismember Germany and reduce her to impotence, whatever I could do would be done to prevent such a deed. I would regard it as a frightful calamity to civilization; and if Austria falls to pieces, I very earnestly hope that the German portion and all the other portions that are willing will join the Germanic body — the German Empire. But most emphatically I hope that ample reparation will be made to Belgium and that an effectual guarantee against the repetition of such wrongs as those that she has suffered will be arranged.

Now, as to the Russian. You speak very bitterly of him, and indeed of the Slav as a whole. I freely admit that the Russian is backward. They have a long way to go, those Russians, before they leave far enough behind them the days of Tartar dominion and the days when Tartar dominion was only overthrown through the upgrowth of a government such as that of Ivan the Terrible. The attitude of the Russian toward the Finn, the Caucasian, the Pole, the Jew and the Slavonian German in the past has too often been an evil attitude. But I think that liberal ideas are gaining in Russia. The gain is slow but on the whole it seems to me that it is evident. I do not believe the Russian will become an Asiatic. I think he will in the long run be the most effective means of preventing a recrudescence of Asiatic rule over Europe. Down at bottom, my dear Münsterberg, the Russian is just about like you or like me. The Englishman thinks of the German as an alien by race and innate disposition. I know better, for I have some English and some German blood in me, not to speak of other strains. In exactly the same way I find that here in America the descendants of the Slavonic immigrants become men precisely like ourselves. Surely in the end we can aim for a better understanding between German, Englishman and Slav; and such an understanding must be based on justice and no one of them must feel for the others either fear or contempt.

You will not misunderstand me. I am not an ultrapacificist. I regard the Wilson-Bryan attitude of trusting to fantastic peace treaties, to impossible promises, to all kinds of scraps of paper without any backing in efficient force, as abhorrent. It is infinitely better for a nation and for the world to have the Frederick the Great and Bismarck tradition as regards foreign policy than to have the Bryan or Bryan-Wilson attitude as a permanent national attitude, for the Bryan-Wilson attitude is one that would Chinafy the country and would reduce us to the impotence of Spain when it was under the leadership of Godoy — "The Prince of Peace," as he was officially entitled. A milk-and-water righteousness unbacked by force is to the full as wicked as and even more mischievous than force divorced from righteousness. But surely there is a goal different from either toward which we can strive. Surely we can strive for an international peace of justice, based on ability to guard ourselves from injustice, and determination not to do injustice to others, a peace in which some step shall have been taken toward putting international force behind an international desire to secure at least a reasonable approximation toward justice and fair play. *Sincerely yours*

To Mrs. Ralph Sanger

Oyster Bay, December 22, 1914

My dear Mrs. Sanger:

I am very sorry; but I cannot sign that appeal. I do not approve of it. You are asking Americans to proclaim themselves Anglo-Americans, and to sympathize with England on the ground that England is the motherland and in order to make what you call "hands across the sea" a matter of living policy. I do not believe that this is the right attitude for Americans to take. England is not my motherland any more than Germany is my fatherland. My motherland and fatherland and my own land are all three of them the United States. I am among those Americans whose ancestors include men and women from many different European countries. The proportion of Americans of this type will steadily increase. I do not believe in hyphenated Americans. I do not believe in German-Americans or Irish-Americans; and I believe just as little in English-Americans. I do not approve of American citizens of German descent forming organizations to force the United States into practical alliance with Germany because their ancestors came from Germany. Just as little do I believe in American citizens of English descent forming leagues to force the United States into an alliance with England because their ancestors came from England. We Americans are a separate people. We are separated from, although akin to, many European peoples. The old Revolutionary stock was predominantly English, but by no means exclusively so; for many of the descendants of the Revolutionary New Yorkers, Pennsylvanians and Georgians have, like myself, strains of Dutch, French, Scotch, Irish, Welsh and German blood in their veins. During the century and a quarter that has elapsed since we became a nation there has been far more immigration from Germany and Ireland and perhaps even from Scandinavia than there has been from England. We have a right to ask all of these immigrants and the sons of these immigrants that they become Americans and nothing else; but we have no right to ask that they become transplanted or second-rate Englishmen. Most emphatically I myself am not an Englishman once removed! I am straight United States!

In international matters we should treat each nation on its conduct and without the slightest reference to the fact that a larger or smaller proportion of its blood flows in the veins of our own citizens. I have publicly and emphatically taken ground for Belgium and I wish that the United States would take ground for Belgium, because I hold that this is our duty, and that Germany's conduct toward Belgium demands that we antagonize her in this matter so far as Belgium is concerned, and that we emphatically and in practical shape try to see that Belgium's wrongs are redressed. Because of the British attitude toward Belgium I have publicly and emphatically approved of this attitude and of Great Britain's conduct in living up to her obligations by defending Belgium, even at the cost of war. But I am not doing this on any ground that there is any "hands across the sea" alliance, explicit or implicit, with England. I have never used in peace or in war any such expression as "hands across the sea"; and I emphatically disapprove of what it signifies save in so far as it means cordial friendship between us and any other nation that acts in accordance with the standards that we deem just and right. On this ground, all Americans, no matter what their race origins, ought to stand together. It is not just that they should be asked to stand with any foreign power on the ground of community of origin between some of them and the citizens of that foreign power. *Sincerely yours*

"WILSON'S ABJECT COWARDICE"

To Archibald Roosevelt

Syracuse, New York, May 19, 1915

Dear Archie:

There is a chance of our going to war; but I don't think it is very much of a chance. Wilson and Bryan are cordially supported by all the hyphenated Americans, by the solid flubdub and pacifist vote. Every soft creature, every coward and weakling, every man who can't look more than six inches ahead, every man whose god is money, or pleasure, or ease, and every man who has not got in him both the sterner virtues and the power of seeking after an ideal, is enthusiastically in favor of Wilson; and at present the good citizens, as a whole, are puzzled and don't understand the situation, and so a majority of them also tend to be with him. This is not pardonable; but it is natural. As a nation, we have thought very little about foreign affairs; we don't realize that the murder of the thousand men, women and children on the *Lusitania* is due, solely, to Wilson's abject cowardice and weakness in failing to take energetic action when the *Gulflight* was sunk but a few days previously. He and Bryan are morally responsible for the loss of the lives of those American women and children — and for the lives lost in Mexico, no less than for the lives lost on the high seas. They are both of them abject creatures and they won't go to war unless they are kicked into it, and they will consider nothing whatever but their own personal advantage in the matter. Nevertheless, there is a chance that Germany may behave in such fashion that they will have to go to war. Of course, I will notify you at once if war is declared; but I hope in any event, that it won't be until you and Quentin have had your month in camp. Probably, as you suggest, in the event of war, I would send you out at once to get under Jack Greenway.

As for the libel suit here, the rulings of the Judge have been such that he has refused to let the jury take into account all my most important evidence, evidence which, to my mind, showed Barnes' guilt beyond a shadow of doubt. The rulings are quite incomprehensible from the standpoint of common sense. But whether they will appeal to the legalistic mind as proper, I do not know.

I am much interested in what you tell me about the incident that led up to your conversation with good Mr. Branding, and I grinned over the incident. I need not say I accept absolutely your statement — that goes without saying; I think you are very right, under all the circumstances, not to drink anything more. *Ever yours*

PREPARING FOR WAR

To Kermit Roosevelt

Oyster Bay, August 28, 1915

Dearest Kermit:

The enclosed letter from old Heller explains itself. I thought you would enjoy reading it. I am glad the leisurely Bwano got the spectacled bear.

Quentin is home from the camp, having received a very good certificate from the regular officer over him, Captain Van Horn. In these certificates the regular officers are required to state exactly their opinion as it would be if they were to have the man about whom they write under them in a volunteer regiment. Quentin's certificate read that he had done good work and that with more age and experience he would make an excellent Second Lieutenant. Archie did really very well indeed. He was given a Battalion Second Lieutenancy at the close of the Students' Camp and stayed a fortnight longer with the Businessmen. Rather to my delight he was put over Ted! One Sunday the two regular officers over them, together with Archie and Ted, went to Montreal to look at some of the military preparations there. Archie with glee mentioned to me the fact that at the Club the two regular officers were both always addressed as "Major," he (Archie) as "Captain," and Ted as "Mr. Roosevelt." I shall tactfully and sympathetically question Ted about the matter day after tomorrow when I see him in camp. Archie's recommendation read in the highest terms, stating that he was fit to be Captain in a volunteer regiment now; and if this infernal skunk in the White House can be kicked into war a Captain Archie shall be. Ted has already been promoted to be a Sergeant. When he comes back a supplementary camp is to be held, to which Mac will go, so that I shall have had three sons and a private secretary in the camps. The camps have been very successful. They are starting others in various parts of the country. But of course they represent nothing whatever but makeshifts. We ought to have universal military service. I enclose you a copy of the address I shall make at the camp and also a statement I have just given to the paper about the sinking of the *Arabic*.

I agree with all that you say about the German brutality and ruthlessness. But after all a brute is not any worse than a coward. Wilson is at heart an abject coward; or else he has a heart so cold and selfish that he is entirely willing to sacrifice the honor and the interest of the country to his own political advancement. Think of President Eliot and Lawrence Lowell and Cleve Dodge and men like that supporting Wilson! Well, I am making as stout a fight as I know how; but the old proverb applies: there are no bad regiments but there are plenty of bad colonels. The United States would stand like a unit if we had in the Presidency a man of the stamp of Andrew Jackson. Think of Old Hickory letting our citizens be constantly murdered on the high seas by the Germans and in Mexico by the Greasers! But men are easily puzzled; and it is easy to mislead them, if one chooses to give them high-sounding names to excuse ignoble deeds. This is the evil service that President Wilson has rendered and is now rendering the American nation. Still, the Germans may kick us into war. He has acted in Mexico in simply ludicrous fashion. In order to seem to do something and yet to do nothing he got a number of the South American powers into consultation and of course what they have told him is that America ought not to intervene at all. Naturally if we have not the manhood ourselves to intervene, we cannot expect Bolivia and Guatemala to lead us along the path of manful duty.

Give my darling Belle many kisses for me. Ethel and her baby have gone off to visit Dorothy Straight. Willard Straight, by the way, is in camp and has been made a Lieutenant. The two Bob Bacons, father and son, are also in camp. Mother and I have had some lovely rows recently. *Your loving father*

GRANDCHILDREN AND DUTY

To Marjorie Sterrett

Oyster Bay, February 5, 1916

Dear little Miss Marjorie,

On behalf of my four grandchildren I join in the effort to help you and your schoolfellows put our country in shape to "Fear God, and Take Her Own Part."

I enclose a dollar. Forty cents — a dime apiece — are for: —

Gracie Roosevelt
Richard Derby II
Theodore Roosevelt III
Cornelius Van Schaak Roosevelt

Cornelius is the youngest. He is only about two months old. He is'n't as long as his name. But he will grow up to it. He is named after his great-great-grandfather, who when I was very small, over fifty years ago, helped teach me a Dutch baby-song. Little Richard is the eighth Richard Derby, from father to son, born here in America. He loves the bulldog — a nice, friendly, almost toothless bulldog. Little Ted is really Theodore IV; for my father was Theodore Roosevelt. He was the best man I ever knew; strong, fearless, gentle. *He* "feared God and took his own part"! Gracie is four. The other day her mother was giving her one of her first bible lessons.

Her mother said "Now, Gracie, remember that God made everything."

Gracie (much impressed) "Did He make *everything?*"

Her mother (with emphasis) "Yes; everything!"

Gracie (after a pause) "Well, He did'n't make my leggings fit very well; but I'm sure He meant to, so I wo'n't say anything about it!"

The other sixty cents are for my other six grandchildren. They are not born yet. If they are girls I think some of them will be named Edith, Alice, Ethel, Eleanor and Belle. If they are boys some of them will be named Kermit, Archie, Quentin and Jonathan Edwards. Jonathan Edwards was an ancestor of their grandmother's who lived in Colonial times. He was a great preacher and a strong and good man. I do'n't agree with all his theology; but his life teaches the two lessons which are more important than all others for the Americans of today; for he always acted in accordance with the strongest sense of duty, and there was'n't a touch of the mollycoddle about him. *Your friend*

RIGHTEOUSNESS AND PEACE

To Henry Ford

Port of Spain, Trinidad, February 9, 1916

My dear Mr. Ford:

I am very much pleased at your letter of the 3rd. Of course, when I come to Detroit it will be a great pleasure to see you. I want to go over at length with you this pacifist business. My dear sir, it was a real grief to me when you took the stand that you did about pacifism. I felt you had rendered a great service industrially, and therefore socially, to this people by what you had done in connection with your automobile factory. I hated to see you fall into the trap of pacifism; for in this country pacifism has been the enemy of morality for over fifty years. Don't forget that the pacifists of 1864 were the copperheads; that the men who put peace above righteousness without exception voted against Abraham Lincoln; that Abraham Lincoln had to war most strongly against the men who tried "to take the soldiers out of the trenches" in the Civil War. Righteousness, if triumphant, brings peace; but peace does not necessarily bring righteousness; and you, my dear Mr. Ford, can render the very greatest service to this country if you will stand up for the valor of righteousness and put your great name and great influence back of that movement; and not try to help strike down righteousness in the name of peace — a copperhead peace.

Again cordially thanking you, I am, *Sincerely yours*

P.S. I do'n't object to the professional pacifist movement merely because it is futile; I object to it primarily because it is profoundly mischievous from the moral standpoint.

To William Moody

Oyster Bay, May 18, 1916

My dear Moody:

Charley Washburn has sent me the letter you wrote him on May 11th, and Mrs. Roosevelt and I are so profoundly touched and pleased by it, that I must send you this line to say so.

I have always said there were three men to whom I owed more than to any three others during the time I was President. One was Elihu Root; another was Gifford Pinchot. These two were with me throughout my term of office, and perhaps therefore I should say I owed them the most. As soon as I left office both obeyed the centrifugal tendencies of the time and flew in opposite directions — Root in the direction of sacrificing idealism to an excessive taste and desire to be severely practical, and Gifford in the direction of sacrificing practical achievement to an excessive, and sometimes, twisted, idealism. You were the man with whom I was in most complete sympathy; the man to whom I owed more and more the longer you stayed with me. If I had not felt obliged to put you on the Supreme Court, you would have ended by being far and away the most influential man for progress in the right direction that there was in my administration. It was, however, more important to have you on the court, and had you been able to stay on the court, I believe you would have accomplished more than any man that has ever been on it, with the sole exception of Marshall — and [   ] you would have worked — as Marshall worked — for nationalism and efficiency, and you would have also worked, as he did not work, for the great Democratic principle of sanely, though cautiously and resolutely endeavoring, to make each of us, so far as may be, "his brother's keeper."

What would I not give if we now had high in our governmental counsels your keen intelligence, your high purpose, and your spirit of good humor and moderation in the endeavor to serve great ideals, by enlisting on their behalf men whose service was often and indeed usually conditioned by aptitudes, traits and surroundings that were anything but idealistic.

I heard from Harry Stimson of his visit to you the other day. *Always yours*

"THE SYMPATHY OF ADMIRATION"

To Thomas Herbert Warren

Oyster Bay, June 7, 1916

My dear Doctor Warren:

It has been a real pleasure to receive your letter, and though at the moment I am up to my ears in work, I cannot resist writing a line in response. Indeed, I am very glad if you have taken any satisfaction in anything I have written during the present war. It must be a very special pleasure to you to feel that you supported Lord Roberts.

While I was President I advocated in a message to Congress the Swiss system of universal service as the example which our country should follow; but at that time I seriously questioned if there were as many as five men in the United States who even knew what I meant, and nobody took the trouble to so much as get angry with me, or to ridicule me for having made the suggestion. A year and three quarters ago at the time when I began to hammer into this country the lamentable lessons taught by this great war, I stood very nearly alone; but I have now a considerable following. I do not believe it is anything near a majority, but it is at least a ponderable minority.

I am pleased that you liked the sketch of myself in the volumes on John Hay. I take the liberty of sending you my *Autobiography*. Incidentally, although it has no special reference to my political life, do glance at the chapter called "Outdoors and Indoors."

I wish very much that there were a chance of welcoming you and yours to our house here. Is there the least likelihood of your coming across to this side of the water? Give my warm regards to Mrs. Warren. Mrs. Roosevelt sends love to both of you.

That was a happy quotation from Horace which Hay used. He was one of the very few men I have known who in conversation or in casual notes said or quoted the felicitous things which one reads of as being said by charming men or women of the past, and which one so rarely sees or listens to in real life. I am distinctly ashamed to say that I myself am no longer at home in Greek nor even in Latin; but as I do not wish to fall too much in your estimation, I boastfully state that one of my sons still continues to read his Horace and Lucretius; and the other, when we went through South America, carried the *Iliad* and *Odyssey*, as the only non-Portuguese books which he had with him — except *The Oxford Book of French Verse*, which he lent me, as I was too benighted to read either Greek or Portuguese.

In my autobiography I did not like to speak of the various presents given me by European sovereigns. Next to Hay's gift of the ring with the hair of President Lincoln (and excepting also a silver vase presented to Mrs. Roosevelt, entirely on their own initiative, by the enlisted men of the battleship *Louisiana* after we had gone thereon to Panama) the gift I appreciated most which I received while in the White House was from King Edward. It was a very beautiful miniature of John Hampden, sent me at the time of my inauguration, at the same time that I received the ring from John Hay. It seemed to me to mark King Edward's tact and genuine refinement of feeling that he should have chosen that precise gift for an American President. It is a little ungracious for me to add what I am about to add; but I cannot resist saying that the worthy Kaiser sent me on the same occasion an enormous bronze bust of himself, weighing about a ton, which was brought to the White House on a four-horse dray, and which caused me real anguish until I found an accommodating Art Gallery that was willing to stow it away in a basement.

William Samuel Johnson is a cousin of Mrs. Roosevelt's. He is descended from an old Colonial notable of New York, a Sir William Johnson who, in the middle of the eighteenth century, was the most influential man in controlling the Iroquois in the Mohawk Valley. The old fellow was a Loyalist when the Revolutionary disturbances began, and unquestionably took a very dark view of my own ancestors! Ever since then from father to son the names have gone on alternately as William Samuel and Samuel William. The present man, he who wrote the poem on peace, is a middle-aged lawyer of uneventful life who simply responded to the spur of a deep emotion on this particular occasion. By the way, if you have any knowledge of Calvinist theologians, you may be amused to know that one of Mrs. Roosevelt's ancestors was Jonathan Edwards.

Yes! You are indeed in a grinding struggle. The sympathy I feel for you is the sympathy of admiration. It was Emerson who said, " 'Tis man's perdition to be safe, when for the truth he ought to die." (I doubt if this is verbally correct.) I wish this truth could be driven home to the hearts of the bulk of my fellow countrymen; I am trying so to drive it. *Faithfully yours*

SUPPORTING HUGHES

To James Bryce

Oyster Bay, June 19, 1916

My dear Bryce:

Your letter of June 9th has just come. Indeed, I well remember your bringing Hood to see me, and I was greatly struck by his evident strength and gentleness of character. His illustrious ancestor has always been one of my favorites; because he was one of those men in history of whom we can say with practical certainty that it was fate and chance that prevented his leaving a name equal to the greatest. As soon as I saw the account of Hood's death, I realized who it was. It is a sad and terrible thing to have such a fine young fellow die; but after all, my dear Bryce, inasmuch as we must die, and as it is a mere matter of a very few years whether we die early or late, the vital thing is that our deaths should be such as to help others to live. This is what Hood and the thousands of other officers and enlisted men of the British Navy have accomplished by their deaths in the past two years.

The spirit of Nelson, Hawke, Blake and Drake burns as high as ever in the British Navy today.

The Germans also, while they are fighting in a cause which I abhor, are showing extraordinary qualities of organization and daring. Many of my German friends, when I tell them this, express surprise that I am so against them. I answer them that my own mother was all of her life a thorough Confederate sympathizer; that my kinsfolk on her side fought in the Confederate service. (One of my uncles, an Admiral, built the *Alabama*; another, a Midshipman, was the captain of the last gun which was fired from her before she sank.)

I am immensely proud of the gallantry and the high devotion to right, as they saw the right, which these men showed. I am immensely proud that their blood runs in my veins. I can quite conscientiously say I hold descent from men who wore the Gray as much of a badge of honor, as descent from men who wore the Blue. Yet I believe that never in history was there a war in which right was more entirely on one side and wrong on the other than in our Civil War; and the triumph of the Confederacy would have been not only a death blow to our people but a terrible misfortune for all mankind.

Where I can speak in this fashion of my own blood kin, I have the right to speak in similar fashion of the Germans.

You have, of course, seen the result of the Presidential nominations here. I am having my own troubles with my fellow Progressives. They are wild to have me run on a third ticket. They feel that the Republican Convention was a peculiarly sordid body, a feeling with which I heartily sympathize. They feel that Mr. Hughes was nominated largely in consequence of the German-Americans, who were against me, and largely also for the very reason that nobody knew anything of his views on living subjects of the day — and a nomination made for such a cause is in my own judgment evidence of profound political immorality on the part of those making it. But Hughes is an able, upright man whose instincts are right, and I believe in international matters he will learn with comparative quickness, especially as I hope he will put Root into office as Secretary of State. Under these circumstances there is in my mind no alternative but to support him. At his worst he will do better than Wilson, and there is always the chance that he will do very well indeed.

Wilson is the most lamentable example we have ever seen

of the success of that kind of demagogue who appeals to the educated incompetents of the *Evening Post* and *Atlantic Monthly* type, the President Eliot type. I have always insisted that he is the greatest possible argument in favor of Democracy, of government by the whole people instead of by "the best." He was supported with more enthusiasm by what I may call the professional intellectuals than any President within my memory. He is without exception the worst of these Presidents. Mechanics, farmers, railroad men and the like make frightful blunders in choosing their representatives. But upon my word, highly educated men of the stamp of President Eliot of Harvard, Nicholas Murray Butler of Columbia, Schurman of Cornell, David Starr Jordan of Leland Stanford, and Cyrus Northrop of Minnesota do rather worse from the moral and intellectual standpoint. The men of the stamp of the late E. H. Harriman, and the present Harry Davison are rather the worst of all; that is, the government of the very rich [   ]

There are a good many forms of government to which I peremptorily object. It would be hard to devise a worse government than one completely dominated by the class spirit of the labor unions, for instance. But on the whole the government of a plutocracy, a mere government of men who accept money-making as the highest, and indeed the only higher expression, of man's activities is the worst.

Mr. Wilson exquisitely combines all of the vices consequent upon the effort to pander to whatever is most objectionable in all three classes.

At present we are drifting stern foremost into a war with Mexico, a war for which he has neither the foresight to prepare, nor the courage either to enter into or to avoid. *Sincerely yours*

AN OFFER OF SERVICE

To Newton Diehl Baker

Oyster Bay, July 6, 1916

Sir:

In the event of a war with Mexico and of volunteers being called for, I have the honor to apply for permission to raise and command a division.

My purpose would be to have the division raised by men who as brigade, regimental, squadron or battalion, troop or company, platoon or squad, commanders, would be chosen carefully with a view to their efficiency in warfare, and who would, in at least a large number, probably a large majority, of the cases, raise the men under them.

I would with your permission submit the division to you with its organization practically complete, so far as the personnel is concerned.

I would raise a cavalry division if you so desire; but in view of the possibility that there may be difficulty in connection with obtaining horses, and of the possibility of the attack being made against the City of Mexico by way of Veracruz, I should like your permission to raise the division on the following lines.

I would make it an infantry division, with a brigade of divisional cavalry instead of a regiment of divisional cavalry; I would raise one, and perhaps two of the brigades as mounted infantry. For service in Mexico I do not believe that it would be necessary to have a brigade of artillery, and instead I should ask permission to raise one regiment of artillery, and one motorcycle regiment with machine guns. In addition I should, of course, raise an engineering regiment, an aviation squadron, a division of the signal corps, together with surgical, supply and other services.

I would respectfully ask permission that I be permitted to request the detailing of regular army officers in the proportion of about one to every thousand men. In the event of war being declared and of my being permitted to raise the division I shall immediately submit to you the names of the regular officers I would like to have as divisional chief of staff, brigade commanders, colonels, lieutenant colonels and majors.

I should like to be permitted to assemble the division at Fort Sill, Oklahoma.

I have made conditional offers to various civilians whom I would desire to have as Divisional Quartermaster General, as Colonels, Lieutenant Colonels, and Majors; and to a very few whom I would desire to have as captains or lieutenants.

In most of their cases, these offers depend in the first instance upon their ability to raise the men, no less than upon my belief that they can handle them when raised. I do not suppose that you wish me at this time to go into details of any kind, but I hold myself ready to do so, whenever it is your wish.

Of course, I understand that nothing can be done at the present moment; but I desire to have my application before you for action if the emergency arises.

I have the honor to be, sir, with great respect, *Very truly yours*

SHAKING HANDS WITH TAFT

To Henry Luther Stoddard

Oyster Bay, September 28, 1916

My dear Mr. Stoddard:

Over a year ago Taft and I were both pallbearers at the funeral of Professor Lounsbury of Yale. He came up, spoke to me, and shook hands with me. In my judgment it would have been simply silly for me to refuse to be a pallbearer for Professor Lounsbury on the ground that Taft was also to be one; and it would have been merely bad manners on my part for me to refuse to recognize him when he came up to speak to me. The newspapers made a great hullabaloo about it at the time. They themselves have utterly forgotten the incident, and are now making another hullabaloo over the Union League Club meeting; and in a short time they will forget that exactly as they have forgotten the other incident.

The Union League Club is to give a reception to Mr. Hughes. Among the members of that Club who will be at that reception are a number of men, including Elihu Root, who shared Taft's guilt four years ago. Indeed, if there must be a choice between them, I think that Root's offense was as rank as Taft's and more wanton. It would, in my judgment, have been absurd for me to say that I would refuse to meet Taft, when I have already met Root and many others. My belief is that for me to refuse to come to the Union League Club for the Hughes reception because Taft was to be there, would be a very, very unwise thing.

I shall most certainly not seek him out at the Club. If he comes up to me and wishes to shake hands, I shall shake hands with him precisely as I did over a year ago at Professor Lounsbury's funeral.

As a mere matter of curiosity, I wish you would tell me why you draw a distinction between the funeral of Lounsbury and the reception to Hughes. *Faithfully yours*

"A LUNATIC FRINGE"

To Amos Pinchot

New York, November 3, 1916

Sir:

When I spoke of the Progressive Party as having a lunatic fringe, I specifically had you in mind. On the supposition that you are of entire sound mind, I should be obliged to say that you are absolutely dishonorable and untruthful. I prefer to accept the former alternative. *Yours truly*

DEMOCRACY AND MILITARY SERVICE

To Stanwood Menken

Oyster Bay, January 10, 1917

My dear Mr. Menken:

As it is unfortunately impossible for me to be present in person, I desire in this letter to express my heartiest good wishes for the success of your meeting and my belief that the movement, in which you are engaged, is one of the really vital movements — indeed at the moment it is I think *the* really vital movement — for the ultimate honor and welfare of this country.

We need, more than anything else in this country, thoroughgoing Americanism, — for unless we are Americans and nothing else, we are not a nation at all — and thoroughgoing preparedness in time of peace against war, — for if we are not thus prepared, we shall remain a nation only until some more virile nation finds it worth while to conquer us.

The work of preparedness — spiritual and material, civic, industrial, and military — and the work of Americanization are simply the two paramount phases or elements of the work of constructive patriotism which your Congress has gathered to foster. There can be no real preparedness in this country unless this country is thoroughly Americanized; for only a patriotic people will prepare; and there can be no deep national feeling for America, until we are all of us Americans through and through.

Americanism means many things. It means equality of rights and therefore equality of duty and of obligation. It means service to our common country. It means loyalty to one flag, to our flag, the flag of all of us. It means on the part of each of us respect for the rights of the rest of us. It means that all of us guarantee the rights of each of us. It means free education, genuinely representative government, freedom of speech and thought, equality before the law for all men, genuine political and religious freedom, and the democratizing of industry so as to give at least a measurable quality of opportunity for all, and so as to place before us, as our ideal in all industries where this ideal is possible of attainment, the system of co-operative ownership and management, in order that the tool users may, so far as possible, become the tool owners. Everything is un-American that tends either to government by a plutocracy, or government by a mob. To divide along the lines of section or caste or creed is un-American. All privilege based on wealth, and all enmity to honest men merely because they are wealthy, are un-American — both of them equally so. Americanism means the virtues of courage, honor, justice, truth, sincerity, and hardihood — the virtues that made America. The things that will destroy America are prosperity-at-any-price, peace-at-any-price, safety-first instead of duty-first, the love of soft living, and the get-rich-quick theory of life.

Preparedness must be of the soul no less than of the body. We must keep lofty ideals steadily before us, and must train ourselves in practical fashion so that we may realize these ideals. Throughout our whole land we must have fundamental common purposes, to be achieved through education, through intelligent organization, and through the recognition of the great vital standards of life and living. We must make Americanism and Americanization mean the same thing to the native born and to the foreign born; to the men and to the women; to the rich and to the poor; to the employer and to the wage-worker. If we believe in American standards, we shall insist that all privileges springing from them be extended to immigrants, and that they in return accept these standards with wholehearted and entire loyalty. Either we must stand absolutely by our ideals and conceptions of duty, or else we are against them. There is no middle course, and if we attempt to find one, we insure for ourselves defeat and disaster.

Citizenship must mean an undivided loyalty to America; there can be no citizenship on the 50–50 basis; there can be no loyalty half to America and half to Germany, or England, or France, or Ireland, or any other country. Our citizens must be Americans, and nothing else, and if they try to be something else in addition, then they should be sent out of this country and back to the other country to which, in their hearts, they pay allegiance. We must have one American language; the language of the Declaration of Independence and the Constitution, of Lincoln's Gettysburg speech and Second Inaugural, and of Washington's farewell address. The American standard of living conditions, and the American standard of working conditions, both must be high. We must insist upon them for immigrants, as well as for the native born. We must insist that the people who work here, live here; that they are not mere birds of passage from abroad. We must insist upon industrial justice, and we cannot get it if we let ignorance and need be preyed upon either by vulpine cunning or by wolfish brutality, and if we do not train the ignorant and the needy up to self-reliance and efficiency.

Preparedness does not mean merely a man with a gun. It means that too; but it means a great deal more. It means that in this country we must secure conditions which will make the farmer and the workingman understand that it is in a special sense their country; that the work of preparedness is entered into for the defense of the country which belongs to them, to all of us, and the government of which is administered in their interest, in the interest of all of us. At this moment, Lloyd George is able to do more than any other man in rallying the people of Great Britain to the defense of that Empire, because the workingmen, the men who actually do the manual labor, know that he has their welfare at heart, that the national ideal for which he is fighting is that which will give them the best chance for self-development, and for that happiness which comes to the man who achieves his rights at the same time that he performs his duties. He is followed by the people as a whole because they know that he stands for the people as a whole. We in America who are striving for preparedness must make it evident that the preparedness is to serve the people as a whole. The war on the other side has shown that there can be no efficient army in the field unless the men behind are trained and efficient, and unless they are wholeheartedly loyal in their patriotic devotion to their country. Here in America we must do justice to the workers, or they will not feel that this is the country to which their devotion is due; and we must exact patriotic devotion to the flag from them, for if they fail to render it they are unfit to live in this country at all. I appeal to all Americans to join in the common effort for the common good. Any man who holds back, and refuses to serve his country with wholehearted devotion, on the ground that enough has not been done for him, will do well to remember that any such holding back, or lukewarmness of patriotism, is itself an admission of inferiority, an admission of personal unfitness for citizenship in a democracy, and ought to deprive him of the rights of citizenship. As for the men of means, from whom we have the right to expect a special quality of leadership, let them remember that as much has been given to them, so much will be expected of them, and that they have no moral right whatsoever to the enjoyment of the ease and the comforts of life beyond that their fellows enjoy, unless they render service beyond what their fellows render.

I advocate military preparedness not for the sake of war, but for the sake of safeguarding this nation against war, so long as that is possible, and of guaranteeing its honor and safety if war should nevertheless come. We hope ultimately the day will come on this earth when wars will cease. But at present the realization of that hope seems as far in the future as the realization of that other hope, that some day in the future all crime shall cease. By wise action, based equally on observed good faith and on thoroughly prepared strength — the precise characteristics which during the last few years we have failed to show — we may hope to limit the probable field of wars; but at present it is as certain as anything can be that every great nation will at some time or other, as generations follow generations, have to face war, and that ours will be no exception to the rule. It is therefore not merely folly, but criminal and unpatriotic folly, to fail to prepare, or to preach the ignoble cult of the professional pacifist, the peace-at-any-price man.

We need first and foremost a thoroughly efficient and large Navy; a navy kept under professional guidance; a navy trained at every point with the sole purpose of making it the most formidable possible instrument of war the moment that war comes; a navy, the mismanagement of which shall be treated as a capital offense against the nation. In the next place, we need a small but highly efficient regular army, of say a quarter million men; an army where provision is made for a certain proportion of the promotions to be by merit, instead of merely seniority; an army of short-term soldiers, better paid than at present; and an army which, like the navy, shall be under the guidance of a general staff. Moreover, every year there should be at one time field maneuvers of from fifty to one hundred thousand men, so that the Army Commander, the Corps Commanders, the Division, Brigade, and Regimental Commanders, who would have to face a foe at the outbreak of war, would all have had experience in performing their duties, under actual field conditions, in time of peace.

The events of the last summer have shown that the Hay bill was as foolish and unpatriotic a bit of flintlock legislation as was ever put on the statute book. I have the greatest admiration and respect for the individual militiamen who went to the border. But the system under which they were sent worked rank injustice to most of them, rank favoritism for some of them, and was worse than ineffective from the national standpoint. It is folly, and worse than folly, to pretend that the National Guard is an efficient second line of defense. Remember also that the laws passed nominally for the betterment of the regular army and navy are producing almost no result. The delays in building the ships are extraordinary. The shortage of enlisted men in the navy and army is appalling, nor is it being made good. It cannot wholly be made good under the volunteer system. But much could be done. Our first care should be to make the navy and the regular army thoroughly efficient.

But this is not enough. To trust only to the Navy and the regular Army amounts merely to preparing to let the other men do it. If we ordinary citizens are fit to be citizens of this country, we shall fit ourselves to defend this country. No man has a right to citizenship in a democracy, if, for any cause whatsoever, he is unwilling to fight, or is morally or mentally incapable of fighting, for the defense of that democracy against a powerful alien aggressor. If a man is physically unfit but is right in his soul and in his head, then he can render high service to the nation, although incapable of bearing arms. But, if from any moral or mental causes he is unwilling to train himself to bear arms, and to bear them if necessary in his country's cause, then he has no moral right to vote.

Be it remembered that such a national armed force as that for which I ask, while very powerful for defense, would be almost useless for aggression. I wish to see our Navy second only to that of Great Britain, because Great Britain is the only power whose naval needs are greater than ours. I do not ask that our Army become second, or anywhere near second, to Germany's, because Germany's military needs are far greater than ours; but merely that relatively to our size our army be made to correspond to that of Switzerland.

This would mean that for the last two or three years of school, our boys would have some military training, substantially such as is given in the Swiss and Australian schools; and that at about the age of nineteen they would spend six months in actual service in the field (or at sea with the fleet) with the colors, and would thereafter for three or four years be required to spend a couple of weeks each year with the colors. Each year, among those who had served well for the six months, a number could be chosen to be trained as officers. These would then be given by the nation for two years, free, a training somewhat like that at West Point, although not as rigid or as thorough. They would be required to pay for this training by, for a certain number of months during each of the few following years, doing their part in drilling the recruits of that year. It would probably be necessary to pay the recruits a small minimum wage so as to be sure that the poorest family would not suffer hardship because of the absence of the young man for six months. No man would be allowed to purchase exemption. The sons of the richest men in the land would have to serve exactly like anyone else, and do exactly the same work — which incidently would be a bit of uncommon good fortune for them.

Side by side with this preparation of the manhood of the country must go the preparation of its resources. The Government should keep a record of every factory, or workshop, of any kind which would be called upon to render service in war, and of all the railroads. All the workers in such factories and railroads should be tabulated so that in the event of war they would not be sent to the front if they could do better service where they were — although as far as possible every strong man should be sent to the front, to the position of danger, while work done in safety should be done by women and old men. The transportation system should receive special study. Factories which would be needed in time of war, should be encouraged by the Government to keep themselves properly prepared in time of peace, and should be required to fill specimen orders, so that there would be no chance of their breaking down in the event of a sudden call at the outbreak of war. Industrial preparedness must go hand in hand with military preparedness.

Indeed, this military preparedness and the acceptance by the nation of the principle of universal, obligatory, military training in time of peace, as a basis of universal, obligatory service in time of war, would do more than anything else to help us solve our most pressing social and industrial problems in time of peace. It would Americanize and nationalize our people as nothing else could possibly do. It would teach our young men that there are other ideals besides making money. It would render them alert, energetic, self-reliant, capable of command, and willing to obey; respectful to others, and demanding respect from others for themselves. It would be the best possible way to teach us how to use our collective strength in order to accomplish those social and industrial tasks which must be done by all of us collectively if we are to do them well.

Just before this war began the male and female apostles of folly and fatuity were at their highest pitch of denunciation of preparedness, and were announcing at the tops of their voices that never again would there be a great war. These preachers of professional pacifism, of peace-at-any-price, of peace put before righteousness and honor and duty, temporarily lead astray many good and earnest men and women. These good, honest intelligent men and women can be shown the facts and when shown the facts will ultimately see the profound immorality as well as the utter folly of the professional pacifist or peace-at-any-price position. There is, however, little to hope for as regards the professional pacifists themselves. The antics of their brethren in England have shown that even although brayed in a mortar their folly shall not depart from them. At the moment their clamor is drowned by the thunder of the great war. But when this war comes to an end, their voices will be as loud as ever on behalf of folly and wickedness, and their brazen effrontery will be proof against all shame, as well as against all wisdom. They will unblushingly repeat every prophecy that has just been falsified by the merciless march of events; they will reiterate all the promises that have always been broken in the past and will always be broken in the future. They are in the majority of cases primarily concerned for the safety of their own wretched bodies, and they are physically safe in the course they follow, for if the disaster they court should come upon this nation, they would themselves instantly flee to safety, while their folly and wrongdoing would be atoned for by the blood of better and braver men.

It is useless to appeal to these persons. But it is necessary to warn our people against them. If our people fail to prepare, whatever the real reason may be, and whatever the reason is which they allege, their fate in the end will be the same. Sooner or later, in such case, either we ourselves or our children will tread the stony path of disaster, and eat the bitter bread of shame. *Faithfully yours*

"AN EX-PRESIDENT WITH HIS DIVISION"

To Jean Jules Jusserand

Oyster Bay, February 16, 1917

My dear M. Jusserand:

I cannot tell whether we shall have war or not; yet it seems to me almost impossible to avoid it. I have already applied for permission to raise a division. It may be that the Government will not intend to send an expeditionary force; it may be that if they do they will not permit me to go with it. In such event, what I should like to do is to raise a division of Americans, who would fight in co-operation with the allies, either under the orders of France or of England. I might be able to make the place of raising it Canada. Of course, I would not attempt to raise it so far as I can now see, unless this country went to war, because I gravely doubt the propriety of an ex-President of the United States attempting to go to war, unless his country is at war. But if we were at war, I should be profoundly unhappy unless I got into the fighting line, and I believe I should raise a division of 20,000 men, even if the Government declined to hold out the promise of an expeditionary force, of which I should form part, to go at the earliest moment.

I believe that in six months I could get this division ready for the trenches. Now, I don't want to be a nuisance instead of a help to France and England, but it is barely possible that inasmuch as they want men, it would be an object to them to have these 20,000 men, and that it would be worth their while to have an ex-President with his division in the trenches — and I need hardly tell you that I would not be a political general, and that I would expect no favors of any kind, except the great favor of being sent to the front. Do you care to inquire confidentially of your Government, whether, under the conditions above outlined, it would be likely that they would care to call upon me, and whether I should raise my troops in Canada, and take them over there for final training in France; or, whether it would be better that I should be under the command of English or French Generals? I shall make some inquiry of England also. *Faithfully yours*

"HE IS YELLOW ALL THROUGH"

To Henry Cabot Lodge

Oyster Bay, February 20, 1917

Dear Cabot:

The enclosed letter explains itself. Can you refer the good fellow to the appropriate document?

I have just received your letter of the 13th. What preposterous nonsense of Stimson's to have told you that Root had compelled Wilson to break with Germany. I never heard of such an absurdity. What you say is absolutely true. Wilson won't break definitely with any man of whom he is afraid. Personally, I have begun to doubt whether he will go to war under any circumstances. He is evidently trying his old tactics; he is endeavoring to sneak out of going to war under any conditions. He is a master hand in bullying Congressmen, (including even some Republican Congressmen) and in bullying ordinary Democratic politicians; he is yellow all through in the presence of danger, either physically or morally, and will accept any insult or injury from the hands of a fighting man. Of course, it costs him nothing, if the insult or injury is to the country, because I don't believe he is capable of understanding what the words "pride of country" mean. Well, I never thought the *Evening Post* could be beaten, but the *New Republic* is running it hard from the standpoint of infamy.

I happen to know that nothing is being done for preparedness, just as you know it. Congress is all right. It is the Administration itself that is to blame, and this means not Baker, nor Daniels, nor Lansing, nor Bryan, but Wilson himself. As for La Follette, he has shown himself to be an unhung traitor, and if the war should come, he ought to be hung. *Faithfully yours*

P.S. Mann ought to be put out of the position of leader of the minority. He is rather worse than Wilson.

TERRESTRIAL AND ARBOREAL MONKEYS

To Joseph Barrell

Oyster Bay, March 5, 1917

My dear Professor Barrell:

I was greatly interested in both pamphlets. Permit me to say that it is refreshing to find a man who does not generalize from insufficient data, but who yet recognizes that some generalization, some type of general deduction from observed and accumulated data, is essential if American scientific work is ever to raise above the mere collecting of bricks in wheelbarrows.

May I make one suggestion? In Africa I actually saw certain monkeys apparently in the state of becoming terrestrial, instead of arboreal, creatures. One of these species I met only on open plains, with very thin thorn tree forest scattered over them. They galloped off like hares, or foxes, whenever they saw us approaching; and we obtained only one or two specimens. The other I had found purely arboreal, in the dense wet mountain forests; but to my utter astonishment, I also found it along the White Nile, on plains with thinly scattered thorn trees; and although it took to the trees at times, its normal method of trying to escape was by running away on the ground. *Sincerely yours*

A MESSAGE FROM THE KAISER

To Eleanor Alexander Roosevelt

Oyster Bay, March 20, 1917

Dearest Eleanor,

What happened was as follows.

Within a week of the outbreak of the war, and after the first assault on Liége, a German whose name I have forgotten, but I think a Count, and bearing letters both from the German Embassy and from the head of one of the great German steamship lines on which I have traveled, came to me, at Progressive headquarters, 42d st & Madison Ave. Bowing, he stated that he was the bearer of a message from His Imperial Majesty; that his Majesty wished me to know that he always kept in mind the great pleasure it had given him to receive me as a guest in Berlin and at the palace in Potsdam, and to entertain me, and that he felt assured he could count on my sympathetic understanding of Germany's position and action.

I bowed, looked him straight in the eyes, and answered, in substance, and nearly in words: — "Pray thank His Imperial Majesty from me for his very courteous message; and assure him that I was deeply conscious of the honors done me in Germany, and that I shall never forget the way in which His Majesty the Emperor received me in Berlin, *nor the way in which His Majesty King Albert of Belgium received me in Brussels.*" He looked me straight in the eyes without changing countenance, clicked his heels together, bowed — whereat I bowed in return — and left the room without speaking another word; nor did I speak another word. *Affectionately*

A REQUEST FOR HIS SONS

To John J. Pershing

Oyster Bay, May 20, 1917

My dear General Pershing:

I very heartily congratulate you, and especially the people of the United States, upon your selection to lead the expeditionary force to the front. When I was endeavoring to persuade the Secretary of War to permit me to raise a division or two of volunteers I stated that if you or some man like you were to command the expeditionary force I could raise the divisions without trouble.

I write you now to request that my two sons, Theodore Roosevelt, Jr., aged 27, and Archibald B. Roosevelt, aged 23, both of Harvard, be allowed to enlist as privates under you, to go over with the first troops. The former is a Major, and the latter a Captain in the Officers' Reserve Corps. They are at Plattsburg for their third summer. My own belief is that competent men of their standing and rank can gain very little from a third summer at Plattsburg, and that they should be utilized as officers, even if only as second lieutenants. But they are keenly desirous to see service; and if they serve under you at the front, and are not killed, they will be far better able to instruct the draft army next fall, or next winter, or whenever they are sent home, than they will be after spending the summer at Plattsburg. The President has announced that only regular officers are to go with you; and if this is to be the invariable rule then I apply on behalf of my two sons that they may serve under you as enlisted men, to go to the front with the first troops sent over.

Trusting to hear that this request has been granted, I am, with great respect, *Very sincerely yours*

P.S. If I were physically fit, instead of old and heavy and stiff, I should myself ask to go under you in any capacity down to and including a sergeant; but at my age, and condition, I suppose that I could not do work you would consider worth while in the fighting line (my only line) in a lower grade than brigade commander.

SENDING "LITTLE BEARS" INTO DANGER

To Theodore Roosevelt Jr.

Oyster Bay, May 30, 1917

Dearest Ted,

I loved the "little bear" letter; darling Eleanor almost wept over it, and I gave it to her to keep. The big bear was not, down at the bottom of his heart, any too happy at striving to get the two little bears where the danger is; elderly bears whose teeth and claws are blunted by age can far better be spared; but (to change from allegory to the first person!) I do not sympathize with the proverb: — "God keep you from the werewolf and from your heart's desire!" It is best to satisfy the heart's desire; and then abide the fall of the dice of destiny.

I think I satisfied Kermit. I was able first to get Quentin into the flying squadron — and now there are literally thousands of applicants who can't be reached. Then I was able to make the try for you and Archie. At the end of August I'll do my level best for Kermit, the shape of my effort depending upon the conditions, including especially whether he gets into active service or into the reserve.

The enclosed letter and memorandum are very satisfactory. You see that the Secretary has now approved your detail; of course I shall not be entirely sure that Wilson wo'n't make him change his mind until you have actually gone; but it is now unlikely that you wo'n't go, and you have established a claim for service abroad that can hardly be ignored. Pershing and Harbord have certainly behaved like trumps. Collins is another trump. Only he and the family are to see the correspondence.

Eleanor and the children are out here and I fairly revel in them. *Your loving father*

Send back the enclosures.

"TO WISH YOU EVERY LUCK"

To Theodore Roosevelt Jr.

Oyster Bay, July 8, 1917

Dearest Ted,

Just a line, through Eleanor, to wish you every luck. Like Artemus Ward I am straining every nerve to get all my wife's relations to the front! (My sons *are* my wife's relations, ar'n't they?). Quentin has his commission and hope to sail in ten days. Lord Derby, thanks to Lord Northcliffe, has offered Kermit a staff position with the British General in Mesopotamia, and he'll be sailing immediately. *Your loving father The Slacker Malgré Lui*

THE EAST ST. LOUIS RIOTS

To Victor Olander

Oyster Bay, July 17, 1917

My dear Sir:

I thank you for your courteous letter enclosing the report of the Committee on Labor of the Illinois State Council of Defense, concerning the race riots at East St. Louis. They had nothing to do with any commission or alleged commission of rape or any other crime. Aside from race antipathy, the report seems to show that the riots were due to economic conditions. I was not informed, in any way, as to these economic conditions which it is alleged led up to the riot, until after Mr. Gompers's speech on July 6th. When on that evening I made my first remarks on the riot I supposed the underlying cause to be racial, and in my remarks I made no allusion whatever to organized labor, or indeed to labor at all, in connection with the riots. It was Mr. Gompers's speech which first gave me clearly to understand that the fundamental cause was alleged to be economic, and that organized labor regarded itself as especially concerned with the riots. Then my attention was called to the newspapers of July 4th, which carried an alleged statement by Mr. Michael Whalen, President of the Central Trades and Labor Councils of East St. Louis. If this statement is correctly reported, Mr. Whalen said: "The chief objection to the negroes is that they would not unionize, and would not strike." I hold, with the utmost intensity of conviction, that it is absolutely impossible for us to succeed along the lines of an orderly democracy, a democracy which shall be industrial as well as political, unless we treat the repression of crime, including crimes of violence, and the insistence on justice obtained through the enforcement of law, as prime necessities. I, of course, refuse, under any conditions, to accept the fact that certain persons decline "to unionize and strike" as warranting their murder, or as warranting any kind of violence against them. But I go much further than this. I will aid in every way in my power to secure, by governmental as well as private action, the remedying of all the wrongs of labor, and in so acting I shall pay no heed to any capitalistic opposition. But I refuse to treat any industrial condition as warranting riot and murder; and I condemn all persons, whether representatives of organized labor or not, who attempt to palliate or excuse such crimes, or who fail to condemn them in clear-cut and unequivocal fashion. I heartily believe in organized labor, just as, and even more than, I believe in organized capital; I am very proud of being an honorary member of one labor organization; but I will no more condone crime or violence by a labor organization or by working men than I will condone crime or wrong-doing by a corporation or by capitalists. A square deal for every man! That is the only safe motto for the United States.

This is a democracy, a government by the people, and the people have supreme power if they choose to exercise it. The people can get justice peaceably, if they really desire it; and if they do not desire it enough to show the wisdom, patience, and cool-headed determination necessary in order to get it peaceably, through the orderly process of law, then they haven't the slightest excuse for trying to get it by riot and murder. All the governmental authorities concerned in the East St. Louis situation should have taken notice of that situation in advance and should take notice of it now. The National Government, and all local governmental authorities in places where such a situation is likely to arise, should take notice now, and act now. Nine-tenths of wisdom is being wise in time. If there has been improper solicitation of negroes to come to East St. Louis, or improper housing and working conditions among them after they have come, or an improperly low wage-scale, or if anything else improper has been done by the capitalists and employers, so that injustice has been done the working men, then it was the bounden duty, and is now the bounden duty, of the government authorities to remedy the wrong and see justice done the working men. But the first consideration is to stop, and to punish, lawless and murderous violence. Lawless violence inevitably breeds lawless violence in return, and the first duty of the government is relentlessly to put a stop to the violence and then to deal firmly and wisely with all the conditions that led up to the violence. If black men are lawlessly and brutally murdered, in the end the effect is to produce lawlessness among brutal blacks. Recently the I.W.W. has been guilty of all kinds of misconduct, and has been acting as in effect a potent ally of Germany, with whom we are now at war; and finally their lawlessness produced an explosion of counter-lawlessness. Of course the government should repress both kinds of lawlessness. It should prevent all lawless excesses against the I.W.W. and it should also act on the theory that these excesses are fundamentally due to the previous failure of the government to deal in drastic fashion and with all necessary severity with the turbulent, lawless, murderous, and treasonable practices which have been so common among the I.W.W. and kindred organizations. And then it should deal in thoroughgoing fashion with the social and industrial conditions which have produced such results. We Americans must hold the scales even.

A few years ago certain negro troops shot up a Texas town, and the other members of their companies shielded them from punishment. The government proceeded to the limit of its power against them all, and dismissed them from the army; not because they were black men who had committed a crime against white men, but because they had acted criminally; and justice should be invoked against wrong-doers without regard to the color of their skins, just as it should be invoked against wrong-doers without regard as to whether they are rich or poor, whether they are employers or employees, whether they are capitalists and heads of corporations who commit crimes of cunning and arrogance and greed, or wage workers and members of labor organizations who commit crimes of violence and envy and greed.

I have just received an abusive letter from an organization styling itself "The Industrial Council of Kansas City," and claiming to be affiliated with the Federation of Labor, which states that I accused organized labor of being responsible for the outrages at East St. Louis. I made no such accusation until the fact that there was at least a measure of truth in the accusation had been in effect set forth in the speech by the special representative of organized labor at the meeting at which I spoke and by the telegram quoted in that speech. Whenever I have the power, I will protect the white man against the black wrong-doer, and the black man against the white wrong-doer; I will as far as I have power secure justice for the laboring man who is wronged by the man of property, and for every man, whether he has property or not, if he is menaced by lawless violence; and when I haven't the power, I will at least raise my voice in protest, if there is the least chance of that protest doing good.

We are at this moment at war with a most formidable and ruthless enemy. We are fighting for our own dearest rights; we are also fighting for the rights of all self-respecting and civilized nations to liberty and self-government. We have demanded that the negro submit to the draft and do his share of the fighting exactly as the white man does. Surely, when such is the case we should give him the same protection, by the law, that we give to the white man. All of us who are fit to fight are to serve as soldiers, shoulder to shoulder, whether we are farmers or townsfolk, whether we are working men or professional men, men who employ others or men who are employed by others. We fight for the same country, we are loyal to the same flag, we are all alike eager to pay with our bodies in order to serve the high ideals which those who founded and preserved this nation believed it our mission to uphold throughout the world. Surely, in such case it is our duty to treat all our fellow countrymen, rich or poor, black or white, with justice and mercy, and, so far as may be, in a spirit of brotherly kindness.

The victims of the mob in East St. Louis were very humble people. They were slain, and their little belongings destroyed. In speaking of the draft riots in New York during the Civil War, Lincoln, addressing a working men's association, singled out as the saddest feature of the riots the killing "of some working people by other working people." We have recently entered into a war, primarily it is true to secure our own national honor and vital interest, but also with the hope of bringing a little nearer to all the world the day when everywhere the humble and the mighty shall respect one another's rights and dwell together in the peace of justice. Surely, when we thus go to war against tyranny and brutality and oppression, our own hands must be clean of innocent blood. We hope to advance throughout the world the peace of righteousness and brotherhood; surely we can best do so when we insist upon this peace of righteousness and brotherhood within our own borders.

In securing such a peace the first essential is to guarantee to every man the most elementary of rights, the right to his own life. Murder is not debatable. *Sincerely yours*

"YOU HAVE SEIZED THE GREAT CHANCE"

To Theodore Roosevelt Jr.

Jack Cooper's, Stamford, Connecticut,
October 20, 1917

Dearest Ted,

After some weeks delay the foreign mails came through in a bunch and I received your very interesting letters. I am so very glad you saw darling Eleanor — but I well know how terribly hard it was to say good bye to her again. However, you and your brothers are playing your parts in the greatest of the world's great days, and what man of gallant spirit does not envy you? You are having your crowded hours of glorious life; you have seized the great chance, as it was seized by those who fought at Gettysburg, and Waterloo, and Agincourt, and Arbela and Marathon.

You are indeed to be congratulated on having General Duncan for your brigade commander and General Seibert for your divisional commander. I am sure that your division is now ready for service. I grow hot with indignation over the folly and complacent sloth responsible for the fact that there are not now, as there readily could have been, half a dozen other divisions to go with you to the front. At the moment I am doing what I can to help the liberty loan; I have taken sixty thousand dollars worth of bonds. I am also warring against the Huns within our gates, from La Follette and Hearst to the Socialists and I.W.W, whenever the chance offers.

The things I would like to tell you I do not suppose the censor would pass. *Your loving father*

DISMISSING DISLOYAL TEACHERS

To William T. Hornaday

Oyster Bay, November 25, 1917

Dear Mr. Hornaday:

I heartily approve the effort to secure the dismissal of all teachers who refuse to sign the loyalty pledge or who in any way have shown the slightest symptoms of disloyalty to this nation or of sympathy with Germany and the other foes of this nation at this time. A public school teacher should stand in loyalty and Americanism precisely where we expect an officer of the Army or Navy to stand, and should be held to an equally rigid accountability for the slightest symptom of disloyalty or of failure in thorogoing Americanism. *Sincerely yours*

To Quentin Roosevelt

Oyster Bay, December 24, 1917

Dearest Quentin,

Mother, the adamantine, has stopped writing to you because you have not written to her — or to any of us — for a long time. That will make no permanent difference to you; but I write about something that may make a permanent difference. Flora spoke to Ethel yesterday of the fact that you only wrote rarely to her. She made no complaint whatever. But she knows that some of her friends receive three or four letters a week from their lovers or husbands (Archie writes Gracie rather more often than this — exceedingly interesting letters).

Now of course you may not keep Flora anyhow. But if you wish to lose her, continue to be an infrequent correspondent. If however you wish to keep her write her letters — interesting letters, and love letters — at least three times a week. Write no matter how tired you are, no matter how inconvenient it is, write if you're smashed up in a hospital; write when you are doing your most dangerous stunts; write when your work is most irksome and disheartening; write all the time! Write enough letters to allow for half being lost. *Affectionately A hardened and wary old father*

To Kermit Roosevelt

Oyster Bay, February 2, 1918

Dearest Kermit:

Since my last letter your letter about Tekrit has come, and I am overjoyed. Three cheers! You have proved yourself; you have made good; you have justified the sorrow and worry you and darling Belle have shared. I am more pleased than I can say. You have actually taken part in a big phase of the greatest war in history; you have efficiently done your duty for the right in the times that tried mens' souls. It *is* better than to be drilling drafted men with wooden cannon here at home, isn't it?

Whether or not we shall see the much-heralded tremendous German offensive I have no idea; her army is still very powerful; but there is no question that the economic strain and social and political unrest within her borders have grown very dangerous; and Austria is if anything in worse shape.

My usefulness is very limited. I do fulfil a modest function, that of telling disagreeable truths which ought to be told but which it is very unpopular to tell and which nobody else will tell. This is a factor in making the Administration do about a fifth of what it ought to and could, instead of only a twentieth. But I tend to be regarded as merely a scold. I am no longer in touch with the dominant currents of the American stream of purpose and perception — I can't say "thought," for there is uncommonly little of it at present. All I wish is to keep on until all of you get back and take up your own lives, and until Quentin marries Flora, and then I shall retire; it is not wise to linger superfluous on the stage; and it is worse to be sour and gloomy and forecast all kinds of evil because the new generation must be spoken to in a different manner — for better or worse.

I am writing darling Belle, saying that I do hope she will take thought primarily of the two children (it is useless to ask her to take thought primarily of herself); that so she can serve you best.

I suppose that Ted and Archie are in the trenches for good now. I do not venture to write you about either public or military matters. *Your loving Father*

To Quentin Roosevelt

Oyster Bay, March 17, 1918

Dearest Quentin,

In a Rochester paper appeared a note from one Whaley, a superintendent of a post office "somewhere in France," who writes "Young Quentin Roosevelt is as modest as a school girl, but as game as they make 'em in aviation. Keep tabs on this game young chap."

Early in the week we were greatly depressed to learn that gallant young Tommy Hitchcock had been captured by the Germans; it is said that he was not hurt. Then came the excitement about Archie. The first news — whether true or not we do not know — was that he had been given the croix de guerre by a French General "under dramatic circumstances"; then the War Dept notified us that he was slightly wounded; then Ted cabled that he had been hit in the leg, and his arm broken, by shrapnel, but that he was in no danger, and that Eleanor would take care of him. Our pride and our anxiety are equal — as indeed they are about all of you.

Why do'n't you write to Flora, and to her father and mother, asking if she wo'n't come abroad and marry you? As for your getting killed, or ordinarily crippled, afterwards, why she would a thousand times rather have married you than not have married you under those conditions; and as for the extraordinary kinds of crippling, they are rare, and anyway we have to take certain chances in life. You and she have now passed your period of probation; you have been tried; you are absolutely sure of yourselves; and I would most heartily approve of your getting married at the earliest possible moment.

Mr. Beebe is out here; he has just come from France; on the French front he was allowed to do some flying and bombing — not fighting the German war-planes. *Your loving father*

To Georges Clemenceau

Private; not *for the official files*

Oyster Bay, March 22, 1918

My dear M. Clemenceau:

The most influential and malignant foe of the Allies, and most powerful supporter and friend of the Germans, in this country is Hearst, the newspaper editor. He is far more dangerous than any organization or newspaper of the German-Americans because he has far wider influence of a very base kind, and far more astuteness. He ardently served Germany up to the period when we went into the war. Since that time he has continued to serve her less openly but quite as effectively. He renders the service in many different ways. He ardently champions negotiations which would lead to the complete triumph of Germany, under cover of supporting the Pope's appeal for peace, or under cover of supporting the Russian Bolshevists' appeal for peace, or under cover of supporting efforts to find out if Austria wouldn't like to make peace. He ardently champions our proposing a peace on the basis of the *status quo ante bellum.* He strongly supports every proposal that means delay in sending troops or munitions and war instruments abroad, or any refusal to declare war on Germany's allies. He continually seeks to create prejudice against, and to embroil us with, England or Japan, as the occasion offers. In short he is as sinister and efficient a friend of Germany as is to be found in all the world. In order to cover up his activities he makes a great pretense of patriotism, or of devotion to the Allies' cause on points where no possible damage to Germany is involved. The feeling in this country for France is very strong and he does not venture to go against it, (although he expressed the greatest disapproval of, and strongly protested against, the demand that France receive back Alsace and Lorraine; and he loudly backs the Russian Bolshevists and their no-annexation and no-indemnities proposal). As part of his campaign he has conducted an advertising scheme for a fund to help "rebuild France." If he can get the French Government to accept his help it will immensely increase his power to aid Germany and to hurt the whole allied cause — and therefore especially France — by his actions in the future. To accept the fund would, in my deliberate judgment, be an evil thing for France here; and no possible material benefit from the money, as regards rebuilding France, will offset the aid and comfort France would thereby give to the man who is playing Germany's game, who can be counted upon to do everything possible to divide and weaken the allies, and who openly and industriously works for a "peace without victory" and against the obtaining of Alsace and Lorraine for France. If the French Government, and above all if you, whose name carries such weight here in America, could announce that France would not find it possible to accept a penny from Mr. Hearst, you would strengthen every friend of the Allies and of the war in America, and incidentally in England; you would offend no human being who is a friend of France, and you would greatly limit Mr. Hearst's real power of mischief to the allied cause.

I was very deeply touched by your note to me during my entirely unimportant sickness. I am very proud that all my sons are on your side of the water and fighting beside the troops of France — and of England and Belgium. One of them was wounded the other day in the trenches, his left arm being broken and one knee injured, together with a slight body wound. One of your Generals gave him the Croix de Guerre, and I am prouder of his having received it than of my having been President!

With high regard, *Faithfully yours*

P.S. Of course I immensely admire your administration of the Government. Oh Lord, how I wish you were President of the United States!

To Cleveland Dodge

Oyster Bay, May 11, 1918

My dear Cleve:

It is difficult for me to write you because of the very fact that six members of your immediate family are in Turkey. Now, my dear Cleve, kinsfolk of mine are in Germany. They are suffering at present from being there. My feeling has been from the beginning that they had no business to stay there. As regards Turkey my feeling is even stronger. I do not feel that any men should have permitted their wives and daughters to stay in Turkey since we have gone to war with Germany. Indeed, my feeling is that from the time of the sinking of the *Lusitania* every American in Germany, Austria, Bulgaria or Turkey should have proceeded on the assumption that ultimately this country would go to war with those four embodiments of satanic policies on this globe at this time, and should have governed himself accordingly. Any Americans in Turkey who now suffer will suffer purely from their own fault; and if they plead their presence in Turkey, after the ample warning they have had, as a reason why this nation should not do its duty, they are guilty of grave moral dereliction.

I entirely agree with all that you say about Robert College and Beirut College in the past. I have no doubt that you are right when you say that there are Bulgarians and Turks (a few!) who are opposed to what their two countries have done in joining Germany. There were Germans and Austrians who felt the same way. But all these men have proved utterly powerless to influence the policies of their countries. They are entitled to no consideration from us in shaping our international policy. It is a good deal worse than silly for us to repeat the worse than silly mistake of those Englishmen who kept insisting that there were Turks and Bulgarians who loved England, and so that England ought not to make active war on Turkey or Bulgaria. I do not for one moment believe that any effective body of Turkish opinion is against Germany, save as it is against all Christians — even against the Christians that let them massacre other Christians. There has been no sign whatever of the existence of any such body of effective opposition to Germany. Foolish persons in England kept insisting on its existence, and did much damage by their insistence. In Turkey public opinion is nil and the people always obey any effective executive force, and obey nothing else. The surest way to strengthen the German hold on Turkey is to give the impression that the Allies are in any way divided. The perpetuation of Turkish rule is the perpetuation of infamy, and to perpetuate it on the theory that there are large numbers of Turks who have fine feelings but who never make those feelings in any way manifest, is an absurdity. If Robert and Beirut Colleges are used as props for the Turkish infamy and if they exert directly or indirectly any influence to keep this country from going to war with Turkey, they will more than counterbalance the good they have done in the past, and will make themselves bywords of derision for the future.

So far from "being of assistance to the Allied cause by keeping on nominal terms of friendliness with Bulgaria and Turkey," I am convinced we are of the very greatest damage to the Allied cause by so doing. Moreover, I feel that we are guilty of a peculiarly odious form of hypocrisy when we profess friendship for Armenia and the downtrodden races of Turkey, but don't go to war with Turkey. To allow the Turks to massacre the Americans and then solicit permission to help the survivors, and then to allege the fact that we are helping the survivors as a reason why we should not follow the only policy that will permanently put a stop to such massacres is both foolish and odious.

I have a most interesting letter on the subject from Einstein, formerly with our Embassy in Turkey. I will send it to you by George Perkins. Some suffering would be caused if we went to war with Turkey, just as some suffering was caused when we went to war with Germany. But the Americans now would suffer only as the English and French suffered three years ago, when their nations were doing their duty, and ours was shirking its duty. We have no business to expect the allies to do the fighting which alone will accomplish anything permanent while we play the utterly ignoble part of being neutral and hoping that somehow or other we can thereby both save our own skins and also accomplish something. The arguments advanced against our going to war with Turkey are on a par with those formerly advanced against our going to war with Germany and then with Austria; only they are not quite as good. The Armenian horror is an accomplished fact. Its occurrence was largely due to the policy of pacifism this nation has followed for the last four years. The presence of our missionaries, and our failure to go to war, did not prevent the Turks from massacring between half a million and a million Armenians, Syrians, Greeks and Jews — the overwhelming majority being Armenians. Our declaration of war now will certainly not do one one-hundredth part of the damage already done by our failure to go to war in the past; and it will enable us to render service of permanent value for the future, and incidentally to take another step in regaining our self-respect.

We should go to war because not to do so is really to show bad faith towards our allies, and to help Germany; because the Armenian massacre was the greatest crime of the war, and failure to act against Turkey is to condone it; because the failure to deal radically with the Turkish horror means that all talk of guaranteeing the future peace of the world is mischievous nonsense; and because when we now refuse to war with Turkey we show that our announcement that we meant "to make the world safe for democracy" was insincere claptrap.

With regret, my dear Cleve, that I must so radically and so fundamentally disagree with you, I am *Sincerely yours*

"THEIR TEMPER AND QUALITY"

To King George V

Oyster Bay, July 22, 1918

Your Majesty,
It was very kind and thoughtful of Her Majesty the Queen, and you, Sir, to cable us about the death of our son Quentin,

and Mrs. Roosevelt and I thank you both, with all our hearts. Of his three brothers Ted, who is a Major of Infantry, has been gassed once and is now in hospital with a bullet through his leg; Archie, a Captain of Infantry, has been badly wounded by a shell; both were cited for gallantry, in orders; Kermit has been Captain of an armored machine gun motor battery with your army in Mesopotamia, has been given the Military Cross, and is now with our army under Pershing. Unlike most of their fellow-countrymen they had prepared in advance! They sailed from our shores over a year ago; their mother and I knew their temper and quality; and we did not expect to see all of them come back.

If you are in touch with your brother-in-law, King Haakon, pray present H.M. my regards. I have not written him recently because I have known how very much he has had to cause him anxiety.

If it be true that the bolshevists have executed the Czar, I should think it would give food for reflection to the Kaiser. Until I saw the revelations by that big German steel manufacturer, Thyssen, and by Lichnowsky, I thought that the Kaiser had merely been swept along by the Junker-capitalistic-militaristic-beaurocratic party; but I fear that he was in reality one of the leaders in the movement that has plunged the civilized world into the abyss. At least America is beginning to render some real help to the Allies, and unless Russia behaves even worse than so far she has behaved the strain can not but tell on Germany; but I always fear lest we find the Germans using Russian man power in their army. I am urging our people over here to prepare *now* for putting in France next year an American army bigger than the German army; if so, we can surely finish the war in '19, and may finish it this year.

I hope all your family are well.

I am, Sir, with great regard, *very faithfully yours*

"A VERY SAD THING"

To Georges Clemenceau

Oyster Bay, July 25, 1918

My dear M. Clemenceau:

I have received many messages from rulers of nations and leaders of peoples; but among these there is none I have valued quite as much as yours, because I have a peculiar admiration for you and feel that you have played a greater part than any man not a soldier has played, and a greater part than any soldier, except one or two, has played in this great world war. It is a very sad thing to see the young die when the old who are doing nothing, as I am doing nothing, are left alive. Therefore it is very bitter to me that I was not allowed to face the danger with my sons. But whatever may be their fate, I am glad and proud that my sons have done their part in this mighty war against despotism and barbarism. Of my four boys Quentin, as you know, has been killed, and two of the other three wounded and all three of these have been decorated for gallantry and efficiency in action.

Thank Heaven, it begins to look as if at last Germany had spent her strength, and I thank Heaven also that we now have at least a few hundred thousand Americans to fight beside the French. *Faithfully yours*

"THEIR GOLDEN MORNING"

To Corinne Roosevelt Robinson

Dark Harbor, Maine, August 3, 1918

Darling Corinne,

Indeed it would be the greatest pleasure — I mean that, exactly — to have you take little Douglas to Sagamore in the holidays.

We are thoroly enjoying our visit to Ethel; its a dear little house, very comfortable; all the people are most considerate;

and little Richard's devotion to Edith has done whatever could be done to ease the dull, steady aching of her heart. He is a dear little boy; he always wishes Edith to sleep beside him when he is taking his nap! Edie is as pretty as a picture, and a little darling; she has been very much of a chimney swallow this morning, clinging to whoever will take her up and cuddle her.

I was much touched by the letters you enclosed; the one from Alice Murray I shall keep, or give to Flora; it was a remarkable letter.

Your burden was harder to bear than ours; for Stewarts life was even shorter than Quentins, and he had less chance to give shape to what there was in him. But, after all, when the young die at the crest of life, in their golden morning, the degrees of difference are merely degrees in bitterness; yet there is nothing more foolish and cowardly than to be beaten down by sorrow which nothing we can do will change.

Edith feels that she does not wish the portrait; will you thank the Studio people very warmly for me? I think she is right. Nor does she feel that Quentin's letters are worth publishing; they are very dear to us (and I dread when Edith receives the letters he wrote before his death — the letters from her dead boy); but they are only such letters as many, many other gallant, clever, manly and gentle boys wrote home — just as our loss is merely like countless other such losses. The history of his life would merely be typical, not exceptional, to the world large; it is to Flora, and to his own household, that the tragedy and the heroism stand by themselves.

Love to Douglas, Helen & Teddy; and to Fanny if she is with you. I shall write her later, some time. *Your devoted brother*

PEACE TERMS

To James Bryce

Dark Harbor, Maine, August 7, 1918

Dear Bryce,

I thank you for your kind letter of sympathy; and I value all you say about my boys, and especially about gallant Quentin who has paid with his life for the faith that was in him. He died just as your nephew, just as young Gladstone, just as so many, many other gallant young fellows have died. It is very dreadful that the young should die and the old be left, especially when the young are those who above all others should be the leaders of the next generation. But they have died with high honor, and not in vain; for it is they, and those like them, who have saved the soul of the world. For the world would have had no soul if the efficient swinishness of Germany had triumphed.

My two wounded sons will both recover. My four boys have "proved their truth by their endeavor," have'n't they?

I am greatly pleased by what you say as to the valor of our troops. I am proud beyond measure that at last we really have a fair sized army in the fighting line.

I am steadily preaching that we ought to make our army in France by next spring larger than the combined armies of England and France.

I absolutely agree with what you say about peace. I do not myself think there will be need of so much wisdom as firmness in settling the terms of peace. The principles are in outline simple enough. I have been preaching them here! England and Japan must keep the Colonies they have won, France receive back Alsace-Lorraine, Belgium be restored and indemnified — Italia irredenta must go to Italy, down to Istria. Roumanian Hungary must go to Hungary. The Czecho-Slovak, Polish and Jugo Slav commonwealths must be created as entirely independent; the latter with access to the Adriatic. Albania should be a cantonal state under the protection of France, England and perhaps the United States; the Turk should be driven from Europe, Armenia made independent under a guarantee of the Allies; the Jews given Palestine; the Syrian Christians protected; the Arabs made independent. The separate nationalities of broken-up Russia should be made commonwealths absolutely free from German dominion and probably independent; the Poles, Slavs of Siberia and Danes of North Sleswig should all be freed from the German yoke.
Faithfully yours

"HER HEART WILL ACHE FOR QUENTIN"

To Belle Willard Roosevelt

Dark Harbor, Maine, August 11, 1918

Darling Belle,

I have written you many times, sometimes like this, direct to the Embassy at Madrid, sometimes, as I am going to do in two or three days, through Mr. Love. If you receive either of these letters (for I shall make the same request in both) will you let me know which address to use hereafter?

Your delightful letter to Mother about your trip with Kermit and blessed Willard from Rome to Madrid has just come. It was even more interesting than Kermit's on the same subject. Aunt Emily also wrote us a most enthusiastic letter about you, and the baby, whom she worships. She immensely admires Kermit, but, quite properly, it is *you* to whom her heart especially goes out. I could not overstate, dearest Belle, how very deeply Mother and I appreciate all that your thoughtfulness and sweetness have meant to and have done for Aunt Emily.

Well, Kermit's extraordinary combination of gentleness, of dauntless courage and energy, and of possession of that elusive but most real quality of being extremely interested in matters and interesting to people, has never been more evident than at the present time; and you, darling girl, have shown that the very sweetest traits of the old-style lovely girl can be joined with the finest heroism and capacity. But I am exactly as proud of the wives of my sons, and of Ethel, as I am of my boys and of Dick.

It is no use pretending that Quentin's death is not very terrible. It is most so for poor Flora who is staying here with Ethel, as we are. But it is almost as hard for Mother. They have both been very brave. There is nothing to comfort Flora at the moment; but she is young; I most earnestly hope that time will be very merciful to her, and that in a few years she will keep Quentin only as a loving memory of her golden youth, as the lover of her golden dawn, and that she will find happiness with another good and fine man. But of course it would be all wrong for me to tell her this *now*. As for Mother, her heart will ache for Quentin until she dies. I would not for all the world have had him fail fearlessly to do his duty, and to tread his allotted path, high of heart, even altho it led to the gates of death. But it is useless for me to pretend that it is not very bitter to see that good, gallant, tender-hearted boy, leave life at its crest, when it held Flora, and such happiness, and certainly an honorable and perhaps a distinguished career.

Evidently Archie is crippled, at least for many months to come, and I wish he would come home. Hitherto the rascal has refused. I would'n't suggest it if he could render any service with the army, but to spend months of pain and idleness in Paris, instead of at least being with his wife and baby and his mother does'n't seem worth while.

Ted has apparently recovered from the gassing, and will soon recover from the bullet wounds in his leg; I am so glad he is with Eleanor.

I do'n't yet know just what Kermit is doing, for I have had no letter from him since he got to France.

Your birthday cable to Mother has just come; it was dear of you to remember.

Kim and Willard must be the most adorable small persons! We have been greatly comforted by Richard and little Edie; the former loves Mother, and the latter lets me love her! (There is a somewhat nice distinction between the two). In time of trouble the unconsciousness of children is often a great comfort.

Tell your father how deeply we appreciated the trouble he took, and the information he got for us from Germany; and give our love to all your dear family. *Ever affectionately yours Kermit's father*

QUENTIN'S LAST LETTERS

To Belle Willard Roosevelt

Oyster Bay, August 11, 1918

Darling Belle,

Day before yesterday I wrote you from Dark Harbor, Maine, where we had been for a fortnight with Ethel and the babies; I addressed it direct to the American Embassy, Madrid; this, which is a sketchy note, is being sent through Mr. Love; do write me which gets to you first, as a guide to my future correspondence.

When we reached here we found Quentin's last letters; he was at the fighting front, very proud and happy — and singularly modest, with all his pride, and his pleasure at showing his metal. Of course that was a wonderful company of men, flying in the swift battle planes — not the ordinary observation or bombing planes — at the front; they were bound together in the close ties of men who know that most of them are to die, and who face their fate high of heart and with a gallant defiance; and Quentin wrote that he would not for any consideration have been any where else. Two days before he was killed he was with Eleanor in Paris; and she was so proud of him, and took him round as the young hero. He had his crowded hour of glorious life.

Yet I do not pretend that it is not very dreadful that his young life, of such promise, should be darkened at dawn. And for Flora and his mother the pain is great. When we reached home yesterday afternoon Alice was waiting for us; a real comfort.

Mrs. Tom Page wrote Belle James a dear letter about you and the adorable baby and Kermit in Rome; such a nice letter. Will you write Kipling and tell him about things? He wrote that he had never heard from Kermit; and he is evidently really fond of you both.

Love to your father, mother and Elizabeth. *Devotedly Kermit's father*

I enclose the photo of a preposterous elderly creature, the father of *real* soldiers in a *real* war, at a time when he went to the only war there was in his time!

UNCONDITIONAL SURRENDER

To Henry Cabot Lodge

Oyster Bay, October 24, 1918

Telegram

I am sending this telegram in triplicate to you and to Senators Miles Poindexter and Hiram Johnson, because I make my appeal to the Representatives of the American people from one ocean to the other. As an American citizen I most earnestly hope that the Senate of the United States, which is part of the treaty-making power of the United States, will take affirmative action as regards peace with Germany and in favor of peace based on the unconditional surrender of Germany. I also earnestly hope that on behalf of the American people it will declare against the adoption in their entirety of the fourteen points of the President's address of last January as offering a basis for a peace satisfactory to the United States.

Let us dictate peace by the hammering guns and not chat about peace to the accompaniment of the clicking of typewriters.

The language of the fourteen points and of the subsequent statements explaining or qualifying them, is neither straightforward nor plain, but if construed in its probable sense many and possibly most of these fourteen points are thoroly mischievous and if made the basis of a peace, such peace would represent not the unconditional surrender of Germany but the conditional surrender of the United States. Naturally they are entirely satisfactory to Germany and equally naturally they are in this country satisfactory to every pro-German and pacifist and socialist and anti-American so-called internationalist.

The only peace offer which we should consider from Germany at this time is an offer to accept such terms as the Allies without our aid have imposed on Bulgaria. We ought to declare war on Turkey without an hour's delay. The failure to do so hitherto has caused the talk about making the world safe for democracy, to look unpleasantly like mere insincere rhetoric. While the Turk is left in Europe and permitted to tyrannize over the subject peoples, the world is thoroly unsafe for democracy.

Moreover we should find out what the President means by continually referring to this country merely as the associate, instead of the ally of the nations with whose troops our own troops are actually brigaded in battle. If he means that we are something less than an ally of France, England, Italy, Belgium and Serbia, then he means that we are something less than an enemy of Germany and Austria. We ought to make it clear to the world that we are neither an untrustworthy friend nor an irresolute foe. Let us clearly show that we do not desire to pose as the umpire between our faithful and loyal friends and our treacherous and brutal enemies, but that we are the staunch ally of our friends and the staunch foe of our enemies. When the German people repudiate the Hohenzollerns, then, and not until then, it will be time to discriminate between them and their masters. I hope the Senate and the House will pass some resolution demanding the unconditional surrender of Germany as our war aim and stating that our peace terms have never yet been formulated or accepted by our people, and that they will be fully discussed with our allies and made fully satisfactory to our own people, before they are discussed with Germany.

"THE VICTORY IS TREMENDOUS"

To Arthur Hamilton Lee

Roosevelt Hospital,
New York, November 19, 1918

Dear Arthur:

Well, we have seen the mighty days and you, at least, have done your full share in them. We have lived through the most tremendous tragedy in the history of civilization. We should be sternly thankful that the tragedy ended with a grim appropriateness, too often lacking. All the people directly or indirectly responsible for the tragedy, all those who have preached and practiced the cynical treachery, brutality and barbarism and the conscienceless worshipping of revolting cunning and brute force which made the German people what it was in

1914 (and what, except that it is defeated, it now is) — all these people have come down in the crash. When the war first broke out I did not think the Kaiser was really to blame. I thought he was simply the tool; gradually I was forced to realize that he was one of the leading conspirators, plotters and wrong-doers. The last fortnight has shown that he was not even a valorous barbarian — he was unwilling to pay with his body when his hopes were wrecked. Think of the Kaiser and his six sons saving their own worthless carcasses at the end, leaving their women, like their honor, behind them. If ever there was a case where on the last day of the fighting the leaders should have died, this was the case.

I was able to render substantial service to the allies during the last month by being probably the chief factor in preventing Wilson from doing what he fully intended to do, namely, double-cross the allies, appear as an umpire between them and the Central Powers and get a negotiated peace which would put him personally on a pinnacle of glory in the sight of every sinister pro-German and every vapid and fatuous doctrinaire sentimentalist throughout the world. I knew in advance what Wilson's intentions were. The probably necessary kowtowing performed in front of him by almost all the British leaders, and by the great majority of the French leaders, had made him certain that they would accept whatever he did. His success in fooling and browbeating our own people, the terror which he had impressed on the newspapers, the immense political funds which he used nominally for national, but really for party, purposes, and the natural tendency of good people to stand by the President in wartime made him convinced that he could induce the nation to follow him in another somersault. Accordingly he entered into negotiations with Germany on the basis of a peace, conditioned upon his famous fourteen points. Germany agreed eagerly and absolutely to his demands. The Fourteen Points were thoroughly mischievous and would have meant a negotiated peace with Germany. Moreover, last January when the Fourteen Points were promulgated our people knew so little of the matter and were so accustomed to loose rhetoric that they did not show any discontent with them. But by the first of October when the Wilson-Germany negotiations were on, our people had waked up. They wished unconditional surrender, and there was an outburst of popular feeling such as I have very rarely seen in America. The President was repudiated and threatened by people who had been his slavish adherents. Wilson is utterly shameless and as soon as he became convinced that the people would upset him, he promptly double-crossed Germany instead of the allies, and appeared again as the lofty opponent of the German Government. But the incident caused him to lose his temper, and he thought he would provide himself with a rubber-stamp Congress in the elections that were about to take place. Accordingly he made an appeal for a Democratic Senate and House, saying that although the Republicans were prowar they were anti-Administration and that he would not regard his policies as sustained if either the House or the Senate were Republican. This gave me my chance, and in the last week of the campaign we did the seemingly impossible, — carried the House by a substantial and the Senate by a bare majority. Wilson explicitly stated that he made no test excepting that of support of his administration, by which he meant support of himself at any point where his personal comfort or personal administration was involved. He appealed just as strongly for antiwar Democrats as for prowar Democrats and his whole argument was against prowar Republicans.

The German people thoroughly understood what the issue was and after election thoroughly understood what had happened. The *Berliner Tageblatt* stated with refreshing frankness that the election of a Republican Congress rendered it impossible for Germany to hope that Mr. Wilson would be able to give them the kind of peace that was "reasonable" — in other words, pro-German.

The comparison between Foch's Twenty-three Points which were actually adopted in the armistice and Wilson's Fourteen show the difference between the shifty rhetorician who wants an indecisive peace and the resolute soldier who will accept only the peace of overwhelming victory. By the way, you will be amused to know that in Canada and Australia I am regarded with hearty sympathy in my views as to the retention by the British Empire of all the German Colonies, etc. etc. I have made the Canadians and Australians feel that *my* utterances do not need a key to explain them!

As regards England, I end the war more convinced than ever that there should be the closest alliance between the British Empire and the United States; and also I am more convinced than ever that neither one can afford for one moment to rely on the other in a sufficiently tight place. There would always of course be the chance that the other, in such event, would wake up to the needs of the situation; but there would also be the chance that its own political tricksters and doctrinaires and sentimental charlatans and base materialists would make it false to its duty. There are just two Englishmen, of the civilian class, with whom I now feel in entire sympathy, namely Kipling and yourself — I am not speaking of dear Trevelyan and the other persons to whom I am attached on mere social and literary grounds.

However, all this is of little account. In spite of our pacifists and sentimentalists and tricky politicians at home, and in spite of the aid given to the worst American foes of England by so many well-meaning foolish Englishmen, America did finally play a real part in the war and played it manfully. England of course has suffered and achieved more than ever before in her whole history. The victory is tremendous, the overthrow of Germany complete.

Ted and Kermit have taken part in the last fighting, and I believe they are now walking toward the Rhine. Archie pretty badly crippled is back with us. I doubt if his arm will ever be quite right again, but he will be able to do a great many things with it. Ted has been made Lieutenant Colonel, and commanded his regiment in the final fighting. Dick Derby has done exceedingly well and has been promoted to be Lieutenant Colonel. This is Quentin's birthday. With dearest love to Ruth and Faith, *Always yours*

"THE MELTING-POT IDEA"

To Madison Grant

Oyster Bay, December 30, 1918

Dear Grant:

Frankly, I think your correspondent an addlepated ass — and the alternative is, that he is worse. I can speak with knowledge of what he says about the Americans in the different units. He says that the southerners and the New Englanders are the best in our lot. In the first place I don't for one moment believe that they are better than the men from the western and middle and Pacific Coast states. They are *all* fine. In the next place, as his thesis is that the fighting quality is in direct proportion to the number of men of old native American blood in the various units, he might take the trouble to inform himself of the simple fact that in the New England units the percentage of men of foreign parentage is as big as in those of the middle and most of the western states. But this is not all. If he knows anything at all he knows that the first and second divisions have on the whole stood the heaviest cutting and rendered the longest service, and that no two divisions in the American army, or in any of the allied armies stand above them. I have had three sons in one, and a son-in-law in the other, and I know what I am speaking about. Now, these two divisions exactly represent the melting-pot idea, about which he ignorantly prattles slander. They include the regular infantry regiments and the marines. If he does not know that the regular infantry regiments and the marines have fought well, he doesn't know anything. Yet a majority, and in some cases a very large majority of the men in these regiments are composed of men of foreign parentage, precisely as is the case with the regiments from Illinois, Wisconsin, Minnesota, Oregon, Washington and other states. If the goose would take the trouble to look over the casualty lists and the lists of the men cited or decorated or mentioned for distinguished gallantry, he would realize what a slander he is speaking. Let him go to the official movie where he will see a picture of my son Ted decorating two of his men for marked gallantry. One of these men was named Murphy; I know nothing of his origin. The other is Lieutenant Holmes, from Cincinnati. On his mother's side he is of pure Jewish blood, the Fleishmans. On his father's side he is half Danish and half native American. He looks, and acts, and thinks and is exactly like any other Yale, or Harvard, or Princeton boy of the oldest Colonial stock.

There are some very obvious errors in what he says of the foreign troops, but I speak only of what I know about the American troops. *Faithfully yours*

"ONE SOUL LOYALTY"

To Richard Melancton Hurd

Oyster Bay, January 3, 1919

Dear Mr. Hurd:

I cannot be with you and so all I can do is to wish you Godspeed. There must be no sagging back in the fight for Americanism merely because the war is over. There are plenty of persons who have already made the assertion that they believe the American people have a short memory and that they intend to revive all the foreign associations which most directly interfere with the complete Americanization of our people. Our principle in this matter should be absolutely simple. In the first place, we should insist that if the immigrant who comes here does in good faith become an American and assimilates himself to us, he shall be treated on an exact equality with everyone else, for it is an outrage to discriminate against any such man because of creed, or birthplace, or origin. But this is predicated upon the man's becoming in very fact an American and nothing but an American. If he tries to keep segregated with men of his own origin and separated from the rest of America, then he isn't doing his part as an American. There can be no divided allegiance here. Any man who says he is an American but something else also, isn't an American at all. We have room for but one flag, the American flag, and this excludes the red flag which symbolizes all wars against liberty and civilization just as much as it excludes any foreign flag of a nation to which we are hostile. We have room for but one language here and that is the English language, for we intend to see that the crucible turns our people out as Americans, of American nationality, and not as dwellers in a polyglot boardinghouse; and we have room for but one soul loyalty, and that loyalty is to the American people. *Faithfully yours* against liberty, and an illusion just as much as it excludes any foreign integration to which we are unable. We have come to bury our heritage, hide and that, the English language aspire toward to see that the visible many our people out as Americans, of American citizenship, and does as a dwelling in a popular to distinguish, and we live at room for but one soil loyalty, and that loyalty is to the American people. I shall...

SELECTED SPEECHES

The Strenuous Life

Speech to the Hamilton Club, Chicago, April 10, 1899

I N speaking to you, men of the greatest city of the West, men of the State which gave to the country Lincoln and Grant, men who preëminently and distinctly embody all that is most American in the American character, I wish to preach, not the doctrine of ignoble ease, but the doctrine of the strenuous life, the life of toil and effort, of labor and strife; to preach that highest form of success which comes, not to the man who desires mere easy peace, but to the man who does not shrink from danger, from hardship, or from bitter toil, and who out of these wins the splendid ultimate triumph.

A life of slothful ease, a life of that peace which springs merely from lack either of desire or of power to strive after great things, is as little worthy of a nation as of an individual. I ask only that what every self-respecting American demands from himself and from his sons shall be demanded of the American nation as a whole. Who among you would teach your boys that ease, that peace, is to be the first consideration in their eyes — to be the ultimate goal after which they strive? You men of Chicago have made this city great, you men of Illinois have done your share, and more than your share, in making America great, because you neither preach nor practise such a doctrine. You work yourselves, and you bring up your sons to work. If you are rich and are worth your salt, you will teach your sons that though they may have leisure, it is not to be spent in idleness; for wisely used leisure merely means that those who possess it, being free from the necessity of working for their livelihood, are all the more bound to carry on some kind of non-remunerative work in science, in letters, in art, in exploration, in historical research — work of the type we most need in this country, the successful carrying out of which reflects most honor upon the nation. We do not admire the man of timid peace. We admire the man who embodies victorious effort; the man who never wrongs his neighbor, who is prompt to help a friend, but who has those virile qualities

755

necessary to win in the stern strife of actual life. It is hard to fail, but it is worse never to have tried to succeed. In this life we get nothing save by effort. Freedom from effort in the present merely means that there has been stored up effort in the past. A man can be freed from the necessity of work only by the fact that he or his fathers before him have worked to good purpose. If the freedom thus purchased is used aright, and the man still does actual work, though of a different kind, whether as a writer or a general, whether in the field of politics or in the field of exploration and adventure, he shows he deserves his good fortune. But if he treats this period of freedom from the need of actual labor as a period, not of preparation, but of mere enjoyment, even though perhaps not of vicious enjoyment, he shows that he is simply a cumberer of the earth's surface, and he surely unfits himself to hold his own with his fellows if the need to do so should again arise. A mere life of ease is not in the end a very satisfactory life, and, above all, it is a life which ultimately unfits those who follow it for serious work in the world.

In the last analysis a healthy state can exist only when the men and women who make it up lead clean, vigorous, healthy lives; when the children are so trained that they shall endeavor, not to shirk difficulties, but to overcome them; not to seek ease, but to know how to wrest triumph from toil and risk. The man must be glad to do a man's work, to dare and endure and to labor; to keep himself, and to keep those dependent upon him. The woman must be the housewife, the helpmeet of the homemaker, the wise and fearless mother of many healthy children. In one of Daudet's powerful and melancholy books he speaks of "the fear of maternity, the haunting terror of the young wife of the present day." When such words can be truthfully written of a nation, that nation is rotten to the heart's core. When men fear work or fear righteous war, when women fear motherhood, they tremble on the brink of doom; and well it is that they should vanish from the earth, where they are fit subjects for the scorn of all men and women who are themselves strong and brave and high-minded.

As it is with the individual, so it is with the nation. It is a base untruth to say that happy is the nation that has no history. Thrice happy is the nation that has a glorious history.

Far better it is to dare mighty things, to win glorious triumphs, even though checkered by failure, than to take rank with those poor spirits who neither enjoy much nor suffer much, because they live in the gray twilight that knows not victory nor defeat. If in 1861 the men who loved the Union had believed that peace was the end of all things, and war and strife the worst of all things, and had acted up to their belief, we would have saved hundreds of thousands of lives, we would have saved hundreds of millions of dollars. Moreover, besides saving all the blood and treasure we then lavished, we would have prevented the heartbreak of many women, the dissolution of many homes, and we would have spared the country those months of gloom and shame when it seemed as if our armies marched only to defeat. We could have avoided all this suffering simply by shrinking from strife. And if we had thus avoided it, we would have shown that we were weaklings, and that we were unfit to stand among the great nations of the earth. Thank God for the iron in the blood of our fathers, the men who upheld the wisdom of Lincoln, and bore sword or rifle in the armies of Grant! Let us, the children of the men who proved themselves equal to the mighty days, let us, the children of the men who carried the great Civil War to a triumphant conclusion, praise the God of our fathers that the ignoble counsels of peace were rejected; that the suffering and loss, the blackness of sorrow and despair, were unflinchingly faced, and the years of strife endured; for in the end the slave was freed, the Union restored, and the mighty American republic placed once more as a helmeted queen among nations.

We of this generation do not have to face a task such as that our fathers faced, but we have our tasks, and woe to us if we fail to perform them! We cannot, if we would, play the part of China, and be content to rot by inches in ignoble ease within our borders, taking no interest in what goes on beyond them, sunk in a scrambling commercialism; heedless of the higher life, the life of aspiration, of toil and risk, busying ourselves only with the wants of our bodies for the day, until suddenly we should find, beyond a shadow of question, what China has already found, that in this world the nation that has trained itself to a career of unwarlike and isolated ease is bound, in the end, to go down before other nations which have not lost the manly and adventurous qualities. If we are to be a really great people, we must strive in good faith to play a great part in the world. We cannot avoid meeting great issues. All that we can determine for ourselves is whether we shall meet them well or ill. In 1898 we could not help being brought face to face with the problem of war with Spain. All we could decide was whether we should shrink like cowards from the contest, or enter into it as beseemed a brave and high-spirited people; and, once in, whether failure or success should crown our banners. So it is now. We cannot avoid the responsibilities that confront us in Hawaii, Cuba, Porto Rico, and the Philippines. All we can decide is whether we shall meet them in a way that will redound to the national credit, or whether we shall make of our dealings with these new problems a dark and shameful page in our history. To refuse to deal with them at all merely amounts to dealing with them badly. We have a given problem to solve. If we undertake the solution, there is, of course, always danger that we may not solve it aright; but to refuse to undertake the solution simply renders it certain that we cannot possibly solve it aright. The timid man, the lazy man, the man who distrusts his country, the over-civilized man, who has lost the great fighting, masterful virtues, the ignorant man, and the man of dull mind, whose soul is incapable of feeling the mighty lift that thrills "stern men with empires in their brains" — all these, of course, shrink from seeing the nation undertake its new duties; shrink from seeing us build a navy and an army adequate to our needs; shrink from seeing us do our share of the world's work, by bringing order out of chaos in the great, fair tropic islands from which the valor of our soldiers and sailors has driven the Spanish flag. These are the men who fear the strenuous life, who fear the only national life which is really worth leading. They believe in that cloistered life which saps the hardy virtues in a nation, as it saps them in the individual; or else they are wedded to that base spirit of gain and greed which recognizes in commercialism the be-all and end-all of national life, instead of realizing that, though an indispensable element, it is, after all, but one of the many elements that go to make up true national greatness. No country can long endure if its foundations are not laid deep in the material prosperity which comes from thrift, from business energy and enterprise, from hard, unsparing effort in the fields of industrial activity; but neither was any nation ever yet truly great if it relied upon material prosperity alone. All honor must be paid to the architects of our material prosperity, to the great captains of industry who have built our factories and our railroads, to the strong men who toil for wealth with brain or hand; for great is the debt of the nation to these and their kind. But our debt is yet greater to the men whose highest type is to be found in a statesman like Lincoln, a soldier like Grant. They showed by their lives that they recognized the law of work, the law of strife; they toiled to win a competence for themselves and those dependent upon them; but they recognized that there were yet other and even loftier duties — duties to the nation and duties to the race.

We cannot sit huddled within our own borders and avow ourselves merely an assemblage of well-to-do hucksters who care nothing for what happens beyond. Such a policy would defeat even its own end; for as the nations grow to have ever wider and wider interests, and are brought into closer and closer contact, if we are to hold our own in the struggle for naval and commercial supremacy, we must build up our power without our own borders. We must build the isthmian canal, and we must grasp the points of vantage which will enable us to have our say in deciding the destiny of the oceans of the East and the West.

So much for the commercial side. From the standpoint of international honor the argument is even stronger. The guns that thundered off Manila and Santiago left us echoes of glory, but they also left us a legacy of duty. If we drove out a mediæval tyranny only to make room for savage anarchy, we had better not have begun the task at all. It is worse than idle to say that we have no duty to perform, and can leave to their fates the islands we have conquered. Such a course would be the course of infamy. It would be followed at once by utter chaos in the wretched islands themselves. Some stronger, manlier power would have to step in and do the work, and we would have shown ourselves weaklings, unable to carry to successful completion the labors that great and high-spirited nations are eager to undertake.

The work must be done; we cannot escape our responsibility; and if we are worth our salt, we shall be glad of the chance to do the work — glad of the chance to show ourselves equal to one of the great tasks set modern civilization. But let us not deceive ourselves as to the importance of the task. Let us not be misled by vainglory into underestimating the strain it will put on our powers. Above all, let us, as we value our own self-respect, face the responsibilities with proper seriousness, courage, and high resolve. We must demand the highest order of integrity and ability in our public men who are to grapple with these new problems. We must hold to a rigid accountability those public servants who show unfaithfulness to the interests of the nation or inability to rise to the high level of the new demands upon our strength and our resources.

Of course we must remember not to judge any public servant by any one act, and especially should we beware of attacking the men who are merely the occasions and not the causes of disaster. Let me illustrate what I mean by the army and the navy. If twenty years ago we had gone to war, we should have found the navy as absolutely unprepared as the army. At that time our ships could not have encountered with success the fleets of Spain any more than nowadays we can put untrained soldiers, no matter how brave, who are armed with archaic black-powder weapons, against well-drilled regulars armed with the highest type of modern repeating rifle. But in the early eighties the attention of the nation became directed to our naval needs. Congress most wisely made a series of appropriations to build up a new navy, and under a succession of able and patriotic secretaries, of both political parties, the navy was gradually built up, until its material became equal to its splendid personnel, with the result that in the summer of 1898 it leaped to its proper place as one of the most brilliant and formidable fighting navies in the entire world. We rightly pay all honor to the men controlling the navy at the time it won these great deeds, honor to Secretary Long and Admiral Dewey, to the captains who handled the ships in action, to the daring lieutenants who braved death in the smaller craft, and to the heads of bureaus at Washington who saw that the ships were so commanded, so armed, so equipped, so well engined, as to insure the best results. But let us also keep ever in mind

that all of this would not have availed if it had not been for
the wisdom of the men who during the preceding fifteen years
had built up the navy. Keep in mind the secretaries of the navy
during those years; keep in mind the senators and congressmen who by their votes gave the money necessary to build and
to armor the ships, to construct the great guns, and to train
the crews; remember also those who actually did build the
ships, the armor, and the guns; and remember the admirals
and captains who handled battle-ship, cruiser, and torpedo-
boat on the high seas, alone and in squadrons, developing the
seamanship, the gunnery, and the power of acting together,
which their successors utilized so gloriously at Manila and off
Santiago. And, gentlemen, remember the converse, too. Remember that justice has two sides. Be just to those who built
up the navy, and, for the sake of the future of the country,
keep in mind those who opposed its building up. Read the
"Congressional Record." Find out the senators and congressmen who opposed the grants for building the new ships; who
opposed the purchase of armor, without which the ships were
worthless; who opposed any adequate maintenance for the
Navy Department, and strove to cut down the number of men
necessary to man our fleets. The men who did these things
were one and all working to bring disaster on the country.
They have no share in the glory of Manila, in the honor of
Santiago. They have no cause to feel proud of the valor of our
sea-captains, of the renown of our flag. Their motives may or
may not have been good, but their acts were heavily fraught
with evil. They did ill for the national honor, and we won in
spite of their sinister opposition.

Now, apply all this to our public men of to-day. Our army
has never been built up as it should be built up. I shall not
discuss with an audience like this the puerile suggestion that
a nation of seventy millions of freemen is in danger of losing
its liberties from the existence of an army of one hundred
thousand men, three fourths of whom will be employed in
certain foreign islands, in certain coast fortresses, and on
Indian reservations. No man of good sense and stout heart
can take such a proposition seriously. If we are such weaklings as the proposition implies, then we are unworthy of
freedom in any event. To no body of men in the United States

is the country so much indebted as to the splendid officers and enlisted men of the regular army and navy. There is no body from which the country has less to fear, and none of which it should be prouder, none which it should be more anxious to upbuild.

Our army needs complete reorganization, — not merely enlarging, — and the reorganization can only come as the result of legislation. A proper general staff should be established, and the positions of ordnance, commissary, and quartermaster officers should be filled by detail from the line. Above all, the army must be given the chance to exercise in large bodies. Never again should we see, as we saw in the Spanish war, major-generals in command of divisions who had never before commanded three companies together in the field. Yet, incredible to relate, Congress has shown a queer inability to learn some of the lessons of the war. There were large bodies of men in both branches who opposed the declaration of war, who opposed the ratification of peace, who opposed the upbuilding of the army, and who even opposed the purchase of armor at a reasonable price for the battle-ships and cruisers, thereby putting an absolute stop to the building of any new fighting-ships for the navy. If, during the years to come, any disaster should befall our arms, afloat or ashore, and thereby any shame come to the United States, remember that the blame will lie upon the men whose names appear upon the roll-calls of Congress on the wrong side of these great questions. On them will lie the burden of any loss of our soldiers and sailors, of any dishonor to the flag; and upon you and the people of this country will lie the blame if you do not repudiate, in no unmistakable way, what these men have done. The blame will not rest upon the untrained commander of untried troops, upon the civil officers of a department the organization of which has been left utterly inadequate, or upon the admiral with an insufficient number of ships; but upon the public men who have so lamentably failed in forethought as to refuse to remedy these evils long in advance, and upon the nation that stands behind those public men.

So, at the present hour, no small share of the responsibility for the blood shed in the Philippines, the blood of our brothers, and the blood of their wild and ignorant foes, lies at the thresholds of those who so long delayed the adoption of the treaty of peace, and of those who by their worse than foolish words deliberately invited a savage people to plunge into a war fraught with sure disaster for them — a war, too, in which our own brave men who follow the flag must pay with their blood for the silly, mock humanitarianism of the prattlers who sit at home in peace.

The army and the navy are the sword and the shield which this nation must carry if she is to do her duty among the nations of the earth — if she is not to stand merely as the China of the western hemisphere. Our proper conduct toward the tropic islands we have wrested from Spain is merely the form which our duty has taken at the moment. Of course we are bound to handle the affairs of our own household well. We must see that there is civic honesty, civic cleanliness, civic good sense in our home administration of city, State, and nation. We must strive for honesty in office, for honesty toward the creditors of the nation and of the individual; for the widest freedom of individual initiative where possible, and for the wisest control of individual initiative where it is hostile to the welfare of the many. But because we set our own household in order we are not thereby excused from playing our part in the great affairs of the world. A man's first duty is to his own home, but he is not thereby excused from doing his duty to the State; for if he fails in this second duty it is under the penalty of ceasing to be a free-man. In the same way, while a nation's first duty is within its own borders, it is not thereby absolved from facing its duties in the world as a whole; and if it refuses to do so, it merely forfeits its right to struggle for a place among the peoples that shape the destiny of mankind.

In the West Indies and the Philippines alike we are confronted by most difficult problems. It is cowardly to shrink from solving them in the proper way; for solved they must be, if not by us, then by some stronger and more manful race. If we are too weak, too selfish, or too foolish to solve them, some bolder and abler people must undertake the solution. Personally, I am far too firm a believer in the greatness of my country and the power of my countrymen to admit for one moment that we shall ever be driven to the ignoble alternative.

The problems are different for the different islands. Porto Rico is not large enough to stand alone. We must govern it wisely and well, primarily in the interest of its own people. Cuba is, in my judgment, entitled ultimately to settle for itself whether it shall be an independent state or an integral portion of the mightiest of republics. But until order and stable liberty are secured, we must remain in the island to insure them, and infinite tact, judgment, moderation, and courage must be shown by our military and civil representatives in keeping the island pacified, in relentlessly stamping out brigandage, in protecting all alike, and yet in showing proper recognition to the men who have fought for Cuban liberty. The Philippines offer a yet graver problem. Their population includes half-caste and native Christians, warlike Moslems, and wild pagans. Many of their people are utterly unfit for self-government, and show no signs of becoming fit. Others may in time become fit but at present can only take part in self-government under a wise supervision, at once firm and beneficent. We have driven Spanish tyranny from the islands. If we now let it be replaced by savage anarchy, our work has been for harm and not for good. I have scant patience with those who fear to undertake the task of governing the Philippines, and who openly avow that they do fear to undertake it, or that they shrink from it because of the expense and trouble; but I have even scanter patience with those who make a pretense of humanitarianism to hide and cover their timidity, and who cant about "liberty" and the "consent of the governed," in order to excuse themselves for their unwillingness to play the part of men. Their doctrines, if carried out, would make it incumbent upon us to leave the Apaches of Arizona to work out their own salvation, and to decline to interfere in a single Indian reservation. Their doctrines condemn your forefathers and mine for ever having settled in these United States.

England's rule in India and Egypt has been of great benefit to England, for it has trained up generations of men accustomed to look at the larger and loftier side of public life. It has been of even greater benefit to India and Egypt. And finally, and most of all, it has advanced the cause of civilization. So, if we do our duty aright in the Philippines, we will add to that national renown which is the highest and finest part of national life, will greatly benefit the people of the Philippine Islands, and, above all, we will play our part well in the great work of uplifting mankind. But to do this work, keep ever in mind that we must show in a very high degree the qualities of courage, of honesty, and of good judgment. Resistance must be stamped out. The first and all-important work to be done is to establish the supremacy of our flag. We must put down armed resistance before we can accomplish anything else, and there should be no parleying, no faltering, in dealing with our foe. As for those in our own country who encourage the foe, we can afford contemptuously to disregard them; but it must be remembered that their utterances are not saved from being treasonable merely by the fact that they are despicable.

When once we have put down armed resistance, when once our rule is acknowledged, then an even more difficult task will begin, for then we must see to it that the islands are administered with absolute honesty and with good judgment. If we let the public service of the islands be turned into the prey of the spoils politician, we shall have begun to tread the path which Spain trod to her own destruction. We must send out there only good and able men, chosen for their fitness, and not because of their partizan service, and these men must not only administer impartial justice to the natives and serve their own government with honesty and fidelity, but must show the utmost tact and firmness, remembering that, with such people as those with whom we are to deal, weakness is the greatest of crimes, and that next to weakness comes lack of consideration for their principles and prejudices.

I preach to you, then, my countrymen, that our country calls not for the life of ease but for the life of strenuous endeavor. The twentieth century looms before us big with the fate of many nations. If we stand idly by, if we seek merely swollen, slothful ease and ignoble peace, if we shrink from the hard contests where men must win at hazard of their lives and at the risk of all they hold dear, then the bolder and stronger peoples will pass us by, and will win for themselves the domination of the world. Let us therefore boldly face the life of strife, resolute to do our duty well and manfully; resolute to uphold righteousness by deed and by word; resolute to be both honest and brave, to serve high ideals, yet to use practical methods. Above all, let us shrink from no strife, moral or physical, within or without the nation, provided we are certain that the strife is justified, for it is only through strife, through hard and dangerous endeavor, that we shall ultimately win the goal of true national greatness.

National Duties

Speech at the Minnesota State Fair,
St. Paul, September 2, 1901

I N his admirable series of studies of twentieth-century problems, Dr. Lyman Abbott has pointed out that we are a
nation of pioneers; that the first colonists to our shores were
pioneers, and that pioneers selected out from among the descendants of these early pioneers, mingled with others selected
afresh from the Old World, pushed westward into the wilderness and laid the foundations for new commonwealths. They
were men of hope and expectation, of enterprise and energy;
for the men of dull content or more dull despair had no part
in the great movement into and across the New World. Our
country has been populated by pioneers, and therefore it has
in it more energy, more enterprise, more expansive power
than any other in the wide world.

You whom I am now addressing stand for the most part but
one generation removed from these pioneers. You are typical
Americans, for you have done the great, the characteristic, the
typical work of our American life. In making homes and carv-
ing out careers for yourselves and your children, you have
built up this State. Throughout our history the success of the
home-maker has been but another name for the upbuilding
of the nation. The men who with ax in the forests and pick in
the mountains and plow on the prairies pushed to completion
the dominion of our people over the American wilderness
have given the definite shape to our nation. They have shown
the qualities of daring, endurance, and far-sightedness, of
eager desire for victory and stubborn refusal to accept defeat,
which go to make up the essential manliness of the American
character. Above all, they have recognized in practical form
the fundamental law of success in American life — the law of
worthy work, the law of high, resolute endeavor. We have but

767

little room among our people for the timid, the irresolute, and the idle; and it is no less true that there is scant room in the world at large for the nation with mighty thews that dares not to be great.

Surely in speaking to the sons of the men who actually did the rough and hard and infinitely glorious work of making the great Northwest what it now is, I need hardly insist upon the righteousness of this doctrine. In your own vigorous lives you show by every act how scant is your patience with those who do not see in the life of effort the life supremely worth living. Sometimes we hear those who do not work spoken of with envy. Surely the wilfully idle need arouse in the breast of a healthy man no emotion stronger than that of contempt — at the outside no emotion stronger than angry contempt. The feeling of envy would have in it an admission of inferiority on our part, to which the men who know not the sterner joys of life are not entitled. Poverty is a bitter thing; but it is not as bitter as the existence of restless vacuity and physical, moral, and intellectual flabbiness, to which those doom themselves who elect to spend all their years in that vainest of all vain pursuits — the pursuit of mere pleasure as a sufficient end in itself. The wilfully idle man, like the wilfully barren woman, has no place in a sane, healthy, and vigorous community. Moreover, the gross and hideous selfishness for which each stands defeats even its own miserable aims. Exactly as infinitely the happiest woman is she who has borne and brought up many healthy children, so infinitely the happiest man is he who has toiled hard and successfully in his life-work. The work may be done in a thousand different ways — with the brain or the hands, in the study, the field, or the workshop — if it is honest work, honestly done and well worth doing, that is all we have a right to ask. Every father and mother here, if they are wise, will bring up their children not to shirk difficulties, but to meet them and overcome them; not to strive after a life of ignoble ease, but to strive to do their duty, first to themselves and their families, and then to the whole State; and this duty must inevitably take the shape of work in some form or other. You, the sons of the pioneers, if you are true to your ancestry, must make your lives as worthy as they made theirs. They sought for true success, and therefore they did not seek ease. They knew that success comes only to those who lead the life of endeavor.

It seems to me that the simple acceptance of this fundamental fact of American life, this acknowledgment that the law of work is the fundamental law of our being, will help us to start aright in facing not a few of the problems that confront us from without and from within. As regards internal affairs, it should teach us the prime need of remembering that, after all has been said and done, the chief factor in any man's success or failure must be his own character — that is, the sum of his common sense, his courage, his virile energy and capacity. Nothing can take the place of this individual factor.

I do not for a moment mean that much cannot be done to supplement it. Besides each one of us working individually, all of us have got to work together. We cannot possibly do our best work as a nation unless all of us know how to act in combination as well as how to act each individually for himself. The acting in combination can take many forms, but of course its most effective form must be when it comes in the shape of law — that is, of action by the community as a whole through the law-making body.

But it is not possible ever to insure prosperity merely by law. Something for good can be done by law, and a bad law can do an infinity of mischief; but, after all, the best law can only prevent wrong and injustice, and give to the thrifty, the far-seeing, and the hard-working a chance to exercise to best advantage their special and peculiar abilities. No hard-and-fast rule can be laid down as to where our legislation shall stop in interfering between man and man, between interest and interest. All that can be said is that it is highly undesirable, on the one hand, to weaken individual initiative, and, on the other hand, that in a constantly increasing number of cases we shall find it necessary in the future to shackle cunning as in the past we have shackled force. It is not only highly desirable but necessary that there should be legislation which shall carefully shield the interests of wage-workers, and which shall discriminate in favor of the honest and humane employer by removing the disadvantage under which he stands when compared with unscrupulous competitors who have no conscience and will do right only under fear of punishment.

Nor can legislation stop only with what are termed labor questions. The vast individual and corporate fortunes, the vast combinations of capital, which have marked the development of our industrial system create new conditions, and necessitate a change from the old attitude of the State and the nation toward property. It is probably true that the large majority of the fortunes that now exist in this country have been amassed not by injuring our people, but as an incident to the conferring of great benefits upon the community; and this, no matter what may have been the conscious purpose of those amassing them. There is but the scantiest justification for most of the outcry against the men of wealth *as such*; and it ought to be unnecessary to state that any appeal which directly or indirectly leads to suspicion and hatred among ourselves, which tends to limit opportunity, and therefore to shut the door of success against poor men of talent, and, finally, which entails the possibility of lawlessness and violence, is an attack upon the fundamental properties of American citizenship. Our interests are at bottom common; in the long run we go up or go down together. Yet more and more it is evident that the State, and if necessary the nation, has got to possess the right of supervision and control as regards the great corporations which are its creatures; particularly as regards the great business combinations which derive a portion of their importance from the existence of some monopolistic tendency. The right should be exercised with caution and self-restraint; but it should exist, so that it may be invoked if the need arises.

So much for our duties, each to himself and each to his neighbor, within the limits of our own country. But our country, as it strides forward with ever-increasing rapidity to a foremost place among the world powers, must necessarily find, more and more, that it has world duties also. There are excellent people who believe that we can shirk these duties and yet retain our self-respect; but these good people are in error. Other good people seek to deter us from treading the path of hard but lofty duty by bidding us remember that all nations that have achieved greatness, that have expanded and played their part as world powers, have in the end passed away. So they have; and so have all others. The weak and the stationary have vanished as surely as, and more rapidly than, those whose citizens felt within them the lift that impels generous souls to great and noble effort. This is only another way of stating the universal law of death, which is itself part of the universal law of life. The man who works, the man who does great deeds, in the end dies as surely as the veriest idler who cumbers the earth's surface; but he leaves behind him the great fact that he has done his work well. So it is with nations. While the nation that has dared to be great, that has had the will and the power to change the destiny of the ages, in the end must die, yet no less surely the nation that has played the part of the weakling must also die; and whereas the nation that has done nothing leaves nothing behind it, the nation that has done a great work really continues, though in changed form, to live forevermore. The Roman has passed away exactly as all the nations of antiquity which did not expand when he expanded have passed away; but their very memory has vanished, while he himself is still a living force throughout the wide world in our entire civilization of to-day, and will so continue through countless generations, through untold ages.

It is because we believe with all our heart and soul in the greatness of this country, because we feel the thrill of hardy life in our veins, and are confident that to us is given the privilege of playing a leading part in the century that has just opened, that we hail with eager delight the opportunity to do whatever task Providence may allot us. We admit with all sincerity that our first duty is within our own household; that we must not merely talk, but act, in favor of cleanliness and decency and righteousness, in all political, social, and civic matters. No prosperity and no glory can save a nation that is rotten at heart. We must ever keep the core of our national being sound, and see to it that not only our citizens in private life, but, above all, our statesmen in public life, practise the old commonplace virtues which from time immemorial have lain at the root of all true national well-being. Yet while this is our first duty, it is not our whole duty. Exactly as each man, while doing first his duty to his wife and the children within his home, must yet, if he hopes to amount to much, strive mightily in the world outside his home, so our nation, while first of all seeing to its own domestic well-being, must not shrink from playing its part among the great nations without.

Our duty may take many forms in the future as it has taken many forms in the past. Nor is it possible to lay down a hard-and-fast rule for all cases. We must ever face the fact of our shifting national needs, of the always-changing opportunities that present themselves. But we may be certain of one thing: whether we wish it or not, we cannot avoid hereafter having duties to do in the face of other nations. All that we can do is to settle whether we shall perform these duties well or ill.

Right here let me make as vigorous a plea as I know how in favor of saying nothing that we do not mean, and of acting without hesitation up to whatever we say. A good many of you are probably acquainted with the old proverb: "Speak softly and carry a big stick — you will go far." If a man continually blusters, if he lacks civility, a big stick will not save him from trouble; and neither will speaking softly avail, if back of the softness there does not lie strength, power. In private life there are few beings more obnoxious than the man who is always loudly boasting; and if the boaster is not prepared to back up his words his position becomes absolutely contemptible. So it is with the nation. It is both foolish and undignified to indulge in undue self-glorification, and, above all, in loose-tongued denunciation of other peoples. Whenever on any point we come in contact with a foreign power, I hope that we shall always strive to speak courteously and respectfully of that foreign power. Let us make it evident that we intend to do justice. Then let us make it equally evident that we will not tolerate injustice being done to us in return. Let us further make it evident that we use no words which we are not prepared to back up with deeds, and that while our speech is always moderate, we are ready and willing to make it good. Such an attitude will be the surest possible guaranty of that self-respecting peace, the attainment of which is and must ever be the prime aim of a self-governing people.

This is the attitude we should take as regards the Monroe Doctrine. There is not the least need of blustering about it. Still less should it be used as a pretext for our own aggrandizement at the expense of any other American state. But, most emphatically, we must make it evident that we intend on this point ever to maintain the old American position. Indeed, it is hard to understand how any man can take any other position, now that we are all looking forward to the building of the Isthmian Canal. The Monroe Doctrine is not international law; but there is no necessity that it should be. All that is needful is that it should continue to be a cardinal feature of American policy on this continent; and the Spanish-American states should, in their own interests, champion it as strongly as we do. We do not by this doctrine intend to sanction any policy of aggression by one American commonwealth at the expense of any other, nor any policy of commercial discrimination against any foreign power whatsoever. Commercially, as far as this doctrine is concerned, all we wish is a fair field and no favor; but if we are wise we shall strenuously insist that under no pretext whatsoever shall there be any territorial aggrandizement on American soil by any European power, and this, no matter what form the territorial aggrandizement may take.

We most earnestly hope and believe that the chance of our having any hostile military complication with any foreign power is very small. But that there will come a strain, a jar, here and there, from commercial and agricultural — that is, from industrial — competition, is almost inevitable. Here again we have got to remember that our first duty is to our own people, and yet that we can best get justice by doing justice. We must continue the policy that has been so brilliantly successful in the past, and so shape our economic system as to give every advantage to the skill, energy, and intelligence of our farmers, merchants, manufacturers, and wage-workers; and yet we must also remember, in dealing with other nations, that benefits must be given where benefits are sought. It is not possible to dogmatize as to the exact way of attaining this end, for the exact conditions cannot be foretold. In the long run, one of our prime needs is stability and continuity of economic policy; and yet, through treaty or by direct legislation, it may, at least in certain cases, become advantageous to supplement our present policy by a system of reciprocal benefit and obligation.

Throughout a large part of our national career our history has been one of expansion, the expansion being of different kinds at different times. This expansion is not a matter of regret, but of pride. It is vain to tell a people as masterful as ours that the spirit of enterprise is not safe. The true American has never feared to run risks when the prize to be won was of sufficient value. No nation capable of self-government, and of developing by its own efforts a sane and orderly civilization, no matter how small it may be, has anything to fear from us. Our dealings with Cuba illustrate this, and should be forever a subject of just national pride. We speak in no spirit of arrogance when we state as a simple historic fact that never in recent times has any great nation acted with such disinterestedness as we have shown in Cuba. We freed the island from the Spanish yoke. We then earnestly did our best to help the Cubans in the establishment of free education, of law and order, of material prosperity, of the cleanliness necessary to sanitary well-being in their great cities. We did all this at great expense of treasure, at some expense of life; and now we are establishing them in a free and independent commonwealth, and have asked in return nothing whatever save that at no time shall their independence be prostituted to the advantage of some foreign rival of ours, or so as to menace our well-being. To have failed to ask this would have amounted to national stultification on our part.

In the Philippines we have brought peace, and we are at this moment giving them such freedom and self-government as they could never under any conceivable conditions have obtained had we turned them loose to sink into a welter of blood and confusion, or to become the prey of some strong tyranny without or within. The bare recital of the facts is sufficient to show that we did our duty; and what prouder title to honor can a nation have than to have done its duty? We have done our duty to ourselves, and we have done the higher duty of promoting the civilization of mankind. The first essential of civilization is law. Anarchy is simply the handmaiden and forerunner of tyranny and despotism. Law and order enforced with justice and by strength lie at the foundations of civilization. Law must be based upon justice, else it cannot stand, and it must be enforced with resolute firmness, because weakness in enforcing it means in the end that there is no justice and no law, nothing but the rule of disorderly and unscrupulous strength. Without the habit of orderly obedience to the law, without the stern enforcement of the laws at the expense of those who defiantly resist them, there can be no possible progress, moral or material, in civilization. There can be no weakening of the law-abiding spirit here at home, if we are permanently to succeed; and just as little can we afford to show weakness abroad. Lawlessness and anarchy were put down in the Philippines as a prerequisite to introducing the reign of justice.

Barbarism has, and can have, no place in a civilized world. It is our duty toward the people living in barbarism to see that they are freed from their chains, and we can free them only by destroying barbarism itself. The missionary, the merchant, and the soldier may each have to play a part in this destruction, and in the consequent uplifting of the people. Exactly as it is the duty of a civilized power scrupulously to respect the rights of all weaker civilized powers and gladly to help those who are struggling toward civilization, so it is its duty to put down savagery and barbarism. As in such a work human instruments must be used, and as human instruments are imperfect, this means that at times there will be injustice; that at times merchant or soldier, or even missionary, may do wrong. Let us instantly condemn and rectify such wrong when it occurs, and if possible punish the wrongdoer. But shame, thrice shame to us, if we are so foolish as to make such occasional wrongdoing an excuse for failing to perform a great and righteous task. Not only in our own land, but throughout the world, throughout all history, the advance of civilization has been of incalculable benefit to mankind, and those through whom it has advanced deserve the highest honor. All honor to the missionary, all honor to the soldier, all honor to the merchant who now in our own day have done so much to bring light into the world's dark places.

Let me insist again, for fear of possible misconstruction, upon the fact that our duty is twofold, and that we must raise others while we are benefiting ourselves. In bringing order to the Philippines, our soldiers added a new page to the honor-roll of American history, and they incalculably benefited the islanders themselves. Under the wise administration of Governor Taft the islands now enjoy a peace and liberty of which they have hitherto never even dreamed. But this peace and liberty under the law must be supplemented by material, by industrial development. Every encouragement should be given to their commercial development, to the introduction of American industries and products; not merely because this will be a good thing for our people, but infinitely more because it will be of incalculable benefit to the people in the Philippines.

We shall make mistakes; and if we let these mistakes frighten us from our work we shall show ourselves weaklings. Half a century ago Minnesota and the two Dakotas were Indian hunting-grounds. We committed plenty of blunders, and now and then worse than blunders, in our dealings with the Indians. But who does not admit at the present day that we were right in wresting from barbarism and adding to civilization the territory out of which we have made these beautiful States? And now we are civilizing the Indian and putting him on a level to which he could never have attained under the old conditions.

In the Philippines let us remember that the spirit and not the mere form of government is the essential matter. The Tagalogs have a hundredfold the freedom under us that they would have if we had abandoned the islands. We are not trying to subjugate a people; we are trying to develop them and make them a law-abiding, industrious, and educated people, and we hope ultimately a self-governing people. In short, in the work we have done we are but carrying out the true principles of our democracy. We work in a spirit of self-respect for ourselves and of good will toward others, in a spirit of love for and of infinite faith in mankind. We do not blindly refuse to face the evils that exist, or the shortcomings inherent in humanity; but across blundering and shirking, across selfishness and meanness of motive, across short-sightedness and cowardice, we gaze steadfastly toward the far horizon of golden triumph. If you will study our past history as a nation you will see we have made many blunders and have been guilty of many shortcomings, and yet that we have always in the end come out victorious because we have refused to be daunted by blunders and defeats, have recognized them, but have persevered in spite of them. So it must be in the future. We gird up our loins as a nation, with the stern purpose to play our part manfully in winning the ultimate triumph; and therefore we turn scornfully aside from the paths of mere ease and idleness, and with unfaltering steps tread the rough road of endeavor, smiting down the wrong and battling for the right, as Greatheart smote and battled in Bunyan's immortal story.

Citizenship in a Republic

Address at the Sorbonne, Paris, April 23, 1910

STRANGE and impressive associations rise in the mind of a man from the New World who speaks before this august body in this ancient institution of learning. Before his eyes pass the shadows of mighty kings and war-like nobles, of great masters of law and theology; through the shining dust of the dead centuries he sees crowded figures that tell of the power and learning and splendor of times gone by; and he sees also the innumerable host of humble students to whom clerkship meant emancipation, to whom it was well-nigh the only outlet from the dark thraldom of the Middle Ages.

This was the most famous university of mediæval Europe at a time when no one dreamed that there was a New World to discover. Its services to the cause of human knowledge already stretched far back into the remote past at the time when my forefathers, three centuries ago, were among the sparse bands of traders, ploughmen, wood-choppers, and fisher-folk who, in hard struggle with the iron unfriendliness of the Indian-haunted land, were laying the foundations of what has now become the giant republic of the West. To conquer a continent, to tame the shaggy roughness of wild nature, means grim warfare; and the generations engaged in it cannot keep, still less add to, the stores of garnered wisdom which once were theirs, and which are still in the hands of their brethren who dwell in the old land. To conquer the wilderness means to wrest victory from the same hostile forces with which mankind struggled in the immemorial infancy of our race. The primæval conditions must be met by primæval qualities which are incompatible with the retention of much that has been painfully acquired by humanity as through the ages it has striven upward toward civilization. In conditions so primitive there can be but a primitive culture. At first only the rudest schools can be established, for no others would meet the needs of the hard-driven, sinewy folk who thrust forward the frontier in the teeth of savage man and savage nature; and many years elapse before any of these schools can develop into seats of higher learning and broader culture.

The pioneer days pass; the stump-dotted clearings expand into vast stretches of fertile farm land; the stockaded clusters of log cabins change into towns; the hunters of game, the fellers of trees, the rude frontier traders and tillers of the soil, the men who wander all their lives long through the wilderness as the heralds and harbingers of an oncoming civilization, themselves vanish before the civilization for which they have prepared the way. The children of their successors and supplanters, and then their children and children's children, change and develop with extraordinary rapidity. The conditions accentuate vices and virtues, energy and ruthlessness, all the good qualities and all the defects of an intense individualism, self-reliant, self-centred, far more conscious of its rights than of its duties, and blind to its own shortcomings. To the hard materialism of the frontier days succeeds the hard materialism of an industrialism even more intense and absorbing than that of the older nations; although these themselves have likewise already entered on the age of a complex and predominantly industrial civilization.

As the country grows, its people, who have won success in so many lines, turn back to try to recover the possessions of the mind and the spirit, which perforce their fathers threw aside in order better to wage the first rough battles for the continent their children inherit. The leaders of thought and of action grope their way forward to a new life, realizing, sometimes dimly, sometimes clear-sightedly, that the life of material gain, whether for a nation or an individual, is of value only as a foundation, only as there is added to it the uplift that comes from devotion to loftier ideals. The new life thus sought can in part be developed afresh from what is roundabout in the New World; but it can be developed in full only by freely drawing upon the treasure-houses of the Old World, upon the treasures stored in the ancient abodes of wisdom and learning, such as this where I speak to-day. It is a mistake for any nation merely to copy another; but it is an even greater mistake, it is a proof of weakness in any nation, not to be anxious to learn from another, and willing and able to adapt that learning to the new national conditions and make it fruitful and productive therein. It is for us of the New World to sit at the feet of the Gamaliel of the Old; then, if we have the right stuff in us, we can show that Paul in his turn can become a teacher as well as a scholar.

To-day I shall speak to you on the subject of individual citizenship, the one subject of vital importance to you, my hearers, and to me and my countrymen, because you and we are citizens of great democratic republics. A democratic republic such as each of ours — an effort to realize in its full sense government by, of, and for the people — represents the most gigantic of all possible social experiments, the one fraught with greatest possibilities alike for good and for evil. The success of republics like yours and like ours means the glory, and our failure the despair, of mankind; and for you and for us the question of the quality of the individual citizen is supreme. Under other forms of government, under the rule of one man or of a very few men, the quality of the rulers is all-important. If, under such governments, the quality of the rulers is high enough, then the nation may for generations lead a brilliant career, and add substantially to the sum of world achievement, no matter how low the quality of the average citizen; because the average citizen is an almost negligible quantity in working out the final results of that type of national greatness.

But with you and with us the case is different. With you here, and with us in my own home, in the long run, success or failure will be conditioned upon the way in which the average man, the average woman, does his or her duty, first in the ordinary, every-day affairs of life, and next in those great occasional crises which call for the heroic virtues. The average citizen must be a good citizen if our republics are to succeed. The stream will not permanently rise higher than the main source; and the main source of national power and national greatness is found in the average citizenship of the nation. Therefore it behooves us to do our best to see that the standard of the average citizen is kept high; and the average cannot be kept high unless the standard of the leaders is very much higher.

It is well if a large proportion of the leaders in any republic, in any democracy, are, as a matter of course, drawn from the classes represented in this audience to-day; but only provided that those classes possess the gifts of sympathy with plain people and of devotion to great ideals. You and those like you have received special advantages; you have all of you had the opportunity for mental training; many of you have had leisure; most of you have had a chance for the enjoyment of life far greater than comes to the majority of your fellows. To you and your kind much has been given, and from you much should be expected. Yet there are certain failings against which it is especially incumbent that both men of trained and cultivated intellect, and men of inherited wealth and position, should especially guard themselves, because to these failings they are especially liable; and if yielded to, their — your — chances of useful service are at an end.

Let the man of learning, the man of lettered leisure, beware of that queer and cheap temptation to pose to himself and to others as the cynic, as the man who has outgrown emotions and beliefs, the man to whom good and evil are as one. The poorest way to face life is to face it with a sneer. There are many men who feel a kind of twisted pride in cynicism; there are many who confine themselves to criticism of the way others do what they themselves dare not even attempt. There is no more unhealthy being, no man less worthy of respect, than he who either really holds, or feigns to hold, an attitude of sneering disbelief toward all that is great and lofty, whether in achievement or in that noble effort which, even if it fails, comes second to achievement. A cynical habit of thought and speech, a readiness to criticise work which the critic himself never tries to perform, an intellectual aloofness which will not accept contact with life's realities — all these are marks, not, as the possessor would fain think, of superiority, but of weakness. They mark the men unfit to bear their part manfully in the stern strife of living, who seek, in the affectation of contempt for the achievements of others, to hide from others and from themselves their own weakness. The rôle is easy; there is none easier, save only the rôle of the man who sneers alike at both criticism and performance.

It is not the critic who counts; not the man who points out how the strong man stumbles, or where the doer of deeds could have done them better. The credit belongs to the man who is actually in the arena, whose face is marred by dust and sweat and blood; who strives valiantly; who errs, and comes short again and again, because there is no effort without error and shortcoming; but who does actually strive to do the deeds; who knows the great enthusiasms, the great devotions; who spends himself in a worthy cause; who at the best knows in the end the triumph of high achievement, and who at the worst, if he fails, at least fails while daring greatly, so that his place shall never be with those cold and timid souls who know neither victory nor defeat. Shame on the man of cultivated taste who permits refinement to develop into a fastidiousness that unfits him for doing the rough work of a workaday world. Among the free peoples who govern themselves there is but a small field of usefulness open for the men of cloistered life who shrink from contact with their fellows. Still less room is there for those who deride or slight what is done by those who actually bear the brunt of the day; nor yet for those others who always profess that they would like to take action, if only the conditions of life were not what they actually are. The man who does nothing cuts the same sordid figure in the pages of history, whether he be cynic, or fop, or voluptuary. There is little use for the being whose tepid soul knows nothing of the great and generous emotion, of the high pride, the stern belief, the lofty enthusiasm, of the men who quell the storm and ride the thunder. Well for these men if they succeed; well also, though not so well, if they fail, given only that they have nobly ventured, and have put forth all their heart and strength. It is war-worn Hotspur, spent with hard fighting, he of the many errors and the valiant end, over whose memory we love to linger, not over the memory of the young lord who "but for the vile guns would have been a soldier."

France has taught many lessons to other nations; surely one of the most important is the lesson her whole history teaches, that a high artistic and literary development is compatible with notable leadership in arms and statecraft. The brilliant gallantry of the French soldier has for many centuries been proverbial; and during these same centuries at every court in Europe the "freemasons of fashion" have treated the French tongue as their common speech; while every artist and man of letters, and every man of science able to appreciate that marvellous instrument of precision, French prose, has turned toward France for aid and inspiration. How long the leadership in arms and letters has lasted is curiously illustrated by the fact that the earliest masterpiece in a modern tongue is the splendid French epic which tells of Roland's doom and the vengeance of Charlemagne when the lords of the Frankish host were stricken at Roncesvalles.

Let those who have, keep, let those who have not, strive to attain, a high standard of cultivation and scholarship. Yet let us remember that these stand second to certain other things. There is need of a sound body, and even more need of a sound mind. But above mind and above body stands character — the sum of those qualities which we mean when we speak of a man's force and courage, of his good faith and sense of honor. I believe in exercise for the body, always provided that we keep in mind that physical development is a means and not an end. I believe, of course, in giving to all the people a good education. But the education must contain much besides book-learning in order to be really good. We must ever remember that no keenness and subtleness of intellect, no polish, no cleverness, in any way make up for the lack of the great solid qualities. Self-restraint, self-mastery, common sense, the power of accepting individual responsibility and yet of acting in conjunction with others, courage and resolution — these are the qualities which mark a masterful people. Without them no people can control itself, or save itself from being controlled from the outside. I speak to a brilliant assemblage; I speak in a great university which represents the flower of the highest intellectual development; I pay all homage to intellect, and to elaborate and specialized training of the intellect; and yet I know I shall have the assent of all of you present when I add that more important still are the commonplace, every-day qualities and virtues.

Such ordinary, every-day qualities include the will and the power to work, to fight at need, and to have plenty of healthy children. The need that the average man shall work is so obvious as hardly to warrant insistence. There are a few people in every country so born that they can lead lives of leisure. These fill a useful function if they make it evident that leisure does not mean idleness; for some of the most valuable work needed by civilization is essentially non-remunerative in its character, and of course the people who do this work should in large part be drawn from those to whom remuneration is an object of indifference. But the average man must earn his own livelihood. He should be trained to do so, and he should be trained to feel that he occupies a contemptible position if he does not do so; that he is not an object of envy if he is idle, at whichever end of the social scale he stands, but an object of contempt, an object of derision.

In the next place, the good man should be both a strong and a brave man; that is, he should be able to fight, he should be able to serve his country as a soldier, if the need arises. There are well-meaning philosophers who declaim against the unrighteousness of war. They are right only if they lay all their emphasis upon the unrighteousness. War is a dreadful thing, and unjust war is a crime against humanity. But it is such a crime because it is unjust, not because it is war. The choice must ever be in favor of righteousness, and this whether the alternative be peace or whether the alternative be war. The question must not be merely, Is there to be peace or war? The question must be, Is the right to prevail? Are the great laws of righteousness once more to be fulfilled? And the answer from a strong and virile people must be "Yes," whatever the cost. Every honorable effort should always be made to avoid war, just as every honorable effort should always be made by the individual in private life to keep out of a brawl, to keep out of trouble; but no self-respecting individual, no self-respecting nation, can or ought to submit to wrong.

Finally, even more important than ability to work, even more important than ability to fight at need, is it to remember that the chief of blessings for any nation is that it shall leave its seed to inherit the land. It was the crown of blessings in Biblical times; and it is the crown of blessings now. The greatest of all curses is the curse of sterility, and the severest of all condemnations should be that visited upon wilful sterility. The first essential in any civilization is that the man and the woman shall be father and mother of healthy children, so that the race shall increase and not decrease. If this is not so, if through no fault of the society there is failure to increase, it is a great misfortune. If the failure is due to deliberate and wilful fault, then it is not merely a misfortune, it is one of those crimes of ease and self-indulgence, of shrinking from pain and effort and risk, which in the long run Nature punishes more heavily than any other. If we of the great republics, if we, the free people who claim to have emancipated ourselves from the thraldom of wrong and error, bring down on our heads the curse that comes upon the wilfully barren, then it will be an idle waste of breath to prattle of our achievements, to boast of all that we have done. No refinement of life, no delicacy of taste, no material progress, no sordid heaping up of riches, no sensuous development of art and literature, can in any way compensate for the loss of the great fundamental virtues; and of these great fundamental virtues the greatest is the race's power to perpetuate the race.

Character must show itself in the man's performance both of the duty he owes himself and of the duty he owes the state. The man's foremost duty is owed to himself and his family; and he can do this duty only by earning money, by providing what is essential to material well-being; it is only after this has been done that he can hope to build a higher superstructure on the solid material foundation; it is only after this has been done that he can help in movements for the general well-being. He must pull his own weight first, and only after this can his surplus strength be of use to the general public. It is not good to excite that bitter laughter which expresses contempt; and contempt is what we feel for the being whose enthusiasm to benefit mankind is such that he is a burden to those nearest him; who wishes to do great things for humanity in the abstract, but who cannot keep his wife in comfort or educate his children.

Nevertheless, while laying all stress on this point, while not merely acknowledging but insisting upon the fact that there must be a basis of material well-being for the individual as for the nation, let us with equal emphasis insist that this material well-being represents nothing but the foundation, and that the foundation, though indispensable, is worthless unless upon it is raised the superstructure of a higher life. That is why I decline to recognize the mere multimillionaire, the man of mere wealth, as an asset of value to any country; and especially as not an asset to my own country. If he has earned or uses his wealth in a way that makes him of real benefit, of real use — and such is often the case — why, then he does become an asset of worth. But it is the way in which it has been earned or used, and not the mere fact of wealth, that entitles him to the credit. There is need in business, as in most other forms of human activity, of the great guiding intelligences. Their places cannot be supplied by any number of lesser intelligences. It is a good thing that they should have ample recognition, ample reward. But we must not transfer our admiration to the reward instead of to the deed rewarded; and if what should be the reward exists without the service having been rendered, then admiration will come only from those who are mean of soul. The truth is that, after a certain measure of tangible material success or reward has been achieved, the question of increasing it becomes of constantly less importance compared to other things that can be done in life. It is a bad thing for a nation to raise and to admire a false standard of success; and there can be no falser standard than that set by the deification of material well-being in and for itself. The man who, for any cause for which he is himself accountable, has failed to support himself and those for whom he is responsible, ought to feel that he has fallen lamentably short in his prime duty. But the man who, having far surpassed the limit of providing for the wants, both of body and mind, of himself and of those depending upon him, then piles up a great fortune, for the acquisition or retention of which he returns no corresponding benefit to the nation as a whole, should himself be made to feel that, so far from being a desirable, he is an unworthy, citizen of the community; that he is to be neither admired nor envied; that his right-thinking fellow countrymen put him low in the scale of citizenship, and leave him to be consoled by the admiration of those whose level of purpose is even lower than his own.

My position as regards the moneyed interests can be put in a few words. In every civilized society property rights must be carefully safeguarded; ordinarily, and in the great majority of cases, human rights and property rights are fundamentally and in the long run identical; but when it clearly appears that there is a real conflict between them, human rights must have the upper hand, for property belongs to man and not man to property.

In fact, it is essential to good citizenship clearly to understand that there are certain qualities which we in a democracy are prone to admire in and of themselves, which ought by rights to be judged admirable or the reverse solely from the standpoint of the use made of them. Foremost among these I should include two very distinct gifts — the gift of money-making and the gift of oratory. Money-making, the money touch, I have spoken of above. It is a quality which in a moderate degree is essential. It may be useful when developed to a very great degree, but only if accompanied and controlled by other qualities; and without such control the possessor tends to develop into one of the least attractive types produced by a modern industrial democracy. So it is with the orator. It is highly desirable that a leader of opinion in a democracy should be able to state his views clearly and convincingly. But all that the oratory can do of value to the community is to enable the man thus to explain himself; if it enables the orator to persuade his hearers to put false values on things, it merely makes him a power for mischief. Some excellent public servants have not the gift at all, and must rely upon their deeds to speak for them; and unless the oratory does represent genuine conviction based on good common sense and able to be translated into efficient performance, then the better the oratory the greater the damage to the public it deceives. Indeed, it is a sign of marked political weakness in any commonwealth if the people tend to be carried away by mere oratory, if they tend to value words in and for themselves, as divorced from the deeds for which they are supposed to stand. The phrase-maker, the phrase-monger, the ready talker, however great his power, whose speech does not make for courage, sobriety, and right understanding, is simply a noxious element in the body politic, and it speaks ill for the public if he has influence over them. To admire the gift of oratory without regard to the moral quality behind the gift is to do wrong to the republic.

Of course all that I say of the orator applies with even greater force to the orator's latter-day and more influential brother, the journalist. The power of the journalist is great, but he is entitled neither to respect nor admiration because of that power unless it is used aright. He can do, and he often does, great good. He can do, and he often does, infinite mischief. All journalists, all writers, for the very reason that they appreciate the vast possibilities of their profession, should bear testimony against those who deeply discredit it. Offenses against taste and morals, which are bad enough in a private citizen, are infinitely worse if made into instruments for debauching the community through a newspaper. Mendacity, slander, sensationalism, inanity, vapid triviality, all are potent factors for the debauchery of the public mind and conscience. The excuse advanced for vicious writing, that the public demands it and that the demand must be supplied, can no more be admitted than if it were advanced by the purveyors of food who sell poisonous adulterations.

In short, the good citizen in a republic must realize that he ought to possess two sets of qualities, and that neither avails without the other. He must have those qualities which make for efficiency; and he must also have those qualities which direct the efficiency into channels for the public good. He is useless if he is inefficient. There is nothing to be done with that type of citizen of whom all that can be said is that he is harmless. Virtue which is dependent upon a sluggish circulation is not impressive. There is little place in active life for the timid good man. The man who is saved by weakness from robust wickedness is likewise rendered immune from the robuster virtues. The good citizen in a republic must first of all be able to hold his own. He is no good citizen unless he has the ability which will make him work hard and which at need will make him fight hard. The good citizen is not a good citizen unless he is an efficient citizen.

But if a man's efficiency is not guided and regulated by a moral sense, then the more efficient he is the worse he is, the more dangerous to the body politic. Courage, intellect, all the masterful qualities, serve but to make a man more evil if they are used merely for that man's own advancement, with brutal indifference to the rights of others. It speaks ill for the community if the community worships these qualities and treats their possessors as heroes regardless of whether the qualities are used rightly or wrongly. It makes no difference as to the precise way in which this sinister efficiency is shown. It makes no difference whether such a man's force and ability betray themselves in the career of money-maker or politician, soldier or orator, journalist or popular leader. If the man works for evil, then the more successful he is the more he should be despised and condemned by all upright and far-seeing men. To judge a man merely by success is an abhorrent wrong; and if the people at large habitually so judge men, if they grow to condone wickedness because the wicked man triumphs, they show their inability to understand that in the last analysis free institutions rest upon the character of citizenship, and that by such admiration of evil they prove themselves unfit for liberty.

The homely virtues of the household, the ordinary workaday virtues which make the woman a good housewife and housemother, which make the man a hard worker, a good husband and father, a good soldier at need, stand at the bottom of character. But of course many others must be added thereto if a state is to be not only free but great. Good citizenship is not good citizenship if exhibited only in the home. There remain the duties of the individual in relation to the State, and these duties are none too easy under the conditions which exist where the effort is made to carry on free government in a complex industrial civilization. Perhaps the most important thing the ordinary citizen, and, above all, the leader of ordinary citizens, has to remember in political life is that he must not be a sheer doctrinaire. The closet philosopher, the refined and cultured individual who from his library tells how men ought to be governed under ideal conditions, is of no use in actual governmental work; and the one-sided fanatic, and still more the mob-leader, and the insincere man who to achieve power promises what by no possibility can be performed, are not merely useless but noxious.

The citizen must have high ideals, and yet he must be able to achieve them in practical fashion. No permanent good comes from aspirations so lofty that they have grown fantastic and have become impossible and indeed undesirable to realize. The impracticable visionary is far less often the guide and precursor than he is the embittered foe of the real reformer, of the man who, with stumblings and shortcomings, yet does in some shape, in practical fashion, give effect to the hopes and desires of those who strive for better things. Woe to the empty phrase-maker, to the empty idealist, who, instead of making ready the ground for the man of action, turns against him when he appears and hampers him as he does the work! Moreover, the preacher of ideals must remember how sorry and contemptible is the figure which he will cut, how great the damage that he will do, if he does not himself, in his own life, strive measurably to realize the ideals that he preaches for others. Let him remember also that the worth of the ideal must be largely determined by the success with which it can in practice be realized. We should abhor the so-called "practical" men whose practicality assumes the shape of that peculiar baseness which finds its expression in disbelief in morality and decency, in disregard of high standards of living and conduct. Such a creature is the worst enemy of the body politic. But only less desirable as a citizen is his nominal opponent and real ally, the man of fantastic vision who makes the impossible better forever the enemy of the possible good.

We can just as little afford to follow the doctrinaires of an extreme individualism as the doctrinaires of an extreme socialism. Individual initiative, so far from being discouraged, should be stimulated; and yet we should remember that, as society develops and grows more complex, we continually find that things which once it was desirable to leave to individual initiative can, under the changed conditions, be performed with better results by common effort. It is quite impossible, and equally undesirable, to draw in theory a hard-and-fast line which shall always divide the two sets of cases. This every one who is not cursed with the pride of the closet philosopher will see, if he will only take the trouble to think about some of our commonest phenomena. For instance, when people live on isolated farms or in little hamlets, each house can be left to attend to its own drainage and water-supply; but the mere multiplication of families in a given area produces new problems which, because they differ in size, are found to differ not only in degree but in kind from the old; and the questions of drainage and water-supply have to be considered from the common standpoint. It is not a matter for abstract dogmatizing to decide when this point is reached; it is a matter to be tested by practical experiment. Much of the discussion about socialism and individualism is entirely pointless, because of failure to agree on terminology. It is not good to be the slave of names. I am a strong individualist by personal habit, inheritance, and conviction; but it is a mere matter of common sense to recognize that the State, the community, the citizens acting together, can do a number of things better than if they were left to individual action. The individualism which finds its expression in the abuse of physical force is checked very early in the growth of civilization, and we of to-day should in our turn strive to shackle or destroy that individualism which triumphs by greed and cunning, which exploits the weak by craft instead of ruling them by brutality. We ought to go with any man in the effort to bring about justice and the equality of opportunity, to turn the tool-user more and more into the tool-owner, to shift burdens so that they can be more equitably borne. The deadening effect on any race of the adoption of a logical and extreme socialistic system could not be overstated; it would spell sheer destruction; it would produce grosser wrong and outrage, fouler immorality, than any existing system. But this does not mean that we may not with great advantage adopt certain of the principles professed by some given set of men who happen to call themselves Socialists; to be afraid to do so would be to make a mark of weakness on our part.

But we should not take part in acting a lie any more than in telling a lie. We should not say that men are equal where they are not equal, nor proceed upon the assumption that there is an equality where it does not exist; but we should strive to bring about a measurable equality, at least to the extent of preventing the inequality which is due to force or fraud. Abraham Lincoln, a man of the plain people, blood of their blood and bone of their bone, who all his life toiled and wrought and suffered for them, and at the end died for them, who always strove to represent them, who would never tell an untruth to or for them, spoke of the doctrine of equality with his usual mixture of idealism and sound common sense. He said (I omit what was of merely local significance):

"I think the authors of the Declaration of Independence intended to include all men, but that they did not mean to declare all men equal *in all respects*. They did not mean to say all men were equal in color, size, intellect, moral development, or social capacity. They defined with tolerable distinctness in what they did consider all men created equal — equal in certain inalienable rights, among which are life, liberty, and the pursuit of happiness. This they said, and this they meant. They did not mean to assert the obvious untruth that all were then actually enjoying that equality, or yet that they were about to confer it immediately upon them. They meant to set up a standard maxim for free society which should be familiar to all — constantly looked to, constantly labored for, and, even though never perfectly attained, constantly approximated, and thereby constantly spreading and deepening its influence, and augmenting the happiness and value of life to all people, everywhere."

We are bound in honor to refuse to listen to those men who would make us desist from the effort to do away with the inequality which means injustice; the inequality of right, of opportunity, of privilege. We are bound in honor to strive to bring ever nearer the day when, as far as is humanly possible, we shall be able to realize the ideal that each man shall have an equal opportunity to show the stuff that is in him by the way in which he renders service. There should, so far as possible, be equality of opportunity to render service; but just so long as there is inequality of service there should and must be inequality of reward. We may be sorry for the general, the painter, the artist, the worker in any profession or of any kind, whose misfortune rather than whose fault it is that he does his work ill. But the reward must go to the man who does his work well; for any other course is to create a new kind of privilege, the privilege of folly and weakness; and special privilege is injustice, whatever form it takes.

To say that the thriftless, the lazy, the vicious, the incapable, ought to have the reward given to those who are far-sighted, capable, and upright, is to say what is not true and cannot be true. Let us try to level up, but let us beware of the evil of levelling down. If a man stumbles, it is a good thing to help him to his feet. Every one of us needs a helping hand now and then. But if a man lies down, it is a waste of time to try to carry him; and it is a very bad thing for every one if we make men feel that the same reward will come to those who shirk their work and to those who do it.

Let us, then, take into account the actual facts of life, and not be misled into following any proposal for achieving the millennium, for recreating the golden age, until we have subjected it to hardheaded examination. On the other hand, it is foolish to reject a proposal merely because it is advanced by visionaries. If a given scheme is proposed, look at it on its merits, and, in considering it, disregard formulas. It does not matter in the least who proposes it, or why. If it seems good, try it. If it proves good, accept it; otherwise reject it. There are plenty of men calling themselves Socialists with whom, up to a certain point, it is quite possible to work. If the next step is one which both we and they wish to take, why of course take it, without any regard to the fact that our views as to the tenth step may differ. But, on the other hand, keep clearly in mind that, though it has been worth while to take one step, this does not in the least mean that it may not be highly disadvantageous to take the next. It is just as foolish to refuse all progress because people demanding it desire at some points to go to absurd extremes, as it would be to go to these absurd extremes simply because some of the measures advocated by the extremists were wise.

The good citizen will demand liberty for himself, and as a matter of pride he will see to it that others receive the liberty which he thus claims as his own. Probably the best test of true love of liberty in any country is the way in which minorities are treated in that country. Not only should there be complete liberty in matters of religion and opinion, but complete liberty for each man to lead his life as he desires, provided only that in so doing he does not wrong his neighbor. Persecution is bad because it is persecution, and without reference to which side happens at the moment to be the persecutor and which the persecuted. Class hatred is bad in just the same way, and without any regard to the individual who, at a given time, substitutes loyalty to a class for loyalty to the nation, or substitutes hatred of men because they happen to come in a certain social category, for judgment awarded them according to their conduct. Remember always that the same measure of condemnation should be extended to the arrogance which would look down upon or crush any man because he is poor and to the envy and hatred which would destroy a man because he is wealthy. The overbearing brutality of the man of wealth or power, and the envious and hateful malice directed against wealth or power, are really at root merely different manifestations of the same quality, merely the two sides of the same shield. The man who, if born to wealth and power, exploits and ruins his less fortunate brethren is at heart the same as the greedy and violent demagogue who excites those who have not property to plunder those who have. The gravest wrong upon his country is inflicted by that man, whatever his station, who seeks to make his countrymen divide primarily on the line that separates class from class, occupation from occupation, men of more wealth from men of less wealth, instead of remembering that the only safe standard is that which judges each man on his worth as a man, whether he be rich or poor, without regard to his profession or to his station in life. Such is the only true democratic test, the only test that can with propriety be applied in a republic. There have been many republics in the past, both in what we call antiquity and in what we call the Middle Ages. They fell, and the prime factor in their fall was the fact that the parties tended to divide along the line that separates wealth from poverty. It made no difference which side was successful; it made no difference whether the republic fell under the rule of an oligarchy or the rule of a mob. In either case, when once loyalty to a class had been substituted for loyalty to the republic, the end of the republic was at hand. There is no greater need today than the need to keep ever in mind the fact that the cleavage between right and wrong, between good citizenship and bad citizenship, runs at right angles to, and not parallel with, the lines of cleavage between class and class, between occupation and occupation. Ruin looks us in the face if we judge a man by his position instead of judging him by his conduct in that position.

In a republic, to be successful we must learn to combine intensity of conviction with a broad tolerance of difference of conviction. Wide differences of opinion in matters of religious, political, and social belief must exist if conscience and intellect alike are not to be stunted, if there is to be room for healthy growth. Bitter internecine hatreds, based on such differences, are signs, not of earnestness of belief, but of that fanaticism which, whether religious or antireligious, demo-cratic or antidemocratic, is itself but a manifestation of the gloomy bigotry which has been the chief factor in the down-fall of so many, many nations.

Of one man in especial, beyond any one else, the citizens of a republic should beware, and that is of the man who appeals to them to support him on the ground that he is hostile to other citizens of the republic, that he will secure for those who elect him, in one shape or another, profit at the expense of other citizens of the republic. It makes no difference whether he appeals to class hatred or class interest, to religious or an-tireligious prejudice. The man who makes such an appeal should always be presumed to make it for the sake of further-ing his own interest. The very last thing that an intelligent and self-respecting member of a democratic community should do is to reward any public man because that public man says he will get the private citizen something to which this private cit-izen is not entitled, or will gratify some emotion or animos-ity which this private citizen ought not to possess. Let me illustrate this by one anecdote from my own experience. A number of years ago I was engaged in cattle-ranching on the great plains of the western United States. There were no fences. The cattle wandered free, the ownership of each being determined by the brand; the calves were branded with the brand of the cows they followed. If on the round-up an animal was passed by, the following year it would appear as an un-branded yearling, and was then called a maverick. By the custom of the country these mavericks were branded with the brand of the man on whose range they were found. One day I was riding the range with a newly hired cowboy, and we came upon a maverick. We roped and threw it; then we built a little fire, took out a cinch-ring, heated it at the fire; and the cowboy started to put on the brand. I said to him, "It is So-and-so's brand," naming the man on whose range we hap-pened to be. He answered: "That's all right, boss; I know my business." In another moment I said to him: "Hold on, you are putting on my brand!" To which he answered: "That's all right; I always put on the boss's brand." I answered: "Oh, very well. Now you go straight back to the ranch and get what is owing to you; I don't need you any longer." He jumped up and said: "Why, what's the matter? I was putting on your brand." And I answered: "Yes, my friend, and if you will steal *for* me you will steal *from* me."

Now, the same principle which applies in private life applies also in public life. If a public man tries to get your vote by saying that he will do something wrong *in* your interest, you can be absolutely certain that if ever it becomes worth his while he will do something wrong *against* your interest.

So much for the citizenship of the individual in his relations to his family, to his neighbor, to the State. There remain duties of citizenship which the State, the aggregation of all the individuals, owes in connection with other States, with other nations. Let me say at once that I am no advocate of a foolish cosmopolitanism. I believe that a man must be a good patriot before he can be, and as the only possible way of being, a good citizen of the world. Experience teaches us that the average man who protests that his international feeling swamps his national feeling, that he does not care for his country because he cares so much for mankind, in actual practice proves himself the foe of mankind; that the man who says that he does not care to be a citizen of any one country, because he is a citizen of the world, is in very fact usually an exceedingly undesirable citizen of whatever corner of the world he happens at the moment to be in. In the dim future all moral needs and moral standards may change; but at present, if a man can view his own country and all others countries from the same level with tepid indifference, it is wise to distrust him, just as it is wise to distrust the man who can take the same dispassionate view of his wife and his mother. However broad and deep a man's sympathies, however intense his activities, he need have no fear that they will be cramped by love of his native land.

Now, this does not mean in the least that a man should not wish to do good outside of his native land. On the contrary, just as I think that the man who loves his family is more apt to be a good neighbor than the man who does not, so I think that the most useful member of the family of nations is normally a strongly patriotic nation. So far from patriotism being inconsistent with a proper regard for the rights of other nations, I hold that the true patriot, who is as jealous of the national honor as a gentleman is of his own honor, will be careful to see that the nation neither inflicts nor suffers wrong, just as a gentleman scorns equally to wrong others or to suffer others to wrong him. I do not for one moment admit that political morality is different from private morality, that a promise made on the stump differs from a promise made in private life. I do not for one moment admit that a man should act deceitfully as a public servant in his dealings with other nations, any more than that he should act deceitfully in his dealings as a private citizen with other private citizens. I do not for one moment admit that a nation should treat other nations in a different spirit from that in which an honorable man would treat other men.

In practically applying this principle to the two sets of cases there is, of course, a great practical difference to be taken into account. We speak of international law; but international law is something wholly different from private or municipal law, and the capital difference is that there is a sanction for the one and no sanction for the other; that there is an outside force which compels individuals to obey the one, while there is no such outside force to compel obedience as regards the other. International law will, I believe, as the generations pass, grow stronger and stronger until in some way or other there develops the power to make it respected. But as yet it is only in the first formative period. As yet, as a rule, each nation is of necessity obliged to judge for itself in matters of vital importance between it and its neighbors, and actions must of necessity, where this is the case, be different from what they are where, as among private citizens, there is an outside force whose action is all-powerful and must be invoked in any crisis of importance. It is the duty of wise statesmen, gifted with power of looking ahead, to try to encourage and build up every movement which will substitute or tend to substitute some other agency for force in the settlement of international disputes. It is the duty of every honest statesman to try to guide the nation so that it shall not wrong any other nation. But as yet the great civilized peoples, if they are to be true to themselves and to the cause of humanity and civilization, must keep ever in mind that in the last resort they must possess both the will and the power to resent wrong-doing from others. The men who sanely believe in a lofty morality preach righteousness; but they do not preach weakness, whether among private citizens or among nations. We believe that our ideals should be high, but not so high as to make it impossible measurably to realize them. We sincerely and earnestly believe in peace; but if peace and justice conflict, we scorn the man who would not stand for justice though the whole world came in arms against him.

And now, my hosts, a word in parting. You and I belong to the only two republics among the great powers of the world. The ancient friendship between France and the United States has been, on the whole, a sincere and disinterested friendship. A calamity to you would be a sorrow to us. But it would be more than that. In the seething turmoil of the history of humanity certain nations stand out as possessing a peculiar power or charm, some special gift of beauty or wisdom or strength, which puts them among the immortals, which makes them rank forever with the leaders of mankind. France is one of these nations. For her to sink would be a loss to all the world. There are certain lessons of brilliance and of generous gallantry that she can teach better than any of her sister nations. When the French peasantry sang of Malbrook, it was to tell how the soul of this warrior-foe took flight upward through the laurels he had won. Nearly seven centuries ago, Froissart, writing of a time of dire disaster, said that the realm of France was never so stricken that there were not left men who would valiantly fight for it. You have had a great past. I believe that you will have a great future. Long may you carry yourselves proudly as citizens of a nation which bears a leading part in the teaching and uplifting of mankind.

The New Nationalism

Speech at Osawatomie, Kansas, August 31, 1910

W<small>E</small> come here to-day to commemorate one of the epoch-making events of the long struggle for the rights of man — the long struggle for the uplift of humanity. Our country — this great Republic -- means nothing unless it means the triumph of a real democracy, the triumph of popular government, and, in the long run, of an economic system under which each man shall be guaranteed the opportunity to show the best that there is in him. That is why the history of America is now the central feature of the history of the world; for the world has set its face hopefully toward our democracy; and, O my fellow citizens, each one of you carries on your shoulders not only the burden of doing well for the sake of your own country, but the burden of doing well and of seeing that this nation does well for the sake of mankind.

There have been two great crises in our country's history: first, when it was formed, and then, again, when it was perpetuated; and, in the second of these great crises — in the time of stress and strain which culminated in the Civil War, on the outcome of which depended the justification of what had been done earlier, you men of the Grand Army, you men who fought through the Civil War, not only did you justify your generation, not only did you render life worth living for our generation, but you justified the wisdom of Washington and Washington's colleagues. If this Republic had been founded by them only to be split asunder into fragments when the strain came, then the judgment of the world would have been that Washington's work was not worth doing. It was you who crowned Washington's work, as you carried to achievement the high purpose of Abraham Lincoln.

Now, with this second period of our history the name of John Brown will be forever associated; and Kansas was the theatre upon which the first act of the second of our great national life dramas was played It was the result of the struggle in Kansas which determined that our country should be in deed as well as in name devoted to both union and freedom; that the great experiment of democratic government on a national scale should succeed and not fail. In name we had the Declaration of Independence in 1776; but we gave the lie by our acts to the words of the Declaration of Independence until 1865; and words count for nothing except in so far as they represent acts. This is true everywhere; but, O my friends, it should be truest of all in political life. A broken promise is bad enough in private life. It is worse in the field of politics. No man is worth his salt in public life who makes on the stump a pledge which he does not keep after election; and, if he makes such a pledge and does not keep it, hunt him out of public life. I care for the great deeds of the past chiefly as spurs to drive us onward in the present. I speak of the men of the past partly that they may be honored by our praise of them, but more that they may serve as examples for the future.

It was a heroic struggle; and, as is inevitable with all such struggles, it had also a dark and terrible side. Very much was done of good, and much also of evil; and, as was inevitable in such a period of revolution, often the same man did both good and evil. For our great good fortune as a nation, we, the people of the United States as a whole, can now afford to forget the evil, or, at least, to remember it without bitterness, and to fix our eyes with pride only on the good that was accomplished. Even in ordinary times there are very few of us who do not see the problems of life as through a glass, darkly; and when the glass is clouded by the murk of furious popular passion, the vision of the best and the bravest is dimmed. Looking back, we are all of us now able to do justice to the valor and the disinterestedness and the love of the right, as to each it was given to see the right, shown both by the men of the North and the men of the South in that contest which was finally decided by the attitude of the West. We can admire the heroic valor, the sincerity, the self-devotion shown alike by the men who wore the blue and the men who wore the gray; and our sadness that such men should have had to fight one another is tempered by the glad knowledge that ever hereafter their descendants shall be found fighting side by side, struggling in peace as well as in war for the uplift of their common country, all alike resolute to raise to the highest pitch of honor and usefulness the nation to which they all belong. As for the veterans of the Grand Army of the Republic, they deserve honor and recognition such as is paid to no other citizens of the Republic; for to them the republic owes its all; for to them it owes its very existence. It is because of what you and your comrades did in the dark years that we of to-day walk, each of us, head erect, and proud that we belong, not to one of a dozen little squabbling contemptible commonwealths, but to the mightiest nation upon which the sun shines.

I do not speak of this struggle of the past merely from the historic standpoint. Our interest is primarily in the application to-day of the lessons taught by the contest of half a century ago. It is of little use for us to pay lip-loyalty to the mighty men of the past unless we sincerely endeavor to apply to the problems of the present precisely the qualities which in other crises enabled the men of that day to meet those crises. It is half melancholy and half amusing to see the way in which well-meaning people gather to do honor to the men who, in company with John Brown, and under the lead of Abraham Lincoln, faced and solved the great problems of the nineteenth century, while, at the same time, these same good people nervously shrink from, or frantically denounce, those who are trying to meet the problems of the twentieth century in the spirit which was accountable for the successful solution of the problems of Lincoln's time.

Of that generation of men to whom we owe so much, the man to whom we owe most is, of course, Lincoln. Part of our debt to him is because he forecast our present struggle and saw the way out. He said:

"I hold that while man exists it is his duty to improve not only his own condition, but to assist in ameliorating mankind."

And again:

"Labor is prior to, and independent of, capital. Capital is only the fruit of labor, and could never have existed if labor had not first existed. Labor is the superior of capital, and deserves much the higher consideration."

If that remark was original with me, I should be even more strongly denounced as a Communist agitator than I shall be anyhow. It is Lincoln's. I am only quoting it; and that is one side; that is the side the capitalist should hear. Now, let the working man hear his side.

"Capital has its rights, which are as worthy of protection as any other rights. . . . Nor should this lead to a war upon the owners of property. Property is the fruit of labor; . . . property is desirable; is a positive good in the world."

And then comes a thoroughly Lincolnlike sentence:

"Let not him who is houseless pull down the house of another, but let him work diligently and build one for himself, thus by example assuring that his own shall be safe from violence when built."

It seems to me that, in these words, Lincoln took substantially the attitude that we ought to take; he showed the proper sense of proportion in his relative estimates of capital and labor, of human rights and property rights. Above all, in this speech, as in many others, he taught a lesson in wise kindliness and charity; an indispensable lesson to us of to-day. But this wise kindliness and charity never weakened his arm or numbed his heart. We cannot afford weakly to blind ourselves to the actual conflict which faces us to-day. The issue is joined, and we must fight or fail.

In every wise struggle for human betterment one of the main objects, and often the only object, has been to achieve in large measure equality of opportunity. In the struggle for this great end, nations rise from barbarism to civilization, and through it people press forward from one stage of enlightenment to the next. One of the chief factors in progress is the destruction of special privilege. The essence of any struggle for healthy liberty has always been, and must always be, to take from some one man or class of men the right to enjoy power, or wealth, or position, or immunity, which has not been earned by service to his or their fellows. That is what you fought for in the Civil War, and that is what we strive for now.

At many stages in the advance of humanity, this conflict between the men who possess more than they have earned and the men who have earned more than they possess is the central condition of progress. In our day it appears as the struggle of freemen to gain and hold the right of self-government as against the special interests, who twist the methods of free government into machinery for defeating the popular will. At every stage, and under all circumstances, the essence of the struggle is to equalize opportunity, destroy privilege, and give to the life and citizenship of every individual the highest possible value both to himself and to the commonwealth. That is nothing new. All I ask in civil life is what you fought for in the Civil War. I ask that civil life be carried on according to the spirit in which the army was carried on. You never get perfect justice, but the effort in handling the army was to bring to the front the men who could do the job. Nobody grudged promotion to Grant, or Sherman, or Thomas, or Sheridan, because they earned it. The only complaint was when a man got promotion which he did not earn.

Practical equality of opportunity for all citizens, when we achieve it, will have two great results. First, every man will have a fair chance to make of himself all that in him lies; to reach the highest point to which his capacities, unassisted by special privilege of his own and unhampered by the special privilege of others, can carry him, and to get for himself and his family substantially what he has earned. Second, equality of opportunity means that the commonwealth will get from every citizen the highest service of which he is capable. No man who carries the burden of the special privileges of another can give to the commonwealth that service to which it is fairly entitled.

I stand for the square deal. But when I say that I am for the square deal, I mean not merely that I stand for fair play under the present rules of the game, but that I stand for having those rules changed so as to work for a more substantial equality of opportunity and of reward for equally good service. One word of warning, which, I think, is hardly necessary in Kansas. When I say I want a square deal for the poor man, I do not mean that I want a square deal for the man who remains poor because he has not got the energy to work for himself. If a man who has had a chance will not make good, then he has got to quit. And you men of the Grand Army, you want justice for the brave man who fought, and punishment for the coward who shirked his work. Is not that so?

Now, this means that our government, National and State, must be freed from the sinister influence or control of special interests. Exactly as the special interests of cotton and slavery threatened our political integrity before the Civil War, so now the great special business interests too often control and corrupt the men and methods of government for their own profit. We must drive the special interests out of politics. That is one of our tasks to-day. Every special interest is entitled to justice — full, fair, and complete — and, now, mind you, if there were any attempt by mob-violence to plunder and work harm to the special interest, whatever it may be, that I most dislike, and the wealthy man, whomsoever he may be, for whom I have the greatest contempt, I would fight for him, and you would if you were worth your salt. He should have justice. For every special interest is entitled to justice, but not one is entitled to a vote in Congress, to a voice on the bench, or to representation in any public office. The Constitution guarantees protection to property, and we must make that promise good. But it does not give the right of suffrage to any corporation.

The true friend of property, the true conservative, is he who insists that property shall be the servant and not the master of the commonwealth; who insists that the creature of man's making shall be the servant and not the master of the man who made it. The citizens of the United States must effectively control the mighty commercial forces which they have themselves called into being.

There can be no effective control of corporations while their political activity remains. To put an end to it will be neither a short nor an easy task, but it can be done.

We must have complete and effective publicity of corporate affairs, so that the people may know beyond peradventure whether the corporations obey the law and whether their management entitles them to the confidence of the public. It is necessary that laws should be passed to prohibit the use of corporate funds directly or indirectly for political purposes; it is still more necessary that such laws should be thoroughly enforced. Corporate expenditures for political purposes, and especially such expenditures by public-service corporations, have supplied one of the principal sources of corruption in our political affairs.

It has become entirely clear that we must have government supervision of the capitalization, not only of public-service corporations, including, particularly, railways, but of all corporations doing an interstate business. I do not wish to see the nation forced into the ownership of the railways if it can possibly be avoided, and the only alternative is thoroughgoing and effective regulation, which shall be based on a full knowledge of all the facts, including a physical valuation of property. This physical valuation is not needed, or, at least, is very rarely needed, for fixing rates; but it is needed as the basis of honest capitalization.

We have come to recognize that franchises should never be granted except for a limited time, and never without proper provision for compensation to the public. It is my personal belief that the same kind and degree of control and supervision which should be exercised over public-service corporations should be extended also to combinations which control necessaries of life, such as meat, oil, and coal, or which deal in them on an important scale. I have no doubt that the ordinary man who has control of them is much like ourselves. I have no doubt he would like to do well, but I want to have enough supervision to help him realize that desire to do well.

I believe that the officers, and, especially, the directors, of corporations should be held personally responsible when any corporation breaks the law.

Combinations in industry are the result of an imperative economic law which cannot be repealed by political legislation. The effort at prohibiting all combination has substantially failed. The way out lies, not in attempting to prevent such combinations, but in completely controlling them in the interest of the public welfare. For that purpose the Federal Bureau of Corporations is an agency of first importance. Its powers, and, therefore, its efficiency, as well as that of the Interstate Commerce Commission, should be largely increased. We have a right to expect from the Bureau of Corporations and from the Interstate Commerce Commission a very high grade of public service. We should be as sure of the proper conduct of the interstate railways and the proper management of interstate business as we are now sure of the conduct and management of the national banks, and we should have as effective supervision in one case as in the other. The Hepburn

Act, and the amendment to the act in the shape in which it finally passed Congress at the last session, represent a long step in advance, and we must go yet further.

There is a wide-spread belief among our people that, under the methods of making tariffs which have hitherto obtained, the special interests are too influential. Probably this is true of both the big special interests and the little special interests. These methods have put a premium on selfishness, and, naturally, the selfish big interests have gotten more than their smaller, though equally selfish, brothers. The duty of Congress is to provide a method by which the interest of the whole people shall be all that receives consideration. To this end there must be an expert tariff commission, wholly removed from the possibility of political pressure or of improper business influence. Such a commission can find the real difference between cost of production, which is mainly the difference of labor cost here and abroad. As fast as its recommendations are made, I believe in revising one schedule at a time. A general revision of the tariff almost inevitably leads to log-rolling and the subordination of the general public interest to local and special interests.

The absence of effective State, and, especially, national, restraint upon unfair money-getting has tended to create a small class of enormously wealthy and economically powerful men, whose chief object is to hold and increase their power. The prime need is to change the conditions which enable these men to accumulate power which it is not for the general welfare that they should hold or exercise. We grudge no man a fortune which represents his own power and sagacity, when exercised with entire regard to the welfare of his fellows. Again, comrades over there, take the lesson from your own experience. Not only did you not grudge, but you gloried in the promotion of the great generals who gained their promotion by leading the army to victory. So it is with us. We grudge no man a fortune in civil life if it is honorably obtained and well used. It is not even enough that it should have been gained without doing damage to the community. We should permit it to be gained only so long as the gaining represents benefit to the community. This, I know, implies a policy of a far more active governmental interference with social and economic conditions in this country than we have yet had, but I think we have got to face the fact that such an increase in governmental control is now necessary.

No man should receive a dollar unless that dollar has been fairly earned. Every dollar received should represent a dollar's worth of service rendered — not gambling in stocks, but service rendered. The really big fortune, the swollen fortune, by the mere fact of its size acquires qualities which differentiate it in kind as well as in degree from what is possessed by men of relatively small means. Therefore, I believe in a graduated income tax on big fortunes, and in another tax which is far more easily collected and far more effective — a graduated inheritance tax on big fortunes, properly safeguarded against evasion and increasing rapidly in amount with the size of the estate.

The people of the United States suffer from periodical financial panics to a degree substantially unknown among the other nations which approach us in financial strength. There is no reason why we should suffer what they escape. It is of profound importance that our financial system should be promptly investigated, and so thoroughly and effectively revised as to make it certain that hereafter our currency will no longer fail at critical times to meet our needs.

It is hardly necessary for me to repeat that I believe in an efficient army and a navy large enough to secure for us abroad that respect which is the surest guaranty of peace. A word of special warning to my fellow citizens who are as progressive as I hope I am. I want them to keep up their interest in our internal affairs; and I want them also continually to remember Uncle Sam's interests abroad. Justice and fair dealing among nations rest upon principles identical with those which control justice and fair dealing among the individuals of which nations are composed, with the vital exception that each nation must do its own part in international police work. If you get into trouble here, you can call for the police; but if Uncle Sam gets into trouble, he has got to be his own policeman, and I want to see him strong enough to encourage the peaceful aspirations of other peoples in connection with us. I believe in national friendships and heartiest good-will to all nations; but national friendships, like those between men, must be founded on respect as well as on liking, on forbearance as well as upon trust. I should be heartily ashamed of any American who did not try to make the American Government act as justly toward the other nations in international relations as he himself would act toward any individual in private relations. I should be heartily ashamed to see us wrong a weaker power, and I should hang my head forever if we tamely suffered wrong from a stronger power.

Of conservation I shall speak more at length elsewhere. Conservation means development as much as it does protection. I recognize the right and duty of this generation to develop and use the natural resources of our land; but I do not recognize the right to waste them, or to rob, by wasteful use, the generations that come after us. I ask nothing of the nation except that it so behave as each farmer here behaves with reference to his own children. That farmer is a poor creature who skins the land and leaves it worthless to his children. The farmer is a good farmer who, having enabled the land to support himself and to provide for the education of his children, leaves it to them a little better than he found it himself. I believe the same thing of a nation.

Moreover, I believe that the natural resources must be used for the benefit of all our people, and not monopolized for the benefit of the few, and here again is another case in which I am accused of taking a revolutionary attitude. People forget now that one hundred years ago there were public men of good character who advocated the nation selling its public lands in great quantities, so that the nation could get the most money out of it, and giving it to the men who could cultivate it for their own uses. We took the proper democratic ground that the land should be granted in small sections to the men who were actually to till it and live on it. Now, with the water-power, with the forests, with the mines, we are brought face to face with the fact that there are many people who will go with us in conserving the resources only if they are to be allowed to exploit them for their benefit. That is one of the fundamental reasons why the special interests should be driven out of politics. Of all the questions which can come before this nation, short of the actual preservation of its existence in a great war, there is none which compares in importance with the great central task of leaving this land even a better land for our descendants than it is for us, and training them into a better race to inhabit the land and pass it on. Conservation is a great moral issue, for it involves the patriotic duty of insuring the safety and continuance of the nation. Let me add that the health and vitality of our people are at least as well worth conserving as their forests, waters, lands, and minerals, and in this great work the national government must bear a most important part.

I have spoken elsewhere also of the great task which lies before the farmers of the country to get for themselves and their wives and children not only the benefits of better farming, but also those of better business methods and better conditions of life on the farm. The burden of this great task will fall, as it should, mainly upon the great organizations of the farmers themselves. I am glad it will, for I believe they are all well able to handle it. In particular, there are strong reasons why the Departments of Agriculture of the various States, the United States Department of Agriculture, and the agricultural colleges and experiment stations should extend their work to cover all phases of farm life, instead of limiting themselves, as they have far too often limited themselves in the past, solely to the question of the production of crops. And now a special word to the farmer. I want to see him make the farm as fine a farm as it can be made; and let him remember to see that the improvement goes on indoors as well as out; let him remember that the farmer's wife should have her share of thought and attention just as much as the farmer himself.

Nothing is more true than that excess of every kind is followed by reaction; a fact which should be pondered by reformer and reactionary alike. We are face to face with new conceptions of the relations of property to human welfare, chiefly because certain advocates of the rights of property as against the rights of men have been pushing their claims too far. The man who wrongly holds that every human right is secondary to his profit must now give way to the advocate of human welfare, who rightly maintains that every man holds his property subject to the general right of the community to regulate its use to whatever degree the public welfare may require it.

But I think we may go still further. The right to regulate the use of wealth in the public interest is universally admitted. Let us admit also the right to regulate the terms and conditions of labor, which is the chief element of wealth, directly in the interest of the common good. The fundamental thing to do for every man is to give him a chance to reach a place in which he will make the greatest possible contribution to the public welfare. Understand what I say there. Give him a chance, not push him up if he will not be pushed. Help any man who stumbles; if he lies down, it is a poor job to try to carry him; but if he is a worthy man, try your best to see that he gets a chance to show the worth that is in him. No man can be a good citizen unless he has a wage more than sufficient to cover the bare cost of living, and hours of labor short enough so that after his day's work is done he will have time and energy to bear his share in the management of the community, to help in carrying the general load. We keep countless men from being good citizens by the conditions of life with which we surround them. We need comprehensive workmen's compensation acts, both State and national laws to regulate child labor and work for women, and, especially, we need in our common schools not merely education in book-learning, but also practical training for daily life and work. We need to enforce better sanitary conditions for our workers and to extend the use of safety appliances for our workers in industry and commerce, both within and between the States. Also, friends, in the interest of the working man himself we need to set our faces like flint against mob-violence just as against corporate greed; against violence and injustice and lawlessness by wage-workers just as much as against lawless cunning and greed and selfish arrogance of employers. If I could ask but one thing of my fellow countrymen, my request would be that, whenever they go in for reform, they remember the two sides, and that they always exact justice from one side as much as from the other. I have small use for the public servant who can always see and denounce the corruption of the capitalist, but who cannot persuade himself, especially before election, to say a word about lawless mob-violence. And I have equally small use for the man, be he a judge on the bench, or editor of a great paper, or wealthy and influential private citizen, who can see clearly enough and denounce the lawlessness of mob-violence, but whose eyes are closed so that he is blind when the question is one of corruption in business on a gigantic scale. Also remember what I said about excess in reformer and reactionary alike. If the reactionary man, who thinks of nothing but the rights of property, could have his way, he would bring about a revolution; and one of my chief fears in connection with progress comes because I do not want to see our people, for lack of proper leadership, compelled to follow men whose intentions are excellent, but whose eyes are a little too wild to make it really safe to trust them. Here in Kansas there is one paper which habitually denounces me as the tool of Wall Street, and at the same time frantically repudiates the statement that I am a Socialist on the ground that that is an unwarranted slander of the Socialists.

National efficiency has many factors. It is a necessary result of the principle of conservation widely applied. In the end it will determine our failure or success as a nation. National efficiency has to do, not only with natural resources and with men, but it is equally concerned with institutions. The State must be made efficient for the work which concerns only the people of the State; and the nation for that which concerns all the people. There must remain no neutral ground to serve as a refuge for lawbreakers, and especially for lawbreakers of great wealth, who can hire the vulpine legal cunning which will teach them how to avoid both jurisdictions. It is a misfortune when the national legislature fails to do its duty in providing a national remedy, so that the only national activity is the purely negative activity of the judiciary in forbidding the State to exercise power in the premises.

I do not ask for overcentralization; but I do ask that we work in a spirit of broad and far-reaching nationalism when we work for what concerns our people as a whole. We are all Americans. Our common interests are as broad as the continent. I speak to you here in Kansas exactly as I would speak in New York or Georgia, for the most vital problems are those which affect us all alike. The National Government belongs to the whole American people, and where the whole American people are interested, that interest can be guarded effectively only by the National Government. The betterment which we seek must be accomplished, I believe, mainly through the National Government.

The American people are right in demanding that New Nationalism, without which we cannot hope to deal with new problems. The New Nationalism puts the national need before sectional or personal advantage. It is impatient of the utter confusion that results from local legislatures attempting to treat national issues as local issues. It is still more impatient of the impotence which springs from overdivision of governmental powers, the impotence which makes it possible for local selfishness or for legal cunning, hired by wealthy special interests, to bring national activities to a deadlock. This New Nationalism regards the executive power as the steward of the public welfare. It demands of the judiciary that it shall be interested primarily in human welfare rather than in property, just as it demands that the representative body shall represent all the people rather than any one class or section of the people.

I believe in shaping the ends of government to protect property as well as human welfare. Normally, and in the long run, the ends are the same; but whenever the alternative must be faced, I am for men and not for property, as you were in the Civil War. I am far from underestimating the importance of dividends; but I rank dividends below human character. Again, I do not have any sympathy with the reformer who says he does not care for dividends. Of course, economic welfare is necessary, for a man must pull his own weight and be able to support his family. I know well that the reformers must not bring upon the people economic ruin, or the reforms themselves will go down in the ruin. But we must be ready to face temporary disaster, whether or not brought on by those who will war against us to the knife. Those who oppose all reform will do well to remember that ruin in its worst form is inevitable if our national life brings us nothing better than swollen fortunes for the few and the triumph in both politics and business of a sordid and selfish materialism.

If our political institutions were perfect, they would absolutely prevent the political domination of money in any part of our affairs. We need to make our political representatives more quickly and sensitively responsive to the people whose servants they are. More direct action by the people in their own affairs under proper safeguards is vitally necessary. The direct primary is a step in this direction, if it is associated with a corrupt-practices act effective to prevent the advantage of the man willing recklessly and unscrupulously to spend money over his more honest competitor. It is particularly important that all moneys received or expended for campaign purposes should be publicly accounted for, not only after election, but before election as well. Political action must be made simpler, easier, and freer from confusion for every citizen. I believe that the prompt removal of unfaithful or incompetent public servants should be made easy and sure in whatever way experience shall show to be most expedient in any given class of cases.

One of the fundamental necessities in a representative government such as ours is to make certain that the men to whom the people delegate their power shall serve the people by whom they are elected, and not the special interests. I believe that every national officer, elected or appointed, should be forbidden to perform any service or receive any compensation, directly or indirectly, from interstate corporations; and a similar provision could not fail to be useful within the States.

The object of government is the welfare of the people. The material progress and prosperity of a nation are desirable chiefly so far as they lead to the moral and material welfare of all good citizens. Just in proportion as the average man and woman are honest, capable of sound judgment and high ideals, active in public affairs — but, first of all, sound in their home life, and the father and mother of healthy children whom they bring up well — just so far, and no farther, we may count our civilization a success. We must have — I believe we have already — a genuine and permanent moral awakening, without which no wisdom of legislation or administration really means anything; and, on the other hand, we must try to secure the social and economic legislation without which any improvement due to purely moral agitation is necessarily evanescent. Let me again illustrate by a reference to the Grand Army. You could not have won simply as a disorderly and disorganized mob. You needed generals; you needed careful administration of the most advanced type; and a good commissary — the cracker line. You well remember that success was necessary in many different lines in order to bring about general success. You had to have the administration at Washington good, just as you had to have the administration in the field; and you had to have the work of the generals good. You could not have triumphed without that administration and leadership; but it would all have been worthless if the average soldier had not had the right stuff in him. He had to have the right stuff in him, or you could not get it out of him. In the last analysis, therefore, vitally necessary though it was to have the right kind of organization and the right kind of generalship, it was even more vitally necessary that the average soldier should have the fighting edge, the right character. So it is in our civil life. No matter how honest and decent we are in our private lives, if we do not have the right kind of law and the right kind of administration of the law, we cannot go forward as a nation. That is imperative; but it must be an addition to, and not a substitution for, the qualities that make us good citizens. In the last analysis, the most important elements in any man's career must be the sum of those qualities which, in the aggregate, we speak of as character. If he has not got it, then no law that the wit of man can devise, no administration of the law by the boldest and strongest executive, will avail to help him. We must have the right kind of character — character that makes a man, first of all, a good man in the home, a good father, a good husband — that makes a man a good neighbor. You must have that, and, then, in addition, you must have the kind of law and the kind of administration of the law which will give to those qualities in the private citizen the best possible chance for development. The prime problem of our nation is to get the right type of good citizenship, and, to get it, we must have progress, and our public men must be genuinely progressive.

Chronology

1858   Born October 27 at 28 East 20th Street, New York City, second child of Theodore Roosevelt and Martha Bulloch Roosevelt. (Grandfather Cornelius Van Schaack Roosevelt, born 1794, founded a prosperous plate-glass importing business and then made successful investments in Manhattan real estate and banking. Father, born 1831, worked for the family firm of Roosevelt & Son while involving himself in civic and philanthropic affairs, including the Children's Aid Society and the YMCA. Mother, born 1835, came from a family of slave-owning Georgia planters. Parents met in 1850 when father visited the Bulloch family home in Roswell, Georgia, and were married there on December 22, 1853. Their first child, Anna, was born on January 18, 1855.) Household includes aunt Anna Bulloch and grandmother Martha Stewart Elliott Bulloch.

1860   Brother Elliott born on February 28.

1861   Father does not enlist in the Union Army because of the objections of his wife, who supports the Confederacy, but does help establish an allotment system allowing Union soldiers to send a portion of their pay home to their families. (His work on the Allotment Commission will keep him away from home for much of the first two years of the war as he lobbies the government and visits army camps.) Sister Corinne born on September 27.

1862   Roosevelt begins to suffer acute asthma attacks, usually at night. Uncle James Bulloch, a Confederate naval officer, arranges the construction of commerce raiders in British shipyards, and uncle Irvine Bulloch serves on the Confederate raider *Alabama*.

1863–65   Father hires a substitute to avoid conscription. Roosevelt begins to be tutored at home by his aunt Anna Bulloch. Grandmother Martha Bulloch dies in October 1864. Roosevelt watches funeral procession for Abraham Lincoln on April 25, 1865, from the window of his grandfather's house at Broadway and 14th Street. Attends Presbyterian services with his family.

1866–68   Continues to suffer from severe asthma attacks as well as frequent headaches and stomach pain. Becomes friends with Edith Kermit Carow (b. 1861), a playmate of his sister Corinne, who is tutored along with the Roosevelt children. Enjoys reading and becomes fascinated with natural history. Father plays leading role in founding the New York Orthopedic Hospital.

1869–70   Father helps found the American Museum of Natural History. Family sails for England on May 12, 1869. They visit with James and Irvine Bulloch in Liverpool, then tour England, Scotland, Belgium, the Netherlands, the German Rhineland, Switzerland, northern Italy, Austria, Bavaria, Prussia, and France. Roosevelt keeps a detailed diary during the trip and takes long walks in the Alps despite his health problems. Family spends winter in Italy, then returns to France and England before sailing from Liverpool on May 14, 1870. Roosevelt continues to be tutored at home along with his siblings and begins lifting weights. Father joins in founding of the Metropolitan Museum of Art.

1871   Grandfather Cornelius Van Schaack Roosevelt dies on July 17, leaving an estate valued at between $3 million and $7 million. Family vacations in Adirondacks and White Mountains.

1872–73   Roosevelt is given a shotgun and his first set of spectacles, which greatly improve his vision. Becomes an enthusiastic bird hunter and studies taxidermy. Family sails for England on October 16, 1872, and travels through Belgium, the Netherlands, Germany, France, and Italy before arriving in Alexandria, Egypt, on November 28. In Cairo they charter a boat, then sail up the Nile as far as Aswan; during the Nile trip Roosevelt shoots almost 200 birds. Family tours Palestine, Lebanon, and Syria before sailing to Greece and Turkey and then traveling up the Danube, arriving in Vienna on April 19, 1873. While father returns to the United States and mother and Anna go to Paris, Roosevelt, Elliott, and Corinne spend five months living with a German family in Dresden. Returns to New York on November 5, 1873, and moves into new family home at 6 West 57th Street.

1874   Studies for Harvard College entrance examinations. Family begins spending summer in Oyster Bay on the north shore of Long Island; Edith Carow becomes a frequent visitor.

1876   Father becomes active in Republican reform politics. Roosevelt enters Harvard in late September. Moves into boarding house at 16 Winthrop Street, Cambridge, where he will live throughout his college years. Studies Greek, Latin, German, geometry, physics, and chemistry during his freshman year.

1877   Asthma improves. Studies rhetoric, German, French, Anglo-American history, vertebrate physiology and anatomy (taught by William James), and botany during his sophomore year. Father falls ill in December.

1878   Father dies of stomach cancer on February 9; Roosevelt describes his death in his diary as "the blackest day of my life." Inherits $125,000. Goes on hunting trip in northern Maine in late summer and continues to enjoy rowing at Oyster Bay and in Cambridge. Studies German, Italian, forensics, logic, metaphysics, political economy, geology, and zoology during his junior year. Meets Alice Hathaway Lee (b. 1861), cousin of his college friend Richard Saltonstall, at her home in Chesnut Hill, Massachusetts, on October 18.

1879   Returns to northern Maine in March for winter hunting trip and climbs Mt. Katahdin in late summer. Studies Italian, forensics, political economy, geology, and zoology during his senior year.

1880   Becomes engaged to Alice Lee on January 25. Writes senior thesis, "The Practicability of Equalizing Men and Women Before the Law," and begins naval history of the War of 1812. Graduates from Harvard on June 30, ranking 21 in a class of 177. Goes hunting in Minnesota with Elliott in the summer. Marries Alice Lee on October 27 at the Unitarian Church in Brookline, Massachusetts. After honeymoon at Oyster Bay, they move into the family home on West 57th Street. Roosevelt enters Columbia Law School.

1881   Sails for Europe with Alice on May 12. During their
            trip they visit Ireland, England, France, Italy, Austria,
            Switzerland, Germany, the Netherlands, and Belgium; in
            Switzerland Roosevelt climbs the Matterhorn. Returns to
            New York on October 2. Nominated as the Republican
            candidate for the state assembly in the 21st District on Oc-
            tober 28. Defeats Democrat William Strew 3,502–1,974 in
            the election on November 8.

1882   Assembly meets in Albany on January 3. Roosevelt accuses
            state supreme court judge T. R. Westbrook of corrupt
            dealings with financier Jay Gould and succeeds in having
            the assembly authorize an investigation of Westbrook.
            Supports bill to ban home manufacture of cigars after
            touring tenements in New York City with labor leader
            Samuel Gompers. Sister Corinne marries Douglas Robin-
            son in April. *The Naval War of 1812* is published to favor-
            able reviews. Effort to impeach Westbrook fails when
            assembly approves committee report clearing him of seri-
            ous wrongdoing. Assembly session ends on June 2. Roo-
            sevelt ends his legal studies. Moves with Alice to house at
            55 West 45th Street. Reelected to the assembly on No-
            vember 7 with 63 percent of the vote.

1883   Assembly meets January 2. Roosevelt is elected Republi-
            can minority leader. Works with Democratic governor
            Grover Cleveland to pass a civil service reform bill; the bill
            prohibiting home cigar manufacture also becomes law. In
            a speech in the assembly Roosevelt calls Jay Gould and his
            associates "the most dangerous of all classes, the wealthy
            criminal class." Assembly session ends May 4. Roosevelt
            plans to build a house in Oyster Bay. In early September
            he travels to the Dakota Badlands along the Little Missouri
            to hunt buffalo and invests $14,000 in two cattle ranches
            near Medora (investment will eventually total $85,000).
            Returns to New York in late September. Reelected to
            the assembly with 67 percent of the vote on November 6.
            Elliott marries Anna Hall on December 1. Roosevelt is
            defeated in voting for Republican assembly leader on
            December 31.

1884   Assembly session begins January 1. Roosevelt leads investigation into corruption in New York City. Alice moves back to West 57th Street while awaiting the birth of their first child. Alice Lee Roosevelt is born on February 12. Roosevelt returns to New York City from Albany on February 13. His mother dies of typhoid fever at 3 A.M. on February 14, and his wife dies of kidney failure at 2 P.M. the same day. Roosevelt writes in his diary: "The light has gone out of my life." Gives Alice to his sister Anna to raise and sells his house on West 45th Street. Wins passage of bill giving the mayor of New York the power to make appointments independently of the aldermen. Declines renomination for the assembly. Forms lifelong friendship with Henry Cabot Lodge of Massachusetts, a fellow supporter of Senator George Edmunds for the Republican presidential nomination. Roosevelt and Lodge attend the Republican convention in Chicago, June 3–7, where they unsuccessfully try to prevent the nomination of James G. Blaine. After the convention they declare their support for Blaine, angering the Republican reformers ("mugwumps") who consider Blaine corrupt and support Democratic candidate Grover Cleveland. In late July Roosevelt goes to the Dakota Badlands and begins building a house on the Elkhorn Ranch north of Medora. Hunts grizzly bears, elk, and deer in the Big Horn Mountains of Wyoming. Campaigns for Blaine in New York and Massachusetts. Cleveland wins election on November 4. Roosevelt goes to the Badlands, then returns to New York in December and stays with his sister Anna.

1885   Travels to the Badlands in April and rides the range during the spring roundup. Returns to New York in June and spends eight weeks with Anna and Alice at Sagamore Hill, newly finished house in Oyster Bay built for $45,000. *Hunting Trips of a Ranchman* published in July. Visits Elkhorn Ranch in August. Returns in September to New York, where he encounters Edith Carow while visiting his sister Anna. They become secretly engaged on November 17.

1886   Travels to the Elkhorn Ranch in March. With two ranch hands, Roosevelt pursues three thieves down the Little Missouri and captures them. Works on biography of Thomas Hart Benton. Returns to New York in July, then goes hunting in the northern Idaho mountains in the late summer. Nominated as Republican candidate for mayor of New York on October 15. In election on November 2, Democrat Abram Hewitt receives 90,552 votes; independent Labor candidate Henry George, 86,110; and Roosevelt, 60,435. Sails for England on November 6. Marries Edith Carow at St. George's, Hanover Square, London, on December 2. They begin their honeymoon in France.

1887   Visits Italy, France, and London with Edith before returning to New York on March 27. Travels to Dakota Badlands in April and learns that more than half his cattle died in the unusually harsh winter of 1886–87. Ends active participation in ranching, though he will return to Elkhorn Ranch during hunting trips. (When he finally liquidates his cattle investments in 1898, Roosevelt will calculate his total loss at about $20,000.) Moves into Sagamore Hill with Edith and Alice. *Life of Thomas Hart Benton* published. Son Theodore Roosevelt Jr. (Ted) born September 13. Hunts in the Dakota Badlands in November. Returns to New York, where he founds the Boone and Crockett Club, dedicated to the hunting, study, and conservation of large American game mammals (will serve as its president until 1894).

1888   *Gouverneur Morris* published. Roosevelt begins work on a multi-volume history of American westward expansion, and becomes a prolific writer of magazine articles on politics, literature, history, natural history, and other subjects (many of his books will also be serialized). Hunts in northern Idaho in August and September. *Essays in Practical Politics*, collecting two essays on New York state and municipal politics, published. Campaigns for Republican nominee Benjamin Harrison in Illinois, Michigan, and Minnesota. Harrison defeats Grover Cleveland on November 6. *Ranch Life and the Hunting Trail* published in December.

1889   Works on *The Winning of the West*. President Harrison appoints Roosevelt as one of three members of the Civil Service Commission, and he takes office on May 13. Travels to Indianapolis and Milwaukee to investigate corruption in the Post Office. The first two volumes of *The Winning of the West*, covering the period from 1769 to

1783, are published in June. Hunts grizzlies in Montana in August. Son Kermit Roosevelt born October 10. Roosevelt rents house at 1820 Jefferson Place N.W., Washington, D.C., where he is joined in December by his wife and children. Becomes part of social circle that includes Lodge, John Hay, House Speaker Thomas Reed, and Henry Adams.

1890   Continues work on Civil Service Commission, but is frustrated by lack of funds and authority (the commission can only recommend the dismissal of corrupt officeholders). House committee investigates his conduct during the Milwaukee Post Office investigation but eventually exonerates him. Reads *The Influence of Sea Power upon History, 1660–1783*, by Alfred Thayer Mahan; the book strengthens his belief in the need for a larger navy. Visits Yellowstone National Park in September on behalf of the Boone and Crockett Club. Becomes increasingly concerned by Elliott's worsening alcoholism and deteriorating mental condition.

1891   Visits Baltimore to investigate involvement of federal officeholders in primary elections, then writes 146-page report calling for the dismissal of 25 postal employees. *History of the City of New York* published. Learns that Elliott has fathered a child with Katy Mann, a servant, and attempts unsuccessfully to have him declared legally insane. Daughter Ethel Carow Roosevelt born August 13. Hunts elk in the northern Rockies in September. Moves to 1215 19th Street N.W. in Washington.

1892   Travels to France in January to see Elliott and succeeds in getting him to place his assets in a trust, enter a sanitarium, and agree to live apart from his family for at least two years. Calls for a congressional investigation into Postmaster General John Wanamaker's failure to dismiss the 25 Baltimore postal workers cited in his 1891 report. Hunts wild pigs in southern Texas. Testifies before the House Civil Service Reform Committee, which issues report on June 22 severely criticizing Wanamaker. Roosevelt investigates corruption on Indian reservations in the northern plains in September. Cleveland defeats Harrison in the presidential election on November 8.

1893   Roosevelt remains in office at the request of President
            Cleveland. Publishes *The Wilderness Hunter*.

1894   Son Archibald Bulloch Roosevelt (Archie) born April 9.
            Elliott dies on August 14 from a seizure during delirium
            tremens; Roosevelt writes to his sister Anna: "he was
            hunted by the most terrible demons that ever entered
            a man's body and soul." The third volume of *The Win-
            ning of the West*, covering the period from 1784 to 1790, is
            published.

1895   Appointed to the New York City Police Commission by
            Republican reform mayor William Strong on April 17.
            Takes office on May 6 and is elected president of the four-
            member commission. Forces the resignation of Chief
            Thomas Byrnes, who is widely suspected of corruption,
            on May 27. Begins making night tours to check on police-
            men walking their beats. Orders strict enforcement of law
            closing saloons on Sundays, a policy that proves highly
            unpopular among traditionally Republican German-
            American voters. Publishes *Hero Tales from American His-
            tory*, a book for children written with Henry Cabot Lodge.
            Sister Anna marries William Sheffield Cowles, an Ameri-
            can naval officer, in November.

1896   Roosevelt continues efforts to expand and modernize
            the police department, but is frustrated when opposition
            by Commissioner Andrew Parker and Chief Peter Con-
            lin blocks the promotion of senior officers he favors.
            Fourth volume of *The Winning of the West*, covering
            years from 1791 to 1807, published. Hunts pronghorn in
            North Dakota in late summer, then campaigns for Re-
            publican nominee William McKinley in New York, Illi-
            nois, Michigan, Minnesota, New Jersey, Delaware, and
            Maryland. McKinley defeats William Jennings Bryan on
            November 3.

1897   Appointed Assistant Secretary of the Navy by President
            McKinley on April 6 and takes office on April 19. Serves
            as deputy to Secretary John D. Long, but soon takes the
            leading role in the department. Becomes an advocate
            within the administration for the annexation of Hawaii
            and intervention in Cuba. Gives widely reported speech
            at the Naval War College in Newport, Rhode Island, on

June 2 in which he calls for the rapid expansion of the navy and praises the willingness to wage war: "It is through strife, or the readiness for strife, that a nation must win greatness." Publishes *American Ideals*, a collection of essays and speeches. Serves as acting secretary during Long's summer vacation in August and September. Secures appointment of Commodore George Dewey as commander of the Asiatic Squadron. Son Quentin Roosevelt born on November 19.

1898   Battleship *Maine* is destroyed in Havana harbor on February 15 by an explosion that kills 262 of its crew. On February 25 Roosevelt alerts all squadrons to prepare for possible war with Spain and orders Dewey to attack the Philippines if war is declared. Edith falls dangerously ill, but recovers after undergoing surgery for an abdominal abscess on March 7. War with Spain is declared on April 25. Roosevelt resigns from the navy department and is appointed deputy commander of the First U.S. Volunteer Cavalry with the rank of lieutenant colonel; his friend Leonard Wood is made the regimental commander. Arrives in San Antonio, Texas, on May 15 and trains with the regiment, which soon becomes known as the Rough Riders. Regiment sails from Florida for Cuba on June 14. It lands at Daiquirí on June 22 and fights in skirmish at Las Guásimas on June 24. Wood is made a brigade commander on June 30 and Roosevelt becomes the regimental commander. On July 1 Roosevelt leads the Rough Riders in successful attacks on Kettle Hill and San Juan Hill during the battle for San Juan Heights. The regiment serves in the siege lines outside Santiago until the city surrenders on July 17. Armistice ending hostilities between Spain and the United States is signed on August 12. Regiment lands in Montauk, Long Island, on August 15 and is mustered out on September 15. Roosevelt is nominated for governor by the Republican state convention on September 27 and campaigns by train throughout the state. In the election on November 8, Roosevelt receives 661,715 votes, and Democratic candidate Augustus van Wyck, 643,921. Peace treaty is signed in Paris on December 10 under which Spain cedes Puerto Rico, Guam, and the Philippines to the United States and renounces all claim to Cuba. Roosevelt begins his two-year term as governor on December 31.

1899   Makes appointments to office in consultation with U.S.
          Senator Thomas Platt, the boss of the state Republican
          machine. Insurrection against American rule begins in the
          Philippines on February 4. Roosevelt supports taxation of
          corporate transit and utility franchises, a measure strongly
          opposed by Platt. Franchise tax bill is passed on April 28
          at the end of a session in which Roosevelt also wins
          passage of legislation improving sweatshop conditions,
          strengthening factory inspections, and limiting the work-
          ing hours of women, children, and state employees. Recalls
          legislature in May and secures passage of a strengthened
          version of the franchise tax bill. Greeted by enthusiastic
          crowds while traveling to Rough Riders reunion in Las
          Vegas, New Mexico, in late June. *The Rough Riders* is pub-
          lished in early summer. Vice-President Garret Hobart dies
          on November 21.

1900   Despite opposition from Platt, Roosevelt replaces the
          state superintendent of insurance, who had received large
          unsecured loans from a New York bank. *Oliver Cromwell*
          published. Roosevelt wins passage of conservation legis-
          lation and works to preserve state forests and wildlife
          through administrative measures. Opposes Hay-Paunce-
          fote treaty, Anglo-American agreement signed on Febru-
          ary 5 that permits the United States to build and maintain
          a canal across Central America, because it does not allow
          the U.S. to fortify the canal. (Treaty is ratified with amend-
          ments by the Senate in December 1900, but then rejected
          by the British in March 1901.) Movement to nominate
          Roosevelt for vice-president is backed by Platt, who
          wishes to remove him from the governorship. Roosevelt
          attends Republican national convention in Philadelphia,
          where on June 21 he is unanimously nominated for vice-
          president. While McKinley remains at home in Canton,
          Ohio, during the campaign, Roosevelt travels 21,000
          miles and makes 673 speeches in 24 states, defending the
          annexation of the Philippines and attacking Democratic
          nominee William Jennings Bryan. *The Strenuous Life*, a
          collection of essays, is published during the campaign. On
          November 6 McKinley is reelected with 292 electoral
          votes, while Bryan receives 155.

1901   Hunts cougars in Colorado. Takes oath of office as vice-
          president on March 4 and presides over the Senate until

its adjournment on March 9. Spends spring and summer at Sagamore Hill; with few official duties, he considers resuming his legal studies. William Howard Taft becomes the first civil governor of the Philippines on July 4 as American troops continue to fight Filipino guerillas. President McKinley is shot by Leon Czolgosz, an anarchist, in Buffalo, New York, on September 6 and dies from his wounds on September 14. Roosevelt takes the oath of office as president in Buffalo on the afternoon of September 14. Keeps George Cortelyou, who had served McKinley, as his presidential secretary, and retains McKinley's cabinet: John Hay (secretary of state), Lyman Gage (secretary of treasury), Elihu Root (secretary of war), Philander Knox (attorney general), Charles Emory Smith (postmaster general), John Long (secretary of the navy), Ethan Hitchcock (secretary of the interior), and as secretary of agriculture, James Wilson (the only cabinet member to serve throughout Roosevelt's presidency). Invites Booker T. Washington to have dinner with the Roosevelt family at the White House on October 16; the dinner is widely condemned in the South as a move toward "social equality." Although Roosevelt continues to consult with Washington and has other African-Americans as guests at White House receptions, he does not have dinner with an African-American again while president. Secretary of State John Hay signs a second treaty with Lord Pauncefote on November 18 after Britain agrees to permit fortification of a future canal. In his first annual message to Congress, December 3, Roosevelt calls for the creation of a department of commerce and labor, the regulation of large corporations, forest conservation, federal irrigation of western lands, and the expansion of the navy (during his presidency the battleship fleet is increased from 17 to 27 ships). Forms close relationship with Gifford Pinchot, chief of the Bureau of Forestry in the Department of Agriculture.

1902   Lyman Gage and Charles Emory Smith both retire; Roosevelt appoints Leslie Shaw as secretary of the treasury and Henry Payne as postmaster general. Department of Justice files anti-trust suit on March 10 against the Northern Securities Company, a recently formed holding company that controls the three major railroads in the northwestern United States. John Long retires and is replaced as secretary of the navy by William Moody. In response to recent allegations of widespread American atrocities in the Philippines, Roosevelt defends the general conduct of U.S. troops during the insurrection while ordering an investigation. Anthracite coal miners in Pennsylvania go on strike on May 12. U.S. administration of Cuba ends May 20 under terms that restrict Cuban sovereignty. Roosevelt signs bill on May 22 creating Crater Lake National Park in Oregon; during his presidency the number of national parks increases from five to ten. On June 17 he signs the National Reclamation Act, which provides for the first federal irrigation projects; 24 projects are established in 14 western states during his presidency. Congress rejects proposal for a Nicaraguan canal while approving plan for building one through the isthmus of Panama, the route favored by Roosevelt, and authorizes the administration to enter into negotiations with Colombia (at the time Panama is a Colombian state). Leaves Washington in early July and goes to Sagamore Hill, where he will spend every summer during his presidency. Officially declares an end to the Philippine insurrection on July 4 after fighting ends in the northern and central islands of the archipelago. (U.S. troops will continue to fight Moro rebels in the southern Philippines until 1913.) Orders Brigadier General Jacob Smith to be retired from the army for his brutal actions in the Philippines; several other officers charged with atrocities are acquitted by military courts. Appoints Oliver Wendell Holmes, chief justice of the Massachusetts Supreme Judicial Court, to the U.S. Supreme Court on August 11. During a visit to Pittsfield, Massachusetts, on September 3, the presidential carriage is struck by a trolley car, killing a Secret Service agent and throwing Roosevelt onto the pavement. Continues speaking tour, but undergoes two operations in late September to treat his injured left leg. Returns to Washington, staying at 22 Jackson Place while the White House undergoes extensive renovations. Meets with United Mine Workers president John Mitchell and mine owners on October 3 in attempt to avert a winter coal shortage. After extensive negotiations, Roosevelt names an investigating commission on October 16 and the miners return to work on October 23. (Commission report on March 18, 1903, results in settlement favorable to the miners, but not in union recognition.) Moves back into the White House on November 4.

Makes hunting trip to Mississippi during which he refuses to shoot a bear tied to a tree (cartoon depicting the
incident inspires the term "teddy bear"). Nominates Dr.
William Crum, an African-American, as collector of customs in Charleston, South Carolina; the appointment is
resisted by southern senators, and Roosevelt makes a
series of recess appointments until Crum is finally confirmed in 1905. On December 9 Britain and Germany
begin a naval blockade of Venezuela in an attempt to force
its government to pay its foreign debt. Concerned about
possible German expansion in Latin America, Roosevelt
reinforces the U.S. fleet in the Caribbean and obtains the
agreement of Germany to submit the dispute to international arbitration (blockade ends in February 1903).

1903   Hay-Herrán treaty, signed January 22, provides for a canal
zone six miles wide under Colombian sovereignty but
with American regulations and courts. After Roosevelt insists that dispute over the Alaska-Canada border not be
arbitrated by outside powers, the Hay-Herbert treaty is
signed on January 24, providing for a commission with
American, Canadian, and British members. Congress es-
tablishes Department of Commerce and Labor, February
14, and Roosevelt appoints George Cortelyou as its first
secretary; William Loeb succeeds Cortelyou as Roosevelt's
secretary. Congress also passes legislation reorganizing the
army and establishing a general staff, a measure advocated
by Roosevelt and Elihu Root, and the Elkins Act, prohibiting railroads from giving or receiving rebates. Roosevelt appoints William Day, a federal appellate judge
from Ohio, to the Supreme Court on February 19. Cre-
ates the first national wildlife refuge on March 14; will establish 54 other wildlife refuges by executive order on
federally owned land during his presidency. Leaves Washington April 1 on western trip during which he visits 25
states and travels 14,000 miles. Goes camping in Yellowstone National Park with nature writer John Burroughs
and in Yosemite National Park with John Muir. Returns
to Washington on June 5. Colombian senate rejects canal
treaty on August 12. Alaska-Canada border commission
proposes settlement favorable to the United States on
October 20. Roosevelt appoints Public Lands Commission to study the use of federal lands. Rebellion in Panama
begins on November 3. U.S. Navy prevents Colombia

from sending reinforcements, and on November 14 the United States formally recognizes the new Panamanian regime. On November 18 Hay signs a convention with Panamanian envoy Philippe Bunau-Varilla; under its terms, the United States guarantees Panamanian independence, while Panama cedes perpetual sovereignty over a zone ten miles wide in return for $10 million and an annuity of $250,000 (financial terms are the same as those in the earlier treaty with Colombia).

1904 Roosevelt appoints William Howard Taft as secretary of war when Root returns to his law practice. Russo-Japanese War begins on February 8. Senator Mark Hanna of Ohio, Roosevelt's main rival for leadership of the Republican party, dies on February 15. Supreme Court rules 5–4 for the government in the Northern Securites antitrust case on March 14. Roosevelt orders warships to Tangier after Ion Perdicaris, a former American citizen, is kidnapped in Morocco on May 18 by Raisuli, a Berber insurgent. Republican national convention nominates Roosevelt by acclamation on June 23, chooses Senator Charles Fairbanks of Indiana as the vice-presidential candidate, and makes Cortelyou national chairman of the party. Perdicaris is released by Raisuli on June 24. Roosevelt appoints Victor Metcalf to succeed Cortelyou as secretary of commerce and labor, names Secretary of the Navy William Moody as attorney general when Knox is elected to the Senate, and replaces Moody with Paul Morton. Democrats nominate Alton B. Parker, a New York judge, for president on July 9. In accordance with tradition, Roosevelt does not actively campaign. Postmaster General Henry Payne dies on October 4; Roosevelt appoints Robert Wynne as his successor. In election on November 8 Roosevelt wins 336 electoral votes and 56 percent of the popular vote; Parker receives 140 electoral votes. Roosevelt declares on election night that he will not seek another term. In his annual message to Congress, December 6, states that in cases of "chronic wrongdoing" or general lawlessness in Latin America the United States should be prepared to intervene and exercise "an international police power" in order to prevent European intervention. (Policy becomes known as the Roosevelt Corollary to the Monroe Doctrine.) Injures left eye while boxing with a military officer at the White

House; over the course of several years he loses sight in the affected eye.

1905 Signs bill on February 1 creating the U.S. Forest Service within the Department of Agriculture and giving it authority over national forest reserves previously controlled by the Department of the Interior. Names Gifford Pinchot as its first chief; during his presidency Roosevelt expands the forest reserves from 43 million to 194 million acres. On February 7 the United States and the Dominican Republic sign a diplomatic protocol under which the U.S. assumes responsibility for collecting Dominican customs and managing the payment of its foreign debt. After the Senate twice adjourns without voting on its ratification, Roosevelt continues to implement the protocol by executive action (American management of Dominican customs and debt payments continues until July 31, 1907). Roosevelt is inaugurated on March 4. Appoints George Cortelyou to succeed Robert Wynne as postmaster general. Gives away niece Eleanor Roosevelt at her marriage to her fifth cousin, Franklin Delano Roosevelt, in New York on March 17. Leaves Washington on western trip, April 3; hunts wolves in Oklahoma and bears in Colorado before returning to the capital on May 11. After the Japanese win decisive naval victory in Tsushima Strait, May 27–28, they ask Roosevelt to mediate peace with Russia, and he agrees. Czar Nicholas II accepts mediation offer on June 7. Roosevelt makes his first visit to Pine Knot, a small wooden cabin near Charlottesville, Virginia, that Edith has bought for him; returns for seven more short visits during his presidency. Kaiser William II writes to Roosevelt warning of a possible war between Germany and France over foreign intervention in Morocco. Roosevelt suggests holding an international conference to resolve the dispute, and Germany and France agree (conference opens in Algeciras, Spain, on January 16, 1906). John Hay dies on July 1, and Roosevelt names Elihu Root as his successor. Appoints Charles Bonaparte as secretary of the navy after Paul Morton resigns over controversy concerning his past actions as a railroad executive. Russo-Japanese peace negotiations begin at the Portsmouth, New Hampshire, navy yard on August 9. Roosevelt follows the talks from Sagamore Hill and helps persuade the Japanese not to press for an indemnity and to claim only the southern half

of Sakhalin Island. Becomes the first president to descend
in a submarine when he dives in Long Island Sound on
August 25 onboard the *Plunger*. Peace treaty is signed at
Portsmouth on September 5. *Outdoor Pastimes of an American Hunter* published in October. In his annual message
to Congress, December 5, Roosevelt calls for legislation
regulating railroad rates and protecting food and drugs
against adulteration and fraudulent labeling.

1906   Daughter Alice marries Nicholas Longworth, a Republican congressman from Ohio, at the White House on February 17. Algeciras conference on Morocco ends on April
6 with the signing of an agreement favorable to France.
Roosevelt orders an investigation of the meatpacking industry after reading Upton Sinclair's *The Jungle*. Signs
Antiquities Act, June 8, giving the president authority to
create national monuments on federally owned land; Roosevelt will establish 18 national monuments during his
presidency. Signs the Hepburn Act, giving the Interstate
Commerce Commission power to regulate railroad rates,
June 29; the Pure Food and Drug Act, June 30; and a federal meat inspection act, June 30. Roosevelt follows investigation into incident in Brownsville, Texas, where on
August 13 one white man is shot to death and two others
are wounded, allegedly by black soldiers from the 25th Infantry Regiment. Orders American intervention in Cuba
on September 28 after the Cuban government collapses
(occupation lasts until a new government is inaugurated
on January 28, 1909). Decision by the San Francisco board
of education on October 11 to segregate Japanese schoolchildren causes crisis in U.S.-Japanese relations. Roosevelt
orders the dishonorable discharge of 167 black soldiers for
not identifying the alleged perpetrators of the Brownsville
shootings, November 5, and subsequently defends decision from public criticism by Republican senator Joseph
Foraker and others. Inspects the construction of the canal
in Panama, November 14–17, becoming the first president
to leave the continental United States while in office. Justice Department files suit to dissolve Standard Oil of New
Jersey (company is dissolved in 1911 after the Supreme
Court rules for the government). Appoints Attorney General William Moody to the Supreme Court on December
3, leading to cabinet reorganization in which Charles
Bonaparte replaces Moody, Victor Metcalf replace Bona-

parte as secretary of the navy, and Metcalf is succeeded as secretary of commerce and labor by Oscar Straus, who becomes the first Jewish cabinet member. Roosevelt is awarded the Nobel Peace Prize on December 10 for his role in the Portsmouth Treaty.

1907   Replaces Ethan Hitchcock with James Garfield as secretary of the interior and Leslie Shaw with George Cortelyou as secretary of the treasury; George von Lengerke Meyer succeeds Cortelyou as postmaster general. In February Roosevelt reaches "gentlemen's agreement" with the Japanese government, under which San Francisco ceases segregation of Japanese schoolchildren in return for severe restrictions on Japanese immigration to the continental United States. Appoints Inland Waterways Commission on March 14 to study the use and control of river systems. During the spring and summer Roosevelt begins actively supporting Taft's bid to win the Republican presidential nomination. Administration files anti-trust suit against the American Tobacco Company in July (in 1911 the Supreme Court orders the company to be broken up). Roosevelt's advocacy of progressive policies and assertions of executive power lead to increasing tension with conservative Republicans in Congress. Collapse of the Knickerbocker Trust Company on October 22 causes major financial panic. Cortelyou works with financier J. P. Morgan to avert further bank failures, and on November 4 Roosevelt gives his approval to the acquisition of Tennessee Coal and Iron by U.S. Steel after being told the purchase will prevent the collapse of a major brokerage house (transaction is later criticized as being unduly favorable to U.S. Steel). Economic situation improves in November after Cortelyou issues $150 million in government bonds. Roosevelt orders 16 battleships on around-the-world cruise to demonstrate American naval power to Japan and other nations, and goes to Hampton Roads, Virginia, on December 16 to view the departure of the "Great White Fleet."

1908   Begins planning African hunting expedition to collect wild-life specimens for the Smithsonian. Holds national conservation conference at the White House, May 13–15, attended by governors from 45 states and territories. Names National Conservation Commission, with Gifford Pinchot as its chairman, on June 8; the commission conducts the first systematic national inventory of American natural resources. Republicans nominate Taft for president on June 18. Roosevelt appoints Luke Wright to succeed Taft as secretary of war. In the election on November 3, Taft wins 321 electoral votes and William Jennings Bryan 162.

1909   Roosevelt watches return of the Great White Fleet at Hampton Roads on February 22. Taft is inaugurated on March 4. Roosevelt and Kermit sail for British East Africa on March 23 and join expedition in Kenya on April 24. Shoots lion, elephant, rhinoceros, hippopotamus, buffalo, giraffe, zebra, and more than 20 different species of antelope while on safari. Travels to Uganda in December.

1910   Learns that Taft has dismissed Gifford Pinchot as head of the forestry service. Hunts in the Belgian Congo, then boards a steamer in southern Sudan and sails down the White Nile. Arrives on March 14 in Khartoum, where he meets Edith and Ethel. Lands in Naples on April 2, beginning European tour that takes him to Rome, Vienna, Budapest, Paris, Brussels, Amsterdam, and Copenhagen. Formally accepts Nobel Peace Prize in Christiana (Oslo) on May 5. Visits Stockholm and attends military maneuvers near Berlin with Kaiser William II. Serves as special American ambassador at the funeral of Edward VII in London on May 20. Returns to New York City on June 18, where he is greeted by a crowd of 100,000 people. Ted marries Eleanor Alexander in New York on June 20. Roosevelt becomes contributing editor to *The Outlook*. Endorses progressive positions in widely reported "New Nationalism" speech given at Osawatomie, Kansas, on August 31. *African Game Trails* published. Flies as passenger in airplane at St. Louis on October 11. Campaigns for Henry L. Stimson, the unsuccessful Republican candidate for governor of New York. *African and European Addresses* and *The New Nationalism* published.

1911   Writes series of articles for *The Outlook* on progressive nationalism as he becomes increasingly critical of Taft's administration. Goes on western speaking tour, March 8–April 16, during which he gives five lectures at the Pacific Theological Seminary in Berkeley (published as *Realizable Ideals* in 1912). Publishes "Revealing and Concealing Coloration in Birds and Mammals," a 112-page monograph, in the *Bulletin of the American Museum of Natural History*. Granddaughter Grace Roosevelt born August 17. Edith suffers serious head injury when she is thrown from her horse on September 30 and slowly recovers during autumn.

1912   Roosevelt declares his candidacy for the Republican nomination on February 21. Campaigns in 21 states during the spring and wins nine of the 12 Republican primaries, including the contest in Ohio, Taft's home state. Control of the party national committee allows Taft loyalists to unseat many Roosevelt delegates, and on June 22 Taft is renominated in Chicago as Roosevelt supporters walk out of the convention. Democrats nominate New Jersey governor Woodrow Wilson for president on July 2. Progressive Party convention meets in Chicago, August 15–17, nominates Roosevelt for president and California governor Hiram Johnson for vice-president, and adopts platform calling for woman suffrage, the direct election of U.S. senators, and legislation prohibiting child labor and limiting women's working hours. (Progressives become widely known as the "Bull Moose Party" after Roosevelt's frequent remark that he feels "as fit as a bull moose.") Roosevelt publishes *The Conservation of Womanhood and Children*. While campaigning in Milwaukee on October 14, Roosevelt is shot in the chest by a mentally unbalanced saloonkeeper; despite having a broken rib, he addresses a rally that evening for 90 minutes. Recovers in a Chicago hospital for eight days, then makes his final campaign speech in New York City on October 30. In the election on November 5, Wilson wins 42 percent of the popular vote and 435 electoral votes; Roosevelt, 27 percent and 88 electoral votes; Taft, 23 percent and eight electoral votes. Delivers address "History as Literature" in Boston on December 27 as he begins one-year term as president of the American Historical Association.

1913   Speaks at Progressive Party meetings. Daughter Ethel marries Richard Derby, a physician, in Oyster Bay on April 4. Roosevelt wins libel action on May 31 against George Newett, a Michigan newspaper editor who had accused him of frequent drunkenness. Hunts cougars in northern Arizona in late July. *An Autobiography* and *History as Literature* published. Sails for South America with

Edith on October 4. Gives speeches in Brazil, Uruguay, Argentina, and Chile, then crosses the Andes on horseback with Kermit in late November and travels through Argentina and Paraguay to Corumbá in southern Brazil. Joins Brazilian expedition led by Colonel Candido Rondon that is planning to explore the uncharted course of the Rio da Dúvida (River of Doubt) in western Brazil. Hunts jaguars and wild boars.

1914   Travels by boat to Tapirapuan, then by mule through the Mato Grosso to the headwaters of the Rio da Dúvida. Party of 22 men begin descent of the river, which the Brazilian government renames the Rio Roosevelt, on February 27. Grandson Richard Derby Jr. born March 6. Roosevelt injures his left leg on March 27. Suffering from abscesses, high fever, and severe dysentery, he recites Coleridge's "Kubla Khan" in his delirium and urges Kermit to leave him behind as the entire party becomes imperiled by a shortage of food and series of boat accidents. Expedition reaches Manaus on the Amazon on April 30, having lost three men during the trip. *Life Histories of African Game Animals*, written with Edmund Heller, published. Roosevelt returns to New York on May 19, his health permanently weakened. Attends wedding in Madrid on June 11 of Kermit and Belle Willard, the daughter of the American ambassador to Spain. Grandson Theodore Roosevelt III born June 14. Returns to New York in late June after visiting France and England. Leaves *The Outlook* and becomes a contributor to *Metropolitan* and the *Philadelphia North American*. At outbreak of war in Europe in early August Roosevelt is initially neutral, but he is soon angered by the German invasion of Belgium and reports of German atrocities. Makes more than 100 speeches for Progressive congressional candidates in the Midwest and Northeast during the fall campaign. *Through the Brazilian Wilderness* published.

1915   *America and the World War* published. Criticizes Wilson for ignoring the violation of Belgian neutrality, neglecting military preparedness, and failing to protect American citizens threatened by the civil war in Mexico. Travels in April to Syracuse, New York, where he is being sued for accusing Republican boss William Barnes of corruption. Publicly denounces the German sinking of the British liner *Lusitania* on May 7, in which 128 American passengers are killed, as an act of piracy and privately calls Wilson a coward for his attempts to avoid war with Germany. Acquitted in Barnes libel case on May 22. Becomes prominent public advocate of increased military preparedness. Goes hunting in Quebec in September. Grandson Cornelius Van Schaak Roosevelt born October 23.

1916 Grandson Kermit Roosevelt Jr. born February 16. Roosevelt visits British West Indies in February and March. Publishes *Fear God and Take Your Own Part*, collection of articles attacking Wilson's conduct of foreign policy, and *A Book-Lover's Holiday in the Open*. Declines presidential nomination of the Progressive Party on June 10 and endorses Republican candidate Charles Evan Hughes. Harshly criticizes Wilson while campaigning for Hughes in October. In the election on November 7 Wilson wins 277 electoral votes, Hughes 254.

1917 Germany resumes unrestricted submarine warfare against neutral shipping on February 1. Wilson sends war message to Congress on April 2, and the United States declares war on Germany on April 6. Roosevelt meets with Wilson at the White House on April 10 to request permission to raise a volunteer division and lead it into battle in France; the administration eventually declines the offer. Attends wedding in Boston on April 14 of Archie and Grace Lockwood. Granddaughter Ethel Roosevelt Derby born June 17. Ted and Archie are commissioned as officers and sail to France to serve with the 1st Infantry Division; Quentin sails for France in late July after training as a pilot on Long Island; and Kermit joins the British forces fighting the Turks in Mesopotamia (he will later serve as an artillery officer in France). Roosevelt continues to advocate progressive social policies while harshly criticizing the administration for failing to adequately equip American troops and for attempting to suppress criticism of its shortcomings. Publishes collection *The Foes of Our Own Household* in October and begins writing column for the *Kansas City Star*.

1918 Grandson Joseph Willard Roosevelt born January 16. Roosevelt has surgery in New York City on February 6 for severe ear infection and abscess related to Brazilian trip. Grandson Archibald Roosevelt Jr. born February 18. Roosevelt leaves hospital on March 4. Archie is severely wounded in the knee and arm by shell fragments on March 11. Quentin joins 95th Aero Squadron in June; on July 14 he is shot down and killed by German fighters near Reims. Ted is wounded in the leg on July 19. Archie returns from France on September 4. Roosevelt speaks at Liberty Loan rallies in September and October. Makes last public appearance on November 2, appearing with W.E.B. Du Bois at a benefit for Negro War Relief in New York City. *The Great Adventure: Present-Day Studies in American Nationalism* published. Suffering from rheumatism and gout, Roosevelt enters hospital in New York on November 11 as the war ends in Europe. Returns to Sagamore Hill on December 25.

1919   Dies in his sleep from a coronary embolism at 4:15 A.M. on January 6. After an Episcopal funeral service at Christ Church in Oyster Bay, he is buried in the nearby Youngs Memorial Cemetery on January 8.

Note on the Texts

This volume prints the texts of 367 letters written by Theodore Roosevelt between 1881 and 1919, as well as the texts of four speeches delivered by Roosevelt between 1899 and 1910. The texts of the letters are taken from *The Letters of Theodore Roosevelt*, selected and edited by Elting E. Morison with associate editor John M. Blum (8 volumes, Cambridge: Harvard University Press, 1951–54), and the texts of the speeches are taken from *The Works of Theodore Roosevelt*, National Edition, edited by Hermann Hagedorn (20 volumes, New York: Charles Scribner's Sons, 1926).

Roosevelt wrote more than 100,000 letters during his lifetime. A very small number of them were written for publication and were printed in newspapers and magazines. When Roosevelt joined the Civil Service Commission in 1889 he began to dictate his correspondence to stenographers, and for the rest of his life most of his letters were typed by secretaries, although he continued to write in longhand to his family. In December 1916 Roosevelt arranged to donate his papers to the Manuscripts Division of the Library of Congress, and the first shipment of documents was sent from Oyster Bay, Long Island, to Washington, D.C., in January 1917. After Roosevelt's death additional shipments were prepared and sent between 1919 and 1922 by Joseph Bucklin Bishop, his literary executor and authorized biographer. Further donations were made by the Roosevelt family, and the Theodore Roosevelt Papers at the Library of Congress now contain approximately 250,000 documents, including about 100,000 letters written by Roosevelt, approximately 90 percent of which are letter-press or carbon copies of dictated letters.

Several collections of Roosevelt's letters were published soon after his death, including *Theodore Roosevelt's Letters to His Children* (1919) and *Theodore Roosevelt and His Time, Shown in His Own Letters* (2 volumes, 1920), both edited by Joseph Bucklin Bishop; *Letters from Theodore Roosevelt to Anna Roosevelt Cowles, 1870–1918* (1924), edited by Anna Roosevelt Cowles; and *Selections from the Correspondence of Theodore Roosevelt and Henry Cabot Lodge, 1884–1918* (2 volumes, 1925), edited by Henry Cabot Lodge and Charles F. Redmond. The editors of these editions sometimes omitted or altered words or passages in the letters they printed to protect the privacy of the Roosevelt family, or to soften some of Roosevelt's critical remarks.

In 1946 work began on *The Letters of Theodore Roosevelt*, an edition sponsored by the Roosevelt Memorial Association (known since 1953 as the Theodore Roosevelt Association), supported by the Massachusetts Institute of Technology, and published by the Harvard University Press. The editors of *The Letters of Theodore Roosevelt* located about 4,000 letters in more than 150 manuscript collections other than the Theodore Roosevelt Papers at the Library of Congress. Although most of these additional documents were typed originals of letters also found in letter-press or carbon copy form in the Theodore Roosevelt Papers, a significant number of them were autograph manuscripts. From the letters available to them the editors of *The Letters of Theodore Roosevelt* selected about 6,500, which were published in four two-volume sets as follows: volume I, *The Years of Preparation, 1868–1898*, and volume II, *The Years of Preparation, 1898–1900* (Cambridge: Harvard University Press, 1951); volume III, *The Square Deal, 1901–1903*, and volume IV, *The Square Deal, 1903–1905* (Cambridge: Harvard University Press, 1951); volume V, *The Big Stick, 1905–1907*, and volume VI, *The Big Stick, 1907–1909* (Cambridge: Harvard University Press, 1952); volume VII, *The Days of Armageddon, 1909–1914*, and volume VIII, *The Days of Armageddon, 1914–1919* (Cambridge: Harvard University Press, 1954).

Wherever possible, the editors of *The Letters of Theodore Roosevelt* used an autograph manuscript or an original typescript as the source of their text. In cases where no autograph manuscript, original typescript, or letter-press or carbon copy version of a letter was available, the editors of *The Letters of Theodore Roosevelt* took their text from a printed source, such as *Theodore Roosevelt's Letters to His Children* or *Selections from the Correspondence of Theodore Roosevelt and Henry Cabot Lodge, 1884–1918*. (The Henry Cabot Lodge papers were closed to the editors of *The Letters of Theodore Roosevelt*, although they did have access to copies of letters sent by Roosevelt to Lodge after 1901.) Autograph manuscript letters were transcribed and printed by the editors of *The Letters of Theodore Roosevelt* without alteration of their spelling, punctuation, and capitalization, while letters typed by secretaries were printed with spelling errors corrected, but without change to their punctuation and capitalization. The editors of *The Letters of Theodore Roosevelt* also omitted Roosevelt's name from the closing of the letters they printed.

This volume prints texts as they appeared in *The Letters of Theodore Roosevelt*, but with a few alterations in editorial procedure. The conjectural readings presented within guillemets (French quotation marks) by the editors of *The Letters of Theodore Roosevelt* in cases where original manuscripts, typescripts, or copies were damaged or difficult to read are accepted without guillemets in this volume. Where a word or words in a source text were "irrevocably obliterated," the editors of *The Letters of Theodore Roosevelt* used three dots to indicate a missing word and four dots to indicate two or more missing words; in this volume, the missing word or words are indicated by a bracketed two-em space, i.e., [   ]. In cases where *The Letters of Theodore Roosevelt* supplied in brackets letters or words that were omitted from the source text by an obvious slip of the pen or by a typist's or printer's error, this volume removes the brackets and accepts the editorial emendation. Bracketed editorial insertions used in *The Letters of Theodore Roosevelt* to clarify meaning have been deleted in this volume. In some cases where Roosevelt made handwritten changes to a letter, the canceled text, if decipherable, was presented in *The Letters of Theodore Roosevelt* within single angle brackets; this volume omits the canceled material. Roosevelt sometimes added handwritten postscripts to typed letters. *The Letters of Theodore Roosevelt* used "[*Handwritten*]" to indicate these postscripts; this volume prints the autograph material and omits the "[*Handwritten*]." Five of Roosevelt's errors in manuscript letters are treated as slips of the pen and corrected in this volume, even though they were not corrected in *The Letters of Theodore Roosevelt*: at 73.26, "see in" is changed to "see you in"; at 728.3, "those fought" is changed to "those who fought"; at 740.24, "Alsace-Lorraine" is changed to "Alsace-Lorraine"; at 740.24, "retorsed" is changed to "restored"; and at 740.34, "seperate" is changed to "separate."

The texts of the speeches "The Strenuous Life," "National Duties," "Citizenship in a Republic," and "The New Nationalism" printed in this volume are taken from the National Edition of *The Works of Theodore Roosevelt*, prepared under the auspices of the Roosevelt Memorial Association. "The Strenuous Life" was delivered at the Appomattox Day banquet of the Hamilton Club, Chicago, Illinois, on April 10, 1899, and first published in *The Strenuous Life: Essays and Addresses* (New York: The Century Co., 1900). "National Duties" was delivered at the Minnesota State Fair, St. Paul, on September 2, 1901, and first published in the "enlarged edition" of *The Strenuous Life: Essays and Addresses* (New York: The Century Co., 1901). The text of "The Strenuous Life" presented here is taken from pages 319–31, and of "National Duties" from pages 469–80, of volume XIII of the National Edition, *American Ideals, The Strenuous Life, Realizable Ideals*, which prints the text of the "enlarged edition" of *The Strenuous Life* published in 1901.

"Citizenship in a Republic" was delivered at the Sorbonne in Paris, April 23, 1910. It appeared in *The Independent* on April 28, 1910, as "Duties of the Citizen" and in *The Outlook* on April 30, 1910, as "Citizenship in a Republic," and was first published in book form in *African and European Addresses* (New York: G. P. Putnam's Sons, 1910). The text presented here is taken from pages 506–29 of volume

XIII of the National Edition, *American Ideals, The Strenuous Life, Realizable Ideals*, which prints the text that appeared in *African and European Addresses*. "The New Nationalism" was delivered at the dedication of the John Brown Memorial State Park in Osawatomie, Kansas, on August 31, 1910, and was first published in *The New Nationalism* (New York: The Outlook Company, 1910). The text presented here is taken from pages 5–22 of volume XVII of the National Edition, *Social Justice and Popular Rule: Essays, Addresses, and Public Statements Relating to the Progressive Movement (1910–1916)*. In presenting "Citizenship in a Republic" and "The New Nationalism" in the National Edition, Hagedorn made a few minor alterations in the spelling and capitalization used in *African and European Addresses* and *The New Nationalism*.

This volume presents the texts of the original printings chosen for inclusion here, but it does not attempt to reproduce nontextual features of their typographic design. The texts are presented without alteration except for the changes previously discussed and for the correction of typographical errors. Spelling, punctuation, and capitalization are often expressive features and are not altered, even when inconsistent or irregular. The following is a list of typographical errors corrected, cited by page and line number: 29.13, your; 30.27, so-many; 81.23, to to; 103.6, know; 124.34, think; 130.25, army; 160.24, champaions; 198.4, drunkeness; 253.3, of needless; 313.27, spech; 414.30, an; 639.14, orioles scarlet; 708.18, respect.; 765.25, firmnes.

Notes

In the notes below, the reference numbers denote page and line of this volume (the line count includes headings). No note is made for material included in standard desk-reference books. Biblical quotations are keyed to the King James Version. Quotations from Shakespeare are keyed to *The Riverside Shakespeare*, ed. G. Blakemore Evans (Boston: Houghton Mifflin, 1974). Footnotes in the text are Roosevelt's own. For further biographical background, references to other studies, and more detailed notes, see *The Letters of Theodore Roosevelt*, selected and edited by Elting E. Morison (8 vols., Cambridge: Harvard University Press, 1951–54); Lewis L. Gould, *The Presidency of Theodore Roosevelt* (Lawrence: University Press of Kansas, 1991); Louis Auchincloss, *Theodore Roosevelt* (New York: Henry Holt and Company, 2001); Edmund Morris, *The Rise of Theodore Roosevelt* (revised edition, New York: The Modern Library, 2001) and *Theodore Rex* (New York: Random House, Inc., 2001); and Kathleen Dalton, *Theodore Roosevelt: A Strenuous Life* (New York: Alfred A. Knopf, 2002).

EARLY PUBLIC CAREER, 1881–1898

4.23   Van Helst] Bartholomeus van der Helst (c. 1613–1670).

4.32   life of that period] The 17th century.

5.6   *To Voters . . . District*] This message was printed in a campaign circular.

5.14   *Charles Washburn*] Washburn (1857–1928) was a Harvard classmate of Roosevelt's. He later served as a Republican representative from Massachusetts, 1906–11.

6.2   *Henry Hull*] Hull was the editor of the *Steuben Courier*, a weekly newspaper published in Bath, New York; this letter appeared in that newspaper on October 27, 1882.

6.7–8   that bill] A bill granting a tax exemption to the Manhattan Elevated Railway, owned by Jay Gould.

6.22   *Van Duzer*] An assemblyman from Chemung County in western New York.

7.1–2   "half breed" nor a "stalwart"] "Half-Breeds" were Republicans who supported strong protective tariffs, anti-inflationary "hard money" policies, and limited civil service reform; they had backed James G. Blaine of

Maine for the 1880 presidential nomination. "Stalwarts" were Republicans who opposed civil service reform and the end of Reconstruction during the Hayes administration and who had supported the attempt to nominate Ulysses S. Grant for a third term in 1880. (The term "Half-Breed," referring to their supposed "half-breed" Republicanism, originated with the "Stalwarts.")

7.16   *Carl Schurz*]   Schurz (1829–1906), a German émigré, had served as a Union general, 1862–65, as a Republican senator from Missouri, 1869–75, and as secretary of the interior, 1877–81. He was editor of the New York *Evening Post*, 1881–83, and was later president of the National Civil Service Reform League, 1892–1901. In 1872 Schurz had been a leader of the Liberal Republican opposition to Grant's reelection.

8.2   *Simon Dexter North*]   The editor of the Utica *Morning Herald*, 1869–86, North (1848–1924) later served as director of the U.S. Census Bureau, 1903–9.

8.16   politicians who at Utica]   At the 1884 Republican state convention, held in Utica on April 23, Roosevelt had succeeded in securing all four at-large delegates to the national convention for his presidential candidate, Senator George F. Edmunds of Vermont.

9.2   *an Unknown Correspondent*]   This letter, sent to an unidentified newspaper reporter, appeared in facsimile in *Cosmopolitan* in November 1907.

9.11   Governor Bulloch]   Archibald Bulloch was elected "president and commander-in-chief of Georgia" under the temporary state constitution adopted in April 1776 and served from May 1, 1776, until his death in February 1777.

10.9–10   Senator Miller]   Warner Miller (1838–1918) was a U.S. senator from New York, 1881–87.

10.20   followers of Blaine]   James G. Blaine (1830–1893) served as a representative from Maine, 1863–76, as a senator, 1876–81, and as secretary of state in 1881 and from 1889 to 1892. He was Speaker of the House, 1869–75, and an unsuccessful candidate for the Republican presidential nomination in 1876 and 1880.

10.30   Douglass]   Douglas Robinson (1855–1918), a New York businessman who was the husband of Roosevelt's sister Corinne.

11.30   Logan . . . Hawley]   John A. Logan (1826–1886) was a Democratic representative from Illinois, 1859–62, a general in the Union army, 1862–65, a Republican representative, 1867–71, and a senator, 1871–77 and 1879–86. John Sherman (1823–1900), brother of General William T. Sherman, was a Republican representative from Ohio, 1855–61, a senator, 1861–77 and 1881–97, secretary of the treasury, 1877–81, and secretary of state, 1897–98. Joseph R. Hawley (1826–1905) was a representative from Connecticut, 1872–75 and 1879–81, and a senator, 1881–1905.

12.25   Cabot Lodge] Henry Cabot Lodge (1850–1924) was an unsuccessful Republican candidate for Congress in 1882 and 1884, a representative
from Massachusetts, 1887–93, and a senator, 1893–1924, as well as the author
of a number of biographies and historical studies.

12.35   White, Curtis and Wadsworth] Andrew D. White (1832–1918) was
the founding president of Cornell University, 1868–85, as well as the American minister to Germany, 1879–81 and 1897–1902, and Russia, 1892–94.
George William Curtis (1824–1892) was editor of *Harper's Weekly*, 1863–92,
and president of the National Civil Service Reform League, 1881–92. James
W. Wadsworth (1846–1926) was a Republican representative from New York,
1881–85 and 1891–1907.

13.2   Governor Long] John Davis Long (1838–1915) was governor of
Massachusetts, 1880–83, a U.S. representative, 1883–89, and secretary of the
navy, 1897–1902.

13.4   Judge West] William H. West (1824–1911), known as "the blind
man eloquent," was attorney general of Ohio, 1866–68, and a judge on the
Ohio supreme court, 1872–73; he lost his eyesight while serving on the court.

16.1   Independent . . . Godkin] Edwin Lawrence Godkin (1831–1902)
was the founder and editor of *The Nation*, 1865–81, and of the New York
Evening Post (into which *The Nation* was merged), 1881–99. In 1884 Godkin
was a leader of the "Independent Republicans," also known as "mugwumps,"
who supported Democratic candidate Grover Cleveland over Blaine in the
presidential election.

16.33–34   Mr. Davis compares . . . Arnold] Roosevelt had made the comparison in an article published in the October 1885 *North American Review*.

17.11–12   three thieves] The three men had stolen a boat from Roosevelt's
Elkhorn Ranch and were also suspected of stealing horses.

17.20   Seawall and Dow] William Sewell and his nephew Wilmont Dow,
Maine hunting guides whom Roosevelt had invited to become partners in his
ranching business.

18.6   Griselda] Character in Geoffrey Chaucer's *The Canterbury Tales*.

18.21   Mr. Weller] Sam Weller, character in Charles Dickens' *The Posthu-
mous Papers of the Pickwick Club* (1837).

20.7   Dawes] Henry L. Dawes (1816–1903) was a Republican representative from Massachusetts, 1857–75, and a senator, 1875–93.

20.8   Black] John Charles Black (1839–1915), an attorney prominent in
Illinois Democratic politics, served as U.S. commissioner of pensions during
the first Cleveland administration, 1885–89.

20.12   Your Hamilton] Lodge edited *The Works of Alexander Hamilton*
(9 volumes, 1885–86) and published a biography of Hamilton in 1882.

21.3   Benton]   Roosevelt was writing his *Life of Thomas Hart Benton* (1887).

22.34   Secretary Endicott]   William C. Endicott (1826–1900) was secretary of war, 1885–89.

23.1   trouble with Mexico]   Captain Emmett Crawford was fatally wounded by Mexican militia in the Sierra Madre on January 11, 1886, while leading Apache scouts in pursuit of Geronimo and his Chiracahua Apache. Despite the claim by an American officer present during the incident that the Mexican attack was "deliberate, dishonorable, and treacherous," the U.S. government eventually declared the shooting to be accidental.

23.17   Nannie]   Anna Cabot Mills Davis Lodge (1850–1915), the wife of Henry Cabot Lodge.

23.18   Childe Harold]   In a letter to Lodge of August 20, 1886, Roosevelt acknowledged that he had confused "Childe Roland" in Robert Browning's poem (1855) with the hero of Lord Byron's *Childe Harold's Pilgrimage* (1812–18).

23.22   *Denis Donahue Jr.*]   Donahue was the president of the Newspaper Men's Henry George Campaign Club.

25.4   White]   Horace White (1834–1916) was an editor of the New York *Evening Post*, 1881–99, and its editor-in-chief, 1899–1903.

27.16   dedicate this to you.]   Parkman gave his permission for the dedication.

28.11   *Cecil Spring-Rice*]   Spring-Rice (1859–1918) was a British diplomat who served at the embassy in Washington, D.C., 1887–88, 1889–92, and 1894–95; in Germany, 1895–98; in Persia, 1898–1901; and in Russia, 1903–6. He was minister to Persia, 1906–8, to Sweden, 1908–13, and the British ambassador to the United States, 1913–18.

28.20   spar with Germany]   In the spring of 1889 Germany and the United States were supporting rival factions in the Samoan civil war. A treaty signed on June 14, 1889, by the U.S., Germany, Great Britain, and Samoa placed the islands under a tripartite protectorate. A second treaty, signed in 1899, divided control over the islands between Germany and the U.S. In 1914 the islands controlled by Germany were occupied by New Zealand, which received a mandate over them from the League of Nations in 1920.

29.1   new minister, Bob Lincoln]   Robert Todd Lincoln (1843–1926), son of Abraham Lincoln, was the U.S. minister to Great Britain, 1889–93.

29.24   Bancroft or Hildreth]   George Bancroft (1800–1891), author of *History of the United States* (10 volumes, 1834–74); Richard Hildreth (1807–1865), author of *History of the United States* (6 volumes, 1849–52).

29.33   Gilmore]   James R. Gilmore (1822–1903) was the author of *The Rear-Guard of the Revolution* (1886), *John Sevier as a Commonwealth-Builder*

(1887), and *The Advance-Guard of Western Civilization* (1888), all published under the pseudonym Edmund Kirke.

30.3   Mr. Draper]   Lyman C. Draper (1815–1891), secretary of the Wisconsin State Historical Society, 1854–86, author of *King's Mountain and its Heroes* (1882), and a leading collector of American historical documents.

30.34   Ferghie]   Robert Ferguson, who later served as a trooper in the Rough Riders.

31.14   *William Warland Clapp*]   Clapp (1826–1891) was the editor, 1865–91, of the Boston *Journal*, where this letter appeared on August 10, 1889.

35.6   *Charles A. Dana*]   Dana (1819–1897) was the owner and editor of the New York *Sun*, 1868–97. This letter and the following one both appeared in the *Sun*, although the texts printed in *The Letters of Theodore Roosevelt* are taken from manuscript sources.

36.20   Ramsey in his history]   James G. M. Ramsey (1797–1884), *The Annals of Tennessee to the End of the Eighteenth-Century* (1853).

37.26   Collin's history]   *Historical Sketches of Kentucky* (2 volumes, 1874), edited by Richard Henry Collins (1824–1888), an expanded version of a single-volume work published in 1847 by Collins' father, Lewis Collins (1797–1870).

38.5   Haywood]   John Haywood (1762–1826), author of *The Natural and Aboriginal History of Tennessee* (1823) and *The Civil and Political History of Tennessee* (1823).

38.7   Putnam's history]   A. W. Putnam, *History of Middle Tennessee: or, Life and Times of Gen. James Robertson* (1859).

44.17   Filson]   John Filson (?1753–1788), author of *The Discovery, Settlement, and Present State of Kentucke* (1784).

45.25   reading your book]   *The Influence of Sea Power upon History, 1660–1783* (1890).

46.29   you and Emily coming over]   Gertrude Carow (1835–1895), Roosevelt's mother-in-law, and Emily Carow (1865–1939), his sister-in-law, had lived in Italy since 1887.

48.2   *Arthur Gorman*]   Arthur P. Gorman (1839–1906) was a Democratic senator from Maryland, 1881–99 and 1903–6, and chairman of the Democratic senate caucus, 1890–98 (in 1891 the Democrats were in the minority in the Senate).

50.2   *Thomas Raynesford Lounsbury*]   Lounsbury (1838–1915) was professor of English at the Sheffield Scientific School at Yale, 1871–1906.

50.8   your "Chaucer."]   *Studies in Chaucer: His Life and Writings* (3 volumes, 1892).

50.37   the *Saturday Review*]   An English periodical, published 1855–1938.

52.10   Winwood Reade]   William Winwood Reade (1838–1875), a British writer whose works included *The Martyrdom of Man* (1872) and *African Sketch-Book* (1873).

53.11   *Richard Watson Gilder*]   Gilder (1844–1909) was the editor of *The Century Illustrated Monthly Magazine*, 1881–1909.

54.2   Napier's *Peninsular War*]   Sir William Napier (1785–1860), *History of the War in the Peninsula and in the South of France* (6 volumes, 1828–40).

54.18   *Madison Grant*]   Grant (1865–1937) was an attorney, a member of the Boone and Crockett Club, and a founder of the New York Zoological Society. In *The Passing of the Great Race, or The Racial Basis of European History* (1916) he advocated eugenics, restrictions on immigration, and the superiority of the "Nordic race."

54.28   our next volume]   Roosevelt and the naturalist George Bird Grinnell (1849–1938) edited three volumes that were published as books of the Boone and Crockett Club: *American Big Game Hunting* (1893), *Hunting in Many Lands* (1895), and *Trail and Camp Fire* (1897).

56.19   *Charles Henry Pearson*]   Pearson (1830–1894) was a British historian and the author of *National Life and Character: A Forecast* (1893), which Roosevelt had reviewed.

58.19   *James Brander Matthews*]   Matthews (1852–1929), a playwright, was professor of literature, 1892–1900, and of dramatic literature, 1900–24, at Columbia University.

59.26   Edgar Fawcett]   Fawcett (1847–1904) was a poet, essayist, and writer of satirical novels and plays set in New York society.

59.39   London *Yellow Book*]   The first issue of *The Yellow Book*, an illustrated quarterly, appeared in April 1894, with contributions by Henry James, Max Beerbohm, and Edmund Gosse, and drawings by Aubrey Beardsley, its art director. The magazine ceased publication in 1897.

61.10–11   died instead of Anna!]   Anna Hall Roosevelt, Elliott's wife and Eleanor Roosevelt's mother, had died of diphtheria on December 7, 1892, at the age of 29.

62.9   *John Joseph Keane*]   Keane (1839–1918) was bishop of Richmond, 1878–87, served as the first rector of the Catholic University of America, 1887–96, and was archbishop of Dubuque, 1900–11.

62.20   A.P.A.]   American Protective Association, an anti-Catholic secret society founded in 1887 that achieved its greatest influence in the early 1890s. It declined after 1897 and dissolved in 1911.

64.2   *John William Fox*]   Fox (1862–1919) was the author of *A Mountain Europa* (1894), *A Cumberland Vendetta and Other Stories* (1896), *"Hell fer Sartain" and Other Stories* (1897), and other works of fiction set in the Tennessee mountains. In 1898 he covered the Cuban campaign for *Harper's Weekly*.

64.16–17   Borrows . . . *Lavengro*]   *Lavengro, The Scholar — The Gypsy — The Priest* (1851), narrative by British writer George Henry Borrow (1803–1881).

64.32   Milfort]   Louis Milfort (1752–1820), author of *Memoirs; or, a quick glance at my various travels and my sojourn in the Creek Nation* (1802).

65.11   *Henry Childs Merwin*]   Merwin (1853–1929) was a Massachusetts lawyer.

66.1   President Eliot's]   Charles William Eliot (1834–1926) was president of Harvard University, 1869–1909.

68.1   Senator Morgan]   John Morgan (1824–1907) was a Democratic senator from Alabama, 1877–1907.

69.14   Senator Cameron]   James Cameron (1833–1918), a Republican, served in the Senate, 1877–97.

69.15   Senator Quay]   Matthew Quay (1833–1904) was a Republican senator from Pennsylvania, 1887–1899 and 1901–4.

75.37   G. G. Club]   Good Government Club.

76.4   *To Preble Tucker*]   In a letter printed in the New York *Times* on October 22, 1895, Tucker had criticized Roosevelt for supporting fusion candidates backed by the Republican machine in the municipal elections instead of an independent reform slate. Roosevelt's reply appeared in the *Times* on October 23, 1895.

78.8–9   Abolitionists nominated a third ticket]   John C. Frémont was nominated for president by a "Radical Democratic" convention that met in Cleveland on May 31, 1864. Although Wendell Phillips supported Frémont, his candidacy was opposed by many prominent abolitionists. Frémont withdrew from the race on September 22.

78.30   the Venezuelan question]   In a note sent to the British government on July 20, 1895, Secretary of State Richard Olney stated that the dispute between Great Britain and Venezuela over the boundary of British Guiana (Guyana) fell under the Monroe Doctrine and should be settled by arbitration. After Lord Salisbury, the British prime minister and foreign secretary, rejected arbitration, President Cleveland sent a message to Congress on December 17 in which he proposed the creation of a commission to determine the boundary and warned that the United States would treat a British refusal to accept the new boundary as an act of aggression. The resulting crisis lessened when Joseph Chamberlain, the British colonial secretary, described a possible Anglo-American war as "an absurdity" on January 24, 1896. Britain and Venezuela agreed on February 2, 1897, to submit the dispute to arbitration, and a settlement was reached in 1899.

80.23   *Francis Markoe Scott*]   Scott was serving as the corporation counsel for New York City. This letter was printed in the New York *Times* on February 12, 1896.

81.4   The "Molly Maguires"]   A secret society of Irish coal miners who engaged in violence against mine owners and operators. James McParlan, a Pinkerton agency detective, lived undercover in the Pennsylvania coal region from October 1873 to March 1876 and gathered evidence that was used in trials held in 1876–77. In 1877–79 a total of 20 men were hanged after being convicted of ten murders committed between 1862 and 1875.

81.14   green-goods men]   Counterfeiters and dealers in counterfeit currency.

83.12   Gerry Society]   The Society for the Prevention of Cruelty to Children, founded in 1874 by Elbridge T. Gerry (1837–1927).

83.30   Tom Reed]   Thomas Reed (1839–1902) was a Republican representative from Maine, 1877–99, and served as Speaker of the House, 1889–90 and 1895–98.

84.19   Governor Morton]   Levi P. Morton (1824–1920) was a Republican representative from New York, 1879–81, vice-president of the United States, 1889–93, and governor of New York, 1895–96.

84.21   Platt]   Thomas Collier Platt (1833–1910) served as a Republican representative from New York, 1873–77, and in the Senate in 1881 and from 1897 to 1909; by 1896 he had established himself as the boss of the state Republican party.

84.22   the bill putting me out]   The bill would have shifted the power to appoint and dismiss New York City police commissioners from the mayor to the governor.

85.2   support Morton . . . Reed]   Morton and Reed were both seeking the 1896 Republican presidential nomination.

85.33–34   volumes by Gustave LeBon]   *Les Premières Civilisations* (1889) by Gustave Le Bon (1841–1931), a French psychologist and sociologist.

86.3–4   Brooks Adams']   Brooks Adams (1848–1927), brother of Henry Adams, was the author of *Law of Civilization and Decay* (1895).

88.9   Speck]   Hermann Speck von Sternberg (1852–1908) was the German military attaché in Washington, 1885–90. He joined the diplomatic service in 1890 and served as first secretary in the Washington embassy, 1898–1900, and as ambassador to the United States, 1903–8.

90.38–39   free silver . . . movement]   The movement for expansion of the monetary supply through the "free and unlimited coinage of silver." Silver proponents, including William Jennings Bryan, advocated backing the currency with silver as well as gold, with their relative value fixed at a ratio of 16 to 1. Opponents of "free silver" denounced it as dangerously inflationary, since the market value of silver was well below the proposed 16 to 1 ratio, and harmful to American interests in international finance and trade, which were conducted on a gold basis.

92.3   Altgeld, Peffer]   John Peter Altgeld (1847–1902) was the Democratic governor of Illinois, 1893–97. In 1893 he pardoned the three survivors of the eight men who had been sentenced to death for their alleged role in the bombing at Haymarket Square in Chicago that killed seven policemen in 1886. Altgeld had also protested the deployment of federal troops in Illinois during the 1894 Pullman railroad strike. William A. Peffer (1831–1912) was a Populist senator from Kansas, 1891–97.

94.33   Cleveland's action]   Following the overthrow of Queen Liliuo-kalani on January 17, 1893, a treaty annexing Hawaii to the United States was signed on February 14 and submitted to the Senate by President Harrison the next day. Cleveland withdrew the treaty on March 9, 1893, and formally recognized the Republic of Hawaii on August 7, 1894.

96.20   Dr. Merriam's article]   Clinton Hart Merriam (1855–1942) was chief of the biological survey of the Department of Agriculture, 1885–1910. His article appeared in *Science* on May 14, 1897; Roosevelt wrote a response that *Science* printed on June 4.

99.27   *Frederick Courtney Selous*]   Selous (1851–1917) was a British hunter and explorer in southern central Africa, especially in what is now Zimbabwe.

102.34–35   my contribution . . . Royal Navy]   Roosevelt's chapter appeared in volume 6 (1901) of *The Royal Navy: a history from the earliest times to the present* by Sir William Laird Clowes (1856–1905) and others (7 volumes, 1897–1903).

106.11–12   address I made . . . Newport]   See Chronology, 1897.

107.2   *George Bird Grinnell*]   Grinnell (1849–1938) was the editor of *Field and Stream*, 1876–1911.

108.15–16   collection of my essays]   *American Ideals* (1897).

114.27   *Russell Alexander Alger*]   Alger (1836–1907) was secretary of war, 1897–99, and later served as a Republican senator from Michigan, 1902–7. A colonel in the Union army, Alger was breveted a major general in 1865 for his service.

114.32   revive the football games]   The first Army-Navy game was played in 1890, but the games were suspended after 1893 by President Cleveland because of fighting between spectators. In 1899 the game was resumed and, with the exception of 1917–18 and 1928–31, has been played every year since then.

116.21   Secretary Bliss]   Cornelius N. Bliss (1833–1911) was secretary of the interior, 1897–99.

117.5   Donaldson Smith's book]   Arthur Donaldson Smith (1866–1939), *Through Unknown African Countries; the first expedition from Somaliland to Lake Lamu* (1897).

117.29   *Francis Vinton Greene*]   Greene (1850–1921) was a colonel in the New York National Guard. A graduate of West Point and author of several works on military history, he had served in the army, 1870–86, before resigning to go into the asphalt business. In 1898 he commanded a brigade of volunteers in the Philippines.

119.2   *John Hay*]   Hay (1838–1905) served as ambassador to Great Britain, 1897–98, and as secretary of state, 1898–1905.

119.7   frigate *President* . . . 1815]   The captured ship had actually been broken up at Portsmouth in 1817, although the name *President* was then given to a series of ships in the Royal Navy.

122.19   *William Wirt Kimball*]   Kimball, a lieutenant commander in the navy, was organizing its first torpedo flotilla.

128.9   Sidney Low]   Low (1857–1932), a British journalist, was the editor of the *St. James Gazette*, 1888–97.

137.5   de Lome affair]   On February 9, 1898, the New York *Journal* published a private letter sent to Cuba in December 1897 by Enrique Dupuy de Lome (1851–1904), the Spanish minister to the United States, in which de Lome described President McKinley as "weak and a bidder for the admiration of the crowd, besides being a would-be politician who tries to leave a door open behind himself while keeping on good terms with the jingoes of his party." De Lome immediately resigned his position.

137.16   Captain Sigsbee]   Charles D. Sigsbee (1845–1923), the captain of the *Maine*, who had survived the destruction of his ship.

137.28   Secretary Tracy]   Benjamin F. Tracy (1830–1915), secretary of the navy, 1889–93.

139.25   *William Peterfield Trent*]   Trent (1862–1939) was professor of English at the University of the South, 1892–1900, and at Columbia University, 1900–29. In 1892 Trent founded *Sewanee Review*, which he edited until 1900.

140.31   Moses Coit Tyler]   Tyler (1835–1900) was professor of English at the University of Michigan, 1867–81, and professor of history at Cornell University, 1881–1900. His works included *History of American Literature During the Colonial Time, 1607–1763* (2 volumes, 1878) and *The Literary History of the American Revolution, 1763–1783* (2 volumes, 1897).

142.7–8   Professor Langley's . . . machine has worked] Samuel Pierpont Langley (1834–1906), an astronomer and physicist, was secretary of the Smithsonian, 1887–1906. In 1896 he successfully tested a pilotless, catapult-launched aircraft with a steam engine; in one test the aircraft flew for 4,790 feet. After receiving $50,000 from the War Department in 1898 Langley designed and built a piloted aircraft with a gasoline engine, but test flights on October 7 and December 8, 1903, failed when the aircraft crashed immediately after leaving the catapult. Langley then abandoned aeronautical research.

142.24   *William Sturgis Bigelow*] Bigelow (1850–1926) was a physician who lived in Japan, 1882–89, and subsequently donated his extensive collection of Japanese art to the Museum of Fine Arts in Boston.

144.1–2   Crowninshield, whose position] Arent S. Crowninshield (1843–1908) was chief of the Bureau of Navigation, which controlled fleet operations.

ROUGH RIDER, GOVERNOR, VICE-PRESIDENT, 1898–1901

148.3   Wood] Leonard Wood (1860–1927) commanded the 1st U.S. Volunteer Cavalry (Rough Riders) until June 30, 1898, when he was made a brigade commander. He was military governor of the city, and then province, of Santiago, July 1898–December 1899, and military governor of Cuba, December 1899–May 1902. Wood served in the Philippines, 1903–8, and was chief of staff of the army, 1910–14. He retired in 1921 with the rank of major general.

150.9   Gen. Shafter] William Shafter (1835–1906) commanded V Corps, the expeditionary force sent to Cuba in 1898.

151.8   Richard Harding Davis] Davis (1864–1916) was covering the campaign as a correspondent for the New York *Herald*.

152.22–24   campaign of Crassus . . . expedition against Walcheren] In 53 B.C. a Roman army of 30,000 men led by Marcus Licinius Crassus was defeated at Carrhae by approximately 10,000 Parthians. Crassus and 20,000 of his men were killed, and the Parthians captured 10,000 prisoners and seven legionary standards. On July 30, 1809, the British landed an expeditionary force of 39,000 men on the islands of Walcheren and South Beveland in the Scheldt estuary. Although Walcheren was known for outbreaks of fever, the expedition had little medical support. By the time the force was withdrawn on December 9, 1809, nearly 4,000 men had died from malaria, typhus, typhoid, and dysentery, while only 106 men were killed in combat.

155.36   "grouse in a gunroom"] See Oliver Goldsmith (?1730–1774), *She Stoops to Conquer* (1773), Act II.

156.7   "crowded hour"] Cf. Thomas Osbert Mordaunt (1730–1809), "Verses Written During the War": "One crowded hour of glorious life / Is worth an age without a name."

156.31   *John Jay Chapman*]   Chapman (1862–1933) was a New York City attorney active in reform movements.

158.26   *James Bryce*]   Bryce (1832–1922) was professor of civil law at Oxford, 1870–93, a Liberal member of Parliament, 1880–1907, British ambassador to the United States, 1907–13, and the author of *The American Commonwealth* (1888, revised 1910).

159.6   Low-Tracy failure]   In the 1897 New York mayoral election the Tammany-backed Democratic candidate Robert A. Van Wyck defeated Seth Low, the independent Citizens Union candidate, and Republican candidate Benjamin Tracy.

159.20   Parkhurst]   Charles H. Parkhurst (1842–1933), a Presbyterian minister, was president of the Society for the Prevention of Crime, 1891–1909, and author of *Our Fight with Tammany* (1895).

160.2   *Helen Kendrick Johnson*]   Johnson (1844–1917) was the author of several books for children and editor of *American Woman's Journal*, 1894–96. In *Woman and the Republic* (1897) she argued against woman suffrage.

160.18   Birney]   James G. Birney (1792–1857) became corresponding secretary of the American Anti-Slavery Society in 1837, but soon split with William Lloyd Garrison over the issue of whether abolitionists should shun electoral politics. Birney then founded the Liberty party and was its presidential candidate in 1840 and 1844.

162.32–33   a story as . . . Mother,"]   The story first appeared in *Harper's Bazaar* in 1890 and was collected in *A New England Nun and Other Stories* (1891). Wilkins (1852–1930) was known as Mary Wilkins Freeman after her marriage in 1902.

164.6   case of Mrs. Place]   Martha Place had been sentenced to death for the murder of her stepdaughter in Brooklyn on February 7, 1898. She was executed on March 20, 1899, becoming the first woman to die in the electric chair.

164.25   *George F. R. Henderson*]   Henderson (1854–1903), a British army officer and military historian, was a professor at the Staff College at Camberley, 1892–99, and the author of *The Campaign of Fredericksburg* (1886) and *Stonewall Jackson and the American Civil War* (2 volumes, 1898).

166.7   Bradley T. Johnson]   Johnson (1829–1903) was a brigadier general in the Confederate army.

166.10   Ropes' second volume]   John Codman Ropes (1836–1899), *The Story of the Civil War* (2 volumes, 1894–98).

166.29   Wolfe Victorious."]   British major general James Wolfe (1727–59) was mortally wounded during his victory over the French at the Plains of Abraham outside Quebec.

167.5   *Frank Michler Chapman*]   Chapman (1864–1945) was an ornithological curator at the American Museum of Natural History and the author of *Handbook of Birds of Eastern North America* (1895).

168.2   *William Bayard Cutting*]   Cutting (1850–1912) was a wealthy New York businessman with investments in banking, railroads, and ferry services.

168.5   my entire speech]   Roosevelt's speech in Chicago on April 10, 1899; see pp. 755–66 in this volume.

170.36–37   trouble . . . in Buffalo]   Dockworkers in Buffalo went on strike in April 1899; the strike ended in May.

172.11–12   veto . . . labor bill]   Roosevelt had vetoed a bill for protecting tenement workers on technical grounds and then signed a different bill with the same aim.

172.13   the 71st Regiment]   Roosevelt had strongly supported a court of inquiry into charges that senior officers of the 71st Infantry Regiment, New York Volunteers, had remained in the rear during the attack on the San Juan Heights.

172.30   Odell]   Benjamin B. Odell Jr. (1854–1926) was a Republican congressman, 1895–99, and governor of New York, 1901–4.

175.28   your history]   *The War with Spain* (1899).

175.33   Admiral Schley]   A public controversy had broken out over whether Rear Admiral Winfield Scott Schley (1839–1909) or Rear Admiral William Sampson (1840–1902) deserved the credit for the destruction of the Spanish fleet at Santiago on July 3, 1898.

176.15   Depew]   Chauncey M. Depew (1834–1928) was president of the New York Central Railroad, 1885–99, and a Republican senator from New York, 1899–1911.

176.28   Frank Platt]   A son of Thomas Collier Platt.

177.20–23   Captain Dreyfus . . . Colonel Picquart]   On June 3, 1899, the French court of appeals overturned the 1894 conviction for espionage of Alfred Dreyfus (1859–1935) and ordered a new trial. Dreyfus was convicted on September 9, 1899, but was pardoned by President Émile Loubet ten days later. He was fully exonerated in 1906. Lieutenant Colonel Georges Picquart (1854–1914) had discovered evidence in 1896 of Dreyfus's innocence and the guilt of Major Ferdinand Esterhazy. In 1898 he was dismissed from the army and imprisoned on charges of improperly giving military information to civilians. Picquart was released from prison on June 5, 1899, and was reinstated in the army in 1906.

177.28   the Duffield incident]   Brigadier General Henry Martin Duffield was ordered on July 1, 1898, to make an attack along the coast with the aim of drawing Spanish troops away from the San Juan Heights. His brigade was late in deploying and did not advance across the Aguadores River, one and a half miles from Morro Castle, which commanded the entrance to Santiago harbor.

178.14   Las Vegas] Las Vegas, New Mexico.

179.21   President's civil service order] McKinley had removed 4,000 government positions from civil service classification in January 1899.

179.24   Kerr, Grosvenor] Winfield Scott Kerr (1852–1917), Republican representative from Ohio, 1895–1901; Charles Henry Grosvenor (1833–1917), Republican representative from Ohio, 1885–91 and 1893–1907.

180.2   *Charles E. S. Wood*] Charles Erskine Scott Wood (1852–1944), a former army officer, was an attorney in Portland, Oregon. He later published *A Book of Tales, Being Myths of the North American Indian* (1901) and several volumes of poetry, essays, and satirical dialogues.

180.8   Senator Simon] Joseph Simon (1851–1935), Republican senator from Oregon, 1897–1903.

180.34   Hanna] Marcus Alonzo Hanna (1837–1904), a Republican senator from Ohio, 1897–1904, was McKinley's strongest political supporter.

183.2   encountered at Ladysmith] The British lost 1,200 casualties in a failed attempt to break the Boer lines at Ladysmith on October 30, 1899.

185.36   the Mahdists] The Islamic rebels in the Sudan who revolted against Egyptian rule and captured Khartoum in January 1885. They controlled the Sudan until their defeat by an Anglo-Egyptian army in 1898.

186.11   Beveridge] Albert Beveridge (1862–1927) was a Republican senator from Indiana, 1899–1911.

187.28   Woodruff] Timothy L. Woodruff (1858–1913) was lieutenant-governor of New York, 1897–1902.

188.9   Black] Frank S. Black (1853–1913) was the governor of New York, 1897–98. His unpopularity with independent voters and a canal scandal made him politically vulnerable, and on September 27, 1898, the Republican state convention rejected his bid for renomination and chose Roosevelt as their candidate, 753–218.

189.10   President Schurman] Jacob Gould Schurman (1854–1942), president of Cornell University, 1892–1920, served as president of the First Philippine Commission, 1899–1900. The commission, appointed by President McKinley, investigated the situation in the Philippines and issued a report.

190.4   the Payn matter] Roosevelt had succeeded in replacing Louis F. Payn, the state superintendent of insurance, despite the opposition of Platt.

190.7   Villards] Henry Villard (1835–1900) was president of the Northern Pacific Railroad, 1881–84, and the chairman of its board of directors,

1889–93. He had purchased the New York *Evening Post* in 1881. His son Oswald Garrison Villard (1872–1949) was vice-president, 1897–1900, and president, 1900–18, of the *Evening Post*.

190.27 Mason, Hale] William Mason (1850–1921) was a Republican representative from Illinois, 1887–91 and 1917–21, and a senator, 1897–1903. Eugene Hale (1836–1918) was a Republican representative from Maine, 1869–79, and a senator, 1881–1911.

191.6–7 "atheist" . . . "filthy"] In *Gouverneur Morris* (1888) Roosevelt had referred to Thomas Paine as "the filthy little atheist."

192.15 the treaty] See Chronology, 1900.

193.26 *Josephine Shaw Lowell*] Lowell (1843–1905) was the first woman to serve as a commissioner on the New York State Board of Charities, 1876–89. She helped found the Charity Organization Society of the City of New York in 1882 and was actively involved with it until her death.

194.20 Sheriff Davidson] In 1884 an assembly committee chaired by Roosevelt recommended that Alexander Davidson, the sheriff of New York County, be dismissed from office. David Hill, Cleveland's Democratic successor, announced in 1885 that Davidson would keep his position.

197.9 Mrs. Kelley] Florence Kelley (1859–1932) worked with Jane Addams at Hull House in Chicago, 1891–99, and was the first Illinois state factory inspector, 1895–97. She was the general secretary of the National Consumers' League, 1899–1932.

197.13–14 appointment of McRoberts] Roosevelt had appointed Hugh McRoberts to be quarantine commissioner for the port of New York.

199.14 Mr. Croker] Richard Croker (1841–1922) was the head of Tammany Hall, 1886–1902.

202.6 Guiteau] Charles Guiteau, the assassin of President Garfield.

203.12–13 the Ramapo job] The Ramapo Water Company was attempting to gain control of the New York City water supply.

207.22 *William Allen White*] White (1868–1944) was editor and publisher of the Emporia (Kansas) *Gazette*, 1895–1944.

209.18 *Seth Low*] Low (1850–1916) was president of Columbia University, 1890–1901. He was elected mayor of New York on a reform ticket in 1901 but was defeated for reelection in 1903.

211.19 Weed instead of Seward] Weed (1797–1882) was publisher of the Albany *Evening Journal*, 1830–63, and a founder of the Whig and Republican parties in New York. William H. Seward (1801–1872) was the Whig governor of New York, 1839–42, a Whig and Republican senator, 1849–61, and secretary of state, 1861–69.

213.24   *John M. Palmer*]   Palmer (1817–1900), a Union army general, had been the Republican governor of Illinois, 1869–73, and a Democratic senator, 1891–97. In 1896 he ran for president as a Gold Democrat.

214.8–9   Vallandigham]   Clement L. Vallandigham (1820–1871) was a Democratic representative from Ohio, 1858–63, and a leader of the "Peace Democrats" opposed to Lincoln and the war.

215.29   late General Lawton]   Major General Henry W. Lawton (1843–1899) was killed during a skirmish in central Luzon on December 19, 1899.

217.15–16   Van Wyck . . . trouble in New York]   On November 5 Roosevelt had written to Mayor Robert A. Van Wyck, demanding that Chief of Police William S. Devery follow the orders of the state elections bureau after Devery had announced that he would disregard the bureau's instructions.

217.23   *Edward Sanford Martin*]   Martin (1856–1939) was a humorous writer who had co-founded the satiric magazine *Life* in 1883.

221.2   *William L. Llewellyn*]   Llewellyn was a former Rough Rider; see also p. 286.6–35 in this volume.

223.8   *William Carey Brown*]   Brown (1854–1939) was an army major serving in the Philippines.

223.13   getting the bandit chief]   Brown had shot Tomas Tagunton, a rebel leader, during a skirmish in central Luzon on January 25, 1901.

224.5–6   John Kendrick Bangs]   Bangs (1862–1922) was a humorous writer whose works included *A Houseboat on the Styx* (1896).

224.25–26   Dewey's lamentable fall]   In an interview given on April 4, 1900, Dewey had announced that he would accept the nomination of either party and described the office of president as "not such a very difficult one to fill."

226.9   the *Journal*]   The New York *Journal* was owned by William Randolph Hearst.

226.15   Bishop]   Joseph Bucklin Bishop (1847–1928), who later edited *Theodore Roosevelt's Letters to His Children* (1919) and *Theodore Roosevelt and His Time, Shown in His Own Letters* (2 volumes, 1920).

226.25   young Villard's mother]   Helen Garrison Villard, the wife of Henry Villard and the daughter of abolitionist William Lloyd Garrison.

227.5   *Frederic Harrison*]   Harrison (1831–1923) was a British legal scholar who had published a biography of Oliver Cromwell in 1888. In 1900 he gave the Rede Lecture at Cambridge.

229.2   *Alton B. Parker*]   Parker (1852–1926) was chief justice of the New York state court of appeals, 1898–1904, and Roosevelt's Democratic opponent in the 1904 election.

233.13   Smalley]   George Washburn Smalley (1833–1916), an American journalist, was the American correspondent for the London *Times*, 1895–1906.

235.23   Jacob Schiff]   Schiff (1847–1920) was a New York banker and philanthropist.

238.6   Ernest Howard Crosby]   Crosby (1856–1907), a New York attorney, became a follower of social reformer Henry George after meeting Tolstoi in the 1890s.

239.19   Fairbanks]   Charles W. Fairbanks (1852–1918) was a Republican senator from Indiana, 1897–1905, vice-president of the United States, 1905–9, and the Republican vice-presidential candidate in 1916.

PRESIDENT, 1901–1909

244.14   *Albion W. Tourgée*]   Tourgée (1838–1905) was an attorney and novelist whose works included *A Fool's Errand* (1879) and *Bricks Without Straw* (1880), both inspired by his experiences as a carpetbagger in North Carolina during Reconstruction. In 1896 he unsuccessfully challenged the Louisiana railroad segregation law when he represented Homer Plessy before the Supreme Court in *Plessy* v. *Ferguson*.

244.20–21   Booker T. Washington to dinner]   See Chronology, 1901.

245.16   *Endicott Peabody*]   Peabody (1857–1944) was the founder and headmaster, 1884–1940, of Groton School.

246.11   General Miles]   Nelson Miles (1839–1925) was commanding general of the army, 1895–1903.

247.16   Aguinaldo]   Emilio Aguinaldo (1869–1964), the leader of the Philippine independence movement, had been captured on March 23, 1901.

247.32   Governor Taft and General Chaffee]   William Howard Taft served as governor of the Philippines, 1901–4. Major General Adna R. Chaffee (1842–1914) was the commander of American forces in the Philippines from July 1901 to October 1902.

248.2   *Cleveland Dodge*]   Dodge (1860–1926), a vice-president of the Phelps Dodge mining company, was a college classmate of Woodrow Wilson.

248.5–6   Wilson . . . election]   Wilson had been chosen to be the new president of Princeton University.

250.8–13   The minority . . . the Philippines.]   In three cases decided in 1901, the Supreme Court ruled 5–4 that Congress had the power to determine the constitutional status of overseas possessions. The dissenters in the "insular cases" held that the Constitution fully applied to any territory under U.S. sovereignty.

250.21–22   Judge Gray . . . Knowlton]   Horace Gray (1828–1902) was an associate justice of the Supreme Court, 1882–1902. Hosea M. Knowlton was attorney general of Massachusetts, 1894–1902.

252.12   Brigadier General Smith]   Jacob H. Smith had allegedly ordered Major Littleton Waller in 1901 to make the interior of Samar "a howling wilderness" and to kill every Filipino male over the age of ten. A court-martial in the spring of 1902 had found Smith guilty of conduct prejudicial to "good order and military discipline" and sentenced him to be "admonished by the reviewing authority." In July 1902 Roosevelt ordered that Smith be retired from the army.

252.23–26   Major Waller . . . murder of ten]   Waller, a Marine Corps officer, had led a party of 56 Marines and 35 Filipinos in a march across southern Samar in January 1902. During the march 11 Marines died or disappeared, and at its conclusion Waller ordered the execution of 11 of the expedition porters. Waller was acquitted at court-martial in the spring of 1902 and retired in 1920 as a major general.

253.23   great work . . . Nicolay]   Hay and John G. Nicolay, who had served as secretaries to Lincoln during his presidency, were the authors of *Abraham Lincoln: A History* (10 volumes, 1890) and the editors of *Complete Works of Abraham Lincoln* (2 volumes, 1894).

254.20–21   Wade and Davis . . . Seymour]   Senator Benjamin F. Wade and Representative Henry W. Davis were Radical Republicans who opposed Lincoln's Reconstruction policies. Horatio Seymour was the Democratic governor of New York, 1863–64, and an opponent of the Emancipation Proclamation and the federal conscription law.

254.26   Charles Francis Adams]   Adams (1835–1915), the brother of Brooks and Henry Adams, was an anti-imperialist.

256.16   *Robert Bacon*]   Bacon (1860–1919), a member of Roosevelt's Harvard class, was a partner at J. P. Morgan & Co., 1894–1903. He later served as assistant secretary of state, 1905–9, and as secretary of state from January 27 to March 5, 1909.

256.23   letter ex-President Cleveland]   Cleveland had written on October 4 to express support for Roosevelt's efforts to end the coal strike.

257.6   John Mitchell]   Mitchell (1870–1919) was president of the United Mine Workers, 1898–1908.

257.21–22   Cleveland's . . . Debs' riots]   The American Railway Union, headed by Eugene Debs, called a strike against railroads using Pullman cars on June 21, 1894. Cleveland used federal troops and a federal court injunction to break the strike, which ended on July 20, 1884.

258.21   Carroll D. Wright]   Wright (1840–1909) was U.S. Commissioner of Labor, 1885–1905.

259.2   *Bessie Van Vorst*] Van Vorst (1873–1928) and her sister-in-law Marie Van Vorst (1867–1936) were the authors of *The Woman Who Toils: Being the Experiences of Two Ladies as Factory Girls* (1903), which first appeared in *Everybody's Magazine*, September–December 1902. Portions of this letter were published.

260.28   *Robert Goodwyn Rhett*] Rhett was a banker in Charleston, South Carolina.

260.32–33   Mr. Waring] Thomas Waring was the editor of the Charleston *Evening Post*, 1897–1935.

261.33   Mr. Crum] See Chronology, 1902.

262.23   *Maria Longworth Storer*] Storer and her husband, Bellamy Storer, were friends of McKinley, who had helped secure Roosevelt's appointment as assistant secretary of the navy in 1897. Bellamy Storer was the American minister to Belgium, 1897–99, and to Spain, 1899–1902; in September 1902 Roosevelt appointed him as minister to Austria-Hungary. Maria Longworth Storer's nephew, Nicholas Longworth, married Alice Roosevelt in 1906.

264.8   the Astor House] A hotel in lower Manhattan.

266.31   *Pierre de Coubertin*] Coubertin (1863–1937), a French historian and educator, was the author of *Notes sur L'Education publique* (1901). He served as the president of the International Olympic Committee, 1894–1925.

271.19   *Winfield Taylor Durbin*] Durbin (1847–1928) was the Republican governor of Indiana, 1901–5. Durbin called out the National Guard on July 6, 1903, to protect the Evansville jail against a mob attempting to lynch a black man accused of the murder of a white policeman. During the night the guardsmen and deputies opened fire, killing or fatally wounding nine people. This letter was written for publication and was released to the newspapers.

275.7   Moody's] William Henry Moody (1853–1917) was secretary of the navy, 1902–4, attorney general, 1904–6, and an associate justice of the Supreme Court, 1906–10.

276.14   Carter Harrison] Harrison (1860–1953), a Democrat, was mayor of Chicago, 1897–1905 and 1911–15.

278.27   Faith, Hope and Charity text] 1 Corinthians 13.

290.13   Heinze] Frederick Augustus Heinze (1869–1914) organized the Montana Ore Purchasing Company in 1893. After 1899 he engaged in a struggle with the Amalgamated Copper Company, which was controlled by Standard Oil, for supremacy in Montana copper mining. In October 1903 Amalgamated Copper was able to weaken his influence over the local court system, and in 1906 Heinze sold most of his Montana holdings. His unsuccessful attempt to fight Amalgamated Copper on Wall Street helped start the Panic of 1907.

290.14   ex-Senator Carter and Senator Clark]   Thomas Carter (1854–1911) was a Republican senator, 1895–1901 and 1905–11; William Clark (1839–1925) was a Democratic senator, 1899–1900 and 1901–7.

290.28–29   Coeur d'Alene strike]   In 1892 and 1899 violent strikes in the silver mines of northern Idaho were suppressed by federal troops.

291.26   "The Golliwoggs,"]   A series of 13 children's books published between 1895 and 1909, written in verse by Bertha Upton (1849–1912) and illustrated by her daughter Florence Upton (1873–1922).

293.2   Loeb]   William Loeb (1866–1937) was secretary to Roosevelt, 1899–1901, assistant secretary, 1901–3, and secretary, 1903–9.

293.28   the Danites]   A Mormon paramilitary organization.

293.25–26   Senator Ankeny's]   Levi Ankeny (1844–1921) was a Republican senator from Washington, 1903–9.

294.22   Senator Dietrich]   Charles Dietrich (1853–1924), a Republican senator from Nebraska, 1901–5.

296.20   Uncle Joe Cannon and Secretary Wilson]   Joseph Cannon (1836–1926) was a Republican representative from Illinois, 1873–91, 1893–1913, and 1915–23, and Speaker of the House, 1903–11. James Wilson (1836–1920) was secretary of agriculture, 1897–1913.

298.40   Garfield]   James R. Garfield (1865–1950) was a civil service commissioner, 1902–3, commissioner of the bureau of corporations in the department of commerce and labor, 1903–7, and secretary of the interior, 1907–9.

299.17   *Nicholas Murray Butler*]   Butler (1862–1947) was president of Columbia University, 1902–45.

299.20   dog has returned to his vomit]   See Proverbs 26:11.

300.25   Gaston]   William A. Gaston (1859–1927) was the unsuccessful Democratic candidate for governor of Massachusetts in 1903. He was the son of William Gaston (1820–1894), a Democrat who had served as governor, 1875–76.

307.2   *John Morley*]   Morley (1838–1923) was a Liberal member of Parliament, 1883–95 and 1896–1908, secretary of state for Ireland, 1892–95, and secretary of state for India, 1905–8. His three-volume biography of Gladstone was published in 1903.

307.24   Finlay]   George Finlay (1799–1875), a British historian, was the author of *A History of Greece* (7 volumes, 1877), which covered the period from 146 B.C. to 1864.

309.9   Chesterfield's-letters-to-his-son]   The letters, written from 1732 to 1768 by the Earl of Chesterfield (1694–1773), were published in 1774.

309.18   the Wood controversy]   Roosevelt had promoted Leonard Wood
to major general in 1903 but, because of the opposition of Mark Hanna
and others, the promotion was not approved by the Senate until March 18,
1904.

314.29   Hoar]   George F. Hoar (1826–1904), a Republican senator from
Massachusetts, 1877–1904.

315.4   Lansdowne]   The Marquis of Lansdowne (1845–1927), British foreign secretary, 1900–5.

315.9   David Harum's famous gloss]   In *David Harum: A Story of American Life*, a novel (1898) by Edward Noyes Westcott (1846–1898): "Do unto
the other feller the way he'd like to do unto you, an' do it fust."

315.17   Upton's book]   *The Military Policy of the United States* (1904),
posthumously published study by Colonel Emory Upton (1839–1881).

316.2   *Theodore Elijah Burton*]   Burton (1851–1929) was a Republican representative from Ohio, 1889–91, 1895–1909, and 1921–28, and a senator,
1909–15 and 1928–29.

316.12   Mr. Williams]   John Sharp Williams (1854–1932) was a Democratic representative from Mississippi, 1893–1909, and a senator, 1911–23.

318.17   The Hague Tribunal]   The Hague Permanent Court of Arbitration, established by the 1899 Hague peace conference.

318.29   *Francis Bennett Williams*]   Williams was the chairman of the
Louisiana Republican party. At the 1904 national convention his all-white
delegation was unseated in favor of a delegation that included African-
Americans.

320.4   *Lawrence Fraser Abbott*]   Abbott (1859–1933) was president of
The Outlook company, 1891–1923.

323.5–6   Cockrell . . . McRae]   Francis M. Cockrell (1834–1915), Democratic senator from Missouri, 1875–1905; Thomas C. McRae (1851–1929),
Democratic representative from Arkansas, 1885–1903.

325.6   Hadley's admirable volume]   Arthur Twining Hadley, *The Relations Between Freedom and Responsibility in the Evolution of Democratic Government* (1903). Hadley (1856–1930), an economist, was the president of Yale
University, 1899–1921.

325.18   Luke Wright]   Wright (1846–1922) was vice-governor, 1901–4,
and governor, 1904–6, of the Philippines; ambassador to Japan, 1906–8; and
secretary of war, 1908–9.

327.3   Cromer in Egypt]   Evelyn Baring (1841–1917), first Earl of Cromer,
was the British plenipotentiary in Egypt, 1883–1907.

330.3 poor sister] Alice Roosevelt, later Alice Roosevelt Longworth (1884–1980).

330.5 Uncle Will] William Sheffield Cowles (1846–1923).

334.10 Baron Kaneko] Kentaro Kaneko (1853–1942), an unofficial Japanese envoy to the United States.

337.25 Jusserand] Jean-Jules Jusserand (1855–1932), French ambassador to the United States, 1902–25.

338.16 *Lyman Abbott*] Abbott (1835–1922), a Congregational clergyman, was editor of *The Outlook*, 1893–1922.

341.17 *Oliver Otis Howard*] Howard (1830–1909) was a Union corps commander, 1863–64, and commander of the Army of the Tennessee, 1864–65.

343.3–4 Blifil . . . Black George] Characters in *Tom Jones* (1749) by Henry Fielding.

344.29 Slabsides!] Burroughs' cabin in the Hudson Valley hills near Esopus, New York.

345.2 *Robert Grant*] Grant (1852–1940) was a novelist whose works included *Unleavened Bread* (1900) and *The Undercurrent* (1904).

346.2 *Eugene A. Philbin*] Philbin (1857–1920) was a lawyer active in New York Catholic organizations. He later served as a state supreme court judge, 1913–20.

346.28 removal of Asa Bird Gardiner] In December 1900 Roosevelt removed Gardiner as district attorney of New York County and replaced him with Philbin, who served until January 1901.

347.2 *George McClellan Harvey*] Harvey (1864–1928) was editor of *The North American Review*, 1899–1926, and *Harper's Weekly*, 1901–13.

347.27 Scott's *Memoirs*] Winfield Scott, *Memoirs of Lieut.-General Scott, LL.D. Written by himself* (2 volumes, 1864).

348.1 of Wilkinson, of Floyd] General James Wilkinson (1757–1825) was a paid Spanish agent who was also involved in the Burr conspiracy. John Floyd (1806–1863), a former governor of Arkansas, was secretary of war from March 1857 until his resignation on December 29, 1860. He was subsequently accused of having ordered the transfer of arms to Southern armories so that they could be seized by secessionists.

349.27 Sydney Smith] Smith (1771–1845), an Anglican clergyman, helped found the *Edinburgh Review* in 1802 and wrote numerous essays, many of them in support of Catholic emancipation and other reform causes.

351.39   so-called Miller case]   William A. Miller was a foreman in the Government Printing Office who was fired after being expelled from his union. In 1903 Roosevelt had publicly supported the ruling by the Civil Service Commission that Miller should be rehired.

353.9–24   California . . . Missouri]   In the election Roosevelt carried all the states he mentioned with the exception of Maryland, where he won one of its eight electoral votes.

354.18   *Augustus Peabody Gardner*]   Gardner (1865–1918) was a Republican representative from Massachusetts, 1902–17.

358.15   *Philander Chase Knox*]   Knox (1853–1921) was attorney general, 1901–4, a senator from Pennsylvania, 1904–9 and 1917–21, and secretary of state, 1909–13.

358.21–22   Murray Crane]   Winthrop Murray Crane (1853–1920) was the Republican governor of Massachusetts, 1900–2, and a senator, 1904–13.

360.20   Peabody]   James H. Peabody, the Republican governor of Colorado, 1903–5, used the National Guard to violently suppress the Western Federation of Miners in 1903–4. He failed to win reelection in 1904.

362.26   the heroine, Selma]   In the novel Selma White marries a merchant in a small western town, divorces him and marries a New York architect, then again divorces and marries a congressman, whom she helps make a senator through unethical dealings.

363.2   *Frederick William MacMonnies*]   MacMonnies (1863–1937) was an American sculptor.

364.18   Cortelyou]   George B. Cortelyou (1862–1940) was secretary to McKinley, 1900–1, and Roosevelt, 1901–3; secretary of commerce and labor, 1903–4; chairman of the Republican national committee, 1904; postmaster general, 1905–7; and secretary of the treasury, 1907–9.

366.34   "vacuity trimmed with lace,"]   The phrase appears as a chapter epigraph in the novel *With Edged Tools* (1894) by Henry Seton Merriman.

366.36   Bourke Cockran]   William Bourke Cockran (1854–1923) was a Democratic representative from New York, 1887–89, 1891–95, 1904–9, and 1921–23.

367.9   Carmack]   Edward Ward Carmack (1858–1908) was a Democratic representative from Tennessee, 1897–1901, and a senator, 1901–7.

371.22   Abraham Lincoln's speeches]   The speech was given in Washington, D.C., on November 10, 1864.

371.19   *William Emlen Roosevelt*]   A banker and a first cousin of Theodore Roosevelt.

371.23   Townsend]   Lawrence Townsend (1860–1954) was U.S. minister to Portugal, 1897–99, and to Belgium, 1899–1905.

373.6   *James Ford Rhodes*]   Rhodes (1848–1927) was the author of *History of the United States from the Compromise of 1850* (7 volumes, 1893–1906).

373.12–13   Macaulay's *History*]   Thomas Babington Macaulay (1800–59), *The History of England from the Accession of James II* (5 volumes, 1849–61).

374.30   Timoleon and John Hampden]   Timoleon was a Corinthian general and statesman who defended Greek cities in Sicily against tyrants and Carthaginian invaders, 344–337 B.C. A leader of the parliamentary opposition to Charles I, John Hampden (1594–1643) was killed in the English Civil War.

375.5–6   Trumbull or Fessenden]   Lyman Trumbull and William Fessenden were moderate Republicans who voted to acquit President Andrew Johnson at his impeachment trial.

375.28   Norman Hapgood]   Hapgood (1868–1937) was editor of *Collier's Weekly*, 1903–12, and *Harper's Weekly*, 1913–16.

375.29   Hill]   David B. Hill (1843–1910) was Democratic governor of New York, 1885–91, and a senator from New York, 1892–97.

375.31   Rollo Ogdens]   Ogdens (1856–1937) was editor of the New York *Evening Post*, 1903–20.

376.6   Judge Jones]   Thomas G. Jones (1844–1914) was governor of Alabama, 1890–94. A Gold Democrat, he was appointed U.S. district judge for Alabama by Roosevelt in 1901 and served until his death.

377.9   President Eliot's little book]   Charles William Eliot, *John Gilley, Maine Farmer and Fisherman* (1904).

378.2   Ware]   Eugene Fitch Ware (1841–1911), author of *Rhymes of Ironquill* (1885), was U.S. pensions commissioner, 1902–5.

379.9   *Michael Joseph Donovan*]   Donovan worked as a boxing instructor at the New York Athletic Club.

379.24   *George von Lengerke Meyer*]   Meyer (1858–1918) was U.S. ambassador to Italy, 1900–5, and to Russia, 1905–7; postmaster general, 1907–9; and secretary of the navy, 1909–13.

380.31   an Englishman]   Cecil Spring-Rice.

380.36   Harry White]   Henry White (1850–1927) served as a secretary in the London legation, 1883–93 and 1897–1905, as ambassador to Italy, 1905–7, and as ambassador to France, 1907–9.

380.39   John Riddle]   Riddle (1864–1941) served as a secretary at the legation in Constantinople; as minister to Romania and Serbia; and as ambassador to Russia, 1907–9.

382.23   Wilson]   Henry Lane Wilson (1857–1932) was minister to Chile, 1897–1904, to Belgium, 1905–9, and to Mexico, 1909–13.

382.25   In Spain . . . a novelist]   Arthur Sherburne Hardy (1847–1930) served as minister to Persia, 1897–99, to Greece, Romania, and Serbia, 1899–1901, to Switzerland, 1901–3, and to Spain, 1903–5. His novels included *But Yet a Woman* (1883) and *The Wind of Destiny* (1886).

382.31   Loomis]   Francis Loomis (1861–1948) was minister to Venezuela, 1897–1901, to Portugal, 1901–3, and assistant secretary of state, 1903–5.

383.5   Griscom]   Lloyd Griscom (1872–1959) was minister to Persia, 1901–2, and to Japan, 1902–6, and ambassador to Brazil, 1906–7, and to Italy, 1907–9.

383.24   *Rafael Reyes*]   Reyes (1850–1921) was president of Colombia, 1904–9.

385.8   I have enjoyed your poems]   Roosevelt praised *The Children of the Night* in a review published in *The Outlook* on August 12, 1905.

389.17   Long]   William Joseph Long (1867–1952), whose works included *Beasts of the Field* (1901) and *A Little Brother to the Bear, and Other Animal Studies* (1903).

390.33   Hudson]   William Henry Hudson (1841–1922), whose works included *The Purple Land* (1885), *The Naturalist in La Plata* (1892), and *Green Mansions* (1904).

391.7–8   defeat Rojestvensky]   The Baltic Fleet commanded by Admiral Zinovi P. Rozhestvenski was almost completely destroyed by the Japanese navy in the battle of Tsushima Strait, May 27–28, 1905.

391.9–10   Evans . . . Beresford]   Robley Evans (1846–1912) was an American admiral; Lord Charles Beresford (1846–1919) was an admiral in the Royal Navy.

395.22   Whitelaw Reid]   Reid (1837–1912) was publisher of the New York *Tribune*, 1872–1912, and ambassador to Great Britain, 1905–12.

396.8   Ambassador Tower]   Charlemagne Tower (1848–1923) was ambassador to Germany, 1902–8.

397.2   *Frank Charles Bostock*]   Bostock (1866–1912) was a British animal trainer and circus performer.

397.23   *James Hulme Canfield*]   Canfield (1847–1909) was president of Ohio State University, 1895–99, and chief librarian of Columbia University, 1899–1909.

397.28   *Captain Craig*]   A book of poetry published by Edward Arlington Robinson in 1902.

398.3–5   tell it not . . . Askelon]   Cf. 2 Samuel 1:20.

399.28   Count Lamsdorff]   Vladimir N. Lamsdorff (1844–1907) was the Russian foreign minister, 1901–6.

401.26   *Charles Joseph Bonaparte*]   Bonaparte (1851–1921) was secretary of the navy, 1905–6, and attorney general, 1906–9.

404.28–29   the Turks . . . the Armenians]   In 1894–96 approximately 100,000 Armenians were killed in a series of massacres in the Ottoman Empire, and another 100,000 died from hunger and disease.

407.14   Durand]   Henry Durand (1850–1924), British ambassador to the United States, 1903–6.

409.20–22   Swettingham . . . *The Real Malay*]   Frank Swettenham, *The Real Malay: Pen Pictures* (1900). Swettenham (1850–1946) was the British resident-general in the Malay States, 1895–1901, and high commissioner to the Malay States and governor of the Straits Settlement, 1901–4.

412.19   McCall and Perkins]   John A. McCall (1849–1906) was president of the New York Life Insurance Company, 1892–1905. George W. Perkins (1862–1920) was vice-president of New York Life, 1893–1905, and a senior financial adviser to J. P. Morgan, 1901–10. In 1912 he became the chairman of the Progressive party national committee.

415.2   *George Herbert Locke*]   Locke (1870–1937) was an editor at Ginn & Company.

415.10   Mr. Long's book]   William Joseph Long, *Northern Trails: Some Studies of Animal Life in the Far North* (1905), which was published by Ginn.

419.21   Mr. Colton]   Arthur Colton (1868–1943), a novelist and essayist.

420.24–25   Bulkeley . . . Dryden]   Morgan Bulkeley (1837–1922) was president of the Aetna Life Insurance Company, 1879–1922, and a Republican senator from Connecticut, 1905–11. John Dryden (1839–1911) was president of the Prudential Insurance Company, 1881–1911, and a Republican senator from New Jersey, 1902–7.

424.24   *Henry Melville Whitney*]   Whitney (1839–1923) was a financier of streetcar and railroad companies in the northeast.

425.28   *Nevada Northrop Stranahan*]   Stranahan was collector of customs for the port of New York.

425.33   Governor Higgins]   Frank W. Higgins (1856–1907) was the Republican governor of New York, 1905–7.

426.23   *Ray Stannard Baker*]   Baker (1870–1946) was a contributor to *McClure's Magazine*, 1897–1905, and an editor of *American Magazine*, 1906–15.

429.7   *Clarence Don Clark*]   Clark (1851–1930) was a Republican representative from Wyoming, 1890–93, and a senator, 1895–1917.

429.11   Daniels . . . recess appointment] Daniels' appointment was confirmed.

433.26   Cardinal Merry del Val] Merry del Val (1865–1930) was secretary of state of the Roman Curia, 1903–14.

433.27   Farley] John Farley (1842–1920), archbishop of New York, 1902–20.

433.30   Ireland] John Ireland (1838–1918), archbishop of St. Paul, 1888–1918.

437.6   dismissal of Hurst] Carlton Bailey Hurst, American consul in Vienna.

438.3   my letters returned to me] Storer did not return the letters, and after Roosevelt dismissed him in March 1906, he published them in a pamphlet in November 1906.

439.27   Swayne's book] Harald G. C. Swayne (1860–1940), *Through the Highlands of Siberia* (1904).

441.2   *Melville Weston Fuller*] Fuller (1833–1910) was chief justice of the Supreme Court, 1888–1910; by law the chief justice serves as a regent of the Smithsonian, and by tradition as its chancellor.

443.2   *James Wolcott Wadsworth Jr.*] Wadsworth (1877–1952), a Republican, was speaker of the New York assembly, 1906–10, a senator, 1915–27, and a representative, 1933–51.

445.35   Soapy Sponge] The hero of *Mr Sponge's Sporting Tour* (1853) by English novelist Robert Smith Surtees (1805–1864).

446.30–31   Oklahoma and Indian Territory] In 1906 present-day Oklahoma was divided into Oklahoma Territory and Indian Territory. The two territories were merged and admitted as the state of Oklahoma in 1907.

447.7   *Ian Hamilton*] Hamilton (1853–1947) headed the British military mission with the Japanese army, 1904–5, and described his experiences in *A Staff Officer's Scrapbook* (2 volumes, 1905–7). He later commanded the expeditionary force that landed on the Gallipoli peninsula in April 1915, but was relieved of command in October 1915.

450.2   *Oscar Solomon Straus*] Straus (1850–1926) was minister to Turkey, 1887–89 and 1898–1900, secretary of commerce and labor, 1906–9, and ambassador to Turkey, 1909–10.

451.8   Bay and Bessie] The Lodges' son, the poet George Cabot Lodge (1873–1909), and his wife, Elizabeth Frelinghuysen Davis Lodge.

451.20   your book] *The Jungle* (1906).

452.5–6   Holmes . . . Teacups] Oliver Wendell Holmes Sr., *Over the Teacups* (1891).

452.28   Wyckoff's account]   Walter A. Wyckoff (1865–1908), *The Workers: An Experience in Reality — The East* (1897) and *The Workers: An Experience in Reality — The West* (1898).

454.39–40   Lawson . . . Phillips]   Thomas Lawson (1857–1925), a Boston stockbroker, wrote "Frenzied Finance," a series of articles for *Everybody's Magazine* in 1904–5. David Graham Phillips (1867–1911) wrote novels and magazine articles about corruption in business and politics.

461.29   French]   American sculptor Daniel Chester French (1850–1931).

461.30   Crothers and Hyde]   Samuel McChord Crothers (1857–1927) was a Unitarian minister and the author of *The Gentle Reader* (1903), a collection of essays. William De Witt Hyde (1858–1917) was president of Bowdoin College, 1885–1917, and the author of *From Epicurus to Christ: A Study in the Principles of Personality* (1904).

462.10–11   Lecky's . . . Revolutionary war?]   In William Lecky, *A History of England in the Eighteenth Century* (8 volumes, 1878–90). Lecky (1838–1903) was an Irish historian.

463.8   *Chapter of Erie*]   "A Chapter of Erie," an account by Charles Francis Adams (see note 254.26) of the struggle to control the Erie Railway, appeared in *North American Review* in July 1869.

466.10   "waving the bloody shirt,"]   A term for the political tactic of arousing anti-Southern feeling and pro-Republican sentiment by invoking the suffering of Union soldiers during the Civil War.

469.25   *Democracy*]   The novel was published anonymously by Henry Adams in 1880.

472.2   *George Horace Latimer*]   Latimer (1867–1937) was editor of *The Saturday Evening Post*, 1899–1936.

475.19   Mr. Whitney]   Henry C. Whitney (1841–1902) was secretary of the navy, 1885–89.

475.26   Mr. Griggs]   John W. Griggs (1849–1927) was attorney general, 1898–1901.

475.36   Foraker]   Joseph Foraker (1846–1917), Republican senator from Ohio, 1896–1909.

476.32   Sam Parks]   Parks became the leader of the iron workers union in New York in 1895. He was convicted of extorting contractors in 1903 and died in Sing Sing prison in 1904.

476.39–40   Moyer . . . Kearny]   Charles Moyer was the president, and William Haywood the secretary-treasurer, of the Western Federation of Miners. Denis Kearney (1847–1917) headed the Workingmen's Party of California, 1877–80.

477.4 Tillman] Benjamin Tillman (1847–1918), known as "Pitchfork Ben," was the Democratic governor of South Carolina, 1890–94, and a senator, 1895–1918.

477.5 Mr. Aldrich] Nelson Aldrich (1841–1915) was a Republican representative from Rhode Island, 1879–81, and a senator, 1881–1911.

478.1–2 Jim Reynolds . . . Alfred Henry Lewis] James B. Reynolds (1861–1924) was a New York lawyer who served on the commission Roosevelt sent to investigate the Chicago meatpacking industry in 1906. Alfred Henry Lewis (c.1858–1914) was a journalist and writer whose works included *Wolfville* (1897), the first of his six volumes of stories about the Southwest.

478.4 Octave Thanet, Laura Richards] Octave Thanet was the pen name of Alice French (1850–1934), a short story writer whose works included *Stories of a Western Town* (1893) and *The Captured Dream* (1899). Laura Richards (1850–1943) was a writer of popular children's books.

479.14 Phillips' . . . the Senate.] The series, "The Treason of the Senate," began appearing in *Cosmopolitan* in March 1906.

480.40 "red fool fury of the Seine,"] Alfred Lord Tennyson, *In Memoriam A.H.H.* (1850), canto 127.

483.5 *Henry Bryant Bigelow*] Bigelow (1879–1967) was a marine zoologist at the Harvard Museum of Comparative Zoology.

483.30 John Luther Long] A playwright who Roosevelt had confused with the nature writer William Joseph Long.

485.9 *Calvin Cobb*] Cobb was the publisher of the Boise *Idaho Daily Statesman*.

485.13 Governor Gooding] Frank R. Gooding (1859–1928) was the Republican governor of Idaho, 1905–9, and a senator, 1921–28.

485.16 murder . . . Steunenberg] Frank Steunenberg, the Democratic governor of Idaho (1897–1901) who had used federal troops to suppress the 1899 strike in the Coeur d'Alene mining region, was killed by a bomb on December 30, 1905. William Haywood, the secretary-treasurer of the Western Federation of Miners; Charles Moyer, its president; and George Pettibone, a union member, were charged with the murder after being implicated by Harry Orchard, who had confessed to setting the bomb. Defended by a team headed by Clarence Darrow, Haywood was acquitted on July 29, 1907. After Pettibone was acquitted in January 1908 the charges against Moyer were dropped.

485.34–486.1 procuring from Colorado the men] Haywood, Moyer, and Pettibone were arrested in Denver on the night of February 17, 1906, and sent by train to Idaho early the next morning without an extradition hearing.

The U.S. Supreme Court upheld the legality of their arrest and removal in a 7–1 decision on December 3, 1906.

487.15   *James Albertus Tawney*]   Tawney (1855–1919) was a Republican representative from Minnesota, 1893–1911.

487.18–19   Mr. Williams]   John Sharp Williams.

489.25–26   the next Hague conference]   The conference was held in 1907.

490.3   Congo Free State]   The Congo Free State was established in 1885 as the personal domain of Leopold II of Belgium. An international campaign against the atrocities committed under Leopold's administration resulted in the annexation of the Free State by Belgium in 1908.

490.15   O. H. Platt]   Orville Hitchcock Platt (1827–1905) was a Republican senator from Connecticut, 1879–1905.

490.30–31   Senate . . . Santo Domingo treaty]   Opposition by Senate Democrats delayed ratification of the customs agreement signed by the U.S. and the Dominican Republic on February 7, 1905. The treaty was finally ratified on February 25, 1907.

491.12   Gussie]   Augustus Peabody Gardner; see note 354.18.

491.25   Dick]   Charles W. F. Dick (1858–1945) was a Republican representative from Ohio, 1898–1904, and a senator, 1904–11.

491.26   Penrose]   Boies Penrose (1860–1921) was a Republican senator from Pennsylvania, 1897–1921.

491.29–30   Hearst . . . elected]   In 1906 William Randolph Hearst was the Democratic candidate for governor of New York. He was defeated by Charles Evans Hughes.

492.26   *Frederick Scott Oliver*]   Oliver (1864–1934), a successful London merchant, published a biography of Alexander Hamilton in 1906. His later works included arguments in favor of tariff reform and Irish Home Rule.

495.5   Sumner]   William Graham Sumner (1840–1910), professor of political and social science at Yale, 1872–1910, had published a biography of Hamilton in 1890.

497.2   *Charles Arthur Stillings*]   Stillings was the head of the Government Printing Office.

498.14   *Florence La Farge*]   Florence Bayard Lockwood La Farge was the wife of the architect Grant La Farge.

499.14   Day]   William R. Day (1849–1923), associate justice of the Supreme Court, 1903–22.

499.16   Lurton business]   Roosevelt was considering appointing federal appellate judge Horace H. Lurton (1844–1914) to the vacancy on the Supreme

Court created by the retirement of Justice Henry B. Brown, but eventually decided to name Attorney General William H. Moody to the open seat. Lurton was later appointed by President Taft and served as an associate justice, 1910–14.

499.21   Littlefield]   Charles E. Littlefield (1851–1915) was a Republican representative from Maine, 1899–1908.

499.25   McCall]   Samuel W. McCall (1851–1923) was a Republican representative from Massachusetts, 1893–1913.

500.4   Winston Churchill's life of his father]   *Lord Randolph Churchill* (2 volumes, 1906).

500.22–23   Mr. Bates]   John Lewis Bates (1859–1946) was the Republican governor of Massachusetts, 1903–5.

500.26   Moran]   John B. Moran, the unsuccessful Democratic candidate for governor of Massachusetts in 1906.

500.32   Jim Sherman . . . Harriman]   James S. Sherman (1855–1912) was a Republican representative from New York, 1887–91 and 1893–1909, and vice-president of the United States, 1909–12. Edward Henry Harriman (1848–1909) controlled the Union Pacific, Central Pacific, and Southern Pacific railroads.

501.28–29   election of Parsons over Quigg]   Congressman Herbert Parsons (1869–1925) defeated former congressman Lemuel Quigg (1863–1919) in the contest for chairman of the New York County Republican committee.

501.31   Ryan]   Thomas F. Ryan (1851–1928) controlled the street railways in New York City through his holding company, Metropolitan Securities, and had major investments in banking and insurance.

502.2   *John St. Loe Strachey*]   A British journalist, Strachey (1860–1927) was editor of *The Spectator*, 1898–1925.

504.34   Secretary Metcalf]   Victor H. Metcalf (1853–1936) was a Republican representative from California, 1899–1904, secretary of commerce and labor, July 1904–December 1906, and secretary of the navy, December 1906–December 1908.

506.30   *Curtis Guild Jr.*]   Guild (1860–1915) was the Republican governor of Massachusetts, 1906–9.

506.33   the order in question]   Roosevelt's order dismissing 167 black soldiers from the army; see Chronology, 1906.

507.32   *Jörn Uhl*]   The novel (1902) was written by Gustav Frenssen (1863–1945).

510.11   the French canal company]   The company was founded in 1879, went bankrupt in 1889, and was reorganized as the New Panama Canal Company in 1894 with the aim of selling its concession to the United States.

512.2   *Silas McBee*]   McBee (1853–1924) was the editor of *The Churchman*, an Episcopalian journal, 1896–1912.

512.31–32   my message about lynching]   See pp. 271–74 in this volume.

512.35   hideous Atlanta race riots]   After a series of sensational reports about alleged assaults on white women by black men appeared in the Atlanta newspapers, white mobs began attacking African-Americans on September 22, 1906. By the time the rioting ended on September 27, one white person and 25 African-Americans had been killed.

513.11   Judge Dickerson . . . Judge Townsend]   Joseph T. Dickerson and Hosea Townsend were federal district judges in Indian Territory. Their judgeships were eliminated in 1907 when Oklahoma became a state, and neither man was reappointed to the federal bench.

517.2   *William Crary Brownell*]   Brownell (1851–1928) was a literary critic and essayist.

517.24   *E. H. Merrell*]   Merrell was president of the New York State Assembly of Mothers.

518.29   *Henry Lee Higginson*]   Higginson (1834–1919) was a Boston banker.

520.6   *Albert Shaw*]   Shaw (1857–1947) was editor of the *American Monthly Review of Reviews*, 1891–1937. This letter appeared in the *Review of Reviews*, May 1907.

521.28   Finot's *Race Prejudice*]   A book published in 1906 by Jean Finot (1858–1922).

523.2   *Thomas McDonald Patterson*]   Patterson (1839–1916) was a Democratic representative from Colorado, 1877–1879, and a senator, 1901–7.

523.9   the Webster letter]   A letter written by Harriman to his associate Sidney Webster regarding contributions Harriman made in 1904 to the Roosevelt campaign was published in the New York *World* on April 2, 1907. Roosevelt responded by releasing a letter he had written to Congressman James S. Sherman on October 8, 1906, in which he quoted from the correspondence he had conducted with Harriman in the fall of 1904.

523.24   urged Depew's appointment]   As ambassador to France.

523.30   Hyde]   James H. Hyde, the owner of a controlling interest in the Equitable Company, who testified in 1905 that Harriman and Odell had solicited him for campaign contributions in 1904 and promised to use their influence to have him appointed ambassador to France.

524.33   "By their fruits . . . know them."]   Cf. Matthew 7:20.

525.24   Senator Curtis]   Charles Curtis (1860–1936) was a Republican representative from Kansas, 1893–1907, a senator, 1907–13 and 1915–29, and vice-president of the United States, 1929–33.

525.26   Long]   Chester Long (1860–1934) was a Republican representative from Kansas, 1895–97 and 1899–1903, and a senator, 1903–9.

527.3   Kittredge]   Albert B. Kittredge (1861–1911) was a Republican senator from South Dakota, 1901–9.

527.40–528.1   whether Borah ought to come on]   William E. Borah (1865–1940), a Republican attorney, was elected to the Senate by the Idaho legislature in January 1907. While serving as a special prosecutor in the Haywood murder trial (see note 485.16), Borah was indicted on federal timber fraud charges on April 12, 1907. Borah asked White, a college friend, to intercede with Roosevelt and allow him to plead in person for a dismissal of the indictment on the grounds that the grand jury had been prejudiced against him.

528.15   Ruick]   Norman Ruick, the U.S. attorney for Idaho.

528.28–30   meet me . . . August 9th]   On August 9 Roosevelt and Attorney General Bonaparte met with White, attorney John Yerkes, and Christopher Connolly, a writer for *Collier's*. Roosevelt and Bonaparte refused to dismiss the indictment but agreed to grant Borah a speedy trial. Borah was acquitted on October 3, 1907, and served in the Senate until 1940.

531.32–33   John Greenway]   Greenway had been a first lieutenant in the Rough Riders.

534.33   Judge Amidon]   In a speech to the American Bar Association, Charles F. Amidon had said that court decisions "must be tested by the way they work in actual application to the national life." Amidon (1856–1937) was a federal district judge in North Dakota, 1896–1928.

540.5   Curtin's book on the Mongols]   Jeremiah Curtin, *The Mongols: A History* (1908). Curtin (1835–1906) was an American linguist and ethnologist who wrote on Celtic, Slavonic, Mongol, and American Indian mythology and folklore.

544.28   *Charles Edward Magoon*]   Magoon (1861–1920) was minister to Panama and governor of the Canal Zone, 1905–6. In 1906 Roosevelt appointed him provisional governor of Cuba during the second American occupation (see Chronology, 1906).

545.15   *Arthur Hamilton Lee*]   Lee (1868–1947) served as an officer in the British army, 1888–1900, and first met Roosevelt in Cuba while observing the Spanish-American War. In 1900 Lee became a Conservative member of Parliament, and from 1906 to 1914 was the opposition spokesman on naval affairs. Lee returned to active military duty in 1914, then served as a parliamentary secretary to Lloyd George, 1915–17, and as director-general of food production, 1917–18.

547.8–9   portrait painter, Laszló]   Philip Alexius Laszló de Lombos (1869–1938).

547.25   three . . . American friends.]   The cup was inscribed by Roosevelt, Henry Cabot Lodge, and Elihu Root.

547.26   your next volume]   *The American Revolution* was published in four volumes, 1899–1907, and concluded with *George III and Charles Fox* (2 volumes, 1912–14).

548.16–19   Rawdon . . . Captain Crawley]   Lord Rawdon (1754–1826) was a British officer who fought in Massachusetts, New York, New Jersey, and South Carolina, 1775–81. Rawdon Crawley is a character in *Vanity Fair* (1848) by William Makepeace Thackeray.

550.10–11   Stephen Lee]   Lee (1833–1908), a Confederate general, was not related to Robert E. Lee.

550.19   Bannockburn]   In 1314 a Scottish army led by Robert Bruce defeated the English under Edward II at Bannockburn and secured Scottish independence.

550.34   Locke's absurd constitution]   The constitution for the Carolinas written by John Locke in 1669 established a hereditary aristocracy, but the plan proved unworkable.

554.15   *Melville Davisson Post*]   Post (1871–1930), a lawyer in West Virginia, wrote mystery and crime stories.

554.19   Madame Versay]   A character in a story by Mason that involved the passing of Confederate currency.

556.21   Miss Addams' book]   *Newer Ideals of Peace* (1907).

556.23–24   Dr. Rainsford]   William Stephen Rainsford, rector of St. George's Church in New York City.

558.9   Justice Brewer]   David J. Brewer (1837–1910), associate justice of the Supreme Court, 1890–1910.

559.16   Tom Pinch]   Character in *Martin Chuzzlewit* (1844).

559.19–20   "made him . . . the pathetic."]   The phrase was applied to Dickens by the English critic Andrew Lang (1844–1912) in *Letters to Dead Authors* (1886).

560.11   *Grafton Dulany Cushing*]   Cushing (1864–1939), a Boston lawyer, served in the Massachusetts house of representatives, 1906–14, and was its speaker, 1912–14.

561.3   The July monarchy]   The regime of King Louis-Philippe, 1830–48.

562.9   *Arthur James Balfour*]   Balfour (1848–1930), a Conservative, was prime minister, 1902–5, leader of the opposition, 1906–11, first lord of the admiralty, 1915–16, and foreign secretary, 1916–19.

566.36   Selim]   Selim II (1524–1574) was the Ottoman sultan, 1566–74.

567.29   Hill]   David J. Hill (1850–1932) was minister to Switzerland, 1903–5, to the Netherlands, 1905–8, and ambassador to Germany, 1908–11.

568.24   James J. Hill]   Hill (1838–1916) was president, 1882–1907, and chairman of the board of directors, 1907–12, of the Great Northern Railway Company.

568.26   Professor Bury]   John Bagnall Bury (1861–1927), a historian of ancient Greece and Rome, was Regius professor at Cambridge, 1902–27.

569.25   Charlie Taft]   A son of William Howard Taft.

572.8   *John Wolcott Stewart*]   Stewart (1825–1915) was a Republican representative from Vermont, 1883–91, and served in the Senate from March to October, 1908.

572.17 18   Senator Rayner]   Isidor Rayner (1850–1912) was a Democratic representative from Maryland, 1887–89 and 1891–1895, and a senator, 1905–12.

572.24   William Alden Smith]   Smith (1859–1932) was a Republican representative from Michigan, 1895–1907, and a senator, 1907–19.

572.27   Colonel Stewart]   William F. Stewart enlisted the help of Rayner and other senators in his attempts to be promoted and reassigned away from his post in Arizona. Rayner introduced a resolution calling on the president to hold a court of inquiry into Stewart's case, but it failed to pass, and in October 1908 Roosevelt placed Stewart on the list of retired officers.

573.3–4   Senators from Maryland]   Rayner and John Walter Smith (1845–1925), a Democrat who served in the House, 1899–1900, and in the Senate, 1908–21.

573.9   Thaw]   Harry K. Thaw (1880–1947), the wealthy son of a Pittsburgh industrialist, fatally shot architect Stanford White (1853–1906) in the rooftop theater at Madison Square Garden on June 25, 1906. At trial Thaw claimed the shooting was in revenge for White's alleged rape in 1901 of Evelyn Nesbit (1884–1967), the showgirl Thaw had married in 1905. After his first trial ended in a deadlocked jury, Thaw was found not guilty for reasons of insanity in January 1908 and was committed to a mental hospital. He was set free in 1915.

574.16–17   Pine Knot]   The Roosevelts' cabin near Charlottesville, Virginia; see Chronology, 1905.

574.28   the Shontses]   Theodore Shonts was a railroad manager who had worked on the Panama Canal.

576.23   Vardaman, and Jefferson Davis]   James K. Vardaman (1861–1930) was the Democratic governor of Mississippi, 1904–8, and a senator, 1913–19. Jeff Davis (1862–1913) was the Democratic governor of Arkansas, 1901–7, and a senator, 1907–13.

580.20   Mr. Cosgrave's]   John Cosgrave was the editor of *Everybody's Magazine*.

581.12   Robert Hunter]   Hunter (1874–1942), a member of the American Socialist Party, was the author of *Poverty* (1904) and *Socialist at Work* (1908).

584.11–12   Oliver P. Morton]   Morton (1823–1877) was the Republican governor of Indiana, 1861–67, and a senator, 1867–77.

584.26   *To Joel Chandler Harris*]   This letter was printed in *Uncle Remus's Home Magazine* in August 1908.

586.11   *French Ensor Chadwick*]   Chadwick (1844–1919) had retired from the U.S. Navy as a rear admiral in 1906.

590.19   Red Top]   A Harvard training facility on the Thames River in Gales Ferry, Connecticut.

594.6–7   *Verdant Green . . . Tom Brown at Oxford*]   Edward Bradley (1827–1889), *The Adventures of Mr Verdant Green* (1857), a novel about an Oxford undergraduate; novel (1861) by Thomas Hughes (1822–1896).

595.29   *Mark Sullivan*]   Sullivan (1874–1952) was a writer for *Collier's*.

596.3–4   article . . . Jack London]   "The Other Animals," September 5, 1908.

596.10–11   the Ananias Club]   The liars' club, from Ananias in Acts 5:1–5.

596.26   what I said on nature faking]   Roosevelt had discussed the subject in an interview with Edward Clark that appeared in *Everybody's Magazine*, June 1907, and in an article, "Nature-Fakers," published in *Everybody's Magazine* in September 1907.

599.2   *Harriet Taylor Upton*]   Upton (1853–1945) was treasurer of the National American Woman Suffrage Association.

600.14   *Henry Stimson*]   Henry Stimson (1867–1950) was U.S. attorney for the Southern District of New York, 1906–10. He later served as secretary of war, 1911–13 and 1940–45, and as secretary of state, 1929–33.

600.17–19   criminal libel . . . *World*]   Joseph Pulitzer (1847–1911) was publisher of the New York *World*, 1883–1911. An editorial in the *World* on December 8, 1908, accused Roosevelt of making "deliberate misstatements of fact" while publicly denying earlier allegations, published in the Indianapolis *News*, that his brother-in-law Douglas Robinson had profited from the government purchase of New Panama Canal Company bonds. In February and March 1909 federal grand juries in Washington, D.C., and New York City issued indictments for criminal libel against the New York *World* and the Indianapolis *News*. Although there was no federal libel statute, the indictments claimed jurisdiction on the grounds that the newspapers had been sent through the mail and sold in areas under federal jurisdiction, such as the

District of Columbia and federal property in New York. In 1910 federal district judges in New York and Indianapolis found the jurisdictional claim inadequate, and the indictments were dismissed or dropped.

600.24–25   Laffan and Delavan Smith]   William M. Laffan (1848–1909) was the publisher of the New York *Sun*, 1902–9. Delavan Smith (1861–1922) was the publisher of the Indianapolis *News*, 1892–1922.

600.30   Macaulay's article about Barère]   Macaulay had described the French revolutionary Bertrand Barère as a "Renegade, traitor, slave, coward, liar, slanderer, murderer, hack writer, police-spy."

602.11   letters of John Hay]   *Letters of John Hay and Extracts from Diary* (3 volumes, 1908). The edition, selected by Henry Adams and edited by Clara Stone Hay, his widow, was privately printed and distributed.

604.7   Davis . . . Allison]   Cushman K. Davis (1838–1900), Republican senator from Minnesota, 1887–1900; William B. Allison (1829–1908), Republican senator from Iowa, 1873–1908.

605.24–25   Julian Pauncefote and Michael Herbert]   Pauncefote (1828–1902) was the British minister, 1889–93, and ambassador, 1893–1902, to the United States. Herbert succeeded Pauncefote as ambassador, 1902–3.

606.17   Choate]   Joseph H. Choate (1832–1917), U.S. ambassador to Great Britain, 1899–1905.

607.5   Turner]   George Turner (1850–1932) was a senator from Washington, 1897–1903. He was elected by a coalition of Democrats, Silver Republicans, and Populists.

607.16   Chamberlain]   Joseph Chamberlain (1836–1914), British colonial secretary, 1895–1903.

611.25   Peirce]   Herbert Peirce (1849–1916) was third assistant secretary of state, 1901–6, and minister to Norway, 1906–11.

FORMER PRESIDENT, 1909–1919

617.3   Juja Farm]   In Kenya, about 25 miles northeast of Nairobi.

618.15–16   my Scribner's articles]   Roosevelt's articles on his African trip appeared in *Scribner's*, October 1909–September 1910, and were collected in *African Game Trails: An Account of the African Wanderings of an American Hunter-Naturalist* (1910).

619.9–10   heavy burden of sorrow]   Stewart Douglas Robinson, Corinne's 21-year-old son, had fallen to his death from a Harvard dormitory window in February 1909.

620.5   *Charles Doolittle Walcott*]   Walcott (1850–1927), a geologist and paleontologist, was director of the geological survey, 1894–1907, and secretary of the Smithsonian Institution, 1907–27.

620.12   Enclave]   The Lado Enclave, a territory north of Lake Albert and west of the White Nile that was leased to Belgium by Great Britain, 1894–1910; it is now divided between Uganda and Sudan. Roosevelt traveled there in January 1910 to hunt white rhinoceros.

620.16–19   Mearns . . . Heller]   The three expedition naturalists, Edgar A. Mearns (1856–1916), John Alden Loring (1871–1947), and Edmund Heller (1875–1939). Heller and Roosevelt wrote *Life Histories of African Game Animals* (1914) together.

621.15   Mr. Carnegie]   Andrew Carnegie, who helped fund the expedition.

623.7   by Bay's death]   George Cabot Lodge had died on August 21, 1909, following an attack of ptomaine poisoning.

623.24   Tarlton]   Leslie Tarlton, an Australian hunter and professional expedition guide.

624.6–7   Peary . . . fake.]   Robert Peary's claim to have reached the North Pole on April 6, 1909, was accepted, while the claim by explorer Frederick Cook (1865–1940) that he had reached the Pole on April 21, 1908, was rejected. Cook's earlier claim of having climbed to the summit of Mount McKinley (Denali) in 1906 was widely challenged, and was proven fraudulent in 1910.

624.12   Ward]   William Ward, a member of the Republican national committee from New York.

625.14   Hughes' nomination]   President Taft appointed Charles Evan Hughes, then governor of New York, to the Supreme Court in 1910. Hughes served as an associate justice until 1916, when he resigned after receiving the Republican presidential nomination. In 1930 President Herbert Hoover appointed him as chief justice of the Court; Hughes served until 1941, when he retired.

627.7   trouble that Halbert caused]   Hugh Halbert, a St. Paul attorney, had urged the Minnesota Republican convention to associate itself with conservationists strongly opposed to Taft's secretary of the interior, Richard Ballinger.

627.23   your disappointment in Taft]   Pinchot's criticism of Ballinger had caused Taft to dismiss him as chief of the U.S. Forestry Service in January 1910.

627.37   Jim]   James Garfield.

628.14   his brother Charley]   Charles P. Taft (1843–1929), President Taft's half-brother, was an attorney and, after 1880, the owner and editor of the Cincinnati *Times-Star*.

628.19   Wickersham]   George W. Wickersham (1858–1936) was attorney general, 1909–13.

629.10   *Sydney Brooks*]   Brooks (1872–1937) was an English journalist and editor.

629.14–15   Buckle . . . Jeffries]   In a letter of October 5, 1911, to the writer David Gray, Roosevelt described his encounter with George Buckle, the editor of the London *Times*, during his visit to England in the spring of 1910: "A number of editors were invited to meet me at lunch. The first five or six spoke to me with the utmost solemnity, and by the time the editor of *The Times* had come up, I felt that the occasion had grown too funereal, and so I said to him, 'It does not seem to me that you and I ought to waste our time in talking of merely frivolous subjects, and I should like to discuss with you the possible outcome of the controversy between Mr. Johnson and Mr. Jeffries.' He looked at me perfectly solemnly, muttered something, and went on. Some months afterwards Sydney Brooks wrote me that this same editor had remarked to him after the Nevada prize ring fiasco that he had always been much puzzled by my remarks, and thought I must have been laboring under some delusion because he did not know whether I referred to Dr. Johnson or Ben Jonson, and to Lord Jeffreys or the editor of the *Quarterly*, and anyhow they were not any of them contemporaries, but he was now much struck by the coincidence that a negro and a white man who possessed the names I had mentioned were engaged in a prize fight in America, and it was such an odd coincidence that he really thought he would have to write to me about it!" In the fight held in Reno, Nevada, on July 4, 1910, Jack Johnson retained his heavyweight title by scoring a technical knockout of Jim Jeffries in the 14th round.

630.27   strike . . . Columbus.]   Roosevelt had spoken in Columbus, Ohio, on September 9, 1910, during a transit strike.

631.30   *Simeon Eben Baldwin*]   Baldwin (1840–1927) was an associate justice, 1897–1907, and chief justice, 1907–10, of the Connecticut supreme court, and the Democratic governor of Connecticut, 1911–15.

636.6   *Charles Atwood Kofoid*]   Kofoid (1865–1947) taught zoology at the University of California at Berkeley, 1900–36.

636.9   Mr. Tracy's pamphlet]   Henry C. Tracy, "Significance of White Markings in Birds of the Order *Passeriformes*," written as a master's thesis under Kofoid's direction.

637.11   my criticisms of Mr. Thayer's article]   In an appendix to *African Game Trails*, Roosevelt had criticized some of the conclusions expressed in *Concealing-Coloration in the Animal Kingdom; an exposition of the laws of disguise through color and pattern: being a summary of Abbott H. Thayer's discoveries* (1909) by Gerald H. Thayer (1883–1939), which contained an introductory essay by his father, Abbott H. Thayer (1849–1921), a painter and naturalist.

637.20   Hudson]   William Henry Hudson; see note 390.33

638.21–22   Allen's pamphlet] Joel A. Allen (1838–1921), curator of ornithology and mammalogy at the American Museum of Natural History,
published the paper in 1905.

638.23   Nelson's] Edward William Nelson (1855–1934) was a naturalist
with the U.S. bureau of biological survey, 1890–1929, and the author of
The Rabbits of North America (1909).

640.19   *Mary Ella Lyon Swift*] Swift was an opponent of woman suffrage
who lived in Indiana.

642.1   John McIlhenny] McIlhenny had been a second lieutenant in the
Rough Riders.

642.29   *Charles Dwight Willard*] Willard was a Los Angeles journalist.

647.17   Governor Bass] Robert P. Bass (1873–1960), Republican governor of New Hampshire, 1911–13.

647.20   Governor Johnson] Hiram W. Johnson (1866–1945) was the
Republican governor of California, 1911–17, and a Republican senator,
1917–45. In 1912 he was the Progressive vice-presidential candidate.

653.2   *Florence Kelley*] See note 197.9.

653.5   that book] Kelley's *Some Ethical Gains Through Legislation* (1905).

653.11   Lindsey in Denver] Benjamin B. Lindsey (1869–1943) was a county
court judge in Denver, 1901–27, and established the first Colorado juvenile
court in 1903. He was the author with Harvey O'Higgins of *The Beast* (1910),
an exposé of political corruption in Colorado.

653.16   *Francis Hobart Herrick*] Herrick (1858–1940) was a professor of
biology at Western Reserve University.

654.14   *Elihu Root*] After leaving the state department in 1909 Root had
been elected to the Senate from New York; he served one term, 1909–15.

654.19–20   letter to Munsey] On January 16, 1912, Roosevelt had written to Frank Munsey, a New York magazine and newspaper editor, that he
would continue to decline to say whether he would accept the Republican
nomination for president.

654.20   request of the nine Governors] On February 10, 1912, Roosevelt
was sent a public appeal by governors William Glasscock (West Virginia),
Chester Aldrich (Nebraska), Robert Bass (New Hampshire), Joseph Carey
(Wyoming), Chases Osborn (Michigan), William Stubbs (Kansas), and Herbert Hadley (Missouri), urging him to declare his willingness to be nominated for president. South Dakota governor Robert Vessey publicly endorsed
the appeal, and Hiram Johnson, the governor of California, had also urged
Roosevelt to run.

656.11–13   Columbus speech . . . the judges]   In a speech at Columbus, Ohio, on February 21, Roosevelt had said that state court decisions declaring legislation unconstitutional should be made subject to popular recall.

656.24   *Albert Cross*]   The physical education director at Groton School.

658.22   *Paul A. Ewert*]   Ewert worked for the Department of Justice in Oklahoma.

658.27   Hadley]   Herbert Hadley (1872–1927) was attorney general, 1905–9, and governor, 1909–13, of Missouri.

658.31   Senator Cummins]   Albert Cummins (1850–1926) was governor of Iowa, 1902–8, and a senator, 1908–26.

658.16   Senator Dixon]   Joseph Dixon (1867–1934) was a representative from Montana, 1903–7, and a senator, 1907–13.

659.27   day I spoke at Osawatomie]   August 31, 1910; see pp. 799–814 in this volume.

659.40   Fairbanks cocktail incident]   Vice-president Fairbanks had served cocktails at a Memorial Day luncheon attended by Roosevelt in 1907.

660.25–26   Frankfurter . . . Lawrence Murray]   Felix Frankfurter was then serving as a lawyer with the bureau of insular affairs; Herbert Knox Smith was the commissioner of corporations; Robert Valentine was commissioner of Indian affairs; and Lawrence Murray was comptroller of the currency. Smith and Valentine both resigned their positions during the summer of 1912 in order to publicly support the Progressive cause.

662.2   *Julian La Rose Harris*]   Harris (1874–1963) was a Georgia journalist. This letter was made public.

670.15   Edith . . . great shape]   After being shot in Milwaukee on October 14, Roosevelt had sent a telegram to Edith Carow Roosevelt, which was published in the New York *Evening Mail* on October 15, 1912: "Am in excellent shape. Made an hour and a half speech. The wound is a trivial one. I think they will find that it merely glanced on a rib and went somewhere into a cavity of the body; it certainly did not touch a lung and isn't a particle more serious than one of the injuries any of the boys used continually to be having. Am at the Emergency Hospital at the moment, but anticipate going right on with my engagements. My voice seems to be in good shape. Best love to Ethel."

670.20   Joe Alsop]   Alsop was the husband of Roosevelt's niece, Corinne Douglas Robinson, and the father of political columnists Joseph Alsop (1910–1989) and Stewart Alsop (1914–1974).

671.2   *Edward Grey*]   Grey (1862–1933) was a Liberal member of Parliament, 1884–1916, and foreign minister of Great Britain, 1905–16.

672.24–25   Bulgars during the last month]   Bulgaria, Serbia, and Greece had gone to war with Turkey on October 18, 1912.

672.27   The Life of Sir Harry Smith]   *The Autobiography of Lieutenant-General Sir Harry Smith, baronet of Aliwal on the Sutlej, G.C.B.* (1901), edited by G. C. Moore Smith.

673.9   my assailant]   John Schrank, a former New York saloonkeeper who had been following Roosevelt around the country. He was declared insane and died in a mental hospital in 1943 at the age of 67.

675.2   *Michael A. Schaap*]   Schaap was the Progressive floor leader in the New York assembly. This letter was published in several New York newspapers.

680.5–6   appointed . . . Navy]   Franklin Delano Roosevelt served in the navy department until his nomination for vice-president by the 1920 Democratic national convention.

680.26   I feel . . . against Root]   As temporary chairman of the 1912 Republican national convention, Root made rulings on the seating of contested delegates that were crucial to Taft's victory.

681.4–5   the wedding]   Ethel Carow Roosevelt (1891–1977) married Dr. Richard Derby on April 4, 1913.

681.13–14   Cushing . . . Guggenheim]   Grafton Dulany Cushing (see note 560.11); William Barnes (1866–1930), chairman of the New York State Republican party, 1911–14; Senator Boies Penrose (see note 491.26); Simon Guggenheim (1867–1941), Republican senator from Colorado, 1907–13.

681.31   poor Hall]   Hall Roosevelt (1891–1941), Theodore Roosevelt's nephew and Eleanor Roosevelt's younger brother, had recently lost his first child in infancy.

682.2   *Lauro Müller*]   Müller (1863–1926) was foreign minister of Brazil, 1912–17.

682.10   Colonel Rondon]   Cândido Mariano da Silva Rondon (1865–1938), a military engineer, had explored the Amazon basin for the Brazilian Telegraphic Commission since 1890. In 1910 he became the first head of the Indian Protection Service.

684.7   Bryan]   William Jennings Bryan served as secretary of state from March 1913 to June 1915.

684.24   danger from the Home Rule question]   Unionists in Ulster had threatened to engage in armed resistance if an Irish Home Rule bill was passed, and by the summer of 1914 there was widespread concern that Ireland was on the brink of civil war.

684.32–34   Winston Churchill]   Churchill was First Lord of the Admiralty from October 1911 to May 1915.

685.38–40   doing injury to Japan . . . nineteen years] Following its defeat in 1894–95 China ceded Liaodong to Japan, but Germany, Russia, and France forced the Japanese to give up their claim to the territory.

688.21   Chequers] The Lees' country home in Buckinghamshire. In 1921 they donated it to the nation to be used by the prime minister as a country residence.

690.5   *Hugo Münsterberg*] Münsterberg (1863–1916) was professor of psychology at Harvard, 1892–95 and 1897–1916.

690.9   your very interesting book] *The War and America* (1914).

691.22–23   Admiral Diederichs at Manila] Otto von Diederichs, the commander of the German Asiatic squadron, arrived with his flagship in Manila Bay on June 12, 1898, while Commodore Dewey was blockading the city. Dewey became apprehensive that the Germans were planning to intervene in the Philippines, although the stated purpose of their naval presence was the protection of German nationals and property. The German squadron began to withdraw after the surrender of Manila on August 13.

693.23–24   Spain . . . Godoy] Manuel de Godoy (1767–1851), prime minister of Spain 1792–98 and 1801–8, became known as "the prince of the peace" after negotiating the Treaty of Basel in 1795, under which Spain ceded Santo Domingo to France while regaining Catalonian territory occupied by the French.

696.10–11   murder . . . *Lusitania*] The British liner *Lusitania* was sunk by a German submarine off the coast of Ireland on May 7, 1915, with the loss of 1,198 lives, including 128 American citizens.

696.13   the *Gulflight*] The American tanker *Gulflight* was torpedoed by a German submarine off the Scilly Isles on May 1, 1915, with the loss of three lives.

696.27   the libel suit] On July 23, 1914, William Barnes (see note 681.13–14) sued Roosevelt for having written that Barnes was on the side of "corrupt and machine ruled government." The case went to trial on April 19, 1915, and Roosevelt was acquitted on May 22.

696.34–36   the incident . . . Mr. Branding] Archibald Roosevelt had been involved as a passenger in a minor automobile accident. Edward Brandgee was the regent of Harvard College.

697.6   the leisurely Bwano] Edmund Heller.

697.32   Mac] Roosevelt's secretary John McGrath.

698.1–2   statement . . . sinking of the *Arabic*] On August 19, 1915, the British liner *Arabic* was sunk without warning by a submarine off the Irish coast with the loss of 44 lives, two of them American. In his statement Roosevelt called for an immediate break in diplomatic relations with Germany.

Johann von Bernstorff, the German ambassador to the United States, announced on September 1 that Germany would no longer attack passenger ships without warning, and on October 5 the German government agreed to pay an indemnity for the Americans lost on the *Arabic*.

698.8   Lawrence Lowell] Abbott Lawrence Lowell (1856–1943), a political scientist, was president of Harvard, 1909–33.

698.29   Willard Straight] Straight (1880–1918) had served as consul-general at Mudken, Manchuria, 1906–8, and as acting chief of the Far Eastern division of the state department, 1908–9. In 1914 Straight and his wife, Dorothy, had financed the establishment of *The New Republic*. Straight died of influenza in Paris in December 1918.

699.2   *Marjorie Sterrett*] A 13-year-old girl living in Brooklyn, Marjorie Sterrett had sent a dime to the New York *Tribune* with a note asking that a fund be established to build a new battleship. Roosevelt's letter was printed in the *Tribune* on February 12, 1916.

699.7   "Fear God . . . Own Part."] In February 1916 Roosevelt published a collection of his recent articles under the title *Fear God and Take Your Own Part*.

701.25   able to stay on the court] Moody had been forced by severe rheumatism to retire from the Supreme Court in 1910.

702.6   *Thomas Herbert Warren*] Warren (1853–1930) was president of Magdalen College, Oxford, 1885–1928, and vice-chancellor of Oxford, 1906–10.

702.14   supported Lord Roberts] After retiring from active duty in 1905, Field Marshal Lord Roberts (1832–1914) became an advocate of universal military service in preparation for British involvement in a European war. Roberts had previously distinguished himself by his command of successful campaigns in Afghanistan (1878–80) and South Africa (1900).

704.3   the poem on peace] "Buttadeus (A Battle Episode of July, 1915)."

704.20   Hood] Rear Admiral Horace Hood (1870–1916) was killed at the battle of Jutland on May 31, 1916, when his flagship, the battle cruiser *Invincible*, was destroyed by a magazine explosion after being hit by German shells.

704.21–22   His illustrious ancestor] Admiral Samuel Hood, first Viscount Hood (1724–1816), fought in the Seven Years' War and in the American and French Revolutionary wars.

706.16   Harry Davison] Davison (1867–1922) was a partner in J. P. Morgan and Company and vice-president of the First National Bank of New York.

707.2   *Newton Diehl Baker*] Baker (1871–1937) was secretary of war, 1916–21.

707.5   war with Mexico] After supporters of Pancho Villa killed 24 Americans during a raid on Columbus, New Mexico, on March 9, a punitive expedition commanded by Brigadier General John J. Pershing entered Mexico on March 15, 1916. Tensions increased after 12 American cavalrymen were killed and 23 taken prisoner at Carrizal on June 21 while fighting troops loyal to President Carranza, but the prisoners were released on July 1 and war was averted. The last U.S. troops left Mexico on February 5, 1917, with Villa still at large.

708.21   *Henry Luther Stoddard*] Stoddard (1861–1947) was the owner and editor of the New York *Evening Mail*.

709.20   *Amos Pinchot*] The brother of Gifford Pinchot, Amos Pinchot (1873–1944) was an attorney. He had publicly accused George W. Perkins of corrupting the Progressive party, and had privately charged that Roosevelt, Perkins, U.S. Steel, and J. P. Morgan and Company were conspiring to gain control of the government.

710.2   *Stanwood Menken*] Solomon Stanwood Menken, a New York attorney, was vice-president of the National Security League.

716.32–33 although brayed . . . from them.] Cf. Proverbs 27:22.

717.18   we shall have war or not] Germany had resumed unrestricted submarine warfare on February 1, 1917, and Wilson had broken diplomatic relations with Germany on February 3.

719.10   Daniels, nor Lansing] Josephus Daniels (1862–1948), secretary of the navy, 1913–21; Robert Lansing (1864–1928), secretary of state, 1913–20.

719.14   Mann] James R. Mann (1856–1922), Republican representative from Illinois, 1897–1922, and House minority leader, 1911–19.

719.17   *Joseph Barrell*] Barrell (1869–1919) was professor of geology at Yale, 1908–19.

720.5   *Eleanor Alexander Roosevelt*] Eleanor Alexander Roosevelt was the wife of Theodore Roosevelt Jr.

722.28–29 Harbord . . . Collins] Lieutenant Colonel James G. Harbord (1866–1947) was chief of staff of the American Expeditionary Force, May 1917–May 1918. Edgar Collins was an army officer Roosevelt had met at the Plattsburg training camp.

723.9   Lord Derby . . . Lord Northcliffe] Edward Stanley, Earl of Derby (1865–1948), was secretary of state for war, 1916–18. Alfred Harmsworth, first Viscount Northcliffe (1865–1922), was the owner of the London *Times*, 1908–22.

723.12   *Malgré Lui*]   In spite of himself.

723.14   *Victor Olander*]   Olander (1873–1949) was secretary-treasurer of the Illinois State Federation of Labor, 1914–49. This letter was printed in Roosevelt's *The Foes of Our Own Household* (1917).

723.19   race riots at East St. Louis]   Following the fatal shooting of two police detectives on July 1, white mobs attacked African-Americans in East St. Louis on July 2, 1917, while the police and National Guard did little to stop the violence. At least 39 African-Americans and nine whites were killed in the riot.

727.7–9   Lincoln . . . other working people."]   In his reply to the New York Workingmen's Democratic Republican Association, Washington, D.C., March 21, 1864.

727.26   Jack Cooper's]   A sanitarium and physical training camp, run by former prize fighter Jack Cooper, where Roosevelt had gone to lose weight.

728.4   Arbela]   In 331 B.C. Alexander the Great decisively defeated the Persian army led by Darius III at Gaugamela, about 30 miles from the city of Arbela (present-day Arbil, Iraq).

728.7   your division]   The 1st Infantry Division.

728.19   *William T. Hornady*]   Hornady (1854–1937) was director of the New York Zoological Park (Bronx Zoo), 1896–1926.

729.9   Flora]   Flora Whitney, Quentin Roosevelt's fiancée.

729.29   Tekrit]   The British armored car unit Kermit Roosevelt was serving with in Mesopotamia had helped capture Tikrit in early November 1917.

730.7–8   tremendous German offensive]   The German offensive on the Western front, which had been anticipated since the collapse of Russia in the fall of 1917, began on March 21, 1918.

732.2   *Georges Clemenceau*]   Clemenceau was premier of France from November 1917 to January 1920.

734.23–24   Robert College and Beirut College]   Robert College in Constantinople, founded in 1863, and Beirut College, founded in 1866. Dodge was a major benefactor of both institutions.

735.22–23   profess friendship for Armenia]   In September 1915 Dodge had helped found the Committee on Armenian Atrocities, which later became Near East Relief.

736.4   then with Austria]   The United States declared war on Austria-Hungary on December 7, 1917.

736.25   "to make . . . for democracy"]   In his war message to Congress on April 2, 1917, Wilson had said: "The world must be made safe for democracy."

736.34   death of our son Quentin]   Quentin Roosevelt (1897–1918) was shot down and killed over France on July 14, 1918.

737.19–20   revelations . . . Thyssen, and by Lichnowsky]   In 1918 the American press published a forged document, allegedly written by German steel manufacturer August Thyssen, that described how in 1912 the Kaiser had planned a war of global conquest. The memorandum by Karl von Lichnowsky, also published in the U.S. in 1918, was authentic. In it Lichnowsky, the German ambassador to Britain from 1912 to 1914, reflected on the mistakes of German policy and acknowledged German responsibility for the outbreak of war in 1914.

740.12   "proved their truth by their endeavor,"]   From the introduction to *Hero Tales From American History* (1895), by Roosevelt and Henry Cabot Lodge.

741.13   Aunt Emily]   Emily Carow (1865–1939).

743.21   with Eleanor in Paris]   Eleanor Alexander Roosevelt was serving as a volunteer with the Y.M.C.A.

744.6   Miles Poindexter]   Poindexter (1868–1946) was a Republican representative from Washington, 1909–11, and a senator, 1911–23.

748.23–25   Ted and Kermit . . . Archie pretty badly crippled]   Despite his wounds Archibald Roosevelt (1894–1979) served as a lieutenant colonel in World War II and commanded an infantry battalion in New Guinea, where he was wounded by grenade fragments in the same knee that had been hit in 1918. Kermit Roosevelt (1889–1943) served as a major in Alaska where, after suffering for years from depression and alcoholism, he shot himself. Brigadier General Theodore Roosevelt (1887–1944) served as assistant commander of the 1st Infantry Division in Algeria, Tunisia, and Sicily, 1942–43, then landed with the 4th Infantry Division in the first wave on Utah Beach on June 6, 1944. He died of a heart attack in Normandy on July 12, 1944, and was posthumously awarded the Medal of Honor for his leadership under fire on D-Day.

748.28   Dick Derby]   Roosevelt's son-in-law Richard Derby served as a surgeon with the American Expeditionary Force in France, 1917–18.

750.11   *Richard Melancton Hurd*]   Hurd was the president of the American Defense Society. This letter was read aloud at a benefit concert held in New York City on January 5, 1919.

SELECTED SPEECHES

758.25   "stern men . . . in their brains"]   James Russell Lowell, "Mason and Slidell," in *The Biglow Papers*, second series (1867).

780.4–5   Gamaliel . . . Paul]   See Acts 22:3.

782.29–32   Hotspur . . . been a soldier."]   See *1 Henry IV*, I.iii.29–64.

782.39   "freemasons of fashion"]   From the review (1833) by Thomas Macaulay of the letters of Horace Walpole to Sir Horace Mann.

791.37–792.13   "I think the authors . . . all people, everywhere."]   From Lincoln's speech on the Dred Scott decision at Springfield, Illinois, June 26, 1857.

798.20   Malbrook]   The Duke of Marlborough.

799.32–33   name of John Brown]   Roosevelt was speaking at the dedication of the John Brown Memorial State Park.

800.26   as through a glass, darkly]   See 1 Corinthians 13:12.

801.30–32   "I hold . . . ameliorating mankind."]   From Lincoln's speech at Cincinnati, Ohio, February 12, 1861.

801.34–802.4   "Labor is prior to . . . any other rights]   The quotations are from Lincoln's annual message to Congress, December 3, 1861.

802.4–11   "Nor should this lead . . . violence when built."]   The quotations are from Lincoln's reply to the New York Workingmen's Democratic Republican Association, Washington, D.C., March 21, 1864.

805.40–806.2   The Hepburn Act . . . the last session]   The Hepburn Act, giving the Interstate Commerce Commission power to regulate railroad rates, was signed by Roosevelt on June 29, 1906. The I.C.C. was strengthened by the Mann-Elkins Act, passed on June 18, 1910, which gave the commission the power to set original rates.

Index

Library of Congress Cataloging-in-Publication Data

Roosevelt, Theodore, 1858–1919.
  [Selections. 2004]
  Letters and speeches / Theodore Roosevelt.
      p. cm. — (Library of America) ; 154)
  ISBN 1–931082–66–9
  1. Roosevelt, Theodore, 1858–1919 — Correspondence.   2. Presidents —
United States — Correspondence.   3. United States — Politics and
government — 1865–1933.   4. Speeches, addresses, etc., American.
I. Title.   II. Series.

E757.A4 2004
973.91'1'092 — dc22   2004044205

THE LIBRARY OF AMERICA SERIES

The Library of America fosters appreciation and pride in America's literary heritage by publishing, and keeping permanently in print, authoritative editions of America's best and most significant writing. An independent nonprofit organization, it was founded in 1979 with seed money from the National Endowment for the Humanities and the Ford Foundation.

This book is set in 10 point Linotron Galliard,
a face designed for photocomposition by Matthew Carter
and based on the sixteenth-century face Granjon. The paper
is acid-free Domtar Literary Opaque and meets the requirements
for permanence of the American National Standards Institute. The
binding material is Brillianta, a woven rayon cloth made by Van
Heek-Scholco Textielfabrieken, Holland. The composition is by
Publishers' Design and Production Services, Inc. Printing
and binding by R.R. Donnelley & Sons Company.
Designed by Bruce Campbell.

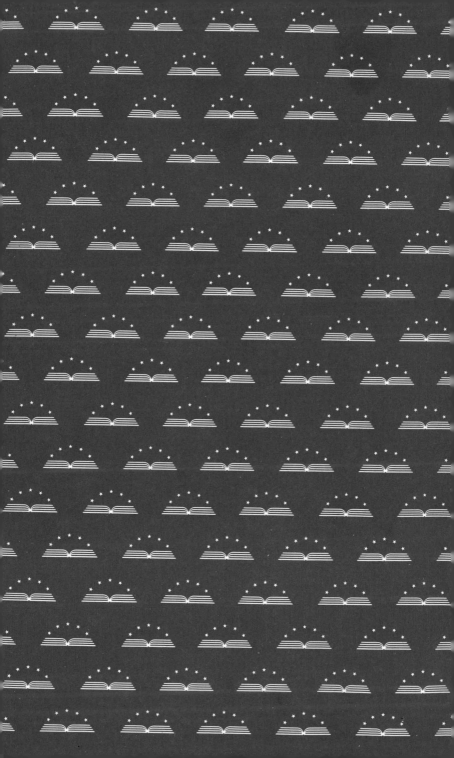